Municipal Accounting
for Developing Countries

Municipal Accounting for Developing Countries

David C. Jones

The Chartered Institute of Public Finance and Accountancy
London, England

The World Bank
Washington, D.C., U.S.A.

Copyright © 1984 by the Chartered Institute of Public
Finance and Accountancy and the International Bank for
Reconstruction and Development / The World Bank,
1818 H Street, N.W., Washington, D.C., 20433, U.S.A.

All rights reserved
Manufactured in the United States of America
First printing September 1984

The views and interpretations in this book are those of the
author and should not be attributed to the Chartered Institute
of Public Finance and Accountancy or the World Bank, to their
affiliated organizations, or to any individual acting on their behalf.

Library of Congress Cataloging in Publication Data

Jones, David C., 1935–
   Municipal accounting for developing countries

   Includes index.
   1. Municipal finance—Accounting. 2. Municipal
finance—Developing countries—Accounting. I. Title.
HJ9773.J66   1984   352.1′71′091724   84-3623
ISBN 0-8213-0350-3

Contents

Chapter number		Page
	Preface	vii
	Acknowledgements	ix
	Joint foreword	xi
1	Basic accountancy principles	1
2	Ledger accounts	21
3	Cash transactions	59
4	Journals and subsidiary records	87
5	Errors and adjustments	118
6	Simple non-profit accounts	137
7	Municipal accounts - introduction	190
8	Fixed assets - introduction	246
9	Municipal budgets	282
10	Income accounting	307
11	Expenditure accounting	361
12	Income and expenditure analysis	411
13	Stores and costing	445
14	Capital expenditure	483
15	Capital expenditure (continued)	535
16	Final accounts	610
17	Internal borrowing	695
18	Temporary borrowing	716
19	Replacement borrowing and sinking funds	734
20	Loans pooling	749
21	Depreciation and capital funds	819
	Index	893

Preface

In many parts of the developing world, the urban population explosion is creating an ever increasing demand for more efficient management of urban institutions providing public services. This is especially true of municipal governments. Outside the urban areas, local government systems vary considerably, depending on circumstances.

In many countries, it is increasingly recognized that local government institutions, with some degree of local financial autonomy, have an important part to play in national development and in urban management. Such autonomy can rarely be absolute. Often it may be rather limited, as each nation searches for its own balance of responsibilities and struggles to allocate scarce financial resources among competing public services.

If local government institutions are to be responsible partners with central governments, financial discipline and accountability are required. This is often sadly lacking - although the lack is not always confined to the developing world!

Crucial to any system of financial management is a sound accounting system. For municipal accounting, there is a paucity not only of skills, but also of good understanding, information and instruction with which to improve skills.

This handbook is an attempt to fill a part of that need. It is ambitious, but cannot be all-embracing. Based on many years of practical experience in developed and developing countries, it leans heavily on the practices and terminology of the United Kingdom, modified to suit the needs of developing countries. Indeed, it is written specifically with developing countries in mind, and much of the material has application far beyond the "sphere of influence" of the UK.

The book is based mainly on teaching material I prepared whilst working in Uganda in the mid-1960s.(1) It has been extensively revised and updated for publication in its present form.

The principles underlying the book are those of fund accounting. These principles differ somewhat from those of commercial accounting. They are, however, the most appropriate ones for use, in a variety of forms, by non-profit-seeking public authorities, particularly local government units with a degree of financial autonomy.

A basic principle of fund accounting, as its name implies, is accountability for public funds. It is not a mere euphemism for "good stewardship", important though this is. Fund accounting seeks to identify the sources of different funds and the purpose for which they may lawfully be used.

First, it necessitates the specific recognition of, and control over, separate inflows of funds, be they tax revenues, user charges, grants or loans. The freedom to use some of these funds may often be seriously curtailed. For example, revenue from a specific betterment charge may often be usable only to improve adjacent streets; revenues from a specific service may, perhaps, be usable only for expenditure on that service; a special tax assessment may sometimes be levied only in an area where a specific service is provided; and a loan or grant may often be authorized only for a specific capital development project.

---

(1) The Ugandan names used in the examples follow a standard pattern of pronunciation. The emphasis is placed on the second syllable and the last vowel is sounded, as in the word "Uganda" itself. Thus, for example, the name "Musoke" is pronounced "Moo-soke-ee" and not Mew-soak".

Municipal Accounting for Developing Countries

Second, once inflows have been properly segregated and accounted for, expenditure from these various funds can usually be made only under conditions of tight financial control, based upon budgets which have been subjected to a formal administrative process.

A principal difference between fund accounting and commercial accounting is in the treatment of depreciation. Commercial accounting practice provides for depreciation, as a periodic charge against revenues, for the gradual using up of the cost (or value) of fixed assets. Fund accounting practice also provides for periodic charges against revenues, but the charges are for the gradual provision of specific funds. These funds are used to discharge obligations incurred to finance the cost of fixed assets, or they are used to provide for the replacement of fixed assets, depending on how each was originally financed. Apart from this important difference, other generally accepted accounting principles apply as much to fund accounting as to commercial accounting.

This system of accounting is not necessarily appropriate for revenue-earning municipal enterprises or public utilities, though it is often used for some of them. Furthermore, its use for such utilities represents a considerable improvement over simple cash accounting.

Because of the shortage of good teaching material in this field, the book provides comprehensive information for the beginner, as well as for the more experienced. Thus, Chapters 1-6 are a very basic introduction to bookkeeping and may be ignored by those already familiar with such concepts. Chapter 6 uses the familiar situation of a simple nonprofit organization to lead into municipal accounting, which starts in Chapter 7.

An important feature of this work is the large number of practical applications and examples. The handbook takes the reader from basic principles of municipal accounting to some of the most advanced concepts currently in use, including the pooling of loans. It also provides illustrations and applications of forms and records covering most circumstances likely to be encountered. The only notable exclusion is the detailed procedure for borrowing through municipal stock (bond) issues. Although common in more developed countries, this is not likely to be a normal method of raising capital funds in many developing countries for the time being.

In the final chapter, I depart somewhat from the conventions of municipal accounting and try to deal comprehensively with the application of depreciation concepts to the accounts of non-revenue-earning services financed largely from taxes. The need for such a practice has long been asserted by many in the accountancy profession, although there is a lack of unanimity on this subject. The potential unwillingness of governmental bodies to raise tax revenues for non-cash expenditures is often seen as a constraint. I demonstrate how this objection might be overcome. The final chapter also provides a framework for a complete accounting system for a "local government loans fund", or a "municipal bank".

Little reference is made to the use of data processing equipment. Where computers or other electronic systems are in use, however, it will be a simple matter to adapt them to the concepts presented here. To limit the number of significant figures in ledger entries, many of the transactions will appear to be lower in value than would normally be the case for the majority of currencies represented by the unit. The principles are in no way affected.

David C. Jones

Water Supply and Urban Development Department
World Bank
Washington DC
USA

Acknowledgments

Much of this book is based on training material used in Uganda. As part of a comprehensive program, I handled the subject matter relevant here, and I accept sole responsibility for the content of this book. The work was part of a team effort, however, and would not have been accomplished without it. In particular, the annex to chapter 11 (overseas purchases) is based on the work of Eric R. Williams, a former World Bank staff member and my personal friend and colleague for many years.

Reg Cobley, our team leader in Uganda, inspired our work. George Mukasa, our first counterpart, was one of its earliest beneficiaries. Both of these dear friends have sadly passed away, each on active duty in the public service. Maurice Shackmaster and John Ridley completed our team in Uganda with one notable exception, to whom special reference must be made.

It is hard to believe, in these days of electronic word processing, that the original text on which this book is based, including all its many charts and tables, was typed on a now old-fashioned machine. This work was done by a Ugandan whom I remember, with affection, only as Paulino. His was a sterling task, performed good-naturedly under the most difficult of circumstances.

More recently, the major responsibility for editing and updating my material has been that of Michael Davis, working for Public Finance International, the international consultancy and training division of CIPFA. Like Paulino, he has proved to be a real workhorse. In the final stages of the preparation of this book, our work together has been ably assisted by Mrs. Amy Glade, my World Bank secretary, and by the staff of Public Finance International, who prepared the final document for publication.

I acknowledge the kindness, patience and support of our many Ugandan friends and colleagues. The five years which my family and I spent in their country were among the happiest we have known.

World Bank colleagues who read the book's final chapter may recognize it as the Madras Model. It is so named because the concepts, long of concern to me, were finally put on paper in Madras, India, where I found that they might be relevant to the needs of Madras Municipality. They were discussed at length with officials and consultants of both the Municipality and the Development Authority. I am particularly grateful for the opportunity to discuss the ideas with a group of chartered accountants from the Madras office of A.F. Ferguson & Co. My friend and guru, J.B. Woodham, would argue that this still does not go far enough and should allow for inflation, through the use of current cost accounting. I would agree, but until professional unanimity emerges, we must rely on tried and tested methods. In the meantime, a compromise, to deal with inflation, has been included.

Finally, I acknowledge the love and support of my wife Gabrielle, my sons Stephen and Philip and my daughter Catherine. They have endured my many absences from home in the service of developing countries but have always made, wherever we have lived, a home to which I am eager to return.

Years ago, as I started out in English local government, two colleagues who have remained firm friends, taught me my craft, which I now attempt to pass on. They were Harry Enever and Dennis Ayress. My son, Philip, was a budding craftsman of a different kind, whose life was tragically lost to us at the very threshold of his intended career. To him this book is dedicated.

Joint Foreword

by Noel Hepworth
Director, Chartered Institute of
Public Finance and Accountancy

and

His Excellency John Lwamafa, Ugandan
Ambassador to the U.S.A.

Without local urban and rural infrastructure such as roads, schools and public health services, the task of economic development is virtually impossible. Without proper accounting and the adequate provision of accurate and timely financial information to management, success in properly maintaining and using that infrastructure will prove to be limited.

These needs can only be met by people trained in the basic skills and ideas. Until the publication of this book, there has been no training programme specifically geared to these particular requirements in the developing countries. The Chartered Institute of Public Finance and Accountancy - which is the United Kingdom professional body specifically organised to meet the accounting and financial management training requirements of the public sector - is therefore very pleased to be associated with this work. Its author is a CIPFA member. The World Bank, which employs Mr. Jones, has also undertaken a major role in ensuring that this project has reached completion.

Money can be poured into development projects (wherever they are in the world) but without the ability or the intention to produce and use good financial information, high ambitions will founder and resource effort will be largely wasted.

The book is based on correspondence course material which Mr. Jones originally prepared for students of municipal finance in Uganda. This material is so comprehensive and thorough that the scope for its wider application seems obvious. This book, therefore, takes students stage by stage through each of the skills needed in accountancy, from the basic general concepts to the more specialist and specific. Guidance throughout is practical and down to earth, with plenty of examples; and the book has the needs and feel of the developing countries at heart. It is not just another adaptation of a Western textbook. The book uses as its underlying theme the accounting needs of a municipality in a developing country but the ideas that it discusses are of wide application throughout all institutions concerned with service delivery and the provision of infrastructure.

A thorough study of this book will enable the student to master all the basic accounting skills. This will, in itself, leave him or her a valuable and highly employable person, with the option of following a good career in public finance. Furthermore, for those who wish to develop formal qualifications in accountancy and financial management, the book will provide most of the specialised knowledge needed in its subject-area. Thus, combining a study of the book with such related subjects as auditing, financial management and economics, should result in a well-balanced set of skills, essential for public sector financial management at the highest level.

Municipal Accounting for Developing Countries

CIPFA, which is itself increasingly involved in giving advice to third world countries, feels that this book is therefore a valuable contribution in stimulating better financial management in the developing world, leading to a more effective and efficient use of very scarce resources.

Any book of this type is only useful whilst it remains relevant to the circumstances of those who want to develop their skills. Therefore we at CIPFA and the author would welcome ideas from readers for improvements or alterations to the text, which could be incorporated in later editions. We would also welcome ideas about parallel training courses that might be developed by using or expanding on the material in this book. Such courses might include, for example, training in audit and in the use of computers (particularly micro-computers) to provide better financial management systems.

So we would hope that you, as readers, would not only treat this book as a study text but as one stage of a dialogue which we hope you will create and which in turn will lead to further developments in training.

Noel Hepworth OBE IPFA DPA
Director
Chartered Institute of Public Finance and Accountancy
3 Robert Street
London WC2N 6BH

During his service in Uganda, Mr. Jones worked for the Ministry of Regional Administrations, the government department for which I was, for some time, the responsible minister. I am pleased that his work, based on his experience in my country, will now be made available, in its present form, for the benefit of others.

John Lwamafa
Embassy of Uganda
Washington, D.C. U.S.A.

1. Basic Accountancy Principles

Section		Page
1.	Accountancy Defined.	2
2.	Financial Records - The Ledger.	3
3.	Variations in Financial Position.	3
4.	Money Values.	4
5.	Results.	4
6.	Period of Time.	4
7.	The State of Balance.	4
8.	Net Results and Net Resources.	5
9.	Opening the Ledger.	8
10.	Posting.	10
11.	Balancing.	12
12.	Trial Balance.	14
13.	Balance Sheet.	14
14.	Gains and Losses.	15
15.	Basic Rules for Accounting.	19

1. **ACCOUNTANCY DEFINED**

   Accountancy is the science dealing with financial information. A person who is trained and qualified to deal with financial information is called an accountant.

   Accountancy includes:

   (a) designing financial records;

   (b) recording financial information;

   (c) producing statements from the recorded information;

   (d) giving advice on financial matters; and

   (e) interpreting and using financial data to assist in making the best of management decisions.

   The recording of financial information according to definite rules is known as book-keeping.

   The accountant carries out his work according to well-established principles, most of which can be emphasized if his work is described as follows:

   "An accountant records and interprets variations in financial position. He records, in money values, the results of variations during any period of time, at the end of which he can balance net results (of past operations) against net resources (available for future operations)".

   As book-keeping and accounting varies from country to country as does its terminology, British practice has been used in this book. However, a fictitious currency namely a UNIT (U) which contains 100 cents has also been used in this book. As this is an international work, the UNIT can be thought of as "UNITED NATIONS INTERNATIONAL TOKEN".

   In order that the reader with little accounting experience may more easily understand municipal accounting, the first six chapters consider simplified book-keeping examples designed to illustrate basic book-keeping and accounting practices and principles.

Basic Accountancy Principles

2. **FINANCIAL RECORDS - THE LEDGER**

    The essential accounting record dealing with variations in financial position is called a ledger. This record is the basis of all financial information. Every change in financial position will be recorded in the ledger in greater or lesser detail. From this record, financial statements will be prepared. This is what a traditional ledger page looks like:

DR.				Title of Account			CR.
(1)	(2)	(3)	(4)	(1)	(2)	(3)	(4)

    The ledger consists of many similarly ruled pages used together, usually bound in the form of a book. Each page records the information of a particular account. The title of each account is written at the top of the appropriate ledger page. Below the heading, the page is divided into two equal and identical sides by a centre line. Each of these identical sides has four columns:

    (1) date;

    (2) details;

    (3) reference; and

    (4) amount.

    The purpose of these columns will be explained later. The columns on the left-hand side of the centre line comprise the debit side and those on the right comprise the credit side. As you will see, the two sides are headed "DR" and "CR"; DR is short for "debit" and CR is short for "credit". Increasingly, much book-keeping work is now handled by computers. As costs and sizes of computers become more manageable to smaller institutions, it may be that the ledger, as we know it, will gradually be phased out as a practical book-keeping tool. However, although computers have now been handling the book-keeping of some organisations for over a quarter of a century, this has resulted in few if any changes in accounting principles. Any such changes have come about largely independently of the computer. Computer developments have been concerned with the increasing speed, accuracy and variety of accounting information. All that the computer really does, therefore, is to produce ledgers and other documents in a more convenient format.

3. **VARIATIONS IN FINANCIAL POSITION**

    The accountant records all variations in financial position, whether or not cash changes hands at the time. He is concerned with every event affecting the financial position, at the time that the event occurs. For example, if a man has his house repaired, a change in his financial position occurs when the repairs are carried out. He suffers a loss in incurring the expense of the repairs and incurs a liability to pay for

Municipal Accounting for Developing Countries

(a) what you own (including legal rights); and

(b) what you owe (the legal rights of others against you).

Accountants give each of these two classes a special name. What you own are called assets. What you owe are liabilities. Persons who owe you money are called debtors. The persons to whom you owe money are called creditors. We often refer to what we own as our resources. We can do the same here. If we refer to your assets (what you own) as your positive (or plus) resources, claims against these assets, called liabilities (what you owe), must be negative (or minus) resources. Your financial position can now be stated as:

Assets	Units
Bicycle	20.00
Debtors:	
John Musoke	3.00
Peter Kibule	.75
Cash at Bank	10.00
Cash in Hand	5.25
Total positive resources	39.00

Liabilities

Creditors:	
Electricity Board	1.80
Water Board	.50
Total negative resources	2.30
Net resources	36.70

By taking your negative resources from your positive resources, or your liabilities from your assets, you are left with your net resources which is what you are worth. Your financial position shows a surplus of assets over liabilities of U 36.70. We have now seen what is meant by net resources. According to our definition in Section 1 they must be balanced against net results. How is this done?

Let us again picture a pair of scales. Supposing for example a trader has a pile of potatoes and he wishes to know how many potatoes he has. He will measure them by weight. He will put the potatoes on one side of the scales and add a metal weight or weights to the other side until the scales balance. By reading the values of the metal weights he can determine the weight of the potatoes. Notice that it is the potatoes he wishes to know the weight of and yet he reads the values on pieces of metal.

The potatoes represent his resources. They are real, and have money value. He could sell them for cash.

The metal weights on the other hand do not represent resources. They are merely symbols of weight. They represent the results of measuring the weight of the resources - potatoes.

Basic Accountancy Principles

Suppose that of the pile of potatoes, three kilos belong to a friend. To discover the weight which belonged to himself the trader could:

(a) Put on one side of the scales a three kilo weight to equal the potatoes which he owes to his friend.

(b) Place potatoes on the other side of the scales until they are in balance.

(c) He can then weigh the remainder of the potatoes to discover the weight of those remaining which are his (7 kilos).

Although the trader's position is expressed in weight only we can still show:

	kilos
Assets	
Potatoes owned	10
Liabilities	
Potatoes owed	3
Net Resources	7

The trader has balanced his position on a pair of scales:

Liabilities		Assets	
Potatoes owed	3	Potatoes owned	10
Surplus			
Net Resources)	7		
Net Results)			
	10		10

Set out on paper like this we can say his position is expressed in the form of a balance sheet.

We can now express your financial position in the same way. The trader used a pair of scales because he measures in weight. We, as accountants, will use a ledger as we must measure in money.

Before we use the ledger, let us set out your financial position in balance sheet form:

Balance Sheet as at (date)

LIABILITIES		Units	ASSETS		Units
Creditors:			Bicycle		20.00
Electricity Board	1.80		Debtors:		
Water Board	.50	2.30	John Musoke	3.00	
			Peter Kibule	.75	3.75
SURPLUS		36.70	Cash at Bank	10.00	
			Cash in Hand	5.25	15.25
		39.00			39.00

9. OPENING THE LEDGER

You will notice that the balance sheet shows figures on either side of a central line. But a balance sheet is not an account and does not form part of the ledger. It is merely a statement of the financial position drawn up at a particular point in time. For traditional reasons the balances in a British balance sheet appear on the opposite sides of the page to similar balances in the ledger: American balance sheets show the assets and liabilities the other way round, which is perhaps more logical. In the ledger all the assets and deficiencies will appear as debits on the left-hand side; whereas all liabilities and surpluses will appear as credits on the right-hand side of the ledger.

This gives us two unalterable rules:

(a) all assets and all deficiencies are debits; and

(b) all liabilities and all surpluses are credits.

Let us now, from the balance sheet, and following our two rules, enter your financial position into a ledger. We shall get the following:

DR.   **CR.**

				Electricity Board				1
				19 Jan.1	By Balance	b/f	1.80	

				Water Board				2
				19 Jan.1	By Balance	b/f	0.50	

NOTE: Both these balances are liabilities (what you owe) and therefore by rule (b) above are credit entries.

				Bicycle				3
19 Jan.1	To Balance	b/f	20.00					

				John Musoke				4
19 Jan.1	To Balance	b/f	3.00					

Basic Accountancy Principles

	Peter Kibule							5
19 Jan.1	To Balance	b/f	.75					

	Bank							6
19 Jan.1	To Balance	b/f	10.00					

	Cash							7
19 Jan.1	To Balance	b/f	5.25					

NOTE: These last five balances are all assets (what you own) and therefore by rule (a) above are debit entries.

	Surplus							8
				19 Jan.1	By Balance	b/f	36.70	

NOTE: This balance is a surplus and therefore by rule (b) above is a credit entry.

Every item which was recorded in the balance sheet has now been entered into the ledger. Therefore the ledger as a whole should be in balance. We can easily see if this is so by taking out a trial balance.

To do this we merely list the debit balances separately from the credit balances to see if they agree:

Account	Item	Debit Balances Units	Credit Balances Units
1.	Electricity Board		1.80
2.	Water Board		.50
3.	Bicycle	20.00	
4.	John Musoke	3.00	
5.	Peter Kibule	.75	
6.	Cash at Bank	10.00	
7.	Cash in Hand	5.25	
8.	Surplus		36.70
		39.00	39.00

Municipal Accounting for Developing Countries

A trader's scales do not give proper information unless they are in balance. Similarly the accountant's ledger cannot give proper information unless it, too, is in balance. The trial balance shows that the ledger system as a whole is in balance. It does not prove that the the accounts in the ledger are correct: it only shows that the ledger appears to balance. This point will be referred to later.

10. **POSTING**

When changes in financial position take place they must be recorded in the ledger. This process of recording is known as posting. Information may be posted in many types of record, but for the present we will confine ourselves to the ledger.

We will assume that during the first few days of January, all amounts owing to you are paid in cash and that you then pay cash to clear your accounts for water and electricity, as follows:

		Units
Jan.2	John Musoke paid	3.00
3	Peter Kibule paid	.75
4	Electricity account settled	1.80
5	Water account settled	.50

John Musoke's payment will result in an increase in one of your assets (cash) and a reduction in another asset (the legal claim upon him).

The increase in the cash will, by rule (a) be recorded as a debit entry in the cash book. If increases in assets are recorded as debits it will be reasonable to assume that decreases in assets should be recorded as credits. The entry in John Musoke's account will therefore be a credit.

The two accounts affected will be John Musoke and cash. After recording the receipt of the cash they will appear like this:

				John Musoke			4
19 Jan.1	To Balance	b/f	3.00	19 Jan.2	By Cash	7	3.00

				Cash in Hand			7
19 Jan.1	To Balance	b/f	5.25				
2	To J.Musoke	4	3.00				

What do you notice about this ledger entry? Firstly, each part of the entry refers to its counterpart in the other account. In John Musoke's account we show that it has been cleared by a cash payment and in the cash account we show that cash was received from J. Musoke.

Basic Accountancy Principles

Secondly, against each entry, a number is written next to the cash column. This is called the "folio" and is a reference to the number of the account in which the other half of the ledger entry appears. Thus number 4, the folio of John Musoke's account, appears in the cash account and number 7, the folio of the cash account, appears in John Musoke's account.

Thirdly, it was customary in the accountancy profession to write the word "To" before debit entries and the word "By" before credit entries.

In modern accounting this practice is disappearing and although many accountants may still insist on its use, it does not appear to serve any significant purpose.

Returning to the book-keeping entries, we now deal with the receipt of 75 cents from Peter Kibule. Remember that the cash account is debited to record increases in assets and Peter Kibule's account is credited to record decreases in assets. The appropriate accounts wll appear like this:

Peter Kibule							5
19 Jan.1	To Balance	b/f	.75	19 Jan.3	By Cash	7	.75

Cash							7
19 Jan.1	To Balance	b/f	5.25				
2	To John Musoke	4	3.00				
3	To Peter Kibule	5	.75				

The next entries will deal with your payment of electricity and water accounts. In each case you are going to reduce your cash by paying the account and reduce your liability to the electricity board or to the water board. You must therefore credit your cash account each time and debit the account of the appropriate board.

Payment of the electricity and water accounts will appear like this:

Electricity Board							1
19 Jan.4	To Cash	7	1.80	19 Jan.1	By Balance	b/f	1.80

	Water Board					2
19 Jan.5	To Cash	7	.50	19 Jan.1 By Balance	b/f	.50

	Cash					7
19 Jan.1 2 3	To Balance To John Musoke To Peter Kibule	b/f 4 5	5.25 3.00 .75	19 Jan.4 By Electricity Board 5 By Water Board	1 2	1.80 .50

11. **BALANCING**

Each of the accounts can now be balanced. When balancing accounts the following procedure is carried out:

(a) Add the figures on each side of the ledger account.

(b) Subtract one total from the other to discover the difference.

(c) Insert this difference, a balancing figure, as the next entry on the side of the smallest total.

(d) Again add each side, which should agree or balance with the other, and enter the totals below a single line, ruling off with a double line.

(e) Carry the balance below the line on the opposite side. Here it will represent the opening balance for the next accounting period.

NOTE: Closing balances (stage c) are known as "balance carried forward" or "balance carried down". Opening balances (stage e) are known as "balances brought forward" or "balances brought down".

When balanced, the set of books which you have kept will appear as follows:

	Electricity Board					1
19 Jan.4	To Cash	7	1.80 ====	19 Jan.1 By Balance	b/f	1.80 ====

	Water Board					2
19 Jan.1	To Cash	7	.50 ====	19 Jan.1 By Balance	b/f	.50 ====

Basic Accountancy Principles

		Bicycle						3
19 Jan.1	To Balance	b/f	20.00	19 Jan.5	By Balance	c/d	20.00	
			=====				=====	
Jan.6	To Balance	b/d	20.00					

		John Musoke						4
19 Jan.1	To Balance	b/f	3.00	19 Jan.2	By Cash	7	3.00	
			====				====	

		Peter Kibule						5
19 Jan.1	To Balance	b/f	.75	19 Jan.3	By Cash	7	.75	
			====				====	

		Bank						6
19 Jan.1	To Balance	b/f	10.00	19 Jan.5	By Balance	c/d	10.00	
			=====				=====	
Jan.6	To Balance	b/d	10.00					

		Cash						7
19 Jan.1	To Balance	b/f	5.25	19 Jan.4	By Electricity Board	1	1.80	
2	To John Musoke	4	3.00	5	By Water Board	2	.50	
3	To Peter Kibule	5	.75	5	By Balance	c/d	6.70	
			9.00				9.00	
			====				====	
Jan.6	To Balance	b/d	6.70					

		Surplus						8
19 Jan.5	To Balance	c/d	36.70	19 Jan.1	By Balance	b/f	36.70	
			=====				=====	
				6	By Balance	b/d	36.70	

12. TRIAL BALANCE

A trial balance can now be prepared to discover if the ledger as a whole is still in balance. Only accounts which have balances carried forward will be included in the trial balance. The other accounts, which balance exactly, can be eliminated. The trial balance will appear like this:

Account	Item	Debit Balances Units	Credit Balances Units
3	Bicycle	20.00	
6	Bank	10.00	
7	Cash	6.70	
8	Surplus		36.70
		36.70	36.70

13. BALANCE SHEET

Having proved that the ledger balances, we can arrange the figures once more in the form of a balance sheet:

Balance Sheet as at 5 Jan.19

SURPLUSES	Units	ASSETS	Units
Surplus	36.70	Bicycle	20.00
		Cash at Bank	10.00
		Cash in Hand	6.70
	36.70		36.70

Referring to the previous balance sheet (Section 8) you will see that the "surplus" is the same as that in this balance sheet. This is because the net resources of assets minus liabilities have remained unchanged.

ASSETS (WHAT IS OWNED)	Units
Bicycle	20.00
Cash at Bank	10.00
Cash in Hand	6.70
	36.70
LIABILITIES (WHAT IS OWED)	Nil
Net Resources	36.70

There has been no change in the overall value of resources and results because during the transactions from 1 Jan. to 5 Jan. each asset was exchanged for another asset of equal value and each liability was discharged by an asset of equal value.

Basic Accountancy Principles

For example the debtor asset John Musoke (U 3.00) was exchanged for another asset of cash (U 3.00). The liability to the electricity board (U 1.80) was discharged by an asset of cash (U 1.80). There were therefore no gains or losses to add to or to subtract from, the original results.

14. **GAINS AND LOSSES**

    Gains can only arise by discharging liabilities with assets of lesser value or by exchanging assets for assets of greater value. Losses can only arise by discharging liabilities with assets of greater value or by exchanging assets for assets of lesser value.

    Supposing the U 20 bicycle is now sold. It should be clear that if sold for more than 20 units there will be a gain or profit. If the bicycle is sold for less than 20 units there will be a loss. The problem is how to record these new circumstances in the books. Let us take each transaction in turn:

    (1) The bicycle is sold on 7 Jan. for 22 units. What happens is that a bicycle of value 20 units is exchanged for cash of value 22 units. By rule "a" all assets are debits. Therefore all decreases in assets will be credits. The bicycle account will appear as:

			Bicycle					3
19 Jan.1	To Balance	b/f	20.00 =====	19 Jan.5	By Balance	c/d	20.00 =====	
Jan.6	To Balance	b/d	20.00	Jan.7	By Cash	7	22.00	

The cash received for the bicycle is U 22 and must by rule "a" be debit in the cash book, as an increase in assets. It will be shown as:

			Cash					7
19 Jan.1	To Balance	b/f	5.25	19 Jan.4	By Electricity Board		1.80	
2	To John Musoke	4	3.00	5	By Water Board		.50	
3	To Peter Kibule	5	.75	5	By Balance	c/d	6.70	
			9.00 =====				9.00 ====	
Jan.6	To Balance	b/d	6.70					
7	To Bicycle	3	22.00					

The bicycle account being an asset account cannot retain the U 2 profit as this should be contained in a gains account. It is therefore necessary to set up a gains and losses account and post the U 2 profit to the credit side, the corresponding debit to the bicycle account.

Municipal Accounting for Developing Countries

Therefore the accounts will now become:

Bicycle								3
19 Jan.1	To Balance	b/f	20.00 =====	19 Jan.5	By Balance	c/d	20.00 =====	
6	To Balance	b/d	20.00	Jan.7	By Cash	7	22.00	
7	To Profit on Sale	9	2.00					

Gains and Losses								9
19				19 Jan.7	By Profit on Sale of Bicycle	7	2.00	

The books now balance once more. A trial balance would give:

Account	Item	Debit Balances Units	Credit Balances Units
6	Bank	10.00	
7	Cash	28.70	
8	Surplus		36.70
9	Gains and Losses		2.00
		38.70 =====	38.70 =====

A balance sheet would give:

Balance Sheet as at 7 June 19

SURPLUSES	Units	ASSETS	Units
Surplus	36.70	Cash at Bank	10.00
Gain from Sale of Bicycle	2.00	Cash in Hand	28.70
	38.70 =====		38.70 =====

If this financial position is compared with the one before the sale took place we shall see:

Basic Accountancy Principles

ASSETS (WHAT IS OWNED)	BEFORE SALE Units	AFTER SALE Units
Bicycle	20.00	Nil
Cash at Bank	10.00	10.00
Cash in Hand	6.70	28.70
	36.70	38.70
LIABILITIES (WHAT IS OWED)	Nil	Nil
Net resources	36.70	38.70

The net resources are represented by:

Surplus (original)	36.70	36.70
Gain on Sale of Bicycle	-	2.00
Net results	36.70	38.70

The net results are, of course, the accumulated surplus. In each case resources are balanced by results but after the sale of the bicycle they were both increased by U 2. Remember that this is always, repeat always, the case in accountancy. There are no exceptions to the rule:

Assets minus liabilities *equals* accumulated surplus
    (Net Resources)   (Net Results)

Whenever net resources increase, net results increase at the same time by the same amount and when net resources decrease the net results will similarly decrease.

(2) We can now consider the case where the bicycle is sold for U 18 at a loss. The book-keeping entries will be:

Credit bicycle account with the cash received from the sale U 18 to partially record the disposal of the asset valued at U 20. <u>Debit</u> cash account U 18 to record the receipt of another asset cash.

A debit entry in the gains and losses account will record the loss of U 2, the corresponding credit entry being to the bicycle account to record the final disposal of the asset.

The accounts will now read:

		Cash							7
19 Jan.1	To Balance	b/f	5.25	19 Jan.4	By Electricity Board		1.80
2	To John Musoke	4	3.00	5	By Water Board		.50
3	To Peter Kibule	5	.75	5	By Balance	c/d	6.70
			9.00				9.00
Jan.6	To Balance	b/d	6.70				
7	To Bicycle	3	18.00				

17

Municipal Accounting for Developing Countries

			Bicycle				3
19 Jan.1	To Balance	b/f	20.00 =====	19 Jan.5	By Balance	c/d	20.00 =====
6	To Balance	b/d	20.00	7	By Cash By Loss on Sale	7 9	18.00 2.00
			20.00 =====				20.00 =====

		Gains and Losses					9
19 Jan.7	To Loss on Sale of Bicycle	3	2.00				

The balance sheet after the sale would read:

Balance Sheet as at 7 June 19

SURPLUSES	Units	ASSETS	Units
Surplus	36.70	Cash at Bank	10.00
LESS Loss from Sale of Bicycle	2.00	Cash in Hand	24.70
	34.70 =====		34.70 =====

A comparison between the financial positions before and after this sale will give:

ASSETS	BEFORE SALE Units	AFTER SALE Units
Bicycle	20.00	Nil
Cash at Bank	10.00	10.00
Cash in Hand	6.70	24.70
	36.70	34.70
LIABILITIES	Nil	Nil
Net resources	36.70 =====	34.70 =====
Represented by:		
Surplus (original)	36.70	36.70
LESS Loss on Sale of Bicycle	-	2.00
Net results	36.70 =====	34.70 =====

Basic Accountancy Principles

Note that in this case, net resources and net results have both decreased by U 2.

15. **BASIC RULES FOR ACCOUNTING**

The study of principles outlined in this chapter can lead us to formulate some basic rules for all accounting procedures. These should be remembered and followed at all times. Try as often as possible to discover how these principles apply to your own work in the office. You can be sure that they will apply.

Rule 1

The ledger system as a whole must always be in balance, otherwise it is not correct. The total of all debit entries (or debit balances) must always agree with the total of all credit entries (or credit balances).

Rule 2

To ensure that the ledger is always in balance, every change in the financial position must be recorded in the form of debit and credit entries of equal value. For all debit(s) there must be equal credit(s).

Rule 3

There are two main classes of ledger accounts, with related, but quite different, purposes:

(a) accounts dealing with assets and liabilities; and

(b) accounts dealing with gains and losses.

The net balance of assets over liabilities will always equal the net balance of gains over losses:

NET RESOURCES = NET RESULTS

Rule 4

In accounts dealing with assets and liabilities, all assets are recorded as debits, and liabilities as credits. It follows from this that:

(a) increases in assets are debits;

(b) decreases in assets are credits;

(c) increases in liabilities are credits; and

(d) decreases in liabilities are debits.

Rule 5

In accounts dealing with gains and losses, all gains are recorded as credits and all losses as debits. It therefore follows that:

(a) increases in gains or surpluses are credits;

(b) decreases in gains or surpluses are debits;

16. CLASSIFICATION OF LEDGER ACCOUNTS

We have already seen how ledger accounts can be divided into those for resources and those for results. We can now extend the classification to cover more detail:

(i)	Personal	Creditors Debtors)	Negative Resources	Credits
(ii)	Impersonal	))	Positive Resources	Debits
	(a) Real	Assets)		
	(b) Nominal	Losses	Negative Results	Debits
		Gains	Positive Results	Credits

Personal accounts are those, as the name implies, dealing with persons. They are concerned entirely with legal claims to money, either owed by another person or to another person. We have seen that persons to whom money is owed are creditors - their accounts are credited with the amounts owed - and are classed as liabilities or negative resources. On the other hand, persons who owe money to us are debtors - their accounts are debited - and are classed as assets, forming part of positive resources.

Impersonal accounts cover all those accounts not dealing with persons. The important classification here is the sub-division of impersonal accounts into "real" and "nominal" accounts.

Real accounts are accounts of things owned. They will normally have debit balances at any time. Quite obviously things owned are assets and form part of positive resources. Examples of real accounts are those for cash, stock, premises, land and equipment.

Nominal accounts are quite different. They do not record any details of what is owned or owed. They are accounts recording the results of changes in financial position. They are, in fact, accounts of gains and losses.

The personal accounts in the previous section were "Electricity Board" and "Water Board" (creditors) together with "John Musoke", "Peter Kibule" and "Bank" (debtors). Real accounts were "Bicycle" and "Cash". Nominal accounts were "Surplus" and "Gains and Losses".

Ledger Accounts

To summarise - real and personal accounts record assets and liabilities; nominal accounts record gains and losses.

17. **EFFECT OF CHANGES IN FINANCIAL POSITION**

    So far, we have been considering accounts of an individual person. Of course, accountancy was also designed for use by business and other organisations, so we will now see by way of an example how the principles of accountancy hold good for a business.

Example:

Mr P. Kabale starts off in business with U 500 in cash. He buys equipment for U 150 and stock for resale at U 300. He has not enough money to buy himself any premises but he borrows U 2,000 from his friend Mr J. Mubende and then buys a shop for U 1,500. He pays U 25 for expenses and later sells on credit to Mr L. Enders for U 210 goods which originally cost U 150.

You will notice that this paragraph reads like a story. It is the job of the accountant to classify the information into a form in which it can be used. It can be shown as follows:

    Jan. 1. Mr P. Kabale starts business with U 500 cash.
         2. Purchase of equipment for U 150 cash.
         3. Purchase of stock for U 300 cash.
         4. Borrows U 2,000 from Mr J. Mubende.
         5. Buys shop premises for U 1,500.
         6. Pays U 25 in expenses.
         8. Sells U 150 worth of goods on credit to Mr L. Enders for U 210.

Before these items are posted into the ledger, let us see how each change in financial position affects his business as a whole:

Date	RESOURCES			RESULTS		
	Items	Value	Change	Items	Value	Change
		Units	Units		Units	Units
Jan.1	Cash	500+	500+	Surplus	500+	500+
	TOTAL	500+	500+	TOTAL	500+	500+
Jan.2	Equipment	150+	150+	Surplus	500+	-
	Cash	350+	150-			
	TOTAL	500+	-	TOTAL	500+	-
Jan.3	Equipment	150+	-	Surplus	500+	-
	Stock	300+	300+			
	Cash	50+	300-			
	TOTAL	500+	-	TOTAL	500+	-

Jan.4	Equipment Stock Cash	150+ 300+ 2,050+	- - 2,000+	Surplus	500+	-
		2,500+	2,000+			
	Loan - (J.Mubende)	2,000-	2,000-			
	TOTAL	500+ ======	- ======	TOTAL	500+ ====	- ====
Jan.5	Shop Equipment Stock Cash	1,500+ 150+ 300+ 550+	1,500+ - - 1,500-	Surplus	500+	-
		2,500+	-			
	Loan - (J.Mubende)	2,000-	-			
	TOTAL	500+ ======	- ======	TOTAL	500+ ====	- ====
Jan.6	Shop Equipment Stock Cash	1,500+ 150+ 300+ 525+	- - - 25-	Surplus Expenses	500+ 25-	- 25-
		2,475+	25-			
	Loan - (J.Mubende)	2,000-	-			
	TOTAL	475+ ======	25- ======	TOTAL	475+ ====	25- ====
Jan.8	Shop Equipment Stock Debtor - (L.Enders) Cash	1,500+ 150+ 150+ 210+ 525+	- - 150- 210+ -	Surplus Expenses Profit	500+ 25- 60+	- - 60+
		2,535+	60+			
	Loan - (J.Mubende)	2,000-	-			
	TOTAL	535+ ======	60+ ======	TOTAL	535+ ====	60+ ====

You will notice from the above statements that after each change in financial position the NET RESOURCES and NET RESULTS balance.

18. **POSTING CHANGES TO THE LEDGER**

We can now see how these statements have produced information for posting in the ledger. Remember that accounting is concerned with changes in financial position, so we must concentrate upon the two columns headed "Change" as the source of our book-keeping material. Pay particular attention to the plus and minus signs in the above statement.

Ledger Accounts

Jan.1

Before commencing business, Mr Kabale's business resources were NIL. His business had NO RESOURCES and therefore NO RESULTS. Quite obviously he must have had private resources but as we are dealing with the accounts of his business this does not concern us.

Now, when he starts up his business with U 500 in cash, his business resources increase by U 500 from his original resources of NIL. Under the "RESOURCES" column in the statement is shown "Cash" U 500 and a positive (+) change of U 500 from the former position. If overall RESOURCES increase then overall RESULTS increase by exactly the same amount. The "RESULTS" column therefore shows a "Surplus" of U 500 and a positive change from the former position of NIL.

If the changes are related to the rules of posting we get:

(a) assets (cash) increase (+) by U 500 and must be a DEBIT; and

(b) gains (surplus) increase (+) by U 500 and must be a CREDIT.

The entries are therefore as follows:

		Cash						1
Jan.1	To Surplus	2	500					

		Surplus						2
				Jan.1	By Cash	1	500	

Jan.2

This time Mr Kabale exchanges one asset (cash U 150) for another asset (equipment) of the same value. The "Change" column records the effect on the two assets concerned. Overall, however, there is no change in total RESOURCES and the RESULTS are therefore not affected.

The rules of posting give:

(a) an asset (equipment) increases (+) by U 150 and is therefore a DEBIT; and

(b) another asset (cash) decreases (-) by U 150 and is therefore a CREDIT.

The entries are as follows:

	Cash						1
Jan.1	To Surplus	2	500	Jan.2	By Equipment	3	150

	Equipment						3
Jan.2	To Cash	1	150				

Jan.3

Mr Kabale now buys stock for resale. Again, at this point, he is only exchanging one asset (cash) for another of equal value (stock). The "Change" column records the effect on the two assets but again there is no overall change in RESOURCES and therefore none in RESULTS. We are only concerned with recording changes in the financial position and not the financial position itself: the latter is shown by a BALANCE SHEET.

The postings are as follows:

(a) an asset (stock) increases (+) by U 300 and is therefore a DEBIT; and

(b) another asset (cash) decreases (-) by U 300 and is therefore a CREDIT.

The entries are:

	Cash						1
Jan.1	To Surplus	2	500	Jan.2 3	By Equipment By Stock	3 4	150 300

	Stock						4
Jan.3	To Cash	1	300				

Jan.4

When Mr Kabale borrows U 2,000 from Mr Mubende he increases his assets (cash) by this sum, but he also increases his liabilities by exactly the same sum (legal right of Mr Mubende to have the loan repaid).

Ledger Accounts

Mr Mubende is of course a creditor. The "Change" column for RESOURCES now shows a positive increase (+) which is offset by an equal negative increase (-) but the overall position still remains the same. Total RESOURCES are still unaltered and therefore the RESULTS are unaffected.

The postings will be:

(a) an asset (cash) increases (+) by U 2,000 and is a DEBIT; and

(b) a liability (Mr Mubende) increases (+) by U 2,000 and is a CREDIT.

The entries are:

		Cash					1
Jan.1	To Surplus	2	500	Jan.2	By Equipment	3	150
4	To Mr Mubende (Loan)	5	2,000	3	By Stock	4	300

		J. Mubende - Loan					5
				Jan.4	By Cash	1	2,000

Jan.5

When Mr Kabale buys shop premises for U 1,500 he merely repeats his action in exchanging one asset (cash) for another (shop) of equal value, leaving no change in overall RESOURCES and still no variation in RESULTS:

(a) The increase (+) in assets (shop) of U 1,500 will appear in the ledger as a DEBIT.

(b) The decrease (-) in assets (cash) of U 1,500 will appear in the ledger as a CREDIT.

		Cash					1
Jan.1	To Surplus	2	500	Jan.2	By Equipment	3	150
4	To Mr Mubende (Loan)	5	2,000	3	By Stock	4	300
				5	By Shop	6	1,500

			Shop					6
Jan.5	To Cash	1	1,500					

Jan.6

We now come to a fundamentally different action from that which has previously taken place. Mr Kabale pays cash for expenses. His assets (cash) decrease by U 25 and no other asset increases in return. Almost certainly Mr Kabale has received some services in exchange for his money but whatever services he has received have been used up, leaving nothing of value behind. He has, therefore, incurred a loss representing negative results.

Examine the RESOURCES column for Jan.6. You will notice that there is a change in the assets (cash) and also a change in the overall resources. They are decreased by U 25. In Section 14 it was stated that when net resources decrease there is an equal decrease in net results. This is because NET RESOURCES and NET RESULTS must always balance. In our example the net loss is recorded in the RESULTS column, showing a decrease (-) of U 25 from the previous position.

By the rules of posting:

(a) one asset (cash) is decreased (-) giving a CREDIT entry; and

(b) because no other change takes place in resources there is an increase (+) in losses which is a DEBIT entry.

			Cash					1
Jan.1	To Surplus	2	500	Jan.2	By Equipment	3	150	
4	To Mr Mubende (Loan)	5	2,000	3	By Stock	4	300	
				5	By Shop	6	1,500	
				6	By Expenses	7	25	

			Expenses					7
Jan.6	To Cash	1	25					

Jan.8

This time the opposite occurs to what happened on Jan.6 because assets (stock) valued at U 150 are exchanged for assets of greater value (legal claims upon Mr Enders) at U 210. The statement shows a positive change in debtors of U 210 and a negative change in stock of U 150 thus bringing about an overall positive change in RESOURCES of U 60. This

Ledger Accounts

must be reflected by an overall positive change in RESULTS of exactly the same sum, in the form of profit or gain.

The rules of posting show:

(a) One asset (stock) is decreased (-) giving a CREDIT entry of U 150.

(b) Another asset (Mr Enders) is increased, giving a DEBIT entry of U 210. At this stage the ledger is out of balance until we bring in -

(c) The net increase in assets represents an increase (+) in gains or profits of U 60 thus requiring a CREDIT entry.

The three entries will be:

	Stock						4
Jan.3	To Cash	1	300	Jan.8	By Mr Enders	8	150

	L. Enders						8
Jan.8	To Stock	4	150				
	To Profit	9	60				

	Profit						9
				Jan.8	By Mr Enders	8	60

You will notice that the entry in Mr Enders' account has been apportioned against the two other accounts to which it refers.

The ledger has now been fully posted with all changes in financial position which have occurred. The completed ledger will, before balancing, look like this:

	Cash						1
Jan.1	To Surplus	2	500	Jan.2	By Equipment	3	150
4	To Mr Mubende	5	2,000	3	By Stock	4	300
	(Loan)			5	By Shop	6	1,500
				6	By Expenses	7	25

			Surplus				2
				Jan.1	By Cash	1	500

			Equipment				3
Jan.2	To Cash	1	150				

			Stock				4
Jan.3	To Cash	1	300	Jan.8	By Mr Enders	8	150

			J. Mubende - Loan				5
				Jan.4	By Cash	1	2,000

			Shop				6
Jan.5	To Cash	1	1,500				

			Expenses				7
Jan.6	To Cash	1	25				

			L. Enders				8
Jan.8	To Stock	4	150				
	To Profit	9	60				

Ledger Accounts

					Profit			9
				Jan.8	By Mr Enders		8	60

Notice the types of account in the ledger.
Personal - Mr J. Mubende (5) Mr L. Enders (8).
Impersonal:
Real   - Cash (1) Equipment (3) Stock (4) Shop (6).
Nominal - Surplus (2) Expenses (7) Profit (9).

It is important to understand why the accounts are classified in this way. In our example they are not in any particular order because we wished to see the transactions step by step. Normally the accounts will be grouped in any order suitable to the business.

19. **TRIAL BALANCE**

In Section 12 a trial balance was prepared by listing debit balances separately from credit balances. This was done after the accounts concerned had been balanced. However a trial balance can be taken out of the books at any time, whether the accounts have been balanced or not. If the accounts have not been balanced it is more helpful to include in the trial balance the gross total of postings from each side of each account.

We can demonstrate this with our present example:

Account	No.	DR. Units	CR. Units
Cash	1	2,500	1,975
Surplus	2	-	500
Equipment	3	150	-
Stock	4	300	150
J. Mubende - Loan	5	-	2,000
Shop	6	1,500	-
Expenses	7	25	-
L. Enders	8	210	-
Profit	9	-	60
TOTALS		4,685	4,685

As you can see, the trial balance "agrees" and we can assume that the ledger is in balance. This is not the same thing as being correct. If the U 25 for expenses had been debited to the stock account the ledger would still balance but would be incorrect, because of an error of principle (see later).

20. FINAL ACCOUNTS

Having satisfied ourselves that the ledger balances we now proceed to the final accounts. Preparation of final accounts consists of two main actions:

(a) The bringing together in a single account of all the RESULTS of changes in financial position, to show the NET RESULTS for the period of time. The account concerned can be referred to (at this stage) as a GAINS and LOSSES account. The NET GAIN or NET LOSS for the period on this account will be added to, or subtracted from, the surplus.

(b) The summarising in the balance sheet of all other balances on the accounts, being positive and negative RESOURCES, together with the accumulated surplus. Thus NET RESOURCES are balanced against NET RESULTS.

NOTE:

1. Every item transferred into the gains and losses account (being RESULTS) will come from a NOMINAL account in the ledger.

2. Every item which is summarised in (but not transferred to) the balance sheet (being RESOURCES) will come from a REAL or PERSONAL account in the ledger. The sole exception to this rule is that the balance on the SURPLUS account is included in the balance sheet.

21. GAINS AND LOSSES ACCOUNT

We can now prepare the GAINS and LOSSES account, as at the close of business on Jan.8.

			Expenses				7	
Jan.6	To Cash	1	25 ==	Jan.8	By Gains and Losses	10	25 ==

			Profit				9	
Jan.8	To Gains and Losses	10	60 ==	Jan.8	By Mr Enders	8	60 ==

			Gains and Losses				10	
Jan.8	To Expenses	7	25	Jan.8	By Profit	9	60

Ledger Accounts

The "expenses" and "profit" accounts are now "closed off", as their balances have been transferred to another account, namely the gains and losses account by which we have brought together all the results of variations in financial position. By comparing the total of the debit side with that of the credit side we shall get the NET PROFIT or GAIN for the period which in this case is U 35. This figure will be transferred to the SURPLUS account (2) by debiting GAINS and LOSSES account and crediting SURPLUS account.

		Gains and Losses						10
Jan.8	To Expenses		7	25	Jan.8	By Profit	9	60
	To Net profit or gain transferred to Surplus Account		2	35				
				60				60

		Surplus						2
					Jan.1	By Cash	1	500
					8	By Net profit or gain for period	10	35

22. BALANCING THE LEDGER ACCOUNTS

The remaining accounts in the ledger can now be balanced and their balances carried down, as described earlier. They will then appear as follows:

		Cash						1
Jan.1	To Surplus		2	500	Jan.2	By Equipment	3	150
4	To Mr Mubende (Loan)		5	2,000	3	By Stock	4	300
					5	By Shop	6	1,500
					6	By Expenses	7	25
					8	By Balance	c/d	525
				2,500				2,500
Jan.9	To Balance		b/d	525				

Municipal Accounting for Developing Countries

				Surplus			2
Jan.8	To Balance	c/d	535	Jan.1	By Cash	1	500
				Jan.8	By Net profit or gain for period	10	35
			535				535
				Jan.9	Balance	b/d	535

				Equipment			3
Jan.2	To Cash	1	150	Jan.8	By Balance	c/d	150
Jan.9	To Balance	b/d	150				

				Stock			4
Jan.3	To Cash	1	300	Jan.8	By Mr Enders	8	150
					By Balance	c/d	150
			300				300
Jan.9	To Balance	b/d	150				

				J. Mubende - Loan			5
Jan.8	To Balance	c/d	2,000	Jan.4	By Cash	1	2,000
				Jan.9	By Balance	b/d	2,000

				Shop			6
Jan.5	To Cash	1	1,500	Jan.8	By Balance	c/d	1,500
Jan.9	To Balance	b/d	1,500				

Ledger Accounts

Expenses   7

Jan.6	To Cash	1	25	Jan.8	By Gains and Losses	10	25

L. Enders   8

Jan.8	To Stock	4	150	Jan.8	By Balance	c/d	210
	To Profit	9	60				
			210				210
Jan.9	To Balance	b/d	210				

Profit   9

Jan.8	To Gains and Losses	10	60	Jan.8	By Mr Enders	8	60

Gains and Losses   10

Jan.8	To Expenses	7	25	Jan.8	By Profit	9	60
	To Net profit or gain transferred to Surplus Account	2	35				
			60				60

23. BALANCE SHEET

The accounts which still have balances remaining can now be summarised in the balance sheet as follows:

35

Municipal Accounting for Developing Countries

Balance Sheet as at 8 Jan. 19

	Units		Units
SURPLUS	535	ASSETS	
LIABILITIES		Shop	1,500
Loan - J. Mubende	2,000	Equipment	150
		Stock	150
		Debtors - L. Enders	210
		Cash	525
	2,535		2,535
	=====		=====

If we compare the financial position revealed by this balance sheet with the position on Jan.1 (just after Mr Kabale began business) we shall see:

	Jan.1 Units	Jan.8 Units
Assets (what is owned)		
Shop	-	1,500
Equipment	-	150
Stock	-	150
Debtors - L. Enders	-	210
Cash	500	525
	500	2,535
Liabilities (what is owed)		
Loan - J. Mubende	-	2,000
NET RESOURCES	500	535
	===	
Represented by:		
Surplus	500	500
Gain for period		35
NET RESULTS	500	535
	===	===

Notice that the variation in the financial position shown by these statements (a NET GAIN of U 35) is exactly the same as that produced by the GAINS and LOSSES account. This must be so, because the GAINS and LOSSES account records the RESULTS of all variations in the financial position.

24. APPLICATION OF FINAL ACCOUNTS

In producing a gains and losses account and a balance sheet we have followed the procedure outlined earlier in the definition of the work of an accountant.

We have recorded and interpreted (in the ledger) variations in financial position. We have recorded, in money values, the results of variations (in the nominal accounts - gains and losses account) during a period of time (1 - 8 Jan.) at the end of which (8 Jan.) we have balanced net results against net resources (in the balance sheet).

Ledger Accounts

Every type of organisation keeping accounts must periodically produce these two vital statements, namely a gains and losses account and a balance sheet. This applies to a trader, manufacturing concern, club, charity, public board or local authority.

The two statements may not be the only statements produced but they are the key statements, common to all types of business. Every organisation has a balance sheet (or could produce one if required). Each also has a gains and losses account which is given a special name according to the nature of the business.

25. TYPES OF GAINS AND LOSSES ACCOUNTS

In a trading or manufacturing business the gains and losses account is called a PROFIT and LOSS account. This reflects the hope of a net profit and the possibility of a net loss, either of which would be revealed by this account (Mr Kabale's account of gains and losses (No 10) is quite properly a PROFIT and LOSS account revealing a net profit of U 35).

In a club or charity the account of gains and losses is called an INCOME and EXPENDITURE account. This indicates that the object of the organisation is not profit, as such, but to meet all proper EXPENDITURE out of INCOME received from members or from donations.

In a government, a local authority or a public utility the account for gains and losses is called a REVENUE account. REVENUE expenditure is that incurred in carrying on the day-to-day running of the organisations, sometimes called recurrent expenditure. REVENUE income is the income required to meet this expenditure. The name REVENUE therefore reflects the day-to-day running of services for the public, as opposed to providing buildings, roads and equipment which is CAPITAL expenditure.

26. TYPES OF SURPLUS

So far, in the balance sheet we have used the word SURPLUS. Again, this balance is given a special name according to the nature of the business.

In a trading or manufacturing concern it is called CAPITAL. CAPITAL is accumulated wealth which is used to earn more income. In the case of a trading undertaking it represents the accumulated wealth of the owner or owners which is used in the business. Profits are added to the CAPITAL and losses deducted from it. CAPITAL is often referred to as the sum of money owed by the business to the proprietor. This is not strictly true. The proprietor owns the business as a whole, that is NET RESOURCES - which of course equals NET RESULTS.

Mr Kabale on 8 Jan. owns a business worth U 535 as a going concern. He could only expect to draw this sum from the business if his shop, equipment and stock could be sold for exactly their balance sheet values, which is unlikely. CAPITAL therefore represents ownership but not a liability to the proprietor. If the U 535 were held to be a liability of the business to Mr Kabale, the balance sheet would show:

		Units
ASSETS (Shop Equipment, Stock, Debtors and Cash)		2,535
LIABILITIES		
Loan - Mr Mubende	2,000	
Capital - Mr Kabale	535	2,535
NET RESOURCES		(NIL)

The business is shown as having a net worth of nothing which could well be misleading.

In a club or charity keeping a proper set of accounts, the accumulated net results are often referred to as SURPLUS or ACCUMULATED SURPLUS. Sometimes the words CAPITAL or ACCUMULATED FUND are used instead.

In a local or public authority the usual expressions are REVENUE ACCOUNT SURPLUS or GENERAL REVENUE BALANCE.

In any organisation we may find proportions of the surplus set aside as separate FUNDS eg for reserves. All the funds together represent the overall surplus. This point will be referred to later.

27. **GROSS TRADING PROFIT**

In the example of Mr Kabale's business we saw how profit was earned by the exchange of stock of certain value for cash (or legal rights to cash) of greater value. The stock account was credited with the value of the goods disposed of U 150. Mr L. Enders' account was debited with U 210 and the difference U 60 was credited to a profit account.

This is theoretically correct, but there is a serious practical difficulty which must be overcome. Profit is the difference between selling price and cost price.

In the example we were able to say that selling price U 210 minus cost price U 150 equals profit U 60. Unfortunately, if this principle were always applied to a business it would mean that every time a sale was made, on credit or for cash, the trader would have to record the cost price and selling price of each article sold. Perhaps this is easy

enough if you are selling motor cars, but not if you are a grocer or a trader selling vegetables in the market. However, such a practice is not necessary because, as a rule, a business man does not wish to know the profit on each and every sale but the GROSS TRADING PROFIT for a period of time on all transactions taken together.

Because of this the accountant uses a TRADING ACCOUNT to calculate the GROSS TRADING PROFIT. This trading account uses only information which is readily available. It saves the trader from keeping detailed records of each sale.

Ledger Accounts

28. **TRADING ACCOUNT**

    We have already seen that:

    Selling Price - Cost Price = Profit.

    This is the same as saying:

    Cost Price + Profit = Selling Price.

    What is true for one item of goods is equally true for all goods taken together:

    Cost Price + Profit = Selling Price
    (all goods) (all goods sold) (all goods sold)

    Accountants usually express this equation as:

    Cost of Sales + Gross Profit = Sales.

    In the case of Mr Kabale we can say:

    Cost of Sales + Gross Profit = Sales
    (U 150)   (U 60)   (U 210)

    Notice that it is the cost of goods sold which is important in a trading account, not the cost of goods purchased. However it is necessary to know the cost of goods purchased to help in calculating the cost of goods sold. If we know the cost of the goods we start with and add to this the cost of goods purchased we have the cost of goods available for sale during a period. If we subtract the cost of goods left in store at the end of the period, we shall know the cost of goods disposed of or sold during the period. This can be expressed as:

    Opening Stock + Purchases - Closing Stock = Cost of Sales
    (at cost)   (at cost)   (at cost)   (at cost)

    In the case of Mr Kabale the position is:

    Opening Stock + Purchases - Closing Stock = Cost of Sales
    (NIL)   (U 300)   (U 150)   (U 150)

    It is necessary for purchases and sales to be recorded separately from stock and for the physical stock in hand at the end of a period to be counted and valued. This is known as STOCKTAKING. If these things are done, the preparation of a TRADING ACCOUNT and calculation of GROSS PROFIT is a simple matter.

    To illustrate the point, let us assume that Mr Kabale continues his business on 9 Jan. From now on his "Stock" account will only record the stock in hand as valued at the end of each period and he will open new and separate accounts for "Purchases" and "Sales".

    His trading continues as follows:

    Jan. 9 Buys stock on credit from Nsamizi Trading Co Ltd for U 125. Pays expenses U 2.
    10 Sells stock on credit to F. Mayanja for U 25.
    11 Sells stock for U 33 cash to J. Katera.
    12 Buys stock on credit from Wholesalers Ltd for U 40.
    13 Sells stock on credit to L. Enders for U 110.

14   Pays **U** 35 expenses.
15   Receives **U** 50 from L. Enders as part payment of his account. Sells stock on credit to F. Mayanja for **U** 30.

At the close of business on 15 Jan. Mr Kabale makes a count of his unsold stock and values it at **U** 175.

Jan. 9

The first book-keeping entry must deal with the purchase of stock. Here an asset (stock) is exchanged for a liability (to Nsamizi Trading Co). We shall therefore debit the stock to a PURCHASES account and credit the NSAMIZI TRADING CO with the amount owing to it:

    DR. Purchases.   )
    CR. Nsamizi Trading Co Ltd.   ) **U** 125

Purchases								11
Jan.9	To Nsamizi Trading Co	12	125				

Nsamizi Trading Co Ltd								12
				Jan.9	By Purchases	11	125

The second entry deals with payment of expenses. This procedure has already been explained in Section 18:

    DR. Expenses.)
    CR. Cash.   ) **U** 2

Expenses								7
Jan.9	To Cash	1	2				

Cash								1
Jan.9	To Balance	b/f	525	Jan.9	By Expenses	7	2

Ledger Accounts

Jan.10

The sale of stock to F. Mayanja for U 25 brings in a new principle. We have already seen that it would be difficult for Mr Kabale to make a note of the cost price of every item of goods sold, and he has not done so in this case. All we know is the selling price of U 25. What does the figure of U 25 represent? As a selling price it must include cost price plus profit - but how much of each we do not know. It represents a reduction in assets (cost price) together with an increase in gains (profit). If we knew how much of the U 25 was the cost price and how much was profit, the entries would be:

    DR. F. Mayanja with amount due from him U 25.
    CR. Stock   ) with individual amounts of
    CR. Profit) cost price and profit totalling U 25.

Notice that both the cost price and the profit, if we knew what they were, would be CREDITED in the ledger. This helps us with our bookkeeping because if we do not know how much to credit to each of two separate accounts we can credit the whole sum to a single account - SALES.

The entries will therefore be:

    DR. F. Mayanja.)
    CR. Sales.   ) U 25

F. Mayanja						13
Jan.10	To Sales	14	25			

				Sales		14
			Jan.10	By F. Mayanja	13	25

Jan.11

In this case there is another sale, this time for cash. The principles are exactly as before except that cash is the asset which increases, instead of legal rights (ie debtors).

The entries are:

    DR. Cash.   )
    CR. Sales.) U 33

	Cash					1
Jan.9	To Balance	b/f	525	Jan.9	By Expenses	7	2
11	To Sales	14	33				

	Sales					14
				Jan.10	By F. Mayanja	13	25
				11	By Cash	1	33

The fact that the goods were sold to Mr Katera is of no consequence. There need be no record of his name. He may walk right out of Mr Kabale's shop and never be seen again. This does not matter. He has paid cash for his goods and no further dealings are necessary.

Jan.12

The purchase of stock on credit from Wholesalers Ltd is the same type of transaction as the purchase from Nsamizi Trading Co Ltd:

    DR. Purchases.   )
    CR. Wholesalers Ltd.) U 40

	Purchases				11
Jan.9	To Nsamizi Trading Co	12	125		
12	To Wholesalers	15	40		

	Wholesalers Ltd				15
			Jan.12	By Purchases	11	40

Jan.13

The credit sale to L. Enders is the same type of transaction as the sale to F. Mayanja. There is already an account opened for Mr Enders so of course we continue to use this:

    DR. L. Enders.)
    CR. Sales.   ) U 110

Ledger Accounts

				L. Enders					8
Jan.9	To Balance	b/f	210						
13	To Sales	14	110						

				Sales					14
					Jan.10	By F. Mayanja	13	25	
					11	By Cash	1	33	
					13	By L. Enders	8	110	

Jan.14

The payment of expenses is dealt with as before:

    DR. Expenses.)
    CR. Cash.   )   U 35

				Expenses					7
Jan.9	To Cash	1	2						
14	To Cash	1	35						

				Cash					1
Jan.9	To Balance	b/f	525	Jan.9	By Expenses	7	2		
11	To Sales	14	33	14	By Expenses	7	35		

Jan.15

The receipt of U 50 from L. Enders is the exchange of one asset (legal rights to debt from L. Enders) for another asset (cash) of equal value. No gains or losses are involved, and net resources remain the same:

    DR. Cash (increase in assets).   )
    CR. L. Enders (decrease in assets).)   U 50

	Cash						1
Jan.9	To Balance	b/f	525	Jan.9	By Expenses	1	2
11	To Sales	14	33	14	By Expenses	1	35
15	To L. Enders	8	50				

	L. Enders						8
Jan.9	To Balance	b/f	210	Jan.15	By Cash	1	50
13	To Sales	14	110				

The sale of stock on credit to F. Mayanja for U 30 is dealt with in the same way as the transaction of Jan.10:

DR.   F. Mayanja.   )
CR.   Sales.   )   U 30

	F. Mayanja						13
Jan.10	To Sales	14	25				
15	To Sales	14	30				

	Sales						14
				Jan.10	By F. Mayanja	13	25
				11	By Cash	1	33
				13	By L. Enders	8	110
				15	By F. Mayanja	13	30

The new trading transactions have all been entered into the ledger. It is now possible, with the information available, to:

(a) prove that the ledger is in balance by extracting a TRIAL BALANCE;

(b) calculate the gross trading profit for the period by means of a TRADING ACCOUNT;

(c) bring together gains (profit) and losses (expenses) to calculate net profit in the PROFIT AND LOSS ACCOUNT; and

(d) show the financial position at the close of business on Jan.15 by means of a balance sheet.

Ledger Accounts

The ledger will appear as follows:

		Cash						1
Jan.9	To Balance	b/f	525	Jan.9	By Expenses	1	2
11	To Sales	14	33	14	By Expenses	1	35
15	To L. Enders	8	50				

		Surplus						2
				Jan.9	By Balance	b/f	535

		Equipment						3
Jan.9	To Balance	b/f	150				

		Stock						4
Jan.9	To Balance	b/f	150				

		J. Mubende - Loan						5
				Jan.9	By Balance	b/f	2,000

		Shop						6
Jan.9	To Balance	b/f	1,500				

Expenses 7

Jan.9	To Cash	1	2				
14	To Cash	1	35				

L. Enders 8

Jan.9	To Balance	b/f	210	Jan.15	By Cash	1	50
13	To Sales	14	110				

Purchases 11

Jan.9	To Nsamizi Trading Co	12	125				
12	To Wholesalers	15	40				

Nsamizi Trading Co Ltd 12

				Jan.9	By Purchases	11	125

F. Mayanja 13

Jan.10	To Sales	14	25				
15	To Sales	14	30				

Sales 14

				Jan.10	By F. Mayanja	13	25
				11	By Cash	1	33
				13	By L. Enders	8	110
				15	By F. Mayanja	13	30

Ledger Accounts

				Wholesalers Ltd			15
				Jan.12	By Purchases	11	40

The Trial Balance

As further work is still required in the ledger we shall use "gross" figures and not "balances" for this purpose:

Account	No.	DR. Units	CR. Units
Cash	1	608	37
Surplus	2		535
Equipment	3	150	
Stock	4	150	
J. Mubende - Loan	5		2,000
Shop	6	1,500	
Expenses	7	37	
L. Enders	8	320	50
Purchases	11	165	
Nsamizi Trading Co Ltd	12		125
F. Mayanja	13	55	
Sales	14		198
Wholesalers Ltd	15		40
TOTALS		2,985	2,985

The ledger system is in balance and we can proceed to the next stage.

The Trading Acount

The gross trading profit is calculated as shown previously in two stages.

(1) Opening Stock and Purchases - Closing Stock = Cost of Sales

(2) Sales - Cost of Sales = Gross Profit.

A combined statement will produce the profit for Mr Kabale from 9 - 15 Jan:

		Units
	SALES (from sales account)	198
Less	COST OF SALES:	
	Opening Stock (from Stock Account)	150
	Add Purchases (from Purchases Account)	165
		315
	Less Closing Stock (from Stocktaking)	175	140
	GROSS TRADING PROFIT		58

The same result can be arrived at by posting the appropriate items from their ledger accounts to the TRADING ACCOUNT, as follows:

Sales

The credit balance on the SALES account is transferred to the credit side of the TRADING account:

    DR. Sales.   )
    CR. Trading Account.) U 198

Sales							14
Jan.15	To Trading Account	16	198	Jan.10	By F. Mayanja	13	25
				11	By Cash	1	33
				13	By L. Enders	8	110
				15	By F. Mayanja	13	30
			198				198

Trading Account							16
				Jan.15	By Sales	14	198

Opening Stock

The sum of **U** 150 at present standing as a debit balance in the STOCK account is transferred to the debit of the TRADING account:

    DR. Trading Account.)
    CR. Stock.   ) U 150

Ledger Accounts

Trading Account						16
Jan.15	To Opening Stock	4	150	Jan.15 By Sales	14	198

Stock						4
Jan.9	To Balance	b/f	150 ===	Jan.15 By Trading Account	16	150 ===

Purchases

The total purchases of U 165 at present debited in the PURCHASES account are transferred to the debit of the TRADING account:

    DR.   Trading Account.)
    CR.   Purchases.   ) U 165

Trading Account						16
Jan.15	To Opening Stock To Purchases	4 11	150 165	Jan.15 By Sales	14	198

Purchases						11
Jan.9 12	To Nsamizi Trading Co To Wholesalers	12 15	125 40 165 ===	Jan.15 By Trading Account	16	165 165 ===

Closing Stock

This sum of U 175 represents the value of real assets (resources) in hand and owned by the business at the close of trading on 15 Jan. It must therefore be shown as a DEBIT in an asset account (STOCK). To complete the double entry the same sum must be credited to the TRADING account:

    DR.   Stock.   )
    CR.   Trading Account.) U 175

	Stock						4
Jan.9	To Balance	b/f	150	Jan.15	By Trading Account	16	150
15	To Trading Account	16	175				

	Trading Account						16
Jan.15	To Opening Stock	4	150	Jan.15	By Sales	14	198
	To Purchases	11	165		By Closing Stock	4	175

All the necessary figures have now been transferred to the TRADING account, and the two sides can now be added:

DR. = U 315.
CR. = U 373.

The difference between the two figures U 58 is GROSS TRADING PROFIT which is the amount by which the SALES exceed the COST OF SALES. This profit can be transferred to the PROFIT and LOSS account as follows:

DR. Trading Account.   )
CR. Profit and Loss Account.) U 58

	Trading Account						16
Jan.15	To Opening Stock	4	150	Jan.15	By Sales	14	198
	To Purchases	11	165		By Closing Stock	4	175
	To Gross Profit transferred to Profit and Loss Account	17	58				
			373				373

Ledger Accounts

					Profit and Loss Account			17
				Jan.15	By Gross profit transferred from Trading Account	16	58

The TRADING ACCOUNT as shown above is in the normal form to be found in a ledger. Before passing on to complete the final accounts we can show it in two alternative ways to illustrate certain important points.

First Alternative

					Trading Account			16
Jan.15	To Opening Stock	4	150	Jan.15	By Sales: Cost of Sales	14	140
	To Purchases	11	165		Profit	14	58
	To Gross Profit	17	58		By Closing Stock	4	175
			373				373

The account is, as its name implies, the account of trading activities, or what takes place in the shop.

Opening Stock represents assets (positive resources) with which the trader starts his business activities for the period. Like all other

assets it is a DEBIT.

Purchases represents assets (positive resources) added to the stocks during the period and is also therefore a DEBIT.

Sales (Cost of Sales) represents nothing more than a reduction of assets (negative resources) in the form of stocks (at cost price) disposed of: as a reduction in assets or negative resources it is a CREDIT.

Sales (Profit) represents the difference between the stock disposed of (at cost) and the asset received in exchange (cash or legal rights to cash). It is a gain (or positive result) and therefore a CREDIT. Being a gain or profit it is quite properly a CREDIT to the PROFIT and LOSS account. This is done, as you can see, by a transfer.

Closing Stock represents the un-used stock still in hand at the end of the trading period. In theory it is transferred out of the shop into store for use in the next trading period. It represents therefore un-used (or negative) resources which are a DEBIT in the stock account and a CREDIT in the trading account.

				Surplus (Capital)			2
				Jan.9	By Balance	b/f	535
				15	By Net Profit transferred from Profit and Loss Account	17	21

You will remember that CAPITAL is the special name given to the SURPLUS of a trading business.

A Balance Sheet can now be prepared to show the financial position at the close of business on Jan.15. The complete balanced ledger will appear as follows:

			Cash				1
Jan.9	To Balance	b/f	525	Jan.9	By Expenses	1	2
11	To Sales	14	33	14	By Expenses	1	35
15	To L. Enders	8	50	15	By Balance	c/d	571
			608				608
Jan.16	To Balance	b/d	571				

			Surplus (Capital)				2
Jan.15	To Balance	c/d	556	Jan.9	By Balance	b/f	535
				15	By Net Profit transferred from Profit and Loss Account	17	21
			556				556
				Jan.16	By Balance	b/d	556

			Equipment				3
Jan.9	To Balance	b/f	150	Jan.15	By Balance	c/d	150
16	To Balance	b/d	150				

Ledger Accounts

Stock — 4

Date	Particulars	Folio	Amount	Date	Particulars	Folio	Amount
Jan.9	To Balance	b/f	150	Jan.15	By Trading Account	16	150
			===				===
Jan.15	To Trading Account	16	175				

J. Mubende – Loan — 5

Date	Particulars	Folio	Amount	Date	Particulars	Folio	Amount
Jan.15	To Balance	c/d	2,000	Jan.9	By Balance	b/f	2,000
			=====				=====
				16	By Balance	b/d	2,000

Shop — 6

Date	Particulars	Folio	Amount	Date	Particulars	Folio	Amount
Jan.9	To Balance	b/f	1,500	Jan.15	By Balance	c/d	1,500
			=====				=====
Jan.16	To Balance	b/d	1,500				

Expenses — 7

Date	Particulars	Folio	Amount	Date	Particulars	Folio	Amount
Jan.9	To Cash	1	2	Jan.15	By Profit and Loss	17	37
14	To Cash	1	35				
			37				37
			==				==

L. Enders — 8

Date	Particulars	Folio	Amount	Date	Particulars	Folio	Amount
Jan.9	To Balance	b/f	210	Jan.15	By Cash	1	50
13	To Sales	14	110		By Balance	c/d	270
			320				320
			===				===
Jan.16	To Balance	b/d	270				

Municipal Accounting for Developing Countries

	Purchases						11
Jan.9	To Nsamizi Trading Co	12	125	Jan.15	By Trading Account	16	165
12	To Wholesalers	15	40				
			165				165
			===				===

	Nsamizi Trading Co Ltd						12
Jan.15	To Balance	c/d	125	Jan.9	By Purchases	11	125
			===				===
				Jan.16	By Balance	b/d	125

	F. Mayanja						13
Jan.10	To Sales	14	25	Jan.15	By Balance	c/d	55
15	To Sales	14	30				
			55				55
			==				==
16	To Balance	b/d	55				

	Sales						14
Jan.15	To Trading Account	16	198	Jan.10	By F. Mayanja	13	25
				11	By Cash	1	33
				13	By L. Enders	8	110
				15	By F. Mayanja	13	30
			198				198
			===				===

	Wholesalers Ltd						15
Jan.15	To Balance	c/d	40	Jan.12	By Purchases	1	40
			==				==
				Jan.16	By Balance	b/d	40

56

Ledger Accounts

Trading Account   16

Jan.15	To Opening Stock	4	150	Jan.15	By Sales	14	198
	To Purchases	13	165		By Closing Stock	4	175
	To Gross Profit transferred to Profit and Loss Account	17	58				
			373				373

Profit and Loss Account   17

Jan.15	To Expenses	7	37	Jan.15	By Gross Profit transferred from Trading Account	16	58
	To Net Profit transferred to Surplus (Capital) Account	2	21				
			58				58

The balances carried forward are now classified in the balance sheet as follows:

Balance Sheet as at 15 Jan. 19

	Units		Units
SURPLUS (CAPITAL)	556	ASSETS	
LIABILITIES		Shop	1,500
Loan J. Mubende	2,000	Equipment	150
Creditors		Stock	175
Nsamizi Trading Co	125	Debtors	
Wholesalers	40	L. Enders	270
		F. Mayanja	55
		Cash	571
	2,721		2,721

Municipal Accounting for Developing Countries

Comparing the financial position for three dates gives:

Assets (What is Owned)	Jan.1 Units	Jan.8 Units	Jan.15 Units
Shop		1,500	1,500
Equipment		150	150
Stock		150	175
Debtors		210	325
Cash	500	525	571
	500	2,535	2,721

Liabilities (What is Owed)			
Loans and other creditors	-	2,000	2,165
NET RESOURCES	500	535	556

Represented by:

Surplus (Capital)	500	500	535
Profit for period	-	35	21
NET RESULTS	500	535	556

3. Cash Transactions

Section		Page
30.	Normal Financial Period.	60
31.	Cash Book.	60
32.	Cash Receipts.	61
33.	Cash Payments.	65
34.	Local Authority Receipts and Payments.	71
35.	Banking Arrangements.	71
36.	Bank Deposits.	72
37.	Bank Withdrawals.	72
38.	Current Accounts.	74
39.	Cheques.	75
40.	Two - Column Cash Book.	77
41.	Bank Overdraft.	85

30. **NORMAL FINANCIAL PERIOD**

In Section 6 of Chapter 1 it was pointed out that results must be related to a period of time. In theory, accounts can be made up for any period of time and this has been demonstrated in earlier sections. In practice most organisations keep their accounts for a normal financial period of one year. This need not be a calendar year. Many commercial undertakings use the calendar year as their financial year: others begin their financial years on the first day of a calendar quarter (April, July or October). In the United Kingdom local authorities end their financial years on 31 March and the Central Government closes its annual accounts on 5 April!

Remember that financial years are only introduced for convenience. Work does not stop on the last day of one year and begin again on the first day of the next. Accountancy is a continuous process, and a good system must be able to produce information whenever required, and related to any period of time. For example monthly cost statements may be produced for management purposes. In this book a financial period of much less than a full year is often used as the principles are the same for a short period as for a long one.

31. **CASH BOOK**

Earlier we considered the various types of ledger accounts kept for assets and liabilities: accounts for assets could be either real (things owned) or personal (legal rights to real things - debtors).

One of the most important assets dealt with in book-keeping is cash. Cash is the means by which assets are exchanged for one another and is also a common measure of value. In earlier examples many of the changes in financial position involve the receipt and payment of cash, and also all assets, liabilities, gains and losses are expressed in cash values.

As with all other assets, cash has a separate account in the ledger. RULE 4 Section 15 stated that:

(a) increases in assets are debits; and

(b) decreases in assets are credits.

Cash Transactions

Application of this rule to the cash account will give us:

DR.	CR.
Increases in assets (Receipts of cash)	Decreases in assets (Payment of cash)

The basic rules apply to the cash account as to all other ledger accounts. But, because of the large number of entries which must be made in the cash account, it is normally kept in a separately bound part of the ledger and is referred to as the CASH BOOK. The cash account or cash book is, however, a vital part of the ledger and must be kept according to the BASIC RULES OF ACCOUNTING.

32. **CASH RECEIPTS**

Cash is received (ie it increases) as a result of four main types of change in financial position:

(a) in settlement of an amount owed by a debtor;

(b) in exchange for another asset;

(c) as a gain;

(d) as a loan.

Cash received for cash sales is partly (b) in exchange for goods and partly (c) gross profit on the sale (see Chapter 2).

The alternative types of cash receipt can be shown as follows:

CASH RECEIPTS

Type of Receipt	Debit	Credit
(a) Receipt from a debtor	Cash	Personal account of the debtor
(b) Receipt in exchange for another asset	Cash	Real account of the asset disposed of
(c) Receipt as a gain	Cash	Nominal account recording the particular type of gain
(b) and (c) Receipt for cash sales	Cash	Sales
(d) Receipt of a loan	Cash	Personal account of the lender (creditor)

In the previous transactions of Mr Kabale (Chapter 2) there is on 16 Jan. 19 a balance of cash in hand of U 571. This would appear in his cash book as:

	Cash					1
Jan.16	To Balance	b/f	571			

Notice that as positive resources (assets) the balance is shown as a debit.

Suppose that he now trades as follows:

Jan.16 Receives U 55 from Mr Mayanja.
    17 Sells U 10 worth of equipment (at cost) for cash.
    17 Receives U 2 commission from Nsamizi Trading Co.
    18 Sells some stock for U 22.

    18 Borrows a further U 500 from J. Mubende.

The book-keeping entries will appear as follows:

Jan.16

The receipt of U 55 from Mr Mayanja represents an increase of one asset (cash) in exchange for a decrease in another asset of equal value (legal rights to debt from F. Mayanja):

    DR. Cash (increase in assets).   )
    CR. F. Mayanja (decrease in assets).) U 55

	Cash					1
Jan.16	To Balance	b/f	571			
16	To F. Mayanja	13	55			

	F. Mayanja					13
Jan.16	To Balance	b/f	55	Jan.16 By Cash	1	55

Jan.17

The receipt of U 10 for sale of equipment represents an increase in one asset (cash) in exchange for a decrease in another asset of equal value (equipment):

    DR. Cash (increase in assets).   )
    CR. Equipment (decrease in assets).) U 10

Cash Transactions

	Cash							1
Jan.16	To Balance	b/f	571					
16	To F. Mayanja	13	55					
17	To Equipment	3	10					

	Equipment							3
Jan.16	To Balance	b/f	150	Jan.17	By Cash	1	10	

The receipt of U 2 commission is an increase in assets (cash) without any corresponding decrease in assets or increase in liabilities. Overall resources therefore increase by U 2 representing a gain which must be credited to an appropriate nominal account:

    DR. Cash (increase in assets).)
    CR. Commission (gain).   ) U 2

	Cash							1
Jan.16	To Balance	b/f	571					
16	To F. Mayanja	13	55					
17	To Equipment	3	10					
17	To Commission	18	2					

	Commission							18
				Jan.17	By Cash	1	2	

Jan.18

The cash sale of stock for U 22 will result in an increase in one asset (cash) which will be debited in the cash account. The credit entry will represent partly a decrease in assets (stock at cost) and partly a gain (gross profit). As already explained in Section 28 these two aspects are combined in one entry in a single account (sales) pending analysis in the trading account:

    DR. Cash (increase in assets).   )
    CR. Sales (decrease in assets - at cost -) U 22
         plus an element of gain).   )

	Cash				1
Jan.16 To Balance	b/f	571			
16 To F. Mayanja	13	55			
17 To Equipment	3	10			
17 To Commission	18	2			
18 To Sales	14	22			

	Sales				14
			Jan.18 By Cash	1	22

Jan.18

The receipt of a loan of U 500 from Mr J. Mubende increases assets (Cash) and at the same time increases liabilities (to J. Mubende) by an equal amount:

    DR. Cash (increase in assets).
    CR. J. Mubende Loan (increase in liabilities).

	Cash				1
Jan.16 To Balance	b/f	571			
16 To F. Mayanja	13	55			
17 To Equipment	3	10			
17 To Commission	18	2			
18 To Sales	14	22			
18 To J. Mubende (loan)	5	500			

	J. Mubende - Loan				5
			Jan.16 By Balance	b/f	2,000
			18 By Cash	1	500

Every entry in the cash book has been on the debit side. Following the basic rules of accounting (RULE 2) there has been an equivalent credit entry in another account for every debit entry in the cash book.

The cash book entries are all on the debit side because they represent the cash owned on 16 Jan. (balance brought forward) together with additions to the cash balance through the receipt of various sums of money. If Mr Kabale were to count his cash on 18 Jan. he would have U 1,160 which would agree with his cash book balance.

Cash Transactions

EVERY RECEIPT OF CASH IS A DEBIT IN THE CASH BOOK AND A CREDIT IN SOME OTHER ACCOUNT.

33. CASH PAYMENTS

Cash is paid (ie it decreases) as a result of four main types of change in financial position:

(a) in settlement of an amount owed to a creditor;

(b) in exchange for another asset;

(c) as a loss; and

(d) as a loan.

The alternative types of cash payment can be shown as follows:

CASH PAYMENTS

Type of Payment	Debit	Credit
(a) Payment to a creditor	Personal account of the creditor	Cash
(b) Payment for the purchase of another asset	Real account of the asset purchased	Cash
(c) Payment as a loss or expense	Nominal account recording the particular type of loss or expense	Cash
(d) Payment as a loan	Personal account of the borrower	Cash

We will asume that Mr Kabale's business now proceeds as follows:

Jan.19 Pays U 40 to Wholesalers.
    20 Purchases new equipment for U 35.
    21 Pays expenses of U 4.
    22 Deposits U 750 with National Bank Ltd.

Jan.19

The payment of U 40 to Wholesalers brings about a reduction in liability (to Wholesalers) together with an equal reduction in assets (cash):

    DR. Wholesalers (decrease in liability).)
    CR. Cash (decrease in assets).) U 40

	Cash					1
Jan.16 To Balance	b/f	571	Jan.19 By Wholesalers	15	40
16 To F. Mayanja	13	55
17 To Equipment	3	10
17 To Commission	18	2
18 To Sales	14	22
18 To J. Mubende (loan)	5	500
		1,160

	Wholesalers Ltd					15
Jan.19 To Cash	1	40	Jan.16 By Balance	b/f	40

Jan.20

The purchase of new equipment for U 35 means that an asset (equipment) is increased and another asset (cash) is decreased by the same sum:

    DR. Equipment (increase in assets).)
    CR. CASH (decrease in assets).) U 35

	Cash					1
Jan.16 To Balance	b/f	571	Jan.19 By Wholesalers	15	40
16 To F. Mayanja	13	55	20 By Equipment	3	35
17 To Equipment	3	10
17 To Commission	18	2
18 To Sales	14	22
18 To J. Mubende (loan)	5	500
		1,160

	Equipment					3
Jan.16 To Balance	b/f	150	Jan.17 By Cash	1	10
20 To Cash	1	35

Cash Transactions

Jan.21

The payment of U 4 for expenses brings about a decrease in assets (cash) without any corresponding increase in assets or decrease in liabilities. The payment therefore results in a loss or expense which must be debited to an appropriate nominal account:

    DR. Expenses (loss or expense).)
    CR. Cash (decrease in assets).) U 4

				Cash				1
Jan.16	To Balance	b/f	571	Jan.19	By Wholesalers	15	40
16	To F. Mayanja	13	55	20	By Equipment	3	35
17	To Equipment	3	10	21	By Expenses	7	4
17	To Commission	18	2				
18	To Sales	14	22				
18	To J. Mubende (loan)	5	500				
			1,160				

			Expenses				7
Jan.21	To Cash	1	4				

Jan.22

The deposit of U 750 with National Bank Ltd is nothing more than the making of a loan to the bank. Assets (cash) decrease by U 750 and other assets (legal claims upon the National Bank) increase by exactly the same amount:

    DR. National Bank Ltd (increase in assets).)
    CR. Cash (decrease in assets).) U 750

				Cash				1
Jan.16	To Balance	b/f	571	Jan.19	By Wholesalers	15	40
16	To F. Mayanja	13	55	20	By Equipment	3	35
17	To Equipment	3	10	21	By Expenses	7	4
17	To Commission	18	2	22	By National Bank	19	750
18	To Sales	14	22				
18	To J. Mubende (loan)	5	500				
			1,160				

	National Bank Ltd						19
Jan.22	To Cash	1	750				

Every entry in the cash book has been on the credit side with equivalent debit entries in other accounts. The payment entries are all credits because they represent decreases in assets. Each payment is a reduction of existing resources of cash, and as negative resources is a credit.

    EVERY PAYMENT OF CASH IS A CREDIT IN THE CASH BOOK AND A DEBIT IN SOME OTHER ACCOUNT.

If the cash book is now balanced we shall arrive at:

	Units
DEBIT SIDE (positive)	
Original cash in hand	571
Receipts of cash	589
	1,160
Less CREDIT SIDE (negative)	
Payments of cash	829
BALANCE IN HAND	331

If the balance of U 331 is entered in the cash book it will appear as follows:

	Cash						1
Jan.16	To Balance	b/f	571	Jan.19 By Wholesalers	15	40
16	To F. Mayanja	13	55	20 By Equipment	3	35
17	To Equipment	3	10	21 By Expenses	7	4
17	To Commission	18	2	22 By National		
18	To Sales	14	22	Bank	19	750
18	To J. Mubende			22 By Balance	c/d	331
	(loan)	5	500			
			1,160			1,160
Jan.23	To Balance	b/d	331			

LOCAL AUTHORITY RECEIPTS

Type of Receipt	Debit	Credit	Class	Examples
(a) Receipt from a debtor	Cash	Personal account of the debtor	Credit Income	Rates, water charges and rent (where a debit has been raised against a person before receiving the cash).
(b) Receipt in exchange for another asset	Cash	Real account of the asset disposed of	Sale of Assets	Sale of buildings, vehicles and permanent equipment no longer required.
(In practice a little more than this simple entry is required - see later)				
(c) Receipt as a gain	Cash	Nominal account recording the particular type of gain	Cash income	Market fees, licence fees and sundry charges (where a debit has not been raised against a person before receiving the cash).
(b) and (c) Receipt for cash sales	Cash	Sales	Cash Sales	Sales of farm produce from agricultural schools.
(d) Receipt of a loan	Cash	Personal account of the lender	Loans received	Loans for capital works and for temporary purposes (See Loans Pooling Chapter 20).

LOCAL AUTHORITY PAYMENTS

Type of Payment	Debit	Credit	Class	Examples
(a) Payment to a creditor	Personal account of the creditor	Cash	1. Loan repayment 2. Sundry creditors	Repayment of principal on loans raised from government and other lenders. Payments for goods and services supplied on credit (where a credit has been raised against the suppliers before settlement – such as at the end of the year).
	(Detailed explanations will appear later.)			
(b) Payment for the purchase of an asset	Real account of the asset purchased	Cash	Capital expenditure	Purchase of vehicles and equipment. Construction of buildings and permanent works.
(c) Payment as a loss or expense	Nominal account recording the particular type of loss or expense	Cash	Revenue expenditure	Salaries, loan interest, repairs, electricity charges and expendable supplies.
(d) Payment as a loan	Personal account of the borrower	Cash	Advances and investments	Housing and car purchase loan. Investments in Government securities. Placing cash on deposit with the bank.

Cash Transactions

34. **LOCAL AUTHORITY RECEIPTS AND PAYMENTS**

    In Sections 32 and 33 the principles of the cash book have been shown in relation to a trader. These principles will, of course, apply equally to any type of business or organisation. The application of accounting principles to a local authority will be dealt with in later sections, but it will be useful at this stage to extend the tables shown in Sections 32 and 33 to cover local authority receipts and payments.

35. **BANKING ARRANGEMENTS**

    The last entry in Section 33 dealt with the deposit of U 750 by Mr Kabale in National Bank. From a book-keeping point of view we saw that this was a loan made to the bank by Mr Kabale. However, the bank is not just an ordinary borrower. Banking is a service provided to traders, public bodies, clubs, organisations and private individuals.

    A most important part of this service consists of receiving deposits of money and holding them in safe custody until required. They can then be withdrawn on demand or after notice. There are two main types of account which are available to bank customers:

    (a) Current accounts are used to receive day-to-day deposits of money. Deposits in current accounts can be withdrawn on demand and cheques can be used to transfer specified sums to the credit of other accounts in the same bank or in any other bank. By special arrangement, transfers can be made on a world-wide basis. As the money is available whenever required, generally no interest will be paid by the bank on balances in current accounts. Charges are often made to current account holders by the banks, to cover the expenses incurred in clearing (ie transferring) cheques between accounts and between banks and in recording the movement of cash coming into, or going out from the current account.

    (b) Deposit (or Savings) accounts are used to receive deposits of money for fixed periods of time. Deposits can normally only be withdrawn after a specified period of notice and cheques cannot normally be used for these accounts. Interest is earned on the balance held in a deposit account and charges are not usually made. As a variation of this system, some banks receive fixed sums of money on fixed deposit for an agreed period of time. The bank issues a deposit receipt which is surrendered upon repayment of the deposit.

    The rates of interest on deposits vary. A typical example would be where 10% is paid for a minimum period of 3 months, 10.5% for a minimum period of 9 months and 11% for a minimum period of 12 months.

    In addition to the deposit, withdrawal and cheque services shown above, banks can normally provide customers with a full range of useful services. Among these are:

    (a) temporary loans and overdrafts (by special arrangement with adequate security);

    (b) settlement of foreign debts;

    (c) safeguarding of important documents;

    (d) settlement of periodic accounts, such as subscriptions, insurance premiums, rates, water and electricity charges;

(e) making investments and collecting interest and dividends on these investments;

(f) giving expert advice on the good standing and credit-worthiness of third parties; and

(g) credit cards and mechanical cash withdrawal facilities.

36. **BANK DEPOSITS**

When a deposit is made with the bank, the cash to be deposited is taken to the bank with a completed paying-in slip. This happens, whether the deposit is made in a deposit account or in a current account. In the case of Mr Kabale's deposit on Jan.22 a paying-in slip might well have been made out in duplicate as follows:

```
                    NATIONAL BANK LTD

                                        Deposit Account No 1234

   Notes   10 U .....500    Date ..22 January 19.....
            5 U .....200
            1 U ......50    Paid into the credit of  ..P. Kabale....
   Coin   50 cents ....
          25 cents ....
          10 cents ....     ...UNITS seven hundred and fifty........
           5 cents ....
           1 cent  ....     ..........................................

                                        By..P. Kabale....(signature)
   TOTAL           750
                            Received by.....XYZ..........(initials)

                                        Bank Cashier
```

The bank cashier will take the money over the counter and having stamped one copy of the paying-in slip will return it to Mr Kabale as a receipt.

Remember that from a book-keeping point of view, Mr Kabale's Cash Book is credited (ie his cash is reduced or paid) with U 750. His personal account with the bank is debited (ie the indebtedness of the bank increases). Mr Kabale becomes a creditor of the bank and the bank becomes a debtor of Mr Kabale.

37. **BANK WITHDRAWALS**

Suppose now that Mr Kabale, on 29 Jan. wishes to withdraw U 250 from the bank. If the money is in a deposit account he will make out a withdrawal slip:

Cash Transactions

```
┌─────────────────────────────────────────────────────────────────┐
│              RECEIPT FOR WITHDRAWAL FROM DEPOSIT ACCOUNT         │
│                                                                  │
│         Deposit account No ..1234.... Date ..29 January 19....   │
│  ┌──────────────────────────┐                                    │
│  │ Notes   10 U .....200    │  Name ....P. Kabale....            │
│  │          5 U ......25    │                                    │
│  │          1 U ......20    │  Received from NATIONAL BANK LTD   │
│  │ Coin    50 cents ...5    │                                    │
│  │         25 cents ....    │  the sum of ...UNITS two hundred.. │
│  │         10 cents ....    │                                    │
│  │          5 cents ....    │  ..and fifty...............        │
│  │          1 cent  .....   │                                    │
│  │                          │  to debit my Deposit account       │
│  │ TOTAL          250       │         ...P. Kabale..  | U 250 |  │
│  └──────────────────────────┘         Signature                  │
└─────────────────────────────────────────────────────────────────┘
```

When the slip is presented to the bank cashier Mr Kabale will receive the U 250 after any period of required notice has expired.

If the money is held in a current account instead of in a deposit account Mr Kabale will draw (ie write) a cheque for the U 250 made payable to "Self" or to "Cash" and withdraw the money on demand in exchange for the cheque.

For book-keeping purposes the withdrawal represents a receipt of cash from a debtor. One asset (cash) is increased and another asset (indebtedness of the bank) is decreased:

    DR. Cash.   )
    CR. National Bank.) U 250

		Cash						1
Jan.23	To Balance	b/f	331					
29	To National Bank	19	250					

		National Bank Ltd					19
Jan.22	To Cash	1	750	Jan.29	By Cash	1	250

You will notice that the withdrawal slip requested the bank to debit Mr Kabale's account. This is because the bank itself keeps a set of accounts. When the deposit was made by Mr Kabale, the bank's cash increased and the U 750 was debited in the bank's cash book. An account for Mr Kabale was opened in the bank's ledger and the U 750 was credited in this account as an inrease in the bank's liabilities (to Mr Kabale).

By contrast, when the withdrawal took place the cash book of the bank was credited (reduction of assets) and the account of Mr Kabale was debited (reduction in bank liabilities to Mr Kabale). The accounts in the ledgers of the bank will appear as follows:

LEDGER OF NATIONAL BANK

Cash							1
Jan.22	To Mr Kabale	2	750	Jan.29	By Mr Kabale	2	250

Mr P. Kabale							2
Jan.29	To Cash withdrawal	1	250	Jan.22	By Cash deposit	1	750

Periodically Mr Kabale will receive from the bank a statement of his account. This statement is a copy of Mr Kabale's account in the ledgers of the bank. When compared with the account of the bank in the ledger of Mr Kabale the debits and credits are seen to be reversed. It will be important to remember this fact when considering bank reconciliation statements (see Section 53).

38. CURRENT ACCOUNTS

We have now considered that the relationship of a bank to a customer is that of a debtor to a creditor, and the book-keeping entries have been based upon this fact. A personal account is opened in the name of the bank concerned. Deposits are debited to the bank and withdrawals credited.

For deposit accounts the relationship is the same and the book-keeping entries in Section 36 and 37 are all that are required.

Current accounts, however, introduce a little more than the normal debtor/creditor relationship. Money paid into a current account can be withdrawn on demand at any time and, in addition, the bank can be instructed to make payments from the customer's current account. These withdrawals or payments are made by the use of cheques. Because of the widespread use of cheques for making payments and the duty of the banks to pay out balances on demand, current accounts have come to be regarded by customers as a separate supply of ready cash, administered by banks as agents.

Therefore, from now on, we can regard the cash balance as being in two parts - cash in hand and cash at the bank (current account). The bank is now regarded as a debtor only for deposit accounts. The current account will in future be looked at as a supply of cash held by the bank to be drawn upon as and when required.

Cash Transactions

39. **CHEQUES**

Payments from current accounts are normally made by cheque. A cheque is a written instruction to the banker keeping a current account. The cheque is signed by the current account holder (called the drawer) requiring the banker to pay on demand a certain sum of money to the person named on the cheque (called the payee). This gives authority for the banker to pay the money out of the drawer's account.

Here is an example of a cheque form:

734993		..30 January 19....
	NATIONAL BANK LIMITED	STAMP 3c. DUTY
Pay ......A. B. Kitasa.....	....	..or Bearer
UNITS One and cents seventy	seven...	....
		Us 1/77
....	....	....
		...P. Kabale.....

There are several important points to notice about the cheque:

Number

Cheques are consecutively numbered to enable the bank to keep a check on their issue to various customers.

Date

The banker is not permitted to make a payment from a current account before the date named upon the cheque. Cheques drawn for payment on a future date are known as "post-dated cheques" and cannot be cashed or paid in until the due date.

Bank and Branch

Cheques bear the printed name of the bank and the branch of the bank where the drawer's current account - his bank balance - is kept. It is the manager of this branch who is being instructed to pay funds out of the account.

Stamp Duty

A Government may impose a tax of say three cents on every cheque drawn. A revenue stamp for this sum is embossed upon each cheque and is paid by the customer when purchasing a cheque book from the bank.

Payee

This is the person to whom the sum named upon the cheque is to be paid. When the payee receives the cheque he pays it into his bank account by completing a paying-in slip. The cheque is then sent to the branch holding the drawer's funds and is charged by the bank against the balance in the drawer's current account.

The payee can be a person, firm or corporate body. Bearer cheques can be drawn, in addition, with words such as "Cash", "Wages" or "Petty Cash".

or Bearer

Strictly speaking these words mean that the sum named on the cheque is payable to the payee or any person to whom the payee has passed on the cheque. Legally, any person coming into possession of a "bearer" cheque can pay it into his own account without formality. In practice, many

banks will insist on certain safeguards, such as endorsement (see below). In particular, a bank will not normally pay cash over the counter in exchange for a cheque unless it is endorsed by the payee (or the drawer himself if it is made out "Pay Cash"), despite the fact that bearer cheques (by definition) do not legally require endorsement.

or Order

As an alternative to the words "or Bearer" if the cheque had been made payable to "Mr A.B. Kitasa or Order" the sum named on the cheque would be payable to Mr A.B. Kitasa or any other person at the written order of Mr Kitasa. Such a written order is made on the back of the cheque and signed by the payee. It is called an endorsement. Mr Kitasa might write for example:

```
Pay Mr Y. Kiberu or order
A.B. Kitasa
```

Usually the back of the cheque would merely be signed by Mr Kitasa with no other instructions and it would then become a bearer cheque, having been endorsed "in blank".

All cheques made payable to order must be endorsed - at least in blank before they will be honoured by a bank. There is thus a safeguard that if a cheque is stolen from a payee it is of no value to the thief unless the payee has endorsed it. On the other hand a person who steals a "bearer" cheque might be able to turn it into cash.

"Bearer" cheques are used in some developing countries because there are fewer banks and fewer people having bank accounts than in more developed countries. By contrast, in the United Kingdom for example, order cheques are used almost exclusively.

Amount

The sum to be paid must be written on the cheque in words and in figures. The words and figures must of course agree, or the bank will not honour (ie pay) the cheque.

Signature

No cheque will be honoured unless it is signed by the drawer in accordance with arrangements made with the bank. If Mr Kabale has arranged to sign P. Kabale on cheques the bank will not recognise "P.R. Kabale" or "Peter Kabale" as signatures.

Cash Transactions

Crossing

When, as in the example, two parallel lines are drawn vertically across the face of the cheque it will not be cashed by the bank. It will require to be paid into the account of the payee or bearer. Such a cheque is known as a "crossed" cheque.

In the example shown, Mr A.B. Kitasa would have to pay the cheque into his account, wherever it was kept. If the two lines (or crossing) were not made, Mr Kitasa would be able to take the cheque to the branch on which it is drawn (ie National Bank) and exchange it for cash over the counter. Such a cheque is known as an "uncrossed" or "open" cheque. It cannot normally be cashed except at the branch upon which it is drawn.

A crossing can be cancelled if the drawer writes "please pay cash" across it and signs against these words. By contrast, anyone is entitled to cross an uncrossed cheque or to add "special crossings" (see below) to cheques already crossed.

General and Special Crossings

The two lines across the cheque shown in our example constitute a general crossing. Sometimes the words "& Co" are written between the lines.

Extra protection can be given to cheques by the addition of words written between the two lines. If a "generally crossed" cheque were stolen it might eventually come into the hands of a person who had received it in good faith and given value for it. Such a person would be entitled to claim the money from the drawer, irrespective of the earlier theft.

If, however, the words "Not negotiable" are written between the lines, the cheque will be worthless to anyone who receives it after a theft whether in good faith and for value or not. The drawer is thus protected from a claim. The words do not restrict the transferability of the cheque which can still be passed from one person to another in good faith and for value.

Sometimes the words "a/c payee" are written between the crossing lines. When this occurs the banker may be liable if he pays anyone but the payee named on the cheque. In addition to the words "a/c payee" the name of a bank or even a branch of a bank may be added. Again the banker is, strictly, bound by these instructions. The cheque should only be paid at the branch or the bank named.

NOTE:

Descriptions of crossings are based on British banking practice. American cheques do not use crossings. Instead, the back of the cheque is stamped or written with the words "for deposit only". In most other respects, apart from a few details, American and British banking practice are similar.

40. **TWO - COLUMN CASH BOOK**

The cash account is usually kept in a separate bound book known as the Cash Book. Now that payments to and from a current account are also regarded in the same way as cash payments the two accounts "Cash" and "Bank" can be combined as a single account in a cash book. The various receipts and payments can be subdivided between "Cash" and "Bank" transactions by the use of columns.

Municipal Accounting for Developing Countries

To illustrate this point let us continue with the accounts of Mr Kabale. We will first see a set of transactions as they would affect a "Cash" account and a "Bank" account kept separately. We will then see the two accounts merged into a single cash book.

Suppose then that Mr Kabale's account at National Bank is a current account. We will call the "Cash" account No.1 (as before) and the "Bank" account No.1A (instead of No.19).

A trial balance taken from his books on 29 Jan. will give:

Account	No.	DR. Units	CR. Units
Cash in Hand	1	581	
Cash at Bank	1A	500	
Surplus	2		556
Equipment	3	175	
Stock	4	175	
J. Mubende - Loan	5		2,500
Shop	6	1,500	
Expenses	7	4	
L. Enders	8	270	
Nsamizi Trading Co Ltd	12		125
Sales	14		22
Commission	18		2
TOTALS		3,205	3,205

Only the accounts which have changed since the 15 Jan.19 are set out in Sections 32-37: those that have not changed can be checked back to the Balance Sheet as at 15 Jan.19 at the end of Section 29.

Mr Kabale's cash position is as follows:

Cash in Hand								1
Jan.29	To Balance	b/f	581					

Cash at Bank								1A
Jan.29	To Balance	b/f	500					

Let us suppose that Mr Kabale now trades as follows:

Cash Transactions

Jan. 30 Cash Sales U 32.
    31 Pays Nsamizi Trading Co U 125 by cheque.
Feb. 1 Cash Sales U 15.
    1 Receives cheque from L. Enders for U 150.
    2 Pays into bank U 550 in cash together with the cheque from Mr Enders.
    3 Purchases goods on credit from Wholesalers for U 75.
    4 Pays expenses U 9 in cash.
    4 Cash Sales U 21.
    4 Purchases U 40 worth of stock paying by cheque.
    6 Pays expenses U 13 by cheque.
    7 Draws U 200 in cash from the bank.

Jan. 30

The sale of stock for cash is the same type of transaction as that which took place on Jan.11 (Section 28):

    DR. Cash.   )
    CR. Sales.) U 32

Cash in Hand							1
Jan. 29	To Balance	b/f	581				
30	To Sales	14	32				

Sales							14
				Jan. 29	By Balance	b/f	22
				30	By Cash	1	32

Jan. 31

The payment of a cheque for U 125 to Nsamizi Trading Co. reduces Mr Kabale's Bank balance (asset) and reduces his liability to Nsamizi Trading Co by the same amount:

    DR. Nsamizi Trading Co.)
    CR. Bank.   ) U 125

Nsamizi Trading Co							12
Jan. 31	To Bank	1A	125	Jan. 29	By Balance	b/f	125

	Cash at Bank						1A
Jan.29	To Balance	b/f	500	Jan.31	By Nsamizi Trading Co	12	125

Feb.1

Cash sales are dealt with as before.

	Cash in Hand						1
Jan.29	To Balance	b/f	581				
30	To Sales	14	32				
Feb. 1	To Sales	14	15				

	Sales						14
				Jan.29	By Balance	b/f	22
				30	By Cash	1	32
				Feb. 1	By Cash	1	15

The receipt of the cheque is treated in the same way as a receipt of cash. The cheque is held in Mr Kabale's office until it is banked and is regarded as part of cash in hand. The "Cash at Bank" account is not affected until the cheque is banked (see later). "Cash in Hand" (asset) is therefore increased (debit) and legal claims upon Mr Enders are reduced to U 120 (reduction in assets and therefore a credit):

    DR. Cash in Hand.)
    CR. L. Enders.   ) U 150

	Cash in Hand						1
Jan.29	To Balance	b/f	581				
30	To Sales	14	32				
Feb. 1	To Sales	14	15				
1	To L. Enders	8	150				

	L. Enders						8
Jan.29	To Balance	b/f	270	Feb.1	By Cheque	1	150

Cash Transactions

Feb. 2

By making a payment into the bank Mr Kabale is decreasing one asset (Cash in Hand) and increasing another asset (Cash at Bank). The amount paid in is:

Cheque - L. Enders	150
Cash	550
	U 700

A paying-in slip for this sum will be made out in detail and taken to the bank with the money. The book-keeping entries are:

DR. Cash at Bank.)
CR. Cash in Hand.) U 700

Cash in Hand							1
Jan. 29	To Balance	b/f	581	Feb. 2	By Bank	1A	700
30	To Sales	14	32				
Feb. 1	To Sales	14	15				
1	To L. Enders	8	150				

Cash at Bank							1A
Jan. 29	To Balance	b/f	500	Jan. 31	By Nsamizi		
Feb. 2	To Cash	1	700		Trading Co	12	125

Feb. 3

The purchase of goods on credit has no effect upon Cash or Bank balances. It is dealt with as shown in Section 30:

DR. Purchases.)
CR. Wholesalers.) U 75

Purchases							11
Feb. 3	To Wholesalers	15	75				

				Wholesalers			15
				Feb.3	By Purchases	11	75

Feb.4

The payment of expenses and the treatment of cash sales have already been explained. The purchase of **U** 40 stock by cheque results in an increase in one asset (purchases) and a corresponding decrease in another (cash at bank):

    DR. Purchases.)
    CR. Cash at Bank.) U 40

After all transactions have taken place on Feb.4 the relevant accounts will appear as:

				Cash in Hand			1
Jan.29	To Balance	b/f	581	Feb.2	By Bank	1A	700
30	To Sales	14	32	4	By Expenses	7	9
Feb. 1	To Sales	14	15				
1	To L. Enders	8	150				
4	To Sales	14	21				

				Cash at Bank			1A
Jan.29	To Balance	b/f	500	Jan.31	By Nsamizi Trading Co	12	125
Feb. 2	To Cash	1	700	Feb. 4	By Purchases	11	40

				Expenses			7
Jan.29	To Balance	b/f	4				
Feb. 4	To Cash	1	9				

				Purchases			11
Feb. 3	To Wholesalers	15	75				
4	To Cash (Bank)	1A	40				

Cash Transactions

			Sales			14
		Jan.29	By Balance	b/f	22	
		30	By Cash	1	32	
		Feb. 1	By Cash	1	15	
		4	By Cash	1	21	

Feb.6

The payment of expenses by cheque results in a decrease in an asset (Cash at Bank) which is a credit entry. The resulting loss or expense is a debit to the expenses account:

    DR. Expenses   )
    CR. Cash at Bank.) U 13

		Cash at Bank			1A
Jan.29	To Balance	b/f	500	Jan.31	By Nsamizi Trading Co	12	125
Feb. 2	To Cash	1	700	Feb. 4	By Purchases	11	40
				6	By Expenses	7	13

		Expenses			7
Jan.29	To Balance	b/f	4		
Feb. 4	To Cash	1	9		
6	To Cash (Bank)	1A	13		

Feb.7

When Mr Kabale wishes to draw U 200 from the bank he makes out a cheque for "Self" (order cheque) or "Cash" (bearer cheque) and exchanges it for cash at the bank. His bank balance will decrease by the same amount as his cash balance increases:

    DR. Cash in Hand.)
    CR. Cash at Bank.) U 200

After this final transaction has taken place the two "Cash" accounts will appear as:

Municipal Accounting for Developing Countries

	Cash in Hand							1
Jan.29	To Balance	b/f	581	Feb.2	By Bank	1A	700	
30	To Sales	14	32	4	By Expenses	7	9	
Feb. 1	To Sales	14	15					
1	To L. Enders	8	150					
4	To Sales	14	21					
7	To Bank	1A	200					

	Cash at Bank							1A
Jan.29	To Balance	b/f	500	Jan.31	By Nsamizi Trading Co	12	125	
Feb. 2	To Cash	1	700	Feb. 4	By Purchases	11	40	
				6	By Expenses	7	13	
				7	By Cash	1	200	

Instead of showing the two accounts separately we shall now combine them in the form of a two-column cash book. Below is shown the state of the cash book after it has been balanced:

Date	Details	FO	Cash	Bank	Date	Details	FO	Cash	Bank
Jan.29	To Balance	b/f	581	500	Jan.31	By Nsamizi Trading Co	12		125
30	To Sales	14	32		Feb. 2	By Bank	C	700	
Feb. 1	To Sales	14	15		4	By Purchases	11		40
1	To L. Enders	8	150		4	By Expenses	7	9	
2	To Cash	C		700	6	By Expenses	7		13
4	To Sales	14	21		7	By Cash	C		200
7	To Bank	C	200			Balance	c/d	290	822
			999	1,200				999	1,200
			===	=====				===	=====
Feb. 8	To Balance	b/d	290	822					

Notice that the folio references used in the two-column cash book are the same as those which were used in the separate cash accounts. The exceptions are where cash is paid to, or withdrawn from, the bank. In these cases the letter "C" is used. It stands for "Contra" or "against" and refers to an opposite entry on the same account.

For the sake of completeness it is possible to draw up another trial balance on 8 Feb:

Cash Transactions

Account	No.	DR.	CR.
Cash	C.B.	290	
Bank	C.B.	822	
Surplus	2		556
Equipment	3	175	
Stock	4	175	
J. Mubende - Loan	5		2,500
Shop	6	1,500	
Expenses	7	26	
L. Enders	8	120	
Purchases	11	115	
Sales	14		90
Wholesalers Ltd	15		75
Commission	18		2
TOTALS		3,223	3,223

Notice that the folios for the cash accounts are now "C.B." (Cash Book) indicating that a separate book is used.

41. BANK OVERDRAFT

As already mentioned it is possible to make arrangements with the bank to allow cheques to be drawn for a larger total sum than has been deposited with the bank. When this happens, the bank balance is said to be "overdrawn". Instead of appearing as a debit balance in the cash book (representing an asset) the sum overdrawn will appear as a credit balance (representing a liability to the bank).

For example, suppose on 7 Feb. Mr Kabale had been asked to repay half of his loan from Mr Mubende U 1,250. If he had made suitable arrangements with the bank he would draw a cheque for this sum and the accounts would appear as:

Date	Details	FO	Cash	Bank	Date	Details	FO	Cash	Bank
Jan.29	To Balance	b/f	581	500	Jan.31	By Nsamizi Trading Co	12		125
30	To Sales	14	32		Feb. 2	By Bank	C	700	
Feb. 1	To Sales	14	15		4	By Purchases	11		40
1	To L. Enders	8	150		4	By Expenses	7	9	
2	To Cash	C		700	6	By Expenses	7		13
4	To Sales	14	21		7	By Cash	C		200
7	To Bank	C	200		7	By J. Mubende	5		1,250
	To Balance	c/d		428		By Balance	c/d	290	
			999	1,628				999	1,628
Feb.8	To Balance	b/d	290		Feb. 8	By Balance	b/d		428

				J. Mubende - Loan				5
Feb.7	To Cash	C.B	1,250	Jan.29	By Balance	b/d	2,500

NOTE:

It must be emphasised that bank balances may not be overdrawn without prior arrangement with the bank. To do otherwise is a breach of contract with the bank and may also become a criminal offence. Technically, in American banking practice overdrafts are not used. Instead, a separate line of credit is opened which may be triggered to cover overdrafts arising in the current (checking) account. The loans are usually transferred in round sums of (say) U 50 - U 100. The practical effect is much the same as an overdraft.

4. Journals and Subsidiary Records

Section		Page
42.	Further Notes on Debit and Credit.	88
43.	Sources of Book-Keeping Information.	90
44.	Prime Records and Documents.	92
45.	Journals.	94
46.	The Main Journal.	95
47.	Journalising.	97
48.	Ledger and Journal.	97
49.	Special Purpose Journals.	97
50.	Analysis of Gains and Losses.	100
51.	Alternative Form of Ledger Ruling.	106
52.	Combined Paying-In Book.	108
53.	Bank Reconciliation.	110

42. FURTHER NOTES ON DEBIT AND CREDIT

An accountant must be able to tell the difference between debits and credits. We have already noted that the classification of book-keeping entries into debit and credit entries depends upon the nature of the transactions. There is a fundamental difference between entries dealing with assets and liabilities and those dealing with gains and losses.

In RULE 2 of Section 15 it was pointed out that every change in financial position is recorded by debit and credit entries of equal value. It is from this rule that we get the term "double-entry book-keeping".

It is possible to say, in many cases, that the double entry reflects the "giving" and "receiving" of a benefit. Indeed, it is almost certain that the original purpose of book-keeping was to reflect the "giving" and "receiving" aspect of every commercial transaction. Modern book-keeping is designed to do much more than this, leading to the more complicated rules of procedure already illustrated. Nevertheless the traditional rules of "giving" and "receiving" may enable readers to see book-keeping from a slightly different angle.

If anything is given, it must also be received by someone else.

Let us consider the transactions in Section 17 from the angle of giving and receiving.

Jan. 1

Mr P. Kabale starts business with U 500 in cash. The cash account is debited because cash is received. The surplus account is regarded as being credited in the name of "P. Kabale - Capital" as it is he who has given the money to the business.

Jan. 2

Equipment is purchased for U 150 cash. The equipment account is debited because equipment is received. The cash account is credited as cash has been given.

Journals and Subsidiary Records

The remainder of the entries can be regarded as follows:

Date	Receiving Account (DEBIT)	Giving Account (CREDIT)
Jan.3	Stock (worth U 300)	Cash
4	Cash U 2,000	J. Mubende (who gives the cash)
5	Shop (worth U 1,500)	Cash
6	Expenses (see below)	Cash
8	L. Enders (who receives U 210 worth of goods)	Sales (the goods go out of the business at a selling price of U 210)

On Jan.6, expenses are paid in cash. It is easy to see how cash is given but not so easy, perhaps, to understand how expenses are received. It can be explained by the fact that expenses are paid for services received. For example if the expense was "wages" it could be said that the trader had received a service to the value of the wages paid.

In a local authority, cash is paid to provide services to the public. For example in the case of a payment for road repairs the cash account (which gives) is credited and a "road repairs" account is debited because the public receives the benefit of repairs to the roads.

It is not possible, however, to extend the "giving" and "receiving" principle to every aspect of book-keeping and it is because of this that readers are urged to follow the basic rules, which do cover all aspects.

The main difficulty in a universal application of the "giving" and "receiving" principle comes in nominal accounts where it is possible to incur an expense or loss without receiving any benefit. To continue the example of a local authority, if cash is paid for salaries it is easy to see that a salaries account can be debited. The public receives service, to the value of salaries, from the officials to whom salaries are paid. However, if cash is lost or stolen from the cash office and cannot be recovered, the cash account must be credited with the sum involved (because it is equivalent to being paid or given). An expense (loss of cash) account must be debited with the loss but no benefit whatever is received by the public. Quite the contrary - the public has suffered a loss!

An additional table of rules will perhaps assist readers to combine the "giving" and "receiving" principle (where it applies) with the rules already given.

Type of Account	Dealing With	Debit	Credit
1. Personal	Debtors and Creditors	Receiver	Giver
2. Real	Assets	What is received (e.g. purchased or cash received)	What is given (e.g. goods sold or cash paid)
3. Nominal	Gains and Losses	Expenses or losses	Gains or profits

43. **SOURCES OF BOOK-KEEPING INFORMATION**

In previous chapters we have been posting ledger accounts with the details of given transactions. We have not yet given much thought as to where the original information comes from.

Consider again the transactions in Section 17 of Chapter 2. The number of dealings are so few that Mr Kabale could probably enter them in his ledger as they took place. But what is to happen if he is busy in his shop serving many customers? He will probably prefer to write up his books later, during a quiet period. He may even employ a clerk to keep his books for him.

The person who posts the ledger will need some basic record from which he can work. A trader cannot be expected to remember every transaction in a busy day. The simplest thing is for Mr Kabale to keep a brief daily record of his transactions as they occur, without concerning himself with the correct ledger entries at the time. Such a record is called a journal. The journal (or day-book) would be ruled as:

Date	Details	FO	DR.	CR.

At the time of the transaction Mr Kabale will concern himself only with the first two columns, giving the date and details of any event which will change his financial position. For the transactions in Section 17 he might well have written:

Journals and Subsidiary Records

Date	Details	FO	DR.	CR.
Jan.1	I began business with U 500 in cash			
Jan.2	I purchased equipment for U 150 in cash			
Jan.3	I purchased stock for U 300 in cash			
Jan.4	I borrowed U 2,000 from J. Mubende			
Jan.5	I bought shop premises for U 1,500 cash			
Jan.6	I paid U 25 cash for expenses			
Jan.8	I sold goods to Mr L. Enders on credit for U 210			

Mr Kabale now has a record of his dealings in diary form. He or his book-keeper will later decide which accounts in the ledger are affected by each transaction and the journal will be entered up ready for posting.

A person who fully understands debits and credits might well complete Mr Kabale's journal as follows:

Date	Details	FO	DR.	CR.
Jan.1	I began business with U 500 in cash		Cash	Capital
Jan.2	I purchased equipment for U 150 in cash		Equipment	Cash
Jan.3	I purchased stock for U 300 in cash		Purchases	Cash
Jan.4	I borrowed U 2,000 from J. Mubende		Cash	J. Mubende
Jan.5	I bought shop premises for U 1,500 cash		Shop	Cash
Jan.6	I paid U 25 cash for expenses		Expenses	Cash
Jan.8	I sold goods to Mr L. Enders on credit for U 210		L. Enders	Sales

The process of correctly entering up the two right-hand columns is known as journalising the transactions. This is a most important aspect of the work of an accountant, and will be referred to again later.

When journalising has been completed the journal represents a complete record of dealings from which the ledger can be posted. The value of the journal can be seen by tracing the journal entries in this section to the ledger accounts in Section 18. (Note that entries have now been made in "Purchases" and "Sales" accounts -to comply with the principles stated in Section 29.)

44. **PRIME RECORDS AND DOCUMENTS**

The journal shown above is a basic form of prime or first record, or book of original entry. It is a rule of book-keeping that there must be a prime record to support every ledger entry. Nowadays this prime record is not necessarily in the form of a book. It may well be a document or group of documents. These are known as prime documents.

Because of the number of business transactions which now take place, the journal shown in Section 4 is unsuitable to use for day-to-day trading transactions. Other records are now used and special kinds of journal have developed for particular classes of transaction (eg sales journal, purchases journal, expenditure journal). The main journal or journal proper is now used only for opening and closing the books and for making adjustments. It is written up in a much more formal manner than the one illustrated in Section 43.

Journals and Subsidiary Records

The two basic forms of prime documents are:

(a) Invoices (and copy invoices)

(b) Receipts (and copy receipts).

An invoice is a statement of goods supplied or services rendered on credit. It is normally made out at least in duplicate. Here is an example of a simple invoice:

PO Box 165,		INVOICE	No.1
		P. KABALE	
		General Merchant	
DR. ...L. ENDERS...PO Box 1537.............................			
19 Jan.8	To 20 Tables @ 5.00 10 Desks @ 7.50 10 Chairs @ 3.50		Units 100.00 75.00 35.00 ───── 210.00 ======

The original invoice will be given to the purchaser (Mr L. Enders) as his record. A copy will be used by Mr Kabale as a prime document giving all information necessary to:

(a) Debit the personal account of L. Enders

(b) Credit the sales account.

A receipt is a certificate that a stated amount of cash has been received by the person who gives the receipt. This also is made out at least in duplicate. Here is an example of a simple receipt:

PO Box 165,	RECEIPT	No.1
	P. KABALE	
RECEIVED WITH THANKS FROM ...J. Mubende......................		
THE SUM OF ..two thousand units............................		
....		
U 2,000 ...... ===============	SIGNED ....P. Kabale..........	
DATE ...Jan.4 19...		

The original receipt will be handed to the payer (Mr J. Mubende) as his evidence of payment to Mr Kabale. A copy will be used by Mr Kabale as a prime document giving the required information to:

(a) Debit the cash book

(b) Credit the personal account of J. Mubende.

When cash sales take place, traders often issue to customers a cash sales note, which is a combined invoice and receipt. Then, at the end of the day, the copy sales notes should agree in total with the cash in the till. A cash register is a modern way of recording cash sales. This machine automatically totals the sales as they occur. The trader can then use the information to:

(a) Debit the cash book

(b) Credit the sales account.

We have seen how copies of prime documents are used as a source of information by the person who issued them. The original documents can be used by the persons to whom they were issued.

A person receiving an invoice will use it as a prime document to:

(a) Debit the purchases account

(b) Credit the supplier of goods (ie the creditor).

A person who is given a receipt will use it as a prime document to:

(a) Debit the proper nominal account or personal account

(b) Credit the cash book.

Increasingly, nowadays, many prime records may be electronic entries in a computer. However, it is still necessary for documents to be prepared (invoices and receipts) to deal with the interface between a business and its customers. The use of computers for the initiation and storage of prime records raises important questions regarding security of data and program. These matters will not be further considered here. Prime documents will normally be designed to provide inputs to or outputs from computers, where used.

45. **JOURNALS**

In Section 43 we saw how the original purpose of a journal was to provide a detailed record of each transaction. Section 44 showed how this detailed record can now more easily be provided by documents. Posting of ledger accounts from documents is sometimes known as the "slip system of posting".

The purpose of the modern journal is to classify financial information for easy posting to the ledger.

The basic ruling of a journal is shown in Section 43. This ruling can be used in two ways; for a main journal or for a special purpose journal.

Journals and Subsidiary Records

46. THE MAIN JOURNAL

The main journal is used to record:

(a) opening entries in the ledger;
(b) transfers between accounts;

(c) adjustment of errors;

(d) items not recorded in another prime record (eg purchase of fixed assets on credit; writing off a bad debt); and

(e) entries required for closing the ledger and for preparation of final accounts.

The layout of the journal is:

Date	Details	FO	DR.	CR.
(a)	(b)	(c)	(d)	
	(e)	(f)		(g)
	(h)			

The items which make up each entry are:

(a) date;

(b) account to be debited;

(c) ledger folio of account debited;

(d) amount of the debit;

(e) account to be credited;

(f) ledger folio of account credited;

(g) amount of the credit; and

(h) the narration, or explanation.

Consider the preparation of the trading account in Chapter 2 Section 28, page 45. The entries are transfers between accounts, connected with the preparation of final accounts. It would be correct to enter them in the main journal as follows:

Date	Details	FO	DR.	CR.
Jan.15	Sales Account DR. To Trading Account Being transfer of sales for the period to the trading account	14 16	198	198
Jan.15	Trading Account DR. To Stock Account Being transfer of opening stock to the trading account	16 4	150	150
Jan.15	Trading Account DR. To Purchases Account Being transfer of purchases for the period to the trading account	16 11	165	165
Jan.15	Stock Account DR. To Trading Account Being transfer of closing stock (valued at cost) to the trading account	4 16	175	175

For the transfer of the gross profit from the trading account to the profit and loss account (page 47) the journal entry would be:

Date	Details	FO	DR.	CR.
Jan.15	Trading Account DR. To Profit and Loss Account Being gross profit transferred to profit and loss account	16 17	58	58

When making journal entries a particular conventional style is used. You will notice that the debit entry begins at the left-hand margin, whilst the credit entry is inset; the symbol "DR" is used against the right-hand margin for the debit entry whereas "CR" is not used for the credit entry; the credit entry is preceded by the word "To" but the debit entry is not; the narration always begins with the word "being" and each entry is ruled off.

Journals and Subsidiary Records

47. JOURNALISING

Although not every transaction is now recorded in the journal, an accountant must visualise the theoretical journal entries for every change in financial position. He must be able to journalise.

48. LEDGER AND JOURNAL

The two basic records of book-keeping are the ledger and the journal. The ledger is a set of books containing a balancing system of accounts: the cash book is an integral part of the whole ledger system. The journal is used to classify and explain the changes in financial position before they are recorded in the ledger.

The actual form of the ledger and the journal can be adapted to suit the needs of a particular organisation. The two-column cash book is a variation of the basic form of ledger account. Many other variations can be made to both ledger and journal, provided the accounts comply with the principles of double-entry.

49. SPECIAL PURPOSE JOURNALS

The main journal classifies each financial change into its debit and credit aspects. Each debit and each credit is separately posted to the ledger.

Special purpose journals can be used to speed up book-keeping. Information is classified to enable a number of entries to be posted to the ledger in a single total instead of individually.

Consider credit sales. Each one changes the financial position as follows:

>   DR. Purchaser.
>   CR. Sales.

Each debit entry must be posted to an individual personal account but all credit entries will be entered in the same sales account. A properly designed journal will provide for all sales for a period to be posted in total to the ledger as a single figure.

Such a record would be known as a sales journal and might be entered up as follows:

SALES JOURNAL

			Units	Units
Jan.1	J. Mukasa 3 bicycles @ U 17.50 6 tyres @ .75 cents	26	52.50 4.50 ———	57.00
Jan.1	P. Kirya 10 cycle wheels @ U 3.50 10 tyres @ .75 cents 10 tubes @ .25 cents	24	35.00 7.50 2.50 ———	45.00
Jan.1	M. Obone 3 radio sets @ U 20 30 records @ U 1	28	60.00 30.00 ———	90.00
Jan.1	R. Mubanda 10 bicycles @ U 18.75	25		187.50
Jan.1	B. Kabeho 20 cycle wheels @ U 4 2 radio sets @ U 19 1 record player @ U 15	22	80.00 38.00 15.00 ———	133.00 ——— 512.50 ====== (L.5)

The example shows a trader's credit sales for one day. Customers will be individually debited with the total value of goods sold to them. The folio number of each personal account is entered in the journal against the sum posted.

At the end of the day the main column of the journal is totalled and a single sum of U 512.50 is credited to the sales account. (No.5).

Had each transaction been dealt with separately there would have been ten ledger postings. There would have been five individual debits to personal accounts and five credits to the sales account. By using a sales journal (sometimes known as a sales book or sales day book) only six entries are required in the ledger. Ledger posting is therefore cut by almost one-half.

By the proper use of copy invoices, book-keeping work can be further reduced. Each entry in the sales journal shown above gives full details of each sale. This information already appears on the copy of each invoice prepared at the time of sale.

Journals and Subsidiary Records

Copy invoices can be filed in numerical order and only the total of each one need appear in the sales journal. It would then appear like this:

				35
Date	Invoice Number	Name	FO.	Amount
				Units
Jan.1	2491	J. Mukasa	26	57.00
	2492	P. Kirya	24	45.00
	2493	M. Obone	28	90.00
	2494	R. Mubanda	25	187.50
	2495	B. Kabeho	22	133.00
				512.50
				======
				L.5.

Notice that there is still enough information with which to make the five postings to personal accounts and the single posting to the sales account.

As a further extension of the principle of reducing book-keeping work to a minimum, the personal accounts could be posted direct from the copy invoices. The sales account total would then be obtained by listing the invoice totals.

It must be noted that the elimination of records can increase the scope for error and fraud unless proper safeguards are introduced. This fact will be referred to later in this book.

After posting, the ledger accounts would appear as follows:

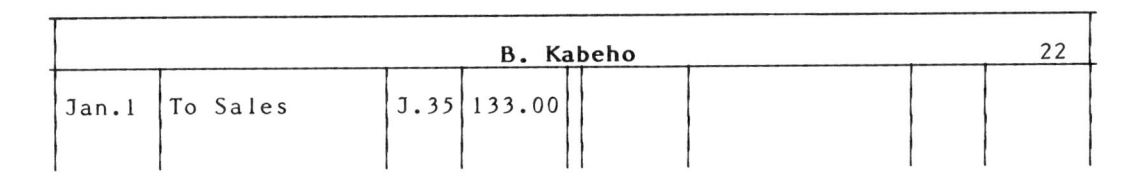

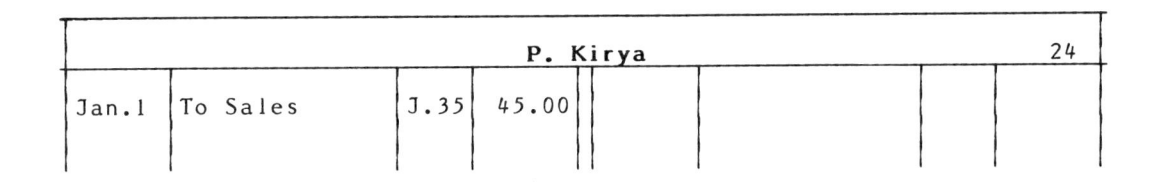

		B. Kabeho				22
Jan.1	To Sales	J.35	133.00			

		P. Kirya				24
Jan.1	To Sales	J.35	45.00			

		R. Mubanda				25
Jan.1	To Sales	J.35	187.50			

				J. Musaka			26
Jan.1	To Sales	J.35	57.00				

				M. Obone			28
Jan.1	To Sales	J.35	90.00				

				Sales			5
				Jan.1	By Sundry Persons	J.35	512.50

The same principles apply to other special journals. Credit purchases would be dealt with by the use of a purchases journal.

Every credit purchase involves the entry:

    CR. Seller (personal account).
    DR. Purchases.

A purchases journal would be in the same form as the sales journal shown above. Had this example been a purchases journal the various individual entries would have been credited to the personal accounts of suppliers and the total **U 512.50** debited to the purchases account.

50. ANALYSIS OF GAINS AND LOSSES

The excess of assets over liabilities is known as net resources. When net resources increase, the result is a gain. When net resources decrease, the result is a loss.

In a trading business, the main type of gain is called "gross profit". This comes about by selling goods for more than they cost. Goods of a certain value are exchanged for cash (or rights to cash) of greater value, bringing about an increase in net resources.

The main losses which occur in a trading business consist of "expenses". Cash is paid (or debts are incurred) thus reducing assets or increasing liabilities. No assets are received in exchange and net resources are reduced, causing the loss or expense.

Until now, we have regarded "expenses" as a single item. However, any person interested in the progress of his business will wish to know how much he has spent upon each type of expense. He will wish to know how much he has spent upon (say) wages, stationery, carriage, electricity, water and other expenses.

Journals and Subsidiary Records

One way of discovering this information would be to make lists of the appropriate items by selecting them in turn from the expenses account at the end of the financial period.

Suppose the "expenses" account of Mr J. Burundi for the month of May was as follows:

		Expenses					25
19 May 1	To Wages	C.B.	25	19 May 31	By Profit and Loss Account		261
2	To Carriage	C.B.	4				
4	To Water	C.B.	6				
4	To Electricity	C.B.	19				
5	To Carriage	C.B.	3				
8	To Wages	C.B.	25				
10	To Stationery	C.B.	19				
15	To Repairs	C.B.	13				
16	To Wages	C.B.	26				
16	To Stationery	C.B.	13				
18	To Carriage	C.B.	7				
21	To Repairs	C.B.	45				
23	To Wages	C.B.	23				
23	To Stationery	C.B.	1				
23	To Carriage	C.B.	6				
27	To Stationery	C.B.	1				
31	To Wages	C.B.	25				
			261				261
			===				===

The double entry would be complete as sums totalling U 261 would appear as credits in the cash book (not illustrated here). Had any expenses been incurred on credit, the personal account of the creditor would have been credited, instead of the cash book.

As in previous examples a single total for "expenses" would be posted to the profit and loss account:

DR. Profit and Loss Account.)
CR. Expenses Account.   ) U 261

The profit and loss account is the summary of gains and losses for a financial period. It would be helpful to Mr Burundi if the figure of U 261 could be analysed over different types of expense. From his "expenses" account, Mr Burundi could extract figures as follows:

Wages	Carriage	Water and Electricity	Stationery	Repairs
25	4	6	19	13
25	3	19	13	45
26	7		1	
23	6	25	1	58
25		==		==
	20		34	
124	==		==	
===				

Municipal Accounting for Developing Countries

From this information a summary could be prepared as follows:

Wages	124
Carriage	20
Water and Electricity	25
Stationery	34
Repairs	58
TOTAL	U 261

The profit and loss account could now be written up in greater detail, giving better information about the running of the business.

The method of analysis shown here is not a good one. It has two distinct disadvantages:

(a) if there were a large number of expense items the work of extraction and listing would be a difficult and time-consuming process; and

(b) the analysis is carried out on a sheet of paper as a memorandum record outside the book-keeping system.

These two disadvantages conflict with two important aims of any good book-keeping system:

(a) a book-keeping system should always be arranged so that clerical work and the possibility of mistake are reduced to a minimum; and

(b) all book-keeping should take place as part of an integrated system in which accounts are interlocked through double-entry.

It is not sufficient for main accounts to be kept on a double-entry system with details in memorandum form. All accounts, including cost accounts, should be capable of being balanced together as an integrated whole.

This can be achieved by opening a separate account in the ledger for each type of expense which is required to be separately shown in the final accounts.

In the above example, Mr Burundi might well open separate accounts for:

(a) wages;

(b) carriage;

(c) water and electricity;

(d) stationery; and

(e) repairs.

Journals and Subsidiary Records

His accounts (assuming his expenses were paid in cash) would appear as follows:

				Cash			51
(The balance brought forward and various receipts would appear on the DEBIT side)				19 May 1	By Wages	31	25
				2	By Carriage	32	4
				4	By Water	33	6
				4	By Electricity	33	19
				5	By Carriage	32	3
				8	By Wages	31	25
				10	By Stationery	34	19
				15	By Repairs	35	13
				16	By Wages	31	26
				16	By Stationery	34	13
				18	By Carriage	32	7
				21	By Repairs	35	45
				23	By Wages	31	23
				23	By Stationery	34	1
				23	By Carriage	32	6
				27	By Stationery	34	1
				31	By Wages	31	25

				Wages			31
19 May 1	To Cash	C.51	25				
8	To Cash	C.51	25				
16	To Cash	C.51	26				
23	To Cash	C.51	23				
31	To Cash	C.51	25				

				Carriage			32
19 May 2	To Cash	C.51	4				
5	To Cash	C.51	3				
18	To Cash	C.51	7				
23	To Cash	C.51	6				

				Water and Electricity			33
19 May 4	To Cash (Water)	C.51	6				
4	To Cash (Elect)	C.51	19				

				Stationery				34
19 May	10	To Cash	C.51	19				
	16	To Cash	C.51	13				
	23	To Cash	C.51	1				
	27	To Cash	C.51	1				

				Repairs				35
19 May	15	To Cash	C.51	13				
	21	To Cash	C.51	45				

NOTE: The folio reference C.51 (or C.B.51) indicates that the credit entry is on page 51 of the cash book.

At the end of the financial period the balances in the various expense accounts will be separately transferred to the profit and loss account as follows:

				Wages				31
19 May	1	To Cash	C.51	25	19 May	31	By Profit and Loss	45	124
	8	To Cash	C.51	25					
	16	To Cash	C.51	26					
	23	To Cash	C.51	23					
	31	To Cash	C.51	25					
				124					124

				Carriage				32
19 May	2	To Cash	C.51	4	19 May	31	By Profit and Loss	45	20
	5	To Cash	C.51	3					
	18	To Cash	C.51	7					
	23	To Cash	C.51	6					
				20					20

Journals and Subsidiary Records

		Water and Electricity						33
19 May 4	To Cash (Water)	C.51	6		19 May 31	By Profit and Loss	45	25
4	To Cash (Elect)	C.51	19					
			25 ==					25 ==

		Stationery						34
19 May 10	To Cash	C.51	19		19 May 31	By Profit and Loss	45	34
16	To Cash	C.51	13					
23	To Cash	C.51	1					
27	To Cash	C.51	1					
			34 ==					34 ==

		Repairs						35
19 May 15	To Cash	C.51	13		19 May 31	To Profit and Loss	45	58
21	To Cash	C.51	45					
			58 ==					58 ==

		Profit and Loss				45
19 May 31	To Wages	31	124		(The gross profit trans-	
31	To Carriage	32	20		ferred from	
31	To Water and Electricity	33	25		the trading account would	
31	To Stationery	34	34		appear on the	
31	To Repairs	35	58		CREDIT side)	

If the gross profit for the month had been (say) U 425 the completed profit and loss account would appear as follows:

			Profit and Loss				45
19 May	31	To Wages	31	124	19 May 31	By Gross Profit transferred from Trading Account	
	31	To Carriage	32	20			
	31	To Water and Electricity	33	25			
	31	To Stationery	34	34			
	31	To Repairs	35	58			425
	31	To Net Profit transferred to Capital Account	1	164			
				425			425

The figures in the profit and loss account are, of course, the same as they would have been if they had been extracted from a single "expenses" account. In the present case, however, analysis takes place automatically as the work proceeds, in accounts which themselves form part of the integrated double-entry system.

The way in which the accounts were analysed would depend entirely upon the wishes of the management. If required, "water" could have been separated from "electricity" or "carriage" could have been combined with "stationery".

The rule is that a separate nominal account should be opened in the ledger for every item of expenditure which is to be separately shown in the profit and loss account.

A non-profit making organisation would keep separate nominal accounts for each item of expenditure (and income - see later) which will be separately shown in the income and expenditure account.

A local or public authority would keep separate accounts for each item of expenditure and income to be shown in the revenue account. This means that a separate nominal account must be kept for each item in the budget, and for each item for which further detailed analysis is required.

51. **ALTERNATIVE FORM OF LEDGER RULING**

Until now, we have considered ledger accounts in conventional form. There is a line down the centre of each account which separates the debit and credit sides. This is often referred to as a "T" Account.

When a balance of any account is required, it is necessary to make separate totals of debit and credit sides and subtract the smaller total from the greater. This practice can be inconvenient if balances are required otherwise than at the end of a financial period.

Journals and Subsidiary Records

A bank, for example, wishes to have an almost continuous knowledge of the balances on a customer's account. If information about balances was not promptly available there would be a danger of accounts becoming overdrawn without proper approval.

An organisation operating a system of budgetary control (eg a local authority) will wish to have up-to-date information about balances on nominal accounts. Without this information, budget allowances could become overspent.

The form of ledger account which will give up-to-date balances after every posting is as follows:

Date	Details	FO	Debit		Credit		Balance	
			Units	Cts.	Units	Cts.	Units	Cts.

This form of ledger page is particularly suitable for use with accounting machines and computers, which will normally calculate the balances automatically after each posting.

Consider the transactions shown in the two-column cash book in Section 41 Chapter 3. It has already been explained that the bank will have in its ledgers a personal account for Mr Kabale. This account will almost certainly be kept in the form shown above and would appear as follows:

P. KABALE - CURRENT A/C   485

			DR. Units	CR. Units	Bal. Units
Jan. 29	Balance				500 (CR)
31	Nsamizi Trading Co		125		375 (CR)
Feb. 2	Cash			700	1,075 (CR)
4	Victory Ltd		40		1,035 (CR)
6	Expenses		13		1,022 (CR)
7	Cash		200		822 (CR)
7	J. Mubende		1,250		428 (DR)

Remember that the account is in the form in which it would appear in the books of the bank. Its entries will be made from the point of view of the bank. Cheque payments or cash withdrawals will decrease the bank's liability to Mr Kabale and by rule 4 Section 15 his account will be debited. Deposits of cash will increase the bank's liability to Mr Kabale and his account will be credited. Whenever Mr Kabale has funds deposited at the bank his account at the bank will have a credit balance. His own cash book will show the bank balance as a debit, because the bank is his debtor and therefore an asset.

When the bank balance is overdrawn, the accounting position is reversed. Mr Kabale becomes a debtor to the bank (ie his account has a debit balance). The bank becomes a creditor of Mr Kabale (ie the "bank" column of his cash book has a credit balance).

The figures in the "balance" column are indicated (DR) or (CR) in our example. Sometimes credit balances will be shown in black ink and debit (ie overdrawn) balances in red ink.

It is usual with this type of ledger form to show normal balances in black and abnormal balances in red. As we have seen, with a bank current account, normal balances are credits (in hand) and abnormal balances are debits (overdrawn). With expenditure accounts, however, a normal balance would be a debit (ie expenditure or loss) whilst an abnormal balance would be a credit (ie income or gain).
NOTE:

We must take care not to confuse the theory of accountancy with the loose terms often used by non-professionals. People talk of being "in the red" when overdrawn and because of this, red ink has become associated with debits. The accountant normally uses red ink to indicate minus quantities whether debit or credit. Cash in hand is sometimes referred to as being "in credit". This is, of course, incorrect when referring to one's own cash book.

A bank statement received from the bank will be an exact copy of the account at the bank. When being compared with the cash book it must be remembered that the debits and credits will be reversed.

The transactions shown above have been assumed to have been recorded by the bank on the same dates as the entries appeared in Mr Kabale's cash book. In practice this would not be the case because cheques paid to other people would not reach Mr Kabale's bank until several days later.

This point is important when we consider bank reconciliation (see Section 53).

52. COMBINED PAYING-IN BOOK

Many banks use a form of paying-in book which combines the deposit of cash and cheques. Cash can always be immediately credited to the account of a depositor. Cheques, on the other hand, will often not be credited to a depositor's account until cleared; that is, until it is known that the drawer's account has sufficient funds.

A paying-in slip might appear as follows:

Journals and Subsidiary Records

```
┌─────────────────────────────────────────────────────────────────┐
│                    CURRENT ACCOUNT                               │
│                                                                  │
│                    BARCLAYS BANKS LTD                            │
│                                                                  │
│                                        ......24 May 19.......    │
│                                                                  │
│    CREDIT .......J. Mukasa...............                        │
│                                                                  │
│    ...PO Box 1658.......................                         │
│                                                                  │
```

		Units	Cents
	.10 units	-	-
Notes	..5 units	10	-
	..1 unit	4	-
Coins	.50 cents	1	50
	.25 cents	1	25
	.10 cents	-	-
	..5 cents	-	85
	..1 cent	-	-
	TOTAL CASH	17	60
Cheques, Postal and Money Orders:			
D. Omari		1	83
J. Smith		3	76
National Government		6	66
	Units	29	85

The form would be made out in duplicate. The bank clerk would stamp and sign one copy indicating that cash had been received and that cheques had been forwarded for clearance.

In the example shown, 17.60 in cash would be credited to Mr W.J. Mukasa on 24 May. The cheques totalling 12.25 might not be credited until (say) 28 May, after they had been cleared. This point must be remembered when dealing with bank reconciliation statements.

Many banks will nowadays credit cheques immediately to a depositor's account. Any cheques which fail to get clearance will later be redebited to the depositor.

Cheques may not be cleared for several reasons. Among these are

(a) The drawer has died since writing the cheque

(b) The drawer has instructed his banker not to pay (ie the cheq has been stopped)

(c) There are insufficient funds in a drawer's account

(d) The cheque may be incorrectly made out - though this will normally be noticed by the receiving cashier.

If a cheque cannot be cleared the banker controlling the account upon which it is drawn will return it to the receiving banker, usually marked R/D (refer to drawer). This means that the person who paid the cheque in should contact the person from whom he received it and ask for an explanation.

If there is an irregularity on the cheque it will probably be indicated, such as:

"words and figures disagree"
"not signed"
"post-dated".

53. BANK RECONCILIATION

When any business is operating a current account every transaction which affects the bank will appear not only in the cash book of the organisation but also in its account at the bank.

In theory a statement received from the bank will agree in detail with every entry made in the bank column of the cash book, (except that debits and credits are reversed).

In practice, the cash book entries will not be made at exactly the same time as the corresponding entries in the bank account. There are several reasons for this:

(a) **Unpresented Cheques**

A cheque will always be entered in the bank column of the cash book before it is given or sent to the payee. It will appear in the bank account only when it has been received and cleared by the bank.

(b) **Uncleared Effects**

Cheques will be debited in the bank column of the cash book on the day they are banked. The bank, as already explained, may not be prepared to credit them in the bank account until they are cleared.

(c) **Bank Charges**

Often a bank will debit charges to a customer's account without informing the customer at the time. Such charges represent payments and are treated in the same way as if a cheque had been drawn in favour of the bank. They must therefore appear as credits in the cash book.

(d) **Direct Debits**

These are payments which may have been made by the bank on instructions from the customer. Until the customer is aware that the payment has actually taken place he cannot make the credit entry in the bank column of the cash book. If the bank has given immediate credit for uncleared cheques, any cheque subsequently dishonoured will be dealt with as a direct debit.

(e) **Direct Credits**

Sometimes money is received direct by the bank for credit to a customer's account. This may happen, for example, where collectors have made direct bankings away from head office. The cash book cannot be debited until the customer is aware of the receipt.

Before accurate accounts can be prepared, the cash book must be agreed with the bank statement (ie with the customer's account at the bank). Every entry in the cash book is checked off against the corresponding entry in the bank statement as far as possible. Then a statement is prepared, setting out all items of disagreement in such a way that the bank balance is reconciled (ie agreed) with the cash book balance.

Journals and Subsidiary Records

As an example, let us assume that a trader, Mr J. Mukasa has entries in his cash book for the first week of April as follows:

19			CASH	BANK	19			CASH	BANK
Apr.1	To Balance	b/f	25	219	Apr.1	By J.Musoke	59		28
1	To Sales	2	73		2	By Bank	C	73	
2	To Cash	C		73	3	By B.Odwara	65		69
2	To Sales	2	184		3	By V.Onaba	68		29
3	To J.Smith	31		24	3	By K.Rutega	72		45
4	To Cash	C		184	4	By Bank	C	184	
4	To Sales	2	126		5	By Bank	C	126	
4	To B.Juma	26		3	6	By Cash	C		25
5	To Cash	C		126	6	By D.Omari	66		140
6	To Bank	C	25		6	By Wages	19	25	
6	To Sales	2	41		6	By Balance	c/f	66	293*
			474	629				474	629

Cash Book 28

* For the purpose of comparing his present cash book balance with the bank statement it is likely that a temporary bank balance will be entered in pencil at this stage. It must be emphasised that the correct balance cannot be inserted until after the cash book has been reconciled with the bank statement.

The bank statement received from the bank might appear as follows:

NATIONAL BANK LTD

Mr J Mukasa,
PO Box 1658,

Date	Details	DR.	CR.	Bal.
Apr.1	Balance			263 (CR)
2	Cash		73	336 (CR)
3	R. Bunyoni	29		307 (CR)
4	J. Musoke	28		279 (CR)
4	Cash		184	463 (CR)
5	D. Kibule	15		448 (CR)
5	Cash		126	574 (CR)
6	Dishonoured Cheque (E. Lobo)	2		572 (CR)
6	B. Odwara	69		503 (CR)
6	V. Onaba	29		474 (CR)
6	Cash (Wages)	25		449 (CR)
6	Charges	1		448 (CR)
6	Branch Sales		30	478 (CR)
6	Rent (Bankers order)	5		473 (CR)
6	J. Smith		24	497 (CR)

Municipal Accounting for Developing Countries

For the sake of illustration we will assume the following:

(a) Cheques received and banked on the same day are entered directly in the bank column of the cash book.

(b) Cheques of over 2 units in value will not be credited to a customer's account until cleared, unless the drawer is of first-class reputation (eg government cheques).

Mr Mukasa must now check his bank statement against the bank column of the cash book as a preliminary step to the preparation of a bank reconciliation statement.

He will notice that the opening balances disagree. The bank statement shows a balance of U 263 which is U 44 more than the cash book figure of U 219. He knows from a previous reconciliation statement that two cheques drawn in March were unpresented at 31 March:

	Units
R. Bunyoni	29
D. Kibule	15
	44

These cheques, having now been presented, have been included in the bank statement on 3 and 5 of April respectively. Mr Mukasa will tick them off against the March cash book entries.

Mr Mukasa can then tick off entries which appear in both cash book and bank statement for April. When he has done this, the records will appear as:

Cash Book 28

19			CASH	BANK	19			CASH	BANK
Apr.1	To Balance	b/f	25	219	Apr.1	By J.Musoke	59		28/
1	To Sales	2	73		2	By Bank	C	73	
2	To Cash	C		73/	3	By B.Odwara	65		69/
2	To Sales	2	184		3	By V.Onaba	68		29/
3	To J.Smith	31		24/	3	By K.Rutega	72		45
4	To Cash	C		184/	4	By Bank	C	184	
4	To Sales	2	126		5	By Bank	C	126	
4	To B.Juma	26		3	6	By Cash	C		25/
5	To Cash	C		126/	6	By D.Omari	66		140
6	To Bank	C	25		6	By Wages	19	25	
6	To Sales	2	41		6	By Balance	c/f	66	293
			474	629				474	629

112

Journals and Subsidiary Records

	NATIONAL BANK LTD			
Mr J. Mukasa, PO Box 1658,				

Date	Details	DR.	CR.	Bal.
Apr.1	Balance			263 (CR)
2	Cash		73 /	336 (CR)
3	R. Bunyoni	29 /		307 (CR)
4	J. Musoke	28 /		279 (CR)
4	Cash		184 /	463 (CR)
5	D. Kibule	15 /		448 (CR)
5	Cash		126 /	574 (CR)
6	Dishonoured Cheque (E. Lobo)	2		572 (CR)
6	B. Odwara	69 /		503 (CR)
6	V. Onaba	29 /		474 (CR)
6	Cash (Wages)	25 /		449 (CR)
6	Charges	1		448 (CR)
6	Branch Sales		30	478 (CR)
6	Rent (Bankers order)	5		473 (CR)
6	J. Smith		24 /	497 (CR)

Items not marked off are as follows:

(a) **In the Cash Book**

   (1) Debit side - B. Juma U 3

   This is a cheque paid in but not yet credited by the bank.

   (2) Credit side - K. Rutega U 45
                  - D. Omari U 140

   These are cheques sent to K. Rutega and D. Omari which have not yet been presented for payment at Mr Mukasa's bank.

(b) **In the Bank Statement**

   (1) Debits - Dishonoured cheque E. Lobo U 2

   This is a cheque which (not being for more than U 2) was immediately credited to Mr Mukasa - probably in March. It has not been paid by Mr Lobo's bank and so the former credit entry in Mr Mukasa's accounts has to be reversed.

      - Charges U 1

   These are payable by Mr Mukasa to the bank for operating his account.

      - Rent (Bankers order) U 5

This is a payment made by the bank acting upon standing instructions of Mr Mukasa.

(2) Credit - Branch Sales U 30

This is a sum collected by a branch shop. It was probably paid in at a branch of the bank, for the credit of Mr Mukasa.

A preliminary bank reconciliation statement can now be drawn up as follows:

BANK RECONCILIATION STATEMENT

		Units	Units
Bank balance as per bank statement			497
Add	Cheque paid in and not credited (B. Juma)		3
Add	Payments not in cash book:		
	Dishonoured Cheque (E. Lobo)	2	
	Charges	1	
	Rent (Bankers order)	5	8
			508
Less	Unpresented Cheques:		
	K. Rutega	45	
	D. Omari	140	
		185	
Less	Receipts not in cash book:		
	Branch Sales	30	215
Bank Balance as per cash book			293

Items appearing in the bank statement which have not yet appeared in the cash book must now be entered in it. The cash book is a complete record of all cash and bank transactions affecting Mr Mukasa's business.

It must also be remembered that the cash book is part of a double-entry system of accounting. Any entry made in the cash book must have a complementary entry in another account:

1. The dishonoured cheque from Mr E. Lobo must be treated as a credit in the cash book because assets (bank balances) have been decreased. Mr Lobo again becomes a debtor for the amount of the cheque. His account is debited:

    DR. E. Lobo.   )
    CR. Cash (Bank).   ) U 2

2. The Charges represent an expense payable by Mr Mukasa to the bank. The cash account must be credited (reduction in assets) and a nominal account - bank charges - debited as a loss or expense:

    DR. Bank Charges.   )
    CR. Cash (Bank).   ) U 1

Journals and Subsidiary Records

3. The rent payment also represents an expense and should be dealt with as follows:

>   DR. Rent (Nominal Account).)
>   CR. Cash (Bank).) U 5

4. The cash paid in by the branch represents "sales" and should be dealt with in the normal manner for cash sales:

>   DR. Cash (Bank).)
>   CR. Sales) U 30

When these entries have been made the cash book and other accounts will appear as:

Cash Book 28

19			CASH	BANK	19			CASH	BANK
Apr.1	To Balance	b/f	25	219	Apr.1	By J.Musoke	59		28
1	To Sales	2	73		2	By Bank	C	73	
2	To Cash	C		73	3	By B.Odwara	65		69
2	To Sales	2	184		3	By V.Onaba	68		29
3	To J.Smith	31		24	3	By K.Rutega	72		45
4	To Cash	C		184	4	By Bank	C	184	
4	To Sales	2	126		5	By Bank	C	126	
4	To B.Juma	26		3	6	By Cash	C		25
5	To Cash	C		126	6	By D.Omari	66		140
6	To Bank	C	25		6	By Wages	19	25	
6	To Sales	2	41		6	By E. Lobo	51		2
6	To Sales (Branch)	2		30	6	By Bank Charges	85		1
					6	By Rent	89		5
					6	By Balance	c/f	66	315
			474	659				474	659
			===	===				===	===
Apr.6	To Balance	b/f	66	315					

Sales 2

					Apr.6	By Cash	28	30

E. Lobo 51

Apr.6	To Cash (Dis. cheque)	28	2				

115

				Bank Charges			85
Apr.6	To Cash	28	1				

				Rent			89
Apr.6	To Cash	28	5				

You will notice that the cash book has now been completed by the inclusion of the final entries.

It can only now be properly balanced and ruled off.

A final reconciliation can now be drawn up as a permanent record. It may be written upon a spare page of the cash book or in a special reconciliation book. It will now include only cash book entries which do not appear in the bank statement:

BANK RECONCILIATION

	Units	Units
Bank balance as per bank statement		497
Add Cheque paid in and not credited (B. Juma)		3
		500
Less Unpresented cheques:		
K. Rutega	45	
D. Omari	140	185
Bank balance as per cash book		315

NOTE:

It does not matter whether the bank statement figure or cash book figure is used first. The above procedure is preferred as it results in a final figure which is in agreement with the accounts being prepared. If the cash book balance were used first in the above example, unpresented cheques would be added and uncleared credits deducted.

The following simple rules may be a useful guide:

(a)   always begin with the bank balance (in hand or overdrawn);

(b)   always add before subtracting; and

(c)   group similar items together.

These two proforma statements may prove a guide in preparing bank reconciliation statements:

Journals and Subsidiary Records

Example 1 (Bank balance in hand)

		Units	Units
Bank balance (in hand) as per statement			x
Add	Deposits not yet cleared:		
	A	x	
	B	x	x
Add	Payments not in cash book:		
	Dishonoured cheques	x	
	Charges	x	
	Bank interest paid	x	
	Direct debits	x	x
			x
Less	Unpresented cheques:		
	A	x	
	B	x	
	C	x	
			* x
(μ) Less	Receipts not in cash book:		
	Direct credits	x	
	Bank interest received	x	x
Bank balance (in hand) as per cash book			x

* If this becomes an overdrawn balance the final adjustment (μ) will be added instead of subtracted.

Example 2 (Bank balance overdrawn)

		Units	Units
Bank balance (overdrawn) as per statement			x
Add	Unpresented Cheques:		
	A	x	
	B	x	
	C	x	x
Add	Receipts not in cash book:		
	Direct credits	x	
	Bank interest received	x	
			x
Less	Deposit not yet cleared:		
	A	x	
	B	x	
			* x
(μ) Less	Payments not in cash book:		
	Dishonoured cheques	x	
	Charges	x	
	Bank interest paid	x	
	Direct debits	x	x
Bank balance (overdrawn) as per cash book			x

* If this becomes a balance in hand the final adjustment (μ) will be added instead of subtracted.

5. Errors and Adjustments

Section		Page
54.	Types of Error.	119
55.	Disagreement of the Trial Balance.	126
56.	Correction of Errors.	127
57.	Suspense Account.	127
58.	Stock Valuation.	134
59.	Marshalling.	134

54. **TYPES OF ERROR**

Complete book-keeping is based upon a system of double-entry (ie every debit entry has a corresponding credit entry or entries) and total debits should always be equal to total credits. The trial balance is the method used to prove that the books as a whole are in balance (ie that total debits equal total credits). The trial balance cannot prove the accuracy of all entries in a set of books because certain errors will not affect the state of balance.

An error which equally affects total debits and total credits will not be detected when a trial balance is prepared. An error which affects only one side of a double entry (debit or credit) will prevent the books balancing. This error will be shown up by a trial balance because the total debits will not equal the total credits.

Errors fall into two categories:

(a) Error of commission (ie making or committing an error) - where a posting is made which should not have been made or where a posting is made incorrectly.

(b) Error of omission - where a posting which should have been made has not been made.

Errors of either type may be further subdivided as follows:

   (i) Error of principle - which will affect the overall financial position of the organisation resulting in the understatement or overstatement of surpluses, deficits, income or expenditure as well as wrongly stating assets and/or liabilities in the balance sheet.

   (ii) Clerical error - which will affect the detailed records of the book-keeping system without mis-stating the financial position.

A further type of error is the:

Compensating error - which is one of two or more separate mistakes which by coincidence cancel out each other so that the books appear to be correct because the trial balance balances.

TABLE OF TYPES OF ERROR

Type of Error	Example	Effect on trial balance (T/B) and final accounts (F/A)	Possible method of detection
A. Commission 1. Principle (a) Capital expenditure treated as revenue expenditure.	Commerce Purchase of equipment for U 25 debited to "purchases".	T/B - no effect F/A - gross and net profit understated by U 50. Balance sheet understates equipment by U 50.	Difficult to detect by normal accounting procedures. Large errors may be detected by comparative statistics of profit ratios and by a skilled inspection of the balance sheet (e.g. by comparison of asset account with inventory of equipment).
	Public authority Construction of a dispensary for U 500 debited to "repairs".	T/B - no effect F/A - revenue account surplus understated by U 500. Balance sheet understates fixed assets by U 500.	By comparison of accounts with revenue and capital budgets and by skilled inspection of the balance sheet (eg by comparison of capital account with register of fixed assets or insurance register).
(b) Cash receipts credited to incorrect class of account.	Commerce Receipt of U 12 from A. in settlement of his account credited to "sales".	T/B - no effect F/A - gross profit will be overstated by U 12. Balance sheet will overstate assets (debtors) by U 12.	Will be brought to light when a reminder is sent to A. to settle his account.

Type of Error	Example	Effect on trial balance (T/B) and final accounts (F/A)	Possible method of detection
	Public authority 1. Receipt of U 24 from A. in settlement of rates is credited to "rate income account" instead of to his personal account	T/B - no effect F/A - rate income will be overstated by U 24 in the revenue account. Balance sheet will overstate assets (debtors) by U 24.	Will be brought to light when a reminder is sent to A. to settle his account.
	2. Receipt of a loan of U 2,500 is credited to an income account.	T/B - no effect F/A - income will be overstated by U 2,500 or if set off against capital expenditure the asset will not appear in the balance sheet. In either event liabilities are understated by U 2,500.	As the sums involved are usually very large the error will be detected by examination of the balance sheet. It will also be revealed when the lender asks for repayment, or doesn't receive the interest.
2. Clerical (a) Cash receipts posted to credit of wrong personal account.	U 43 received from A. is credited to B.	T/B - no effect F/A - no material effect	Will be brought to light when a reminder is sent to A. to settle the balance of his account, or by B's account showing an unusual credit balance.
(b) Posting of expenditure to debit of wrong nominal account.	U 33 for "wages" debited to "electricity and water" account.	T/B - no effect F/A - U 33 wrongly allocated within the profit and loss or revenue account. No effect on overall profit or surplus.	Rather difficult to detect - may be detected by comparison with budget. Large sums more likely to be detected than small sums. May be prevented by insistence that well-qualified and senior staff check the analysis of expenditure and income.

Type of Error	Example	Effect on trial balance (T/B) and final accounts (F/A)	Possible method of detection
(c) Incorrect figure listed in the trial balance.	The debit balance on the wages account of U 180 is listed in the trial balance as U 108.	T/B - debit side will be U 72 short.	Checking extraction of figures from ledger to trial balance.
(d) Incorrect totalling and balancing of ledger account.	The debit side of the account of a debtor is undercast by U 10 thus reducing the balance carried forward.	T/B - debit side will be U 10 short.	Checking additions in all ledger accounts.
(e) Incorrect carrying forward of totals from the foot of one ledger page to the top of the next.	A sub-total of U 187 in a repairs account is carried forward to a new page as U 178.	T/B - debit side will be U 9 short.	Checking all carrying forward of sub-totals in the ledger (note that the error of U 9 divides by 9 - this gives a clue to an error of transposed figures).
(f) Posting an amount to the wrong side of the same account.	A receipt of cash of U 12 from A. is debited to his account, instead of being credited.	T/B - debit side will be U 12 over and the credit side U 12 short - giving a total difference of U 24 (ie twice the amount of the error).	Divide the error by two and search the ledger for an obvious amount - otherwise every ledger posting must be checked.
(g) Error in giving a receipt.	A receipt for a cash remittance of U 503 is made out for U 3.	T/B - no effect - but cash will fail to balance (unless it is fraud!)	1. If an accidental error, the cashier will discover that he is U 500 "over" when he "cashes up".

Type of Error	Example	Effect on trial balance (T/B) and final accounts (F/A)	Possible method of detection
			2. If a fraud (ie the cashier steals the U 500), the payer may complain about his receipt or (if good internal check is in force) will complain when a reminder is sent to him to settle the balance of his account.
(h) Error in making out an invoice (or in posting an invoice to an account).	An invoice for U 24 is made out for U 34 (this may be due to an arithmetical error in calculating prices or charges).	T/B - no effect. (The personal account of the debtor will be debited with the incorrect amount of U 34 - the sales or income account will be credited with U 34.)	Normally such an error can only be discovered by checking the invoice itself or by checking total of individual invoices against an independent control debit. A debtor may, however, complain if he is overcharged.

(NOTE: Errors g. and h. are sometimes known as errors of original entry)

B. Omission

1. Principle

Type of Error	Example	Effect on trial balance (T/B) and final accounts (F/A)	Possible method of detection
(a) Complete omission of journal adjustments.	1. Wages of U 500 incurred for capital expenditure has not been transferred from wages account to the debit of the asset concerned.	T/B - no effect F/A - profit or surplus will be understated by U 500 because revenue expenditure has been overstated. The asset will be understated by U 500 on the balance sheet.	By comparison of accounts with the revenue and capital budgets.

Type of Error	Example	Effect on trial balance (T/B) and final accounts (F/A)	Possible method of detection
	2. Irrecoverable debts of U 18 are not written off.	T/B - no effect F/A - profit or surplus will be overstated by U 18. The balance sheet will overstate assets (debtors) by U 18.	Should be discovered by an independent follow-up of unpaid accounts.
(b) Complete omission of outstanding accounts of certain creditors at the end of a financial period. (Or non-payment of a charge during the year).	Unpaid accounts totalling U 528 have not been debited to nominal accounts or credited to personal accounts of creditors (OR to a creditors control account).	T/B - no effect F/A - profit or surplus will be overstated by U 528 as various items of expenditure totalling this sum have been omitted. The balance sheet will understate liabilities (creditors) by U 528.	1. By comparison of expenditure accounts with the budget. 2. By a proper control over the system of ordering goods and services under the control of a chief financial officer, or by customer complaints.
(c) Complete omission of an invoice from the books or failure to make out an invoice for a debt due.	1. An account for U 18 sent to B. is not posted to the debit of his personal account nor credited to an income account. 2. No account is made out for a charge of U 18 due from C.	T/B - no effect F/A - income (and therefore surplus) will be understated by U 18 in profit and loss or revenue account. The balance sheet will understate assets (debtors) by U 18.	Very difficult to detect if a proper system of internal control is not in operation. In the case of (1) it may come to light when the debtor pays and in the case of (2) if he asks to pay.

(NOTE: All the above are errors of complete omission)

Type of Error	Example	Effect on trial balance (T/B) and final accounts (F/A)	Possible method of detection
2. Clerical (a) Complete omission of cash receipt from the books.	No receipt is issued for cash paid by A. of U12.	T/B - no effect - but cash will fail to balance (unless fraud).	1. If an accidental error, the cashier will discover that he is U 12 over when he "cashes up". 2. If a fraud (ie the cashier steals the money) the payer may complain about not getting a receipt or (if good internal check) will complain when a reminder is sent to him to settle his account.

Municipal Accounting for Developing Countries

The Table in this section gives examples of various types of error together with possible methods of detection. The Table deals with:

(a) Errors of commission

    (i) Errors of Principle

    (ii) Clerical Errors.

(b) Errors of omission

    (i) Errors of Principle

    (ii) Clerical Errors.

Compensating errors occur when any error, including those referred to in this Table, is prevented from upsetting the trial balance by the effect of another error. Note that each error in a set of two or more compensating errors falls into one of the other classes.

Although errors are, for convenience, classified, it is more important to be able to detect and recognise an error and to be able to correct it. In practice, an accountant would waste little time in attempting to classify an error; he would be more concerned to correct it and to discover others. The above classification, although helpful, is somewhat arbitrary and even accountants cannot always agree whether a particular error is of one type or another. The classification should be used only as a guide.

55. DISAGREEMENT OF THE TRIAL BALANCE

If the ledger as a whole is not in balance, the trial balance will not agree. The debit total will not be the same as the credit total. When this occurs the following steps should be taken in an attempt to discover the error.

(a) Cast again the trial balance itself, to ensure that totals have been added correctly.

(b) Subtract one total from the other to discover the amount of the difference.

(c) Look quickly through the ledger for an obvious error equal to the amount of the difference. Sometimes a ledger figure will be omitted in error from the trial balance.

(d) Halve the amount of the difference. The resulting amount will perhaps represent a posting to the wrong side of the ledger (ie a debit posted as a credit or vice versa).

(e) Check individual balances from the ledger to the trial balance. If the difference is divisable by nine it may be that figures have been transposed (eg a ledger balance of 23.50 is included in the trial balance as 25.30).

(f) Check the totals and balances on each ledger account by again casting debit and credit sides and paying particular attention to sub-totals carried forward from one page to another. Transposition of figures is a common error (eg 253.20 at the foot of one page is carried forward as 523.20 to the top of the next).

Errors and Adjustments

(g) If the errors have still not been detected the double entry of individual ledger postings must be checked. This is often a laborious job, but there is usually no alternative when other methods of attempting to find the error have failed to reveal it.

NOTE: Although it is sometimes possible to discover quickly an obvious error by the procedures given above, experience shows that too much time is wasted in searches for specific amounts, instead of pursuing detailed checking.

56. CORRECTION OF ERRORS

When an error has been made which is immediately discovered, the incorrect figure should be neatly crossed out with a single line and the correct figure inserted above it. Errors discovered subsequently must be adjusted by journal entries.

57. SUSPENSE ACCOUNT

It is sometimes necessary to make an entry in a suspense account. A suspense account should normally only be used to keep the ledger system in balance whilst a decision is made about the correct treatment of a doubtful item. Entries in suspense accounts should be cleared as quickly as possible to their correct accounts. Ideally suspense account balances should not appear in balance sheets.

If a remittance has been received, but there is no accompanying indication for which account it is intended, it is permissible to use a "Suspense Account". For example, let us suppose that on 3 May Mr P. Nimule sends by post to Kambale Municipal Council a cheque for U 3 without information about the nature of the payment. The cheque should be banked in the normal way and will therefore appear as a debit in the cash book. To complete the double entry a suspense account could be opened and credited with the amount of the cheque.

Cash (Bank)						1
19 May 3	To Suspense (P. Nimule)	2	3			

Suspense						2
			19 May 3	By Cash (P. Nimule)	1	3

On 7 May it is ascertained that the U 3 was in payment of water charges. The payment must therefore be posted to the credit of Mr P. Nimule (personal account) in the water consumers ledger. The suspense account is cleared by the debit. The relevant journal entry would be made as follows:

| 19 May 7 | Suspense Account DR. To P. Nimule Account Being receipt from P. Nimule (receipt No....) placed in suspense on 3 May 19... and now transferred to correct account. | | 2 3 | 3 | | 3 |

The ledger accounts would appear as:

		Suspense						2
19 May 7	To P. Nimule	J.1	3	19 May 3	By Cash (P. Nimule)	1	3

	P. Nimule - Water Consumer					3
			19 May 7	By Suspense	J.1	3

The amount of the difference in a trial balance is sometimes recorded in a suspense account whilst a search is made for errors.
In this way the suspense account is used as a starting point for the subsequent correction of errors through the journal.

Consider the following trial balance:

TRIAL BALANCE

Account	FO	DR. Units	CR. Units
Capital	1		1,000
Sales	2		766
Purchases	3	621	
Equipment	4	750	
Stock	5	162	
Debtors: A. Lule	6	3	
B. Musoke	7	8	
C. Mukasa	8	4	
Creditors: M. Ongira	9		13
Y. Lumufu	10		25
Rent	11	40	
Electricity	12	3	
Carriage	13	2	
Cash	C.B.	209	
		1,802	1,804

Errors and Adjustments

It will be seen that there is a difference. Credits exceed debits by U 2. A suspense account could be opened with a debit entry of this amount and the trial balance, including the suspense account debit, would agree.

Suspense

19 June 30	To Difference on trial balance	2	

TRIAL BALANCE

Account	FO	DR. Units	DR. Units
Capital	1		1,000
Sales	2		766
Purchases	3	621	
Equipment	4	750	
Stock	5	162	
Debtors: A. Lule	6	3	
B. Musoke	7	8	
C. Mukasa	8	4	
Creditors: M. Ongira	9		13
Y. Lumufu	10		25
Rent	11	40	
Electricity	12	3	
Carriage	13	2	
Cash	C.B.	209	
Suspense	15	2	
		1,804	1,804

It is important to note that the suspense account is not used to clear the difference but merely to hold it (in suspense) until it can be cleared by discovery of errors.

Let us suppose that a subsequent check of the ledger reveals the following mistakes:

(a) cash receipt U 2 has been credited to the account of A. Lule instead of to B. Musoke;

(b) the purchases journal has been over-added by U 7;

(c) new equipment costing U 50 has been debited to "purchases";

(d) a cash payment of U 7 to Y. Lumufu has been credited to his account, instead of being debited; and

(e) a rent payment of U 11 has been debited in the rent account as U 16.

The errors can now be corrected using journal entries to clear the suspense account and to bring the books into balance.

(a) The amount of U 2 credited to A. Lule instead of to B. Musoke has not upset the trial balance. Any adjustment will therefore not affect the suspense account. All that is required is for the U 2 to be debited to A. Lule and credited to B. Musoke.

(b) The amount of U 7 over-added in the purchases journal has resulted in "purchases" being over by U 7 in the trial balance. The error is adjusted by crediting purchases with U 7 and debiting the suspense account.

(c) The U 50 equipment debited to purchases has not upset the trial balance. An adjustment is required crediting the purchases account and debiting the equipment account.

(d) The sum of U 7 has been posted to the wrong side of an account. This has caused the trial balance to disagree by twice the amount of the error (ie U 14). It is adjusted by debiting U 14 to Y. Lumufu and crediting the suspense account (ie U 7) to clear the wrong credit and U 7 to record the correct debit).

(e) The rent payment of U 11 debited as U 16 means that rent has been overstated by U 5. The trial balance is U 5 over on the debit side. The error is adjusted by crediting the rent account by U 5 and debiting the suspense account.

After all adjustments have been made, the journal, ledger and correct trial balance will appear as:

Errors and Adjustments

JOURNAL

19					
June 30	A. Lule DR. To B. Musoke Being correction of error – receipt posted to the credit of A. Lule instead of B. Musoke.	6 7	2	2
June 30	Suspense DR. To Purchases Being correction of error – purchases journal over-added.	15 3	7	7
June 30	Equipment DR. To Purchases Being correction of error – capital expenditure wrongly treated as "purchases".	4 3	50	50
June 30	Y. Lumufu DR. To Suspense Being correction of error – payment of U 7 credited to Y. Lumufu instead of being debited.	10 15	14	14
June 30	Suspense DR. To Rent Being correction of error – U 16 debited to rent account instead of U 11.	15 11	5	5

LEDGER

(adjusted accounts only)

Purchases								3
19 June 30	To Balance *	b/f	621	19 June 30 30 30	By Suspense By Equipment By Balance	J J c/d	7 50 564
			621				621
June 30	To Balance	b/d	564				

Equipment 4

19				19			
June 30	To Balance *	b/f	750	June 30	By Balance	c/d	800
30	To Purchases	J	50				
			800				800
June 30	To Balance	b/d	800				

A. Lule 6

19				19			
June 30	To Balance *	b/f	3	June 30	By Balance	c/d	5
30	To B. Musoke	J	2				
			5				5
June 30	To Balance	b/d	5				

B. Musoke 7

19				19			
June 30	To Balance *	b/f	8	June 30	By A. Lule	J	2
				30	By Balance	c/d	6
			8				8
June 30	To Balance	b/d	6				

Y. Lumufu 10

19				19			
June 30	To Suspense	J	14	June 30	By Balance *	b/f	25
30	To Balance	c/d	11				
			25				25
				June 30	By Balance	b/d	11

Errors and Adjustments

Rent								11
19 June 30	To Balance *	b/f	40	19 June 30 30	By Suspense By Balance	J c/d		5 35
			40 ==					40 ==
June 30	To Balance	b/d	35					

Suspense								15
19 June 30 30	To Difference on trial balance To Purchases To Rent	 J J	2 7 5	19 June 30	By Y. Lumufu	J		14
			14 ==					14 ==

* In practice the balances used for the trial balance, marked * will have been entered in the ledger in pencil.

TRIAL BALANCE

Account		FO	DR. Units	CR. Units
Capital		1		1,000
Sales		2		766
Purchases		3	564	
Equipment		4	800	
Stock		5	162	
Debtors:	A. Lule	6	5	
	B. Musoke	7	6	
	C. Mukasa	8	4	
Creditors:	M. Ongira	9		13
	Y. Lumufu	10		11
Rent		11	35	
Electricity		12	3	
Carriage		13	2	
Cash		C.B.	209	
			1,790 =====	1,790 =====

58. STOCK VALUATION

Before final accounts of an organisation are prepared it is often necessary to value the stock of goods or expendible materials. This is done by stocktaking at the close of business on the last day of the financial period or as soon as possible afterwards. A stocktaking list is prepared as follows:

Item	Price Units	Number	Value Units
A	35.00	10	350
B	11.00	8	88
C	5.00	5	25
D	2.50	150	375
E	0.25	824	206
F	8.00	25	200
G	13.50	2	27
H	10.00	40	400
	TOTAL VALUE OF STOCK		1,671

The prices used for the valuation of stock will normally be the cost prices of the goods or materials, that is, the prices at which they were purchased. Other methods of valuation are sometimes used and these will be referred to later in the book.

59. MARSHALLING

It has already been shown that the balance sheet is a statement of the financial position of an organisation at a point in time.

The financial position can be stated in the form:

Net resources = Net results.

Which is another way of saying:

Assets minus liabilities = Surpluses minus deficiencies.

The balance sheet re-states the position as:

Surplus plus liabilities = Assets plus deficiencies.

BALANCE SHEET

SURPLUS + LIABILITIES	ASSETS + DEFICIENCIES

To arrive at the financial position, the balance sheet classifies and summarises the balances remaining in the books after final accounts have been prepared. The logical classification of balances is known as "marshalling" and follows two main rules:

Errors and Adjustments

(a) Assets, liabilities, surpluses and deficiencies are grouped separately.

(b) Assets and liabilities are arranged in order of permanence or liquidity.

A simplified layout of a commercial balance sheet, with assets and liabilities arranged in order of permanence, might be:

Balance Sheet as at

	Units		Units
CAPITAL		FIXED ASSETS	
LONG-TERM LIABILITIES		Land	
Mortgage Loans		Buildings	
CURRENT LIABILITIES		Equipment	
Cash Overdrawn		INVESTMENTS	
Sundry Creditors		CURRENT ASSETS	
		Stock	
		Sundry Debtors	
		Cash	
	=====		=====

Notice that assets are listed starting with the most permanent (land) and finishing with the least permanent (cash). Assets which would not normally be sold or exchanged in day-to-day trading transactions are called fixed assets. Current assets are those which are continuously circulating during normal business activity.

Long-term liabilities are those which do not require immediate settlement, as opposed to current liabilities which are expected to be settled within a short time of being incurred.

Sometimes, as in the case of banks, an organisation will wish to emphasise its liquidity, that is the ease with which assets can, if necessary, be turned into cash. The balance sheet will then be presented in the order of liquidity:

Balance Sheet as at

	Units		Units
CURRENT LIABILITIES		CURRENT ASSETS	
Sundry Creditors		Cash	
Cash Overdrawn		Sundry Debtors	
LONG-TERM LIABILITIES		Stock	
Mortgage Loans		INVESTMENTS	
CAPITAL		FIXED ASSETS	
		Equipment	
		Buildings	
		Land	
	=====		=====

Municipal Accounting for Developing Countries

A simplified layout of a local authority or public utility balance sheet (arranged in order of permanence) might be:

Balance Sheet as at

	Units	Units		Units	Units
LONG-TERM LIABILITIES			FIXED ASSETS		
Loans Outstanding			Land		
CURRENT LIABILITIES			Buildings		
Creditors			Permanent Works		
Temporary Loans			Equipment		
Cash Overdrawn	___		CURRENT ASSETS		
PROVISIONS			Stocks		
Renewals Funds			Debtors		
Repairs Funds	___		Investments		
OTHER BALANCES			Cash	___	
Capital Discharged			OTHER BALANCES		
Sinking Funds			Deferred Charges		
Capital Receipts			Revenue Account		
Unapplied			Deficiency	___	
Reserve Accounts					
Revenue Account					
Surplus	___				
		___			___
		=====			=====

Notice that assets and liabilities are arranged in much the same way as for commercial balance sheets. The "other balances" on the left hand side represent accumulated surpluses and those on the right hand side are accumulated losses.

For presentation purposes balance sheets may take many different formats, for example see narrative balance sheet (page 238). Presentation will not affect accounting principles.

6. Simple Non-Profit Accounts

Section		Page
60.	The Cash Book as a Prime Record.	138
61.	Receipts and Payments Book-Keeping.	140
62.	Analysis of Cash Book.	144
63.	The Imprest System.	149
64.	The Abstract System.	151
65.	Conversion of Single-Entry to Double-Entry (Basic Principles).	151
66.	Analysis of Surplus.	165
67.	Complete Set of Accounts.	165
68.	Conclusion.	189

60. THE CASH BOOK AS A PRIME RECORD

One of the most important accounts in the ledger system is the cash account. Its importance lies in the fact that it records all dealings affecting money. Cash is an asset and is treated in the double-entry system like any other asset:

(a) increases (receipts) are DEBITS; and

(b) decreases (payments) are CREDITS.

Because cash transactions are so numerous the cash account is often kept in a special book, called the CASH BOOK which forms part of the double-entry system.

Cash, however, is a different kind of asset from others in the ledger.

Its value lies in the assets or services which it can buy. Economists suggest that the uses of cash are:

(a) as a means of exchange;

(b) as a measure of value;

(c) as a store of value;

(d) as a measure of indebtedness.

(a) Means of Exchange

Assets can be sold for cash, which can in turn be used to purchase new assets or services.

(b) Measure of Value

The science of accountancy deals with many aspects of business life. These the accountant seeks to express in a common measure of value - cash.

(c) Store of Value

Savings in the form of bank deposits and investments are measured in terms of cash.

Simple Non-Profit Accounts

(d) **Measure of Indebtedness**

Debts which are owed to us or those which we owe to others are expressed in cash values - although the indebtedness may arise, for example, through the supply of equipment, goods, labour or services.

Because of the importance of cash it is usually the first thing to be recorded. Even the ordinary man is concerned with how much cash he has. His only exercise in accounting may be to count his supply of cash from time to time to discover whether he has enough for his immediate needs. If he wishes to advance further in his records he must keep a cash book. Receipts of cash will be recorded as debits and payments of cash, as credits. Periodically he will balance his book and the debit balance should agree with the cash in his pocket. A simple example might appear as:

Cash Book

19			Units	19			Units
Apr.1	To Balance	b/f	8	Apr.3	By Food		7
	To March Salary		25	5	By Tax		3
13	To Sale of Garden Produce		2	9	By Electricity		2
				17	By Savings		5
17	To Repayment of loan made to R. Musoke in March		3	25	By Bicycle		17
				30	By Balance	c/d	4
			38				38
			==				==
May 1	To Balance	b/d	4				

Notice that he has concerned himself only with the "cash" aspect of his transactions. There is no system of double-entry book-keeping, as the cash book is sufficient for his needs. He will count his cash of **U 4** on 30 April and be satisfied if it agrees with his cash book. The cash book has recorded various kinds of receipts as debits. His payments, whether for expenses (electricity and tax), consumable stores (food), capital equipment (bicycle) or investments (savings), have all been treated in the same way - as credits in the Cash Book.

If asked for a statement of his financial position, this man might be satisfied to say that he had **U 4** in cash. Of course, a complete double-entry system of book-keeping would reveal that he owned a bicycle (valued at cost) worth **U 17** and might perhaps also indicate that he owed **U 2** for water charges; that a friend owed him **U 1**; that the tax payment was in arrears and he still owed **U 5** for the current year.

A complete double-entry system is not necessary here. He is, in fact, keeping his accounts on the "receipts and payments" or "single-entry" system. The cash book does not, in this case, act as part of a ledger system but forms a basic record from which, if necessary, a complete set of accounts could be drawn up.

Municipal Accounting for Developing Countries

In the same way, almost all organisations, including traders, clubs, companies, local authorities and public bodies, can use a cash book as a basic record. The extent to which cash book entries are used for the preparation of further information depends upon the nature and size of the organisation. The small club or trader or a local or public authority in its early stages of development, may be satisfied to use the information in the cash book to produce a statement of "receipts and payments". A more mature organisation will use the cash book as part of a complete double-entry system or as a basis for preparing a complete set of double-entry accounts. It is quite possible for an accountant to take a cash book as his basic record and by combining it with certain other information, convert the statement of "receipts and payments" to an account of "income and expenditure". Such a process is sometimes called "converting single-entry to double-entry" and it is a recognised short-cut in the science of accountancy.

A statement of receipts and payments deals only with cash received and cash paid. An income and expenditure account (or revenue account) takes into account income due (or accrued) and expenditure incurred, even though some of the income and expenditure may not, at the time, have been received or paid in cash.

The remainder of this Chapter will be concerned with the development of an accounting system from a basic cash book, through several stages to complete double-entry final accounts. It uses the example of a sports club so as to provide a close analogy with the requirements of a local authority accounting system, the principal purpose of this book.

61. RECEIPTS AND PAYMENTS BOOK-KEEPING

Let us suppose that a small club is formed, known as the Victory Sports Club. It is to have a membership of 80 persons who are to pay a subscription of U 2.50 per month. Casual memberships are allowed at U 1.50 per month. There is a football match every Saturday, each player contributing 50 cents per match towards expenses. There is a bar at which beer costing 80 cents per bottle is sold for U 1 and soft drinks costing 30 cents per bottle are sold for 50 cents. The club hut costs U 1,500 which is financed from a gift of U 600 and a loan of U 900. The loan is repayable in 36 monthly instalments together with interest at the rate of 12% per annum. U 10 per month is to be used to buy equipment and U 15 per month is to be set aside in a savings account for repairs to the club hut.

The finances of the club for the first month might appear as follows:

Jan. 1 Received gift of U 600 for the club hut.
    2 Received loan of U 900 for club hut.
    3 Received 20 subscriptions @ U 2.50.
  *3 Purchased on credit from Breweries Ltd 200 bottles of soft drink @ 30 cents each.
    4 Purchased for cash 100 bottles of beer @ 80 cents each.
    5 Received 9 subscriptions @ U 2.50.
    6 Bar sales U 12.50.
    6 Paid for hire of football pitch U 15.
    6 Received from 11 footballers 50 cents each (home game).
    8 Paid for club hut U 1,500.
  12 Received 23 subscriptions @ U 2.50.
  13 Received from 11 footballers 50 cents each (away match - no pitch hire).
  15 Received 5 subscriptions @ U 2.50.
  16 Bar sales U 26.
  18 Paid water account U 14.

Simple Non-Profit Accounts

19 Received donation towards general expenses U 50.
19 Bar sales U 4.
20 Received from 11 footballers 50 cents each.
20 Paid for hire of football pitch U 15.
22 Spent monthly allowance on equipment U 10.
23 Received 12 subscriptions @ U 2.50.
24 Received 20 casual membership subscriptions @ U 1.50.
24 Bar sales U 32.50.
25 Paid loan instalment:

		Units	
$\frac{900}{36}$	=	25	(i.e. Principal)
Interest on U 900 @ 12% per annum (ie 1% per month)	=	9	(i.e. Interest)
	TOTAL	34	

26 Paid repairs fund contribution to savings account U 15.
27 Received from 11 footballers 50 cents each.
28 Received U 20 from a draw - to be paid out later as prize money.
30 Paid club steward U 70 and part-time porter U 30.
31 Advanced U 15 to porter in respect of Feb wages.
*31 Received account for month's electricity U 24.

(Here is a partial analogy to a local authority. Here you will find the equivalent of Rates (general subscriptions), Taxes (casual members), rate fund services (general expenses), services partly met by charges (football), trading undertaking (bar); also capital and revenue grants, contributions to renewals funds, loans, loan charges and revenue contributions to capital outlay. You will also find investments, cash and credit income, and sundry creditors).

Municipal Accounting for Developing Countries

The cash book might appear (in its most simple form) as follows:

Cash Book						
19		Units	19			Units
Jan.1	To Gift for Hut	600.00	Jan.4	By 100 Bottles of Beer @ 80 cents		80.00
2	To Loan for Hut	900.00	6	By Hire of Football Pitch		15.00
3	To 20 Subscriptions @ 2.50	50.00	8	By Club Hut		1,500.00
5	To 9 Subscriptions @ 2.50	22.50	18	By Water Account		14.00
6	To Bar Sales	12.50	20	By Hire of Football Pitch		15.00
6	To Football Fees	5.50	22	By Equipment		10.00
12	To 23 subscriptions @ 2.50	57.50	25	By Loan Charges Principal		25.00
13	To Football Fees	5.50		Interest		9.00
15	To 5 Subscriptions @ 2.50	12.50	26	By Savings Accounts Repairs Fund		15.00
16	To Bar Sales	26.00	30	By Wages Steward		70.00
19	To Donation	50.00		Porter		30.00
19	To Bar Sales	11.00	31	By Wages Advance - Porter - Feb		15.00
20	To Football Fees	5.50	31	By Balance	c/d	78.50
23	To 12 subscriptions @ 2.50	30.00				
24	To 20 Casual Members @ 1.50	30.00				
24	To Bar Sales	32.50				
27	To Football Fees	5.50				
28	To Draw Receipts	20.00				
		1,876.50				1,876.50
		========				========
Feb.1	To Balance	b/d 78.50				

It has been assumed that all receipts and payments were in cash and that a bank account was not opened - except the savings account for repairs. Notice that only cash transactions appear in the books. No record is made of credit transactions (marked *). For this reason a cash book, (ie a record of receipts and payments) is, by itself, an incomplete record. A dirt road is incomplete. It is capable of being very fully used up to a point and is capable of being converted into a complete tarmac road. But in certin circumstances (such as after heavy rain) the dirt road may be very unreliable. In the same way, a record of

Simple Non-Profit Accounts

receipts and payments is incomplete. It can be used in many ways and (as we shall see later) it can be converted to a complete (double-entry) system. But also, in certain circumstances, its partial information may be extremely unreliable.

From the above cash account the club treasurer can prepare a simple statement of "receipts and payments". This is nothing more than a summary of the cash book. Taking a sheet of paper he might analyse the information as follows:

Receipts	Units	Units	Payments	Units	Units
Donations	600.00		Bar Purchases		80.00
	50.00		Hire of Football		
		650.00	Pitches	15.00	
Loan		900.00		15.00	
Subscriptions	50.00				30.00
	22.50		Club Hut		1,500.00
	57.50		Water		14.00
	12.50		Equipment		10.00
	30.00		Loan Charges		34.00
		172.50	Savings Account		15.00
Bar Sales	12.50		Wages	70.00	
	26.00			30.00	
	11.00			15.00	115.00
	32.50	82.00			
Football Fees	5.50				1,798.00
	5.50		Balance in Hand		78.50
	5.50				
	5.50	22.00			
Casual Subs		30.00			
Draw Receipts		20.00			
		1,876.50			1,876.50
		========			========

He can then produce to the club committee, a statement as follows:

Victory Sports Club
Statement of Receipts and Payments for the Month of January 19

Receipts		Units	Payments	Units
Donations		650.00	Bar Purchases	80.00
Loan		900.00	Hire of Football Pitches	30.00
Subscriptions			Club Hut	1,500.00
Full	172.50		Water Charges	14.00
Casual	30.00		Equipment	10.00
		202.50	Loan Charges	34.00
Bar Sales		82.00	Savings Account	15.00
Football Fees		22.00	Wages	115.00
Draw Receipts		20.00	Balance - Cash in Hand	78.50
		1,876.50		1,876.50
		========		========

143

Municipal Accounting for Developing Countries

From this statement, the committee can see how the treasurer has been dealing with the club funds and how much cash remains at the end of the month. However, the record is incomplete, and to give members a fuller explanation of the club's financial affairs the treasurer might add all or some of the following explanatory notes:

NOTE:

(a) The club owns a hut (valued at cost) worth U 1,500 upon which there is a loan outstanding at 31 Jan amounting to U 875.

(b) Of the 80 full members, only 69 have paid their subscriptions leaving arrears of U 27.50 (11 @ 2.50).

(c) Draw receipts totalling U 20 will be paid out as prize money when the draw is held on 6 Feb.

(d) The club now owns equipment (valued at cost) worth U 10.

(e) In addition to the cash in hand there is U 15 deposited in a savings account as a provision for repairs.

(f) Wages include a sum of U 15 advanced to the porter against his wages for February.

(g) There are outstanding accounts for bar purchases U 60 and electricity U 24.

(h) Unsold stock of drinks.

62. **ANALYSIS OF CASH BOOK**

We saw in the above example that by making an analysis of the cash book information, the treasurer could prepare his statement of receipts and payments. He made his analysis on a rough sheet of paper. He would have found it easier to analyse the information in a specially designed cash book drawn up with suitable columns.

An example of such a cash book is given below. We will now assume that certain of the receipts are banked and that certain payments are made by cheque.

Section 62 is important because the principles outlined are exactly the same as those concerned with local and public authority accounts.

(NOTE: The significance of ledger folio numbers (marked *) will be seen in Section 67, page 165).

When both the receipts and payments sides of the cash book have been entered up and analysed, it is a simple matter to prepare a statement of receipts and payments. Each analysis column is totalled to provide the required information. The totals of the analysis columns, when added across, must of course agree with the combined totals of the "cash" and "bank" columns. Contra entries of U 300 appear on both the receipts and payments sides. These cancel out each other and are ignored. The statement of receipts and payments will be drawn up exactly as before, except that the balance carried forward will be split between "Cash at Bank" U 11 and "Cash in Hand" U 67.50.

CASH RECEIPTS

DR.

Date	From Whom Recieved	Details	Receipts Cash	Receipts Bank	Contra	Donations Equip-ment	Donations General	Loans	Subscriptions Full	Subscriptions Casual	Bar Sales	Football Fees	Draw Receipts	Balance
19 Jan.1	J.Mukasa	Gift for Hut	U	600.0	U	600.0	U	U	U	U	U	U	U	U
2	National Sports Union	Loan for Hut		900.0				900.0						
3	Sundry Members	Subs 20 @ 2.50	50.0						50.0					
5	Sundry Members	Subs 9 @ 2.50	22.5						22.5					
6	Steward	Bar Sales	12.5								12.5			
6	Football Team	Match Fees	5.5									5.5		
6	Cash	Banking		75.0	75.0									
12	Sundry Members	Subs 23 @ 2.50	57.5						57.5					
13	Football Team	Match Fees	5.5									5.5		
15	Sundry Members	Subs 5 @ 2.50	12.5						12.5					
16	Steward	Bar Sales	26.0								26.0			
17	Cash	Banking		75.0	75.0									
19	M.Patel	Donation		50.0			50.0							
19	Steward	Bar Sales	11.0								11.0			
20	Football Team	Match Fees	5.5									5.5		
23	Sundry Members	Subs 12 @ 2.50	30.0						30.0					
24	Visitors	Casual Subs 20 @ 1.50	30.0							30.0				
24	Steward	Bar Sales	32.5								32.5			
25	Cash	Banking		50.0	50.0									
27	Football Team	Match Fees @ 1.50	5.5									5.5		
28	Secretary	Draw Receipts	20.0										20.0	

145

CASH RECEIPTS

DR.

Date	From Whom Recieved	Details	Receipts			Analysis of Receipts							
			Cash	Bank	Contra	Donations		Loans	Subscriptions		Bar Sales	Football Fees	Draw Receipts	Balance
						Equipment	General		Full	Casual				
			U	U	U	U	U	U	U	U	U	U	U	U
19 30	Bank	Cheque Cashed	100.0		100.0									
			426.5	1,750.0	300.0	600.0	50.0	900.0	172.5	30.0	82.0	22.0	20.0	
			=====	======	=====	(L. 6)*	(L. 19)*	(L. 3)*	(L. 11)*	(L. 21)*	(L. 15)*	(L. 18)*	(L. 5)*	====
Total Balance brought down			67.5	11.0										78.5

146

CASH PAYMENTS

Date	To Whom Paid	Details	Payments Cash	Payments Bank	Contra	Bar Purchases	Football Pitch	Club Hut	Water Charges	Equipment	Loan Charges Principal	Loan Charges Interest	Savings	Wages	Balance
19 Jan. 4	Breweries	100 beers @ 80c		80.0		80.0									
6	National Sports Club	Hire of Pitch	15.0				15.0								
6	Bank	Bankings	75.0		75.0										
8	Builders	Club Hut		1500.0				1500.0							
17	Bank	Banking	75.0		75.0										
18	Water Board	Water Charges	14.0						14.0						
20	National Sports Club	Hire of Pitch	15.0				15.0								
22	National Sports Store	Equipment		10.0						10.0					
25	Bank	Banking	50.0		50.0										
25	National Sports Union	Loan Charges		34.0							25.0	9.0			
26	National Bank	Savings A/C Repairs		15.0									15.0		
30	Cash	Cheque Cashed		100.0	100.0										
30	Steward	Salary	70.0											70.0	
30	Porter	Salary	30.0											30.0	

147

CASH PAYMENTS

Date	To Whom Paid	Details	Payments			Analysis of Payments										
			Cash	Bank	Contra	Bar Purchases	Football Pit-	Club Hut	Water Charges	Equipment	Loan Charges Principal	Interest	Savings	Wages	Balance
19			U	U	U	U	U	U	U	U	U	U	U	U	U
31	Porter	Salary Advance	15.0											15.0	
31	Balance	Carried Down	67.5	11.0											78.5
			426.5	1750.0	300.0	80.0	30.0	1500.0	14.0	10.0	25.0	9.0	15.0	115.0	78.5
			=====	======	=====	=====	=====	======	=====	=====	=====	=====	=====	=====	=====
						(L.14)*	(L.17)*	(L.1)*	(L.23)*	(L.2)*	(L.3)*	(L.27)*	(L.13)*	(L.22)*	

Simple Non-Profit Accounts

63. THE IMPREST SYSTEM

What happens if on 1 Feb. the club secretary asks the treasurer for an advance to meet small items of expense? The treasurer can do one of several things:

(a) He can tell the secretary to incur expenses on credit and ask for accounts to be sent to the treasurer for settlement. Generally this is sound practice but it can be irksome and inconvenient where the items involved amount only to a few cents each.

(b) He can ask the secretary to meet the expenses initially from his own pocket and to submit periodical claims for reimbursement. Although this is a fairly common practice it is not to be recommended, if only because official money and private money should never be mixed.

(c) He can make an advance to the secretary telling him to ask for a further advance when it is exhausted. This is a better system but is untidy and haphazard. The treasurer would not be certain how much cash at any time was in the hands of the secretary.

(d) He can introduce an "imprest system", which is the recommended method of dealing with petty cash expenses.

Suppose the treasurer and the secretary decide that a normal month's minor expenses would amount to no more than U 8. They would fix an "imprest" at (say) U 10 to cover contingencies. This sum would be advanced to the secretary on 1 Feb. as a permanent "float" of cash, out of which the secretary would meet expenses during the month. At the end of the month the secretary would submit to the treasurer a claim for these expenses. The treasurer would reimburse the secretary the amount spent, to restore his "imprest" to the original U 10. The secretary would be required to keep a separate "Petty Cash Book" in which he would enter the receipt of his imprest, details of his expenses and the amount reimbursed.

Let us assume the following transactions concerning the secretary:

Feb. 1 Imprest of U 10 received from treasurer.
    3 Paid postage of U 1.50.
    4 Purchased a bottle of ink U 1.
    7 Paid postage 50 cents.
  13 Purchased tea and sugar for committee meeting U 1.
*15 Received U 15 for draw tickets.
  17 Paid postage U 1.
*18 Received 5 subscriptions @ U 2.50 = U 12.50.
  21 Purchased table tennis balls U 1.50.
  27 Purchased drawing pins for notice board 50 cents.
  28 Expenses reimbursed by treasurer.

Municipal Accounting for Developing Countries

His Petty Cash Book will appear as follows:

Receipts	Date	Details	Payments	\multicolumn{7}{c}{Analysis of Payments}						
				Postage	Stationery	Meetings	Equipment	Etc.	Etc.	Etc.
U	19		U	U	U	U	U	U	U	U
10.00	Feb. 1	Advance								
	3	Postages	1.50	1.50						
	4	Ink	1.00		1.00					
	7	Postages	.50	.50						
	13	Tea and Sugar	1.00			1.00				
	17	Postage	1.00	1.00						
	21	Table Tennis Balls	1.50				1.50			
	27	Drawing Pins	.50		.50					
		TOTAL EXPENDITURE	7.00	3.00	1.50	1.00	1.50			
			=====	========	=====	======	====	====	====	
7.00	28	Reimbursement								
	28	Balance c/d	10.00							
17.00			17.00							
=====			=====							
10.00	Mar. 1	Balance b/d								

To save space in the petty cash book the same "date" and "details" columns are used for both debit and credit entries. Some books in use have separate columns for debit entries but this appears to be superfluous. The only debit entries normally occurring are advances and reimbursements. Space saved on the "receipts" side leaves room for a greater number of analysis columns on the "payments" side.

You will notice that receipts by the secretary of "draw ticket money" and "subscriptions" (marked *) have been ignored. These monies should be paid in to the main cashier (in this case the treasurer) without deduction and he will issue official receipts. It would have been far preferable of course, if the secretary had not accepted incoming money at all, but instead had referred the persons concerned to the treasurer.

The expenses incurred by the secretary must be recorded in the main accounts in the same way as other expenses.

The petty cash book is a subsidiary record. The original advance of the imprest is debited against the secretary in a personal account and all future reimbursements treated as part of the payments in the main cash book. In this case the petty cash payments are not posted independently to the main accounts or statement because they go through the main cash book.

Simple Non-Profit Accounts

The main cash book (part of credit side) might appear as:

CASH PAYMENTS

Date	Details	Payments		Analysis of Payments					
		Cash	Bank	Contra	Secretary Imprest	Postage	Stationery	Meetings	Equipment
19 Feb.1	Cheque for advance of imprest	U	U 10.00	U	U 10.00	U	U	U	U
	OTHER PAYMENTS MADE DIRECT BY THE TREASURER 1 FEB - 28 FEB.								
Feb.28	Cheque for reimbursement of petty cash		7.00			3.00	1.50	1.00	1.50

The amount in the "imprest" column would be debited against the secretary. The various items of reimbursed expenditure would be included with the totals of similar payments made from the main cash book.

64. **THE ABSTRACT SYSTEM**

In our study of the cash analysis system we have assumed that the cash book would contain enough columns to analyse all receipts and all payments. With the petty cash book this would probably be true because the variety of such payments is limited. With the main cash book the situation might be different. Where there are many types of receipts and payments to be dealt with, the pages of the cash book are not wide enough to produce a sufficiently detailed analysis. When this occurs, an ordinary two-column cash book is used to record the actual receipts and payments, whilst the analysis is carried out on separate sheets of specially ruled paper sometimes known as "abstracts". The totals of the receipts and payments abstracts are agreed respectively with the totals of receipts and payments entered in the cash book.

As the abstract system is used for many government and local authority accounts, readers may have experience of this system.

Like all receipts and payments systems the abstract system is not a complete system of double-entry book-keeping, though it forms the basis from which such a system could, if required, be drawn up. Although the terms "income (revenue) abstracts" and "expenditure abstracts" are often used in referring to government-type accounting systems, they do not, strictly speaking, record "income and expenditure" but merely "receipts and payments".

65. **CONVERSION OF SINGLE-ENTRY TO DOUBLE-ENTRY**

It was explained in Section 61 that a cash book, or record of receipts and payments, kept on single-entry principles can be used as a basis for the preparation of a complete set of double-entry accounts.

Municipal Accounting for Developing Countries

The steps required to carry out this exercise are normally as follows:

(a) Draw up a statement of affairs setting out the financial position as known at the beginning of the period. A statement of affairs is the term applied to a statement purporting to disclose the financial position. If the books have been kept on the single-entry method, the accountant cannot be sure that the complete financial position is revealed. On the other hand, the term "Balance Sheet" implies that accounts have been kept upon the double-entry system and that the financial position is fully revealed by the Balance Sheet.

(b) Journalise the opening balances and post them to a set of ledger accounts.

(c) Post cash receipts, in total, to the credit of appropriate ledger accounts.

(d) Post cash payments, in total, to the debit of appropriate ledger accounts.

(e) Take out a trial balance.

(f) Journalise final adjustments, posting, in total or in detail, to appropriate ledger accounts.

(g) Draw up revenue accounts.

(h) Prepare balance sheet.

Let us return to the man referred to in Section 60. His record of receipts and payments is reproduced below:

Cash Book

19			Units	19			Units
Apr.1	To Balance	b/f	8	Apr.3	By Food	6	7
	To March Salary	4	25	5	By Tax	2	3
13	To Sale of Garden Produce	5	2	9	By Electricity	7	2
				17	By Savings	8	5
17	To Repayment of loan made to R. Musoke in March	1	3	25	By Bicycle	9	17
				30	By Balance	c/d	4
			38				38
May 1	To Balance	b/d	4				

We can now go through the steps necessary to convert his accounts to double-entry.

(a) **Opening Statement of Affairs**

All we know of his financial position at 1 April is that he has U 8 in cash and R. Musoke owes him U 3. He owes tax arrears of U 3.

Simple Non-Profit Accounts

	Units
Assets (what is owned*)	
Cash	8
R. Musoke	3
	11
Less **Liabilities (what is owed)**	
Tax	3
Surplus	8

(*including legal claims)

The Statement of Affairs then reads:

Mr Ogwang
Statement of Affairs as at 1 April 19

	Units		Units
Surplus	8	**Assets**	
Liability		Debtors - R. Musoke	3
Creditor - Tax Authority	3	Cash	8
	11		11

(b) **Opening Journal and Ledger Entries**

The journal entries will appear as:

				Units	Units
19 Apr.1	Debtor - R. Musoke DR.	1	3		
	Cash DR.	C.B.	8		
	To Creditor - Tax Authority	2		3	
	To Surplus	3		8	
	Being known assets liabilities and surplus of Mr Ogwang at this date.				

The cash has already been debited in the cash book (above). The other ledger accounts will appear as follows:

	R. Musoke			1
19 Apr.1	To Balance	5	3	

153

Municipal Accounting for Developing Countries

				Tax Authority			2
				19 Apr.1	By Balance	J	3

				Surplus			3
				19 Apr.1	By Balance	J	8

(c) Post Cash Receipts to Ledger

Apr. 1   The receipt of salary represents a gain and is posted to the credit of a nominal account (Salary).

    13   The receipt from the sale of garden produce also represents a gain and is posted similarly to a nominal account (Sales of Produce).

    17   The receipt from R. Musoke discharges a debt. Mr. Musoke's personal account is credited.

The accounts will appear as follows:

				Salary			4
				19 Apr.1	By Cash	C.B.	25

				Sales of Produce			5
				19 Apr.13	By Cash	C.B.	2

				R. Musoke			1
19 Apr.1	To Balance	J	3 =	19 Apr.17	By Cash	C.B.	3 =

Simple Non-Profit Accounts

(d) Post Cash Payments to Ledger

Apr. 3 The purchase of food represents a loss (or expense) to be debited to a nominal account (Food).

5 The payment of tax discharges a liability and is debited to the personal account of the tax authority (NOT - please note - to a "tax account").

9 The payment of electricity charges is a loss (or expense) to be debited to a nominal account (Electricity).

17 The payment for savings is the exchange of one asset (cash) for another asset of equal value (bank deposit). It must be debited to the personal account of the bank concerned.

25 The purchase of the bicycle represents the exchange of one asset (cash) for another of equal value (bicycle). It must be debited to a real account (Bicycle).

The accounts will appear as follow:

				Food			6
19 Apr.3	To Cash	C.B.	7				

				Tax Authority			2
19 Apr.5	To Cash	C.B.	3	19 Apr.1	By Balance	J	3

				Electricity			7
19 Apr.9	To Cash	C.B.	2				

				National Bank Ltd			8
19 Apr.17	To Cash	C.B.	5				

				Bicycle			9
19 Apr.25	To Cash	C.B.	17				

Notice that the journal is not used in posting the receipts and payments. This is because the cash book itself acts as a prime record and as a source of posting, as well as being part of the ledger.

(e) **Trial Balance**

The trial balance should appear as follows:

Account	FO	DR. Units	CR. Units
Cash	C.B.	4	
Surplus	3		8
Salary	4		25
Sales of Produce	5		2
Food	6	7	
Electricity	7	2	
National Bank Ltd	8	5	
Bicycle	9	17	
		35	35

(f) **Journalising and Posting Final Adjustments**

The U 2 which has become due for water charges is a loss (or expense) which must be debited to a nominal account (water charges). It is also a liability to be credited to the personal account of the Water Board.

The U 1 which becomes due from his friend, Mr A. Masemba, represents a gain to be credited to a nominal account. Let us suppose that the debt arises from the sale of garden produce on credit. It must be credited to Sales of Produce account. It is also an asset (debtor) which must be debited to the personal account of Mr Masemba.

The U 5 which was assessed for tax in April represents a loss (or expense) to be debited to a nominal account (Tax). It is also a liability which must be credited to the personal account of the tax authority.

Simple Non-Profit Accounts

The journal entries will appear as follows:

Apr.30	Water Charges DR. To Water Board Being water charges due but unpaid to date		10 11	2	2
Apr.30	A. Masemba DR. To Sales of Produce Being sale of produce on credit		10 5	1	1
Apr.30	Tax DR. To Tax Authority Being tax assessed and due but unpaid to date		13 2	5	5

(g) **Draw up Revenue Accounts**

When the ledger posting (including the above journal entries) has been completed the various accounts will appear as:

Cash Book

19			Units	19			Units
Apr.1	To Balance	b/f	8	Apr.3	By Food	6	7
	To March			5	By Tax	2	3
	Salary	4	25	9	By Electricity	7	2
13	To Sale of			17	By Savings	8	5
	Garden			25	By Bicycle	9	17
	Produce	5	2	30	By Balance	c/d	4
17	To Repayment of loan made to R. Musoke in March	1	3				
			38 ==				38 ==
May 1	To Balance	b/d	4				

Tax Authority 2

19				19			
Apr.5	To Cash	C.B.	3	Apr.1	By Balance	J	3
				30	By Current Assessment	J	5

Municipal Accounting for Developing Countries

								Surplus			3
							19 Apr.1	By Balance	J		8

								Salary			4
							19 Apr.1	By Cash	C.B.		25

								Sales of Produce			5
							19 Apr.13	By Cash	C.B.		2
							30	By A. Masemba	J		1

					Food						6
19 Apr.3	To Cash	C.B.	7								

					Electricity						7
19 Apr.9	To Cash	C.B.	2								

					National Bank Ltd						8
19 Apr.17	To Cash	C.B.	5								

					Bicycle						9
19 Apr.17	To Cash	C.B.	17								

Simple Non-Profit Accounts

		Water Charges						10
19 Apr.30	To Water Board		J	2				

		Water Board						11
					19 Apr.30	By Charges	J	2

		A. Masemba						12
19 Apr.30	To Sales of Produce		J	1				

		Tax						13
19 Apr.30	To Current Assessment		J	5				

The above ledger accounts can be classified into the types shown in the table in Section 16 as follows:

1.	Personal	Creditors	(2) Tax Authority (11) Water Board	Liabilities (negative resources) which are CREDIT balances.
		Debtors	(8) National Bank Ltd (12) A. Masemba	Assets (positive resources) which are DEBIT balances.
2.	Impersonal	(a) Real	(C.B.) Cash (9) Bicycle	Assets (positive resources) which are DEBIT balances.
		(b) Nominal Losses	(6) Food (7) Electricity (10) Water Charges (13) Tax	Losses or expenditure (negative results) which are DEBIT balances.
		Gains	(3) Surplus (4) Salary (5) Sales of Produce	Gains or income (positive resources) which are CREDIT balances.

Municipal Accounting for Developing Countries

The REVENUE ACCOUNT or INCOME AND EXPENDITURE ACCOUNT deals only with GAINS and LOSSES. The only balances to be included in the Revenue Account are those of NOMINAL accounts. The balances of PERSONAL and REAL accounts do not appear in the Revenue account. They are carried down in the ledger and appear in the balance sheet.

The balances on Mr Ogwang's nominal accounts (except at this stage, the SURPLUS) will be transferred to the Revenue Account through the journal as follows:

				Units	Units
Apr.30	Salary	DR.	4	25	
	Sales of Produce	DR.	5	3	
	To Revenue Account		14		28
	Being various items of income now transferred				
Apr.30	Revenue Account	DR.	14	16	
	To Food		6		7
	To Electricity		7		2
	To Water Charges		10		2
	To Tax		13		5
	Being various items of expenditure now transferred.				

The accounts concerned will then appear as:

\multicolumn{8}{c}{**Salary**}	4
19 Apr.30	To Revenue Account	J	25 ==	19 Apr.1	By Cash	C.B.	25 ==

\multicolumn{8}{c}{**Sales of Produce**}	5
19 Apr.30	To Revenue Account	J	3 =	19 Apr.13 30	By Cash By A. Masemba	C.B. J	2 1 — 3 =

\multicolumn{8}{c}{**Food**}	6
19 Apr.3	To Cash	C.B.	17 ==	19 Apr.30	By Revenue Account	J	17 ==

160

Simple Non-Profit Accounts

		Electricity						7
19 Apr.9	To Cash	C.B.	2	19 Apr.30	By Revenue Account	J	2	
			=				=	

		Water Charges						10
19 Apr.30	To Water Board	J	2	19 Apr.30	By Revenue Account	J	2	
			=				=	

		Tax						13
19 Apr.30	To Current Assessment	J	5	19 Apr.30	By Revenue Account	J	5	
			$\overline{5}$ =				$\overline{5}$ =	

		Revenue Account					14
19 Apr.30	To Food	J	7	19 Apr.30	By Salary	J	25
	To Electricity	J	2		By Sale of Produce	J	3
	To Water Charges	J	2				
	To Tax	J	5				
			$(\overline{16})$				$(\overline{28})$

If the debit and credit sides of the Revenue Account are now totalled as shown, we can see that credits (gains or income) exceed debits (losses or expenditure) by **U** 12 (ie **U** 28 - **U** 16). This represents the surplus for the financial period (the month of April) which is transferred through the journal to the Surplus account:

				Units	Units
19 Apr.30	Revenue Account DR.	4		12	
	To Surplus Account	3			12
	Being net surplus of income over expenditure now transferred to Surplus Account.				

Municipal Accounting for Developing Countries

The accounts will appear as:

				Surplus			3
				19 Apr.1 30	By Balance By Surplus for Month	J J	8 12

				Revenue Account			14

19
Apr.30
	To Food
	To Electricity
	To Water
	    Charges
	To Tax
	To Surplus
		J
		J
		
		J
		J
		J
			7
			2
			
			2
			5
			12
			$\overline{28}$
			==
				19
				Apr.30
					By Salary
					By Sale of
					    Produce
						J
						
						J
							25
							
							3
							
							$\overline{28}$
							==

The combined effect of all nominal account balances has now been summarised and transferred to the Surplus account. This account, together with the Personal and Real accounts, can now be balanced and their balances carried down in the ledger as follows:

			Cash Book				
			Units				Units

19
Apr.1
 	
13
 	
17
	To Balance
	To March
	    Salary
	To Sale of
	    Garden
	    Produce
	To Repayment
	    of loan
	    made to
	    R. Musoke
	    in March
		b/f
		
		4
		
		5
		
		1
			8
			
			25
			
			2
			
			3
			$\overline{38}$
			==
				19
				Apr.3
				    5
				    9
				   17
				   25
				   30
					By Food
					By Tax
					By Electricity
					By Savings
					By Bicycle
					By Balance
						6
						2
						7
						8
						9
						c/d
							7
							3
							2
							5
							17
							4
							
							$\overline{38}$
							==

May 1	To Balance	b/d	4				

162

Simple Non-Profit Accounts

		Tax Authority						2
19 Apr.5	To Cash		C.B.	3	19 Apr.1	By Balance	J	3
30	To Balance		c/d	5	30	By Current Assessment	J	5
				8̄				8̄
					May 1	By Balance		5

		Surplus						3
19 Apr.30	To Balance		c/d	20	19 Apr.1	By Balance	J	8
					30	By Surplus for Month	J	12
				20				20
					May 1	By Balance	b/d	20

		National Bank Ltd						8
19 Apr.17	To Cash		C.B.	5	19 Apr.30	By Balance	c/d	5
May 1	To Balance		b/d	5				

		Bicycle						9
19 Apr.17	To Cash		C.B.	17	19 Apr.30	By Balance	c/d	17
May 1	To Balance		c/d	17				

		Water Board						11
19 Apr.30	To Balance		c/d	2	19 Apr.30	By Water Charges	J	2
					May 1	By Balance	b/d	2

			A. Masemba			12
19 Apr.30	To Sale of Produce	J	1	19 Apr.30	By Balance	c/d	1
			=			=
May 1	To Balance	b/d	1			

(h) **Balance Sheet**

The balances carried down in the ledger can now be summarised in the form of a balance sheet setting out Mr Ogwang's financial position on 30 April:

Mr Ogwang
Balance sheet as at 30 April 19

	Units			Units
SURPLUS		FIXED ASSETS		
At 1st April	8	Bicycle		17
Add Profit for April	12	CURRENT ASSETS		
	20	Investment	5	
CURRENT LIABILITIES		Debtors	1	
Creditors		Cash	4	10
Tax Board	5			
Water Board	2			
	7			
	27			27
	==			==

A comparative statement of Mr Ogwang's financial position at the beginning and at the end of the period can be drawn up in narrative form:

	1 April Units	30 April Units
ASSETS		
Bicycle	-	17
Investment	-	5
Debtors	3	1
Cash	8	4
	11	27
Less LIABILITIES		
Creditors	3	7
NET RESOURCES	8	20
	==	==
Represented by:		
Original Surplus	8	8
Add Surplus for period	-	12
NET RESULTS	8	20
	=	==

Simple Non-Profit Accounts

66. ANALYSIS OF SURPLUS

It will be noted that Mr Ogwang not only began the month with a surplus but added considerably to it during the month. His surplus of assets over liabilities at 30 April is U 20. This does not necessarily mean, however, that he is, in every respect, in a sound financial position.

Consideration must be given to the form in which the surplus is held. It will be seen that most of the surplus is held in the form of a bicycle, which is a fixed asset resulting from capital expenditure. U 17 of the surplus therefore represents capital expenditure which has been fully financed or discharged.

The technical name given to this kind of surplus is "Capital Discharged".

The surplus can therefore be analysed as:

	Units
Capital discharged	17
Revenue fund surplus	3
	20

The current assets U 10 are barely more than sufficient to cover the current liabilities U 7. If the creditors demanded immediate payment, the investment (savings) would have to be withdrawn from the bank in order to settle the debts in cash.

If Mr Ogwang wished to use a large part of his U 20 surplus to meet future day-to-day (ie revenue) expenditure he could do so - but only if he was prepared to sell his bicycle. This would leave him with no capital equipment.

What is true for Mr Ogwang is also true for any organisation. Manufacturers do not sell factory buildings and machinery in order to pay workmen; railways do not meet running expenses by selling engines, coaches and railway track; and the City Council does not sell its roads, sewers, houses and other buildings in order to pay staff salaries. It is therefore necessary to show how much surplus is held in the form of net current (liquid) assets and this is often referred to as the revenue fund (or revenue account) surplus.

67. COMPLETE SET OF ACCOUNTS

In Section 62 we saw the preparation of a Statement of Receipts and Payments for the Victory Sports Club. Because of the nature of this type of statement it was necessary for the treasurer to add several explanatory notes. The club members are able to see from these footnotes that the statement itself is incomplete. The notes give certain explanations of the various matters affecting the finances of the club, but the complete financial position is not clearly set out. This could only be done by a complete set of double-entry accounts leading to a Revenue Account and a Balance Sheet.

Municipal Accounting for Developing Countries

Let us now suppose that the rules of the club include the following:

"Accounts

The Hon Treasurer shall keep proper accounts which will enable him to produce at the end of each month:

(a) a revenue (income and expenditure) account for the General Fund showing the surplus or deficit of income due over expenditure incurred during the month;

(b) separate revenue accounts for -

    (i) bar trading; and

    (ii) football matches;

(c) a balance sheet showing as at the end of the month:

    (i) the value (at cost) of all assets owned by the club;

    (ii) the extent to which the cost of fixed assets has been fully discharged;

  (iii) the amount of loans outstanding;

   (iv) the total amount owed to sundry creditors of the club;

    (v) the total amount owing to the club by sundry debtors; and

   (vi) the accumulated revenue surplus (or deficiency)."

When all receipts and payments have been posted from the cash analysis book the ledger accounts will appear as:

Club Hut							1
19 Jan.31	To Cash	C.B.	1,500.00				

Equipment							2
19 Jan.31	To Cash	C.B.	10.00				

Loan - National Sports Union							3
19 Jan.31	To Cash	C.B.	25.00	19 Jan.31	By Cash	C.B.	900.00

Simple Non-Profit Accounts

					Hon Secretary - Deposit - Draw Receipts			5
				19 Jan.31	By Cash	C.B.	20.00

					Capital Discharged - Donation			6
				19 Jan.31	By Cash	C.B.	600.00

					Sundry Members - Subscriptions			11
				19 Jan.31	By Cash	C.B.	172.50

					Investment - N. & G. Bank - Savings			13
19 Jan.31	To Cash	C.B.	15.00					

					Bar Purchases			14
19 Jan.31	To Cash	C.B.	80.00					

					Bar Sales			15
				19 Jan.31	By Cash	C.B.	82.00

					Football Pitch Hire			17
19 Jan.31	To Cash	C.B.	30.00					

Municipal Accounting for Developing Countries

				Football Fees			18
				19 Jan.31	By Cash	C.B.	22.00

				Donations - General			19
				19 Jan.31	By Cash	C.B.	50.00

				Subscription Income - Casual			21
				19 Jan.31	By Cash	C.B.	30.00

			Wages				22
19 Jan.31	To Cash	C.B.	115.00				

			Water Charges				23
19 Jan.31	To Cash	C.B.	14.00				

			Loan Charges - Interest				27
19 Jan.31	To Cash	C.B.	9.00				

The totals of the analysis columns in the cash book have been posted to the ledger accounts whose folio references appear at the bottom of each column.

(e) **Trial Balance**

A trial balance drawn up from the ledger accounts so far posted, including the cash balances will appear as:

Simple Non-Profit Accounts

TRIAL BALANCE

		Units	Units
Club Hut	1	1,500.00	
Equipment	2	10.00	
Loan - National Sports Union	3	25.00	900.00
Deposit - Draw Receipts	5		20.00
Capital Donation	6		600.00
Sundry Members - Subscription	11		172.50
Investment - Savings Account	13	15.00	
Bar Purchases	14	80.00	
Bar Sales	15		82.00
Football Pitch Hire	17	30.00	
Football Fees	18		22.00
Donations - General	19		50.00
Subscriptions - Casual	21		30.00
Wages	22	115.00	
Water Charges	23	14.00	
Loan Charges - Interest	27	9.00	
Cash at Bank	C.B.	11.00	
Cash in Hand	C.B.	67.50	
		1,876.50	1,876.50

(f) **Journalising and Posting Final Adjustments**

The final adjustments to be dealt with fall into two main classes.

(i) Assets and Liabilities not yet appearing in the books must be properly accounted for.

(ii) The surplus must be correctly allocated to show how much of it relates to the cost of fixed assets which has been fully financed (i.e. Capital Discharged) and how much is General Fund (i.e. Revenue Account) surplus.

(i) **Assets and Liabilities**

The first accrued asset is that of Bar Stocks. The treasurer will count the unsold bottles of beer and soft drinks and draw up a stocktaking list. The items will be priced out at cost to give the value of unsold stocks at 31 Jan. as follows:

Victory Sports Club Bar Stocktaking 31 Jan. 19			
Item	Quantity	Price	Value
Beer	66	80c	52.80
Soft Drinks	112	30c	33.60
			86.40

Municipal Accounting for Developing Countries

The **U** 86.40 will be credited (as shown in Chapter 2 Section 28) to the Bar Trading account as "Closing Stock" and debited to the "Stock" account as an asset, through the journal as follows:

Jan.31	Stock DR.	10	86.40	
	To Bar Trading Account	16		86.40
	Being bar stocks on hand			
	at 31 Jan. (valued at			
	cost)			

The other accrued asset is that of debtors. The 80 members each owing subscriptions of **U** 2.50 have not yet been accounted for. The club will keep a subscription register to show how much is due and received from each member. A collective personal account is opened for the members known as the "Sundry Members - (Subscriptions) account" to which is debited the total collectible for the month. Cash collections are, as shown above, credited to this account. The total amount due for the month is a gain (income) to the club and is credited to a nominal account for "Subscription Income - Full". The journal entry will be:

Jan.31	Sundry Members (Subscriptions) DR.	11	200.00	
	To Subscriptions Income	20		200.00
	(Full)			
	Being subscriptions due			
	for Jan. from 80 full			
	members @ 2.50 each			

We must also deal with the advance of wages to the porter. At 31 Jan. this sum of **U** 15 represents a debt due from the porter and must be debited to a personal account in his name. As it is for wages payable in Feb. the Jan. "Wages" account is at present overstated by **U** 15. The expenditure in this account is reduced by a credit entry. The journal will show:

19 Jan.31	Wages Advance - Porter DR.	12	15.00	
	To Wages	22		15.00
	Being adjustment for Feb.			
	wages paid in advance			

Simple Non-Profit Accounts

The first liabilities to deal with are the unpaid accounts. These can be listed on a "Creditors List" as follows:

\multicolumn{6}{c}{Victory Sports Club Unpaid Creditors 31 Jan. 19}
Date Incurred	Name	Details	Account to be debited	Amount	Date Paid
19 Jan.3	Breweries Ltd	200 bottles of soft drinks @ 30 cents	Bar Purchases	60.00	
Jan.31	Electricity Board	Electricity at Club Hut	Electricity	24.00	
			TOTAL SUNDRY CREDITORS	84.00	

The amounts due represent expenditure which must be debited to appropriate nominal accounts of "Bar Purchases" and "Electricity".

The liabilities could be credited to personal accounts specially opened for the two separate creditors. This is not, however, necessary. The U 84 can be credited IN TOTAL to a single "Sundry Creditors (Control) account".

The journal entries appear as:

19
Jan.31
	Bar Purchases
	Electricity
	   To Sundry Creditors
	   (Control)
	Being expenditure incurred
	and unpaid to date
		DR.
		DR.
			14
			24
			4
				60.00
				24.00
					
					84.00

When settlement is made in Feb. the list will be marked off as paid in the "date paid" column. There will be an analysis column for "Sundry Creditors" on the payment side of the cash analysis book to which will be extended the two payments when they are made. At the end of Feb. the total of this column will be debited to the "Sundry Creditors (Control) account" which will then appear as:

Municipal Accounting for Developing Countries

			Sundry Creditors (Control)				4
19 Jan.31	To Balance	c/d	84.00	19 Jan.31	By Sundry Accounts	J	84.00
			=====				=====
Feb.28	To Cash	C.B.	84.00	Feb.1	By Balance	b/d	84.00

The other liability concerns repairs. A monthly sum of U 15 is being saved to meet a future liability for repairs to the club hut. We know that there will definitely be repairs to the hut in the future. It is a known liability. What is not known is the exact amount. The setting aside of such sums is known as making a "provision".

A provision (in technical terms) is a sum set aside to meet future known liabilities, the exact amount of which cannot be determined with substantial accuracy.

When the club paid the U 15 into the savings account it had only dealt with half the transaction. It had invested the provision, before it had been actually "set aside".

The present use of the club is the cause of future repairs. The sum set aside should therefore be regarded as a current revenue expense of running the club and debited to a nominal account. At the same time a Repairs Fund account is credited with the sum so set aside. Actual repair expenses can then be debited to this fund in the future, as and when they occur.

The journal entries for actually making the provision are:

19 Jan.31	Provision for Repairs DR. To Repairs Fund Being monthly provision for repairs now set aside	25 9	15.00	15.00

(ii) **Capital Discharged**

What are the capital assets of the club and by how much has their cost been fully discharged at 31 Jan?

Simple Non-Profit Accounts

The position is as follows:

	Units
Fixed Assets	
Club Hut	1,500
Equipment	10
TOTAL ASSETS (AT COST)	1,510
Less **Loan Outstanding**	875
CAPITAL DISCHARGED	635 (i.e. NET CAPITAL RESOURCES)
Represented by:	
Donation	600
Contribution from Revenue	10
Loan Repaid	25
CAPITAL DISCHARGED	635 (i.e. NET CAPITAL RESULTS)

The U 600 donation has already been credited to a "Capital Discharged" account. No entries have yet been made for the two other items.

The purchase of equipment represented a decrease in current assets (cash) and an increase in fixed assets (equipment). This has already been recorded in the books. What now must be done is to debit a nominal account - "Revenue Contributions to Capital" with the amount of the revenue loss (or expense) and credit the "Capital Discharged - Revenue Contributions" account.

The repayment of part of the loan represented a decrease in current assets (cash) and an equal decrease in a long-term liability (loan outstanding). This has been recorded in the books. It is now necessary to debit a nominal account "Loan Charges - Principal" with the amount of the revenue loss (or expense) and credit the "Capital Discharged - Loans Repaid" Account.

Journal entries will appear as follows:

19 Jan.31	Revenue Contributions to Capital DR. To Capital Discharged (RCC) Being purchase of fixed assets from Revenue Account	287	10	0

19 Jan.31	Loan Charges - Principal DR. To Capital Discharged (Loan Repaid) Being repayment of loan debt now charged to Revenue Account	268	25	25

173

Municipal Accounting for Developing Countries

When all final adjustments have been made and the "Bar Purchases" and "Bar Sales" accounts have been transferred to the "Bar Trading Account" the ledger accounts will appear as follows:

		Club Hut					1
19 Jan.31	To Cash	C.B.	1,500.00				

		Equipment					2
19 Jan.31	To Cash	C.B.	10.00				

		Loan - Sports Union					3
19 Jan.31	To Cash	C.B.	25.00	19 Jan.31	By Cash	C.B.	900.00

		Sundry Creditors (Control)					4
				19 Jan.31	By Sundry Accounts	J	84.00

		Hon Secretary - Deposit - Draw Receipts					5
				19 Jan.31	By Cash	C.B.	20.00

		Capital Discharged - Donation					6
				19 Jan.31	By Cash	C.B.	600.00

		Capital Discharged - Revenue Contribution					7
				19 Jan.31	By Revenue Account	J	10.00

Simple Non-Profit Accounts

Capital Discharged - Loans Repaid							8
				19 Jan.31	By Loan Charges (Principal)	J	25.00

Repairs Fund							9
				19 Jan.31	By Provision for Month	J	15.00

Stock							10
19 Jan.31	To Trading Account	J	86.40				

Sundry Members - Subscriptions							11
19 Jan.31	To Subscription Income Due	J	200.00	19 Jan.31	By Cash	C.B.	172.50

Wages Advance - Porter							12
19 Jan.31	To Wages	J	15.00				

Investment - N & G Bank - Savings							13
19 Jan.31	To Cash	C.B.	15.00				

Bar Purchases							14
19 Jan.31	To Cash	C.B.	80.00	19 Jan.31	By Trading Account	J	140.00
	To Sundry Creditors	J	60.00				
			140.00				140.00

Municipal Accounting for Developing Countries

Bar Sales							15
19 Jan.31	To Trading Account	J	82.00	19 Jan.31	By Cash	C.B.	82.00
			=====				=====

Bar Trading Account							16
19 Jan.31	To Purchases	J	140.00	19 Jan.31	By Sales By Stock (closing)	J J	82.00 86.40

Football Pitch Hire							17
19 Jan.31	To Cash	C.B.	30.00				

Football Fees							18
				19 Jan.31	By Cash	C.B.	22.00

Donations - General							19
				19 Jan.31	By Cash	C.B.	50.00

Subscription Income - Full							20
				19 Jan.31	By Sundry Members	J	200.00

Subscription Income - Casual							21
				19 Jan.31	By Cash	C.B.	30.00

Simple Non-Profit Accounts

			Wages				22
19 Jan.31	To Cash	C.B.	115.00	19 Jan.31	By Wages Advance	J	15.00

			Water Charges				23
19 Jan.31	To Cash	C.B.	14.00				

			Electricity				24
19 Jan.31	To Sundry Creditors	J	24.00				

			Provision for Repairs				25
19 Jan.31	To Repairs Fund	J	15.00				

			Loan Charges - Principal				26
19 Jan.31	To Capital Discharged	J	25.00				

			Loan Charges - Interest				27
19 Jan.31	To Cash	C.B.	9.00				

			Revenue Contributions to Capital				28
19 Jan.31	To Capital Discharged	J	10.00				

Municipal Accounting for Developing Countries

The journal entry for transfer of bar purchases and sales was:

19 Jan.31				
	Bar Sales DR.	15	82.00	
	To Trading Account	16		82.00
	Trading Account DR.	16	140.00	
	To Bar Purchases	14		140.00
	Being transfer of Sales and Purchases to Trading Account			

(g) Draw up Revenue Accounts

The ledger accounts are now complete except for the final work of drawing up Revenue Accounts and extracting a balance sheet.

It will be remembered that three separate revenue accounts are required:

(i) General Fund Revenue Account;

(ii) Bar Revenue Account; and

(iii) Football Matches Revenue Account.

The balances (surplus or deficiency) on the separate revenue accounts will be transferred to the General Fund (Revenue Account) Surplus.

Before drawing up these final accounts it will be useful to check the balance of the books once more by extracting a trial balance. In the trial balance shown below, additional notes have been added to show the revenue account to which each account is to be posted or alternatively that the balance on the account is carried forward and listed in the balance sheet.

Simple Non-Profit Accounts

Also indicated is the type of account.

TRIAL BALANCE

Account	FO	DR. Units	CR. Units	Type of Account	Revenue Account or Balance Sheet
Cash	C.B.	78.50		Real	Balance Sheet
Club Hut	1	1,500.00		Real	Balance Sheet
Equipment	2	10.00		Real	Balance Sheet
Loan S.U.	3	25.00	900.00	Personal	Balance Sheet
Sundry Creditors	4		84.00	Personal	Balance Sheet
Deposit - Draw	5		20.00	Personal	Balance Sheet
Capital Discharged Donation	6		600.00	Nominal	Balance Sheet
Capital Discharged Revenue	7		10.00	Nominal	Balance Sheet
Capital Discharged Loan Repaid	8		25.00	Nominal	Balance Sheet
Repairs Fund	9		15.00	Nominal	Balance Sheet
Stock	10	86.40		Real	Balance Sheet
Sundry Members	11	200.00	172.50	Personal	Balance Sheet
Wages Advance	12	15.00		Personal	Balance Sheet
Investment	13	15.00		Personal	Balance Sheet
Bar Trading	16	140.00	168.40	Nominal	Bar Trading A/C
Football Pitch Hire	17	30.00		Nominal	Football Revenue Account
Football Fees	18		22.00	Nominal	Football Revenue Account
Donations General	19		50.00	Nominal	General Revenue Account
Subscription Full	20		200.00	Nominal	General Revenue Account
Subscription Casual	21		30.00	Nominal	General Revenue Account
Wages	22	115.00	15.00	Nominal	General Revenue Account
Water Charges	23	14.00		Nominal	General Revenue Account
Electricity	24	24.00		Nominal	General Revenue Account
Provision for Repairs	25	15.00		Nominal	General Revenue Account
Loan Charges (Principal)	26	25.00		Nominal	General Revenue Account
Loan Charges (Interest)	27	9.00		Nominal	General Revenue Account
Revenue Contributions to Capital	28	10.00		Nominal	General Revenue Account
TOTALS		2,311.90	2,311.90		

Notice as a principle that all Real and Personal account balances are carried forward in the ledger and included in the balance sheet. They represent the RESOURCES of the organisation.

Municipal Accounting for Developing Countries

The nominal account balances (other than those representing sums set aside from surpluses) are included in the Revenue Accounts. These represent the RESULTS of carrying on the business of the organisation and the cumulative results carried forward.

The completed ledger and final accounts will now appear as follows:

\multicolumn{8}{c}{**Club Hut**}	1
19 Jan.31	To Cash	C.B.	1,500.00	19 Jan.31	By Balance	c/d	1,500.00	
			========				========	
Feb.1	To Balance	b/d	1,500.00					

\multicolumn{8}{c}{**Equipment**}	2
19 Jan.31	To Cash	C.B.	10.00	19 Jan.31	By Balance	c/d	10.00	
			=====				=====	
Feb.1	To Balance	b/d	10.00					

\multicolumn{8}{c}{**Loan - National Sports Union**}	3
19 Jan.31	To Cash	C.B.	25.00	19 Jan.31	By Cash	C.B.	900.00	
	To Balance	c/d	875.00					
			900.00				900.00	
			======				======	
				Feb.1	By Balance	b/d	875.00	

\multicolumn{8}{c}{**Sundry Creditors (Control)**}	4
19 Jan.31	To Balance	c/d	84.00	19 Jan.31	By Sundry Accounts	J	84.00	
			=====				=====	
				Feb.1	By Balance	b/d	84.00	

Simple Non-Profit Accounts

		Hon Secretary - Deposit - Draw Receipts						5
19 Jan.31	To Balance	c/d	20.00	19 Jan.31	By Cash	C.B.	20.00
			=====	Feb.1	By Balance	b/d	20.00

		Capital Discharged - Donation						6
19 Jan.31	To Balance	c/d	600.00	19 Jan.31	By Cash	C.B.	600.00
			======	Feb.1	By Balance	b/d	600.00

		Capital Discharged - Revenue Contribution						7
19 Jan.31	To Balance	c/d	10.00	19 Jan.31	By Revenue Account	J	10.00
			=====	Feb.1	By Balance	b/d	10.00

		Capital Discharged - Loan Repaid						8
19 Jan.31	To Balance	c/d	25.00	19 Jan.31	By Loan Charges (Principal)	J	25.00
			25.00 =====	Feb.1	By Balance	b/d	25.00

		Repairs Fund						9
19 Jan.31	To Balance	c/d	15.00	19 Jan.31	By Provision for Month	J	15.00
			15.00 =====	Feb.1	By Balance	b/d	15.00

Municipal Accounting for Developing Countries

		Stock						10
19 Jan.31	To Trading Account	J	86.40	19 Jan.31	By Balance	c/d	86.40	
			=====				=====	
Feb.1	To Balance	b/d	86.40					

		Sundry Members - Subscriptions						11
19 Jan.31	To Subscriptions Income Due	J	200.00	19 Jan.31	By Cash By Balance	C.B. c/d	172.50 27.50	
			200.00				200.00	
			=====				=====	
Feb.1	To Balance	b/d	27.50					

		Wages Advance - Porter						12
19 Jan.31	To Wages	J	15.00	19 Jan.31	By Balance	c/d	15.00	
			=====				=====	
Feb.1	To Balance	b/d	15.00					

		Investment - N & G Bank - Savings						13
19 Jan.31	To Cash	C.B.	15.00	19 Jan.31	By Balance	c/d	15.00	
			=====				=====	
Feb.1	To Balance	b/d	15.00					

		Bar Purchases						14
19 Jan.31	To Cash To Sundry Creditors	C.B. J	80.00 60.00	19 Jan.31	To Trading Account	J	140.00	
			140.00				140.00	
			=====				=====	

Simple Non-Profit Accounts

		Bar Sales					15
19 Jan.31	To Trading Account	J	82.00	19 Jan.31	By Cash	C.B.	82.00

		Bar Trading Account					16
19 Jan.31	To Purchases Gross Profit to Revenue Account	J J	140.00 28.40 168.40	19 Jan.31	By Sales By Stock (closing)	J J	82.00 86.40 168.40

		Football Pitch Hire					17
19 Jan.31	To Cash	C.B.	30.00 30.00	19 Jan.31	By Transfer to Football Revenue Account	J	30.00 30.00

		Football Fees					18
19 Jan.31	To Transfer to Football Revenue Account	J	22.00 22.00	19 Jan.31	By Cash	C.B.	22.00 22.00

		Donations - General					19
19 Jan.31	To Transfer to General Revenue Account	J	50.00 50.00	19 Jan.31	By Cash	C.B.	50.00 50.00

Municipal Accounting for Developing Countries

			Subscription Income - Full				20
19 Jan.31	To Transfer to General Revenue Account	J	200.00	19 Jan.31	By Sundry Members	J	200.00
			200.00				200.00

			Subscription Income - Casual				21
19 Jan.31	To Transfer to General Revenue Account	J	30.00	19 Jan.31	By Cash	C.B.	30.00
			30.00				30.00

			Wages				22
19 Jan.31	To Cash	C.B.	115.00	19 Jan.31	By Wages Advance	J	15.00
					By Transfer to General Revenue Account	J	100.00
			115.00				115.00

			Water Charges				23
19 Jan.31	To Cash	C.B.	14.00	19 Jan.31	By Transfer to General Revenue Account	J	14.00
			14.00				14.00

Simple Non-Profit Accounts

Electricity — 24

Date	Particulars	Fol	Amount	Date	Particulars	Fol	Amount
19 Jan. 31	To Sundry Creditors	J	24.00	19 Jan. 31	By Transfer to General Revenue Account	J	24.00
			24.00				24.00

Provision for Repairs — 25

Date	Particulars	Fol	Amount	Date	Particulars	Fol	Amount
19 Jan. 31	To Repairs Fund	J	15.00	19 Jan. 31	By Transfer to General Revenue Account	J	15.00
			15.00				15.00

Loan Charges – Principal — 26

Date	Particulars	Fol	Amount	Date	Particulars	Fol	Amount
19 Jan. 31	To Capital Discharged	J	25.00	19 Jan. 31	By Transfer to General Revenue Account	J	25.00
			25.00				25.00

Loan Charges – Interest — 27

Date	Particulars	Fol	Amount	Date	Particulars	Fol	Amount
19 Jan. 31	To Cash	C.B.	9.00	19 Jan. 31	By Transfer to General Revenue Account	J	9.00
			9.00				9.00

Revenue Contributions to Capital								28
19 Jan.31	To Capital Discharged	J	10.00	19 Jan.31	By Transfer to General Revenue Account	J	10.00
			10.00 =====				10.00 =====

Bar Revenue Account								29
19 Jan.31	(Here would be debited any expenses specific to operating the bar - eg wages of a bar steward - there are none in this case)			19 Jan.31	By Gross Profit from Trading Account	J	28.40
31	To Surplus Transferred to General Fund	J	28.40				
			28.40 =====				28.40 =====

Football Matches Revenue Account								30
19 Jan.31	To Hire of Pitches	J	30.00	19 Jan.31	By Match Fees By Deficiency - transferred to General Fund	J	22.00 8.00
			30.00 =====				30.00 =====

Simple Non-Profit Accounts

General Fund Revenue Account — 31

19 Jan.31				19 Jan.31			
To Wages	J	100.00		By Donations - General	J	50.00
To Water Charges	J	14.00		By Subscriptions		
To Electricity	J	24.00		Full	J	200.00
To Provision for Repairs	J	15.00		Casual	J	30.00
To Loan Charges						
Principal	J	25.00				
Interest	J	9.00				
To Revenue Contributions to Capital	J	10.00				
To Surplus carried to General Fund	J	83.00				
		280.00				280.00

General Fund Surplus — 32

19 Jan.31				19 Jan.31			
To Deficiency on Football Matches Revenue Account	J	8.00		By Surplus on Bar Revenue Account	J	28.40
To Balance	c/d	103.40		By Surplus on General Revenue Account	J	83.00
		111.40				111.40
				Feb.1 By Balance	b/d	103.40

Transfers between accounts could be made by journal entries.

Victory Sports Club

Balance Sheet as at 31 Jan. 19

	Units	Units	Units		Units	Units	Units
LONG-TERM LIABILITIES				FIXED ASSETS			
Loan Outstanding			875.00	Club Premises		1,500.00	
CURRENT LIABILITIES				Equipment		10.00	1,510.00
Creditors		84.00		CURRENT ASSETS			
Sundry Creditors		20.00		Stocks and Stores		86.40	
Deposits (Receipts in Advance)			104.00	Debtors			
PROVISIONS				Sundry Debtors	27.50		
Repairs Fund			15.00	Payments in Advance	15.00	42.50	
SURPLUS				Investments		15.00	
Capital Discharged	600.00			Cash			
Donations	25.00			At Bank	11.00		
Loans Repaid	10.00	635.00		In Hand	67.50	78.50	222.40
Revenue Contributions							
Revenue Account Surplus		103.40	738.40				
			1,732.40				1,732.40

188

Simple non-profit Accounts

68. **Conclusion**

Examples have been given of "Receipts and Payments" book-keeping single-entry), and "Income and Expenditure" accountancy (double-entry). The first has been shown to be incomplete and poor evidence upon which to make policy decisions. The second has been shown to be complete and sound evidence upon which to make policy decisions.

Upon examining the Bar Revenue account, Football Matches Revenue account and the General Fund Revenue account, shown in Section 68 we can see:

(a) that the Bar makes a profit providing we do not have to employ a barman and pay him wages. If this becomes necessary, we shall either have to increase the selling price of our drinks or sell a lot more.

(b) that the Football Matches show a loss and that we shall have to increase the match fee; or negotiate for lower hiring charges when we want the pitch; or, continue to subsidise this activity.

(c) that the General Fund Revenue account shows an operating surplus, when the donations and casual subscriptions (which may not be received in future months) are deducted.

Upon examining the balance sheet we see that the club is in a strong financial position considering that this has been the first month of operation, but this strength can be traced to the donation of U 600 towards our Club Hut. We also see that something must be done to encourage the 11 members to pay up their January subscriptions quickly. There really ought to be a policy decision made, too, about making advances to employees; and although our Club Hut is new, a committee member ought to be asked to check it over every month in case minor repairs are required. And so on!

Properly prepared accounts give a wealth of information - information which is not available in any records which fall short of complete double-entry book-keeping. Sound policy decisions can be based upon complete accounts.

The principles we have dealt with in the Club Accounts apply also to local authority accounts. If a local authority's accounts are not based upon the complete double-entry system of book-keeping, policy decisions are likely to be made in darkness.

The duty of the finance officer is to prepare accounts in such a form that he can surely and quickly give sound advice to his Finance Committee and Council.

7. Municipal Accounts—Introduction

Section		Page
69.	Introduction to Local and Public Authority Accounts.	191
70.	Application of Accountancy Principles to Local and Public Authorities.	191
71.	Local Authority Cash Books.	193
72.	Local Authority Abstracts.	198
73.	Basic Information.	198
74.	Statement of Receipts and Payments.	202
75.	Classified Statement of Receipts and Payments.	203
76.	Complete Final Accounts.	208
77.	Explanation of Technical Points.	236
78.	Order of Revenue Account.	236
79.	Conclusions.	237
80.	The Balance Sheet.	238
81.	Surplus and Capital Discharged.	239
82.	The Double-Account System.	239

69. INTRODUCTION TO LOCAL AND PUBLIC AUTHORITY ACCOUNTS

In previous chapters the basic principles of book-keeping as applied to both trading and non-trading undertakings were considered, including profit and loss accounts and income and expenditure accounts: these principles of book-keeping apply fully to the accounts of a local or public authority.

The policy decisions of local and public authorities will often be concerned with financial matters and should be based upon complete evidence of the authority's financial position. As explained in Section 68, this suggests that the accounts might well need to be kept on a double-entry system, leading to the preparation of Revenue Accounts (of income and expenditure) and Balance Sheets (showing assets, liabilities, surpluses and deficiencies).

The detailed application of accounting principles to local authorities differs somewhat from commercial accounts. Also, as with commercial accounts, practice varies from one country to another and even within a single country. Even where practices are similar, terminology sometimes varies. For example, American and British accountancy practice is broadly similar but much of the terminology quite different. Because this book is based upon practices in former British territories, UK terminology will prevail. To link municipal practice with your knowledge of commercial accounts, this chapter will do two things. First, it will provide a very quick overview of a local authority balance sheet, so that the reader feels comfortable with this concept. Second, the reader will be given a walk-through of a simplified set of municipal accounting transactions, emphasising similarities with commercial accounts and also highlighting and explaining differences. The stage will then be set for subsequent chapters to deal with each concept in depth.

70. APPLICATION OF ACCOUNTANCY PRINCIPLES TO LOCAL AND PUBLIC AUTHORITIES

The chief financial officer of a local or public authority is the accountant and financial adviser to his authority. He designs the financial records and he produces statements from his records to assist him in giving advice to the management. His advice should enable management (eg board, council or finance committee) to make soundly-based decisions.

Consider any Municipal Council. Every day, variations are occurring in its financial position. Houses, roads, markets and water supplies are

Municipal Accounting for Developing Countries

constructed or repaired; salaries are paid; rates, charges and taxes are collected; loans are raised and repaid. The chief financial officer records the results of these variations during a period of time (normally a financial year) by producing accounts of income and expenditure. He produces a balance sheet setting out at the end of each period the resources of the authority against the results of changes in their value.

A simplified version of a hypothetical municipality, say Kambale Municipal Council's balance sheet as at 31 Dec. 19 might appear as:

Balance Sheet as at 31 Dec. 19

	Units		Units
LONG-TERM LIABILITIES		FIXED ASSETS	
Loans outstanding	67,920	Land, buildings,	
CURRENT LIABILITIES		permanent works and	
Sundry creditors	94,220	equipment (at cost)	3,231,800
PROVISIONS		CURRENT ASSETS	
Renewals	594,860	Sundry debtors	70,960
Repairs	30,620	Investments	752,980
Gratuities and Leave	28,840	Cash	257,780
SURPLUS			
Capital Discharged	3,163.880		
General Fund	333,180		
	4,313.520		4,313.520
	=========		=========

This balance sheet is shown in its conventional form. But it does not show clearly how RESOURCES are related to RESULTS. By re-arranging the figures into a narrative form of balance sheet we can show how the RESOURCES of the Municipal Council are related to the cumulative RESULTS of its financial activities; for a fuller description of "RESOURCES" and "RESULTS" see Chapter 1 Section 8.

Municipal Accounts - Introduction

KAMBALE MUNICIPAL COUNCIL

Balance Sheet as at 31 Dec. 19

		Units	Remarks
FIXED ASSETS			
Land, buildings, permanent works and equipment		3,231.800	) The various physical
CURRENT ASSETS			) and monetary resources
Sundry debtors		70,960	) owned by the Municipal
Investments		752,980	) Council and used for
Cash		257,780	) the benefit of the
		4,313,520	) public.
Less			
LONG-TERM LIABILITIES			) The various sums of
Loans outstanding	67,920		) money owed by the
CURRENT LIABILITIES			) Kambale Council.
Sundry creditors	94,220	162,140	)
		4,151,380	
Less			) Sums of money set
PROVISIONS			) aside by the Kambale
Renewals	594,860		) Municipal Council out
Repairs	30,620		) of its resources to
Gratuities and Leave	28,840	654,320	) meet known future
			) commitments (of
NET RESOURCES		3,497,060	) unknown definite
		=========	) amount).
Represented by:			A different way of
SURPLUS			expressing the
Capital Discharged		3,163,880	resources of the
General Fund		333,180	Municipal Council shows how much of it
NET RESULTS		3,497,060	is represented by:
		=========	

(a) fixed assets which have been fully financed;

(b) the accumulated surplus of revenue (recurrent) income over revenue expenditure.

71. **LOCAL AUTHORITY CASH BOOKS**

A local authority is a non profit-seeking organisation, which aims to meet its expenditure out of income. In this respect it is like the club whose accounts were examined in Chapter 6. To apply the principles of book-keeping to a local authority we can use the same methods as we used for the Victory Sports Club.

We will now assume the existence of a small local authority called

Municipal Accounting for Developing Countries

Makale Council. For simplicity we will also assume that its financial period is one month and that rates are assessed, loans repaid and accounts made up, monthly instead of annually. We will use a hypothetical currency of UNITS (U) with a 100 cents to a unit.

Using these assumptions let us hypothesise a simple series of transactions as follows:

Makale Council is formed with a rateable value of U 800,000 on which there is to be a rate levy of 12% per annum (1% per month). This will bring in from 1600 ratepayers an average of U 5 per month each. Licences are issued for U 3 per month. There is a weekly market for which 110 traders pay 10 cents each in cash as they enter the market. The market premises are rented by the Council at a rent of U 60 per month payable in two instalments. The Council has an information centre at which publications costing U 1.50 per 100 are sold at U 2 per 100; other publications costing 50 cents per 100 are sold for 75 cents per 100. Council offices are to be purchased for U 60,000, financed by a government grant of U 24,000 and a loan of U 36,000. The loan is repayable in 36 equal monthly instalments together with interest on the outstanding balance at the rate of 12% per annum. Each month U 400 is to be spent on capital equipment, financed by a revenue contribution to capital. U 600 each month is to be set aside as a contribution to a repairs fund for the Council offices.

The receipts, payments and other transactions for January were as follows:

Jan. 1   Received specific capital grant of U 24,000 for the Council offices.
    2   Received a loan of U 36,000 for the Council offices.
    3   Received rates from 400 ratepayers @ U 5 each.
    3   Purchased on credit from Government Printer 200 packets of publications at 50c each packet.
    4   Purchased for cash from Makale Publications 100 packets of publications at 1.50 per packet.
    5   Received rates from 180 ratepayers @ U 5 each.
    6   Sales of publications for cash U 25.
    6   Paid for rent of market U 30.
    6   Received cash income from market for 110 traders @ 10c each (U 11).
    8   Paid for Council offices U 60,000.
   12   Received rates from 460 ratepayers @ U 5 each. (Two receipts were spoiled and cancelled).
   13   Received cash income from market for 110 traders @ 10c each (U 11).
   15   Received rates from 100 ratepayers @ U 5 each.
   16   Sales of publications for cash U 53.
   18   Paid water charges on Council offices U 560.
   19   Received general revenue grant U 2,000.
   19   Sales of publications for cash U 21.
   20   Received cash income from market for 110 traders @ 10c each (U 11).
   20   Paid market rent U 30.
   22   Purchased office capital equipment U 400.
   23   Received rates from 240 ratepayers @ U 5 each.
   24   Received cash income for issue of 20 licences @ U 3 each.

Municipal Accounts - Introduction

24 Sales of publications for cash U 35.
25 Paid loan instalment:

                                                                Units

$$\frac{36,000}{36} \qquad 1,000 \text{ (ie Principal)}$$

Interest on 36,000 @
12% per annum
(ie 1% per month)   360 (ie Interest)
                                                          1,360
                                                          =====

26 Invested U 600 repairs fund contribution in Government stocks.
27 Received cash income from market for 110 traders @ 10c each (U 11).
28 Received from revenue collectors U 840 in graduated tax to be handed over.
30 Paid salaries of U 3,000 and wages of U 1,200.
31 Advanced U 600 in respect of February wages.
31 Received an account for January's electricity U 960.
31 Stock of publications in hand (valued at cost) U 155.

Let us assume that the Chief Executive Officer operates a petty cash imprest system and that the transactions take place in January as follows:

Jan. 1 Imprest of U 20 received by the Chief Executive Officer from the Chief Financial Officer.
     3 Paid postage U 3.
     4 Purchased stationery U 2.
     7 Paid postage U 1.
   13 Paid expenses for committee meeting U 2.
*15 Received by post a cheque for U 600 graduated tax.
  17 Paid postage U 2.
*18 Received cheques from 100 ratepayers @ U 5 each for February rates.
  21 Paid for typewriter repairs U 3.
  27 Purchased pencils and stamp pads U 1.
  31 Expenses re-imbursed by Chief Financial Officer.

Items marked * will be quickly disposed of by the Chief Executive Officer. He will send the cheques to the finance department main cashier for official receipts to be written and sent direct to the payers.

The items for which the cashier has issued receipts will appear in the main cash book of the finance department and will not appear in the Chief Executive Officer's petty cash book.

Municipal Accounting for Developing Countries

The remaining items will appear in the Chief Executive Officer's petty cash book as follows:

DR.   PETTY CASH BOOK   CR.

Receipts	Date	Details	Payments	Analysis of Payments			
				Postage	Stationery	Meetings	Equipment Maintenance
U	19		U	U	U	U	U
20	Jan.1	Advance					
	3	Postages	3	3			
	4	Stationery	2		2		
	7	Postages	1	1			
	13	Meeting Expenses	2			2	
	17	Postages	2	2			
	21	Typewriter Repairs	3				3
	27	Sundry Office Supplies	1		1		
		TOTAL EXPENDITURE	14	6	3	2	3
14	31	Reimbursement					
	31	Balance c/d	20				
34			34				
======			=======				
20	Feb.1	Balance b/d					

There will be vouchers to support each payment made from petty cash by the Chief Executive Officer. These vouchers will be produced to the expenditure section of the finance department on 31 Jan. when reimbursement is claimed. They will be retained by the expenditure section to support the payment of U 14 from the main cash book.

In a mature authority operating a sound system of internal check, the receipts and the payments would be dealt with and recorded quite separately from one another, by different persons or sections. They would be brought together in the main cash book in total only. This important point will be dealt with later. For the present, just to get the basic ideas, we will assume that a normal two-column cash book is used. We shall, however, assume three important principles of internal check:

(a) all payments (other than petty cash) will be made by cheque;

(b) all receipts will be banked intact as soon as possible after collection; and

(c) petty cash payments will be controlled by an imprest system and made by a person other than the one making cheque payments.

If we make these assumptions, the main cash book will appear as:

Municipal Accounts - Introduction

DR. CASH BOOK CR.

Date	Details	Receipt No.	Cash	Bank	Date	Details	Voucher No.	Cash	Bank
19			U	U	19			U	U
Jan.1	Government Capital Grant	1	24,000		Jan.1	Bank	C	24,000	
1	Cash	C		24,000	1	CEO Imprest	1		20
2	Loan	2	36,000		3	Bank	C	38,000	
3	Rates 400 @ U 5	3-22	2,000		4	Publications	2		150
3	Cash	C		38,000	6	Properties - Market Rent	3		30
5	Rates 180 @ U 5	23-31	900		6	Bank	C	936	
6	Information Centre Sales of Publications	32	25		8	Builders - Offices	4		60,000
6	Market Master - Market Fees	33	11		13	Bank	C	2,311	
6	Cash	C		936	16	Bank	C	1,153	
12	Rates 460 @ U 5	34-56	2,300		18	Water Board - Water Charges	5		560
12	(Cancelled) Receipts	57-58	-	-	20	Bank	C	2,532	
13	Market Master - Market Fees	59	11		20	Properties - Market Rent	6		30
13	Cash	C		2,311	22	Office - Supplies Ltd - Equipment	7		400
14	Rates 100 @ U 5	60-64	500		24	Bank	C	1,295	
15	Graduated Tax	65	600		25	Loan Charges U P.1,000 I. 360	8 9		1,360
16	Information Centre - Sales of Publications	66	53		26	Admin - Repairs Fund Investment	10		600
16	Cash	C		1,153	28	Bank	C	851	
18	Rates 100 @ U 5 (Feb.)	67-71	500		30	Salaries	11		3,000
19	Government - Block Grant	72	2,000		30	Wages	12		1,200
19	Information Centre Sales of Publications	73	21		31	Wages Advance	13		600
20	Market Master - Market Fees	74	11		31	Chief Executive Officer - Petty Cash U Postage 6 Stationery 3 Meetings 2 Equipment 3 (Maintenance)	14 15 16 17		14
					31	Balance	c/d		3,114

197

DR.					CASH BOOK					CR.
Date	Details	Rec-eipt No.	Cash	Bank	Date	Details	Vou-cher No.	Cash	Bank
			U	U					U	U
20	Cash	C		2,532						
23	Rates 240 @ U 5	75-86	1,200							
24	Licences 20 @ U 3	87-106	60							
24	Information Centre - Sales of Public-ations	107	35							
24	Cash	C		1,295						
27	Market Master - Market Fees	108	11							
28	Graduated Tax	109	840							
28	Cash	C		851						
			71,078	71,078				71,078	71,078
			======	======				======	======
Feb.1	Balance	b/d		3,114						

In this cash book we use a column to show receipt numbers (for cash received) or voucher numbers (for cheques paid). Where several types of expenditure are included in a single cheque (ie loan charges and reimbursement of petty cash) an analysis has been given as an inset. In practice the voucher itself would record the analysis (see later).

Cancelled receipts can be dealt with in various ways. Here we have shown them noted in the cash book.

72. **LOCAL AUTHORITY ABSTRACTS**

The receipts and payments are analysed on abstracts, as shown on the next page. The abstracts are really nothing more than analysis columns which have been separated from the cash book because of the large number of columns required. The "abstract of receipts" is sometimes called (less correctly) a "revenue abstract" and the "abstract of payments" is sometimes called (less correctly) an "expenditure abstract".

When each item is entered in the abstract it is given a reference (receipt or voucher) number to link it with the cash book entry.

When totalled at the end of the month, each abstract gives an analysis of the cash receipts or payments during the month, and must balance in total with the cash book.

Municipal Accounts - Introduction

73. BASIC INFORMATION

The cash book, together with the abstracts of receipts and payments, represents the basic book-keeping information from which the accountant can work. The accountant must now apply his skill to the information to make it yield facts upon which sound decisions can be based.
The correct approach would be to:

(a) analyse the information;

(b) classify the information;

(c) combine the information with other known facts;

(d) summarise the facts; and

(e) draw conclusions.

The book-keeping information shown above has already been analysed. We shall now see how the accountant may proceed through the various other stages until sound conclusions can be drawn from the facts set down in the final accounts and balance sheet.

ABSTRACT OF RECEIPTS

Vo	Capital Grant Amt	Vo	Loan Amt	Vo	Rates Amt	Vo	Sales of Publications Amt	Vo	Market Fees Amt	Vo	Graduated Tax Amt	Vo	Block Grant Amt	Vo	Licences Amt	Vo	Amt	Vo	Amt	Vo	Amt	Vo	Amt
1	U 24,000	2	U 36,000	3	U 2,000	32	U 25	33	U 11	65	U 600	72	U 2,000	87	U 60								
				23	900	66	53	59	11	109	840												
				34	2,300	73	21	74	11														
				60	500	107	35	108	11														
				67	500																		
				75	1,200																		
	24,000		36,000		7,400		134		44		1,440		2,000		60								
	L.6		L.3		L.11		L.16		L.19		L.5		L.20		L.22								

200

ABSTRACT OF PAYMENTS

	Imp-rest		Pub-lica-tions		Mar-ket Rent		Council Offices		Water Char-ges		Equip-ment		Loan Char-ges (Prin-cipal)		Loan Char-ges (Inte-rest)		Re-pairs Fund		Sal-aries		Wages		Wages Ad-vance	
Vo	Amt	Vo	Amt	Vo	Amt	Vo	Amt	Vo	Amt	Vo	Amt	Vo	Amt	Vo	Amt	Vo	Amt	Vo	Amt	Vo	Amt	Vo	Amt
	U		U		U		U		U		U		U		U		U		U		U		U
1	20	2	150	3	30	4	60,000	5	560	7	400	8	1,000	9	360	10	600	11	3,000	12	1,200	13	600
				6	30																		
	20		150		60		60,000		560		400		1,000		360		600		3,000		1,200		600
L.13		L.15		L.18		L.1		L.25		L.2		L.3		L.31		L.12		L.23		L.24		L.14	

	Post-age		Stat-ion-ery		Meet-ings		Equip-ment Maint-enance	
Vo	Amt	Vo	Amt	Vo	Amt	Vo	Amt
	U		U		U		U
14	6	15	3	16	2	17	3
	6		3		2		3
L.26		L.27		L.28		L.34	

Vo = Voucher (or Receipt) Number.

74. STATEMENT OF RECEIPTS AND PAYMENTS

The simplest form of statement which could be set down from the basic books would be a statement of receipts and payments. The totals of the various abstract columns would be listed with the bank balance to give the following:

MAKALE COUNCIL

Statement of Receipts and Payments for the month of Jan. 19

Receipts	Units	Payments	Units
Capital Grant	24,000	Imprest	20
Loan	36,000	Publications	150
Rates	7,400	Market Rent	60
Sales of Publications	134	Council Offices	60,000
Market Fees	44	Water Charges	560
Graduated Tax	1,440	Equipment	400
Block Grant	2,000	Loan Charges (P.1000 + I.360)	1,360
Licenses	60	Repairs Fund	600
		Salaries	3,000
		Wages	1,200
		Wages Advances	600
		Postage	6
		Stationery	3
		Meetings	2
		Equipment Maintenance	3
		Balance - Cash at Bank	3,114
	71,078		71,078

If such a statement were presented to (say) a finance committee it would need to be explained by many notes, such as:

(a) The Council owns offices (valued at cost) worth U 60,000 upon which there is a loan outstanding at 31 Jan. amounting to U 35,000.

(b) Rate income due for the month is U 8,000 (1% of R.V. 800,000). At 31 Jan. there were rate arrears totalling U 1,100. U 500 has been received in advance for rates due in February.

(c) Graduated tax receipts totalling U 1,440 are to be paid to the Government.

(d) The Council owns equipment (valued at cost) worth U 400.

(e) In addition to cash in hand the Council holds investments of U 600 as a provision for office repairs.

(f) Wages advances of U 600 will be recovered from wages due in February.

(g) There are outstanding accounts for the purchase of publications (U 100) and electricity supply (U 960).

(h) The unsold stock of publications (valued at cost) is worth U 155.

Municipal Accounts - Introduction

A member of a finance committee, or in fact, anyone else, could be forgiven if he was unable to interpret the council's financial position from the above information - he would rightly argue that it is the job of the Chief Financial Officer to set out the figures so that they can be interpreted. Unhappily, many local government units and public authorities in developing countries (perhaps the majority) do little more than provide for this basic kind of cash accounting.

The statement shows what the Council has received in cash; what cash has been paid out; and how much cash is left at the bank. It does not show, for example, whether any of the receipts are to be repaid; whether all sums due have been collected; whether payments are for fixed assets (capital expenditure) or current expenses (revenue expenditure); whether or not sums paid by the Council are to be repaid to it later on; or whether there are outstanding accounts that the Council has not paid. All these facts are given, not as part of the accounts, but in a separate written statement.

75. **CLASSIFIED STATEMENT OF RECEIPTS AND PAYMENTS**

    How could the accountant present the facts more clearly? The cash receipts and payments have been analysed, and a simple statement prepared. The items in the statement could be more clearly understood if they were classified into some order. Perhaps the first thing to do would be to separate the day-to-day (recurrent) payments from the others to see whether they can be met from the day-to-day (recurrent) receipts. This would give some idea of whether the finances were operating on a sound basis.

    After recurrent items have been separated from other items, the classified statement might appear as:

Municipal Accounting for Developing Countries

MAKALE COUNCIL

Statement of Receipts and Payments for the Month of Jan. 19

Recurrent Receipts*	Units	Recurrent Payments*	Units
Rates	7,400	Publications	150
Sales of Publications	134	Market Rent	60
Market Fees	44	Water Charges	560
Block Grant	2,000	Equipment	400
Licences	60	Equipment Maintenance	3
		Salaries	3,000
		Wages	1,200
		Loan Charges	1,360
		Postage	6
		Stationery	3
		Meetings	2
TOTAL RECURRENT RECEIPTS*	9,638	TOTAL RECURRENT PAYMENTS*	6,744
Other Receipts		**Other Payments**	
Capital Receipts:		Capital Payments:	
Loan	36,000	Council Offices	60,000
Grant	24,000	Advances:	
Deposits:		Imprest	20
Graduated Tax	1,440	Wages	600
		Investments:	
		Government Stock	600
		Balance - Cash in Hand	3,114
	71,078		71,078

* Often referred to (less correctly) as "recurrent revenue" and "recurrent expenditure".

The above statement is based on the system of book-keeping used by many central governments.

Now that the figures are arranged in order, certain conclusions can be drawn about the receipts and payments of the Council:

(a) Recurrent receipts U 9,638 exceed recurrent payments U 6,744 by U 2,894;

(b) Capital (sometimes called non-recurrent) receipts from grants U 24,000 and loans U 36,000 have been correctly used to finance capital payments on the Council offices U 60,000;

(c) Cash received for graduated tax U 1,440 has been treated as a "deposit" to be repaid by the Council. It is owed to the Government and is therefore a liability (creditor);

(d) Cash paid for the imprest (U 20) and wages advance U 600 have been treated as "advances". They will be recovered by the Council at a later date, and are therefore assets (debtors); and

(e) Investments of U 600 will be held in addition to cash balances.

No distinction has been drawn between the purchase of new equipment and repairs to existing equipment. The new equipment purchased from revenue has been treated as a normal recurrent payment.

Municipal Accounts - Introduction

Notice that a line has been drawn across the statement of receipts and payments. This separates what are sometimes referred to as "above-the-line" receipts and payments, from "below-the-line" receipts and payments.

If the accounts were to be prepared on the lines required by some Governments the various items of receipts and payments would be posted to accounts as follows:

	Revenue Account						1
19			Units	19			Units
Jan.31	To Publications	C.B.	150	Jan.31	By Rates		7,400
	To Market Rent	C.B.	60		By Sales of Publications		134
	To Water Charges	C.B.	560		By Market Fees		44
	To Equipment	C.B.	400		By Block Grant		2,000
	To Equipment Maintenance	C.B.	3		By Licences		60
	To Loan Charges	C.B.	1,360				
	To Salaries	C.B.	3,000				
	To Wages	C.B.	1,200				
	To Postage	C.B.	6				
	To Stationery	C.B.	3				
	To Meetings	C.B.	2				
	To Revenue Account Surplus	2	2,894				
			9,638				9,638
			=====				=====

	General Revenue Balance						2
19				19			
Jan.31	To Balance	c/d	2,894	Jan.31	By Surplus for Jan.	1	894
			2,894				894
			=====				===
				Feb.1	By Balance	b/d	894

205

Municipal Accounting for Developing Countries

			Suspense Account				3
19 Jan.31	To Capital Account	4	60,000	19 Jan.31	By Loan (cash) By Grant (cash)	C.B. C.B.	36,000 24,000
			60,000 ======				60,000 ======

			Capital Account - Offices				4
19 Jan.31	To Cash	C.B.	60,000	19 Jan.31	By Transfer from Suspense Account	3	60,000
			60,000 ======				60,000 ======

			Advance - Imprest				5
19 Jan.31	To Cash	C.B.	20 ==	19 Jan.31	By Balance	c/d	20 ==
Feb. 1	To Balance	b/d	20				

			Advance - Wages				6
19 Jan.31	To Cash	C.B.	600 ===	19 Jan.31	By Balance	c/d	600 ===
Feb.1	To Balance	b/d	600				

			Deposit - Graduated Tax				7
19 Jan.31	To Balance	c/d	1,440 =====	19 Jan.31	By Cash	C.B.	1,440 =====
				Feb.1	By Balance	b/d	1,440

Municipal Accounts - Introduction

Investment - Government Stock								8
19 Jan.31	To Cash	C.B.	600 ===	19 Jan.31	By Balance	c/d	600 ===
Feb.1	To Balance	b/d	600					

A statement of receipts and payments would be published and the balances on the various accounts would be listed in a statement known as a "Statement of Assets and Liabilities".

Statement of Assets and Liabilities as at 31 Jan. 19

Liabilities		Assets	
	Units		Units
Deposits	1,440	Cash	-
Suspense	-	Bank	3,114
*General Account	2,894	Investments	600
*Reserve Account	-	Fixed Deposits	-
*Vehicle Advances Fund	-	Advances	
		(a) Personal	600
		(b) Motor Vehicles	-
		(c) Imprests	20
	4,334		4,334

The statement includes only "Current Assets" and "Current Liabilities" and the heading "Liabilities" covers certin balances (*) which are in fact surpluses. Notice also that a "Suspense" account has been used in a different way to that normally used in a complete double-entry system. Here it is used to eliminate fixed assets and long-term liabilities from the accounts.

The publication of a classified "Statement of Receipts and Payments" together with the "Statement of Assets and Liabilities" shown above is a vast improvement on the unclassified "Statement of Receipts and Payments" shown earlier.

To complete the financial picture we should still require certain notes of explanation as follows:

(a) The Council owns offices (valued at cost) worth U 60,000 and equipment (at cost) worth U 400.

(b) There is a loan of U 36,000 outstanding.

(c) There are arrears of rates totalling U 1,100 and U 500 has been received in advance.

(d) There are outstanding accounts for the purchase of publications U 100 and electricity supply U 960.

(e) The unsold stock of publications (valued at cost) is worth U 155.

76. COMPLETE FINAL ACCOUNTS

If the Chief Financial Officer wishes to present to his Council a full set of final accounts, giving the complete financial position without the need for detailed explanatory notes, he must use a complete double-entry system.

The procedure necessary to convert "single-entry" accounts to "double-entry" accounts is as follows:

(a) Draw up a statement of affairs setting out the financial position as known at the beginning of the period.

(b) Journalise the opening balances and post them to a set of ledger accounts.

(c) Post cash receipts during the period (in total) to the credit of appropriate ledger accounts.

(d) Post cash payments during the period (in total) to the debit of appropriate ledger accounts.

(e) Take out a trial balance.

(f) Journalise final adjustments, posting (in total or in detail) to appropriate ledger accounts.

(g) Draw up revenue accounts.

(h) Prepare balance sheet.

The procedure, which is similar to that used for the Victory Sports Club in Chapter 6, is as follows:

(a) **Opening Statement of Affairs.**

(b) **Opening Journal and Ledger Entries.**

As the Council is starting on 1 Jan. 19 no opening entries are required.

(c) **Post Cash Receipts to Ledger.**

The amounts are posted in total from the various columns of the abstract of receipts. Cash receipts are all debits in the cash book and must therefore be posted to the credit of other ledger accounts.

Capital Grant

The grant of U 24,000 is a "specific grant" to help in financing the purchase of Council offices. It is a gain (or capital income) used to discharge capital expenditure (on fixed assets) and is credited to a "Capital Discharged - Grant" account.

Loan

The loan of U 36,000 incurs a liability to the lender which must be credited to a personal account.

Municipal Accounts - Introduction

Rates

As we shall see in the final adjustments - the actual rate income due to the Council is a 1% levy on R.V. of U 800,000 that is U 8,000. Receipts of cash from individual ratepayers will be credited against their names in a subsidiary record known as a "Rate Book" (see later). The total collections will be credited in the ledger to a collective personal account known as a "Ratepayers (Rates) Control Account".

Sales of Publications
Market Fees

These are all items of cash income to be posted to nominal accounts.

Graduated Tax

This is not the authority's income. It is money collected on behalf of another authority. There is a liability to pay the graduated tax over, and a personal account must be opened in the name of this authority.

Revenue Grant

Unlike the Capital Grant, which was for a specific purpose, the revenue grant is given to finance normal revenue expenditure. It is therefore posted to a nominal account as normal revenue income. (We assume at this stage that the grant paid in the financial period is the grant due.)

(d) Post Cash Payments to Ledger.

As with receipts, the amounts are posted in total. Cash payments are credits in the cash book and the payments abstract provides totals to be posted to the debit of ledger accounts.

Imprest

This sum is advanced as a "float" to the Chief Executive Officer. The Chief Executive Officer is expected to be responsible for this sum and to account for it from time to time. In one way it represents a debt due to the Council to be posted to a personal account in the name of the imprest-holder. However, it is normal to regard it as a separate part of the Council's stock of cash and to treat it as a real (asset) account to be listed with other cash in the balance sheet.

Publications Market Rent

These are both items of revenue expenditure to be debited to nominal accounts.

Council Offices

This is capital expenditure for the purchase of a fixed asset. The U 60,000 is debited to a real account for "Council Offices".

Water Charges

Revenue expenditure to be debited to a nominal account for "Water Charges".

Municipal Accounting for Developing Countries

Equipment

Capital expenditure on fixed assets. U 400 to be debited to a real account for "Equipment".

Loan Charges

The repayment of principal of U 1,000 reduces the loan outstanding from U 36,000 to U 35,000. As a reduction in a liability it is debited to the personal account of the lender.

The interest of U 360 represents a charge made by the lender for the use of one month of U 36,000 cash. It is a loss (or expenses) to be debited to a nominal account for "Loan Charges - Interest". For simplicity we have assumed an instalment loan - more normally local government loans are repaid by the annuity method. Interest is calculated only on the balance outstanding at the end of the previous month. In Feb. the interest would be 1% of U 35,000 (i.e. U 350); in March 1% of U 34,000 (i.e. U 340) and so on.

When all receipts and payments have been posted from the abstracts the ledger accounts will appear as:

		Council Offices					1
19 Jan 31	To Cash	C.B.	60,000				

		Equipment					2
19 Jan.31	To Cash	C.B.	400				

		Loan					3
19 Jan.31	To Cash	C.B.	1,000	19 Jan.31	By Cash	C.B.	36,000

		Government Graduated Tax					5
				19 Jan.31	By Cash	C.B.	1,440

Municipal Accounts - Introduction

						Capital Discharged - Grant					6
						19 Jan.31	By Cash	C.B.	24,000

					Ratepayers (Rates) Control				11
					19 Jan.31	By Cash	C.B.	7,400

				Repairs Fund Investment - Government Stock					12
19 Jan.31	To Cash	C.B.	600					

				Imprest - Chief Executive Officer					13
19 Jan.31	To Cash	C.B.	20					

				Wages Advances					14
19 Jan.31	To Cash	C.B.	600					

				Publications - Purchases					15
19 Jan.31	To Cash	C.B.	150					

					Publications - Sales					16
					19 Jan.31	By Cash	C.B.	134

Market Rent 18

19 Jan.31	To Cash	C.B.	60				

Market Fees 19

				19 Jan.31	By Cash	C.B.	44

Block Grant 20

				19 Jan.31	By Cash	C.B.	2,000

Licences 22

				19 Jan.31	By Cash	C.B.	60

Salaries 23

19 Jan.31	To Cash	C.B.	3,000				

Wages 24

19 Jan.31	To Cash	C.B.	1,200				

Water Charges 25

19 Jan.31	To Cash	C.B.	560				

Municipal Accounts - Introduction

				Postages					26
19 Jan.31	To Cash	C.B.	6						

				Stationery					27
19 Jan.31	To Cash	C.B.	3						

				Meetings					28
19 Jan.31	To Cash	C.B.	2						

				Loan Charges - Interest					31
19 Jan.31	To Cash	C.B.	360						

				Equipment Maintenance					34
19 Jan.31	To Cash	C.B.	3						

If you will now refer to the abstracts you will see that under each column is the folio number of the account in the ledger to which it has been posted. The abstracts have formed a basis for posting in the same way as journals. Later in the Course we shall see how this simple form of abstract is developed to become an "income journal" or "expenditure journal".

(e) **Trial Balance**

A trial balance extracted from the ledger accounts so far posted, (including the bank balance) will appear as:

Municipal Accounting for Developing Countries

TRIAL BALANCE

		Units	Units
Cash at Bank	C.B.	3,114	
Council Offices	1	60,000	
Equipment	2	400	
Loan	3	1,000	36,000
Graduated Tax	5		1,440
Capital Discharged - Grant	6		24,000
Ratepayers (Rates) Control	11		7,400
Repairs Fund Investment -Government Stock	12	600	
Imprest - Chief Executive Officer	13	20	
Wages Advances	14	600	
Publications - Purchases	15	150	
Publications - Sales	16		134
Market Rent	18	60	
Market Fees	19		44
Block Grant	20		2,000
Licences	22		60
Salaries	23	3,000	
Wages	24	1,200	
Water Charges	25	560	
Postages	26	6	
Stationery	27	3	
Meetings	28	2	
Loan Charges - Interest	31	360	
Equipment Maintenance	34	3	
		71,078	71,078

The accountant has thus analysed and classified the information. His next step is to combine the information with other known facts. He does this in making the final adjustments.

(f) Journalising and Posting Final Adjustments

The final adjustments fall into two main classes:

(i) Assets and liabilities not yet appearing in the books must be properly accounted for.

(ii) The surplus must be correctly allocated to show how much of it relates to the cost of fixed assets which has been fully financed (i.e. Capital Discharged) and how much is General Fund (i.e. Revenue Account) surplus.

The detailed procedure is as follows:

(i) Assets and Liabilities

The first asset not yet accounted for is the stock of unsold publications. A count of the stocks will be made and a stocktaking list drawn up. The items will be priced at cost to give the value of unsold stocks (at cost) at 31 Jan. as follows:

Municipal Accounts - Introduction

```
┌─────────────────────────────────────────────────────────────┐
│                      MAKALE COUNCIL                         │
│                    INFORMATION CENTRE                       │
│                                                             │
│               Stationery Stock at 31 Jan. 19                │
├──────────────────┬──────────┬────────────┬─────────────────┤
│      Item        │ Quantity │ Cost Price │     Value       │
│                  │   PKTS   │  PER PKT   │                 │
│                  │          │   Units    │     Units       │
│ Town Guide Books │    66    │    1.50    │      99         │
│ Town Maps        │   112    │    0.50    │      56         │
│                  │          │            │     ___         │
│                  │          │            │     155         │
│                  │          │            │     ===         │
└──────────────────┴──────────┴────────────┴─────────────────┘
```

The U 155 will be credited to the Information Centre Trading Account as "Closing Stock" and debited to the "Stock" account, through the journal as follows:

```
┌──────────┬────────────────────────────────┬────┬─────┬──────┐
│ 19       │                                │    │     │      │
│ Jan.31   │ Stock                      DR. │ 10 │ 155 │      │
│          │   To Information Centre        │    │     │      │
│          │      Trading Account           │ 17 │     │ 155  │
│          │   Being stationery stocks      │    │     │      │
│          │   on hand at 31 Jan.           │    │     │      │
│          │   (valued at cost).            │    │     │      │
└──────────┴────────────────────────────────┴────┴─────┴──────┘
```

The other outstanding asset is that of debtors. The 220 ratepayers owing U 5 each have not been accounted for. The Council will keep a rate book to show how much is due and received from each ratepayer. As a control over the rate collection the total rate debit will be calculated as:

Rateable Value U 800,000

Rate levy for Jan. 1% (ie $\underline{\text{Annual Levy - 12\%)}}$
12

Total rates due for Jan. U 800,000 x 1% = U 8,000

This sum is the income to be accounted for in January and to be debited against the ratepayers in total. The rating section will have recorded in detail that this U 8,000 is to be collected or otherwise accounted for in January. In fact U 7,400 has already been collected and credited to the account. The debit to the ratepayers will be recorded in the main ledger by a journal entry as follows:

```
┌──────────┬────────────────────────────────┬────┬───────┬───────┐
│ 19       │                                │    │       │       │
│ Jan.31   │ Ratepayers (Rates) Control DR. │ 11 │ 8,000 │       │
│          │   To Rate Income               │ 21 │       │ 8,000 │
│          │   Being rates due for January  │    │       │       │
│          │   (1% of U 800,000 R.V.)       │    │       │       │
└──────────┴────────────────────────────────┴────┴───────┴───────┘
```

Municipal Accounting for Developing Countries

The first liabilities to deal with are the unpaid accounts. These can be listed in a creditors list as follows:

<table>
<tr><td colspan="6" align="center">MAKALE COUNCIL

Unpaid Creditors 31 Jan. 19</td></tr>
<tr><td>Date of Invoice</td><td>Name</td><td>Details</td><td>Account to be Debited</td><td>Amount
Units</td><td>Date Paid</td></tr>
<tr><td>19
Jan.3</td><td>Government Printer</td><td>200 PKTS publications @ 50 cents each pkt</td><td>Publications Purchases</td><td>100</td><td></td></tr>
<tr><td>31</td><td>Electricity Board</td><td>Electricity @ Council Offices</td><td>Electricity</td><td>960</td><td></td></tr>
<tr><td colspan="4" align="center">TOTAL SUNDRY CREDITORS</td><td>1,060
=====</td><td></td></tr>
</table>

The amounts due to be paid represent expenditure which must be debited to appropriate nominal accounts for "Publications - Purchases" and "Electricity".

The liabilities could be credited to personal accounts, specially opened for the two separate creditors. This is not necessary however. The U 1,060 can be credited IN TOTAL to a single "Sundry Creditors (Control) Account".

The journal entry is:

19
Jan.31
	Publications - Purchases DR.
	Electricity DR.
	  To Sundry Creditors (Control)
	  Being expenditure incurred
	  and unpaid to date.
		15
		29
		4
			100
			960
				1,060

The Sundry Creditors (Control) account will appear as:

		Sundry Creditors (Control)			4
			19 Jan.31 By Sundry Accounts	J	1,060

When settlement is made in February the list will be marked off as paid in the "date paid" column. There will be an analysis column for "Sundry Creditors" on the payments abstract for February. At the end of

Municipal Accounts - Introduction

February the total of this column will be debited to the Sundry Creditors (Control) account, which will then show:

\multicolumn{6}{c}{Sundry Creditors (Control)}		4
19 Jan.31	To Balance	c/d	1,060	19 Jan.31	By Sundry Accounts	J	1,060
			=====				=====
Feb.28	To Cash	C.B.	1,060	Feb.1	By Balance	b/d	1,060

The other liability concerns repairs. A monthly sum of U 600 is being invested to meet a future liability for repairs to the Council offices. We know that there will definitely be repairs to the offices in the future - what we do not know is the exact cost of these repairs. We must therefore make provision for the liability. This can be defined as:

"Amounts set aside to meet specific commitments, known contingencies and diminutions in values of assets existing as at the date of the balance sheet where the amounts involved cannot be determined with substantial accuracy".

When the Council invested U 600 it had only dealt with half the transaction. It had invested the provision before it had been "set aside".

The present use of the Council offices is the cause of future repairs The sum set aside to meet these future costs is regarded as revenue expenditure to be debited to a nominal account. The provision will be credited to the Repairs Fund. The journal will appear as:

19 Jan.31	Provision for Repairs
	  To Repairs Fund
	  Being the setting aside of
	  provision for repairs to
	  the Council offices.
		DR.	30
			9
				600	600

When actual repairs are carried out their cost will be debited to the Repairs Fund.

(ii) Capital Discharged

What are the capital assets of the Council and by how much has their cost been fully discharged at 31 Jan?

Municipal Accounting for Developing Countries

The position is:

Fixed Assets
	Council offices		60,000
	Equipment		400
	TOTAL ASSETS (AT COST)		60,400
Less **Loan Outstanding**			35,000
	CAPITAL DISCHARGED		25,400 (ie NET CAPITAL RESOURCES)

Represented by:
Capital Grant		24,000
Contribution from Revenue		400
Loan Repaid		1,000
CAPITAL DISCHARGED		25,400 (ie NET CAPITAL RESULTS)

The U 24,000 grant has already been credited to a "Capital Discharged" account. No entries have yet been made for the two other items.

The purchase of equipment represented a decrease in current (cash) and an increase in fixed assets (equipment). Capital expenditure has been paid for with current revenue money. The purchase has already been recorded in the books - but the financing of the purchase out of current income must still be dealt with (see Section 82). A nominal account "Revenue Contributions to Capital" is debited with the amount of the revenue loss (or expense) and a "Capital Discharged - Revenue Contributions to Capital" account is credited with the capital surplus. The financing of the equipment is now shown as revenue expenditure. It will appear in the Revenue account as expenditure to be met from revenue income.

The repayment of the loan represented a decrease in current assets (cash) and an equal decrease in long-term liability (loan outstanding). This has been recorded in the books. To charge the loan repayment against current income it is now necessary to debit a nominal account "Loan Charges - Principal" with the amount of the revenue loss (or expense) and credit the "Capital Discharged - Loans Repaid" account.

The journal entries will be:

19				
Jan.31	Revenue Account (R.C.C.) DR. To Capital Discharged (R.C.C.) Being purchase of fixed assets now financed by a Revenue Contribution to Capital Outlay.	337	400	400
Jan.31	Loan Charges - Principal DR. To Capital Discharged (Loan Repaid) Being repayment of loan debt now charged to Revenue Account	318	1,000	1,000

When all final adjustments have been made and the "Publications - Purchases" and "Publications - Sales" accounts have been transferred to

Municipal Accounts - Introduction

the "Information Centre Trading Account" the ledger accounts will appear as follows:

				Council Offices			1
19 Jan.31	To Cash	C.B.	60,000				

				Equipment			2
19 Jan.31	To Cash	C.B.	400				

				Loan			3
19 Jan.31	To Cash	C.B.	1,000	19 Jan.31	By Cash	C.B.	36,000

				Sundry Creditors Control			4
				19 Jan.31	By Sundry Accounts	J	1,060

				Government - Graduated Tax			5
				19 Jan.31	By Cash	C.B.	1,440

				Capital Discharged			6
				19 Jan.31	By Cash	C.B.	24,000

Capital Discharged - Revenue Contribution to Capital — 7

				19 Jan.31	By Revenue Account (R.C.C.)	J	400

Capital Discharged - Loan Repaid — 8

				19 Jan.31	By Loan Charges (Principal)	J	1,000

Repairs Fund — 9

				19 Jan.31	By Provision for Month	J	600

Stock of Publications — 10

19 Jan.31	To Trading Account	J	155				

Ratepayers (Rates) Control — 11

19 Jan.31	To Rate Income	J	8,000	19 Jan.31	By Cash	C.B.	7,400

Repairs Fund Investment - Stock — 12

19 Jan.31	To Cash	C.B.	600				

Municipal Accounts - Introduction

Imprest - Chief Executive Officer   13

| 19 Jan.31 | To Cash | C.B. | 20 | | | | |

Wages Advance   14

| 19 Jan.31 | To Cash | C.B. | 600 | | | | |

Publications - Purchases   15

19 Jan.31	To Cash	C.B.	150	19 Jan.31	By Trading Account	J	250
	To Sundry Creditors	J	100				
			250				250
			===				===

Publications - Sales   16

19 Jan.31	To Trading Account	J	134	19 Jan.31	By Cash	C.B.	134
			134				134
			===				===

Information Centre Trading Account   17

| 19 Jan.31 | To Purchases | J | 250 | 19 Jan.31 | By Sales | J | 134 |
| | | | | | By Stock (closing) | J | 155 |

Market Rent   18

| 119 Jan.31 | To Cash | C.B. | 60 | | | | |

Municipal Accounting for Developing Countries

				Market Fees			19
				19 Jan.31	By Cash	C.B.	44

				Block Grant			20
				19 Jan.31	By Cash	C.B.	2,000

				Rate Income			21
				19 Jan.31	By Rate-payers	J	8,000

				Licences			22
				19 Jan.31	By Cash	C.B.	60

				Salaries			23
19 Jan.31	To Cash	C.B.	3,000				

				Wages			24
19 Jan.31	To Cash	C.B.	1,200				

				Water Charges			25
19 Jan.31	To Cash	C.B.	560				

Municipal Accounts - Introduction

			Postages					26
19 Jan.31	To Cash	C.B.	6					

			Stationery					27
19 Jan.31	To Cash	C.B.	3					

			Meetings					28
19 Jan.31	To Cash	C.B.	2					

			Electricity					29
19 Jan.31	To Sundry Creditors	J	960					

			Provision for Repairs					30
19 Jan.31	To Repairs Fund Contribution	J	600					

			Loan Charges - Principal					31
19 Jan.31	To Capital Dis-charged	J	1,000					

			Loan Charges - Interest					32
19 Jan.31	To Cash	C.B.	360					

		Revenue Contributions to Capital				33
19 Jan.31	To Capital Dis- charged (R.C.C.)	J	400			

		Equipment Maintenance				34
19 Jan.31	To Cash	C.B.	3			

The journal entries for transfer of puchases and sales of publications to the "Information Centre Trading Account" were:

19 Jan.31	Publications - Sales DR.	16	134	
	To Trading Account	17		134
	Trading Account DR.	17	250	
	To Publications - Purchases	15		250
	Being transfer of Sales and Purchases to Trading Account.			

The cash book information has now been analysed, classified and combined with other known facts. The next step is to summarise the facts. The accountant does this by producing final accounts and a balance sheet. These are often referred to as financial statements.

(g) **Draw up Revenue Accounts**

Remember that the accountant produces information in a form which assists in making better decisions. For the Kambale Council it would be wise to produce the following revenue accounts:

(i)   General Revenue Account.

(ii)   Information Centre Revenue Account.

(iii)   Market Revenue Account.

The balances (surplus or deficiency) on the separate revenue accounts will (in this case) be transferred to the General Fund. This is not always done, as will be seen later. Housing and trading undertaking accounts, for example, usually carry their balances forward separately.

Before preparing the final accounts, a second trial balance could be drawn up as follows:

Municipal Accounts - Introduction

Account	FO.	DR.	CR.	R/A or B/S
		Units	Units	
Cash	C.B.	3,114		B/S
Council Offices	1	60,000		B/S
Equipment	2	400		B/S
Loan	3	1,000	36,000	B/S
Sundry Creditors - Control	4		1,060	B/S
Government - Graduated Tax	5		1,440	B/S
Capital Discharged - Grant	6		24,000	B/S
Capital Discharged - Revenue Contributions to Capital	7		400	B/S
Capital Discharged - Loan Repaid	8		1,000	B/S
Repairs Fund	9		600	B/S
Stock of Publications	10	155		B/S
Ratepayers (Rates) Control	11	8,000	7,400	B/S
Repairs Fund Investment	12	600		B/S
Imprest - Chief Executive Officer	13	20		B/S
Wages Advances	14	600		B/S
Information Centre Trading Account	17	250	289	I/C/R
Market Rent	18	60		M/R
Market Fees	19		44	M/R
Block Grant	20		2,000	G/R
Rate Income	21		8,000	G/R
Licences	22		60	G/R
Salaries	23	3,000		G/R
Wages	24	1,200		G/R
Water Charges	25	560		G/R
Postages	26	6		G/R
Stationery	27	3		G/R
Meetings	28	2		G/R
Electricity	29	960		G/R
Provision for Repairs	30	600		G/R
Loan Charges - Principal	31	1,000		G/R
Loan Charges - Interest	32	360		G/R
Revenue Contributions to Capital	33	400		G/R
Equipment Maintenance	34	3		G/R
		82,293	82,293	

Key

B/S - Balances carried forward and included in Balance Sheet.
I/C/R - Balances transferred to Information Centre Revenue Account.
M/R - Balances transferred to Markets Revenue Account.
G/R - Balances transferred to General Fund Revenue Account.

The completed ledger and final accounts will now appear as follows:

	Council Offices						1
19 Jan.31	To Cash	C.B.	60,000	19 Jan.31	By Balance	c/d	60,000
Feb.1	To Balance	b/d	60,000				

Municipal Accounting for Developing Countries

		Equipment						2
19 Jan.31	To Cash	C.B.	400	19 Jan.31	By Balance	c/d	400	
Feb.1	To Balance	c/d	400					

		Loan						3
19 Jan.31	To Cash	C.B.	1,000	19 Jan.31	By Cash	C.B.	36,000	
31	To Balance	c/d	35,000					
			36,000				36,000	
				Feb.1	By Balance	b/d	35,000	

		Sundry Creditors Control						4
19 Jan.31	To Balance	c/d	1,060	19 Jan.31	By Sundry Accounts	J	1,060	
			1,060				1,060	
				Feb.1	By Balance	b/d	1,060	

		Government - Graduated Tax						5
19 Jan.31	To Balance	c/d	1,440	19 Jan.31	By Cash	C.B.	1,440	
				Feb.1	By Balance	b/d	1,440	

		Capital Discharged - Grant						6
19 Jan.31	To Balance	c/d	24,000	19 Jan.31	By Cash	C.B.	24,000	
				Feb.1	By Balance	b/d	24,000	

Municipal Accounts - Introduction

									7
\multicolumn{10}{c}{Capital Discharged - Revenue Contribution to Capital}
19 Jan.31	To Balance	c/d	400	19 Jan.31	By Revenue Account (R.C.C.)		J		400
			400 ===						400 ===
				Feb.1	By Balance		b/d		400

									8
\multicolumn{10}{c}{Capital Discharged - Loan Repaid}
19 Jan.31	To Balance	c/d	1,000	19 Jan.31	By Loan Charges - (Principal)		J		1,000
			1,000 =====						1,000 =====
				Feb.1	By Balance		b/d		1,000

									9
\multicolumn{10}{c}{Repairs Fund}
19 Jan.31	To Balance	c/d	600	19 Jan.31	By Provision for Month		J		600
			600 ===						600 ===
				Feb.1	By Balance		b/d		600

									10
\multicolumn{10}{c}{Stock of Publications}
19 Jan.31	To Trading Account	J	155	19 Jan.31	By Balance		c/d		155
			155 ===						155 ===
Feb.1	To Balance	b/d	155						

Ratepayers (Rates) Control — 11

19				19			
Jan.31	To Rate Income	J	8,000	Jan.31	By Cash	C.B.	7,400
31	To Balance (advance receipts)	c/d	500	31	By Balance (arrears)	c/d	1,100
			8,500				8,500
			=====				=====
Feb.1	To Balance (arrears)	b/d	1,100	Feb.1	By Balance (advance receipts)	b/d	500

Repairs Fund Investment - Stock — 12

19				19			
Jan.31	To Cash	C.B.	600	Jan.31	By Balance	c/d	600
			===				===
Feb.1	To Balance	b/d	600				

Imprest - Chief Executive Officer — 13

19				19			
Jan.31	To Cash	C.B.	20	Jan.31	By Balance	c/d	20
			==				=
Feb.1	To Balance	b/d	20				

Wages Advances — 14

19				19			
Jan.31	To Cash	C.B.	600	Jan.31	By Balance	c/d	600
			===				===
Feb.1	To Balance	b/d	600				

Publications - Purchases — 15

19				19			
Jan.31	To Cash	C.B.	150	Jan.31	By Trading Account	J	250
	To Sundry Creditors	J	100				
			250				250
			===				===

Municipal Accounts - Introduction

Publications - Sales   16

Date	Particulars	Folio	Amount	Date	Particulars	Folio	Amount
19 Jan.31	To Trading Account	J	134	19 Jan.31	By Cash	C.B.	134
			134 ===				134 ===

Information Centre Trading Account   17

Date	Particulars	Folio	Amount	Date	Particulars	Folio	Amount
19 Jan.31	To Purchases	J	250	19 Jan.31	By Sales	J	134
	Gross Profit to Revenue Account	35	39		By Stock (closing)	J	155
			289 ===				289 ===

Market Rent   18

Date	Particulars	Folio	Amount	Date	Particulars	Folio	Amount
19 Jan.31	To Cash	C.B.	60	19 Jan.31	By Revenue Account	36	60
			60 ==				60 ==

Market Fees   19

Date	Particulars	Folio	Amount	Date	Particulars	Folio	Amount
19 Jan.31	To Revenue Account	36	44	19 Jan.31	By Cash	C.B.	44
			44 ==				44 ==

Block Grant   20

Date	Particulars	Folio	Amount	Date	Particulars	Folio	Amount
19 Jan.31	To Revenue Account	37	2,000	19 Jan.31	By Cash	C.B.	2,000
			2,000 =====				2,000 =====

Municipal Accounting for Developing Countries

			Rate Income				21
19 Jan.31	To Revenue Account	37	8,000 =====	19 Jan.31	By Rate-payers	J	8,000 =====

			Licences				22
19 Jan.31	To Revenue Account	37	60 — 60 ==	19 Jan.31	By Cash	C.B.	60 — 60 ==

			Salaries				23
19 Jan.31	To Cash	C.B.	3,000 — 3,000 =====	19 Jan.31	By Revenue Account	37	3,000 — 3,000 =====

			Wages				24
19 Jan.31	To Cash	C.B.	1,200 — 1,200 =====	19 Jan.31	By Revenue Account	37	1,200 — 1,200 =====

			Water Charges				25
19 Jan.31	To Cash	C.B.	560 — 560 ===	19 Jan.31	By Revenue Account	37	560 — 560 ===

Municipal Accounts - Introduction

								26
		Postages						
19 Jan.31	To Cash	C.B.	6	19 Jan.31	By Revenue Account		37	6
			6					6

								27
		Stationery						
19 Jan.31	To Cash	C.B.	3	19 Jan.31	By Revenue Account		37	3
			3					3

								28
		Meetings						
19 Jan.31	To Cash	C.B.	2	19 Jan.31	By Revenue Account		37	2
			2					2

								29
		Electricity						
19 Jan.31	To Sundry Creditors	J	960	19 Jan.31	By Revenue Account			960

								30
		Provision for Repairs						
19 Jan.31	To Repairs Fund Contribution	J	600	19 Jan.31	By Revenue Account			600
			600					600

Municipal Accounting for Developing Countries

\multicolumn{8}{c	}{Loan Charges - Principal}	31
19 Jan.31	To Capital Dis- charged	J	1,000	19 Jan.31	By Revenue Account	37	1,000
			1,000 =====				1,000 =====

\multicolumn{8}{c	}{Loan Charges - Interest}	32
19 Jan.31	To Cash	C.B.	360	19 Jan.31	By Revenue Account	37	360
			360 ===				360 ===

\multicolumn{8}{c	}{Revenue Contributions to Capital}	33
19 Jan.31	To Capital Dis- charged (R.C.C.)	J	400	19 Jan.31	By Revenue Account	37	400
			400 ===				400 ===

\multicolumn{8}{c	}{Equipment Maintenance}	34
19 Jan.31	To Cash	C.B.	3	19 Jan.31	By Revenue Account	37	3
			3 =				3 =

Municipal Accounts - Introduction

	Information Centre Revenue Account							35
19 Jan.31	Here would be debited any expenses specific to the Information Centre			19 Jan.31	By Gross Profit on Sales of Publications			39
31	To Surplus transferred to General Fund	38	39					
			$\overline{39}$ ==					$\overline{39}$ ==

	Market Revenue Account							36
19 Jan.31	To Hire of Market Premises (Rent)	18	60	19 Jan.31	By Market Fees	19	44	
					By Deficiency transferred to General Fund	38	16	
			$\overline{60}$ ==					$\overline{60}$ ==

MAKALE COUNCIL

Balance Sheet as at 31 Jan. 19

	Units	Units	Units		Units	Units	Units
LONG-TERM LIABILITIES				FIXED ASSETS			
Loan Outstanding			35,000	Council Offices		60,000	
				Equipment		400	60,400
CURRENT LIABILITIES							
Creditors		1,060		CURRENT ASSETS			
Sundry Creditors		500		Stocks and Stores		155	
Receipts in Advance (Rates)		1,440		Debtors			
Graduated Tax Deposits			3,000	Sundry Debtors (Rates)	1,100		
				Payments in Advance (Wages)	600	1,700	
PROVISIONS							
Repairs Fund			600	Investments		600	
SURPLUS				Cash			
Capital Discharged	24,000			at Bank	3,114		
Grants	1,000			Petty Cash (Imprest)	20	3,134	
Loans Repaid	400						
Revenue Contributions		25,400					5,589
General Fund Surplus		1,989	27,389				
			65,989				65,989

Municipal Accounts - Introduction

				General Revenue Account				37
19 Jan.31	To Salaries	23	3,000	19 Jan.31	By Block Grant	20	2,000
	To Wages	24	1,200		By Rate Income	21	8,000
	To Water Charges	25	560		By Licence Fees	22	60
	To Electricity	29	960				
	To Provision for Repairs	30	600				
	To Equipment Maintenance	34	3				
	To Postages	26	6				
	To Stationery	27	3				
	To Meetings	28	2				
	To Loan Charges Principal	31	1,000				
	Interest	32	360				
	To Revenue Contributions to Capital Outlay	33	400				
	To Surplus carried to General Fund	38	1,966				
			10,060				10,060
			======				======

				General Fund				38
19 Jan.31	To Deficiency on Market Revenue Account	36	16	19 Jan.31	By Surplus on Information Centre Revenue Account	35	39
	To Balance	c/d	1,989		By Surplus on General Revenue Account	37	1,966
			2,005				2,005
			=====				=====
				Feb.1	By Balance	b/d	1,989

In theory journal entries should be used to transfer to the final Revenue Accounts. In practice this procedure is often omitted - the post-

235

ings being made direct from the detailed ledger accounts as shown above. The final balance sheet appears on page 234.

77. **EXPLANATION OF TECHNICAL POINTS**

In the above set of accounts there are one or two technical matters which require explanation.

You will notice that the ledger accounts are drawn up only at the end of the financial period. This is standard practice in local and public authorities. Many types of subsidiary record are used to record detailed transactions during the financial period.

Certain accounts are known as "Control" accounts. These are used mainly to record in total only the many individual transactions of exactly the same type which are recorded in subsidiary books. For example, Kambale Council has 1,600 ratepayers. The details of rates due and paid by each ratepayer are best recorded in a specially designed "rate book". For final accounts the entries are in total only in the Ratepayers (Rates) Control account. This is quite sufficient for the double-entry system. The word "control" emphasises internal check. The total rate debit was independently calculated at U 8,000 and debited in the control account. The income section would have to see that the whole of this sum was accounted for. Similarly the total of all creditors U 1,060 has been credited to a Sundry Creditors Control Account. Eventually accounts totalling to this amount must be paid and debited to the account.

Another thing to notice is that there is both a debit and a credit balance brought down on the Ratepayers (Rates) Control Account (folio 11). The debit balance is for arrears and the credit balance for receipts in advance. This information is not readily available from the final accounts but would be obtained from the detailed records of the income (or rating) section. The chief of the income section would submit a statement accounting for the rate debit as follows:

Rate Collection - Jan. 19

		Units
Cash Collected		7,400
Arrears	1,100	
Less Receipts in Advance	500	600
TOTAL RATES DUE		8,000

Notice in the above accounts that the purchase of new equipment (fixed asset) is treated as capital expenditure, whereas repairs to existing equipment is treated as revenue expenditure.

78. **ORDER OF REVENUE ACCOUNT**

With the drawing up of revenue accounts and a balance sheet, the accountant has set out the summary of the facts from which conclusions can now be drawn.

It has been shown in an earlier chapter how the Balance Sheet is

Municipal Accounts - Introduction

prepared in a particular form to illustrate the financial position.

The Revenue Account, too, should be set out with its figures in a logical order. Notice in our example that the expenditure items in the General Fund Revenue Account have not been thrown together in a haphazard fashion. They are not merely in the order in which they appear in the ledger - but are grouped as follows:

Employees	Salaries
	Wages
Premises	Water Charges
	Electricity
	Provision for Repairs
Equipment	Equipment Maintenance
Establishment Expenses	Postages Stationery
	Stationery
	Meetings
Capital Finance	Loan Charges
	Revenue Contributions to Capital.

79. **CONCLUSIONS**

What conclusions can be drawn from the Revenue Accounts and Balance Sheet of Makale Council?

The Revenue Accounts show:

(a) That the Information Centre makes a surplus providing it is staffed by voluntary workers. If the Council employs staff, or pays rent for the premises, the selling prices of publications will have to be increased or more will have to be sold.

(b) That the market is operating at a loss and the Council will have to increase the market fees; or attract more traders to the market; or open the market more frequently than once a week; or negotiate for a lower rent; or continue to subsidise the activity.

(c) That the General Fund Revenue Account shows a considerable surplus and there might be a case for reducing rates; there would probably be a better case for using surpluses to build up a capital fund; to expand services; to meet increased loan charges on further capital expenditure; to make more revenue contributions to capital outlay, or to pay off the existing loan more quickly to save interest charges.

(d) The General Fund has built up quite a large net surplus - this will be required by the chief financial officer as a working balance to retain a margin of cash to meet future payments without having to wait for receipts. It may still not be enough. On the other hand it may be more than enough, in which case idle cash should be invested.

Upon examining the Balance Sheet we see that the Council appears to be in a sound financial position, considering this has been only the first month of operation - but some of the strength is due to the grant of U 24,000 towards the Council Offices. Loan interest on this sum would have been about another U 240 per month. We see that the rate collection procedure is not yet working smoothly - nearly 14% of the rates due are already in arrears. Wages advances appear high when related to the total monthly wages payable - the Council should lay down a policy about advances.

Many other conclusions can be drawn from the Balance Sheet - in fact if the Council's activities are to expand, the financial position may not be so strong as it first appears.

Properly prepared accounts give a wealth of information which is not available unless a complete double-entry system is used. Sound policy decisions can be more easily made where complete accounts are kept. As an example of the danger of making decisions based on incomplete information, consider the Information Centre in the above accounts. The accounts show that a profit of U 39 was made. On the other hand the statement of receipts and payments shows that payments for publications (U 150) exceeded receipts from sales (U 134) by U 16. By ignoring the creditors and the closing stock the impression has been given that the Information Centre is making a "loss". A decision might well have been made to close down an activity which was earning income for the Council!

80. **THE BALANCE SHEET**

How can we determine from the Balance Sheet the RESOURCES of the Council and the accumulated RESULTS of its activities? This can be achieved by re-arranging the figures in the form of a NARRATIVE Balance Sheet, as follows:

MAKALE COUNCIL

Balance Sheet as at 31 Jan. 19

	Units	Units
FIXED ASSET		
Council Offices	60,000	
Equipment	400	60,400
CURRENT ASSETS		
Stocks and Stores	155	
Debtors	1,700	
Investments	600	
Cash	3,134	5,589
		65,989
Less		
LONG-TERM LIABILITIES		
Loan Outstanding	35,000	
CURRENT LIABILITIES		
Creditors	3,000	
PROVISIONS		
Repairs Fund	600	38,600
NET RESOURCES		27,389
Represented by:		
SURPLUS		
Capital Discharged		25,400
General Fund Surplus		1,989
NET RESULTS		27,389

Municipal Accounts - Introduction

81. **SURPLUS AND CAPITAL DISCHARGED**

Although the Council holds net surplus balances totalling U 27,389, most of this sum U 25,400 is held in the form of fixed assets. Only the Revenue Account surplus U 1,989 is available for future spending, unless the Council was prepared to sell the Council Offices or the equipment!

This distinction between the "Capital" and "Revenue" aspects of a local or public authority's accounts is most important.

A Local Authority normally meets capital payments from capital receipts (eg loans, grants, sales of old assets).
Some of these receipts (i.e. grants and receipts from sales of old assets) represent true capital income. Loans, however, are liabilities which are repaid over a period by charges against revenue income. As stated previously, direct revenue contributions to capital are also met out of revenue income.

To illustrate the distinction between the Capital and Revenue aspects of the Council's financial position the Balance Sheet of Makale Council could be shown in two separate parts as follows:

MAKALE COUNCIL

Balance Sheet as at 31 Jan. 19

Capital

	Units		Units
LONG-TERM LIABILITIES		FIXED ASSETS	
Loans Outstanding	35,000	Council Offices	60,000
SURPLUS		Equipment	400
Capital Discharged	25,400		
	60,400		60,400

Revenue

	Units		Units
CURRENT LIABILITIES		CURRENT ASSETS	
Creditors	3,000	Stocks and Stores	155
PROVISIONS		Debtors	1,700
Repairs Fund	600	Investments	600
SURPLUS		Cash	3,134
General Fund - Surplus	1,989		
	5,589		5,589
	65,989		65,989

82. **THE DOUBLE-ACCOUNT SYSTEM**

The separate accounting for the "Capital" and "Revenue" aspects is known as the "double-account" system. The "double-account" system should not be confused with the "double-entry" system.

The "double-entry" system is the technical system upon which all complete book-keeping is based - summed up in the rule that "all debit entries must be balanced by credit entries". The "double-account" system goes beyond this - to separate the "Capital Accounts" from the "Revenue Accounts".

Municipal Accounting for Developing Countries

There is, however, a relationship between "double-entry" and "double-account" systems.

In "double-entry" all that is required is that TOTAL DEBITS equal TOTAL CREDITS whereas in "double-account" the TOTAL CAPITAL DEBITS must equal TOTAL CAPITAL CREDITS and TOTAL REVENUE DEBITS must equal TOTAL REVENUE CREDITS.

If transactions take place wholly within the "Capital Accounts" or wholly within the "Revenue Accounts" then double-entry is sufficient to record the transaction.

But when transactions affect both the "Capital Accounts" and the "Revenue Accounts" then "quadruple-entry" (four entries) is required. In other words a "double-entry" is required for each of the "double accounts".

Consider the "Capital" transactions of the Kambale Council (above). Imagine the Balance Sheet in its "Revenue" form only before the "Capital" transactions take place.

Revenue

	Units		Units
Current Liabilities	3,000	Current Assets (excluding	
Provisions	600	Cash)	2,455
Revenue Surplus	3,389	Cash	4,534
	6,989		6,989

After the receipt of the grant (capital income) the balance sheet would show:

Capital

	Units		Units
Grant	24,000		

Revenue

Current Liabilities	3,000	Current Assets (excluding	
Provisions	600	Cash)	2,455
Revenue Surplus	3,389	Cash (4,534 + 24,000)	28,534
	30,989		30,989

The double-entry to arrive at the above position was:

    DR. Cash.   )
    CR. Grant.   ) U 24,000

but although the Balance Sheet as a whole balances, the separate Capital and Revenue sections are out of balance. Balance is restored by allocating U 24,000 cash to the Capital Account:

    DR. Cash (Capital).   )
    CR. Cash (Revenue).   ) U 24,000

after which the Balance Sheet appears as:

Municipal Accounts - Introduction

Capital

	Units		Units
Grant	24,000	Cash (Capital)	24,000
	======		======

Revenue

	Units		Units
Current Liabilities	3,000	Current Assets (excluding	
Provisions	600	Cash)	2,455
Revenue Surplus	3,389	Cash (Revenue)	4,534
	6,989		6,989
	30,989		30,989
	======		======

Each section now balances separately.

The receipt of the loan affects both the Capital and Revenue Accounts and also requires four entries:

```
DR.  Cash (Revenue).    )
CR.  Loan Outstanding.  )  U 36,000

DR.  Cash (Capital).    )
CR.  Cash (Revenue).    )  U 36,000
```

after which the Balance Sheet would read:

Capital

	Units		Units
Grant	24,000	Cash (Capital) (U 24,000	
Loan Outstanding	36,000	+ U 36,000)	60,000
	60,000		60,000
	======		======

Revenue

	Units		Units
Current Liabilities	3,000	Current Assets (excluding	
Provisions	600	Cash)	2,455
Revenue Surplus	3,389	Cash (Revenue) (U 4,534	
		+ U 36,000 - U 36,000)	4,534
	6,989		6,989
	66,989		66,989
	======		======

The purchase of the Council Offices is made with capital cash. The transaction does not concern the Revenue Account and can be dealt with by a straight-forward double-entry:

```
DR.  Council Offices.  )
CR.  Cash (Capital).   )  U 60,000
```

after which the Capital section of the Balance Sheet would show:

Municipal Accounting for Developing Countries

Capital

	Units		Units
Grant	24,000	Council Offices	60,000
Loan Outstanding	36,000		
	60,000		60,000
	======		======

What happens when the first instalment of the loan is repaid? A revenue asset (cash) is used to discharge a capital liability (loan outstanding) as follows:

    DR. Loan Outstanding.)
    CR. Cash   ) U 1,000

leaving both sections of the Balance Sheet out of balance by U 1,000 as follows:

Capital

	Units		Units
Grant	24,000	Council offices (at cost)	60,000
Loan Outstanding (36,000 - 1,000)	35,000		
	59,000		60,000
	======		======

Revenue

Current Liabilities	3,000	Current Assets (excluding Cash)	2,455
Provisions	600		
Revenue Surplus	3,389	Cash (4,534 - 1,000)	3,534
	6,989		5,989
	65,989		65,989
	======		======

The lack of balance is corrected by the second part of the "quadruple" entry as follows:

    DR. Loan Charges (Principal).)
    CR. Loan Repaid   ) U 1,000

The debit for Loan Charges (Principal) will be an expense (loss) to be deducted from the Revenue Account Surplus - reducing it to U 989. The Balance Sheet will appear as follows:

Municipal Accounts - Introduction

Capital

	Units		Units
Grant	24,000	Council Offices (at cost)	60,000
Loan Repaid	1,000		
Loan Outstanding	35,000		
	60,000		60,000
	======		======

Revenue

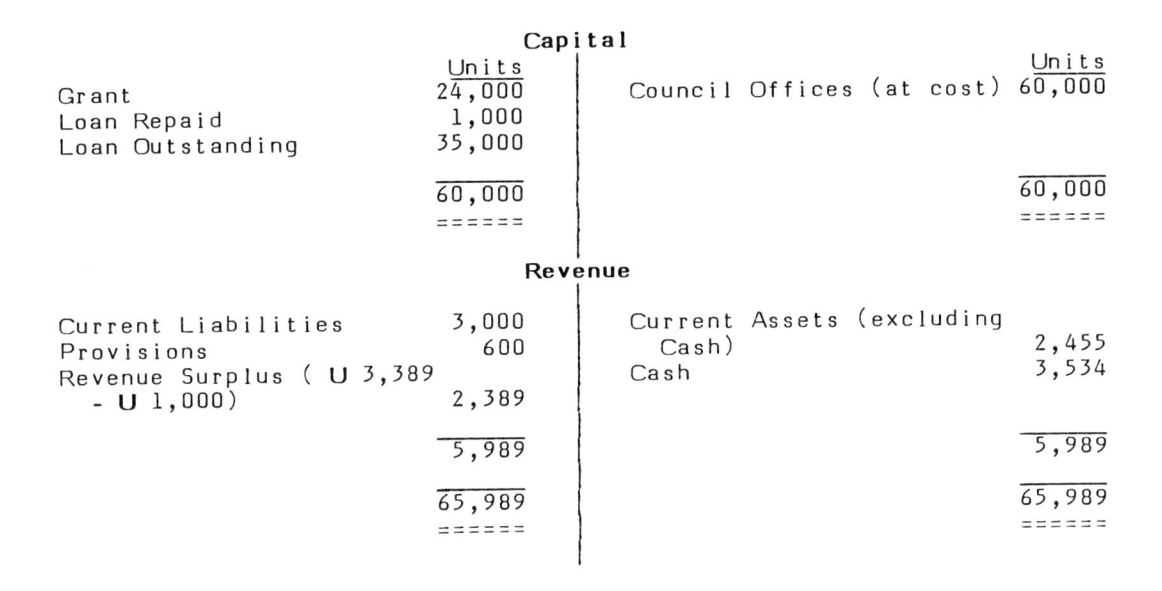

	Units		Units
Current Liabilities	3,000	Current Assets (excluding Cash)	2,455
Provisions	600	Cash	3,534
Revenue Surplus (U 3,389 − U 1,000)	2,389		
	5,989		5,989
	65,989		65,989
	======		======

The final capital transaction in our example is the purchase of equipment. A revenue asset (cash) is exchanged for a capital asset (equipment) as follows:

    DR. Equipment.)
    CR. Cash.   ) U 400

leaving both sections of the Balance Sheet out of balance again as follows:

Capital

	Units		Units
Grant	24,000	Council Offices	60,000
Loan Repaid	1,000	Equipment	400
Loan Outstanding	35,000		
	60,000		60,400
	======		======

Revenue

	Units		Units
Current Liabilities	3,000	Current Assets (excluding Cash)	2,455
Provisions	600	Cash (3,534 − 400)	3,134
Revenue Surplus	2,389		
	5,989		5,589
	65,989		65,989
	======		======

Again, the lack of balance is corrected by the second part of the quadruple entry as follows:

    DR. Revenue Account.   )
    CR. Revenue Contributions to Capital.   ) U 400

The debit to the Revenue Account will reduce its surplus balance by another U 400 to U 1989. The Balance Sheet will appear as follows:

Municipal Accounting for Developing Countries

Capital

	Units		Units
Grant	24,000	Council Offices (at cost)	60,000
Loan Repaid	1,000	Equipment (at cost)	400
Revenue Contribution	400		
Loan Outstanding	35,000		
	60,400		60,400
	======		======

Revenue

	Units		Units
Current Liabilities	3,000	Current Assets (excluding	
Provisions	600	Cash)	2,455
Revenue Surplus	1,989	Cash	3,134
	5,589		5,589
	65,989		65,989
	======		======

Now compare this with the Balance Sheet shown on page 239.

Of the balances on the left hand side of the capital section of the balance sheet, the Loan Outstanding is a liability. The remaining items represent the cost of assets which have been fully financed or discharged. The balances can therefore be shown as:

		Units
LONG-TERM LIABILITY		
Loan Outstanding		35,000
SURPLUS		
Capital Discharged		
Grant	24,000	
Loan Repaid	1,000	
Revenue Contributions	400	25,400
		60,400
		======

The double-account system had its origins in the accounts of public companies operating monopoly services, such as railway and waterworks companies. The law required that the money raised as capital funds be spent only on fixed assets, leaving revenue expenditure to be financed from revenue income.

The double-account system was followed in the United Kingdom by local authorities for many years, although it was modified from its original form to deal with such things as loan repayments and revenue contributions.

Nowadays the trend is towards presenting the Balance Sheet in its integrated form without the separate self-balancing Revenue and Capital sections. The principles of the double-account system are still of great importance to local and public authorities and a competent municipal accountant must be able to convert a Balance Sheet from one form to the other as a matter of course.

Not all the quadruple-entries shown above are always made in practice

Municipal Accounts - Introduction

because certain entries (in particular - cash) often cancel out each other. However the principle of quadruple-entry is important and if you are in any doubt about the entries to make in any given circumstances you should draft all four entries. You will then be able to see which entries cancel out and which require to be posted into the books.

8. Fixed Assets—Introduction

Section		Page
83.	Financing the Cost of Fixed Assets.	247
84.	Depreciation - General.	249
85.	Depreciation - Detailed Methods.	249
86.	Loan Charges.	257
87.	Renewals Funds.	263
88.	Reserves and Provisions.	271
89.	Capital and Revenue.	279
90.	Capital Expenditure.	281

83. FINANCING THE COST OF FIXED ASSETS

In Section 3 of Chapter 1 we saw that an accountant is concerned with all changes in financial position whether or not cash changes hands at the time. During previous chapters we have dealt with transactions which occur when cash changes hands, either at the time or after a period of credit. The exact sum due to be paid is known and can be accurately recorded.

We must now consider changes in financial position which occur, not by cash or credit transactions, but by the gradual passing of time and by use of equipment, buildings, tools and machinery in the normal course of business. These changes in financial position are not so obvious, or so easy to measure, as those which take place by cash or credit.

Furthermore, the income from charges must cover (as far as possible) the full costs of providing the service. This is an important principle in accountancy and costing.

Every form of business receives income. Trading companies receive cash from sales, professional firms from fees, clubs from subscriptions, charities from donations and public authorities from taxes, rates, rents, charges and grants. Whatever kind of business we consider, the amount collected in overall income must, in the long run, cover all the expenditure incurred in running the business including the cost of financing its fixed assets. If income is insufficient to meet expenditure (and to allow for profits where appropriate) sooner or later the business will stop; this is a straightforward economic fact.

To illustrate the above point let us consider the simple case of a taxi proprietor who owns a vehicle which cost U 10,000 and employs one driver. His annual running expenses might work out at (say):

	Units
Driver's wages	1,200
Petrol and Oil	4,500
Repairs and Maintenance	1,000
Licence and Insurance	1,300
TOTAL	8,000

He might assume that if he collected more than U 8,000 from passengers in one year he would make a profit. However, he will have failed to consider that his vehicle will wear out. If he continues in business it will eventually need replacement. Let us suppose that at the end of five years (a reasonable life for a motor vehicle) his vehicle is worn out. His full costs over five years would be:

	Units
Annual Running Costs for five years (U 8,000 x 5)	40,000
Cost of Vehicle	10,000
TOTAL COST	50,000
Average Annual Cost	10,000

He will therefore need to collect an average of not less than U 10,000 from passengers in each of the five years to cover his costs.

In practice the taxi owner will wish to know whether it is more profitable for him to invest his money in a taxi or, for example, in an interest-earning bank deposit. In addition to the costs shown above he will take into account the loss of investment interest plus risk and profit in order to fix his charges - but this is ignored in our example for the sake of simplicity.

Exactly the same principle would apply to a vehicle owned and run by a public authority. A vacuum tanker service, for example, might be operated incurring similar costs, say:

	Units
Wages	2,500
Fuel and Oil	6,500
Repairs and Maintenance	2,000
Licence and Insurance	1,000
TOTAL	12,000

At first sight it appears that charges could be fixed to bring in an average of U 1,000 per month (U 12,000 per year) but these charges would not cover the finance of the tanker lorry itself. If it cost (say) U 40,000, had a life of four years, the full costs over that period would be:

	Units
Annual Running Costs for four years (U 12,000 x 4)	48,000
Cost of Vehicle	40,000
TOTAL COST	88,000
Average Annual Cost	22,000

Charges would have to be fixed to bring in an average of U 1,834 per month (U 22,000 per year) if the service were to be run on an economic basis. The original charges would have to be almost doubled to cover the capital cost of the vehicle. If a lesser charge were made,

Fixed Assets - Introduction

the expenses would still be incurred and to the extent to which they were not met from charges they would be subsidised, that is, paid for out of general income such as rates and taxes.

What applies to a vehicle applies to other fixed assets, such as buildings, permanent works, plant and equipment. All must in some way be financed before the period of their useful life expires. Although the above principles have been used to illustrate the fixing of charges, they apply in every case where costs are calculated, even where the whole cost is met from rates or taxes.

(Again - for simplicity - loss of interest on capital has been ignored.)

84. **DEPRECIATION - GENERAL**

The gradual using up or wearing out of fixed assets over a period of time is called depreciation. In commercial accounting practice an amount for depreciation is shown as an expense in the profit and loss account, but this practice is not common in the accounts of local authorities. The simplest way of calculating the annual charge for depreciation is the "straight line" (or fixed instalment) method and operates as follows:

(a) take the original cost of the asset;

(b) deduct the estimated price for which the asset could be sold for scrap at the end of its useful life;

(c) estimate the working life of the asset; and

(d) divide the net cost (after deducting scrap value) by the estimated life in years.

The result is the annual charge for depreciation.

Example

A motor vehicle costing U 10,500 has an estimated life of 5 years at the end of which it is expected to be sold as scrap for U 500.

$$\frac{\text{Cost - Scrap Value}}{\text{Years of Working Life}} = \text{Annual Depreciation}$$

$$\frac{U\ 10,500 - U\ 500}{5} = \frac{U\ 10,000}{5} = U\ 2,000 \text{ per annum.}$$

85. **DEPRECIATION - DETAILED METHODS**

Having calculated depreciation, how is it shown in the accounts? Consider the taxi owner in Section 83. We will assume that he began business with U 10,000 capital in cash which he used for the purchase of the vehicle. Before he begins business his balance sheet is:

Municipal Accounting for Developing Countries

Balance Sheet as at 1 Jan. (year 1)

	Units		Units
Capital	10,000	Fixed Asset Vehicle	10,000
	10,000		10,000

Assuming a nil scrap value at the end of the five years the annual depreciation will be U 2,000. At the end of the first year he will reduce the value of his vehicle in the books from U 10,000 to U 8,000 and record the loss as depreciation. The journal entry would be:

19 Dec.31	Depreciation Account DR. To Vehicle Being annual depreciation on motor vehicle (1/5 of U 10,000)	Units 2,000	Units 2,000

The ledger accounts would appear as:

Depreciation

19 Dec.31	To Vehicle	J	2,000	19 Dec.31	By Profit and Loss	J	2,000
			2,000				2,000

Vehicle

19 Jan.1	To Cash	C.B.	10,000	19 Dec.31	By Depreciation By Balance	J c/d	2,000 8,000
			10.000				10,000
19 Jan.1	To Balance	b/d	8,000				

The U 2,000 depreciation is transferred to the Profit and Loss account as an expense. The U 8,000 is carried forward as a debit balance on the vehicle account and will be included in the balance sheet.

The Profit and Loss account (assuming a profit of U 2,000) would appear as:

Fixed Assets - Introduction

Profit and Loss Account
for the year ended 31 Dec. 19

	Units		Units
Wages	1,200	Income from Passengers	12,000
Petrol and Oil	4,500		
Repairs and Maintenance	1,000		
Licence and Insurance	1,300		
Depreciation	2,000		
Net Profit	2,000		
	12,000		12,000

If we assume that all running expenses have been paid in cash and the U 2,000 profit is drawn from the business by the owner, the cash transactions could be summarised as:

Statement of Receipts and Payments

	Units		Units
Capital	10,000	Purchase of Vehicle	10,000
Income from Passengers	12,000	Expenses - Wages	1,200
		- Petrol and Oil	4,500
		- Repairs and Maintenance	1,000
		- Licence and Insurance	1,300
		Drawings - Profit for Year	2,000
		Balance - Cash in Hand	2,000
	22,000		22,000

There is a cash balance in hand of U 2,000. This occurs because although U 2,000 has been provided for as depreciation in the profit and loss account the cash has been retained in the business. This is another example of a provision where an estimated sum is set aside to meet a known future liability of an unknown precise amount.

The balance sheet at the end of the first year would appear as:

Balance Sheet as at 31 Dec. 19

	Units	Units		Units	Units
Capital			Fixed Asset		
Balance 1 Jan	10,000		Vehicle (at cost)	10,000	
Add Net Profit	2,000		Less Depreciation	2,000	8,000
	12,000		Current Asset		
Less Drawings	2,000	10,000	Cash		2,000
		10,000			10,000

Each following year the journal and ledger entries will be repeated. In the second year accounts the ledger will appear as:

			Depreciation				
19 Dec.31	To Vehicle	J	2,000	19 Dec.31	By Profit and Loss	J	2,000
			2,000				2,000

			Vehicle				
19 Jan.1	To Cash	C.B.	10,000	19 Dec.31	By Depreciation By Balance	J c/d	2,000 8,000
			10,000				10,000
19 Jan.1	To Balance	b/d	8,000	19 Dec.31	By Depreciation By Balance	J c/d	2,000 6,000
			8,000				8,000
19 Jan.1	To Balance	b/d	6,000				

At the end of the second year, and still assuming he draws only profit in cash, assuming a profit of (say) U 2,300, the balance sheet might appear as:

Balance Sheet as at 31 Dec. 19

	Units	Units		Units	Units
Capital			Fixed Asset		
Balance 1 Jan.	10,000		Vehicle (at cost)	10,000	
Add Net Profit	2,300		Less Depreciation	4,000	6,000
	12,300		Current Asset		
Less Drawings	2,300	10,000	Cash		4,000
		10,000			10,000

Fixed Assets - Introduction

Assuming the life of the vehicle to be from 1 Jan.19_0 to 31 Dec. 19_4 the complete vehicle account will be:

Vehicle							
19_0 Jan.1	To Cash	C.B.	10,000	19_0 Dec.31	By Depreciation By Balance	J c/d	2,000 8,000
			10,000				10,000
19_1 Jan.1	To Balance	b/d	8,000	19_1 Dec.31	By Depreciation By Balance	J c/d	2,000 6,000
			8,000				8,000
19_2 Jan.1	To Balance	b/d	6,000	19_2 Dec.31	By Depreciation By Balance	J c/d	2,000 4,000
			6,000				6,000
19_3 Jan.1	To Balance	b/d	4,000	19_3 Dec.31	By Depreciation By Balance	J c/d	2,000 2,000
			4,000				4,000
19_4 Jan.1	To Balance	b/d	2,000	19_4 Dec.31	By Depreciation	J	2,000
			2,000				2,000

Assuming that all income and expenditure (except depreciation) is received and paid in cash, and all profits are drawn in cash, the successive balance sheets (in brief form) will appear as:

Balance Sheet as at 31 Dec. 19_0

	Units		Units
Capital	10,000	Vehicle Cash	8,000 2,000
	10,000		10,000

Municipal Accounting for Developing Countries

Balance Sheet as at 31 Dec. 19_1

Capital	10,000	Vehicle	6,000
		Cash	4,000
	10,000		10,000

Balance Sheet as at 31 Dec. 19_2

Capital	10,000	Vehicle	4,000
		Cash	6,000
	10,000		10,000

Balance Sheet as at 31 Dec. 19_3

Capital	10,000	Vehicle	2,000
		Cash	8,000
	10,000		10,000

Balance Sheet as at 31 Dec. 19_4

Capital	10,000	Cash	10,000

The value of the vehicle has been written down (ie reduced) each year until at the end of its life it has been written off (ie eliminated from the books). This keeps the books in line with known facts, as at the end of the five years the taxi is assumed to be worthless.

By setting aside depreciation the taxi owner has only drawn cash from the business for the profits earned from operating the taxi and has kept his capital intact. At the end of the five years (disregarding inflation) he is in no worse position than when he began business. He could buy a new vehicle (assuming the same price) or withdraw his capital.

If he had failed to make provision for depreciation or had drawn out the cash set aside, he would have been left with a virtually worthless pile of scrap (his worn-out taxi) and no money to replace it!

Instead of the straight-line method of calculating depreciation the reducing (declining) balance method is sometimes used. The book-keeping entries are similar to those used in the straight-line method: the difference is in the calculation of the annual depreciation. In the straight-line method a fixed percentage of the original cost is annually provided for depreciation. In our example, 20% was used. Had the life of the asset been 10 years, the provision would have been 10%; for 20 years, 5% and so on.

In the reducing balance method the percentage is applied to the cost of the asset as reduced by previous depreciation.

Fixed Assets - Introduction

If this method had been applied in the above example, using a rate of 30% the vehicle account would have appeared as:

Vehicle								
19_0 Jan.1	To Cash	C.B.	10,000	19_0 Dec.31	By Depreciation By Balance	J c/d	3,000 7,000	
			10,000				10,000	
19_1 Jan.1	To Balance	b/d	7,000	19_1 Dec.31	By Depreciation By Balance	J c/d	2,100 4,900	
			7,000				7,000	
19_2 Jan.1	To Balance	b/d	4,900	19_2 Dec.31	By Depreciation By Balance	J c/d	1,470 3,430	
			4,900				4,900	
19_3 Jan.1	To Balance	b/d	3,430	19_3 Dec.31	By Depreciation By Balance	J c/d	1,030 2,400	
			3,430				3,430	
19_4 Jan.1	To Balance	b/d	2,400	19_4 Dec.31	By Depreciation By Balance	J c/d	720 1,680	
			2,400				2,400	

Depreciation calculations were:

Year	1	U 10,000 x 30%	=	U 3,000
	2	7,000 x 30%	=	2,100
	3	4,900 x 30%	=	1,470
	4	3,430 x 30%	=	1,030
	5	2,400 x 30%	=	720

A much higher percentage has to be used than in the straight line method and yet after five years there is still a considerable balance on the asset account. This method can never arrive at a completely NIL balance because by deducting from any figure a proportion of itself - something must always remain.

The advantage claimed for this method is that depreciation is high to start with, but reduces year by year, thus compensating for the increasing repair costs as the asset gradually wears out. With careful calculation by a formula the balance at the end of the period may be nearly the same as the scrap value of the asset when finally disposed of. A common system is to use a percentage which is double that for straight-line methods. It is then known as the "double-declining" system.

Other methods of depreciation sometimes found include:

(a) annuity system;

(b) depreciation fund;

(c) insurance policy; and

(d) revaluation.

It is not necessary to consider these methods in detail at this stage.

The depreciation method of financing the cost of fixed assets is used almost universally in business and has the following advantages:

(a) the book value of the asset is reduced annually, thus keeping it more in line with the true value of the asset;

(b) cash is retained in the business to keep the capital intact. This cash is then available to help in the purchase of replacements; and

(c) the asset is financed during its lifetime out of the income which it earns.

When applied to a local authority the method has not generally been considered satisfactory. Among the reasons often asserted for this different treatment, have been:

(a) it is often extremely difficult to assess the true value or working life of assets used for public benefit. Many public works (e.g. roads, sewers, lake defences, street lighting cables) are often unidentifiable after construction and in any case could not be sold. Those assets which have a realisable value (e.g. buildings) are rarely sold (except perhaps houses) because they are provided for public benefit;

(b) whereas many commercial assets are financed from the proprietor's, partners' or shareholders' capital, most large public assets are originally financed by the raising of loans. The cash to repay these loans is later raised from rates, taxes or charges, and these repayments are broadly equivalent to depreciation;

(c) public assets are not normally provided to earn income but to give social benefits. Whilst some assets (eg waterworks and markets) earn income to finance themselves, most (eg roads, schools, sewers, bridges and dispensaries) are financed from various forms of taxation; and

(d) governments and public authorities have a natural reluctance to set taxes to cover costs not represented by immediate cash payments.

The capital expenditure accounts of a public authority are prepared, not to show the value of assets for trading purposes, but to show:

(a) the cost of assets provided for public use;

Fixed Assets - Introduction

(b) the extent to which the capital cost has been fully discharged from grants, rates, taxes, charges and other revenue income; and

(c) the extent to which the capital cost has still to be met by the repayment of loans.

86. LOAN CHARGES

By far the most common method of the annual financing of the cost of fixed assets in a public authority is by the payment of loan charges on borrowed money.

Consider the case of the vacuum tanker lorry in Section 83. Unlike the taxi owner the local authority has no "capital" from which to buy the vehicle and will probably raise a loan to purchase it.

Let us assume that a loan of U 40,000 is raised on 1 Jan. 19_1 @ 10% for 4 years. Interest, as well as principal, must be paid annually (or half yearly) to the lender. To make an equal charge in each of the four years an annuity system would probably be used.

To repay a loan of U 40,000 over 4 years @ 10% would require (in round figures) an annuity of U 12,619. This figure is obtained from standard loan tables or by using a financial calculator. A table of loan charges could be prepared as follows:

Date	Annuity	Interest	Principal	Principal Outstanding
	Units	Units	Units	Units
1.1._1	-	-	-	40,000
31.12._1	12,619	4,000	8,619	31,381
31.12._2	12,619	3,138	9,481	21,900
31.12._3	12,619	2,190	10,429	11,471
31.12._4	12,619	1,148	11,471	-

The loan table is prepared as follows:

(a) calculate 10% of U 40,000 (4,000);

(b) deduct interest (U 4,000) from annuity (U 12,619) to give principal repayment (U 8,619);

(c) deduct principal repayment (U 8,619) from principal outstanding (U 40,000) to give new principal outstanding (U 31,381);

(d) calculate 10% of U 31,381 (U 3,138);

(e) deduct interest (U 3,138) from annuity (U 12,619) to give principal repayment (U 9,481);

(f) deduct principal repayment (U 9,481) from principal outstanding (U 31,381) to give new principal outstanding (U 21,900);

(g) and so on.

After the purchase of the vehicle the balance sheet would show:

Municipal Accounting for Developing Countries

Balance Sheet as at 1 Jan.19_1

	Units		Units
Long Term Liability		Fixed Asset	
Loan Outstanding	40,000	Vacuum Tanker Lorry	40,000

At the end of 19_1 the loan charges would be paid. Shown in journal form (not necessary in practice) this transaction would appear as:

19_1					
Dec.31	Loan Charges - Interest	DR.	5	4,000	
	Loan Outstanding	DR.	3	8,619	
	To Cash	C.B.			12,619
	Being payment of annual loan charges on vacuum tanker lorry (USJ 488)				

The principal repaid will now be charged in the revenue account and credited to a capital discharged account by a journal entry as follows:

19_1					
Dec.31	Loan Charges - Principal	DR.	4	8,619	
	To Capital Discharged (Loan Repaid)		2		8,619
	Being capital discharged by repayment of loan on vacuum lorry (USJ 488)				

Assuming charges were collected and all expenses paid in cash the ledger accounts at the end of 19_1 would appear as follows:

	Vacuum Tanker Lorry (USJ 488)							1
19_1 Jan.1	To Cash	C.B.	40,000	19_1 Dec.31	By Balance	c/d	40,000	
19_2 Jan.1	To Balance	b/d	40,000					

258

Fixed Assets - Introduction

		Capital Discharged (Loan Repaid)						2
19_1 Dec.31	To Balance	c/d	8,619	19_1 Dec.31	By Loan Charges (Principal)	J	8,619
			8,619 =====				8,619 =====
				19_2 Jan.1	By Balance	b/d	8,619

		Loan Outstanding						3
19_1 Dec.31	To Cash To Balance	C.B. c/d	8,619 31,381	19_1 Jan.1	By Cash	C.B.	40,000
			40,000 ======				40,000 ======
				19_2 Jan.1	By Balance	b/d	31,381

		Loan Charges - Principal						4
19_1 Dec.31	To Capital Discharged	J	8,619	19_1 Dec.31	By Revenue Account	6	8,619
			8,619 =====				8,619 =====

		Loan Charges - Interest						5
19_1 Dec.31	To Cash	C.B.	4,000	19_1 Dec.31	By Revenue Account	6	4,000
			4,000 =====				4,000 =====

Revenue Account							6
19_1 Dec.31	To Wages	C.B.	2,500	19_1 Dec.31	By Charges	C.B.	24,619
	To Fuel and Oil	C.B.	6,500				
	To Repair and Maintenance	C.B.	2,000				
	To Licence and Insurance	C.B.	1,000				
	To Loan Charges Principal	4	8,619				
	Interest	5	4,000				
			24,619				24,619
			======				======

Cash Book (Summary)							C.B.
19_1 Jan.1	To Loan	3	40,000	19_1 Jan.1	By Lorry	1	40,000
Dec.31	To Charges	6	24,619	Dec.31	By Wages	6	2,500
					By Fuel and Oil	6	6,500
					By Repair and Maintenance	6	2,000
					By Licence and Insurance	6	1,000
					By Loan Charges Principal		8,619
					Interest	5	4,000
			64,619				64,619
			======				======

The balance sheet would appear as:

Fixed Assets - Introduction

Balance Sheet as at 31 Dec. 19_1

	Units		Units
Long-Term Liability		Fixed Asset	
Loan Outstanding	31,381	Vacuum Tanker Lorry	
Capital Discharged		(at cost)	40,000
Loan Repaid	8,619		
	40,000		40,000

There is no cash balance in hand in this case because cash raised from charges has been used to pay the loan charges. The fixed asset remains in the books at cost and the equivalent of depreciation (capital discharged) is carried forward as a separate balance.

In the case of a vehicle there could be little objection to writing down its cost annually by the amount of capital discharged and showing the balance sheet in commercial form as follows:

Balance Sheet as at 31 Dec. 19_1

	Units		Units
Long-Term Liability		Fixed Asset	
Loan Outstanding	31,381	Vacuum Tanker Lorry	
		(at cost)	40,000
		Less Capital Discharged	8,619
	31,381		31,381

The advantage here is that the vehicle is shown at a book value nearer to its actual worth at the end of 19_1 (approximately 25% has been written off the cost).

Unfortunately this does not hold good for the majority of public assets, especially for permanent works. Who could confidently say for example that a road improvement costing U 40,000 will last for four years, or a sewer or lake defences costing U 40,000 will be worth approximately U 31,381 after one year?

For this reason, to be consistent and to avoid rather ludicrous assumptions, the first method of presenting the balance sheet is to be preferred. Here only facts are stated:

(a) the asset cost U 40,000 (no attempt is made to assess its present value);

(b) the loan outstanding is U 31,381; and

(c) part of the cost (U 8,619) has been discharged by repayment of the loan.

Similar journal entries will be made in the second, third and fourth years using the figures in the loan repayment table. The lorry will remain in the books at cost, the loan outstanding will be progressively reduced and the capital discharged progressively increased. Balance sheets (in brief form) will appear at the end of the second and third years as follows:

Balance Sheet as at 31 Dec. 19_2

	Units		Units
Loan Outstanding	21,900	Lorry (at cost)	40,000
Loan Repaid	18,100		
	40,000		40,000

Balance Sheet as at 31 Dec. 19_3

	Units		Units
Loan Outstanding	11,471	Lorry (at cost)	40,000
Loan Repaid	28,529		
	40,000		40,000

The full balance sheet at the end of 19_4 would appear as:

Balance Sheet as at 31 Dec. 19_4

	Units		Units
Capital Discharged		Fixed Asset	
Loan Repaid	40,000	Vacuum Tanker Lorry (at cost)	40,000
	40,000		40,000

Once the asset has been fully financed, the two equal balances will be carried forward in the books until the asset is disposed of or falls out of use. Balances like this occur frequently, because loans are often raised for a shorter period than the estimated life of the asset. Permission to borrow must usually be obtained through a specific process (eg from a controlling government department). Maximum periods for repayment are thus often fixed on a conservative basis (ie fixed on the short side, for safety).

When the asset is disposed of, it is written out of the books by a simple journal entry. For example:

19_4 Dec.31	Capital Discharged DR.	2	40,000	
	To Vacuum Tanker Lorry	1		40,000
	Being lorry No.USJ 488 now written off as scrap.			

Fixed Assets - Introduction

87. RENEWALS FUNDS

Sometimes it is not necessary to raise a loan to pay for a fixed asset. This happens when the cost is met from a capital receipt, capital grant, direct revenue contribution or where the asset has been taken over from Central Government. In these cases the cost is fully financed right from the beginning and in strict theory no other accounting work is necessary.

Suppose for example that our tanker lorry had been financed in one of these ways. After purchase the balance sheet would show:

Balance Sheet as at 1 Jan. 19_1

	Units		Units
Capital Discharged Grant*	40,000	Fixed Asset Vacuum Tanker Lorry (at cost)	40,000
	40,000		40,000

* or (Revenue Contributions to Capital) as the
   (Capital Receipt applied   ) case may
   (Take-over from Government   ) be.

The above balances will remain in the books until the asset is disposed of. However, when this happens it will be necessary to raise a loan to finance a replacement unless other funds are available. These can be set aside in a renewals fund. Contributions can be made during the life of an existing asset to provide funds for its replacement.

The simplest way of doing this would be to divide the cost of the tanker (U 40,000) by its estimated life (say 4 years) and to contribute U 10,000 each year to a renewals fund. In the first year a journal entry will be made as follows:

| 19_1 Dec.31 | Revenue Account   DR. To Renewals Fund Being annual contribution towards replacement of vacuum tanker lorry (USJ 488) | 4 3 | 10,000 | 10,000 |

The ledger accounts will appear as follows:

Municipal Accounting for Developing Countries

		Vacuum Tanker Lorry (USJ 488)				1
19_1 Jan.1	To Cash	C.B.	40,000	19_1 Dec.31	By Balance	c/d	40,000
			======				======
19_2 Jan.1	By Balance	b/d	40,000				

		Capital Discharged (Grant)				2
19_1 Dec.31	To Balance	c/d	40,000	19_1 Jan.1	By Cash	C.B.	40,000
			======				======
				19_2 Jan.1	By Balance	b/d	40,000

		Renewals Fund				3
19_1 Dec.31	To Balance	c/d	10,000	19_1 Dec.31	By Revenue Account	J	10,000
			10,000				10,000
			======				======
				19_2 Jan.1	By Balance	b/d	10,000

		Renewals Fund Contribution				4
19_1 Dec.31	To Renewals Fund	J	10,000	19_1 Dec.31	By Revenue Account	6	10,000
			======				======

Fixed Assets - Introduction

Revenue Account								6
19_1 Dec.31	To Wages	C.B.	2,500	19_1 Dec.31	By Charges	C.B.		22,000
	To Fuel and Oil	C.B.	6,500					
	To Repair and Maintenance	C.B.	2,000					
	To Licence and Insurance	C.B.	1,000					
	To Renewals Fund Contribution	4	10,000					
			22,000					22,000

Cash Book (Summary)								C.B.
19_1 Jan.1	To Grant	2	40,000	19_1 Jan.1	By Lorry	1		40,000
Dec.31	To Charges	6	22,000	Dec.31	By Wages	6		2,500
					By Fuel and Oil	6		6,500
					By Repair and Maintenance	6		2,000
					By Licence and Insurance	6		1,000
					By Balance	c/d		10,000
			62,000					62,000
19_2 Jan.1	To Balance	b/d	10,000					

The balance sheet will appear as:

Balance Sheet as at 31 Dec. 19_1

	Units		Units
Capital Discharged		Fixed Asset	
Grant	40,000	Vacuum Tanker Vehicle (at cost)	40,000
Provision Renewals Fund	10,000	Current Asset Cash	10,000
	50,000		50,000

Municipal Accounting for Developing Countries

This time there is a cash balance, representing the sum charged against the revenue account but not paid in cash. This is another example of a provision.

To ensure that the cash is available when required, it is sound financial practice to invest it. The U 10,000 cash will be used to purchase suitable investments which will earn interest. The journal entry would be:

19_1 Dec.31	Renewals Fund Investment DR. To Cash Being investment of renewals fund in National Bank 10% deposit account	5 C.B.	10,000	10,000

Similar entries will be made in subsequent years and if interest added by the bank to the deposit account is credited to the fund annually the "Renewals Fund Account" and "Renewals Fund Investment Account" will build up like this:

Renewals Fund   3

19_1 Dec.31	To Balance	c/d	10,000	19_1 Dec.31	By Revenue Account	J	10,000
			10,000				10,000
19_2 Dec.31	To Balance	c/d	21,000	19_2 Jan.1 Dec.31	By Balance By Interest By Revenue Account	b/d 5 J	10,000 1,000 10,000
			21,000				21,000
19_3 Dec.31	To Balance	c/d	33,100	19_3 Jan.1 Dec.31	By Balance By Interest By Revenue Account	b/d 5 J	21,000 2,100 10,000
			33,100				33,100
19_4 Dec.31	To Balance	c/d	46,410	19_4 Jan.1 Dec.31	By Balance By Interest By Revenue Account	b/d 5 J	33,100 3,310 10,000
			46,410				46,410
				19_5 Jan.1	By Balance	b/d	46,410

Fixed Assets - Introduction

	Renewals Fund Investment (National Bank 10% Deposit Account)							5
19_1 Dec.31	To Cash	C.B.	10,000	19_1 Dec.31	By Balance	c/d	10,000	
19_2 Jan.1	To Balance	b/d	10,000	19_2 Dec.31	By Balance	c/d	21,000	
Dec.31	To Interest	3	1,000					
	To Cash	C.B.	10,000					
			21,000				21,000	
19_3 Jan.1	To Balance	b/d	21,000	19_3 Dec.31	By Balance	c/d	33,100	
Dec.31	To Interest	3	2,100					
	To Cash	C.B.	10,000					
			33,100				33,100	
19_4 Jan.1	To Balance	b/d	33,100	19_4 Dec.31	By Balance	c/d	46,410	
Dec.31	To Interest	3	3,310					
	To Cash	C.B.	10,000					
			46,410				46,410	
19_5 Jan.1	To Balance	b/d	46,410					

Because of accumulated interest the fund has built up to U 46,410 instead of to U 40,000. This will help to meet any increase in costs which may have occurred over the four years - a replacement vehicle may cost more than the original one purchased four years earlier.

There are, in fact, more complex methods of calculating renewals fund contributions to take into account both interest and changes in money values. These need not concern us at this stage.

The successive balance sheets (second and third years in brief) will appear as follows:

Balance Sheet as at 31 Dec. 19_1

	Units		Units
Capital Discharged		Fixed Asset	
Grant	40,000	Vacuum Tanker Lorry	40,000
Provision		Current Asset	
Renewals Fund	10,000	Renewals Fund Investment	10,000
	50,000		50,000

Balance Sheet as at 31 Dec. 19_2

	Units		Units
Capital Discharged	40,000	Vehicle	40,000
Renewals Fund	21,000	Investment	21,000
	61,000		61,000

Balance Sheet as at 31 Dec. 19_3

	Units		Units
Capital Discharged	40,000	Vehicle	40,000
Renewals Fund	33,100	Investment	33,100
	73,100		73,100

Balance Sheet as at 31 Dec. 19_4

	Units		Units
Capital Discharged Grant	40,000	Fixed Asset Vacuum Tanker Lorry	40,000
Provision Renewals Fund	46,410	Current Asset Renewals Fund – Investment	46,410
	86,410		86,410

If the original vehicle were scrapped on 31 Dec. 19_4 its cost would be written off against capital discharged and the balance sheet would show:

Balance Sheet as at 31 Dec. 19_4

	Units		Units
Provision Renewals Fund	46,410	Current Asset Renewals Fund Investment	46,410
	46,410		46,410

The investment could then be turned into cash and used to purchase a new vehicle (assuming it cost U 46,410). The Renewals Fund, having been used for its intended purpose, would be closed and the balance transferred to a "capital discharged" account. Journal entries would be:

Fixed Assets - Introduction

19_4				
Dec.31	Capital Discharged (Grant) DR. To Vacuum Tanker Lorry Being worn-out vehicle USJ 488 now scrapped	2 1	40,000	40,000
Dec.31	Cash DR. To Renewals Fund Investment Being realisation of investment	C.B. 5	46,410	46,410
Dec.31	Vacuum Tanker Lorry DR. To Cash Being purchase of replacement vehicle USN 546	7 C.B.	46,410	46,410
Dec.31	Renewals Fund DR. To Capital Discharged (Renewals Fund) Being purchase of vehicle USN 546 now financed from Renewals Fund.	3 8	46,410	46,410

The accounts will appear as:

Vacuum Tanker Lorry (USJ 488)   1

19_4				19_4			
Jan.1	To Balance	b/f	40,000	Dec.31	By Capital Discharged	J	40,000
			40,000				40,000
			======				======

Capital Discharged (Grant)   2

19_4				19_4			
Dec.31	To Vacuum Tanker Lorry	J	40,000	Jan.1	By Balance	b/f	40,000
			40,000				40,000
			======				======

Municipal Accounting for Developing Countries

				Renewals Fund			3
19_4 Dec.31	To Capital Dis- charged	J	46,410	19_4 Jan.1	By Balance By Interest By Revenue Account	b/f 5 J	33,100 3,310 10,000
			46,410				46,410

				Renewals Fund Investment			5
19_4 Jan.1 Dec.31	To Balance To Interest To Cash	b/f 3 C.B.	33,100 3,310 10,000	19_4 Dec.31	By Cash	C.B.	46,410
			46,410				46,410

				Vacuum Tanker Lorry (USN 546)			7
19_4 Dec.31	To Cash	C.B.	46,410	19_4 Dec.31	By Balance	c/d	46,410
19_5 Jan.1	To Balance	b/d	46,410				

				Capital Discharged (Renewals Fund)			8
19_4 Dec.31	To Balance	c/d	46,410	19_4 Dec.31	By Renewals Fund	J	46,410
			46,410				46,410
				19_5 Jan.1	By Balance	b/d	46,410

Fixed Assets - Introduction

	Cash Book			C.B.
19_4 Dec.31 To Renewals Fund Investment	J	46,410	19_4 Dec.31 By Vacuum Tanker Lorry	J	46,410
		46,410 ======			46,410 ======

The final balance sheet would show:

Balance Sheet as at 31 Dec. 19_4

	Units		Units

Capital Discharged
  Renewals Fund applied
	46,410
	======
		Fixed Asset
		  Vacuum Tanker Lorry
			46,410
			======

The process will now be repeated for the renewal of the new vehicle.

88. RESERVES AND PROVISIONS

(a) Provisions

As we have already seen in a previous chapter, provisions are:

"Amounts set aside to meet specific commitments, known contingencies and diminutions in values of assets ..... where the amounts involved cannot be determined with substantial accuracy".

We have already studied various examples of provisions, as follows:

1. Specific Commitments   Renewals Fund
2. Known Contingencies   Repairs Fund
3. Diminutions in Value of Assets   Depreciation

The book-keeping entries for setting aside a provision follow a standard pattern, expressed in journal form as follows:

Revenue Account   DR.
  To (Provision)
  Being the setting aside
  of provision for
  (repairs, renewals,
  depreciation etc.)

If the provision is invested, this is a quite separate transaction, dealt with as follows:

```
Fund (Investment)                 DR.
   To Cash
   Being investment of
   (repairs, renewals
   etc.) fund
```

Investment affects neither the fund itself nor the revenue account. It merely changes the form of assets in which the fund is held.

Depreciation deals with the diminution in value of fixed assets. Current assets do not normally depreciate, though there are important exceptions. One of these concerns debtors.

Until now we have assumed that all debts will be collected and the figure for "debtors" has been shown in the accounts at its gross value. The unfortunate fact must now be faced that not all debts are settled by those who owe them. Debtors may die, become insolvent, or just wilfully refuse to pay. Because of this it is sometimes necessary to write off bad debts as irrecoverable or to reduce the book value of debts to a more realistic figure by setting aside a provision.

An individual debt is written off when it becomes impossible to collect, for one of the various reasons shown in the last paragraph.

Suppose, for example, on 15 Jan. 19 a local authority carries out rechargeable work for a Mr J. Musoke costing **U** 120. An account (invoice) will be sent to Mr Musoke demanding payment of the sum due. The **U** 120 will be taken into the accounts as income and debited to Mr Musoke's account.

The journal entry would be:

```
19
Jan.15  J. Musoke                          DR.  121   120
            To Rechargeable Works Income               120
            Being sum due for rechargeable
            works as follows:
                                   U
            Labour                80
            Materials             10
            Transport             20
            Overheads             10
                                 ___
                                 120
                                 ===
```

The ledger accounts would show:

```
                 Rechargeable Works Income                       1
                                       19
                                       Jan.15  By J. Musoke   J   120
```

Fixed Assets - Introduction

	J. Musoke			12
19 Jan.15	To Recharge- able Works Income	J	120	

If Mr Musoke failed to pay his account after a reasonable period of credit (say one month) various reminders would be sent to him. If he still did not pay, the Council's legal department or lawyers would take the matter over, perhaps leading to a case being brought to Court. At some point in the recovery procedure one of three things must happen:

(a) Mr Musoke settles the whole of his debt in cash;

(b) a decision is reached that none of the money will ever be recovered; or

(c) Mr Musoke settles part of his debt, the remainder being irrecoverable.

To the extent to which cash is paid, the cash book will be debited and Mr Musoke's account credited. To the extent to which cash is not paid the debt must be written off as "bad". Mr Musoke's account would be credited (reduction in assets) and the income account debited (loss).

Suppose in August 19 a decision is taken to write off the U 120 as a bad debt. The journal entry would appear as:

19 Aug.31	Rechargeable Works Income DR. To J. Musoke Being bad debt now written off as authorised by Finance Committee minute 25/653.	1 12	120	120

The ledger accounts would show:

	Rechargeable Works Income						1
19 Aug.31	To J. Musoke	J	120	19 Jan.15	By J. Musoke	J	120

Municipal Accounting for Developing Countries

	J. Musoke						12
19 Jan.15	To Rechargeable Works Income	J	120 ===	19 Aug.31	By Rechargeable Works Income	J	120 ===

Although we write off actual bad debts the remaining debts may still not be shown in the books at a realistic figure. Suppose that during 19 the total amount due for rechargeable works is U 11,620 of which the U 120 due from Mr Musoke has been written off. At 31 Dec. 19 the ledger accounts will appear as:

	Rechargeable Works Income						1
19 Aug.31	To Sundry Debtors (J. Musoke)	J	120	19 Dec.31	By Various Sundry Debtors (including J. Musoke)	J	11,620

	Sundry Debtors Control (Including J. Musoke)						12
19 Dec.31	To Rechargeable Works Income	J	11,620	19 Aug.31	By Rechargeable Works Income (J. Musoke)	J	120

The debtors now due to the authority are:

	Units
Total sums due	11,620
Less Written off	120
	11,500

However, whilst none of the remaining U 11,500 has yet been written off, the Chief Financial Officer may know from experience that about (say) 10% of the sums due will never be collected and will have to be written off at a later date.

Fixed Assets - Introduction

Because of this he may find it prudent to make provision for the expected loss. This is done by reducing the amount of the income by a debit in the "Rechargeable Works Income" account and setting aside the sum as a credit in the "Provision for Bad and Doubtful Debts" account.

The journal entry in this case would be:

19 Dec.31	Rechargeable Works Income DR. To Provision for Bad and Doubtful Debts Being 10% of total debtors U 1,150 now set aside against possibility of non-settlement	1 15	1,150	1,150

The ledger accounts would then show:

Rechargeable Works Income   1

19 Aug.31	To Sundry Debtors (J. Musoke)	J	120	19 Dec.31	By Various Sundry Debtors (including J. Musoke)	J	11,620
Dec.31	To Provision for Bad and Doubtful Debts	J	1,150				

Sundry Debtors Control (Including J. Musoke)   12

19 Dec.31	To Rechargeable Works Income	J	11,620	19 Aug.15	By Rechargeable Works Income (J. Musoke)	J	120

Provision for Bad and Doubtful Debts   15

				19 Dec.31	By Rechargeable Works Income	J	1,150

Only U 10,350 would be transferred to the Revenue Account as income - arrived at as follows:

	Units	Units
Total amount due		11,620
Less Bad debts written off	120	
Less Provision for bad and doubtful debts on remainder	1,150	1,270
		10,350

As an alternative, the Revenue Account of any particular fund might show the gross income due on the Income side and the Bad Debts and Provisions for Bad Debts as expenditure.

If this were done in the above case the journal entries would have been:

19 Aug.31	Revenue Account (Bad Debts) DR. To J. Musoke Being bad debt now written off as authorised by Finance Committee Minute 25/653	18 12	120	120
Dec.31	Revenue Account (Provision for Bad and Doubtful Debts) DR. To Provision for Bad and Doubtful Debts Being 10% of total debtors U 11,150 now set aside against possibility of non-settlement	19 15	1,150	1,150

The Debtors and Provisions accounts would appear in the ledger as before but the Revenue account would (using assumed figures) be shown as:

Rechargeable Works Revenue Account						25
19 Dec.31	To Wages	5	5,000	19 Dec.31	By Charges (Transfer from Rechargeable Works Income Account)	11,620
	To Materials	6	3,000			
	To Transport	7	1,000			
	To Works Department Overheads	8	1,350			
	To Bad Debts	18	120			
	To Provision for Bad and Doubtful Debts	19	1,150			
			11,620			11,620

In practice the Revenue account rarely balances exactly because charges

Fixed Assets - Introduction

are often fixed before exact costs are known - any debit or credit balance is carried forward or transferred to the General Fund.

Provisions for specific commitments and known contingencies are normally shown on the left hand side of the balance sheet and are often invested. Provisions for diminutions in values of assets are normally shown on the right hand side of the balance sheet as deductions from the assets to which they refer: they are rarely invested.

Examples have already been given of how Renewals Funds, Repairs Funds and Depreciation are shown in balance sheets. Provision for bad debts is normally shown like this:

Balance Sheet (Right hand side)

	Units	Units
Sundry Debtors	11,500	
Less Provision for Bad and Doubtful Debts	1,150	10,350

(b) Reserves

Sometimes funds are set aside from surplus balances, not as provisions for known liabilities, but to increase general financial stability. These funds are known as reserves.

Suppose Kambale and District Water Board had a Revenue Account Surplus of U 460,000 and wished to transfer U 200,000 to a Reserve Fund. The journal entry would appear as:

19 Dec.31	Revenue Account DR. To Reserve Fund Being transfer of surplus balances to reserves	1 2	200,000	200,000

If the Reserve Fund were invested the journal entry would be:

19 Dec.31	Reserve Fund Investment DR. To Cash Being investment of Reserve Fund - purchase of 6% Government Stock	3 C.B.	200,000	200,000

Ledger accounts would appear as:

		Revenue Account					1
19 Dec.31	To Reserve Fund	J	200,000	19 Dec.31	By Balance	b/f	460,000
	To Balance	c/d	260,000				
			460,000				460,000
			======				======
				19 Jan.1	By Balance	b/d	260,000

		Reserve Fund					2
19 Dec.31	To Balance	c/d	200,000	19 Dec.31	By Revenue Account	J	200,000
			200,000				200,000
			======				======
				19 Jan.1	By Balance	b/d	200,000

		Reserve Fund (10% Government Stock)					3
19 Dec.31	To Cash	J	200,000	19 Dec.31	By Balance	c/d	200,000
			======				======
19 Jan.1	To Balance	b/d	200,000				

		Cash Book					4
19 Dec.31	To Balance	b/f	460,000	19 Dec.31	By Investment	J	200,000
					By Balance	c/d	260,000
			460,000				460,000
			======				======
19 Jan.1	To Balance	b/d	260,000				

The balance sheet would show:

Fixed Assets - Introduction

Balance Sheet as at 31 Dec. 19

	Units		Units
Surplus		Current Assets	
Reserve Fund	200,000	Reserve Fund	
General Fund	260,000	Investments	200,000
		Cash	260,000
	460,000		460,000

Reserves can only be set aside out of surplus balances, whereas provisions are a charge against income in the revenue account and must be set aside whether there are surpluses or not, even to the extent of increasing a revenue account deficiency or converting a surplus into a deficiency.

89. **CAPITAL AND REVENUE**

    In relation to local and public authority accounting the following terms are normally used:

    (a) **Capital Expenditure**

    All expenditure incurred (by cash payment or on credit) in the provision of fixed assets which give a future flow of benefit to the authority. Examples include construction of roads, schools, houses and acquisition of heavy plant and machinery.

    (b) **Capital Payments**

    All cash actually paid for the acquisition or construction of a capital asset.

    (c) **Capital Income**

    All income due to the authority (whether received in cash or not) which represents a true gain to the authority and is to be used exclusively for financing capital expenditure. Examples include land premiums, receipts from the sale of fixed assets and specific capital grants (but not loans - see below).

    (d) **Capital Receipts**

    All cash actually received which is to be used to meet capital payments. Capital receipts include items which do not represent a gain to the authority. The most important items in this category are loans, which, although received in cash, represent a liability of the authority to the lender.

    (e) **Revenue Expenditure**

    All expenditure incurred (by cash payment or on credit) in the provision of day-to-day services and normal running expenses of the authority and in the acquisition of current assets (e.g. stores). Examples normally include salaries and wages, repairs and maintenance, rent, general office expenses and loan charges. Unallocated stores (inventories) are normally regarded as revenue (i.e. current) assets but stores subsequently issued for the constructon of fixed assets become capital expenditure. Wages and salaries paid for the construction of fixed assets also become capital expenditure.

(f) **Revenue Payments**

All cash actually paid for day-to-day services, normal running expenditure and unallocated stores.

(g) **Revenue Income**

All income due to the authority (whether received in cash or not) which is not specifically earmarked to finance the acquisition or construction of capital assets, but which is to be used to finance revenue expenditure. Such income includes rates, taxes, fees, charges and normal government grants.

(h) **Revenue Receipts**

All cash actually received in respect of Revenue Income.

(i) **Deferred Charge**

Expenditure which, by its nature, would normally be regarded as revenue expenditure but which because of its heavy cost is financed over a number of years, usually by the raising of a loan. For example, heavy expenditure might have been incurred by a local authority to meet an emergency such as famine, or widespread damage by rain. In such exceptional circumstances a loan might be authorised to meet the expenditure and a deferred charge (i.e. an accumulated loss) would be carried forward in the accounts until the loan was repaid and the loan charges debited in the revenue account (see subsequent chapters).

It should be emphasised that, although a deferred charge is financed in the same way as capital expenditure and appears on the same side of the balance sheet, it is not a fixed asset but an accumulated loss.

Sometimes alternative terms are used, especially where central government accounting systems have been in use.

Term used in the accountancy profession	Term used outside the accountancy profession	Alternative terms sometimes used
Capital	Capital or non-recurrent	Development or re-development
Revenue+	Recurrent	Operation and/or Maintenance
Income	Revenue+	Incomings or receipts*
Expenditure	Expenditure	Outgoings or payments*

* The terms "receipts" and "payments" are sometimes used indiscriminately for "income" and "expenditure". The terms are not in fact synonymous and should be used with great care.

Fixed Assets - Introduction

+ Note that the word "Revenue" can have two entirely different meanings.

90. **CAPITAL EXPENDITURE**

    What constitutes a fixed asset which gives a future flow of benefit is sometimes a matter of opinion. The provision of a school or a house is obviously capital expenditure but someone might argue that a typewriter was an asset giving a future flow of benefit and its purchase should therefore be treated as capital expenditure. At what point does a road repair (revenue expenditure) become a road improvement (capital expenditure)?

    A further difficulty is that what might be considered as capital expenditure by a small authority might be treated as revenue expenditure by a large municipality.

    To solve these difficulties each authority should decide for itself what it considers to be capital expenditure using the following definition for guidance:

    Capital expenditure is all expenditure incurred in the provision of fixed assets which give a future flow of benefit to the authority and which the authority would normally expect to finance over a number of years by loans, renewals fund contributions or regular revenue contributions to capital.

    This does not preclude an authority from financing any particular capital asset (or a proportion of its capital investment programme) by a direct revenue contribution. Furthermore, there should be consistency regarding classification. It would normally be inconsistent for assets of the same category to be distinguished solely on grounds of cost.

    Examples

    A typewriter is clearly not capital expenditure, because, although it is technically an asset, no local authority would finance it over a period of years. All would finance it as normal revenue expenditure.

    A vehicle can normally be regarded as capital expenditure because it has a working life of several years and a small authority might raise a loan to finance it. Although a large local authority might not need to raise a loan, the purchase should still be regarded as capital expenditure. The vehicle will be shown as an asset (ie capitalised) and the charge to the revenue account shown not as a purchase of the vehicle but as a "revenue contribution to capital outlay".

9. Municipal Budgets

Section		Page
91.	Accountancy Practice.	283
92.	The Local Authority in Practice.	283
93.	The Budget.	284
94.	Capital Programmes and Capital Budgets.	286
95.	Revenue Budget.	286
96.	Working Papers.	295
97.	Manpower Budgets.	298
98.	Working Balance.	299
99.	Cash Forecasts.	302
100.	Legal Requirements.	305

91. **ACCOUNTANCY PRACTICE**

All book-keeping should take place as part of an integrated system in which accounts are interlocked through double-entry. All accounts, including cost accounts, should be capable of being balanced together as an integrated whole.

In the organisation of a practical system of accountancy for a local or public authority, these principles must be borne firmly in mind.

The basic considerations in the organisation of a finance department are:

(a) efficiency and maximum service to employing authority, spending departments and the public;

(b) prevention of expensive duplication of work, of fraud and irregularities; and

(c) internal financial control.

In practice, therefore, accountancy records must be designed to provide the greatest possible efficiency in operation. Thus, it is likely that much of the detailed record-keeping will be carried out by computer systems. However, it is still necessary, whatever the detailed system, to observe the basic principles of double-entry book-keeping.

92. **THE LOCAL AUTHORITY IN PRACTICE**

To show how the principles of accountancy are put into practice, we shall study an imaginary local authority, which we shall call Kambale Municipal Council. We shall not assume any particular type of authority because the systems in use could apply to any.

We shall however assume that the Kambale Council operates more on the lines of an urban authority than a rural authority, because it is in the urban areas that greater development has taken place, rating systems are widely used, and more advanced procedures are generally in operation. In addition, we shall assume that Kambale Council has a Finance Committee, with specific responsibility to oversee the council's financial activities, together with other committees to oversee the running of various services. This is a common practice, especially where there is a large council. Where it is necessary to demonstrate points of rural practice we shall show these separately.

Let us suppose that the balance sheet of Kambale Council on 31 Dec. 19_5 is as shown on page 285. We shall show, in due course, how each of the balances is brought into the accounts; how it is dealt with in detail; how the activities of the Council are recorded in the accounts for 19_6 and how the final accounts for the year ended 31 Dec. 19_6 can be prepared.

93. **THE BUDGET**

During 19_5 the Kambale Council will prepare its Budget for 19_6. This should consist of several stages:

(a) **Capital Programme**

An authority should plan its capital programme giving forecasts of expenditure for a period of 3 - 5 years, and a programme will be drawn up accordingly for the years 19_6 - 19_0.

(b) **Capital Budget**

That part of the capital programme which sets out the expenditure estimated for the immediately ensuing year (in our case 19_6) represents the Capital Budget and although the various schemes may not yet be approved they will be known in greater detail than those of later years, thus allowing loan charges and other revenue expenditure to be determined for the 19_6 revenue budget.

(c) **Revenue Budget (General)**

This is a comprehensive and detailed statement showing how much the council intends to spend on its current services during 19_6 and where the income to finance the expenditure is to come from. Having determined its estimated expenditure and deducted government grants and miscellaneous income, the Council will almost certainly be left with a budget deficiency which must be financed from rates (property tax) or other taxes. In considering its budget, the Council will determine the percentage rate levy (or graduated tax scales) necessary to raise the required sum to cover the deficiency.

(d) **Revenue Budget (Special)**

Although the Revenue Budget reflects the intended level of day-to-day running expenditure it will almost certainly contain many items of a special or non-recurrent nature which should receive separate consideration and approval. These items can either be listed separately in the main budget or, preferably, shown in a separate supporting statement.

(e) **Cash Forecast**

A forecast of cash requirements should be made to cover 19_6, and continually be kept up to date. The flow of cash into and out of the authority's bank account will fluctuate during the year yet the Chief Financial Officer will wish to be sure that at all times there is enough cash to meet current obligations. Alternatively if the authority is prepared to have a bank overdraft at certain "difficult" periods of the year the Chief Financial Officer will wish to know when, for how long, and to what extent the overdraft will occur. This is so that it will not exceed proper limits; so that it can be arranged in good time; and so that bank interest can be calculated in advance.

KAMBALE COUNCIL

Balance Sheet as at 31 Dec. 19_5

	Units	Units	Units		Units	Units	Units
LONG-TERM LIABILITIES				FIXED ASSETS			
Loans Outstanding			15,009,300	Buildings		10,093,740	
CURRENT LIABILITIES				Permanent Works		9,686,520	
Creditors				Equipment		512,900	20,293,160
Sundry Creditors		316,460					
Receipts in Advance		30,720		CURRENT ASSETS			
Government Graduated Tax		144,160	491,340	Stocks and Stores		310,460	
				Debtors			
PROVISIONS				Sundry Debtors	110,320		
Repairs Funds		63,000		Payments in Advance	4,840	115,160	
Renewals Funds		85,000					
				Investments		148,000	
SURPLUS				Cash			
Capital Discharged				At Bank	410,780		
Grants	1,008,400			In Hand	3,660	414,440	988,060
Takeover Values	3,000,000						
Loans Repaid	1,032,460						
Revenue Contributions	243,000	5,283,860					
General Fund Surplus		348,720	5,632,580				
			21,281,220				21,281,220

Municipal Accounting for Developing Countries

94. CAPITAL PROGRAMMES AND CAPITAL BUDGETS

The summary of the Capital Programme might appear as shown on page 287. Part of the programme, showing individual estimates and forecasts of expenditure for some of the services covered by the Works Committee might appear as shown on page 288.

The programme covers the capital budget for 19_6 and the detail shown is often sufficient. However the authority may choose to draw up a more detailed budget for 19_6. Part of the capital budget for the works department might appear as shown on page 289.

Notice that only schemes beginning or in progress before the end of 19_6 are included in the detailed Budget. (Refuse Collection has therefore been left out in our example.) The allocation of expenditure to each quarter of the year assists in raising loans, calculating loan charges and cash forecasting.

In addition to loan charges, an estimate of other revenue expenditure should be shown, to determine how much additional revenue expenditure will be incurred as a result of the capital project. A new dispensary will generate additional annual costs for medical staff, drugs and maintenance, but a replacement vehicle should add no additional annual costs. The purchase of machinery to take over work formerly done by hand may reduce annual running costs for the service.

95. REVENUE BUDGET

The next step is to produce a revenue budget. The summary of the revenue budget might appear as shown on page 290.

Presentation of the summary varies in its form. The example has been prepared in a way which will show the net expenditure on various services after specific income has been deducted from the costs of those services.

From the net expenditure has been deducted the Council's general income. After allowing for contributions to and from the general balances the resulting net expenditure must be met from rates or other local tax.

In the case of Kambale Council, rates must be levied to bring in an estimated U 3,840,000 in 19_6. The levy for 19_5 was originally estimated to bring in U 3,540,000. Due to new building and revaluations of existing buildings and sites the income is now likely to be U 3,600,000. Supplementary estimates in 19_5 have caused an overall increase in net expenditure of U 147,700. Only U 60,000 of this is covered by extra rate income so instead of a planned surplus of U 51,000 on the year's working there will be a probable deficit of U 36,700 reducing the Council's general fund balance from U 379,680 to U 342,980.

(A glance at the balance sheet shows that the general fund balance was eventually U 348,720 on 31 Dec. 19_5 (1 Jan. 19_6) so the actual deficit must have been U 30,960.)

It will be seen that U 64,920 was taken from balances in 19_4 and a further U 36,700 is estimated to be taken in 19_5. Thus, at the time the estimates are prepared it appears that balances will be reduced by U 101,620 in 19_4 and 19_5. The Council has therefore estimated for an increase in balances during 19_6 to bring the surplus balance to U 477,680 on 31 Dec. 19_6 compared with U 444,600 on 1 Jan. 19_4 (U 379,680 + U 64,920).

CAPITAL BUDGET 19_6
WORKS COMMITTEE

Ref No	Project	Life of Asset (YRS)	Source of Finance	Total Estimated Cost U	Actual to 31.12._4 U	Probable 19_5 1st Half U	Probable 19_5 3rd Qtr U	Expenditure 19_5 4th Qtr U	Estimate 19_6 1st Qtr U	Estimate 19_6 2nd Qtr U	Estimate 19_6 3rd Qtr U	Estimate 19_6 4th Qtr U	Loan Charges 19_5 U	Loan Charges 19_6 U
1.	CAR PARKING Central Car Park	20	Loan	118,000	-	-	-	18,000	90,000	10,000	-	-	-	10,400
	TOTAL			118,000	-	-	-	18,000	90,000	10,000	-	-	-	10,400
2.	LAND DRAINAGE Northern Swamp Area	30	Grant	140,000	-	-	-	-	-	-	10,000	100,000	-	-
	TOTAL			140,000	-	-	-	-	-	-	10,000	100,000	-	-
5.	REFUSE DISPOSAL Extension and Levelling Tip (Stage I)	10	Rev	49,000	900	48,100	-	-	-	-	-	-	-	-
6.	Extension and Levelling Tip (Stage II)	10	Rev	44,000	-	-	-	44,000	-	-	-	-	-	-
	TOTAL			93,000	900	48,100	-	44,000	-	-	-	-	-	-
7.	ROADS West Street/South Street Junction - Major Improvement	20	Loan	774,900	763,900	11,000	-	-	-	-	-	-	68,300	68,300
8.	Dwonga Road - Complete Tarmac to Boundary	20	Loan	1,449,100	1,326,500	110,600	12,000	-	-	-	-	-	127,700	127,700
9.	Church Road - Re-alignment	20	Loan	448,000	-	-	18,000	380,000	50,000	-	-	-	-	39,500
10.	North Street/Park Road - New Road	20	Loan	970,000	-	-	-	-	-	30,000	440,000	420,000	-	42,700
	TOTAL			3,642,000	2,090,400	121,600	30,000	380,000	50,000	30,000	440,000	420,000	196,000	278,200

287

KAMBALE COUNCIL
CAPITAL EXPENDITURE PROGRAMME 19_6/_0 - SUMMARY

Committee and Service	Total Estimated Cost	Actual to 31.12.-4	Probable 19_5	Expenditure Estimate 19_6	19_7	Forecast 19_8	19_9
	Units	Units	Units	Units	Units	Units	Units
GENERAL PURPOSES							
Administrative Buildings	426,000	-	-	-	116,000	310,000	-
HEALTH							
Abattoir	90,000	-	-	-	90,000	-	-
Ambulances	229,000	-	91,000	-	46,000	46,000	46,000
Clinics and Dispensaries	904,000	105,200	258,800	180,000	180,000	-	180,000
Markets	518,000	-	288,000	230,000	-	-	-
Parks	110,000	94,000	16,000	-	-	-	-
HOUSING							
General Estates	2,560,000	-	-	-	480,000	1,000,000	1,080,000
Staff	250,000	163,100	1,900	85,000	-	-	-
WORKS							
Car Parking	118,000	-	18,000	100,000	-	-	-
Land Drainage	140,000	-	-	110,000	30,000	-	-
Refuse Collection	102,000	-	-	-	51,000	-	51,000
Refuse Disposal	93,000	900	92,100	-	-	-	-
Roads	3,642,000	2,090,400	531,600	940,000	80,000	-	-
Sewage Disposal	2,203,500	1,125,700	569,800	-	244,000	168,000	96,000
Sewerage	1,389,000	504,900	428,100	-	264,000	192,000	-
Street Lighting	565,800	76,900	318,900	-	-	-	170,000
Surface Water Drainage	110,000	-	110,000	-	-	-	-
Vacuum Tanker Service	57,000	-	-	57,000	-	-	-
Water Supply	1,308,000	979,600	328,400	-	-	-	-
TOTAL	14,815,300	5,140,700	3,052,600	1,702,000	1,581,000	1,716,000	1,623,000

CAPITAL EXPENDITURE PROGRAMME 19_6/_0
WORKS COMMITTEE

Ref No	Project	Life of Asset (YRS)	Source of Finance	Total Estimated Cost Units	Actual to 31.12._4 Units	Probable 19_5 Units	Expenditure Estimate 19_6 Units	Expenditure 19_7 Units	Forecast 19_8 Units	19_9 Units
1.	CAR PARKING Central Car Park TOTAL	20	Loan	118,000 118,000	- -	18,000 18,000	100,000 100,000	- -	- -	- -
2.	LAND DRAINAGE Northern Swamp Area TOTAL	30	Grant	140,000 140,000	- -	- -	110,000 110,000	30,000 30,000	- -	- -
3.	REFUSE COLLECTION Refuse Vehicle to replace - Vehicle purchased 19_2	5	V.R.F.	51,000	-	-	-	51,000	-	-
4.	Vehicle purchased 19_4 TOTAL	5	V.R.F.	51,000 102,000	- -	- -	- -	51,000 51,000	- -	51,000 51,000
5.	REFUSE DISPOSAL Extension and level-ling tip (Stage I)	10	Rev.	49,000	900	48,100	-	-	-	-
6.	Extension and levelling tip (Stage II) TOTAL	10	Rev.	44,000 93,000	- 900	44,000 92,100	- -	- -	- -	- -
7.	ROADS West St/South St Junction - Major Improvement	20	Loan	774,900	763,900	11,000	-	-	-	-
8.	Dwonga Rd - Complete Tarmac to Boundary	20	Loan	1,449,100	1,326,500	122,600	-	-	-	-
9.	Church Rd - Re-alignment	20	Loan	448,000	-	398,000	50,000	-	-	-
10.	North St/Park Rd - New Road TOTAL	20	Loan	970,000 3,642,000	- 2,090,400	- 531,600	390,000 940,000	80,000 80,000	- -	- -

(similar details for other services)

V.R.F. = Vehicles Renewals Fund

Municipal Accounting for Developing Countries

The summary is prepared from the detailed estimated expenditure and income of the various committees and services.

The Finance Committee estimates will cover the running of the finance department and might also include a central buying and stores section, as this is often under the control of the Chief Financial Officer.

Assuming only a finance department, the Finance Committee estimates of Kambale Council might appear as shown on page 291. Totals are taken direct to the main summary.

The Health Committee estimates will cover the running of several different services. These would be summarised on a committee summary as shown on page 292. The totals of this committee summary would be taken to the main summary.

Whilst most services are a net charge against rates or taxes some are (or could be) self supporting. Although the abattoir made a modest surplus in 19_4 and was originally estimated to "break even" in 19_5 it now seems likely that the service will be subsidised in 19_5 and to greater extent in 19_6. It may be that a revision of charges should be considered before the estimates are finalised.

KAMBALE COUNCIL
REVENUE BUDGET 19_6
MAIN SUMMARY

Actual 19 4	Committee	Page No.	Estimate 19 5	Probable 19 5	Estimate 19 6
Units			Units	Units	Units
1,462,580	Education	2	1,489,600	1,524,900	1,567,300
456,860	Finance	6	429,200	450,800	473,600
685,740	General Purposes	8	685,700	683,300	735,300
1,362,880	Health	12	1,334,900	1,463,600	1,544,800
382,780	Housing	26	398,800	382,500	404,800
(296,520)	Land Control (Credit)	30	(292,000)	(305,700)	(330,500)
2,728,740	Works	32	2,624,300	2,655,200	2,679,600
6,783,060	TOTAL NET EXPENDITURE OF COMMITTEES		6,670,500	6,854,600	7,074,900
	Deduct General Income:				
167,260	Licences - Trading		169,000	171,300	178,000
51,800	- Liquor		50,600	53,400	52,000
4,820	- Miscellaneous		5,000	5,000	5,000
8,720	Investment Income		9,700	9,000	9,600
2,916,520	Government Grants		2,947,200	2,979,200	3,125,000
3,149,120	TOTAL GENERAL INCOME		3,181,500	3,217,900	3,369,600
3,633,940	TOTAL NET EXPENDITURE OF COUNCIL		3,489,000	3,636,700	3,705,300
-	Add Increase in Surplus Balances		51,000	-	134,700
64,920	Deduct Decrease in Surplus Balances		-	36,700	-
3,569,020	NET REQUIREMENTS FROM RATES/GRADUATED TAX		3,540,000	3,600,000	3,840,000

Municipal Budgets

Statement of Balances

		Units
	General Fund Surplus 1.1._5	379,680
Deduct	Probable Deficiency 19_5	36,700
	Probable General Fund Surplus 31.12._5	342,980
Add	Estimated Surplus 19_6	134,700
	Estimated General Fund Surplus 31.12._6	477,680

Municipal Accounting for Developing Countries

FINANCE COMMITTEE

Actual 19-4	Details	Ref No.	Estimate 19-5	Probable 19-5	Estimate 19-6
Units			Units	Units	Units
	FINANCE DEPARTMENT				
	Expenditure				
	Employees				
367,880	Salaries	1	346,600	365,000	368,200
29,340	Provident Fund and Gratuities	2	30,400	31,200	31,600
37,800	Housing	3	39,000	39,000	43,000
6,420	Wages	4	7,000	8,000	8,000
	Premises				
2,720	Furniture and Fittings	5	2,500	3,000	6,000
	Supplies and Services				
900	Books and Journals	6	800	1,000	2,000
10,240	Equipment	7	2,200	2,000	4,000
	Transport				
8,560	Vehicle Expenses	8	8,500	9,000	9,500
6,500	Car and Cycle Allowances	9	6,600	6,600	7,000
	Establishment Expenses				
32,820	Printing and Stationery	10	33,000	33,000	33,000
2,720	Advertising	11	2,500	3,000	3,000
2,040	Postages	12	2,000	2,200	2,200
6,560	Telephones	13	6,500	6,500	6,500
540	Insurance	14	600	600	600
	Miscellaneous Expenses				
8,700	Audit Fees	15	8,700	8,700	8,700
1,860	Study Grants	16	2,000	2,000	4,000
3,100	Cash Security	17	300	300	300
1,420	Bank Charges	18	1,500	1,500	1,500
530,120			500,700	522,600	539,100
	Income				
72,820	Graduated Tax Agency Fees	19	71,000	71,300	65,000
380	Sales of Publications	20	400	400	400
60	Miscellaneous	21	100	100	100
73,260			71,500	71,800	65,500
	NET EXPENDITURE TO MAIN SUMMARY				
456,860			429,200	450,800	473,600
=======			=======	=======	=======

Municipal Budgets

HEALTH COMMITTEE

Actual 19-4 Units		Page No.	Estimate 19_5 Units	Probable 19_5 Units	Estimate 19_6 Units
	Summary				
282,460	Administration	14	263,000	317,000	333,600
(3,080)	Abattoir	16	-	11,000	25,200
30,940	Ambulances	18	30,000	33,000	35,000
716,600	Clinics and Dispensaries	20	677,200	711,100	739,600
(27,020)	Markets	22	(25,000)	(18,900)	(6,400)
362,980	Parks	24	389,700	410,400	417,800
1,362,880	NET EXPENDITURE TO MAIN SUMMARY		1,334,900	1,463,600	1,544,800

The modest surplus being made by the markets is also gradually falling, and it will not be long before a revision of charges is also necessary here.

The detailed estimates for the health department (administration) will appear in a similar form to those of the finance department. The estimates for clinics and dispensaries might appear as shown on page 294 and those for markets as shown on page 295

The estimates of the detailed services will include salaries for all staff engaged on those particular services. Where staff are directly engaged on two or more services, their salaries are apportioned. Salaries of staff not engaged on any specific service will be included under administration (eg medical officers, health inspectors and administrative staff).

Municipal Accounting for Developing Countries

HEALTH COMMITTEE

Actual 19-4 Units	Details	Ref No.	Estimate 19-5 Units	Probable 19-5 Units	Estimate 19-6 Units
	CLINICS AND DISPENSARIES				
	Expenditure				
	Employees				
283,260	Salaries	53	308,700	312,100	321,200
20,620	Provident Fund	54	20,200	21,200	21,500
4,860	Housing	55	5,000	5,000	5,000
42,980	Wages	56	43,000	43,600	49,100
	Premises				
5,040	Repair and Maintenance of Buildings	57	1,000	1,000	3,000
6,300	Electricity	58	6,000	6,600	7,600
3,920	Water	59	3,400	4,000	5,000
1,940	Cleaning Materials	60	2,000	2,000	2,700
860	Rates	61	900	900	1,800
	Supplies and Services				
65,640	Equipment	62	22,900	31,600	25,000
252,720	Drugs and Medical Supplies	63	231,000	251,000	257,000
5,000	Uniform	64	5,000	5,200	5,200
	Establishment Expenses				
2,460	Printing and Stationery	65	2,400	2,400	2,800
940	Telephones	66	900	1,000	1,100
500	Insurance	67	500	500	500
17,060	Loan Charges	68	20,300	20,300	27,100
2,500	Revenue Contributions to Capital Outlay	69	4,000	2,700	4,000
716,600	NET EXPENDITURE TO SUMMARY		677,200	711,100	739,600

The budget items have been numbered consecutively throughout each committee. The advantage of this is that Council members and officers of other departments have a simple and straightforward reference to any particular item.

As an alternative, accountancy code numbers could be used, thus linking the estimates with the accounts. However, in a large authority the coding system may be somewhat complex and might be difficult for laymen to follow.

The estimates prepared in this form show clearly the net cost of each service, and services are grouped for presentation to each committee. After each committee has approved its own estimates, they can be combined for presentation to the Finance Committee.

Municipal Budgets

HEALTH COMMITTEE

Actual 19_4 Units	Details	Ref No.	Estimate 19_5 Units	Probable 19_5 Units	Estimate 19_6 Units
	MARKETS				
	Expenditure				
	Employees				
46,160	Salaries	70	68,900	65,000	66,100
2,540	Provident Fund	71	2,600	2,600	2,600
71,620	Wages	72	81,000	83,600	88,000
	Premises				
9,020	Repair and Maintenance of Buildings	73	11,200	11,200	11,200
700	Electricity	74	800	800	800
19,620	Water	75	19,000	21,000	21,000
5,260	Cleaning Materials	76	5,000	5,400	5,400
35,100	Rates	77	35,100	35,100	35,100
	Supplies and Services				
1,220	Equipment Maintenance	78	2,000	2,000	2,000
2,940	Uniform	79	3,000	3,000	3,000
660	Transport	80	1,000	1,000	1,000
	Establishment Expenses				
3,220	Printing and Stationery	81	3,000	3,500	3,500
860	Insurance	82	900	900	900
33,620	Loan Charges	83	33,600	33,600	40,800
232,540			267,100	268,700	281,400
	Income				
259,560	Rents and Dues	84	292,100	287,600	287,800
	NET INCOME TO SUMMARY				
27,020			25,000	18,900	6,400

The budget can also be used for monitoring and controlling expenditure and income. Output statistics, which are designed to assist these processes, are often an integral part of the budget documentation. These monetary and/or physical indicators of output may take the form of numbers of clinics, numbers and types of patients, and patient day costs etc.

96. **WORKING PAPERS**

Before any figures can be included in the budget as estimates, calculations will be made by finance officers preparing the budget, in consultation with officers of the department concerned.

These detailed workings are often prepared on rough sheets of paper but it is good practice to have some specially printed working papers kept

Municipal Accounting for Developing Countries

in a file for each service. For items 63 - 66 of the Health Committee estimates for Kambale Council the working papers might be as follows.

The papers can be prepared in outline long before the budget is prepared and the following items typed in readiness:

(a) committee, service and item;

(b) actual 19_4; and

(c) original estimate 19_5.

As soon as figures are available, the actual expenditure to date can be inserted.

Working figures are only given to the extent to which they will assist preparation of estimates. There is often little justification for a breakdown of "actual 19_4" figures but this may be required sometimes.

COMMITTEE: Health
SERVICE: Clinics and Dispensaries REF.No: 63
ITEM: Drugs and Medical Supplies

Actual 19_4		Estimate 19_5	Probable 19_5			Estimate 19_6
			Actual to 31/8	Estimate to 31/12	Total	
Units		Units	Units	Units	Units	Units
252,720	TOTAL	231,000	162,400	88,600	251,000	257,000
=======		=======	=======	======	=======	=======
	Drug Allowances:					
	Mabale	40,000	32,520	4,480	37,000	40,000
	Gutoka	40,000	24,820	12,180	37,000	40,000
	Toroti	30,000	22,520	4,980	27,500	30,000
	Enoto	30,000	18,860	8,640	27,500	30,000
	Midwifery Supplies	45,000	31,620	12,380	44,000	44,000
	Disposable Surgical Masks	13,000	3,000	9,000	12,000	12,000
	Disposable Syringes	12,000	12,000	2,000	14,000	14,000
	Typhoid Vaccine (Ministry of Health Circular 25)			32,000	32,000	22,000
	Dental Supplies	21,000	17,060	2,940	20,000	25,000
	Note:					
	Due to typhoid epidemic - cuts made in normal drug allowances to help finance cost of vaccine.					
	Supplementary estimate approved 2/7/_5 (U 20,000) for balance.					

Municipal Budgets

COMMITTEE: Health
SERVICE: Clinic and Dispensaries
ITEM: Uniform

REF. No: 64

| Actual 19_4 | | Estimate 19_5 | Probable 19_5 ||| Estimate 19_6 |
			Actual to 31/8	Estimate to 31/12	Total	
Units 5,000 =====		Units 5,000 =====	Units 3,260 =====	Units 1,940 =====	Units 5,200 =====	Units 5,200 =====
	Original Price Increase 19_5	5,000			200	

COMMITTEE: Health
SERVICE: Clinics and Dispensaries
ITEM: Printing and Stationery

REF. No: 65

| Actual 19_4 | | Estimate 19_5 | Probable 19_5 ||| Estimate 19_6 |
			Actual to 31/8	Estimate to 31/12	Total	
Units 2,460 =====		Units 2,400 =====	Units 1,520 =====	Units 880 ===	Units 2,400 =====	Units 2,800 =====
	Normal Requirements Index Cards 19_6	2,400			2,400	2,400 400

COMMITTEE: Health
SERVICE: Clinics and Dispensaries
ITEM: Telephones

REF. No: 66

| Actual 19_4 | | Estimate 19_5 | Probable 19_5 ||| Estimate 19_6 |
			Actual to 31/8	Estimate to 31/12	Total	
Units 940 ===		Units 900 ===	Units 500 ===	Units 500 ===	Units 1,000 =====	Units 1,100 =====
	4 Clinics @ U 180 p.a.	720				)
	1 Dental Clinic @ U 180 p.a.	180				)
	Actual for] year		500	500		) 1,000))
	1 New Clinic] year 19_6					100

(Notice that working papers shown above are added upwards instead of downwards. Totals occupy a standard position at the top of each sheet to reduce the possibility of wrong figures being taken to the main estimates.)

97. MANPOWER BUDGETS

One of the most important documents prepared in support of a main budget is a manpower budget, setting out details of staff establishment in each department. This part of the budget is so important that it is often included in summary form in the main estimates in many authorities. In large authorities this is not possible and there are in any case certain objections to the practice.

(a) The extra figures in the main budget make it less digestible to the lay council member.

(b) It is often bad from the point of view of public relations and staff relations to show salaries of individual officers on public documents.

(c) Council and Committee members may be tempted to discuss individual salaries and gradings when they should be dealing with overall control (detailed matters should be dealt with by negotiation between officers concerned - or trade unions - and an appropriate committee), separately from the budget process.

The manpower budget for the Finance Department of Kambale Council might appear as shown on page 299.

The probable salaries can be calculated from individual records, allowing for vacancies and sickness so far during 19_5.

A supplement to the published estimates should set out the authorised staff establishment for each department, if necessary broken down over the various posts, and stating the authority for any increases in staff.

The list for the health department might begin as follows:

Establishment 1.1._5	Post	Grade	Authorised Establishment Original 19-5	Revised 19-5	Approved 19-6
1	Medical Officer of Health	A	1	1	1
3	Assistant Medical Officers	B	3	3	4(a)
1	Chief Administrative Officer	C	1	1	1
1	Chief Public Health Inspectors	D	1	1	1
4	Public Health Inspectors	E	4	5(b)	5
5	Clerical Assistants	J	5	5	5
(etc)	etc.		(etc)	(etc)	(etc)
25	TOTAL		25	26	27

(a) authorised 13/6/_5

(b) authorised 25/2/_5

Municipal Budgets

Some authorities give this information in the main budget.

FINANCE DEPARTMENT
MANPOWER BUDGET

Post	Present Holder	Annual Salary 1.1._6	Probable 19_5 Salary	Probable 19_5 Prov Fund	Estimated 19_6 Salary	Estimated 19_6 Prov Fund
		Units	Units	Units	Units	Units
Chief Financial Officer	Musoke	24,500	23,500	1,180	24,500	1,230
Deputy	Kibule	18,200	17,600	880	18,200	910
Principal Assistant	Kilama	15,500	15,000	750	15,500	780
Chief Accountant	Mukasa	12,800	12,300	-	12,800	-
Chief Auditor	(etc)	12,800	10,100	510	12,800	640
Chief Paymaster		8,200	7,900	-	8,200	-
Chief Collector		8,200	7,750	-	8,200	-
Chief Cashier		8,200	7,900	400	8,200	410
Assistant Accountant 1		(etc)	(etc)	(etc)	(etc)	(etc)
Assistant Accountant 2						
Assistant Auditor (etc)						
			365,000	17,100	368,200	17,800

98. **WORKING BALANCE**

How does the Chief Financial Officer of Kambale Council decide to recommend that the General Fund Surplus should be U 477,680 on 31 Dec. 19_6? He wants to be sure that at all times during a financial year he has enough cash to meet commitments.

He knows from experience that there are certain times of the year when cash balances are likely to be lower than at other times. In Kambale Council this will probably be at the beginning of January and the beginning of June, before the half yearly rate income begins to come in.

The probable surplus on 31 Dec. 19_5 is (from estimates) U 342,980. The probable level of creditors, debtors and stocks will be known from experience, based on past balance sheets and known variations.

Municipal Accounting for Developing Countries

The probable cash balance at 31 Dec. 19_5 can therefore be calculated as (in round figures):

	Units	Units
Probable Surplus		350,000
Probable Creditors		490,000
		840,000
Less Probable Stocks	310,000	
Probable Debtors	120,000	430,000
Balance held in Cash		410,000
Additional Funds		
Repairs Funds	63,000	
Renewals Funds	85,000	
	148,000	
Less Investments	148,000	-
Overall Cash Balance		410,000

The Chief Financial Officer is, in fact, preparing an estimated balance sheet (for revenue balances only) which would appear as follows:

Estimated Balance Sheet as at 31 Dec. 19_5
Revenue

	Units		Units
Sundry Creditors	490,000	Stocks and Stores	310,000
Repairs Funds	63,000	Sundry Debtors	120,000
Renewals Funds	85,000	Investments	148,000
General Fund Surplus	350,000	Cash at Bank and In Hand	410,000
	988,000		988,000

Earlier chapters showed how results are related to resources and this is re-emphasised here by a narrative balance sheet:

	Units	Units
Assets		
Stocks and Stores		310,000
Sundry Debtors		120,000
Investments		148,000
Cash		410,000
		988,000
Less **Liabilities and Provisions**		
Sundry Creditors	490,000	
Repairs Funds	63,000	
Renewals Funds	85,000	638,000
NET RESOURCES		350,000
Represented by:		
Opening Surplus 1.1._5 (approximately)		380,000
Less Deficiency during 19_5 (approximately)		30,000
NET RESULTS		350,000

Municipal Budgets

Results (i.e. fund surpluses) cannot be considered in isolation from resources (i.e. the assets in which surpluses are held).

In the above example the surplus might be said to be satisfactory but exactly the same surplus could be considered a highly unsatisfactory state of affairs in a position such as:

	Units	Units
Assets		
Stocks and Stores		400,000
Sundry Debtors		300,000
Investments		568,000
Cash in Hand		30,000
		1,298,000
Less **Liabilities and Provisions**		
Sundry Creditors	490,000	
Bank Overdraft	310,000	
Repairs Funds	63,000	
Renewals Funds	85,000	948,000
NET RESOURCES		350,000
Represented by:		
Opening Surplus 1.1._5		320,000
Add Surplus during 19_5		30,000
NET RESULTS		350,000

Here, although a surplus (instead of a deficiency) has been made during 19_5, the accumulated results are by no means adequate to cover the resources in which they are held, thus probably paying (say) 10% on the overdraft and earning (say) 10% on its investments. Some investments should either be turned into cash to eliminate the overdraft or (if this could not be done except at a considerable loss) the surplus will have to be increased.

In much the same way it is no good estimating for (say) a surplus of U 400,000 if, as a result of inefficient tax (or rate) collections, U 100,000 of the estimated tax (or rate) income is still uncollected at the end of the year. The surplus will certainly exist on paper in the revenue account, but will be held in book debts and not in cash.

The working balance calculation shown on page 300 could be confirmed by preparing a cash forecast from the date the estimates are prepared (August or September) to the end of December, by the method shown later.

Because the end of December (beginning of January) is known to be the most difficult cash period the Chief Financial Officer can be fairly certain, all other things being equal, that his cash balance will not fall below **U** 410,000 during 19_6.

Suppose he now makes certain decisions:

(a) to speed up payment of creditors accounts so that no more than an estimated U 400,000 is outstanding at any time. This might be in response to complaints by suppliers of goods and services who have been kept waiting too long for their money;

(b) to cut maximum stocks to an overall limit of U 260,000 as a result of an efficiency audit;

(c) to improve debt collection procedure, so that no more than U 100,000 is outstanding at the year end; and

(d) always to have in hand a minimum of U 500,000 in cash to meet unforseen eventualities and to ensure that wages and salaries can always be paid on the due dates.

The projected cash position at the end of 19_6 would be:

	Units
Stocks and Stores (maximum)	260,000
Sundry Debtors (maximum)	100,000
Cash at Bank (minimum)	500,000
Cash in Hand	4,000
	864,000
Less Sundry Creditors (minimum)	400,000
Working Balance Requirements	464,000
Less Uninvested Cash on other Revenue Funds (eg Repairs and Renewals)	-
General Fund Surplus required	464,000

The total requirements to build up such a surplus in 19_6 must be, and have in fact been, included in the estimates for that year. The figures in the estimates differ slightly from those shown above - this is always the case because in practice the rate levy is estimated to yield a certain fixed sum - no council would reduce its site rate from (say) 2% to (say) 1.9854% just for the sake of hypothetical precision.

Notice how the art of approximation has been used in the above example.

The working balance in practice is also used as a cushion against possible lost income and unavoidable expenditure increases. It should involve borrowing strategy (payment of loan charges, temporary loans, fundings and interest on internal balances); collections on behalf of other authorities; and the flow of government grants.

99. CASH FORECASTS

These should be made continuously during the year and projected for as long a period as possible. Minimum requirements would probably be to prepare a forecast at the beginning of each quarter and project it for six months. Some authorities might well prepare monthly forecasts and project them for a twelve month period.

Advantages of a careful cash forecast are:

(a) to plan in advance for temporary investment of surplus cash;

(b) to plan in advance for temporary borrowing, bank overdraft or realisation of investments;

(c) to plan the timing of loan raising operations for capital works so that unproductive loan charges are minimised;

(d) to plan the payment of creditors and bulk ordering of goods for stores;

Municipal Budgets

(e) to take advantage of cash discount allowed by suppliers for prompt payment;

(f) to take steps to improve procedure for collection of income, especially at difficult periods; and

(g) to minimise bank charges and interest on overdrafts.

Payments (and to some extent receipts) fall into six main types:

(a) regular - eg wages, salaries, electricity, routine expenses;

(b) periodical - eg loan charges, insurance premiums, licence fees;

(c) seasonal - eg grass cutting, road repairs, control of bush fires, flood control;

(d) individual - eg contract payments, purchase of equipment;

(e) irregular or uneven - eg bulk purchase of stores, gratuities; and

(f) payments to other authorities of revenues collected on their behalf.

A cash forecast prepared at the beginning of January and projected to the end of June for Kambale Council might appear in skeleton form as shown on page 304. Cash sums entered in the forecast are shown by the symbol "x". Where no such sums occur during any month the symbol "-" appears. In practice, of course, actual figures would be used, based on experience.

KAMBALE COUNCIL
CASH FORECAST
Jan - Jun 19_6

Item	Type	Months Due	Jan	Feb	Mar	Apr	May	Jun
			U	U	U	U	U	U
Receipts								
Bank Balance brought forward	-	-	x	x	x	x	x	x
Rates	P/U	all	x	x	x	x	x	x
Graduated Tax	U	all	x	x	x	x	x	x
Rents	R	all	x	x	x	x	x	x
Water Charges	P/U	all	x	x	x	x	x	x
Investment Interest	P	MAR/JUN	-	-	x	-	-	x
Miscellaneous	U	all	x	x	x	x	x	x
Loans	U	APR	-	-	-	x	-	-
Grants - General	P	JAN/MAR/MAY	x	-	x	-	x	-
- Specific	U	APR/MAY	-	-	-	x	x	-
Total Receipts			x	x	x	x	x	x
Payments								
Salaries at U x per month	R	all	x	x	x	x	x	x
Wages at U x per month	R	all	x	x	x	x	x	x
Electricity at U x per month	R	all	x	x	x	x	x	x
Routine Expenses	R	all	x	x	x	x	x	x
Car Allowances U x per month	R	all	x	x	x	x	x	x
Road Repairs	S	(dry)	x	x	x	-	-	-
Grass Cutting	S	(wet)	-	-	x	x	x	-
Vehicle Licences	P	JAN	x	-	-	-	-	-
Insurance Premiums	P	MAR	-	-	x	-	-	-
Municipal Rates	P	JAN/JUL	x	-	-	-	-	-
Loan Charges	P	JAN/MAR	x	-	x	-	-	-
Telephones U x quarter	P	FEB/MAY	-	x	-	-	x	-
Contract - Church Road Re-alignment U x due	I	JAN-MAR	x	x	x	-	-	-
New Vehicle expected April	I	APR	-	-	-	x	-	-
Gratuities - Staff Retiring	U	FEB/MAY	-	x	-	-	x	-
Audit Fee	P	MAY	-	-	-	-	x	-
Graduated Tax	U	FEB/APR/JUN	-	x	-	x	-	x
Bulk Purchase - Stores	U	APR/JUN	-	-	-	x	-	x
Total Payments			x	x	x	x	x	x
Estimated Bank Balance at Month End			x	x	x	x	x	x

R = Regular
P = Periodical
S = Seasonal
I = Individual
U = Irregular (uneven)

Municipal Budgets

In drawing up the cash forecast the following points should be considered:

(a) Rates and water charges will be levied periodically but the flow of cash receipts will tend to be uneven.

(b) Graduated tax will be assessed annually but the flow of cash will be uneven, probably reaching its peak just before the date when prosecution and penalties are applied.

(c) Loan receipts will cause temporary large increases in cash balances which will fall again as capital payments are made - consideration should be given to the practice of delaying loan-raising operations for as long as possible to save unproductive loan charges.

(d) Payments for road repairs and grass cutting should only include extra materials or additional temporary staff - wages of permanent staff employed on these duties will be included under normal wages and they must not be counted twice.

(e) No cash is actually paid or received when the council pays rates on its own property as it is merely a book transfer. The figure for "Rates" shown in the "Receipts" forecast is the gross figure (including Council property) and the "Payments" forecast includes the Council's rates as a payment. Alternatively the figure for "Rates" in the "Receipts" forecast could be shown as excluding Council property and nothing would appear as payments.

(f) Payments of graduated tax to the goverment would reflect the flow of receipts.

(g) Bulk purchase of stores might depend upon delivery dates, advantageous prices, contract arrangements and other factors - they could also perhaps be planned in advance so that payment could be made when cash balances were higher than at other times.

100. LEGAL REQUIREMENTS

The forms used in budget preparation are many and varied. The examples given are only a general guide, based on experience.

The form in which the estimates of particular local authorities are submitted to higher authority (eg government departments) for approval are often governed by financial regulations or financial instructions. These must be adhered to and readers are urged to study for themselves the regulations relating to their own countries and/or authorities.

NOTE:

Revenue estimates are prepared about four or five months before the year to which they relate. Sixteen or seventeen months may elapse before an estimated sum is actually spent. Experience has shown that there is little use in trying to estimate more accurately than to the nearest U 100 for any single item.

For capital estimates, prepared several years in advance, accuracy to the nearest U 500 is all that can be expected for schemes in progress. For schemes not yet started it is usually only possible to estimate to the nearest U 1,000 or U 2,000.

Although for illustrative purposes the budget has been presented as an annual exercise, in practice supplementary estimates may be prepared

Municipal Accounting for Developing Countries

when required or otherwise as the authority reacts to changing circumstances.

10. Income Accounting

Section		Page
101.	Receipt and Payment of Cash.	308
102.	Book-Keeping Procedures.	310
103.	Costing.	310
104.	Books and Records.	313
105.	Cash and Credit Income.	313
106.	Credit Income.	314
107.	The Rate Book (Property Tax Register).	315
108.	The Rate (Property Tax) Demand.	323
109.	Sundry Debtors (Miscellaneous Receivables) Invoices.	325
110.	Periodical Income Register.	326
111.	Sundry Debtors Book.	327
112.	The Slip System.	331
113.	Rents.	334
114.	Ticket Income.	336
115.	Remittance List.	337
116.	Licences.	338
117.	Receipts.	341
118.	The Cash Book.	343
119.	Collection and Deposit Book.	344
120.	Graduated Personal Tax.	349

101. RECEIPT AND PAYMENT OF CASH

Having prepared and approved its budget for 19_6, Kambale Council will, on 1 Jan. 19_6, begin to collect its estimated income and to incur its estimated expenditure. A chart showing the receipt and payment of cash is shown on page 309.

The Central Government, other public authorities and the general public will pay cash to the authority as taxpayers, ratepayers and payers of fees, charges and grants. Some of this cash will be paid at branch cash offices and will later be paid in to the main cashier. Other cash will be paid direct to the main cashier. Money on loan or deposit or repaid by borrowers will also be paid to the main cashier. Sometimes money will be paid direct to the bank by branch cashiers and others, but this is not shown on the chart.

On the payments side, cheques are drawn on the authority's bankers to pay suppliers, contractors and employees. Cheques are also drawn to provide petty cash, which in turn is used to make small payments. All cheques will be drawn by the expenditure section under the control of an officer who might be known as "chief paymaster", to distinguish him from the "chief cashier" (receiving cash) and the "chief collector" (controlling credit income). Cheques drawn by the expenditure section will include advances to borrowers and repayments to lenders. As with payers of cash the receivers of cheques and cash will be the Central Government, other public authorities and the general public. Sometimes money will be paid by direct bank transfer, but this is not shown on the chart.

For the purpose of internal check, receipts of cash should be separated from payments, all receipts being deposited at the bank intact, and all payments drawn from the bank by cheque. Not all authorities follow this practice - often the officer known as the cashier collects cash and makes payments out of the collected cash, merely banking the surplus, to be drawn upon by cheque at a later date.

Differences in procedure are inevitable, especially where banking facilities are limited. Chief financial officers will realise that internal financial control is considerably weakened by non-separation of receipts and payments and will weigh this against the possible advantages of allowing both functions to be dealt with by a single cashier.
The main point is that records and book-keeping procedures must be designed to allow for the efficient collection and disbursement of cash

LOCAL AUTHORITY
RECEIPT AND PAYMENT OF CASH

and to record the effect of receipts and payments upon the authority's finances.

102. BOOK-KEEPING PROCEDURES

The chart on page 311 shows the book-keeping procedures necessary in a typical authority.

The Central Government, public authorities or the general public will represent sources of either cash income (eg market fees, licence fees) or credit income (eg for rates, taxes, rents or water charges). Cash income will be recorded by the cashier as it arises, whereas for credit income, invoices will be sent to debtors by the income section, which will keep records of the amounts due. Sometimes other departments of the authority will send invoices to debtors - either direct (not recommended) or (preferably) through the income section. In either case the income section will receive a copy of the invoice and thus have a record of the debt.

Cash payment by debtors will be recorded by the income section from copies of receipts issued by the cashier. All copy receipts, whether for cash or credit income, will be recorded by the accountancy section in its income analysis. This section will provide control totals of the various types of credit income against which the income section must balance its detailed records of debtors.

Orders will be issued by various departments of the authority to suppliers of goods and services, either direct (not recommended) or (preferably) through the expenditure section of the finance department. If a central purchasing system is operated, the buying and stores section will issue the orders against requisitions from departments. In any case, the expenditure section will receive a copy of each order issued. Invoices will be received from suppliers of goods and services, to be paid by the expenditure section. This section will mark off copy orders to avoid duplicate payment. Employees will be listed on payrolls (or muster rolls) and will also be paid by the expenditure section. Sometimes goods are purchased for (unallocated) stores or for vehicles and plant. When this happens, details of prices and quantities will be required by those keeping stores and plant accounts. This information will be supplied by the expenditure section from paid invoices. All paid invoices and payrolls, together with details of stores and plant actually used, will be made available to the accountancy section for expenditure analysis. This section will provide control totals against which detailed stores and vehicle records will be balanced.

Borrowers and lenders are in many ways no different from other debtors and creditors but their continuing relationship with the authority calls for special records to be kept of their transactions.

Periodically, such as monthly or annually, the accountancy section will prepare summaries of analysed income and expenditure to produce final accounts, to be published as annual financial statements. Summaries and other information for final accounts will also be obtained from cash, debtors, loans, stores, plant, wages and creditors' records and also from other departments. For simplicity this is not fully shown on the chart.

103. COSTING

In the structure of any system to be applied to local authority accounting there are three important objectives:

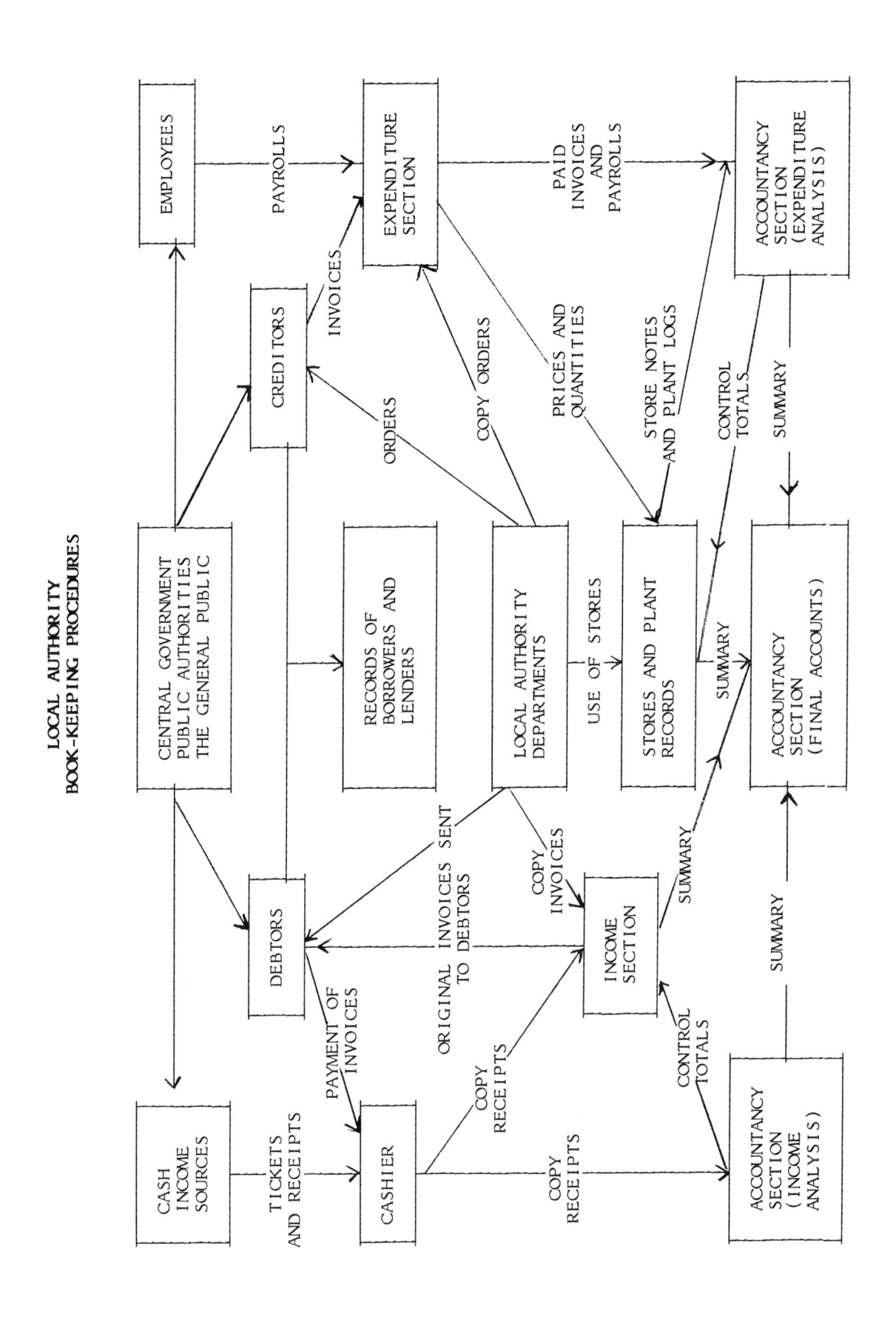

LOCAL AUTHORITY
BOOK-KEEPING PROCEDURES

Municipal Accounting for Developing Countries

(a) the preparation of complete and balanced accounts showing the financial position at the end of an accounting period;

(b) availability of information for compiling all government and other official returns and preparation of statements of account as required by law for audit, for verification of grant claims and for publication; and

(c) measuring and recording activities to produce a detailed analysis and explanation of financial accounts for purposes of budgetary control.

The preparation and use of accounts for purposes (a) and (b) is often known as financial accounting. The extension of accounting procedures into greater detail to provide for purpose (c) is known as cost or management accounting. Emphasis is placed on determination of the costs of individual services or jobs, and equally important, the analysis of these costs.

Financial accounts are not different from cost accounts. Costing is merely an extension of normal accounting procedures. In fact it is sometimes difficult to say where financial accounting ends and costing begins. For example, financial accounting will give the expenditure on (say) "road repair and maintenance" whilst cost accounting will give expenditure on (say) "road repair and maintenance - job number 25" - analysed over wages, materials, transport, plant and overhead expenses.

The main advantages of costing to a local authority are as follows:

(a) the cost of a service is known in detail;

(b) information is available for making estimates and for fixing charges for services;

(c) services which are seen to be costly can be reduced, eliminated, improved or provided in another way;

(d) waste, leakage and inefficiency can be detected;

(e) there is better control over stocks and stores; and

(f) information is disclosed on day-to-day activities, allowing prompt remedial action to be taken if necessary.

Obviously, costing is largely concerned with expenditure, rather than income, and will be dealt with in detail at the same time as expenditure.

At this stage we must understand that the book-keeping procedures for expenditure shown in the chart (ie wages, materials, stores, plant and expenditure analysis) must be designed to produce the necessary costing information.

One sometimes hears of costing being carried out in works departments or elsewhere. Where the work of costing is carried out is not important, but unless the cost accounts are capable of being balanced as an integrated part of the accountancy system they are of limited value. Because of this, it is normally sensible for costing to be carried out within the finance department, and in any case the costing system must be under the control of the Chief Financial Officer.

Income Accounting

104. BOOKS AND RECORDS

In book-keeping theory the main book of account is called a ledger and the subsidiary books are called journals. When considering practical applications of book-keeping we shall see that there is not always a clear division between ledgers and journals or between books of account and memorandum records. We hear of "subsidiary ledgers" and "main journals" and of records which are not referred to by either name, such as cash books or abstracts. Sometimes a record may be used both as a ledger account and a subsidiary book (eg a cash book); sometimes a record, though important, may be neither a ledger nor a journal (eg a periodical receipts register or a votebook).

As a further complication, the same record may be referred to in different ways by different people; what one calls an expenditure ledger, another may call an expenditure journal - and so on.

From what has just been said you may feel that practical "real-life" accounting systems seem to be very complicated. They are complicated, simply because any real-life undertaking or business (of any reasonable size) in this rapidly developing, modern world cannot avoid being complicated and the accounting system likewise has to be complicated to meet the requirements of the business.

However, do not worry unduly about the name given to a particular record. Discover the purpose of the record and see how it fits into the double-entry system. A proper accounting system is not just a lot of debits and credits but an integrated system of accounts, all interlocking with each other like the wheels of a clock, so that figures shown on one account can be tested and checked against figures from another source altogether.

Whatever detailed system is used it should eventually produce in the main ledger a set of final accounts where the appropriate debit and credit aspects of each transaction (or group of transactions) appear once and once only.

In naming a particular record we shall try to show why this name is used and to mention alternative names in common use. But beware of assuming that names not used in this book are wrong. Someone may produce correct and adequate reasons for using them.

In demonstrating systems of accounting we shall try to confine ourselves to records already in use in many authorities. We may also refer to records which could easily be created in locally obtainable books of standard ruling or else produced by a local printer or in the office.

We shall assume that only the simplest mechanical aids to book-keeping are available, such as adding/listing machines or pocket calculators. However, these principles can easily be adapted to various types of electronic data processing.

For purposes of illustration, we shall continue to assume the currency in Units (U), relating to an imaginary local authority "Kambale Municipal Council".

105. CASH AND CREDIT INCOME

For accounting purposes, income may be divided into two main classes - cash income and credit income.

Cash income arises only when the cash is actually received. The authority has no prior knowledge of the exact total amount to be collected and it cannot be precisely calculated in advance. Personal accounts are not required and cannot be used for this type of income, which is often collected at points away from the main cash office. Such income includes casual market fees and cash sales.

Credit income arises where the amount due to the authority can be determined in advance, before cash is actually demanded or received. Personal accounts are kept to record the amounts due from and paid by various persons (debtors).

The personal accounts will be of two kinds. The first kind (sometimes called a rental) is used where income arises regularly and continuously from one person or source such as rates, rents or water charges. The second kind is used where the income arises from individual charges which are calculated as and when necessary, such as sundry debtors income from rechargeable works.

106. CREDIT INCOME

With credit income, because cash is not paid at the time it is due, there is nearly always an outstanding balance of arrears, due but not yet paid in cash. Such a sum, for all sources of credit income, appears in the balance sheet as an asset and as a receivable (sundry debtors).

Sometimes cash is received by an authority before it is due and is treated as receipts in advance. Such a sum appears in the balance sheet as a liability and as a receipt in advance.

Let us now suppose that specific figures can be attributed to various sources of credit income as follows:

	Arrears Units	Receipts in Advance Units
Property Tax (Rates)	23,220	13,540
Water Charges	16,180	9,260
Housing Rents	16,240	6,500
Market Rents	3,020	-
Sundry Debtors	23,040	-
Trading Licences	60	1,060
Liquor Licences	-	360
Motor Advances	27,300	-
Personal Advances	1,260	-
	110,320	30,720

Invoices for the sums in arrears will have already been sent to various debtors and reminders or final notices may have also been sent. Individual sums will appear against their names in the personal ledger (or rental) concerned.

The use of the word "rental" stems from the original use of a book specially designed for the collection of rents. The word now covers many types of books used to keep personal accounts, where the account of each debtor occupies a horizontal line across the page. The rate book (Section 107) and the market rental (Section 113) are both examples of rentals. Sometimes they are referred to as "columnar" or "tabular" ledgers and are also used for such things as water and electricity charges as well as for the obvious case of housing rents. They could

Income Accounting

also be used for graduated tax, as indicated in Section 120. The use of the "rental" system for "rates" has nothing to do with "rents".

107. THE RATE BOOK (PROPERTY TAX REGISTER)

Let us assume that the Revenue Budget for Kambale Council shows that the rate levy for 19_6 is estimated to bring in U 3,840,000 and that the estimate had been prepared as follows:

	Units (000)
Site Values	
Estimated capital values at 1/1/_6	176,000
Estimated increase in values during 19_6 = U 8,000,000 x ½	4,000
Equated values for year	180,000
Improvement Values	
Estimated capital values at 1/1/_6	440,000
Estimated increase in values during 19_6 = U 32,000,000 x ½	16,000
Equated values for year	456,000
Rate Levy	
Site Rate @ 1½% on R.V. U 180,000,000	2,700
Improvements Rate @ ¼ on R.V. U 456,000,000	1,140
Total estimated rate income	3,840

Estimates are made of what the probable total site and improvement capital values will be on 1 Jan. 19_6.

Estimates will then be made of the total increases in value which will take place during 19_6 because of development - which will increase site values and produce new buildings. Because the increases in value will take place during the year they will be effective for only part of the rating period. If the development takes place evenly, an approximate effective value of the increases can be obtained by dividing the total increase by two. In other words, all development is assumed to be effective from the middle of the year, so that, for example, values effective for nine months will be offset by those effective for three months. Large single changes in rateable values (such as the construction of a new factory) must be dealt with separately.

The figures given above are estimates, prepared about 4-5 months before the end of 19_5. Actual values as at 1 Jan. 19_6 might well turn out to be (say):

	Units (000)
Sites	175,108
Improvements	443,136
	618,244

The total rates due from ratepayers on 1 Jan. 19_6 can be calculated as follows:

Municipal Accounting for Developing Countries

			Units
Site Rate @ 1½% on R.V. U 175,108,000	=		2,626,620
Improvements Rate @ ¼% on R.V. U 443,136,000	=		1,107,840
			3,734,460

The figure of U 3,734,460 is known as the "control debit". Individual sums totalling to this amount will be debited to various ratepayers on 1 Jan. The control debit will not remain constant during the year, but will increase from time to time during the year as more properties are assessed for rates or existing properties are revalued. When all additional debits and reductions in assessment have been included, the final figure at 31 Dec. 19_6 will be the debit in a Ratepayers Control Account. This figure, together with net arrears brought forward from 19_5, will have to be cleared either by cash collections, or by properly authorised allowances. The uncleared remainder will be net arrears carried forward to 19_7.

Records of individual sums due from ratepayers will be recorded in a Rate Book (Property Tax Register). It is sometimes called a Ratepayers Ledger because individual sums are debited to ratepayers and subsequent cash collections or allowances are credited. It can be regarded as a subsidiary ledger, the totals of which will be included in the Ratepayers Control Account in the main ledger.

Let us suppose that during 19_6 the rate assessment and collection can be summarised as follows:

	Units	Units
Balance brought forward:		
Arrears	23,220	
Less Receipts in advance	13,540	9,680
Rate Levy for year:		
Site Rate		
R.V. @ 1/1/_6 U 175,108,000 x 1½%	2,626,620	
Additional items	72,960	2,699,580
Improvements Rate		
R.V. @ 1/1./_6 U 443,136,000 x ¼%	1,107,840	
Additional items	57,860	1,165,700
Penalties		4,940
	TOTAL AMOUNT DUE	3,879,900
Cash Collected:		
Gross amount	3,853,020	
Less Refunds	4,860	3,848,160
Allowances:		
Reductions on appeal	7,240	
Empty property	11,880	
Otherwise irrecoverable	1,900	21,020
Balance carried forward:		
Arrears	19,100	
Less Receipts in advance	8,380	10,720
	ACCOUNTED FOR	3,879,900

KAMBALE MUNICIPAL COUNCIL
RATE BOOK SUMMARY

	DR.						CR.				
	Arrears Brought Forward	Site Rate @ 1½%	Improvement Rate @ ¼%	Penalty	Total DR. and CR.	Cash Received		Allowances		Arrears Carried Forward
						Amount	Ref	Amount	Ref	
	U	U	U	U	U	U		U		U
Folio No. 1	480	12,560	8,480	-	21,520	21,520	-	-	-	140CR
2	40CR	37,240	16,660	380	54,240	53,240	-	180	-	960CR
3	120CR	1,080*	2,420*	-	-	940CR	-	-	-	320CR
4	1,060	58,020	31,420	160	94,040	88,360	-	4,300	-	2,640
	-	9,400	4,340	-	13,740	12,920	-	-	-	820
5	660	13,260	6,860	-	20,780	21,400	-	220	-	840CR
(etc)	(etc)	(etc)	(etc)	(etc)	(etc)	(etc)	(etc)	(etc)	(etc)	(etc)
	13,540CR	72,960*	57,860*			4,860CR				8,380CR
	23,220	2,626,620	1,107,840	4,940	3,879,900	3,853,020		21,020		19,100
								7,240 appeals		
								11,880 voids		
								1,900 other		
	(a)	(b)	(c)	(d)	(e)	(f)	(g)	(h)	(i)	(j)

317

Municipal Accounting for Developing Countries

The summary of the Rate Book as it might appear on 31 Dec. 19_6 (after having been balanced) is shown on page 317.

The figures of arrears in column (a) will agree with those carried forward in the 19_5 Ratepayers Control Account and included in the balance sheet. The figures marked (CR) are receipts in advance, which will have been entered in red ink and separately totalled.

The lower figures in columns (b) and (c) are the original control debits calculated on the rateable values at 1 Jan. 19_6. The figures marked * are additional debits calculated on increases in rateable values which have arisen during 19_6. They will either be included in separate columns or (as in the example) entered in (say) green ink and separately totalled.

The figures in column (d) are penalties fixed according to law for late payment.

The figures in column (e) control the balancing of the debit and credit sides of the book, each side being added towards the centre as follows:

(a) + (b) + (c) + (d) = (e) = (f) + (h) + (j).

The lower figure in column (f) is the cash collected from ratepayers during the year and will be agreed with the total amount posted as rate receipts in the analysis of receipts or in the income journal (ledger). The figures marked (CR) are refunds of cash which may have been made for allowances or simply because the ratepayer paid too much by mistake. Sometimes, where a ratepayer has paid rates for a full year he is refunded a proportion of rates when he hands over his property to another ratepayer during the year. The rates will then be recovered from the new ratepayer. The refunds will be entered in red ink and totalled separately. They will be agreed with the total posted as rate refunds in the analysis of payments or expenditure journal (ledger).

Column (g) is not used in the summary. In the main body of the book it is used to show the receipt number or date of payment against individual collections of cash.

Column (h) shows the amount written off the rates due as irrecoverable. Allowances are given where rateable values are reduced on appeal, or for certain periods when property is empty. Sometimes, too, amounts must be written off as bad debts. Where good records and systems are maintained, allowances should be few in relation to the total volume of rates. An analysis of allowances can easily be obtained on an adding/listing machine and agreed with the total.

Column (i) is used in the main body of the book to show the reference to the authority for the allowance.

The lower figures in column (j) are the amounts not collected at 31 Dec. 19_6, known as arrears. It is always advisable to relate the total rate arrears to the total rate debit to test for any unreasonable increase in arrears. The figures marked (CR) are receipts in advance. Both figures will be carried forward as balances in the Ratepayers Control Account and included in the Balance Sheet as at 31 Dec. 19_6.

The Ratepayers Control Account in the main ledger for 19_6 will appear as follows:

Income Accounting

Ratepayers (Rates) Control

Balance b/f (arrears)	23,220	Balance b/f (advance)	13,540
Rate Income Account:		Cash (collections)	3,853,020
Site Rates	2,699,580	Rate Income Account -	
Improvement Rates	1,165,700	Allowances	21,020
Penalties	4,940	Balance c/d (arrears)	19,100
Cash (refunds)	4,860		
Balance c/d (advance)	8,380		
	3,906,680		3,906,680
Balance b/d (arrears)	19,100	Balance b/d (advance)	8,380

Cash postings in this account will come from the analysis of receipts and payments. Other postings will come from the journal, based upon the entries in the rate book summary, as follows:

19_6 Dec.31				
	Ratepayers (Rates) Control:			
	Site Rates	DR.	2,699,580	
	Improvement Rates	DR.	1,165,700	
	To Rate Income Account			3,865,280
	Being rates due for year as shown by Rate Book			
	Ratepayers (Rates) Control:			
	Penalties	DR.	4,940	
	To Rate Income Account			4,940
	Being penalties assessed during year as shown by Rate Book			
	Rate Income Account	DR.	21,020	
	To Ratepayers (Rates) Control:			
	Appeals			7,240
	Voids			11,880
	Other			1,900
	Being allowances for year as shown by Rate Book			

The Rate Income Account will appear as:

Rate Income

Allowances:		Gross Rate Income:	
Appeals	7,240	Site Rates	2,699,580
Voids	11,880	Improvement Rates	1,165,700
Other	1,900	Penalties	4,940
Balance (net rate income) transferred to General Fund Revenue Account	3,849,200		
	3,870,220		3,870,220

Municipal Accounting for Developing Countries

The net rate income is the income due (ie earned) which is taken into the Revenue Account and NOT merely the cash collected.

Sometimes separate accounts are kept of the cost of collecting the rates. Such accounts are essential where the net rate income is to be shared between the rating authority and other authorities.

Although not shown in our example, costs of collection (eg salaries of collectors, printing and stationery, office accommodation) could be shown as additional debits in the Rate Income Account, thus reducing the Net Rate Income transferred to the Revenue Account. If these costs of collection are high, the rating system becomes less effective as an acceptable local tax. If property valuations are carried out by council staff (as opposed to being made by a government department) these costs would also represent a cost of collection.

The rate book summary is prepared from the totals of various pages (folios) in the Rate Book. It is preferable to list each page separately as we have shown, rather than to carry forward sub-totals from page to page (otherwise the correction of an error on the first page might have to be adjusted on every subsequent page of the book!).

Folio 3 of the Rate Book might appear in detail as shown on page 321.

Mr B. Ongira (No.1) was assessed for a site rate of $1\frac{1}{2}$% of U 485,200 and an improvement rate of $\frac{1}{4}$% of 1,658,400. The total, including arrears of U 300, came to U 11,724 which he paid, being issued with receipt No.126. Later his appeal against the valuation of his improvements resulted in it being reduced by U 360,000 from U 1,658,400 to U 1,298,400. Assuming this decision to have been effective from the first day of the rating period, he has been given an allowance of U 900 (i.e. $\frac{1}{4}$% of U 360,000) authorised by the court decision and recorded in file reference A/33. The allowance creates a credit balance on his account which is adjusted by a cash refund of U 900 on payment voucher No.985.

Mr R. Musoke (No.2) pays the amount assessed (U 6,941) and is issued with receipt No.461.

Mr J. Mubanda (No.3) is assessed for site rate of U 2,037 and improvement rate of U 641 but the total amount due is reduced by a credit brought forward from 19_5 making U 2,558 due. He pays only U 2,500 leaving arrears carried forward of U 58.

Mr Matoke (No.4) owns an unoccupied site, originally valued at U 646,800 on 1 January. As there are no improvements, only a site rate of U 9,702 is payable. A new assessment is made to increase its value by U 144,000 to U 790,800. An additional site rate on the increase in value can be calculated as U 144,000 x $1\frac{1}{2}$% = U 2,160 = annual rate. Assuming the new value to be effective from 1 July 19_6 the rate levy in 19_6 will be one half of U 2,160 i.e. U 1,080. Thus, Mr Matoke is obliged to pay nearly U 12,000 in a full year on an undeveloped site. His remedy is to develop the land or sell it for development, so that sufficient rent may be earned to cover the rate levy. Mr Matoke has paid all his rates except for U 350. Perhaps he is holding back some money whilst making an appeal against his assessment.

National Bank Ltd (No.5) have had extensions built on to their premises. The extensions came into use on 5 Oct. 19_5 but had not been valued by 1 Jan. 19_6. The original buildings were valued at U 6,085,600 on 1 Jan. and rates of U 15,214 were levied, together with a site rate of U 23,874. When the value of the extensions is known an additional improvement rate can be levied as follows:

KAMBALE MUNICIPAL COUNCIL
RATE BOOK

Folio 3

Ref	(a) Ratepayer and Address (b) Rateable property	Rateable Values Site	Rateable Values Improvement	Arrears Brought Forward (DR)	Site Rate @ 1½%	Improvements Rate @ ¼%	Penalty	Total DR & CR	Cash Received Amount	Cash Received Ref	Allowances Amount	Allowances Ref	Arrears Carried Forward (CR)
1	B.Ongira Box 153 Shop 1 Mwofu Rd	485,200	360,000CR 1,658,400	300	7,278	4,146	-	11,274	900CR 11,724	985 126	900	A/33	-
2	R.Musoke Box 85 Shop 2 Mwofu Rd	286,600	1,056,800	-	4,299	2,642	-	6,941	6,941	461	-	-	-
3	J.Mubanda Box 283 House 3 Mwofu Rd	135,800	256,400	120CR	2,037	641	-	2,558	2,500	892	-	-	58
4	M.Matoke Box 1046 Land 1 Mwofu Rd	144,000* 646,800	-	540	1,080* 9,702	-	-	11,322	10,972	249	-	-	350
5	N Bank Ltd Box 45 Bank 5 Mwofu Rd	1,591,600	780,000* 6,085,600	-	23,874	2,420* 15,214	-	41,508	41,508	236	-	-	-
6	M.Mukasa Box 2385 Shop 6 Mwofu Rd	255,200	1,439,200	-	3,828	3,598	-	7,426	40CR 7,466	492 381	-	-	-
7	J.Kiboko Box 546 Flat 6A Mwofu Rd	-	445,600	220	-	1,114	-	1,334	-	-	1,334	48/66	-
8	Supplies Ltd Box 651 Shop 7 Mwofu Rd	368,600	1,386,400	-	5,529	3,466	-	8,995	7,249	616	2,066	V/21	-
9	P.Oola Box 92 House 8 Mwofu Rd	98,200	239,600	-	1,473	599	160	2,232	-	-	-	-	320CR 2,232
		144,000* 3,868,000	420,000* 12,568,000	120CR 1,060	1,080* 58,020	2,420* 31,420	160	94,040	940CR 88,360		4,300		320CR 2,640

	Units
Additional Rates for 19_6:	
U 780,000 x ¼%	1,950
Additional Rates for 19_5:	
U 780,000 x ¼% U 1,950	
Proportion from 5/10/_5 = $\frac{1,950 \times 88}{365}$ =	470
	2,420

Strictly speaking the U 470 should have been taken as income for 19_5 but this was impossible in practice because of delays in making assessments.

Mr Mukasa (No.6) assessed in the normal way, wrote out a cheque for U 7,466 instead of for U 7,426. When the error was discovered a refund of U 40 was made on voucher 492.

For various reasons Mr J. Kiboko (No.7) cannot be traced and there are disputes as to whether he was, in fact, in occupation of the flat. After a long period of fruitless enquiries the council has decided to write off the whole of the sum. The finance committee minute was 48/66.

Supplies Ltd (No.8) have been allowed U 2,066 for a period when the shop premises were empty. Voids file V/21 refers to the case. The allowance resulted in an overpayment of cash amounting to U 320. This sum is being carried forward to 19_7 as a receipt in advance.

Mr P. Oola (No.9) has paid nothing and the whole of his rates for 19_6 are therefore in arrears, together with a penalty for non-payment which the Council has imposed.

The page is balanced as follows:

DEBIT (1,060 - 120) + (58,020 + 1,080) + (31,420 + 2,420) + 160 = 94,040

CREDIT 94,040 = (88,360 - 940) + 4,300 + (2,640 - 320).

The original assessments can be proved in total as follows:

		Units
Site Rate U 3,868,000 x 1½%	=	58,020
Improvement Rate U 12,568,000 x ¼%	=	31,420

Additional assessments cannot be proved in total because of the differences in effective dates.

Because of lack of space, we have shown the second column as containing all basic information. In practice, several columns might be used as follows:

Ref.	Description of Property	Situation of Property	Dates of Changes From	Dates of Changes To	Name and Address of Ratepayer

Income Accounting

Sometimes the Rate Book can be divided into two parts. A Rate Charge Book will give standing information and last for several (say) five years, whilst a Rate Account Book will give details of annual rate levies and collections. If valuations are made by the authority's own staff, this information would be combined with the valuation roll (or list).

These records imply normal payments of rates on a half-yearly basis. It might well be more appropriate to allow payments by more frequent instalments, in which case the Rate book would require adaptation to accommodate this or subsidiary collection records would need to be introduced.

108. THE RATE (PROPERTY TAX) DEMAND

To let each ratepayer know how much is due from him the Council will send him an invoice, sometimes known as a Rate Demand.

Such an invoice might be sent to (say) Mr J. Mubanda by Kambale Council in the following form:

	No.10461
KAMBALE MUNICIPAL COUNCIL	

Tel: 1234   **Rates 19_6**   Finance Department,
                                           PO Box 165,
                                           Kambale.

> Mr J. Mubanda,
> PO Box 283,
> Kambale.

The Kambale Council has levied rates for the year 19_6 at one and one half per cent of all site values included in the valuation roll and at one quarter of one per cent of all improvement values included in the valuation roll.

The rates set out below are now due from you and payment should be made within 30 days.

Cheques should be crossed and made payable to "Kambale Municipal Council". Only official receipts will be recognised as proof of payment.

PLEASE PRODUCE THIS INVOICE (OR QUOTE REFERENCE) WHEN PAYING

Ref.	Property	Rateable Value		Amount
		Site	Improvement	
		Units	Units	Units
3/3	House	135,800		2,037
	3 Muwofu Road		256,400	641
	Credit b/f			120CR
	TOTAL DUE			2,558

As you will see, the particulars shown on the demand note are a copy of those in the Rate Book. Although it is not strictly necessary to take a carbon copy of each demand note, copies are often useful for reference purposes and may even be used for posting the receipts, in the same way as described under the sundry debtors system (see later).

The Rate Book is an example of a rental, where income arises continuously from the same persons or sources. Other rentals will be required for water charges and for housing and market rents - these will be dealt with later.

The above illustration of rate accounting, whilst dealing with site and improvement rates on capital values should not be assumed to relate to any particular rating law. The general principles illustrated will apply whatever the detailed provisions of the present laws. Where rental values are used, the procedures are the same. The percentage levies may, however, be somewhat higher.

Income Accounting

109. SUNDRY DEBTORS (MISCELLANEOUS RECEIVABLES) INVOICES

During 19_6, income will be due to Kambale Municipal Council from various kinds of charges, where cash is not paid at the time a service is provided. Such income will include casual lettings of premises, sales of scrap and compost, rechargeable works and night soil fees.

When the charge is made, an invoice will be sent to the person from whom the charge is due. Sometimes the charge will arise in the finance department and sometimes in an outside department such as the works department.

Any office or department which is likely to raise charges should be supplied with a pad of triplicate "sundry debtors invoices". The invoices should be printed with consecutive numbers and unissued stocks stored in the finance department. Invoices should be recorded in a register as soon as received from the printer, together with details of issues to departments.

An account for a charge originating in the works department of Kambale Municipal Council might appear as follows:

```
Dr to:                                          INVOICE No. 15826
                                                30 Jan. 19_6

                 KAMBALE MUNICIPAL COUNCIL
                    PO Box 165, Kambale.

Please quote the above number (or enclosed this account) when
paying. Cheques should be crossed, made payable to "Kambale
Municipal Council" and forwarded to the Chief Financial Officer.

                     Mr B. Kanyama
                      PO Box 481,
                      Kambale.
```

Date	Particulars	Amount Units
24.1._6	To Repairing broken drains at Plot 15 Acacia Drive: Labour Materials Transport Overheads TOTAL	 15 24 16 10 65

The original invoice and the first copy will be forwarded to the finance department. After the charges have been checked by the income section the original will be sent to the debtor and the copy filed in the income section. The second copy of the invoice remains in the works department.

110. PERIODICAL INCOME REGISTER

Sometimes invoices, especially those originating in the finance department, must be sent at regular intervals to the same person, perhaps annually such as for licences, or quarterly such as for special or long-term rents or lettings. It is useful to have a reminder to send the invoices and standing information about charges.

A simple periodical income register can be built up from duplicated numbered sheets filed in a binder. A page of the register for Kambale Municipal Council might appear as:

PERIODICAL INCOME RECORD	No.13
NAME AND ADDRESS OF DEBTOR: A. Kabanda PO Box 3235, Kambale.	ANNUAL AMOUNT: U 12,000 AGREEMENT DATE: 1/1/_3 FILE NO: R.251 MINUTE REF: 79/_2
ACCOUNT TO BE SENT TO: (same)	PAYMENT DUE FROM: 31/3/_3 PAYABLE: Quarterly in arrears
SPECIAL INSTRUCTIONS: (none)	INCOME ANALYSIS: Admin. Buildings - rent
PARTICULARS OF CHARGE Rent of Offices in Council Office Block	MONTHS DUE JAN [ ] JUL [ ] FEB [ ] AUG [ ] MAR [X] SEP [X] APR [ ] OCT [ ] MAY [ ] NOV [ ] JUN [X] DEC [X]

Dates Due	Amount Due
31 Mar. 30 Sept 30 Jun. 31 Dec	U 3,000

The left-hand side of the page contains the details necessary for making out the invoice. The name and address of the debtor are shown, together with the place to which the invoice should be sent. In our example the invoice is sent direct to the debtor, but in some cases it could be sent to an agent or lawyer. In the space for "special instructions" can be shown any information which will help in assessing the charge or collecting the debt such as:

"contact Harris & Smith" (lawyers) tel.36546 before sending reminder"

or in the case of a charge for nightsoil emptying "obtain number of loads from Engineers' department"

or in the case of trading or liquor licences "obtain report from public

Income Accounting

health inspector (police) before licence is issued".

The particulars of charge will be entered on the invoice, which will be sent on the date shown, for the amount due. Sometimes the charge will not be fixed, in which case under "amount due" will be shown (say) " U 2 per load" or " U 5 per journey".

The top right-hand side of the page gives standing information and references, together with the income account which will be credited with the amount due (if a coding system is used the code will be given instead). The bottom right hand corner is a simple "signal" system. A red ink cross is marked in the "box" against the months due and once every month a clerk from the income section will thumb through the pages looking for the red crosses for that month, indicating that accounts must be sent. The pages themselves are filed in alphabetical order of creditor or in any other suitable order. The signal system can be improved upon by using special proprietary systems but these are more expensive than simple duplicated sheets. Of course, this is an ideal subject for computorised records.

The back of the record may show brief details of invoices sent as follows:

Date	Invoice	Date	Invoice	Date	Invoice	Date	Invoice
31/3/_3	9849						
30/6/_3	10325						
30/9/_3	10618						
31/12/_3	11131						
31/3/_4	11327						
(etc)	(etc)						

111. SUNDRY DEBTORS BOOK

When an invoice has been sent to a debtor there must be some system to ensure that he pays. The simplest "system" is for the cashier to notify the income section whenever a sundry debtor pays his account and for the copy account to be marked or stamped "Paid (date)". Periodically, reminders will be sent to debtors whose copy accounts have not been marked off. This system is not a good one because it is based on memorandum records. The records do not interlock through double-entry and there is no system of internal financial control. It is dangerous to rely on such a system.

A sound system can be operated as follows:

(a) all invoices (debit notes) are consecutively numbered and are issued by the finance department to other departments;

(b) invoices are made out in triplicate and distributed as follows:

    (i) original sent to debtor via the income section;

    (ii) first copy retained and filed by income section; and

    (iii) second copy retained and filed by department originating the charge (both copies of invoices originating in finance department are filed by the income section);

Municipal Accounting for Developing Countries

(c) the income section checks copy invoices to ensure that numbers run consecutively and it demands the original and first copy of cancelled invoices (this restricts fraudulent use of invoices by a person attempting to collect money for himself);

(d) the copy invoices are entered by the income section in a sundry debtors book (sometimes called a sundry debtors ledger) in numerical order. It is sometimes convenient to have a separate book for the invoices of each department. An example of a page of such a book for Kambale Council is shown on page 329 and an example of the invoice on page 325.

(e) in the sundry debtors book invoices are analysed according to the type of income under the various "analysis of income" columns. When cross-cast the totals of these columns should agree with the total of the "amount due" column. This analysis of "income due" is the information which will be required by the accountancy section for final accounts. No detailed analysis is made of "cash collected" because this is not required for the final accounts, or for any other purpose, (if a coding system is used the analysis columns will show the various code numbers);

(f) a receipt is issued by the cashier in the normal way for each sundry debtors invoice settled in cash, the receipt quoting the invoice number and the symbol S/DRS;

(g) copy receipts are passed to the income section which extracts those relating to sundry debtors for posting against individual names. For example Mr B. Kanyama paid his invoice and was issued with receipt No.730;

(h) along with all other copy receipts, those issued for sundry debtors will be passed to the accountancy section for analysis of receipts. The receipts for sundry debtors will be posted under a single "sundry debtors" analysis to provide a control total against which individual cash postings in the sundry debtors book can be balanced, (as explained above, the detailed analysis of "income due" is provided by the income section from the sundry debtors' book); and

(i) reminders and threats of legal proceedings will be sent direct to unpaid debtors by the income section. Any sums written off will be properly authorised and amounts unpaid will be carried forward as arrears. Eventually, long-standing arrears will be passed to the Council's legal section or to lawyers for recovery proceedings to be instituted.

The sundry debtors book shows details of arrears brought forward of U 23,040 equal to the total shown on page 329. The invoice numbers do not run consecutively - the missing invoices were paid in 19_5. New invoices are entered daily from copies received by the income section and, as stated above, cash payments are posted from copy receipts. The book is shown as it would appear after balancing on 31 Dec. 19_6. Arrears carried forward will be individually entered at the beginning of the 19_7 book. The book is sometimes known as a "Sundry Debtors Ledger" because the personal account of each debtor is kept in debit and credit form. Each line is really a separate ledger account. For example, the account of Mr Kanyama could be shown in conventional book-keeping form as:

KAMBALE MUNICIPAL COUNCIL
SUNDRY DEBTORS BOOK

Date	Name	Invoice Number	Arrears Brought Forward	Amount Due	Cash Received Amount	Cash Received Ref	Allowances Amount	Allowances Ref	Arrears Carried Forward	Analysis of Income (etc)	Analysis of Income (etc)	Analysis of Income Sewerage Recharge-able	Analysis of Income (etc)	Analysis of Income (etc)
19_6 Jan.1	R. Musoke	15,109	156		156	243								
	P. Otim	15,117	4,825		4,825	839								
	J. Oneko	15,118	25				25	6/66						
	R. Kibule	15,119	682		682	106								
	M. Kuka	15,122	12		12	546								
	J. Odwako	15,124	193						193					
	B. Brown	15,125	1,235		1,235	85								
	(etc)	(etc)	(etc)		(etc)		(etc)		(etc)					
	TOTAL ARREARS		23,040											
Jan.1	P. Odema	15,237		124	124	723				124				
1	B. Kamire	15,238		1,065	1,065	432					1,065			
3	R. Kirya	15,239		81			81				81			
6	T. Bwire	15,240		36					36			36		
7	M. Oloko	16,241		93	50	185	43	32/66					93	
(etc)	(etc)			(etc)	(etc)		(etc)		(etc)	(etc)	(etc)	(etc)	(etc)	(etc)
30	B. Kanyana	15,826		65	65	730						65		
31	S. Patel	15,827		147	147	842							147	
				4,025	26,260		225		580	124	1,326	101	325	2,149

N.B. Amounts shown as "arrears brought forward" are not analysed in the "analysis of income" columns. The income to which they relate has already been included in the 19_5 accounts.

329

	B. Kanyama							15826
19_6 Jan.31	To Sewerage Rech. Works	J	65	19_6 Apr.15	By Cash	C.B.	65	
			65 ==				65 ==	

The page of the sundry debtors book can be balanced in total, also like a ledger, as follows:

Sundry Debtors

Balance b/f	23,040	Cash	26,260
Sundry Income Due	4,025	Allowances	225
		Balance c/d	580
	27,065		27,065
Balance b/d	580		

In the rate book, all income was credited to a single "Rate Income Account" whereas sundry debtors accounts are for income of many different kinds. Because of this, analysis columns are required in the sundry debtors book to provide totals of various types of income to be credited to separate income accounts. These totals can be credited monthly or quarterly to the income accounts concerned or single totals posted to each income account at the year end.

Only part of the Sundry Debtors Book is shown, but as with the Rate Book, the final totals will be used to produce a control account in the main ledger. This is known as a Sundry Debtors Control Account. Using assumed figures, the 19_6 Control Account for Kambale Council might appear as:

Sundry Debtors Control

Balance b/f	23,040	Cash	123,500
Sundry Income Due	126,360	Allowances	1,580
		Balance c/d	24,320
	149,400		149,400
Balance b/d	24,320		

Cash postings will come from the analysis of receipts. The other entries will be made through the journal. The debit for sundry income due will equal the total of individual credits in the various income accounts. The detailed information is obtained from the analysis columns of the sundry debtors book. The credit for allowances will equal the total of individual debits in the various income accounts for sums written off. The detailed information is obtained from an analysis of the figures in the "allowances" column. The control account figures must, of course, agree with the totals of the sundry debtors book.

Income Accounting

112. THE SLIP SYSTEM

If there is a sound system of internal financial control (and this is most important) the copies of the invoices can be used as the sundry debtors book. Instead of the first copies of invoices being entered into a book, they are filed in numerical or alphabetical order on a suitable binder. The copy is specially printed to act as the personal account of the debtor. For example, the copy of Mr Kanyama's invoice would appear as:

CREDIT			INVOICE No. 15826			
Sewerage		Rechargeable	30 Jan. 19_6			
1st REMINDER 28/2/_6 2nd REMINDER 31/3/_6 ACTION: Referred to C.F.O. 25/4/_6			CASH RECEIVED		ALLOWANCES	
			AMOUNT	REF.	AMOUNT	REF.
			65	730		
Mr B. Kanyama PO Box 481, Kambale.							
Date	Particulars					Amount Units

24.1._6	To Repairing broken drains at Plot 15, Acacia Drive:
	   Labour
	   Materials
	   Transport
	   Overheads
						15
						 24
						 16
						 10
						 ──
						 65
						 ==

Whilst the original invoice shows details of the Council's address and instructions for payment, these are not required on the copy. Space is therefore available to show details of cash received and allowances given, together with details of the reminders sent (if any) and action taken for non-payment. Also shown, in the top left-hand corner, is the income account to be credited.

It is very important that the payments and allowances are not merely noted but posted as part of a double-entry system. If such a system were operated by Kambale Municipal Council the Sundry Debtors Book would be replaced by a Control Sheet as shown on page 332. The balance of arrears will be entered in total on the sheet as shown, and the unpaid copy invoices covering the total arrears placed in an "Unpaid Invoices" binder. The system will then proceed as follows:

(a) Copies of all invoices issued during January 19_6 will be placed on the "Unpaid Invoices" binder;

KAMBALE MUNICIPAL COUNCIL
SUNDRY DEBTORS CONTROL SHEET

Date	Partic-ulars	Debit Amount	Debit Total to Date	Credit Amount	Credit Total to date	Balance	Analysis of Income (a)	(b)	(c)	(d)	(e)
19_6											
Jan. 1	Balance	23,040	23,040	–	–	23,040					
31	Invoices	15,420	38,460	–	–	38,460	(Various	sums	totalling	U	15,420)
31	Cash	–	–	12,320	12,320	26,140					
Feb.28	Invoices	23,240	61,700	–	–	49,380	(Various	sums	totalling	U	23,240)
28	Cash	–	–	26,080	38,400	23,300					
Mar.31	Invoices	9,860	71,560	–	–	33,160	(Various	sums	totalling	U	9,860)
31	Cash	–	–	6,420	44,820	26,740					
31	Allowances	–	–	360	45,180	26,380					
Apr.30	Invoices	6,360	77,920	–	–	32,740	(Various	sums	totalling	U	6,360)
30	Cash	–	–	8,440	53,620	24,300					
(etc)	(etc)	(etc)	(etc)	(etc)	(etc)	(etc)					
Dec.31	Invoices	11,320	149,400	–	–	33,600	(Various	sums	totalling	U	11,320)
31	Cash	–	–	9,340	125,080	24,320					
19_7											
Jan. 1	Balance	24,320				24,320					

Income Accounting

(b) Any cash received during January, will be posted to the copy invoice, which is now the debtors personal account. For example if the U 65 from Mr Kanyama had been received in January (in fact it was not) it would have been posted as shown;

(c) At the end of January the amounts on the various invoices issued during January will be totalled on the adding/listing machine (U 15,420). This sum will be debited on the control sheet and added to the previous debit for arrears (U 23,040) to give the total debit to date (U 38,460) and the balance.

(d) The copy invoices for January are now sorted into separate piles for each head of income, according to the analysis (or coding) written under "CREDIT" on each one. Mr Kanyama's invoice would be included in the "Sewerage - rechargeable" pile. Each pile will now be separately listed on the machine to produce totals for the income analysis columns (for eventual credit in various income accounts). The grand total of the analysis columns must come to U 15,420.

(e) After the January invoices have been sorted back into order and replaced in the "Unpaid Invoices" binder all copies with "Cash Received" posted on them will be extracted and listed on the machine to produce a total of U 12,320. This figure (which begins the cumulative credit total) will be entered on the control sheet and deducted from the balance (U 38,460) to give a new net balance of U 26,140. Copies with "allowances" posted on them will be also extracted and totalled. There are none in January but there are allowances of U 360 in March.

(f) After totalling, the invoices which have been fully settled by cash or allowances are transferred to a "Paid Invoices" binder. Any part payment on an invoice will be included in the listed total but marked with a red cross and returned to the "Unpaid Invoices" binder.

(g) The invoices on the "Unpaid Invoices" binder should now represent the arrears at the date of balancing. If listed on the machine they will give a total of U 26,140. Partially paid invoices will be listed at their unpaid balance. Better still, the invoices can be listed gross and the part payments deducted as minuses.

The above procedure will be repeated at the end of each month. The control sheet will be entered up as shown to build up final totals for the Sundry Debtors Control Account. The balance of U 24,320 will agree with the total of invoices on the "Unpaid Invoices" file at 31 Dec. 19_6 and will be the figure included in the balance sheet. Previous part-payments (marked with a red cross) will be ignored when totalling "Cash Received" for subsequent months.

For purposes of internal financial control and internal audit all machine lists should be pasted into a bound book. Each list should be headed in ink to show its purpose, eg:

New debits Feb. 19_6	**Cash Received April 19_6**	**Arrears May 19_6**

113. RENTS

Rents are the charges levied by an owner of property upon occupiers. The property may be land or buildings. Kambale Municipal Council will collect premia and annual ground rents on its land and rents from markets, houses and other buildings.

When land is leased for development a single lump-sum premium will be calculated. After this has been paid, the occupier of the land will pay an annual ground rent. These transactions can be dealt with through the "sundry debtors" system, with the annual ground rent recorded in the periodical income register. Alternatively a rental system can be used.

Let us now consider the collection of charges (including rents) from the markets of Kambale Municipal Council. This will give us an example of the use of a rental for rents and also of the collection of cash income from casual users.

We will assume that for 19_6 there will be rents to be collected from markets as follows:

100 stalls at U 240 p.a.	24,000
100 stalls at U 360 p.a.	36,000
100 stalls at U 600 p.a.	60,000
	120,000

In the same way as for rates the U 120,000 is regarded as the "control debit" which together with any arrears brought forward must be cleared in total either by cash collections or by allowances. The market rental might appear as shown on page 335. We have assumed that the annual rent is payable in monthly instalments. The rental operates on the same principle as the rate book except that instead of being posted direct to the "total cash" column the monthly rent payments are posted in the "monthly rents paid" columns under the month in which they are paid. At the end of each month the "rents paid" column for that month will be totalled and agreed with the total shown as "market rents" in the "analysis of receipts" records in the accountancy section.

At the end of the year the twelve monthly columns (only some of which are shown in the example) will be cross-cast to provide the figure for the "total cash" column. Where the total cash is less than the total debit the difference will normally be arrears to be carried forward to 19_7. However, where a "V" appears in the appropriate "monthly rents paid" column it means that the stall was "void" or "vacant" for that month and the rent is written off as an allowance. When balanced, the market rental (or market tenants ledger) provides information for the Market Tenants Control Account in the main ledger which would appear as follows:

KAMBALE MUNICIPAL COUNCIL
MARKET RENTAL

Stall No	Tenant	Monthly Rent	Arrears Brought Forward	Annual Rent	Total DR & CR	Total Cash	Total Allowances	Arrears Carried Forward	Monthly Rents Paid Jan	Feb	Mar	...	Nov	Dec
1	B. Ogwang	20	20	240	260	260	-	-	40	20	20		20	20
2	J. Odotu	20	-	240	240	220	-	20	20	-	40		20	-
3	R. Alengal	20	-	240	240	200	40	-	20	V	V		20	20
4	M. Musisi	20	-	240	240	240	-	-	20	20	20		20	20
(etc)	(etc)	(etc)	(etc)	(etc)	(etc)	(etc)	(etc)	(etc)	(etc)	(etc)	(etc)		(etc)	(etc)
101	P. Odeke	30	-	360	360	360	-	-	30	30	30		30	30
102	S. Oneko	30	60	360	420	360	-	60	30	60	30		-	30
103	Y. Mukasa	30	-	360	360	360	-	-	30	30	30		30	30
104	F. Kitubya	30	30	360	390	390	-	-	60	30	30		30	30
(etc)	(etc)	(etc)	(etc)	(etc)	(etc)	(etc)	(etc)	(etc)	(etc)	(etc)	(etc)		(etc)	(etc)
201	B. Odoko	50	-	600	600	550	50	-	V	50	50		50	50
202	A. Kibule	50	-	600	600	600	-	-	50	50	-		100	50
203	P. Olwech	50	-	600	600	500	-	100	50	50	50		-	-
204	G. Kalule	50	100	600	700	700	-	-	100	50	100		50	50
(etc)	(etc)	(etc)	(etc)	(etc)	(etc)	(etc)	(etc)	(etc)	(etc)	(etc)	(etc)		(etc)	(etc)
		10,000	3,020	120,000	123,020	118,620	860	3,540	9,840	10,230	9,980		9,760	10,120

Municipal Accounting for Developing Countries

Market Tenants Control

Balance b/f	3,020	Cash	118,620
Total Rent Due	120,000	Allowances	860
		Balance c/d	3,540
	123,020		123,020
	=======		=======
Balance b/d	3,540		

Cash will be posted from the analysis of receipts and the other entries will be made through the journal as follows:

19_6				
Dec.31	Market Tenants (Control) DR. To Market Rent Income Being rents due for year on market stalls as follows: 100 @ U 240 = 24,000 100 @ U 360 = 36,000 100 @ U 600 = 60,000 _____ 120,000 =======		120,000	120,000
Dec.31	Market Rent Income DR. To Market Tenants (Control) Being void allowances for year as shown on file V.11.		860	860

114. TICKET INCOME

We now turn to cash income, which does not arise in the books until it is paid. One of the common ways of controlling cash income is by the use of tickets or fixed value receipts. Other methods include turnstiles, locked boxes and meters.

As an example of the use of tickets let us continue our study of the markets of Kambale Municipal Council. As well as permanent stall holders, paying fixed monthly or annual rents, there will be many casual users of the market who will bring small quantities of goods for sale in the general compound. They will pay a small fee for admission and will be issued with a ticket which entitles them to sell their goods in the market. The price of the ticket issued may depend on the quantity of goods to be sold.

Let us assume that the charges for Kambale market require tickets for 20 cents, 50 cents, U 1, U 5 and U 20. The tickets will be ordered and stored by the finance department. Tickets issued to the market-master or collector will be booked out in the register of receipts. To lessen the possibility of irregularities, separate tickets might be printed for each market, with the name of the market on the ticket. This will also permit the ticket numbers to run consecutively all the time. At the close of each day's business an independent officer (perhaps the senior market-master) will visit the collectors in each market, examine their unused tickets and prepare a return of tickets issued. (A return is a statement prepared by a person who is liable to account for tickets or similar documents - having been issued with tickets he must either

Income Accounting

"return" them or account for the cash which they represent.) The senior market-master will collect the correct amount of cash which will then be paid to the main cashier. The cashier will issue a receipt and stamp one copy of the return which he will hand back to the market-master. The top copy of the return will be passed to the audit section or filed with the copy receipt. A typical ticket return for three markets could appear as follows:

\multicolumn{7}{c}{KAMBALE MUNICIPAL COUNCIL MARKETS RETURN Tickets Sold 15/4/_6}
Details	No. on Last Return	No. on Next Ticket Unissued	No. of Tickets Issued	Amount	Total	Audit
Kibule 20c	10561	10711	150	30		
50c	20315	20355	40	20		
U 1	13612	13682	70	70		
U 5	48325	48325	-	-		
U 20	08912	08913	1	20	140	
Kitoro 20c	48321	48371	50	10		
50c	28403	28463	60	30		
U 1	57925	57965	40	40		
U 5	43687	43704	17	85		
U 20	09463	09466	3	60	225	
Busira 20c	20872	20972	100	20		
50c	54384	54404	20	10		
U 1	10361	10396	35	35		
U 5	28463	28483	20	100		
U 20	6010	6012	2	40	205	
				TOTAL CASH	570	

There can be many variations to the above system, depending on the ability of staff. For example individual collectors could pay in their cash direct to the main cashier, in which case the cashier will check the tickets before receipting the cash. Any system in operation should aim at increasing efficiency and eliminating wasteful duplication of effort. It would be absurd for the cashier in our example to retain a copy of the return and then write all the details again on the receipt.

115. REMITTANCE LIST

Cash received by the Council's cashier will be received either over the counter from the customer (or another council official) or through the postal system. A person paying cash at the counter is in a position to demand an immediate receipt for his payment, but with postal remittances this is not possible. Using remittance lists for postal remittances adds to the effectiveness of financial control. A typical remittance list for Kambale Municipal Council might appear as follows:

				No.5/36
\multicolumn{5}{	c	}{KAMBALE MUNICIPAL COUNCIL REMITTANCE LIST 24.5._6}

No.	Name	Account	Amount		Receipt
			Cheques Etc	Cash	Number
385	J. Musa	Rates 14/12		150	719
386	M. Busa	Water 28/1	25		720
387	Patel Ltd	S/Drs.16121	160		721
388	National Government	Grant	520,000		722
389	R. Smith	Water 13/6	60		723
(etc)		(etc)	(etc)	(etc)	(etc)
396	B. Kanyama	Rates 10/14) S/Drs.15826)	165		730
397	R. Juma	Rates 10/24		400	731
		TOTAL	527,910	550	
\multicolumn{3}{	r	}{Received remittances totalling}	\multicolumn{2}{c	}{U 528,460}	

XYZ
Cashier

Mr B. Kanyama has paid his sundry debtors account and his rates and has been issued with receipt No.730. The receipt numbers are shown in consecutive order because the cashier will probably write them out in a block during slack periods of the day.

Reference 5/ refers to month 5 (May); reference /36 refers to the 36th list of the month (the box will often be emptied twice each day); and the references 385-397 refer to the consecutive numbers of remittances during the month.

A copy of the list will be sent to the internal audit section which will check to ensure that:

(a) receipts are issued promptly for each remittance;

(b) all cheques, money orders and postal orders are promptly banked; and

(c) all cash is in the hands of the cashier or has been banked.

116. LICENCES

The collection of fees for trading licences and liquor licences can be dealt with by the combined use of a "periodical income" register and the "sundry debtors" system.

It would be convenient to keep the periodical income register for licences separate from that for sundry debtors and to use a separate series of sundry debtors invoices, perhaps of a different colour. The basic system will operate in the same way as for sundry debtors. Either a book will be used, with analysis columns for different kinds of licences or the slip system will be used.

Income Accounting

One important problem likely to arise is that of "receipts in advance". Persons requiring licences may have to appear before a licensing board or committee which meets well before the beginning of the year to which the licence relates. Once licences have been granted, the licence holders may pay for them in advance. Cash is therefore received before the income is due, and if there is no proper accounting treatment the result for the year in which the cash is received may be over-stated.

If you look at the figures in Section 106 you will see that **U** 1060 was paid in advance for trading licences and **U** 360 for liquor licences. In other words, a total of **U** 1420 of 19_6 income was received in 19_5.

Kambale Municipal Council can deal with its problems as follows:

(a) as soon as the decisions of the licensing authorities are known, licence invoices will be prepared in duplicate and both copies kept on a file until 31 Dec. 19_5 (the end of the financial year);

(b) licence holders who pay for their licences before 31 Dec. 19_5 will be issued with licences in the normal way;

(c) when the copy licences (which for book-keeping purposes are merely receipts) are received by the income section the appropriate invoice will be located on the file. The top copy will be stamped "PAID IN ADVANCE (DATE)";

(d) the number of the paid invoice and the name of the debtor will be entered in the sundry debtors (licence) book. No debit will be set up but the cash payment will be posted and carried forward as a credit;

(e) on 1 Jan. 19_6, unstamped invoices on the file will be sent to the unpaid licence holders. Stamped invoices will merely be filed with their copies;

(f) all copy invoices will now be debited in the sundry debtors book as income for 19_6, because this is the year to which the income earned relates (even though some of the cash was collected in 19_5);

(g) receipts in advance will be brought forward from the 19_5 book and entered against the debits in the 19_6 book; and

(h) from this point normal sundry debtors procedure will be followed:

Part of the 19_5 book for trading licences might appear as follows:

Date	Name	Invoice Number	Arrears Brought Forward	Amount Due	Cash Received Amount	Ref.	Arrears Carried Forward
19_5	B/f		1,150CR	171,500	170,290		60DR
Oct.17	J.Patel & Son	4859	-	-	150	859	150CR
Nov. 8	R.Musoke Ltd	4861	-	-	150	893	150CR
12	Bango's Bar	4862	-	-	150	902	150CR
Dec. 3	(etc)	(etc)			(etc)		(etc)
		TOTALS	1,150CR	171,500	171,350		60DR 1,060CR

Municipal Accounting for Developing Countries

The control account for 19_5 would have appeared as:

Sundry Debtors (Trading Licences) Control

Trading Licence		Balance b/f	1,150
Income	171,500	Cash	171,350
Balance c/d	1,060	Balance c/d	60
	172,560		172,560
	=======		=======
Balance b/d	60	Balance b/d	1,060

The 19_6 book would then begin as:

Date	Name	Invoice Number	Arrears Brought Forward	Amount Due	Cash Received Amount	Ref.	Arrears Carried Forward
19_6			U		U		
Jan. 1	B.Matoke	3,624	60DR	-	60	125	
1	Fruit Stores	4,858	-	150	150	214	
1	J.Patel & Son	4,859	150CR	150	-	-	
1	Traders Ltd	4,860	-	150	150	316	
1	R.Musoke Ltd	4,861	150CR	150	-	-	
1	Bango's Bar	4,862	150CR	150	-	-	
1	(etc)	4,863	(etc)	(etc)	(etc)		(etc)
			60DR				
			1,060CR				
			=======				

If the slip system were used, it would be a good idea to make out the invoices in triplicate. The two copies would be printed to allow cash postings to be made on them. The system would proceed as follows:

(a) original invoices and first copies would be filed until 31 Dec;

(b) second copies would be used as what are sometimes known as "dummy" debits to set up an "unpaid invoices" file for 19_5;

(c) any cash received in advance for 19_6 licences will be posted against the "dummy debits" on the second copies. Nothing will, however, be debited to the control account or credited to the income account. Cash payments will be machine listed monthly and carried to the control account. Paid invoices will be transferred to a "paid invoices" file;

(d) at 31 Dec. 19_5 any unpaid "dummy" (second copy) invoices will be destroyed. Paid copies will be machine listed and then filed with the original and first copies, which will be stamped "PAID IN ADVANCE". Unpaid invoices will be sent to debtors;

(e) all first copies will now be machine listed and the total debited to the control account and credited to the income account; and

(f) the paid invoices will be transferred to the "paid invoices" file and normal sundry debtors procedure will operate.

Income Accounting

The "dummy" second copy for J. Patel and Son might appear as:

Credit Trading Licences	Invoice No. 4859 1 Jan. 19_6	
	Cash Received		Balance
	Amount	Ref.	
	150	859	150CR

```
            ┌─────────────────┐
            │ J. Patel & Son  │
            │   PO Box 821    │
            │   Kambale       │
            └─────────────────┘
```

| 19_6 | To Trading Licence
    Grocers Shop
        Plot 25, Central Road | <u>Units</u>
150 |

The control sheet might appear as:

Date	Parti- culars	Debit Amount	Debit Total to Date	Credit Amount	Credit Total to Date	Balance
19_5	(etc)	(etc)	170,350	(etc)	170,290	60DR
Oct.31	Cash	-	-	150	170,440	90CR
Nov.30	Cash	-	-	300	170,740	390CR
Dec.31	Cash	-	-	610	171,350	1,000CR
19_6						
Jan. 1	Balance			1,000	1,000	1,000CR
31	Invoices	165,000	165,000	-	-	164,000DR

117. RECEIPTS

The two basic forms of prime document are "invoices" and "receipts". We have already given some consideration to invoices so we shall now consider receipts.

All the income records we have examined are closely related to the receipt of cash. When this happens a receipt will be issued. There are many forms of receipt, all containing certain basic information. The minimum information normally appearing will be:

(a) name and address of the person or body receiving the cash;

(b) reference number;

(c) name of the payer;

(d) amount of cash received (always in figures - and sometimes in words also);

(e) date of the receipt;

(f) signature (or equivalent) acknowledging the cash received; and

(g) revenue stamp if the law so prescribes.

Usually there will be provision for one or more copies of the receipt to be taken, perhaps by carbon paper.

For Kambale Council, it would seem reasonable to issue receipts in triplicate, to be distributed as follows:

(a) original - handed to payer;

(b) duplicate - used for posting income records and analysis of receipts; and

(c) triplicate - remains in the book as a record for the cashier.

The forms may be "general" for use with any type of payment received or "special" for specific kinds of income only, such as for water charges or housing rents. Sometimes the receipt may act as a licence as well as a mere acknowledgement of cash. Sometimes receipts (or tickets) will be for fixed amounts, such as for graduated tax or markets.

We will assume that Kambale Municipal Council has separate receipt books for (among other things):

(a) general purposes;

(b) housing rents;

(c) trading licences;

(d) liquor licences; and

(e) graduated tax (tickets).

The general receipt book will be used for three main classes of receipts:

(a) rates;

(b) water charges; and

(c) other.

Receipts can be specially designed to make totalling and analysis easier. If this is too expensive it is still possible to provide some form of analysis on the copy - even by using a rubber stamp.

Income Accounting

An example of the general receipt used by Kambale Municipal Council for Mr Kanyama might appear as follows:

	Date	Name	Amount	Ref.	Rates	Water	Other
"A"	Apr.15	B. Kanyama	Units 165	10/14 15826	Units 100	Units	Units 65

Received the sum shown in figures "AMOUNT"
XYZ REVENUE STAMP Cashier
CHEQUE/CASH No.B.48739
CODE: S/DRS (U 65)

If the back of the receipt is treated with carbon (or if carbon paper is used) to the width shown by "A" then a cash book sheet could be written up as the receipt is prepared, as follows:

CASH RECEIPTS

Date	Name	Amount	Ref.	Rates	Water	Other
Apr.15	(etc) B. Kanyama (etc)	(etc) 165 (etc)	10/14 15826	(etc) 100 (etc)	(etc) (etc)	(etc) 65 (etc)
Banked 16/4		32,160		14,280	13,140	4,740

118. THE CASH BOOK

Whenever cash is received by an authority it must be recorded, in detail or in total, as a debit entry in a cash account or cash book.

In many authorities each receipt is entered separately, in detail, on the debit side of a main cash book. This has the great advantage of simplicity - there is only one cash book; all receipts are debited in detail; and all payments credited in detail. The effect of the double-entry can be clearly seen.

However, as cash transactions become more numerous, experience shows that the basic systems have to be modified. Internal financial control demands that receipts are separated from payments and detail must be sacrificed for speed and efficiency. Chief financial officers must ask themselves whether the public can afford the cost of duplicating and even triplicating entries in the books. Certainly greater protection is often afforded - but at what cost?

To take an extreme and, hopefully, an imaginary example, consider the return of tickets in Section 106. The return is presented to the cashier who might write out a receipt giving full details of all tickets issued. The receipt is virtually copied into the cash book, again with full details. A little thought could devise a system whereby a receipt was written out for the total amount only, the original receipt attached to the copy ticket return and handed back to the collector. The original ticket return would be filed with the copy of the receipt, thus giving the cashier all the information required. The copy receipt will be entered in the cash book as a brief entry only (or as part of a total - see later).

To take the matter a stage further, there is no real need to write individual entries in the cash book at all. The information is all available on the copy receipt. However, total cash collected must be debited to the cash account and in the next Section we shall see how this is done.

119. COLLECTION AND DEPOSIT BOOK

Let us assume that the main cashier of Kambale Municipal Council is required to collect cash and to bank it intact on the following working day. As he is in no way concerned with payments he will keep a "receipts cash book" or "collections cash book". It is commonly referred to as a "collection and deposit" book to emphasise that all debits are collections and all credits are deposits in the bank.

An example of a page of the collection and deposit book for Kambale Municipal Council is shown on page 345. Collections are shown on the debit side as a single total for each day's work. The credit side shows the disposal of the daily collections.

Let us assume that we are dealing with collections for May 4. The cashier at balancing time will count up his cash and list his cheques, whilst an independent officer (such as an internal auditor) will list the general receipts, rent receipts, licence counterfoils and graduated tax ticket return. The auditor will arrive at the following debit:

	Units
Receipts Issued	115,553
Change Float	100
	115,653

This is the sum which the cashier must account for and he eventually produces cash, (or its equivalent) totalling **U** 115,660.

Subsequent checking fails to reveal the difference and the surplus of U 7 is paid into the Council's funds, a receipt being issued. General receipts will be issued (or will have already been issued) for rents, licences and tax and a daily balance statement can be drawn up as shown on page 347.

Whilst it is not strictly necessary to issue general receipts for amounts already receipted in other ways (eg rents, graduated tax and licences) the cash for these items may be paid in by a sub-cashier (such as a rent collector or district office cashier) who will require a receipt.

One item on the credit side of the daily balance statement is "Direct Banking". In this case an outside collector (eg a district cashier) with a large sum of graduated tax money totalling **U** 8,540 paid it into the bank nearest to his collection point. The receipted bank paying-in slip was produced to the main cashier together with a return of tax

KAMPALE MUNICIPAL COUNCIL
COLLECTION AND DEPOSIT BOOK

Date	Receipts Nbs From	Receipts Nbs To	Collections Accounts Rates	Collections Accounts Water	Collections Accounts Other	Total	Date	Deposits Banked Cash	Deposits Banked Cheques	Direct Bank Credits	Internal Transfer (Contra)	Banking Adjustments Over	Banking Adjustments Under
19_6							19_6						
May 2	549	565	4,060	1,320	940	6,320	May 2	1,460	3,040	-	-	-	-
3	566	584	6,480	840	1,040	8,360	3	4,180	2,130	-	-	-	10
4	585	597	99,240	2,460	13,860	115,560	4	6,240	2,130	-	-	10	-
5	597	621	680	-	4,800	5,480	5	8,460	2,560	8,540	96,000	-	-
6	622	636	1,080	3,600	1,080	5,760	6	5,240	240	-	-	-	-
(etc)	(etc)	(etc)	(etc)	(etc)	(etc)	(etc)	9	3,280	2,480	-	-	-	-
31	849	865	4,620	380	500	5,500	(etc)	(etc)	(etc)	(etc)	(etc)	(etc)	(etc)
			216,460	49,320	50,800	316,580		146,080	48,040	25,460	96,000	10	10
			-	-	-	-	Jun 1	5,100	400	-	-	-	-

tickets. The cashier issued a receipt to the collector and retained a copy of the receipted bank paying-in (deposit) slip as his authority.

Another item on the credit side of the daily balance statement is "Transfers". These arise when income due to one fund of the Council is payable from another fund. In this particular case the rates on the Council's own property must be credited in the rating accounts and debited against the revenue accounts of the appropriate services (for example rates on the Council offices must be debited against "Administrative Buildings").

One way of dealing with this problem would be to draw an ordinary cheque payable to the Council itself, which will be receipted and paid into the bank in the ordinary way. Another way is to do a journal entry but experience shows that this can often upset the smooth book-keeping routine because it always has to be remembered as a special item, particularly for statistical purposes.

A mid-way system is to use an internal cash transfer, as follows:

```
                                                          No.316
              INTERNAL CASH TRANSFER
                   (Contra Entry)

   Pay Kambale Municipal Council
   The sum of U Ninety six thousand              U 96,000


                                             OPQ
                                     Chief Financial Officer

   Details:   Rates on Council property (V.4046)
```

It is written out like a cheque and can sometimes be banked as a cheque. However, many chief financial officers take the view that the bank should not be employed to do the Council's internal book-keeping work, and arrangements are made for internal transfers to be shown as contra entries (as in our case).

In our example the cashier has written a receipt for U 96,000 and he is entitled to use the transfer slip as a credit item in his "cashing up".

When the "cashing up" is complete, the collection side of the collection and deposit book is entered up, totalling U 115,560. Bank paying-in slips are entered up for cash U 8,460 and cheques U 2,560. The cash and cheques are then locked away to await banking the following day.

On 5 May, when the receipted paying-in books are returned from the bank, the "deposits" side of the collection and deposit book is entered up with the appropriate amounts. The direct bank credit slip and the transfer slip, are passed to the accountancy section.

Income Accounting

DAILY BALANCE
(Date) 4/5/_6

	Units		Units
General Receipts (No.585 to 595)	104,430	Cheques (listed)	2,560
Rents (No.596) — Units 2,233		Money Order (listed)	-
Liquor Licences (No.596) — 50		Postal Orders (listed)	-
Trading Licences (No.596) — 300			
Graduated Tax (No.596) — 8,540	11,123	Bank Notes	
		U 100	1,500
Miscellaneous:		U 20	4,200
		U 10	1,940
		U 5	460
		Silver U 1	390
		50 cents	40
SUB-TOTAL	115,553	10 cents	20
Surplus (General Receipt No.597)	7	5 cents	10
		Direct Banking	8,540
TOTAL	115,560		
Cashier's Change Float	100	Transfers	96,000
TOTAL DEBIT	115,660		115,660

Surplus on balancing U 7

Shortage on balancing -

_____ABC_____   _____XYZ_____
Internal Auditor   Cashier

The direct credit of **U 8,540** presents a slight problem in that it is actually banked (direct) on 4 May, but shown in the collection and deposit book as being banked on 5 May. The sum can be regarded as being "in suspense" at the bank for one day and allowed for in the bank reconciliation statement.

At the end of the month, after a bank reconciliation had been carried out, the main cash book (kept in the accountancy section) would be entered up with single monthly totals for May as follows:

CASH BOOK (DEBIT SIDE)

Date	Details	Cash	Cheques	Direct	Contra	Total
May 31	Deposits for Month	146,080	48,040	25,460	96,000	315,580

The activity of the cashier can be controlled by a "Cashier's Account". It will (for the month of May) appear as follows:

Municipal Accounting for Developing Countries

Cashier's Account

19_6				19_6			
May	1	To Balance b/f (unbanked cash at 30/4/_6)	4,500	May	31	By Deposits for month	315,580
	31	To Collections for month	316,580			By Balance c/d (unbanked cash)	5,500
			321,080				321,080
Jun	1	To Balance b/d	5,500				

The balance brought forward is taken from the April account and is the amount banked on 1 May. The total collections would be obtained independently from the receipts analysis in the accountancy section and the total deposits from the main cash book. The balance of U 5,500 is the sum collected on 31 May and banked on 1 June. It represents unbanked money belonging to the Council at the close of business on 31 May. This shows how control accounts are used as part of the system of internal check.

In our example there was (on 4 May) a surplus of U 7 on "cashing-up". This sum was paid in and a receipt was issued. A record would also be made in the "shorts and overs" book. Had there been a shortage of cash on balancing, the cashier would normally be expected to replace the cash from his own pocket. No book-keeping entries are required - he is NOT given a receipt - but an entry will be made in the "shorts and overs" book.

What happens if the cashier has no money immediately available to make up the difference, or if the amount of the difference is too great for him to settle? The "shorts and overs" book must still be entered up, but unless some action is taken, the collection and deposit book will be out of balance. The circumstances would be reported to the Chief Financial Officer who makes a decision as to how the difference is to be dealt with. The Chief Financial Officer might decide to sign an internal cash transfer slip for the difference. No receipt will be issued for this slip which will act as the equivalent of cash to clear the deposit side of the collection and deposit book. The expenditure aspect of the transfer slip will be treated as a personal advance to the cashier, to be usually cleared by cash, or by deduction from salary, unless it is written off on proper authority.

A word about the columns headed "Banking Adjustments". These have nothing at all to do with shorts and overs on cashing up. They deal with mistakes which sometimes arise in banking of remittances. In our example, let us assume that on 3 May an officer went to the bank with remittances of cash and cheques totalling (as he thought) U 6,320. The cheques were found to be correct but when the bank cashier counted the notes he found they were U 10 short. The paying-in book was altered and initialled and the officer returned to the cash office, having under-banked U 10. The deposit side of the collection and deposit book was entered up with the amount banked and the U 10 entered in the "under" column. Almost immediately it was discovered that the U 10 note had slipped behind the lining of the bank bag. By now the bank was closed (or too far away). Next day the U 10 was "over-banked" to put the matter right. The aim should be for the "over" and "under" columns to cancel out as quickly as possible. One fairly common cause of

Income Accounting

"under-banking" is where the bank cashier discovers a "dud" or foreign coin or note in the banking. A possible cause of "over-banking" or "under-banking" would be where the income analysis section discovered an error in the receipts after they had appeared to balance.

120. GRADUATED PERSONAL TAX

One of the greatest difficulties with income records arises over graduated personal tax, which is a simple form of local income tax. The records for the collection of this tax, forming the major source of locally raised income for some local authorities, could cover almost the whole range of records discussed in this chapter. It is unfortunate that the theories of sound income records are hard to reconcile with the extremely difficult circumstances under which graduated tax must be collected. Much of this chapter will apply to "Octroi", a crude form of customs duty levied on goods entering a town, hitherto common in the Indian sub-continent.

Let us first consider the theory. Each rural authority is divided into areas for collection of the tax. Each town or municipal council collects graduated tax from its own residents either to retain or to hand over to the appropriate national, provincial or state governments. Sometimes, this revenue is shared between the authorities.

By 1 Jan. in each year (or soon afterwards) each taxpayer of an area should have been assessed for tax due from him for that year. It should be possible to calculate an overall control debit for the area as follows:

```
    x taxpayers @ (say) U 50    =
    y taxpayers @ (say) U 70    =
    z taxpayers @ (say) U 100   =
        (etc)
             TOTAL CONTROL DEBIT  _____
                                  ========
```

Because the tax is an annual tax, which a taxpayer should expect to pay year after year, it would be reasonable to record the sums due from each taxpayer in a rental, as for rates, with the overall amount due balancing with the control debit. When each taxpayer paid his tax it would be reasonable to credit his personal account in the rental, in the same way as for rates.

These theories do not work out in practice. Some of the reasons are as follows:

(a) not all potential taxpayers are assessed for tax by 1 Jan. - some are never assessed for various reasons. It is obvious that taxes levied upon persons cannot be as certain and definite as rates levied upon fixed and immovable property. In rural communities the population is thinly spread over wide areas, and in large towns there are very large movements of population into and out of the authority's area. Both problems make control very difficult;

(b) potential taxpayers move from area to area and even across national borders leaving behind a large number of bad debts for unpaid tax;

(c) new taxpayers are continually being assessed during the year; and

(d) although strictly credit income, much of the tax is collected "on the spot" as cash income.

Because of these considerable difficulties, it is usual practice for authorities to regard all graduated tax income as "cash income" for book-keeping purposes - controlled (as in the case of markets -above) by the use of tickets. Proof of payment depends entirely upon a person's ability to produce his tax ticket to an authorised person. Of course, records will exist for controlling the printing, issue and use of tax tickets and there will be various records of tax assessments and tax payments. It may be that the present system will have to continue for some time, but it is as well to be aware of its various disadvantages and to be on the alert for ways of improving the system. Some of the accounting difficulties are:

(a) there is no "control debit" either as a basis for controlling the income or for preparing the estimates;

(b) the treating of the tax as "cash income" seriously disrupts the "income and expenditure" method of accounting, so necessary for mature local authorities;

(c) there is much less scope for "internal financial control" and consequently much greater scope for fraud and corruption, where "cash income" arises;

(d) the reliance upon the taxpayer to produce a ticket or receipt as the main proof of payment is clearly second best to a system which is designed to maintain proper records of the sums due and paid; and

(e) the attention of the authority is not drawn to the existence of arrears.

No-one would seriously suggest that the system of accounting for graduated tax is always adequate or efficient. It would be optimistic for us, as finance officers, to suppose that we could make it so overnight. Much lies outside our control, including standards of education and of integrity, but we can perhaps suggest lines along which a possible future system might operate.

Let us suppose that Kambale Municipal Council (an urban authority) collects graduated tax as agent for the national, provincial or state government. Let us also assume that the urban authority (Kambale) retains $17\frac{1}{2}\%$ of the total collected. Taxpayers would normally fall into the following groups.

(a) permanent residents of the area who would pay tax year after year;

(b) others, including casual residents, who are assessed for tax after the original assessments have been made; and

(c) casual taxpayers who pay tax in cash as demanded without prior assessment.

Group (a) are rather like ratepayers and could be controlled by a rental system; group (b) are rather like sundry debtors and group (c) are similar to payers of ticket income.

By 1 Jan., group (a) taxpayers should have all been assessed. Assessment notices will be issued to them and the copies entered in a rental. The total assessments will be agreed with the control debit.

Income Accounting

As group (b) taxpayers are assessed they will be given assessment notices and the copies of these will be entered in numerical order in an "additional assessments" book (like a sundry debtors book).

In either of these cases the "slip" system could be used, subject to adequate safeguards.

When taxpayers in either of these classes pay their taxes they will be issued with a fixed value tax receipt (ticket) for the appropriate amount. A carbon copy will be taken (noting the assessment number) and posted to the taxpayer's personal account in the rental or additional assessments book. The copy receipts will be posted in total under the analysis heading "Graduated Tax - Credit Income".

When taxpayers of group (c) pay their taxes they will be issued with a fixed value tax receipt of a different series to distinguish them from "credit" receipts. Perhaps these tickets could have a diagonal red line across them as a distinctive mark. Carbon copies will be taken and daily totals will be analysed as "Graduated Tax - Cash Income".

Both forms of receipts will be controlled by ticket registers and ticket returns in the ordinary way.

Normal reminder and follow-up procedure can be followed for assessed taxpayers who are in arrears. Among the difficulties which will arise are:

(a) persons originally assessed for tax cannot be traced; and

(b) some persons will be assessed for tax and the amount debited against their personal accounts: later, when the taxpayers actually pay tax, perhaps at the time of a "collection drive" by officials, they do not disclose their original assessments (possibly thinking that they can get away with a lower payment of tax) and are issued with "Cash Income" receipts. Thus there is "cash income" and "credit income" for the same persons.

Where taxpayers who are pursued for arrears of tax produce "Cash Income" receipts, their debits can be written off in the "rental" or "additional assessments" book to the extent of the cash payment made. They will still be liable for legal proceedings on the unpaid balance of the assessed tax.

When an amount is written off in this way, the "Cash Income" receipt number will be quoted as the authority for the write-off.

Where persons originally assessed cannot be traced, unpaid tax on their accounts should NOT be written off immediately but carried forward as arrears (unless, for example, the taxpayer has died or otherwise become exempt - when a write-off can be made).

However, whilst individual unpaid sums are carried forward as arrears it would be most imprudent for any finance officer to regard them all as "good" debts. He will know from experience that perhaps a high proportion of the debts will never be paid. To avoid overstating his assets (debtors) in the balance sheet he will make a provision for bad and doubtful debts, as described in Section 88 of chapter 8 (page 271).

The forms of rental, and other subsidiary records necessary to operate such a system, can easily be adapted from those already described. Where it is known or suspected that "casual" or "on the spot" assessments are for permanent residents of the area, their names should be noted for inclusion in the rental of basic assessments for future years. In this way they will automatically become liable for future assessments of tax.

Sometimes graduated tax will be paid in instalments. If this is done it becomes very like an annual market rent payable in monthly instalments, and a suitable record could be adopted from that shown on page 335.

Sometimes, too, tax will be collected from employers, who will in turn deduct it from the monthly salaries of their employees, paying monthly lump sum instalments to the local authority. Again a suitable record could be adopted from the market rental and used as follows:

(a) a schedule will be prepared in duplicate for each employer on the lines of the market rental page. Headings of columns will be:

    (i) assessment number;

    (ii) name of taxpayer;

    (iii) monthly instalment;

    (iv) arrears brought forward;

    (v) annual tax;

    (vi) total amount due;

    (vii) total cash;

    (viii) total allowances;

    (ix) arrears carried forward; and

    (x) monthly tax paid (number of columns as required);

(b) details of tax assessments for each employee will be extracted from the main rental and listed upon his employer's schedule;

(c) each schedule will be totalled to give the total amount due from each employer, in respect of the tax for his employees;

(d) the original of each schedule will be sent to the employer with a letter requiring him to deduct the monthly instalments of tax from his employees. The copy schedules are kept by the finance department;

(e) cash received from the employer each month will be posted against each taxpayer's name on the finance department copy schedule; and

(f) when all cash has been received from an employer his copy schedule is cross-cast and the "total cash" columns are entered up. A single figure of "cash paid" for each employee can be posted to his account in the main rental, any arrears being in agreement with those shown on the copy schedule.

In book-keeping terms "instalment registers" or "employers' schedules" are merely acting as "suspense" or "holding" accounts until the various instalments paid by each taxpayer are posted, in total, to his personal account.

As a further refinement of the instalment system, a personal account can be opened for each employer and debited with the total amount which he

Income Accounting

is required to collect from his employees.

Cash received from the employer, from time to time, will be credited as lump sum instalments in his personal account. Instalments not collectable because employees have left the service of the employer will also be credited to the employer's personal account (but not written off against the employees' tax liability).

In this system the employer is treated for accounting purposes rather like a district officer.

Sometimes employers buy special tax stamps and affix them to the instalment cards of their employees. When the employer surrenders the stamped cards he is issued with receipts to hand to the employees, equal to the amount of the stamps on their cards.

To see how the tax collections of Kambale Municipal Council for 19_6 will appear in the final accounts we shall assume the following tax collection statistics:

(a) **Basic Assessments**

Assessment			Collection	
Number of Taxpayers	Rate	Amount	Details	Amount
	Units	Units		Units
825	100	82,500	Paid in Cash	266,700
460	200	92,000	Allowances: Died	600
190	300	57,000	Exempt	2,100
50	400	20,000	"Cash	
42	500	21,000	Income"	900
20	600	12,000	Arrears c/f	14,200
	TOTAL	284,500	TOTAL	284,500

Provision is to be made for bad and doubtful debts of 50% of arrears (U 7,100)

Municipal Accounting for Developing Countries

(b) Additional Assessments

| Assessment |||| Collection ||
Number of Taxpayers	Rate	Amount	Details	Amount
	Units	Units		Units
250	100	25,000	Paid in Cash	46,500
65	200	13,000	Allowances: Died	100
25	300	7,500	Exempt	200
40	400	16,000	"Cash	
3	600	1,800	Income"	100
			Arrears c/f	16,400
	TOTAL	63,300	TOTAL	63,300
		======		======

Provision is to be made for bad and doubtful debts of 80% of arrears (U 13,120)

(c) Cash Income

| Assessment |||| Collection ||
Number of Taxpayers	Rate	Amount	Details	Amount
	Units	Units		Units
476	100	47,600	Paid in Cash	60,600
50	200	10,000		
10	300	3,000		
	TOTAL	60,600	TOTAL	60,600
		======		======

(d) The U 144,160 due to the National Government at 31 Dec. 19_5 was paid to it on 15 Jan. 19_6. In addition, U 200,000 was paid on account on 30 June 19_6 (in practice more frequent instalments would be usual).

A complete set of final accounts would show:

Sundry Taxpayers (Basic Assessments) Control				1
To Tax Income Account 19_6 Assessments	284,500	By Cash*	266,700	
		By Tax Income Account Allowances	3,600	
		By Balance c/f	14,200	
	284,500		284,500	
	======		======	

Income Accounting

Sundry Taxpayers (Additional Assessments) Control — 2

To Tax Income Account 19_6 Assessments	63,300	By Cash*	46,500
		By Tax Income Account Allowances	400
		By Balance c/f	16,400
	63,300		63,300

Tax Income Account — 3

To Sundry Taxpayers - Allowances		By Sundry Taxpayers	
Basic	3,600	Basic	284,500
Additional	400	Additional	63,300
To Provision for Bad and Doubtful Debts		By Cash*	60,600
Basic	7,100		
Additional	13,120		
To Tax Income Appropriation Account (Net Tax Income)	384,180		
	408,400		408,400

Tax Income Appropriation Account — 4

To National Government	316,960	By Tax Income Account	384,200
To Revenue Account	67,240		
	384,200		384,200

Provision for Bad and Doubtful Debts — 5

To Balance c/f	20,200	By Tax Income Account Provisions -	
		Basic	7,100
		Additional	13,100
	20,200		20,200

National Government — 6

To Cash*	344,160	By Balance b/f	144,160
To Balance c/f	116,940	By Tax Income Appropriate Account	316,940
	461,100		461,100

Municipal Accounting for Developing Countries

General Revenue Account
Finance Department   7

To (Various Items of Expenditure)	(?)	By Tax Income Appropriate Account (Agency Fee)	67,240
		Sales of Publications	(?)
		Miscellaneous	(?)
	(?)		(?)
	===		======

Cash postings will come from the analyses of receipts and of payments in the accountancy section. Other postings will be based on totals of information provided by the various graduated tax records. The necessary journal entries would appear as follows:

Income Accounting

19_6					

Dec.31	Sundry Taxpayers (Basic) Control DR.
	   To Tax Income Account
	   Being basic assessments
	   of tax as shown by rental
		1
		3
			284,500	284,500

Dec.31	Sundry Taxpayers (Additional) Control DR.
	   To Tax Income Account
	   Being additional assessments
	   of tax as shown by additional
	   assessments book
		2
		3
			63,300	63,300

Dec.31	Tax Income Account DR.
	   To Sundry Taxpayers (Basic)
	     Control
	   Being authorised allowances
	   against basic assessments:
	                    Units
	   Deaths 600
	   Exempt 2,100
	   Paid (Cash Income) 900
	                    3,600
		3
		1
			3,600	3,600

Dec.31	Tax Income Account DR.
	   To Sundry Taxpayers
	    (Additional) - Control
	   Being authorised allowances
	   against additional assessments:
	                    Units
	   Deaths 100
	   Exempt 200
	   Paid (Cash Income) 100
	                    400
		3
		1
			400	400

Dec.31	Tax Income Account DR.
	   To Provision for Bad and
	     Doubtful Debts
	   Being 50% of arrears on basic
	   assessments (U 14,200) now
	   set aside as a provision
	   against non-settlement
		3
		5
			7,100	7.100

Dec.31	Tax Income Account
	   To Provision for Bad and
	     Doubtful Debts
	   Being 80% of arrears on
	   additional assessments
	   (U 16,400) now set aside as
	   a provision against non-
	   settlement
		3
		5
			13,120	13,120

At this stage we have posted to the Tax Income Account the best available estimate by the Chief Financial Officer, based upon his skill and experience, of the net amount of tax income which it is proper to regard as income earned for 19_6. The higher percentage for bad and doubtful debts allowed on additional assessments seems fully justified by the fact that these arrears represent a much higher proportion of total assessments than the arrears for basic assessments, suggesting that the majority will never be collected.

Because of the high percentage which may have to be set aside as provisions for doubtful debts, it might be argued that there is little advantage in treating the tax as credit income at all. Treating the tax as cash income at least has the advantage of giving a book-keeping figure based on facts. Each Chief Financial Officer will decide for himself the most expedient book-keeping treatment but he should be prepared to maintain a flexible attitude towards possible changing circumstances. Treating the debt as credit income maintains the legal liability against the debtor.

| 19_6 Dec.31 | Tax Income Account DR. To Tax Income Appropriation Account Being transfer of net tax income due for year | 3 4 | 384,180 | 384,180 |

Here, the net tax income due is transferred to an appropriation account because it must be shared between the Kambale Municipal Council and the National Government (say) in the ratio of 17½% and 82½%.

| 19_6 Dec.31 | Tax Income Appropriation Account DR. To National Government To Revenue Account Being appropriation of net tax income in the ratios prescribed by law: National Government 82½% Kambale Municipal Council 17½% | 4 6 7 | 384,180 | 316,940 67,240 |

Notice that only the 17½% share of the tax has been included in the Revenue Account of Kambale Municipal Council. As it represents an agency fee to cover collection costs it is reasonable to credit it as income earned by the Finance Department.

As the agency fee has been based upon "income due" and not on "cash collected" it is obvious that the amount of the provision for bad and doubtful debts will have a direct effect upon the amount of tax each authority receives. It might be argued by the government that for any particular year an over-provision has resulted in loss of income to that authority. On the other hand the urban authority could argue that it is paying over the whole of the amount calculated as due to the goverment; that it is carrying all the arrears in its own books, even though 82½% of the sum is owed indirectly to the government; and that it is having to provide a larger working balance entirely out of its own resources perhaps paying (or losing) interest on the cash not collected.

If agreement cannot be reached, the agency fee would have to be

Income Accounting

calculated on the basis of "cash received". In our example it would be 17½% of U 373,800 (ie U 65,415). But if this were done, the government or district authority could only expect to receive the balance of "cash received" (ie U 308,385). It cannot have it both ways.

If none of the tax collected by an authority represents income to any other authority there is no need for a "Tax Income Appropriation" account. The total net tax income can be transferred direct from the "Tax Income" account to the Revenue Account. Assuming (for the moment) that the above figures had related to such an authority the journal entry would have shown:

| 19_6 Dec.31 | Tax Income Account DR. To Revenue Account Being net tax income now transferred | 3 7 | 384,180 | 384,180 |

Sometimes taxes will be assessed and collected at district offices. Control could still be exercised by the headquarters finance department in the following way:

(a) returns are made of all tax assessments made at district level and forwarded to the finance department to form the basis of "control debits";

(b) the finance department will keep separate "Taxpayers Control Accounts" for each tax area and debit these accounts with total tax assessed, according to returns;

(c) additional returns will be required for new assessments taking place during the year and these will be debited against control accounts in the same way as basic assessments;

(d) credit entries in the control accounts will come only from total cash paid in by each district or from properly authorised allowances; and

(e) balances on each control account will represent arrears of tax due from taxpayers of each area. In other words each balance will represent assessed tax uncollected by the appropriate district manager, which he should be required to explain.

It might be possible for control accounts to be kept in tabular (columnar) form as follows (using assumed figures):

Sundry Taxpayers Control

	District "A"	District "B"	(etc)		District "A"	District "B"	(etc)
Balances (arrears of tax) brought forward	58,460	24,280	(etc)	Cash paid to Headquarters Cashier	990,860	835,100	(etc)
Tax assessed for year as shown by returns	986,040	842,900	(etc)	Allowances (properly authorised)	10,240	5,160	(etc)
				Balances (arrears of tax) carried forward	43,400	26,920	(etc)
	1,044,500	867,180	(etc)		1,044,500	867,180	(etc)

Such a system forms a basis of internal financial control. It is considerably strengthened by an efficient internal audit section, making frequent visits to district headquarters.

Apart from possible bad debts, which can be dealt with by making provisions, the graduated tax system suffers from uncertainty, brought about by annual changes in weather, market prices and other factors which affect the incomes of urban and rural communities, out of which taxes are payable. The only long-term solution is to build up adequate reserves which can be added to in good years from budget surpluses. Budget deficits arising in bad years can then be met from these reserves. Two important budgetary controls are necessary:

(a) annual revenue expenditure should be based at levels no greater than average annual income (taking good and bad years together) and NOT expanded to meet maximum income levels;

(b) revenue reserves should be invested as lucratively as possible so as to give maximum liquidity with minimum possibility of capital losses.

11. Expenditure Accounting

Section		Page
121.	Cheque Payments.	362
122.	Petty Cash Payments.	365
123.	Sundry Creditors.	365
124.	Official Order Systems.	377
125.	Periodical Payments.	381
126.	Car Allowances.	381
127.	Contracts and Professional Fees.	384
128.	Occasional Payments.	387
129.	Refunds.	388
130.	Salaries and Wages.	388
131.	Payments in Advance.	400
132.	Advances and Deposits.	402
133.	Overseas Indents.	406

121. CHEQUE PAYMENTS

In the last chapter we saw how the cash and credit income of an authority was collected and paid into the bank. We now deal with the payments which must be made by an authority to run its services.

We have already seen that if a sound system of internal financial control is in operation, all payments will be made either by cheque (or direct bank transfer) or from a petty cash imprest. No payments will be made from the authority's funds unless they have been properly authorised.

Each payment will be supported by a voucher, which may be a supplier's invoice, a payroll or a voucher prepared in the finance department. An authority might establish a definite routine for making payments, so that all invoices from each creditor can be collected together and totalled, and a single cheque sent monthly, weekly, or even daily, for the total amount due. The vouchers supporting the payments will normally contain all the necessary information for book-keeping purposes, so that the "payments cash book" is represented by a simple list of cheques.

By way of example we will assume that Kambale Municipal Council has established a monthly payments routine. Whilst this might be suitable, where normal monthly credit facilities operate among traders it may not be suitable where credit trading is restricted, and more frequent payments (weekly or even daily) may be necessary.

The Kambale Municipal Council cheque list for August 19_6 might appear as follows:

Expenditure Accounting

	Cheque Payments - August 19_6			List.No.8/_6	
Day	Voucher No.	Name	Particulars	Cheque No.	Amount
					Units
1	1646	Chief Financial Officer	Petty Cash - July	48294	245
1	1647	Chief Executive Officer	Petty Cash - July	48295	85
3	1648	Kambale Argus	Advertisement	48296	45
6	1649	B. Odema	Cash Shortage	TR335	90 *
9	1650	Carters Ltd	Carriage	48297	15
9	1651	R. Okumu (etc)	Motor Advance (etc)	48298	10,000 Various
31	1684	Cash	Wages	48331	185,245
31	1685	Badu Ltd	Machinery Repairs	48332	4,860
31	1686	Kambale Supplies	Furniture	48333	530
31	1687	National Government	Loan Charges	48334	65,425
31	1688	Motors Ltd	Motor Spares	48335	1,240
31	1689	Shell Ltd	Petrol and Oil	48336	8,420
31	1690	Kambale Printers (etc)	Stationery (etc)	-	465 Various
31	1863	National Bank Ltd	Bank Charges	-	60 μ
					745,820
				Cheques	745,670
				Direct	60 μ
				Contra	90 *

The list produces a final monthly total of payments, including petty cash reimbursements, amounting to U 745,820 which can be posted to the main cash book in a single total as follows:

CASH BOOK (CREDIT SIDE)

Date	Details	Cheques	Direct	Contra	Total
Aug.31	Cheque List No.8	745,670	60	90	745,820

Cheque payments are entered in the "cheques" column and the other columns are used for "direct" bank debits (eg bank charges) and "contra" entries resulting from the internal cash transfers explained in Chapter 10. These direct debits and contra entries could, if required, be included on the cheque list, as shown in our example. The total of the list would then be analysed by a small entry below the total, as shown. However, if direct debits and contra entries were numerous it would probably be better to list them separately.

During the early part of the month only urgent payments are made. The invoices of creditors giving normal monthly credit terms will be collected together as they arrive and kept for payment on or about the last day of the month.

Voucher No.1649 is for an internal cash transfer to clear a cash shortage of U 90 in the cash collection office. As explained in the last chapter the cashier will use the transfer slip as cash income to clear the shortage but a personal account in his name (ie an advance account) will be debited as a result of the payment.

Where actual cash is required for making payments (eg reimbursement of petty cash imprests and payment of wages) cheques are drawn for the exact amount of cash required.

Sometimes the cheque number can be used also as the voucher number. This system is particularly suitable where the authority uses its own printed series of cheques.

If columns were provided to the right of the "amount" column in the cheque list we should have a "payments analysis" or "expenditure journal" as described in Chapters 6 and 7.

The invoices or vouchers supporting each payment could be attached to and summarised on a summary voucher for each separate creditor. The summary vouchers will be arranged in alphabetical order and consecutively numbered throughout the financial year. It is these summary vouchers which provide the necessary information for analysis of expenditure (see later).

Copies of the cheque list may be used as follows:

(a) as the payments cash book;

(b) as an index, attached to the front of each monthly file of vouchers;

(c) as a cheque list, for marking off presented cheques as they appear in the bank statement, prior to preparing a reconciliation statement;

(d) as a means of reporting payments to the finance committee if required;

(e) for purposes of internal audit (and as a copy for the external auditor if required); and

(f) as a means of producing a total for sundry creditors (see later).

Alternatively, cheques may be specially designed with carbonised strips on the back, so that the cheque list is taken as a copy, automatically, as the cheques are prepared.

In countries following UK banking practice, cheques will normally be crossed before payment is made, except where cash is required, (such as for wages and petty cash) or perhaps for salary cheques. It is a good practice to use cheques with printed crossings, with the additional words "not negotiable" added for protection. Crossings can then be individually cancelled where cash is required, by using the words "pay cash", accompanied by a signature, over the printed crossing. The signature must be the same as that used in signing the cheque. If more than one person signs a cheque, each must sign the cancelled crossing.

Expenditure Accounting

122. PETTY CASH PAYMENTS

Where the amount of a payment is small (say under U 20) it is sometimes more convenient to pay in cash than by cheque, particularly where credit facilities are not granted. An example might be where a parcel was sent from the post office, and paid for in cash.

Such payments are made from petty cash imprests held in the finance department or in other departments as required. The book-keeping procedures would be as described in Chapter 7. The Chief Financial Officer would decide the amount of each imprest, and this would be advanced to a fairly senior officer of the department concerned. Each imprest-holder would have a petty cash book which he would keep in the form shown in Chapter 7. Each payment out of petty cash would be supported by a voucher and these vouchers would be submitted periodically (usually monthly) to the chief paymaster (head of expenditure section) for reimbursement.

The cheque list in Section 121 shows cheques drawn on 1 August to reimburse the Chief Financial Officer and the Chief Executive Officer for the petty cash payments made in their departments during July.

The various items of petty cash expenditure will be listed on a summary voucher attached to the individual petty cash vouchers. The summary voucher will be used for posting the payments analysis in the same way as other cheque payments vouchers.

123. SUNDRY CREDITORS

Earlier chapters indicated that expenditure is incurred as soon as goods or services are supplied on credit and not merely when they are paid for. Every credit transaction entered into by a local authority has two separate parts:

(a) When the goods are supplied or the services are performed the expenditure has been incurred. In other words the benefit of the goods or services has been gained by the authority, which now has a liability to pay for them. In theory the book-keeping treatment (not done in practice) could be journalised as follows:

   DEBIT. Expenditure Account.
   CREDIT. Creditor (supplier of goods or services).

(b) When the goods or services are paid for, the liability of the authority is discharged, journalised (in theory) as follows:

   DEBIT. Creditor (supplier of goods or services)
   CREDIT. Cash.

In theory a personal account could be opened for each creditor with whom the authority deals, his account being credited with the value of invoices for goods and services supplied and debited with subsequent payments by the authority.

The keeping of individual creditors accounts is unnecessary and and expensive in terms of stationery and clerical work and it is therefore often not the practice for such accounts to be kept by local and public authorities.

Consider the purposes of personal accounts with creditors. These accounts act as:

Municipal Accounting for Developing Countries

(a) a statement of the creditors' position with the authority;

(b) a means of preventing duplicate payment of the creditors for the same goods or services;

(c) a record of outstanding liabilities for inclusion in the balance sheet; and

(d) a means of ensuring that expenditure is debited in the nominal accounts of the year (or financial period) in which it is incurred.

It has been found possible, in practice for each of these purposes to be accomplished without individual accounts and yet still maintaining sound principles of double-entry book-keeping, as follows:

(a) the actual possession of an unpaid invoice, is, in itself, a reminder of the debt, whether it is written in a book or not - furthermore if it is not paid within a reasonable time the creditor will send a reminder;

(b) as explained later in this chapter the copy order system, combined with the use of other special records, is an efficient guard against duplicate payments;

(c) although individual amounts of "sundry creditors" must be known in detail for other purposes they are grouped together in a single total for inclusion in the balance sheet; and

(d) correct nominal accounts can be debited by the "short-cut" method of converting "receipts and payments" into "income and expenditure".

The possibility of making a payment to a creditor twice for the same invoice is a very remote risk if an efficient order system is in force. Unfortunately, instead of accepting the risk, officers dealing with public funds sometimes become so obsessed with the possibility of making a duplicate payment that all kinds of costly records are introduced in an attempt to prevent it. The cost of keeping these extra records may far exceed any loss likely to arise from a duplicate payment.

Certain facts should be faced:

(a) no system, even a complete set of individual creditors accounts, can entirely eliminate duplicate payments, because of the human element;

(b) a duplicate payment made to a reputable supplier will almost certainly be returned as a matter of courtesy, or permitted to be deducted from a future payment;

(c) duplicate payments are normally (as "payments made under mistake of fact") legally recoverable;

(d) experience shows that the official order system, combined with the practice of paying only on invoices (never on statements) will almost always prevent duplicate payments on suppliers invoices; and

(e) the few duplicate payments which may occur usually arise on items originating in the finance department (eg refunds, professional fees) - errors can occasionally creep through in any system, however well organised.

Expenditure Accounting

Some authorities keep invoice registers in which are entered all incoming invoices. When the invoices are actually paid the entries in the register are marked off.

In this connection it is interesting to note the comments of a research team investigating accounting practice in United Kingdom authorities in 1959:

"..... Another system was observed, in which memorandum cards are kept for individual creditors on which are recorded details of invoices submitted to the council for payment: previous entries are scrutinized in order to avoid paying an account twice. Such a record inevitably takes time to compile, involves risk of copying errors, with consequent need for checking, and must, of necessity, add to costs. We consider it possesses no advantages over the copy order system .....".

It is the duty of every Chief Financial Officer to see that public funds are not spent on keeping records which serve no useful purpose. It is also his duty to see that necessary information is made available in the most economical way, and it is questionable whether invoice registers are worthwhile.

We can now return to the problem of how to record sundry creditors for book-keeping purposes.

Payments during a financial year will divide themselves into two main classes:

(a) those for expenditure incurred (ie goods or services received) during the current financial year; and

(b) those for expenditure incurred during the previous financial year.

As an example of the first class, let us assume that the payment of U 465 on voucher No.1690, on the cheque list of Kambale Municipal Council in Section 121 related to stationery supplied to the finance department on 20 July 19_6 and chargeable against item No.10 in the finance committee estimates - "Printing and Stationery" (see Chapter 9 page 292). In theory, the journal entry would have been as follows:

19_6 July 20	Finance Department (Printing and Stationery) DR. To Kambale Printers Being goods supplied on credit	2 1	465	465

When the invoice was paid on 31 August 19_6 the correct journal entry would have been (in theory):

19_6 Aug.31	Kambale Printers DR. To Cash Being settlement of invoice No..... dated 20/7/_6	1 3	465	465

In theory the ledger would appear as follows:

	Kambale Printers							1
19_6 Aug.31	To Cash	J	465	19_6 Jul.20	By Finance (Printing and Stationery)	J		465
			465 ===					465 ===

	Finance Department Printing and Stationery							2
19_6 Jul.20	To Kambale Printers	J	465					

				Cash				3
				19_6 Aug.31	By Kambale Printers	J		465

The debit and credit entries in the personal account of Kambale Printers have now cancelled out each other, leaving a cash payment on 31 August balanced against an expenditure debit on 20 July.

Because the expenditure is incurred and the payment is made during the same financial year, substantially the same effect can be produced by eliminating the creditor's account altogether and posting the payment as though it were a cash transaction. The journal entry in theory would be:

19_6 Aug.31	Finance Department (Printing and Stationery) To Cash Being settlement of invoice No..... dated 20/7/_6	2 3	465	465

In practice the credit entry would be dealt with by the inclusion of the U 465 in the cheque list posted in total to the main cash book; the debit entry would come from the expenditure analysis in the expenditure journal or abstract.

The expenditure has been debited to the correct nominal account in the correct year and the cash payment has been recorded as before. As the liability to the creditor no longer exists, a record of it is not required.

Expenditure Accounting

The important theoretical points must be noted:

(a) The payment is not charged against the appropriate budget head until 31 August, whereas the expenditure is incurred on 20 July. At first sight this seems to be poor budgetary control but in fact the expenditure can no more be controlled when the invoice is received than when the payment is made. As we shall see later, effective budgetary control can take place only before the order is issued for the supply of goods and services.

(b) Any balance sheet produced on 30 July (or indeed upon any date between 20 July and 31 August) would overstate the surplus and understate the liabilities by U 465. This would be important if 31 July was the end of the financial year but, as it is not, the authority would be unlikely to produce a complete balance sheet. (Any monthly statements produced are normally capable of being produced from a trial balance, for cash control, for statistical purposes and for the information of government departments in prescribed form.)

Let us now assume that the above expenditure is incurred on 20 December 19_5 and is paid for on 31 January 19_6. Had the expenditure account been posted direct from the payment voucher the expenditure would be charged in 19_6. Also, in the balance sheet as at 31 December 19_5, the authority's liability to its creditor would not be recorded and the accumulated surplus would be overstated through not having been charged with the U 465.

Obviously for this type of transaction, some procedure is necessary to bring the outstanding liabilities into the books in 19_5.

In theory, journal entries would be required as follows:

OLD YEAR JOURNAL

19_5 Dec.20	Finance Department (Printing and Stationery) DR. To Kambale Printers Being goods supplied on credit	2 1	465	465

NEW YEAR JOURNAL

19_6 Jan.31	Kambale Printers DR. To Cash Being settlement of invoice No..... dated 20/12/_6	1 3	465	465

Ledger accounts would appear as:

	Kambale Printers		1
19_5 Dec.31 To Balance c/d 465	19_5 Dec.20 By Finance (Printing and Stat- ionery) J	465

465
                                 ===
	465
	                                                                 ===

19_6 Jan.31 To Cash J 465	19_6 Jan.1 By Balance b/d	465

	Finance Department Printing and Stationery		2
19_5 Dec.20 To Kambale Printers J 465	19_5 Dec.31 By General Revenue Account J	465

465
                                      ===
	465
	                                                                  ===

	Cash		3
	19_6 Jan.31 By Kambale Printers J	465

The **U** 465 (together with all other expenditure on the vote) would be transferred to the General Fund Revenue Account for 19_5. The balance carried down on the account of Kambale Printers will be included in the balance sheet as at 31 Dec. 19_5 under "Sundry Creditors".

We can now see that, whilst we can eliminate creditors accounts during the financial year, they are required at the end of the financial year whenever any goods or services are received in the old financial year and paid for in the new one.

However, to post each unpaid invoice at 31 Dec. to a personal account and clear these accounts against subsequent cash payments would be an expensive and time-consuming process. Because of this, the system of "converting receipts and payments to income and expenditure" has been devised. To see how this would operate in practice let us examine the balance sheet of Kambale Municipal Council on 31 Dec. 19_5 (page 285 of Chapter 9) where we see that the figure for "Sundry Creditors" is **U** 316,460. This represents, of course, expenditure incurred on various services during 19_5 and not paid for at 31 Dec. 19_5. Let us suppose that this figure of **U** 316,460 can be broken down as follows:

Expenditure Accounting

(a) invoices outstanding on 31 Dec. 19_5 but paid before final accounts are prepared (early in 19_6) 195,440

(b) invoices outstanding on 31 Dec. 19_5 and still outstanding when final accounts are prepared 73,460

(c) goods and services supplied during 19_5 for which no invoices have been received when final accounts are prepared 38,340

(d) other expenditure calculated as relating to 19_5 9,220

TOTAL 316,460

We will assume that the programme for preparation of the 19_5 final accounts provides for "sundry creditors" to be dealt with during February 19_6. During the month of January, various invoices will be received for payment in the finance department. Some of these, probably the majority, will relate to goods and services received in the 19_5 financial year. These invoices will go through the checking process in the ordinary way. Those which relate to the 19_5 financial year will be clearly marked "SUNDRY CREDITORS" preferably with a rubber stamp. On the individual invoice the expenditure will be allocated in the normal manner but on the invoice summary for each creditor, separate allocations and totals will be made for each financial year. The cheque list will be drawn up in the normal way with a single cheque for each creditor covering all invoices. For payment purposes it does not matter to which year the invoices relate - they will all be included on the same cheque.

When the cheque list has been completed, two extra columns will be drawn to the right of the "amount" column. In these columns each cheque will be analysed between 19_5 and 19_6 invoices. If copy cheque lists are taken, the analysis could be done on a copy, rather than on the original. This could then be filed with the final accounts working papers.

For Kambale Municipal Council the January cheque list might appear as follows:

	Cheque Payments - January 19_6			List No.1/_6	
Name	Particulars	Cheque No.	Amount	19_5	19_6
R. Musoke	Salary	46785	320		320
Badu Ltd	Machinery Repairs	46786	2,430	1,650	780
Kambale Supplies	Office Materials	46787	820	820	
Motors Ltd	Motor Spares	46788	1,450	940	510
Shell Ltd	Petrol and Oil	46789	9,230	9,230	
Kambale Printers	Stationery	46790	325	325	
	(etc)	(etc)	(etc)	(etc)	(etc)
			431,860	195,440	236,420

Municipal Accounting for Developing Countries

The payment to Motors Ltd on cheque No.46788 might be for three invoices as follows:

A/01369	19_5	Dec. 13	U 360	Works Department	-	spares
A/01423	19_5	Dec. 21	U 580	Works Department	-	tyres
A/01848	19_6	Jan. 7	U 510	Works Department	-	spares

The summary voucher attached to the invoices might appear as:

Name:	Motors Ltd		Vo.No.
Details:	Motor Spares		
Cheque No:	46788	**Dated:**	31/1/_6

Invoice	Amount	Allocation	Amount
A/01369	360	19_5 Works Department - Spares	360
A/01423	580	Works Department - Tyres	580
A/01848	510		940
			===
	1,450		
	=====	19_6 Works Department - Spares	510
			===

When the payments are posted in the expenditure analysis (or abstract) the 19_6 items will be posted in the ordinary way from the summary vouchers. The 19_5 items will be posted in the 19_5 expenditure analysis (or abstracts), as though they had been paid in 19_5. At this stage, the ledger accounts of both years will be out of balance. In 19_5 the sum of U 195,440 will have been debited to nominal accounts from invoices but there has so far been no credit entry. This credit entry will be a single total posted to a Sundry Creditors (Control) Account. A journal entry would be required as follows:

19_5 Dec.31	Sundry Accounts DR. To Sundry Creditors (Control) Being 19_5 invoices paid in Jan. 19_6 as shown on cheque list No.1/_6	V 100	195,440	195,440

The individual debits will be included as expenditure in 19_5 and will find their way into the revenue accounts. The Sundry Creditors (Control) Account will appear as:

Sundry Creditors (Control)			100
	19_5 Dec.31	By Sundry Accounts J	195,440

Expenditure Accounting

In 19_6, cash payments totalling U 195,440 have been credited in the cash book but there is so far no debit entry. The total amount will be debited to a single expenditure analysis headed "Sundry Creditors 19_5" to be dealt with as shown later.

Some invoices for 19_5 will be received in January too late for inclusion in the cheque list and others will be received in the early part of February. By the middle of February the accountancy section is in a position to "close off" this part of the final accounts work. The invoices will be checked and made ready for payment, and could then be included on a "sundry creditors" list as for estimated liabilities (see later).

However, if there are a large number of these invoices a different system might be adopted. The invoices could be collected together in a single bundle and their amounts listed to give a total. In our example the total would be U 73,460. Each invoice would then be posted to the appropriate expenditure analysis for 19_5, the machine-listed total being credited by journal entry to the Sundry Creditors (Control) Account. The journal entry would be as follows:

19_5 Dec.31	Sundry Accounts DR. To Sundry Creditors (Control) Being unpaid 19_5 invoices now charged as expenditure	V 100	73,460	73,460

The Sundry Creditors (Control) Account will now appear as:

	Sundry Creditors (Control)			100
		19_5 Dec.31	By Sundry Accounts J By Sundry Accounts J	195,440 73,460

The individual items of expenditure will now be posted as credit entries in red ink (because they are minuses) in the expenditure analysis for 19_6 under the appropriate allocations or codes and the single total debited to the Sundry Creditors (Control) Account as follows:

19_6 Jan.1	Sundry Creditors (Control) DR. To Sundry Accounts Being unpaid 19_5 invoices charged as expenditure in 19_5 and now written back 19_6	100 V	73,460	73,460

We can now leave aside the "sundry creditors" aspect of these unpaid invoices. When they are eventually paid in 19_6 in the normal course of events they will be posted as debits against the appropriate expenditure analysis, thus cancelling out the credits already in the analysis and leaving nil expenditure charged in 19_6. This is precisely what is wanted, because the expenditure has already been charged in 19_5.

The actual postings of the minus or credit (red ink) entries in the 19_6 expenditure analysis can be done either from the invoices or from the 19_5 expenditure analysis debits.

Another way of looking at this practice is to regard all the invoices as being first posted to nominal accounts in 19_6, expenditure then being transferred back into the 19_5 accounts. Minus entries (red ink) are made in the 19_6 nominal accounts, balanced by plus entries (black ink) in the 19_5 nominal accounts. The double-entry in each year is completed by the appropriate entries in the Sundry Creditors (Control) Account.

So far, we have dealt only with items where the exact amount of the "sundry creditors" liability is known from a paid or unpaid invoice. The next stage is to deal with goods and services supplied during 19_5 for which no invoice has been received and for which the exact amount of the liability is therefore often unknown. As we shall see later, there should be an "unpaid orders" file in the finance department containing copies of all official orders made for goods and services which have not yet been paid for. All unpaid orders relating to goods and services actually received in 19_5 will be listed at an estimated or quoted price on a "sundry creditors list". To comply with the theory of book-keeping, it is emphasised that only goods and services actually received during 19_5 are included. The actual date of the order is quite irrelevant and it does not matter in which year budget provision has been made. Thus goods ordered on 3 Nov. 19_5 and received on 15 Dec. 19_5 will be included as "sundry creditors". So will goods received on 21 Dec. 19_5 and confirmed by a "confirmation order" dated 3 Jan. But goods ordered on 13 Dec. and received on 1 Jan. will not be included, even though there may be budget provision, because the actual benefit is received in 19_6.

The finance department will consult other departments to confirm actual delivery dates. Departments will sometimes try to charge expenditure against the "wrong" year because provision exists in the budget for that year although in fact the actual expenditure has not taken place until the following year. This is wrong in principle and should not be allowed. Preparation of estimates is an attempt to forecast actual expenditure. The final accounts are records of fact, NOT an attempt to conform to the budget.

In addition to unpaid orders, certain other liabilities relating to 19_5 and remaining unpaid will be known from experience. Examples of liabilities falling in this category include such things as legal fees, professional fees and contract payments for revenue expenditure (eg repairs), travelling allowances and retirement benefit contributions.

In our example a single "Sundry Creditors List" could be drawn up for unpaid orders (U 38,340) and other liabilities (U 9,220) totalling U 47,560 as follows:

Expenditure Accounting

Kambale Municipal Council Estimated Creditors 19_5					
Date	Name	Details	Account to be debited	Amount	Date Paid
Nov. 14	R. Kumi	Repairs	Admin. Bldgs	1,160	28/2/_6
21	B. Juma	Stationery	Finance P&S	50	31/3/_6
Dec. 3	C. Madu	Office Supplies	Admin. P&S	100	28/2/_6
12	P. Kanu	Printing	Admin. P&S	200	28/2/_6
		(etc)		(etc)	
31	Brown & Partners	Architects Fees	Admin. Bldgs	130	30/4/_6
		(etc)		(etc)	
				47,560	

The individual items would be debited to the 19_5 expenditure analysis direct from the creditors's list, and the total would be posted to the credit of the Sundry Creditors (Control) Account.

The journal entry would be:

19_5
Dec.31
	Sundry Accounts DR.
	   To Sundry Creditors (Control)
	   Being estimated accrued
	   liabilities to date
		V
		100
			47,560	47,560

The completed Sundry Creditors (Control) Account would appear as follows:

Sundry Creditors (Control)								100
19_5 Dec.31	To Balance	c/d	316,460	19_5 Dec.31	By Sundry Accounts By Sundry Accounts By Sundry Accounts	J J J	195,440 73,460 47,560	
			316,460				316,460	
				19_6 Jan. 1	By Balance	b/d	316,460	

The total of U 316,460 has now been debited as expenditure in 19_5 and is carried forward as an outstanding liability to appear in the balance sheet as at 31 Dec. 19_5.

Municipal Accounting for Developing Countries

The creditors list will be retained in a file. It is an integral part of the accounts and must be produced at audit.

The balance of **U** 316,460 appears as an opening balance in the 19_6 ledger accounts. How is it cleared?

For invoices paid in January we have seen that the total (**U** 195,440) has been debited in a single figure, not to nominal accounts but to a special expenditure analysis "sundry creditors". Unpaid invoices were adjusted by credit (red ink) postings in the new year's accounts through the journal entry shown on pages 372-3. These two categories have now been fully dealt with.

For items appearing on the "Sundry Creditors" list, invoices will be later received for payment or vouchers made out by the finance department. Before payment is made, these invoices will be marked off (with the date paid) on the "Sundry Creditors" list to the extent of the accrued liability). The allocation (or coding) for this sum will be "SUNDRY CREDITORS" to be debited to this item in the expenditure analysis, (not to nominal accounts).

Let us suppose that during February an invoice is received from P. Kanu for printing on 12 Dec. 19_5. The invoice is for **U** 210 whereas the accrued amount (ie the sum set aside to meet the liability) was only **U** 200. Although the extra **U** 10 relates strictly to 19_5, the accounts have now been closed, so there is no alternative to charging it in 19_6 accounts. The grid stamp on the invoice would show:

	Units	Cents
Accounts Chargeable: Sundry Creditors	200	-
Admin. Printing and Stationery	10	-
	210	-

Where an over-provision has been made the odd sum must be "written back" in 19_6. Had the architects' fees for Brown and Partners finally come to **U** 125 the grid stamp on the invoice would show:

	Units	Cents
Accounts Chargeable: Sundry Creditors	130	-
Admin. Buildings	(CR) 5	-
	125	-

Again the **U** 5 should, strictly, be credited in 19_5 but the accounts have now been closed.

Expenditure Accounting

When all the outstanding accounts have been paid in 19_6 the total payments will have been debited to the "Sundry Creditors (Control)" Account. This comes about in two ways. For those invoices which were credited direct to the 19_6 expenditure accounts the entry in the Sundry Creditors (Control) Account will come from the journal entry shown on pages 372-3. The remaining items will have been debited direct to a "Sundry Creditors" item in the expenditure analysis as the cash payments were made. This would have been done either in total (for invoices paid in January) or individually (for items paid later).

The total of this analysis will be posted to the debit of the Sundry Creditors (Control) Account at the end of 19_6. The Control Account will then appear as:

	Sundry Creditors (Control)					100
19_6 Dec.31	To Sundry Accounts To Cash	C.B.	73,460 243,000	19_6 Jan. 1	By Balance	b/d	316,460
			316,460				316,460

The debit entry for "Sundry Accounts" represents item (b) on page 371 whilst that for "Cash" represents the totals of items (a) (c) and (d). You will notice that although the "Control Account" is now balanced, it has not been ruled off. This is because the 19_6 creditors will now be included on the credit side and carried forward on a balance sheet into 19_7.

NOTES:

(a) The above examples have been given to illustrate the variety of possible methods for dealing with sundry creditors. Probably the most common method is to use the "Creditors List" for all creditors, though the other methods may have advantages where data processing machines are used.

(b) The above method of dealing with sundry creditors is normally confined to revenue expenditure. Capital expenditure is normally dealt with on a "receipts and payments" basis. This is because payments relate not to a particular financial year but to a particular scheme for the construction of a fixed asset, which may sometimes take several years to complete.

124. OFFICIAL ORDER SYSTEMS

The officials of Kambale Municipal Council will issue orders for the supply of goods and services provided for in the budget. The issue of an official order commits the Council to pay for goods and services supplied under the order.

The tightest form of budgetary control is obtained by a central purchasing system under the control of the chief financial officer. Departments requiring goods and services would follow this procedure:

(a) Purchase Requisition signed by officer in charge of payment in the spending department and forwarded to the Chief Financial Officer.

Purchase Requisition is certified to effect that budget provision exists.

(b) Accountancy (or Budget) Section (on behalf of Chief Financial Officer) checks available provision.

(c) Buying and Stores Section (on behalf of Chief Financial Officer) after quotation or tendering procedure, issues official order: top copy to trader or contractor; second copy to Accountancy Section; third copy stays in Buying and Stores Section.

(d) When goods are delivered or services are rendered, invoice is sent by trader direct to Chief Financial Officer.

(e) When goods are received or services performed, goods/services received note is completed by Buyer and Stores Controller and is sent to Accountancy Section.

(f) Accountancy Section will match invoice, copy order and G.R.N., and pay trader.

Under the above system the Chief Financial Officer is without doubt acting fully as the Council's accountant and financial controller.

A less efficient, but widely practised, system is where responsibility for ordering and budgetary control rests with the spending department. Under this system the Chief Financial Officer, whilst still acting as the Council's accountant, has delegated some functions of financial control to other officers.

Because of the importance of central purchasing we shall give special consideration to this subject in a later chapter. However, in this chapter we will deal with the system in common use, whereby goods and services are ordered by heads of departments.

Orders should be issued in writing and should be signed by a responsible officer of the department concerned. No person should be permitted to issue orders for goods and services unless he is authorised to do so by the appropriate chief officer.

Orders for goods and services should be issued only on official order forms, consecutively numbered and bound into books which are kept under strict control.

Let us suppose that the works department requires some new tools and some cement. Assuming there is provision in the budget and that any tender regulations have been complied with, the supervisor of works (or a senior officer in his department) will issue an official order from his order book (sometimes known as a local purchase order) as follows:

Expenditure Accounting

(ORIGINAL)	KAMBALE MUNICIPAL COUNCIL	58463

PO Box 165,
Kambale.

To Kambale Building Supplies,
   PO Box 1234,

(Date) 25 Mar. 19_6

Please Supply:

Item No.	Quantity	Units	Description of Goods	Estimated Cost
1	10		Spear & Jackson Type "x" Spades	Units 300
2	100	Cwt bags	Tororo Type "y" cement	600

Deliver to:

Council Yard

Kambale

Invoice to:

Supervisor of Works

PO Box 165

Kambale

Expenditure analysis (code):

1. Works - tools and equipment
2. Stores

Signature: P.Q.R.

Title: Sup of Works

The order will be made out in triplicate, the original and first copy being sent to the finance department (central purchasing or expenditure section) and the remaining copy retained in the book. When the finance department is satisfied that budgetary provision exists, it will send the original to the supplier and file the copy on an "unpaid orders" file. Copy unpaid orders will be filed in numerical order.

In some authorities the original order will be sent direct to the supplier by the department concerned. In this case vote control must be exercised by the departmental chief officer. In some cases, too, the copy order is sent to the finance department together with the invoice when received, but this weakens control over duplicate payments.

Let us suppose that the cement is delivered on 14 April and an invoice is received on 16 April. The works department will stamp the invoice with a "grid stamp" and enter the order number (58463) on the stamp. At the same time the works department will check and certify that the goods are received and that the quality and quantity are satisfactory. The invoice will then be forwarded to the expenditure section of the finance department.

Municipal Accounting for Developing Countries

The finance department will check that prices and calculations are correct and will take the copy order from the "unpaid orders" file. A rubber stamp can be put on the blank space of the copy order, entered with the number and amount of the invoice and marked to show that payment will take place on 30 April 19_6. The order (being uncompleted) will be returned to the "unpaid orders" file to await the invoice for the spades. The "grid stamp" will be completed by the expenditure section and the invoice passed for payment.

Later the invoice for the spades will be received from the works department, dated (say) 17 June, the spades having been delivered on 15 April. Again the copy order will be removed from the "unpaid orders" file and marked to show that payment will take place on 30 June. The order is now completed and will be transferred to a "paid orders" file. Here it will be filed in numerical order or in alphabetical order. If filed in alphabetical order the copy orders in the "paid orders" file will provide a useful index of paid creditors.

The rubber stamp on the completed copy order will now show:

Item	Invoice	Amount	
		Units	
1	2/123456	310	x
2	2/126789	595	V
3			
4			
5			
6			
PAID:			
	V 30/4/_6		
	x 30/6/_6		

Had all the goods been supplied and invoiced at the same time the copy order would merely be stamped (say) "paid 30/4/_6" and immediately transferred to the "paid orders" file.

As an alternative to the paid orders being placed on a "paid orders" file they can be filed with the appropriate paid invoices thus keeping together all documents for the same payment. Difficulties can arise where an order is for several separate purchases which are supplied and invoiced at different times. Either the earlier invoices will be held back until all are received (which is unbusinesslike and discourteous) or there must be a system of cross-reference. It cannot be emphasised too strongly that the issue of an order is the last point at which effective budgetary control can be exercised, because the officer issuing the order is, at that stage, committing the authority to pay for the goods and services supplied. Once the goods or services have been supplied for a lawful purpose, the authority has a legal liability to pay for them (under the law of contract) whether or not funds exist in the budget. Unless budgetary control is exercised at the time of ordering, the Chief Financial Officer might be placed in an impossible position. Because of the lack of budgetary funds he might (under local government law) have to withhold payments which the authority is contractually bound to make (under the law of contract).

To prevent fraud, copy orders should be clearly printed to show that

Expenditure Accounting

they are copies and cannot be used for ordering goods. It is sometimes good practice (though expensive) to have the copies printed on coloured paper. For example, copies of local purchase orders could be coloured and bear the words:

"Copy of LOCAL PURCHASE ORDER. An order placed on this form should not be executed; the white original form only is a valid order to supply".

125. PERIODICAL PAYMENTS

Apart from payments for the supply of goods and services on official orders an authority will make regularly recurring payments of the same amount each time, such as for rents, rates, subscriptions and wayleaves.

Records of such payments should be kept in a "periodical payments" register. Such a register can be in a similar form to the "periodical income register" described in Section 110 of Chapter 10. Slight alteration to wording would produce "name and address of creditor:", "cheque to be sent to:" and so on.

Many periodical payments will be made on suppliers invoices in which case the "special instructions" would be:

"await invoice before making payment".

Sometimes a voucher will have to be made out by the finance department. As invoices or vouchers are passed for payment they will be marked off on the back of the record.

126. CAR ALLOWANCES

Another type of payment which might require a special record is that of car allowances, particularly where these allowances are based upon mileage. A record should be opened for each officer who is authorised to claim a car allowance.

Let us assume that the deputy medical officer of health of Kambale Municipal Council is permitted to claim mileage allowances on the following scale:

    First 2,400 miles per year: 50 cents per mile
    Next 12,000 miles per year: 38 cents per mile
    Remainder: 25 cents per mile.

He would keep log sheets showing the number of miles run on each authorised journey, leading to a total number of miles run during each month. At the end of each month the log sheet would be submitted to the finance department. After checking, the details would be entered in the record, and the payment calculated.

The record, showing payments for the first four months of 19_6 might appear as follows:

Municipal Accounting for Developing Countries

Name: B. Dawa				Per Month			Mileage Rate	
Post: Medical Officer							1.1._6	
Car Reg. No. USJ 488 C.C. 1194				First 200 m			50c	
Date of Committee Approval 27/3/_4				Next 1,000 m			38c	
				Remainder			25c	
Month	Mileo-meter Reading (14329)	Official Miles During Month	Official Miles Run to Date	Allocation Of Miles Run to Date			Allow-ance for Miles Run to Date	Amount Due for Month
				50c	38c	25c		
19_6							Units	Units
Jan.	15,076	360	360	200	160		161	161
Feb.	16,934	1,380	1,740	400	1,340		709	548
Mar.	17,789	520	2,260	600	1,660		931	222
Apr.	19,065	740	3,000	800	2,200		1,236	305

The claim for the April payment might appear on the back of the log sheet for that month in the following form:

Expenditure Accounting

CAR ALLOWANCE CLAIM

Name: B. Dawa   **Dept:** Health

Car Registration No: USJ 488   **c.c.:** 1194   **Make:** V.W.

1. Cumulative official miles run from 1 Jan. to 30/4/_6 = 3,000

2. Allowance for cumulative mileage:

800 miles @ 50 cents	400
2,200 miles @ 38 cents	836
-------- miles @ 25 cents	
3,000	1,236

3. Less total allowance due to end of March — 931

4. Amount now due — 305

CERTIFICATE BY CLAIMANT

I certify that I have included against item (1) above only mileage for official journeys which have been properly authorised.

(Signed) B. Dawa   (Date) 30/4/_6

CERTIFICATE BY HEAD OF DEPARTMENT

I certify the above claim to be for official journeys which were properly authorised.

(Signed) F. Lumu   (Date) 30/4/_6

EXPENDITURE CHARGED TO:
Health Department - Car and Cycle Allowances.

The number of miles permitted to be run annually at different mileage rates has been divided into monthly proportions and the calculation of the allowance is cumulative.

At the end of April the officer has run 3,000 miles on official business and he is entitled to receive payment for the first 800 miles (ie four months at 200 miles per month) at the rate of 50 cents per mile. The next 4,000 miles (ie four months at 1,000 miles per month) is paid for at 38 cents per mile. This is not exceeded in our example. When the cumulative allowance has been calculated, the total previously paid is deducted, leaving the amount due for the current month.

Municipal Accounting for Developing Countries

The mileometer reading is included for audit purposes. An auditor checking the register for the March claim might work out:

Mileometer reading 31/3/_6	=	17,789
Mileometer reading 28/2/_6	=	16,934
Total miles run during March	=	855
Less Official mileage		520
Remainder		335

The auditor would then weigh up whether the remainder, being private running, was credible. On the face of it, 335 miles appears reasonable for one month's private mileage but if the officer was daily travelling 20 miles each way from his home to the office or if the auditor knew that the car had been taken on a trip to the coast during one weekend, he might have some awkward questions to ask!

Some authorities pay all the mileage at the higher rate first, only dropping to lower rates when the initial mileage allowance has been used up. There can be no real objection to this procedure, which is more simple to operate than the one shown above and which gives the same figure for total mileage paid during the year. There are however certain disadvantages as follows:

(a) officers serving for only part of the financial year will get a larger proportion of their allowance at the higher rate per mile unless some adjustment is made;

(b) when the initial mileage runs out, the officer will suffer a drop in actual cash paid to him and might be tempted to inflate future claims in an attempt to maintain his previous level of cash receipts; and

(c) the outward cash flow tends to be heavier during the earlier part of the financial year - to the authority's disadvantage.

The preparation and checking of claims involves a good deal of clerical work. Wherever possible, fixed consolidated allowances should be paid, which will eliminate nearly all of this detailed checking. The fixed allowance should genuinely represent the average mileage run during each month and should be adjusted if the officer is obviously making less use of his car for official business.

For simplicity, details of consolidated mileages have not been shown in the above records and no mention has been made of the problem of differential mileage rates for "tar" and "dirt" roads. In practice, the records would be adapted to take account of these matters.

127. CONTRACTS AND PROFESSIONAL FEES

Contract payments differ from the payments to other creditors in the following important ways:

(a) the contractors are paid by instalments, because building and engineering contracts involve large sums of money and because the work is spread over a comparatively long period;

(b) each instalment paid to a contractor is based on an assessment of the money value of the work which has been carried out by him - the assessment is made by quantity surveyors or other technical

Expenditure Accounting

experts and a certificate is then issued by the architect or engineer in charge, showing the amount to be paid; and

(c) contracts normally provide for a percentage (often 10%) to be deducted from the instalments paid to contractors - to be retained by the authority until the engineer or architect issues a certificate that the contractor has discharged his contractual liabilities.

The only acceptable voucher to support a contract payment is a certificate (interim or final) issued by the appropriate technical officer.

Where the contract is being supervised by the authority's own technical staff the certificate will be signed by the chief officer (ie head of department) concerned, such as the "Town Engineer" or "City Architect".

A contracts register will be kept by the finance department in which will be recorded details of instalments paid to contractors and percentage deductions made from such payments for retention. Most contracts are for capital works. We can therefore take an example from the capital programme shown on page 287 of Chapter 9. Let us assume we are dealing with item No.8 "Roads - Dwonga Road - Complete Tarmac to Boundary" and that the final costs have worked out as follows:

	Units
Contract	1,315,400
Quantity Surveyors Fees	39,500
Proportion of Salaries of Council's Works Department (Capital Salaries)	92,000
Legal Fees, Printing and Stationery etc.	3,700
TOTAL	1,450,600

The contracts register might appear as shown on page 386.

The amounts shown on the left hand side are cumulative amounts. The contractor has been paid in fifteen instalments, the supervising engineer having issued fourteen "interim certificates" and then a final certificate after the checking of the final account. The certificate forms used by the supervising engineer might be in a numbered pad - the consecutive number of each certificate issued appears in column (2). The numbers do not follow one another because there would be several certificates for various other jobs to be issued each month.

To demonstrate how each payment is calculated let us examine instalment No.8.

During July the quantity surveyors will inspect the progress of the work and will calculate as accurately as possible that the value of the work done to date is U 683,000. On 27 July the supervising engineer will issue interim certificate No.8 certifying that an additional U 172,800 is due to Tarmac Ltd calculated as follows:

REGISTER OF CONTRACTS AND PROFESSIONAL FEES

Folio _____

To Whom Payable: Tarmac Ltd
Committee: Works
Address: PO Box 854, Kambale
Date of Contract: 14 October 19_3
Amount of Contract of Fees: U 1,310,000
Min. Ref: FIN.146/_3
Loan Sanction: U 1,360,000
Details of Contract or Fees: Dwonga Road — Complete Tarmac to Boundary

Details of Certificates or Claims

Date	No	Inst No	Value of Work to Date	Retention %	Retention Amount	Net Amount Due to Date
19_3						
Nov.23	463	1	5,000	10	500	4,500
Dec.21	469	2	12,500	10	1,250	11,250
19_4						
Feb.21	496	3	65,000	10	6,500	58,500
Mar.24	504	4	158,000	10	15,800	142,200
Apr.24	510	5	269,000	10	26,900	242,100
May 23	519	6	375,000	10	37,500	337,500
Jun.26	526	7	491,000	10	49,100	441,900
Jul.27	531	8	683,000	10	68,300	614,700
Aug.21	538	9	947,000	10	94,700	852,300
Sep.19	547	10	1,151,000	10	115,100	1,035,900
Oct.22	552	11	1,248,000	10	124,800	1,123,200
Nov.23	560	12	1,312,500	10	131,250	1,181,250
Dec.20	567	13	1,312,500	5	65,625	1,246,875
19_5						
Jul.14	594	14	1,312,500	1	13,125	1,299,375
Dec.21	636	F	1,315,400	-	-	1,315,400
			=========	==	=======	=========

Amounts Paid

Date	Amount	Total To Date	Notes
19_3			
Nov.30	4,500	4,500	
Dec.31	6,750	11,250	
19_4			
Feb.28	47,250	58,500	
Mar.31	83,700	142,200	
Apr.30	99,900	242,100	
May 29	95,400	337,500	
Jun.30	104,400	441,900	
Jul.31	172,800	614,700	
Aug.31	237,600	852,300	
Sep.30	183,600	1,035,900	
Oct.31	87,300	1,123,200	
Nov.30	58,050	1,181,250	
19_5			
Jan. 2	65,625	1,246,875	
Jul.18	52,500	1,299,375	Practical Completion
Dec.31	16,025	1,315,400	Completion of Maintenance
	1,315,400		
	=========	=========	

Expenditure Accounting

Value of work to date as calculated by quantity surveyors	683,000
Less Retention at 10% as provided for in the contract	68,300
Total amount so far due to the contractor	614,700
Less Total cash already paid to the contractor on certificates 1-7	441,900
Amount now due	172,800

Details of the certificate will be entered in the register as shown and a cheque will be drawn on 31 July for U 172,800.

This procedure continues until the work is finished, just before 23 Nov. On this date the work is valued at U 1,312,500 and an interim payment is made as before. During December the supervising engineer satisfies himself that the work is properly completed and issues to the contractor a "certificate of practical completion". At this stage it is common for a proportion of the "retention money" to be released to the contractor. In our example one half has been released, reducing the percentage retained from 10% to 5%. So, although the value of the work is unchanged, the contractor receives an additional U 65,625 on 2 Jan. 19_5 as a result of certificate No.13. For an agreed period after practical completion, the contractor is liable to make good, at his own expense, any defects appearing in the work (eg cracks which may appear in the new road surface). In our example we have assumed a "maintenance period" of six months, although twelve months is not unusual for road works. In July the supervisor inspects the work again and when he is satisfied that all defects have been made good he releases nearly all the balance of retention money on certificate No.14. Only 1% is now retained to cover possible fluctuations in the final account. The contractor will by now have submitted his final account, and after measurement and checking by quantity surveyors and examination by the internal audit section the sum of U 1,315,400 is agreed as the final value of the work. The supervising engineer than issues the final certificate authorising payment of the outstanding balance, including the remainder of the retention money.

The contracts register can be in a bound book or made up of loose leaf sheets filed in alphabetical order of contractor.

In our example, a page in the contracts register could be used to record the payment of professional fees to the quantity surveyors. It is quite common to make an interim payment to quantity surveyors after the "bills of quantities" have been prepared and perhaps other interim payments for measurement of the contractor's work. It is not normal to deduct "retention money" from professional fees.

The same record could be used for instalments of fees paid to private firms of architects or engineers (as appropriate). This does not apply in our example, because the technical supervision has been carried out by officers of the council's own works department. A proportion of their salaries are charged against the capital scheme instead of engineers' fees.

128. OCCASIONAL PAYMENTS

Sometimes payments arise which are not the subject of official orders or contracts; nor are they salaries, car allowances, refunds or periodical payments. Such payments include legal fees, ex gratia payments, damage to crops or public utility services, and other miscellaneous payments authorised in committee minutes. (An ex gratia payment is made to settle a claim made on the authority where no legal liability exists but where there is a strong moral obligation wholly or partially to recompense the claimant).

To avoid the possibility of duplicate payment the details should be entered in chronological order in an "Occasional Payments Register" as shown below:

Date Paid	To Whom Paid	Details	Amount	Authority	Checked by
19_6					
3 May	Brown & Smith	Legal Fees	135	F.13/_6	A.B.
16 Jun.	B. Musoke	Ex-gratia Payment	200	F.21/_6	A.B.
26 Jul.	National Theatre	Donation	500	F.34/_6	C.D.

Payments of this type are normally so few in number that it is a simple matter to scrutinize the register for previous payments before any payment is made. No other records are necessary.

129. REFUNDS

It is sometimes necessary to make refunds of sums originally collected as income, such as for rates or rents. These payments will affect income records as well as expenditure records and care must be taken that the double-entry system is not put out of balance, by dealing with only one aspect. The voucher for refunds will normally be initiated in the income section. This section will record the refund against the appropriate name in its records and then pass the voucher to the expenditure section. The expenditure section might need to record the refund in a suitable register before making the payment. Periodically this Refunds Register will be balanced in total against the records in the income section and against the appropriate analysis of expenditure in the accountancy section.

For example, the U 900 refunded to Mr B. Ongira for rates (see page 320 of Chapter 10) has been entered in the rate book by the income section. The expenditure section might enter up the "Rates Refund Register", giving details of name and address; date of original receipt of the cash; reason for the refund; date and amount of the refund; and a reference to the original entry in the rate book.

The total of the entries in this register for 19_6 will agree with the total refunds figure of U 4,860 in column (f) of the rate book summary shown on page 317 of Chapter 10.

130. SALARIES AND WAGES

In dealing with payments for work done by employees it is usual to distinguish between "salaries" and "wages".

Salaries are usually regarded as payments made to administrative and technical staff who are employed on a permanent basis at agreed annual rates of pay.

Wages are usually regarded as payments made to manual workers who are

Expenditure Accounting

employed on a less permanent basis at agreed hourly, daily or monthly rates of pay.

Salary earners are normally covered by special employment conditions laid down by the authority, whereas wage-earners are normally covered by minimum conditions laid down by law together with trade union agreements.

Initial Information

In order that an employee can be paid, someone must calculate the gross pay due to him for a particular period of work. For salaries, this will normally be 1/12 of the annual salary as shown by the personal record.

For wages each employee might submit a time-sheet, showing the various tasks he has done during the month, the number of hours worked on each job and the calculated amount of his gross pay. Where groups of workers are employed in gangs, or where the workers are illiterate, it will often be the job of a foreman to submit muster rolls for the employees under his control.

When a time-sheet or muster roll is received by the finance department it will be checked to see that hours or days of work are correct; that the rate of pay is correct; that the authorised establishment is not being exceeded; and that the document is properly certified by the foreman. This work will often be carried out by a salaries and wages sub-section of the expenditure section or by a separate establishment section.

Personal Records

A personal record card (or sheet) will be maintained in the establishment section, for each employee, whether salaried or wage-earning. Each personal record will contain some or all of the following information about the employee:

(a) name;

(b) details of employment;

(c) date of appointment;

(d) annual or monthly salary;

(e) scale or grading giving details of increments;

(f) details of provident fund or superannuation deductions;

(g) minute references for appointment or variation of terms of service;

(h) details of leave and sickness;

(i) details of absence from duty;

(j) details of special allowances;

(k) details of deductions to be made from gross pay;

(l) training record; and

(m) examinations passed.

Municipal Accounting for Developing Countries

The gross pay for each employee will be calculated, either from the above information (in the case of salaries) or from time-sheets or muster rolls (in the case of wages) and entered on the personal record. Details of deductions from gross pay will be entered in special columns on the record and deducted from gross pay to give the net pay due. Items to be deducted from gross pay might include:

(a)   graduated tax;

(b)   income tax;

(c)   provident fund contributions;

(d)   superannuation contributions;

(e)   rent;

(f)   vehicle advance repayments;

(g)   personal advances;

(h)   court orders; and

(i)   trade union dues.

A personal record sheet for the Principal Assistant in the Finance Department of Kambale Municipal Council (Mr Kilama) might appear for the month of March 19_6 as follows:

Expenditure Accounting

```
┌─────────────────────────────────────────────────────────────────┐
│                    EMPLOYEE'S PERSONAL RECORD                   │
│                                                                 │
│  Name:   Kilama A.B.                  Dept: Finance             │
│  Post:   Principal Assistant          Date of Appointment: 1/5/_2 │
│  Annual Salary:  U 16,500 (1/1/_6)    Monthly Salary: U 1,375   │
│  Details of Salary Scale:   13,500 x 500 - 16,000 (basic)       │
│                                                                 │
│       Special increment 1,000 p.a. for Municipal Accounting (1st Cert) │
│  -------------------------------------------------------------- │
│  Provident Fund:  5% of basic salary (825 per annum)            │
│                                                                 │
│  Minutes:  F.24/_2, F.121/_5                                    │
│                                              DEDUCTIONS         │
│  Annual Leave:  25 days                                         │
│                                            1.1._6               │
│                                            Units                │
│  Examinations:  Municipal Accounting                            │
│      (1st Cert) (passed Dec. 19_5)   Prov.F   69                │
│  Incremental Date:  1st Jan.         Rent    300                │
│  Allowances:   Housing U 200 month   Vehicle 200                │
│                                                                 │
├─────────────────────────────────────────────────────────────────┤
│  Remarks:  Acted as Deputy Chief Financial Officer during Feb. 19_6 - │
│            allowance U 110                                      │
└─────────────────────────────────────────────────────────────────┘
```

Month	Basic Pay	Addi-tional Items	Gross Pay	Deductions			Total Deduc-tions	Net Pay
				P.F.	Rent	Veh-icle		
19_6								
Jan.	1,375	200	1,575	69	300	200	569	1,006
Feb.	1,375	200 110	1,685	69	300	200	569	1,116
Mar.	1,375	200	1,575	69	300	200	569	1,006

In practice there would be a greater number of columns for deductions.

Payrolls

The monthly salaries and wages will be summarised on payrolls. The payrolls might be divided into sections for each department. For Kambale Municipal Council, part of the payroll for the finance department might appear for the month of March 19_6 as shown on page 392.

For wages payments, the muster rolls sent to the finance department by various other departments might be used as the payrolls to save paper and clerical labour. The establishment section would then confine its work to checking.

Where cheques are drawn (see later) for the payment of individual salaries or wages, the last column of the payroll could be used for recording cheque numbers against each employee. Where payment is made in cash, this column could be used for signatures of employees as they are paid.

If a carbon copy of each payroll is taken, this copy could be perforated into horizontal strips to provide an advice note for each employee. Modern manual and computer systems provide for the personal records, the payroll and the advice notes to be prepared at one writing.

PAYROLL
FINANCE DEPARTMENT
March 19_6

No	Name	Basic Pay	Additional Items	Gross Pay	Provi-dent Fund	Rent	Vehicle Advances	Gradu-ated Tax	Total Deduc-tions	Net Pay
1.	Musoke	2,050	200(H)	2,250	102	350	150	-	602	1,648
2.	Kibule	1,515	200(H)	1,715	76	300	-	-	376	1,339
3.	Kilama	1,375	200(H)	1,575	69	300	200	-	569	1,006
4.	Mukasa	1,067	50(A) 150(H)	1,267	-	-	-	75	75	1,192
	(etc)	(etc)	(etc)	(etc)	(etc)	(etc)	(etc)	(etc)	(etc)	(etc)
	TOTAL	30,650	300(A) 3,580(H)	34,530	1,450	2,850	2,560	1,540	8,400	26,130

(It is assumed that the three most senior officers of the finance department paid their graduated tax in full on 1 January.)

H = Housing Allowance
A = Acting Allowance

Expenditure Accounting

It might be found preferable (particularly where special systems are in use) to show only the minimum of personal details on the "employee's personal record" and to keep the majority of information in a separate permanent record.

Payment of Net Salaries and Wages

When the payrolls have been prepared and totalled, arrangements must be made for the payment of net pay to each employee. There are three main ways of doing this:

(a) by individual cheques to each employee;

(b) by bank transfers; and

(c) by cash.

Salaries are likely to be paid by cheques or bank transfers, whereas wages are more likely to be paid in cash.

Where individual cheques are used, one cheque will be made out for each employee and included in the cheque list like other payments. Each cheque will, of course, be for the amount of "net pay" due. Under UK-type banking systems, it is sometimes the practice for salary payments to be made on uncrossed cheques to enable staff to cash them at the bank. Where the authority uses cheques with printed crossings for its normal payments, the crossings will have to be "opened", if uncrossed cheques are requested by employees. Alternatively a single crossed cheque for total salaries could be drawn and paid into a special "salaries" bank account. A special series of uncrossed cheques would then be drawn on this special account.

Where uncrossed cheques are used, they should be collected personally and signed for by the payees, because uncrossed cheques, whilst not open to quite the same risks as cash, can easily be turned into cash by unauthorised persons. Crossed cheques should be used wherever possible.

If bank transfers are made, the authority's bank will require several copies of a list of the employees concerned and amounts payable, prepared to the bank's instructions. By cheque or otherwise, the bank will require authority to make a single debit in the Council's bank account. The bank will then arrange for individual salaries to be credited to the bank accounts of the employees concerned, either at that branch or at other branches or other banks, as notified. A commission is usually charged by the bank for this service.

Where payments are made in cash, a single cheque will be drawn for the total "net pay" on each payroll or each group of payrolls. Pay packets should always be made up in the finance department. Sometimes the wages cheques might be sent to various outside departments, together with a copy of the payroll or a list of payments due to each employee. This system is not to be recommended because of the serious risks of fraud which can occur when the same persons are responsible for preparing payrolls and paying cash.

Cash payments, whether loose or in pay packets, should be made to employees by at least two officers, one of whom can identify the employees concerned (eg a foreman or supervisor). Unpaid wages should be returned to the finance department and recorded in an unpaid wages book.

Each copy payroll or list of payments should be returned to the finance department bearing certificates in something like the following form:

Municipal Accounting for Developing Countries

I certify that I have today paid to each employee the sum set out against his name as "net pay", except where marked "unpaid". Unpaid wages totalling Units   Cts. have been returned to the finance department.

_____   _____
         (date)   (paying officer)

I certify that the payment of wages to the employees shown above, except where marked "unpaid" was made in my presence. I personally identified each person receiving wages as the employee named on the payroll.

_____   _____
         (date)   (witnessing officer)

The unpaid wages book might be ruled as follows:

Date Due	Name	Department	Amount	Signature or Date Banked	Initials of Payer

Deductions

As well as payments of "net pay" to employees, the various deductions will have to be accounted for, either by cheques to the appropriate authorities or by internal adjustment. Deductions will be dealt with as shown in the following table:

Deduction	Remarks	Procedure
1. Income Tax		Cheque to Income Tax Authority
2. Graduated Tax	a) Tax due to another Authority	Cheque to Graduated Tax Authority
	b) Tax due to own Authority	Internal Adjustment
3. Provident Fund or Superannuation Contributions	a) Outside Fund	Cheque to the appropriate Fund Authority
	b) Internal Fund	Internal Adjustment
4. Court Orders		Cheque to the Registrar of the Court concerned
5. Rents	a) Where Local Authority is not the Landlord	Cheque to the Housing Authority concerned
6. Vehicle Advances		) Internal Adjustment unless
7. Personal Advances		) acting as agent for another) body - when cheques will be) sent to that body
8. Trade Union Dues		Cheque to Trade Union

Expenditure Accounting

Only one cheque should be sent to each authority each month, for the total amount of deductions made from all wages and salaries. Separate cheques should not be sent for deductions from each department.

Generally, the amount on each cheque will be the total deductions made under that item during a particular month. With superannuation or provident fund contributions, however, the cheque must include the amount of the authority's contribution to the fund, as well as that deducted from employees.

In theory internal adjustments could be made by journal entries in the following form:

Salaries DR.
Wages DR.
  To Graduated Tax (own)
  To Provident Fund (internal)
  To Rent
  To Vehicle Advances
  To Personal Advances
Being internal adjustment from
salaries and wages for the month			

In practice it would be better to use "internal cash transfer" slips because income records, as well as expenditure records, are affected.

Accountancy

Whilst the actual payment of salaries and wages is fairly straightforward, some accountancy problems are encountered because:

(a) deductions and employers' contributions must be accounted for;

(b) gross pay plus employers' contributions must be allocated (coded) to appropriate expenditure heads; and

(c) deductions are not always paid over promptly to the appropriate authorities and in particular may be held over the end of the financial year.

It must be appreciated that the cost of wages and salaries which is borne by the authority is not merely the total net payments made to employees, nor yet is it the gross pay and allowances earned by employees. It is the gross pay and allowances earned by employees plus any employers contributions, usually towards pension funds.

Let us suppose that the payment of salaries and wages of Kambale Municipal Council for March 19_6 works out as follows:

Municipal Accounting for Developing Countries

(a) Salaries
    Gross Pay - Basic   285,180
              - Additional Items   31,240   316,420

    Less Provident Fund   13,260
        Rent   15,100
        Vehicle Advances   12,500
        Graduated Tax   5,760   46,620
                                                                           269,800

(b) Wages
    Gross Pay   141,480
    Less Provident Fund   5,320
        Graduated Tax   2,140
        Trade Union Dues   880   8,340
                                                                            133,140

Let us also suppose that the Council contributes to the provident fund an amount equal to the employees' contributions.

The following table shows how payments are related to expenditure:

Expenditure	Amount	Payments	Amount
Salaries:		Salaries:	
Gross Pay	316,420	Net Pay	269,800
Provident Fund		Provident Fund	26,520
(Council's Contribution)	13,260	Rent	15,100
		Vehicle Advances	12,500
		Graduated Tax	5,760
	329,680		329,680
Wages:		Wages:	
Gross Pay	141,480	Net Pay	133,140
Provident Fund		Provident Fund	10,640
(Council's Contribution)	5,320	Graduated Tax	2,140
		Trade Union Dues	880
	146,800		146,800

The left-hand entries show how the expenditure will be debited in the nominal accounts and the right-hand entries show how the corresponding payments are credited in the cash book. Taking salaries as our example we find that, in theory, there are two stages. The first stage, when the salaries have been calculated and become payable, is represented (in theory) by the following journal entry:

Expenditure Accounting

19_6 Mar.31				
	Salaries	DR.	316,420	
	Provident Fund	DR.	13,260	
	To Sundry Employees			269,800
	To Provident Fund			26,520
	To Housing Authority			15,100
	To Vehicle Advances Authority			12,500
	To Graduated Tax Authority			5,760
	Being net pay and deductions now due to employees and other bodies		329,680	329,680

The debit entries represent all the various debits which would be made to nominal accounts (eg Finance Department - salaries, Health Department - provident fund) whilst the credit entries represent postings to personal accounts, pending actual payment.

In each case the amount credited is the amount deducted from salaries except of course that "Sundry Employees" have been credited with net pay and the provident fund has been credited with the amount deducted from salaries (U 13,260) plus the equivalent amount contributed by the Council (another U 13,260) making U 26,520 altogether.

When the actual cash is paid out (or cash transfer slips passed through the books for internal adjustments) the journal entry (in theory) is as follows:

19_6 (Date)				
	Sundry Employees	DR.	269,800	
	Provident Fund	DR.	26,520	
	Housing Authority	DR.	15,100	
	Vehicle Advances Authority	DR.	12,500	
	Graduated Tax Authority	DR.	5,760	
	To Cash			329,680
	Being payment of amounts due to employees and other authorities		329,680	329,680

In practice, the book-keeping would be carried out by short-cut procedures.

The first (and simplest) alternative would be to credit the cash payments in the cash book (via the cheque list) and debit the appropriate nominal accounts direct from the summaries of the payrolls with the gross pay and provident fund contributions. This procedure is only possible where the salary or wages allocation is fairly straightforward (eg a single posting for each department or service) and where deductions are all paid over in the year in which they are made.

Where a complete costing system is in operation or where individual employees have their salaries or wages allocated to several heads of account, more complex accounting arrangements are necessary. This is also true where deductions are not all paid over in the year in which they are made.
Control accounts will be opened for "salaries" and for "wages". The gross pay and employers contributions will be debited to various expenditure heads (or codes) from payrolls, muster rolls or time-sheets as explained later in this book. The totals of these allocations will

be credited to the control accounts. For Kambale Muncipal Council the journal entries (in theory) for March would be:

19_6				
Mar.31	Sundry Expenditure Accounts DR. To Salaries (Control) Being allocation of salaries and provident fund contributions for month as shown by payrolls	V 1	329,680	329,680
Mar.31	Sundry Expenditure Accounts DR. To Wages (Control) Being allocation of wages and provident fund contributions for month as shown by time- sheets and muster rolls	V 2	146,800	146,800

The actual payment of "net pay" internal deductions will be debited to the control accounts and the actual payment of external deductions will be debited to appropriate personal accounts, direct from the cash book (via the cheque list). Journal entries will complete the adjustments between control accounts and personal accounts, which might appear (for March) as follows, (assuming Provident Fund, Graduated Tax and Trade Union authorities to be external and the remaining deductions to be internal):

	Salaries (Control)							1
19_6 Mar.31	To Cash (Net Pay) To Cash Transfers Rent Vehicle Advances To Provident Fund To Graduated Tax	C.B. C.B. C.B. J J	269,800 15,100 12,500 26,520 5,760 ——— 329,680 ======		19_6 Mar.31	By Sundry Accounts	J	329,680 ——— 329,680 ======

398

Expenditure Accounting

Wages (Control) — 2

19_6				19_6			
Mar.31	To Cash (Net Pay)	C.B.	133,140	Mar.31	By Sundry Accounts	J	146,800
	To Provident Fund	J	10,640				
	To Graduated Tax	J	2,140				
	To Trade Union	J	880				
			146,800				146,800

Provident Fund Authority — 3

19_6				19_6			
Mar. 4	To Cash	C.B.	36,880	Mar. 1	By Balance	b/d	36,880
31	To Balance	c/d	37,160	31	By Salaries (Control)	J	26,520
				31	By Wages (Control)	J	10,640
			74,040				74,040
				Apr. 1	By Balance	b/d	37,160

Graduated Tax Authority — 4

19_6				19_6			
Mar. 5	To Cash	C.B.	7,400	Mar. 1	By Balance	b/d	7,400
31	To Balance	c/d	7,900	31	By Salaries (Control)	J	5,760
				31	By Wages (Control)	J	2,140
			15,300				15,300
				Mar.31	By Balance	b/d	7,900

Municipal Accounting for Developing Countries

			General Workers Union				5
19_6 Mar. 5	To Cash	C.B.	860	19_6 Mar. 1	By Balance	b/d	860
31	To Balance	c/d	880	31	By Wages (Control)		880
			1,740				1,740
			=====				=====
				Apr. 1	By Balance	b/d	880

The journal entries (in theory) would have been:

19_6 Mar.31	Salaries (Control) Wages (Control) To Provident Fund Authority Being deductions from gross pay and Council's equivalent contributions	DR. DR.	1 2 3	26,520 10,640	37,160
Mar.31	Salaries (Control) Wages (Control) To Graduated Tax Authority Being deductions from gross pay	DR. DR.	1 2 4	5,760 2,140	7,900
Mar.31	Wages (Control) To General Workers Union Being deductions from gross pay	DR.	2 5	880	880

In practice the cash payments would probably be accumulated month by month in the personal accounts by means of expenditure analysis. A single total for payments made during the year would be posted from the expenditure analysis to each personal account. In addition there could be cumulative summaries of monthly payrolls building up to annual totals. The main journal entries would then need to be done only once, at the end of the financial year, and complete personal accounts would appear only in the final ledger.

131. PAYMENTS IN ADVANCE

From time to time during a financial year, payments are made covering expenditure partly in one year and partly in the next. A good example might be a fire insurance premium paid on (say) 1 October 19_6 to cover the period until 30 September 19_7 and amounting to **U** 120.

According to strict book-keeping theory, the expenditure should be allocated proportionately to each year. The standard procedure suggested in text books is to carry a balance forward on the appropriate nominal account as follows:

Expenditure Accounting

Fire Insurance								
19_6 Jan. 1	To Balance	b/f	90	19_6 Dec.31	By Revenue Account	J	120	
Oct. 1	To Cash	C.B.	120	31	By Balance	c/d	90	
			210				210	
19_7 Jan.1	To Balance	b/d	90					

The sum transferred to the revenue account represents the unexpired payment of U 90 brought forward from 19_5, together with the first U 30 of the payment made in October 19_6. The remaining U 90 of the 19_6 payment relates to 19_7 and is carried forward. (For simplicity, apportionment has been made on a monthly basis and not on a daily basis).

In practice, the above procedure would rarely be used, because where similar payments occur year after year the same effect can be obtained by charging each payment to the revenue account of the year in which it is made. Thus in our example the U 120 paid in October 19_6, would be wholly debited in the 19_6 revenue account, the earlier payment having been debited wholly in 19_5 and so on.

The same could apply to monthly or quarterly payments, whether in arrear or in advance. For example if an electricity meter were read on 15 Dec. 19_6 and the account received on 5 Jan. 19_7 the amount would probably be accrued as a sundry creditor for 19_6. But no attempt would be made to apportion the next account to determine how much of it related to electricity consumed from 16-31 December. It would be charged wholly in Jan. 19_7.

Here is an example of where a finance officer uses the art of approximation and how strict book-keeping theory is modified to solve practical problems. The main rule to follow is to ensure that one annual payment, four quarterly payments or twelve monthly payments fall in the same financial year. Very occasionally a payment will be made in one year which definitely relates to the year following and cannot be covered by the normal practice shown above. In such a case the payment would be debited to a "payments in advance" account and the balance carried forward in the balance sheet instead of being debited to the revenue account. In the following year a journal entry would be made.

For example, if you will refer to the balance sheet of Kambale Municipal Council on page 285 of Chapter 9, you will see an item of "Payments in Advance" amounting to U 4,840. Let us suppose that U 4,000 of this figure was rent for temporary storage accommodation to be occupied only during 19_6 but which was paid for in advance on 30 Nov. 19_5.

The 19_5 accounts would show:

    DR. Payments in Advance (19_6).)
    CR. Cash.   ) U 4,000

The U 4,000 is carried forward as a debit balance and included in the balance sheet (as part of the U 4,840) and in 19_6 a journal entry would show:

19_6				
Jan. 1	Revenue Account (Rent) DR. To Payments in Advance Being advance payment of rent now charged to Revenue Account		4,000	4,000

132. ADVANCES AND DEPOSITS

Where a sum of money is advanced to an employee or other person an "advance account" (ie a debtor's personal account) must be opened in the name of the person concerned. The amount advanced, together with any interest accruing from time to time, will be debited in the advance account and subsequent repayments or recoveries from salary will be credited. Any debit balances at the end of a financial period will be carried forward in the ledger accounts and included in the balance sheet. Such advances will include "motor car" and "personal" advances.

Where a sum of money is received which is not income due to the authority a "deposit account" (ie a creditor's personal account) must be opened in the name of the person paying the money or in the name of the person or body to whom the money will ultimately be paid. The amount received will be credited in the deposit account and subsequent payments will be debited. Any credit balances at the end of a financial period will be carried forward in the ledger accounts and included in the balance sheet. Such deposits will include money collected by a local authority as agent for another body (eg Central Government).

Individual advance and deposit accounts can be kept in conventional ledger form, and will follow ordinary book-keeping procedures. If they are numerous, "advance accounts" will be grouped together in an "advances ledger" and "deposit accounts" will be grouped together in a "deposits ledger".

It will be useful to keep a control account for each group, against which the individual cash transactions can be proved.

In "advance" accounts the original debits will usually come from expenditure vouchers and subsequent credits will come from copy receipts. In "deposit" accounts, the original credits will come from copy receipts and the subsequent debits from expenditure vouchers. Using the balance brought forward as shown on page 314 of Chapter 10, a control account for the motor advances of Kambale Municipal Council for 19_6 might appear as follows:

Motor Advances (Control)

19_6			19_6		
Jan. 1	To Balance b/f	27,300	Dec.31	By Repayments	
Dec.31	To New Advances	90,000		with Interest	36,040
	To Interest	5,440		By Balance c/d	86,700
		122,740			122,740
		=======			=======
19_7					
Jan. 1	To Balance b/d	86,700			

Expenditure Accounting

The item for "new advances" will be posted in total from the expenditure analysis and will agree in total with the individual advances in various accounts. The item for "interest" will be posted by a journal entry, based on the total interest debited to individual accounts as follows:

19_6			
Dec.31	Motor Advances (Control) DR. To Revenue Account (Interest) Being interest on advances accruing for year	5,440	5,440

The item for "Repayments with Interest" will be posted in total from the income analysis and will agree with the individual repayments on various personal accounts.

To simplify the monthly balancing of individual advance accounts a columnar system might be used as shown on page 404. Interest is assumed to be charged at the rate of 6% per annum (i.e. $\frac{1}{2}$% per month) on outstanding individual balances, calculated to the nearest unit. To save space the same column can be used for "advances" and "interest". Advances could be written in different coloured ink and in any case will be comparatively few and easily identified by the large sums involved. The account for Feb. 19_6 would be balanced as follows:

Motor Advances (Control)

19_6			19_6		
Feb. 1	To Balance b/f	41,300	Feb.28	By Repayments	2,406
28	To Advances	12,000		By Balance c/d	51,100
	To Interest	206			
		53,506			53,506
Mar. 1	To Balance b/d	51,100			

As an alternative to calculating monthly interest, it is often the practice to make a "compounded" interest charge on the balance outstanding at the beginning of the year, thus saving work whilst giving substantially the same effect. This can be illustrated by assuming a loan of U 12,000 outstanding at 1 Jan. in any year, being repaid at the rate of U 1,000 per month plus interest @ 6%. The repayment table would be:

REGISTER OF MOTOR ADVANCES

Name	Balance 1.1.6	Advances Interest	Repayments (Including Interest)	Balance 1.2.6	Advances Interest	Repayments (Including Interest)	Balance 1.3.6	Advances Interest	Repayments (Including Interest)	Balance 1.4.6	
Musoke	8,500		300	8,243		300	7,984		300	7,724	(etc)
INT		43			41			40			
Kilama	6,400		200	6,232		200	6,063		200	5,893	(etc)
INT		32			31			30			
Baletta	2,100		–	2,111		–	2,122		2,133	–	(etc)
INT		11			11			11			
Odonga	–	16,000	400	15,600		400	15,278		400	14,954	(etc)
INT					78			76			
Avua	–				12,000	300	11,700		300	11,459	(etc)
INT								59			
(etc)	(etc)	(etc)	(etc)	(etc)	(etc)	(etc)	(etc)	(etc)	(etc)	(etc)	(etc)
	27,300	16,000*	2,136	41,300	12,000*	2,406	51,100		2,355	49,000	
INT		136			206			255			

Expenditure Accounting

Date	Principal Repayment	Interest	Monthly Instalment	Balance
1 Jan.				12,000
31 Jan.	1,000	60	1,060	11,000
28 Feb.	1,000	55	1,055	10,000
31 Mar.	1,000	50	1,050	9,000
30 Apr.	1,000	45	1,045	8,000
31 May	1,000	40	1,040	7,000
30 June	1,000	35	1,035	6,000
31 July	1,000	30	1,030	5,000
31 Aug.	1,000	25	1,025	4,000
30 Sept.	1,000	20	1,020	3,000
31 Oct.	1,000	15	1,015	2,000
30 Nov.	1,000	10	1,010	1,000
31 Dec.	1,000	5	1,005	-
TOTALS	12,000	390	12,390	

Suppose now that instead of interest at 6% per annum being charged on monthly balances, 3% is charged on the opening balance of U 12,000. This will give annual interest of U 400. Instalments will then be

$$\frac{12,000 + 400}{12} = U\ 1,033$$

The slightly higher amount of the interest is justified by the fact that lower instalments are being paid at the beginning of the year, than with the other method.

A further refinement, and probably the best method, would be to calculate an exact annuity and work out a repayment schedule from tables or a financial calculator.

Where a single annual interest calculation is made, where an annuity system is used or where (as in the case of salary advances) no interest is charged, a suitable advances register could be adopted from the market rental shown on page 335 of Chapter 10. The columns would be headed:

(a) Balance brought forward;

(b) Advances;

(c) Annual Interest;

(d) Total;

(e) Cash Received; and

(f) Balance carried forward.

The monthly instalments paid would then be shown in the right-hand columns. Each monthly instalment would be one-twelfth of the annual repayment plus interest (if any).

Municipal Accounting for Developing Countries

133. OVERSEAS INDENTS

Sometimes an authority will need to buy materials from abroad. An explanation of the procedure is given in appendix "A". Some of the details may not become clear to you, until you have studied "costing" and "stores control" later in the book but are included for the sake of completeness.

The appendix is included because it may help you in your work if you should have to buy goods direct from overseas.

It will normally be best to buy imported goods from local agents, rather than direct from overseas sources because commercial importers of goods are usually experienced in dealing with freight, customs, insurance and other matters. The authority merely pays a single charge to the supplier (ie the local price) thus saving the clerical work of keeping separate cost records.

APPENDIX "A"

Overseas Indents _ Accounts and Records

1. Authority's overseas agents (eg World Agents) are requested to obtain a supply of materials - let us say, 150 3-inch bends and 100 4-inch bends. An indent is prepared on special forms giving a full specification of what is required, and sent to the agents.

2. The agents make enquiries, and eventually place an order with (for instance) XYZ Foundries Ltd. (Orders are not necessarily placed in the agents' own country.) They advise the authority by telex, intimating where the order has been placed, and what prices have been quoted - for example U 17 each for the 3-inch bends, and U 19 for the 4-inch.

3. The agents inspect the finished goods, arrange shipping for them, and obtain marine insurance cover. Having done so, they pay the suppliers, and this payment, together with shipping freight, marine insurance, and the agents' fees, will in due course appear as debits to the authority in the periodical statements of account sent by the agents.

4. The goods eventually arrive at a home post. The authority's coast agents clear them from the docks, and send them by rail or road to the authority's store. The coast agents submit an invoice requesting payment of dock, railage, and other local charges paid by them on the goods.

5. Costing and accounting are complicated because the authority may have dozens of indents in progress at any time - some for "Unallocated Stores", some for specific jobs. In addition, charges for the goods may be spread over a period of months (unlike a local purchase, where one invoice is received and paid, and that is the end of the matter). For example, the goods may be paid for this month, freight and insurance next month, the agents' commission partly next month and partly the following month, and the coast agents' disbursements in two months' time. All these charges may arise separately for each of several distinct deliveries under one indent, where the indent covers a number of different kind of goods.

6. Obviously, some accounting system is required whereby the charges relating to one indent, or one consignment, can be collected together and finally transferred in total to the account for which the goods were ordered. To charge the costs piecemeal direct to that account, as

Expenditure Accounting

and when they arise, causes confusion, and prevents full control over costs and deliveries under indent.

7. An account should be opened for each indent in the ledger (specimen A). This is debited with payments and credited with the final costs of each consignment as it is transferred to Stock Account, or other account for which the goods were ordered. Eventually, each Indent Account should, of course, show a "Nil" balance.

8. In addition, a memorandum cost sheet (as specimen B) should be kept, in more detail, for each consignment. This enables close control to be established over charges and deliveries (similar to the control exercised over ordinary invoice payments by using the official order system).

9. Finally, if the goods are for stock, it will be necessary to work out a cost, not only for the consignment as a whole, but also for every item in it which has a separate account in the Stores Ledger (for pricing subsequent issues of the goods from store). A calculation sheet (as specimen C) is useful in this respect.

10. The procedure for the indent for bends, instanced above, would therefore be on the following lines (corresponding entries appear in the specimen forms):

    *(a) The authority is debited via the World Agents' statement, with the invoiced price of U 4,450, subsequent to adjustments for packing, discounts etc. making the final amount payable U 4,352.50.

    *(b) In subsequent World Agent's statements, other charges appear for freight (U 240), insurance (U 37.10) and agency fees (U 185.15).

    (c) Charges (railage etc) total U 415,80.

    (d) All these add up to a total cost of U 5,230.55. This is clearly ascertainable from specimen B, and is the "landed" or delivered cost of the goods to the authority.

    (e) As the goods are for stock, it is necessary to know for pricing purposes, how much of the final cost of U 5,230.55 relates to the 3" bends and how much to the 4". This is ascertained by the calculation sheet C. The total cost is apportioned to the several types of material in the same proportion as their basic cost, as shown by the suppliers' invoice (excluding the adjustments for discount and packing).

    *In practice, these items would be billed in foreign currency (eg US dollars, French francs). The authority would have to make appropriate arrangements to pay these amounts in the foreign currencies, by purchasing foreign currency drafts or by letters of credit.

    NOTE:

    In practice, prices are often wanted before all the costs are in, but it is usually possible to pencil in estimated prices on the cost sheet and work out a provisional price which will differ only by odd cents from the eventual costings.

11. **Short Deliveries**

    The procedure where supplies are received showing losses or damage is as follows:

Municipal Accounting for Developing Countries

(a) As the amount paid by the authority represents the cost of a full and perfect delivery, the stock accounts (if the goods are for stock) must bring on charge the full quantity invoiced.

(b) The value of the goods lost or damaged is then transferred from Stock Account to a "Short Deliveries (Suspense) Account", as a separate operation (if necessary, using a Stores Issue Voucher).

(c) The value remains on the suspense account until cleared by insurance refund, replacement deliveries by the suppliers, or otherwise.

SPECIMEN FORM "A"

Goods in Transit (Indent 12/5/ 6) Account

19_6		Units	Cts	19_6		Units	Cts
Mar.	To World Agents Account	4,352	50	June	By Stock Account Cost Sheet 1 Transferred on Completion	5,230	55
Apr.	To World Agents Account	451	20				
May	To World Agents Account	11	05				
		4,814	75				
June	To Cash Account (Coast Agent's Charges)	415	80				
		5,230	55				

NB: In practice, the debits would probably also include charges relating to other consignments under the same indent. The separate cost sheets, however, facilitate the costing of each individual consignment, so as to transfer the cost of each to Stock Account and eventually clear the Indent Account completely.

Expenditure Accounting

SPECIMEN FORM "B"

INDENT COST SHEET

Indent No. ..12/5/_6.... **Cost Sheet No.** ...1.....

Details ..3" and 4" Steel Bends........................

Suppliers ..XYZ Foundry Co Inc...... **Est. Cost (Basic)** .. U 4,280.

..Birmingham...Al. USA....

Account Chargeable ..Stock Account.. **Agents' Commission Rate** ..4%.

	Cost			Commission			Total	
	Paid	U	Cts	Paid	U	Cts	U	Cts
Purchase	MCH.	4,352	50	APL.	174	10	4,526	60
Freight/Postage	APL.	240	00	MAY	9	55	249	55
Marine Insurance	APL.	37	10	MAY	1	50	38	60
TOTAL C.I.F. VALUE... U							4,814	75

	Date	Ref	U	Cts
CIF Value	-	-	4,814	75
Handling and Wharfage	JUNE)	(	75	95
Customs Duty	JUNE)	Coast (	-	-
Railways - Charges	JUNE)	Agents (	282	50
Coast Agents' Fees and Expenses	JUNE)	Account (	57	35
Other Expenses:		T.214 (		
ALL-IN COST DELIVERED			5,230	55

Transferred to ..Stock Account at U 5,230.55.. Date ..23/6/_6......

Goods Received ..17 JUN 19_6... Stores Received Note No. ...1076...

CHECK CALCULATIONS - HANDLING AND WHARFAGE

	Units	Cents
Handling U 17 per 40 cu.ft. on 37 cu.ft.	15	75
or U 17 per ton on 0t. 17cwt 0 qr. 14lbs.	14	60
(whichever is the higher) (MIN. U 8.50)	15	75 higher
Wharfage 1¼% on CIF Value 1¼% x U 4,814.75	60	20
	75	95 O.K.

Municipal Accounting for Developing Countries

NOTE OF CLAIMS FOR SHORT-DELIVERIES OR DAMAGE

Nil

SPECIMEN FORM "C"

INDENT DELIVERIES - STOCK LEDGER PRICE CALCULATION SHEET

	Details of Purchase Price from Supplier's Invoice	Units	Cents
Indent No: 12/5/_6	Basic Cost	4,450	-
Cost Sheet No: 1	+ Packing etc	14	10
Goods Received 17/6/_6		4,464	10
Stores Recd Note No: 1076	Discounts	111	60
	Total of Invoice	4,352	50

A - Basic Cost: U 4,450

B - All-In Cost Delivered (per Cost Sheet): U 5,230.55

C - Pricing Factor (B - A): 1.1754

Goods Supplied	Qty	Foreign Currency Cost	Convert to Local Currency		X Price Factor = Cost		Unit Cost	Stores Cat No
			Units	Cts	Units	Cts	Each	
3" Bends	150	5,100 -	2,550	-	2,997	28	19/98	643
4" Bends	100	3,800 -	1,900	-	2,233	27	22/33	644
TOTAL (Agreeing Invoice)		8,900	4,450	-				
TOTAL COST (agreeing with cost sheet)...					5,230	55		

12. Income and Expenditure Analysis

Section		Page
134.	Income and Expenditure Analysis.	412
135.	Cash Receipts Analysis.	413
136.	Credit Income Analysis.	414
137.	Income Ledger.	415
138.	Payments Analysis.	417
139.	Wages and Salaries Analysis.	419
140.	Vehicle and Plant Analysis.	421
141.	Stores Analysis.	429
142.	Stores Ledger.	433
143.	Expenditure Ledger.	439
144.	Transfers and Adjustments.	442
145.	Tables of Postings.	443

134. INCOME AND EXPENDITURE ANALYSIS

In the two previous chapters we have studied the various records and procedures concerned with receipt and payment of cash. We saw how these receipts and payments affected the cash book or cash account.

We shall now consider how the receipts and payments are analysed according to the principles outlined in Chapter 7, and how the analysis is used as a basis for preparing a complete set of income and expenditure accounts (revenue accounts) and a balance sheet.

The procedure used to analyse cash receipts and credit income is known as income analysis. The procedure used to analyse payments, creditors, wages, stores, vehicles, and plant is known as expenditure analysis.

Both income and expenditure will be initially analysed according to the services to which they relate. The first stage of the analysis should be into objective headings which will be the same for both income and expenditure. A suitable objective classification based on recommendations of the Chartered Institute of Public Finance and Accountancy (UK) could be carried out in a series of steps, as follows:

Step	Classification	Description
1.	Committee	Services grouped according to committee responsible (eg Health)
2.	Service	Main services under which activities are grouped (eg Health - to distinguish from (say) Markets which may be controlled by the same committee)
3.	Division of Service	Division of the main service (eg Health) into functions (eg Refuse and Collection and Disposal)
4.	Sub-Division of Service	A further break-down if required (eg by separating Refuse Collection from Refuse Disposal

Having first analysed objectively, further analysis will be made subjectively.

The subjective headings used in the income analysis (eg rents, fees)

Income and Expenditure Analysis

will be quite different from those used in the expenditure analysis (eg wages, repairs) and will be considered separately.

135. CASH RECEIPTS ANALYSIS

As shown in Section 30 of Chapter 3:

"every receipt of cash is a debit in the cash book and a credit in some other account".

Section 119 of Chapter 10 shows how cash receipts are brought to the debit of the cash book either directly or through the "collection and deposit" book.

The corresponding credits to other accounts are made through the income analysis system.

Reference to the table on page 61 of Chapter 3 will show that cash receipts are not all of the same type. Some affect personal accounts, some real accounts and some nominal accounts. Only cash receipts affecting nominal accounts are "income" in the strict sense. It is possible to separate the analysis of receipts into three main sections:

Section	Dealing With
1. Personal and Control Accounts	Cash receipts for credit income on revenue account
2. Revenue Accounts	Cash income on revenue account
3. Capital Accounts	Capital receipts

The first section (Personal and Control) will provide analysis for control accounts of "Ratepayers", "Housing Tenants", "Market Tenants", "Sundry Debtors", "Deposits" and any other group of persons against whom debits have been raised in personal accounts. Cash receipts accumulated in this part of the analysis will eventually be totalled and each separate total posted to the appropriate control account, as described in Chapter 10.

The second section (Revenue) will provide analysis for the various types of cash receipts where debits have not been raised in advance against the persons paying the cash. Cash receipts accumulated in this part of the analysis will eventually be totalled and each separate total posted to the appropriate income (nominal) account, for ultimate inclusion in the revenue accounts. These receipts are often known as cash income. The third section (Capital) will provide analysis of the various items of cash received with which to make capital payments. Such receipts will include loans, capital grants, receipts from the sale of assets and land premia. Cash receipts accumulated in this part of the analysis will eventually be totalled and each separate total posted to the capital accounts, to be dealt with as shown later.

The simplest form of analysis of receipts is the "abstract of receipts" or "income journal" illustrated on page 200 of Chapter 7. Each copy receipt is separately posted in the appropriate column, and periodically, usually monthly or annually, the total of each column is posted to the "income ledger". Of course, in practice, many more columns would be required than those shown, but the principles are the same. If a coding system were in use the codes would be written on the copy receipts and used at the heads of the columns of the income journal, with or without detailed descriptions. Columns provided in the collection and deposit book can give a daily analysis of major items, in total, making it unnecessary to post individual copy receipts for these items. For example, the Collection and Deposit book of Kambale Municipal Council shown on page 345 of Chapter 10 gives single monthly totals for "rates" and "water charges", which can be posted direct to the income journal or income ledger. The analysis of "other" items in the income journal, posted from copy receipts, will be proved against the total of the "other" column in the Cash and Deposit book. In our example, the "other" postings for May would have to balance against the Cash and Deposit book figures of U 50,800.

The income analysis of Kambale Municipal Council would largely depend upon the headings in its budget. It could include, for example:

(a) **Personal and Control Accounts**

   Ratepayers (Rates Control)
   Water Consumers (Water Charges) Control
   Housing Tenants (Rents) Control
   Market Tenants (Rents) Control
   Sundry Debtors Control;

(b) **Revenue Accounts**

   Finance - Investment Income
           - Government Grants
           - Sales of Publications
           - Miscellaneous
   Markets - Market Dues; and

(c) **Capital Accounts**

   Land Drainage - Swamp Area - Grant
   Roads - North Street/Park Road - Loan.

136. CREDIT INCOME ANALYSIS

As we saw in Chapter 10, all personal accounts for a particular class of credit income are kept together. For example, all personal accounts of ratepayers are kept in a rate book. The analysis of credit income provides totals of the final control debits for each class of income. These are then posted, often via the journal, to the appropriate income account in the ledger. This posting is done once, at the year end, for each class of credit income.

The postings for Rates, for Kambale Municipal Council, are shown on pages 317-318 of Chapter 10 and those for Markets on pages 335-336. The same system will apply to other classes of credit income.

The only type of credit income normally requiring further analysis is that of "Sundry Debtors". As shown on page 329 of Chapter 10, columns are provided in the "Sundry Debtors" book to give the necessary analysis. As stated in Section 112 (page 331) postings can be made monthly, quarterly or annually to the appropriate income accounts.

Income and Expenditure Analysis

137. INCOME LEDGER

Amounts accumulated in the various columns of the income journal may be totalled at the year end and individual totals posted direct to the main ledger.

Alternatively the income journal may be totalled and posted monthly (or even weekly), in which case an income ledger will be required. There will be a separate folio in the income ledger for each control account, revenue account and capital account for which cash or credit income is received. In other words, each page will correspond to a column of the income journal.

If we assume that Kambale Municipal Council posts monthly to its income ledger, the folio for Market Dues might appear as follows:

```
                        INCOME ACCOUNT

    Code    02/99/58           Estimate    U 167,500

    Head    Health - Market Dues
```

Date	Details		Debit	Credit	Balance
19_6	Source	Reference	Units	Units	Units
Jan.31	Income Journal	5		13,240	13,240
Feb.28	Income Journal	11		13,460	26,700
Mar.31	Income Journal	18		12,820	39,520
31	Sundry Debtors	65		2,480	42,000
Apr.30	Income Journal	24		13,120	55,120
May 31	Income Journal	30		12,960	68,080
Jun.30	Income Journal	34		13,300	81,380
30	Sundry Debtors	73		2,360	83,740
Jul.31	Income Journal	39		13,080	96,820
31	Main Journal	58	160		96,660
Aug.31	Income Journal	44		13,680	110,340
Sep.30	Income Journal	47		13,240	123,580
30	Sundry Debtors	84		2,500	126,080
Oct.31	Income Journal	53		13,120	139,200
Nov.30	Income Journal	59		13,860	153,060
Dec.31	Income Journal	66		12,820	165,880
31	Sundry Debtors	89		2,440	168,320

The code number is interpreted as follows:

```
        02              =   Health Committee
             99         =   Income
                  58    =   Market Dues
```

The estimate of U 167,500 is part of item 84 in the Markets estimates (page 295, Chapter 9) which might have been broken down as:

```
        Rents   120,300
        Dues    167,500
                -------
                287,800
                =======
```

Municipal Accounting for Developing Countries

Items shown as a single total in the main budget are often broken down in the actual accounting system to give closer control.
The actual income collected against item 84 in the budget will be:

Rents (see pages 335-336 of Chapter 10)

Total Rent due		120,000
Less Allowances		860
		119,140
Dues (see income account above)		168,320
	TOTAL	287,460
		=======

The actual figure is therefore U 340 less than the original estimate.

The income ledger has been kept in the same way as that referred to in Section 51 of Chapter 4. This style is recommended for income and expenditure ledgers, because the accumulating balance assists in budgetary control.

Postings from the subsidiary records to the income ledger have been made on the last day of each month. The source of the posting (ie the subsidiary record from which it comes) together with a folio reference, is shown in the "details" column. For example on 30 April U 13,120 was posted from income journal folio 24.

Most of the postings have come from the income journal because most of the market dues will arise as cash (ticket) income. We have assumed, however, that credit arrangements exist with one or two major users of the market (say - transporters of produce) and that monthly or weekly invoices are sent to them through the sundry debtors system. Each invoice will be analysed under the "market dues" column of the sundry debtors book (see page 329 of Chapter 10). Periodically (we shall assume quarterly) the total of this column will be posted to the income account. For example, the U 2,480 posted from the "Sundry Debtors" source (folio 65) on Mar.31 represents the total of all invoices sent during the first quarter.

On Jul.31 there has been a debit posting from the main journal. This refers to an allowance granted on a sundry debtors invoice. After proper authority has been given (by the Chief Financial Officer or committee) the journal entry would be made as follows:

19_6				
Jul.31	Health - Market Dues DR.		160	
	To Sundry Debtors Control			160
	Being allowance on invoice			
	No......(Minute FIN.43/6)			

When the final accounts are prepared the accumulated totals of the various income accounts will be posted as credits to the main ledger (explained in detail later). For example, the U 168,320 for Market Dues will appear on the credit side of the main ledger as follows:

Income and Expenditure Analysis

						CR.
Account Markets Revenue			Main Code	02		
Code	Details	Income Analysis	Expenditure Analysis	Transfers	Balances	Total
02.99.57	Rents	119,140				119,140
02.99.58	Dues	168,320				168,320
		287,460				287,460

Within each objective classification (ie committee, service, division of service, sub-division of service) there should be fairly standard groupings for subjective analysis. The actual classifications will depend upon budgetary (and sometimes legal) requirements but the form set out below may be useful as a guide. It is based upon recommendations of the CIPFA.

Sales

sale of publications
sale of produce
sale of meals and refreshments
sale of materials
sale of old equipment and waste products
other sales.

Fees and Charges

fees, tolls and charges for services
contributions by other local and public authorities.

Rents

rents
letting of halls, rooms etc
hire of equipment.

Interest

Miscellaneous

donations
insurance claims
other.

138. PAYMENTS ANALYSIS

As shown in Section 3 of Chapter 3:

"every payment of cash is a credit in the cash book and a debit in some other account".

Section 121 of Chapter 11 shows how cash payments are brought to the credit of the cash book through the cheque list.

Municipal Accounting for Developing Countries

The corresponding debits to other accounts are made through the expenditure analysis system.

Reference to the table on page 70 of Chapter 3 will show that cash payments are not all of the same type. Some affect personal accounts, some real accounts and some nominal accounts. In addition, some payments (eg wages) will be debited to holding (or suspense) accounts, pending re-allocation to appropriate nominal accounts. As with receipts, it is possible to separate the analysis of payments into three main sections:

Section	Dealing With
1. Personal and Control Accounts	Payments debited to personal accounts (eg sundry creditors) and holding accounts (eg wages)
2. Revenue Accounts	Payments representing revenue expenditure
3. Capital Accounts	Capital payments

The first section (Personal and Control) will provide analysis for personal accounts of "Sundry Creditors", "Income Tax Authority", "Graduated Tax Authority", "Pension Fund Authority", Advances" etc and for holding or suspense accounts of "Wages", "Salaries", "Vehicles and Plant", "Stores" etc. Cash payments accumulated in this part of the analysis will eventually be totalled and each separate total posted to the appropriate control account as described for "Sundry Creditors" and "Wages and Salaries" in Chapter 11.

The second section (Revenue) will provide analysis for the various cash payments which will be treated directly as revenue expenditure because the expenditure is incurred in the same year as the payment takes place. An example of this type of payment appears on pages 367-368 of Chapter 11. Cash payments accumulated in this part of the analysis will eventually be totalled and each separate total posted to the appropriate expenditure (nominal) account for ultimate inclusion in the revenue accounts.

The third section (Capital) will provide analysis of the various payments for the purchase or construction of fixed assets or for deferred charges. Payments accumulated in this part of the analysis will eventually be totalled and each separate total posted to the capital accounts, as shown later.

Initial analysis of payments will normally be made through an "abstract of payments" or "expenditure journal" as illustrated on page 201 of Chapter 7. Each separately analysed (or coded) item on an invoice or invoice summary is individually posted in the appropriate column and periodically (weekly, monthly or annually) the total of each column is posted to the "expenditure ledger". In practice, many more columns would be required than those shown, but the principles are the same. If a coding system were in use, each column would be headed with the appropriate code number instead of the detailed descriptions. As an alternative to using the abstract system the expenditure journal could be formed by having vertical columns to the right of the cheque list, as explained in Section 1 of Chapter 11. The expenditure journal will then be in similar form to the payments cash book shown on page 155 of

Income and Expenditure Analysis

Chapter 6.

The expenditure analysis of Kambale Municipal Council would largely depend upon the headings in its budget. It would include for example:

(a) **Personal and Control Accounts**

Sundry Creditors Control
Salaries Control
Wages Control
Income Tax Authority
Provident Fund Authority
Stores Control
Haulage (Vehicles and Plant) Control;

(b) **Revenue Accounts**

Finance - Salaries
Clinics and Dispensaries - Repair and Maintenance of Buildings
Works - Debt Charges
Markets - Water Charges; and

(c) **Capital Accounts**

Land Drainage - Swamp Area - Contract Payments
Roads - North Road/Park Road - Contract Payments.

139. WAGES AND SALARIES ANALYSIS

Where the allocation of wages or salaries is fairly straightforward, the payments can be analysed direct, through the expenditure journal, as described on pages 396-398 of Chapter 11.

In other cases, the payments will be allocated from the expenditure journal to "Control" or "Holding" accounts as shown on pages 396-398 of Chapter 11. The expenditure will then be re-allocated to appropriate expenditure analysis heads (codes) through an "abstract of salaries (wages)" or "salaries (wages) journal".

As an example, let us refer to the "wages" payment for March 19_6 for Kambale Municipal Council. Reference to account No.2 on page 398-399 (Chapter 11) shows that the total debit to the wages (control) account is U 146,800. Reference to the table on page 396 shows that this is made up of:

Gross Pay	141,480
Provident Fund (Council's Contribution)	5,320
	146,800

Let us suppose that in the works department there is a workman called K. Rubanga earning U 6 per day and that his wages are calculated as

27 working days @ U 6 per day		162
Less Provident Fund @ 5%	8	
Graduated Tax	20	
Trade Union Dues	2	30
NET PAY		132

419

Municipal Accounting for Developing Countries

Let us suppose that he has been employed in March as follows:

	Days
Refuse Collection	10
Road Repairs	8
Sewage Disposal	9
	27

The cost to the Council of employing the workman during March was:

	Gross Pay	162
Add	Provident Fund (Council's Contribution)	8
		170

Although the workman received only U 132 in cash the Council has had to pay out U 170 altogether. This U 170 must be apportioned over the various jobs as follows (for simplicity we shall work to the nearest unit):

			Units
Refuse Collection	$\frac{170}{27} \times 10$	=	63
Road Repairs	$\frac{170}{27} \times 8$	=	50
Sewage Disposal	$\frac{170}{27} \times 9$	=	57
			170

The above calculation will be done on a timesheet or muster roll, and when the calculations have been made for every worker the "wages abstract" or "wages journal" will be drawn up as follows:

WAGES JOURNAL
March 19_6

No	Name	Gross Pay	Provident Fund	Total	Refuse Collection	Road Repairs	Sewage Disposal	etc
1	Rubanga	165	8	170	63	50	57	
2	Kabanda	162	8	170	44	94	32	
3	Ocheng	150	-	150	78			72
4	Otim	150	-	150		117	33	
	(etc)			(etc)				
		141,480	5,320	146,800	55,420	36,860	13,240	41,280

The totals of each analysis column will be posted as debits to the appropriate accounts in the expenditure ledger, the grand total of U 146,800 being credited to the wages control account.

Income and Expenditure Analysis

Where groups of workers (eg road gangs) are employed as teams on the same jobs the wages for the whole group can be apportioned and allocated in total.

For salaries, apportionment is usually less complex than for wages, the payroll summary being allocated according to departments. Sometimes, however, the salaries of individual officers must be apportioned in the same way as for wages. This applies particularly to technical officers (eg architects, engineers) engaged on supervision of capital schemes.

The apportionment of wages and salaries from a control account is part of the process of costing. We are measuring and recording activities to produce a detailed analysis and explanation of financial accounts for purposes of budgetary control.

140. VEHICLES AND PLANT ANALYSIS

The majority of local authorities operate vehicles, such as vans, tipper lorries (trucks) and refuse vehicles. Many will also operate various forms of mechanical equipment, usually referred to as plant, such as graders, dozers, excavators and motor mowers.

Accurate accounting for the operation of vehicles and plant is more complex than accounting for the employment of staff. In the first place, payment of staff is directly related to work done (eg a day's pay for a day's work) whereas payments for operating vehicles and plant are made in a haphazard way. Licence duty may be paid in January, insurance premium paid in May, petrol purchased every day or so, maintenance carried out monthly and so on. Secondly, there are only two direct expenses connected with employment of staff - gross pay and employer's contributions, whereas there are many direct expenses connected with vehicle and plant operation as follows:

(a) licence duty;

(b) insurance premium;

(c) depreciation (or the equivalent);

(d) garaging;

(e) wages of driver;

(f) major repairs;

(g) routine maintenance;

(h) fuel (petrol or diesel);

(i) lubricants;

(j) spares and tyres; and

(k) interest.

To illustrate the difficulties which can arise, let us take an example. Suppose you are employed as a clerk for one month at an agreed monthly rate of pay. At the end of the month you can go to your employer and collect the exact cost of your services, one month's pay, (say) U 500. Now, suppose you have a small car and you agree to drive it on a day trip to a town 20 miles away to collect a parcel for your employer. He agrees in advance to pay the "full actual cost" of the journey. How would you calculate the cost? You might begin your journey by putting

Municipal Accounting for Developing Countries

(say) 2 gallons of petrol in the tank at (say) U 5 per gallon, charging this U 10 to your employer as the cost of the journey - but there must be approximately one gallon still in your tank as you know that your car does roughly 40 miles to the gallon: so you charge for 1 gallon (U 5) - but this is not exact, because it might (on this trip) do 38.65 miles to the gallon or 41.2 miles to the gallon. Then, reflecting further, you realise that every 4,000 miles you pay U 100 for servicing the car - so you decide to charge a proportion of this cost (U $\frac{100 \times 40}{4,000}$) = U 1 to your employer.

Even now you have not covered the full cost, because you cannot anticipate (for example) that a new set of sparking plugs will be required at the next service. You have not yet charged a proportion of the licence, insurance premium, depreciation or garage costs - so you add these up to (say) U 1,825 and divide by the number of days in the year to give a daily rate of U 5, which you add to the charge. Even this is not accurate, because if you used the car for a total of only 73 days a year the daily rate should be U 25. Suppose you have an accident on the journey which involves uninsured repairs expenditure of U 400. Do you charge the whole of this to your employer or spread it over all the journeys in the year (or in five years). Finally, does your employer consider the payment of (say) U 215 for your day's work as part of the cost of the journey (driver's wages) or part of your ordinary pay as his clerk. You might say he would pay it anyhow, but what if you did the journey for an extra day's pay on your day off or he had to employ another clerk to do your work for the day?

Although the above example is simple, it illustrates most of the difficulties which will be encountered by a local authority in calculating and estimating the running costs of vehicles and plant: in particular the following points connected with costing:

(a) the full economic cost of an activity is often different from what is at first apparent; and

(b) it is impossible to calculate exact or "actual" costs, making it necessary to calculate what are known as "ascertained" costs, which are accurate only within defined limits.

The nearest approach to exact allocation of vehicle or plant expenses occurs where a particular group of vehicles or plant is used exclusively on one service. A good example for Kambale Municipal Council might be the "Refuse Collection" service, which will use specially designed refuse vehicles, not generally suitable for other work. The expenditure analysis for this service will include a head for "Transport" and sub-heads for "petrol", "oil", "tyres", "licences", "insurance", "repairs", "contributions to renewals funds" etc. Payments for any of these items will be allocated direct from the invoices through the expenditure journal. Wages of drivers will, in this case, usually be allocated under "Employees - wages" rather than "Transport".

Even here, a share of the cost of garaging or depot expenses may have to be apportioned to the "Refuse Collection" service from a holding account. Also, if the vehicle is used for any other purpose (eg hired out to another authority), a cost will have to be calculated as shown later.

What happens when, for example, the works department operates a number of vehicles and plant which are used from time to time on a wide variety of services, including rechargeable works. Let us suppose that Kambale Municipal Council has vehicles and plant in its works department as follows:

Income and Expenditure Analysis

```
5 cwt vans          2
1-ton lorries       4
3-ton lorries       3
mechanical graders  2
```

The vehicles and plant will be regarded as "pooled" and all expenses relating to their operation will be charged from invoices and sundry creditors to a "Transport and Heavy Plant - Holding Account". Separate cost accounts will be kept for each vehicle or group of vehicles as shown later.

When a vehicle is required by a department or service, the officer responsible will prepare a vehicle requisition and send it to the transport officer in the works department. The requisition will show:

(a) the approximate time for which the vehicle is required;

(b) the job or service upon which it will be used; and

(c) the type and size of the required vehicle.

The driver of the vehicle will normally be provided by the works department and he will be supplied with a log-sheet or log-book in which he will record details of each journey as follows:

(a) date;

(b) starting time;

(c) finishing time;

(d) job or service;

(e) code number (if appropriate);

(f) number of miles; and

(g) number of hours.

At the end of each week or month, the log-sheet for each vehicle will be totalled to show the miles run and hours worked on each job. The charge for the use of the vehicle will then usually be worked out in one of two ways:

(a) multiplying the miles run by a fixed rate per mile; or

(b) multiplying the hours worked by a fixed rate per hour.

When the calculations have been made for each vehicle a "transport and plant" abstract (or journal) will be drawn up as follows:

Municipal Accounting for Developing Countries

WEEKLY VEHICLES AND PLANT JOURNAL W/E 18/6/_6

No	Type	Hourly Rate	Hours Worked	Total Charge	Road Repairs	Sewage Disposal	Housing Repairs	Etc
		U		U	U	U	U	U
UBC.123	5 CWT VAN	8	40	320	100	70	150	
UBJ.627	5 CWT VAN	8	30	240		50	50	140
UBC.625	1 TON TIPPER	15	40	600	400		100	100
UBC.626	1 TON TIPPER	15	40	600	500	50		50
UBC.627	1 TON TIPPER	15	35	525	325	100	50	50
	(etc)			(etc)				
				7,625	3,450	485	520	3,170

The totals of each analysis column will be posted as debits to the appropriate accounts in the expenditure ledger. There will usually be a subjective head "Use of transport and heavy plant" under each service. The grand total of U 7,625 will be credited to the holding account. The rate of charge should be fixed so that all expenditure originally charged during the year to the holding account is eventually re-charged to the various expenditure accounts. If the total cost of the transport pool of Kambale Municipal Council for 19_6 was U 456,460 the ideal position would be represented (in theory) by the following journal entries:

19_6 Dec.31	Vehicles and Plant Holding Account DR. To Cash) To Sundry Creditors) Being cash payments and accrued expenditure on transport and plant for year	456,460	456,460*
19_6 Dec.31	Sundry Accounts (Rev Exp) DR. To Vehicles and Plant Holding Account Being expenditure on vehicles and plant charged out to expenditure accounts	456,460	456,460

* Transfers of renewals fund contributions or depreciation might be included in place of cash payment of loan charges.

In practice, such an ideal situation would rarely be achieved because the rates of charge must be fixed well in advance of costs being incurred and must therefore be based on estimates.

The estimated costs will be drawn up for each group of vehicles of the same type, and a common rate of charge fixed for all vehicles of that type. Though the costs of individual vehicles may be kept separately in cost accounts it is not usual to charge a separate rate for each vehicle.

Income and Expenditure Analysis

One problem which arises is whether to use mileage rates or hourly rates of charge. Mileage rates are more likely to be employed where distance is an important factor. For example, mileage rates will often be used for transport of stores in rural areas and running of ambulances. On the other hand, where distances are relatively short and there is a considerable amount of standing time, hourly rates will be used. This will apply particularly to such services as refuse collection and road repairs where a great deal of loading and unloading is done.

On balance, experience favours the use of hourly rates for local authority work. It encourages departments to make more efficient use of vehicles by keeping them running, because supervisors know that budgets under their control are being charged with hourly rates, whether vehicles are working to full capacity or not. By contrast, where mileage rates are used, the services of an expensive vehicle and driver can be tied up in mere "waiting around", yet no costs are charged to the department using (or rather failing to make use of) the vehicle, unless actual journeys are run.

Another method, perhaps more scientific, would be to charge running expenses (eg petrol) on a mileage basis and fixed charges (eg licence duty) on an hourly basis, thus giving a "composite" rate. This method would involve more clerical work than the other two and it is doubtful whether this would be justified.

To show how the alternative rates are calculated we shall consider the costs of the two 5-cwt vans used by Kambale Municipal Council as follows:

Municipal Accounting for Developing Countries

UBC.123 - purchased in 19_3 for U 18,000 UBJ.627 - purchased in 19_5 for U 22,000					
Item	Estimated Cost		Rate per mile (d)	Rate per hour	Composite Rates
	U	U	U Cts	U Cts	U Cts
Petrol	5,000(a)				
Lubricants	600				
Repairs and Maintenance (including tyres)	6,400	12,000	50	3 00	50 (p. mile)
Drivers Wages (including Provident Fund)	6,000(b)				
Insurance	2,000				
Licences	1,000				
Depreciation (4 year life)	10,000(c)				
Garage	1,000	20,000	85	5 00	5 00 (p. hour)
		32,000	1 35	8 00	

```
Mileage = 12,000 miles per vehicle = 24,000 miles
Hours = 2,000 hours per vehicle = 4,000 hours
(a) = 1,000 gallons - 24 mpg for 24,000 miles
(price of petrol assumed to be U 5 per gallon)
(b) = 2 drivers @ U 238 per month + 5% Provident Fund
(c) = U 18,000 = U 4,500 + 22,000 = U 5,500
        4                       4
(d) = to nearest 5 cents
```

If mileage rates were used, each mile would be charged out at U 1.35 per mile.

If hourly rates were used, each hour of use would be charged out at U 8 per hour as shown in our example.

If composite rates were used, each mile would be charged out at 50 cents per mile and each hour worked (standing or running time) at U 5 per hour.

The charge for depreciation is based in our example on the "straight line" method but, where appropriate, renewals fund contributions or debt charges would be substituted.

In calculating the charge by the above method an attempt has been made to forecast a balanced holding account for the year. If the 15-cwt vans were the only vehicles used, the estimated holding account would appear as follows:

Income and Expenditure Analysis

Vehicles and Plant Holding Account

To Petrol	5,000	By Sundry Accounts	
To Lubricants	600	(4,000 hours @ U 8	
To Repairs and Maintenance	6,400	per hour)	32,000
To Drivers Wages	6,000		
To Insurance	2,000		
To Licences	1,000		
To Depreciation	10,000		
To Garage	1,000		
	32,000		32,000
	======		======

When the actual expenses and the actual number of running hours are known at the end of the year there will inevitably be differences from the estimates. Taking the whole vehicle pool of Kambale Municipal Council, the ideal position, illustrated by the journal entries on page 12 could be shown in account form (abbreviated) as follows:

Vehicles and Plant Holding Account

To Vehicle and Plant Running Expenses	456,460	By Recharges to Services	456,460
	=======		=======

However, if expenses were less than estimated and the number of hours charged out were greater than estimated the position might be:

Vehicles and Plant Holding Account

To Vehicle and Plant Running Expenses	455,820	By Recharges to Services	456,920
To Balance - being Expenses Over-Recovered	1,100		
	456,920		456,920
	=======		=======

Alternatively, if expenses were greater than estimated, and the number of hours charged out were less than estimated, the position might be:

Vehicles and Plant Holding Account

To Vehicle and Plant Running Expenses	457,260	By Recharges to Services	455,280
		By Balance - being Expenses Under-Recovered	1,980
	457,260		457,260
	=======		=======

Municipal Accounting for Developing Countries

In both the above cases there is a balance on the holding account because more (or less) than the full costs have been recharged to (or recovered from) services.

Balances on holding accounts can be dealt with in several ways. The simplest (and also the least accurate) method is to debit under-recoveries and to credit over-recoveries to one special head in the revenue account. This method is sometimes loosely referred to as "writing the balance off to revenue". The second method (where permissible) would be to transfer over-recoveries to the credit of the Vehicles and Plant Renewals Fund. It is less likely that under-recoveries would be debited to this fund. The third method would be to carry the balance forward to the holding account for the following year. Over-recoveries would be credit balances and under-recoveries would be debit balances, necessitating possible adjustments in the charging-out rates for the new year. Fourthly, the under-recoveries could be debited, or over-recoveries credited, to the expenditure accounts which have borne the original charges by making a supplementary re-allocation.

The rates of charge for vehicles should be fixed by the Chief Financial Officer after consulting the appropriate technical officer (e.g. transport officer) about estimated costs, estimated running time and estimated mileage.

The aim should be to recover actual running costs - not, as is sometimes thought, to build up a large credit balance on the holding account. Sometimes, where works department officers are allowed to fix vehicle rates without consulting the Chief Financial Officer, inflated rates of charge are worked out. The works department officer then suggests that his vehicles are running at a "profit" which of course is nonsense, and defeats the purpose of accurate costing.

Sometimes, especially when dealing with heavy plant, such as graders, daily rates of charge are fixed instead of hourly rates.

Whether the wages of vehicle drivers (or plant operators) are included in the costs and charged out in the hourly, daily or mileage rate is a matter to be decided by the Chief Financial Officer. Where vehicles are used on a single service or where heavy overtime at enhanced rates of pay is involved, it is more usual to charge the wages of drivers as "Employees - wages" direct from expenditure or wages journals. This would apply, for example, to the "Refuse Collection" service where anomalies would be created if the pay of loaders were charged to "wages" and the pay of drivers to "transport" particularly as drivers may also assist with loading.

Where vehicles are pooled, and used on many jobs, it is more usual to charge the wages of drivers to the holding account. The charging-out rate will then be calculated for a vehicle and driver operating as a single unit.

Where heavy plant is used, the charge may include the operator's wages where he spends all his time operating the plant. However, some plant (such as a tarsprayer or tarmac machine) is operated by a gang of workers and it would seem more reasonable in this case to charge all labour costs to "wages".

Although we have referred above to a "holding" account it can also be called a "control" account, and sometimes even a "suspense" account.

Income and Expenditure Analysis

141. STORES ANALYSIS

Invariably goods, particularly those purchased in bulk, are held in a store for some time before they are used. For example a large quantity of cement or pipes may be purchased on a particular date and placed in a store. Later, when required for a job, some of the cement or some of the pipes may be issued from the store and used. The rest, for the time being, remain in the store until required.

Among the reasons for this stores procedure are:

(a) some materials, though used in small quantities, may be too small to be purchased except in much larger quantities (e.g. nuts and bolts, stopcocks);

(b) goods purchased in bulk are usually cheaper because of special discounts and lower transport costs (eg it should be more economical to send a lorry to collect 50 bags of cement than to collect 1 bag - also the supplier might give a discount because his clerical work involves a single customer, instead of 50 separate customers for 1 bag each);

(c) unless materials in continuous use are purchased and stored in advance of requirements there may be delays in carrying out urgent work; and

(d) as will be shown later, an efficient stores system aids in costing, budgetary control and control of materials.

According to the theory of book-keeping, when materials are purchased for stores, one asset (cash) is exchanged for another asset (materials) and no expenditure (ie loss) occurs at this stage. Expenditure is incurred when the materials are actually used. For example, if 10 bags of cement at U 6 per bag were purchased for stores on 31 Jan. and used for housing repairs on 18 Feb. the journal entries (in theory) would be:

19_6				
Jan.31	Stores DR.	60	
	To Cash		60
	Being purchase of 10 bags cement @ U 6 per bag		
Feb.18	Housing Repairs DR.	60	
	To Stores		60
	Being use of 10 bags of cement @ U 6 per bag for housing repairs		

If goods purchased for stores were all used on a single service, the only accounting difficulty would be the time delay between the receipt of materials into the stores and their actual use. This could be taken care of by stocktaking, rather on the lines of the trading account in a commercial undertaking, for example:

Municipal Accounting for Developing Countries

Housing Stores		Units
Opening Stock 1/1/_6	35,460
Add	Purchases	43,240
	78,700
Less	Closing Stock 31/12/_6	31,420
Expenditure during year	47,280
	======

This system gives no control over the storage and use of individual commodities and is unsuitable where goods in store are used for a variety of purposes. In these circumstances a complete stores system is required.

Where a complete stores system is in operation all goods purchased for store are debited NOT to an expenditure (nominal) account but to a "Stores Control" account or "Stores Holding" account. The individual commodities will be recorded in a stores ledger as explained later.

When goods are issued from stores for a specific purpose a "stores requisition note" or "stores issue note" will be made out, showing the quantity issued, the job or service on which it is used and the amount to be charged. The amount to be charged will normally be the cost price per unit, multiplied by the number of units issued (eg 7 bags of cement @ U 6 per bag = U 42).

Sometimes goods are returned to the store as unsuitable or surplus to requirements after being issued. When this happens, a "stores returned note" is made out showing the quantity returned, the job or service to which it was originally issued and the amount to be allowed as a credit against that job or service. The amount credited will normally be the issue price per unit, multiplied by the number of units returned (eg 2 bags of cement @ U 6 per bag = U 12).

Priced copies of the "stores issued notes" and "stores returned notes" will be received in the finance department daily, weekly or monthly and will be listed in a "stores journal" or "abstract of stores". For example, the stores issues for Kambale Municipal Council for Feb. 19_6 might appear as follows:

MONTHLY STORES JOURNAL
Feb. 19_6

Stores Return No		Total	Road	Sewage	Housing	etc
Returns	Issues	Amount	Repairs	Disposal	Repairs	
485		25CR	25CR			
486		60CR		60CR		
487		15CR			15CR	
		100CR	25CR	60CR	15CR	
	4825	440	440			
	4826	280			280	
	4827	10				10
	4828	45		45		
	4829	125		125		
	(etc)	(etc)	(etc)	(etc)	(etc)	(etc)
		3,940	685	250	460	2,545
		========	========	=========	========	=======

Income and Expenditure Analysis

The totals of each analysis column will be posted as debits in the appropriate accounts in the expenditure ledger, the grand total of U 3,940 being credited to the stores control account.

You will notice that the "stores returned notes" have been listed first, as credit (ie minus) entries. This would, in practice, probably be done in red ink. Sub-totals are made in each column, which are deducted from the totals of issues, to give net totals.

At the end of the financial year the total purchases will have been debited to the "Stores Control" account and the total net issues (ie issues minus returns) will have been credited.

For Kambale Municipal Council, the final figures for 19_6 might appear as follows:

Stores (Control)

To Balance b/f	310,460	By Issues (Net)	122,920
To Purchases	106,820	By Balance c/d	294,360
	417,280		417,280
	=======		=======
To Balance b/d	294,360		

The debit balance brought forward at the beginning of the year represents the value of the actual stocks in the store at 1 Jan. 19_6 as shown by stocktaking on 31 Dec. 19_5. Reference to the balance sheet on page 285 of Chapter 9 will show this figure of U 310,460 as a current asset.

The figure for purchases (U 106, 820) represents items posted from the expenditure journal and sundry creditors lists for materials purchased for stores during the year.

The figures for issues (U 122,920) represents the net totals of the stores journals, giving an analysis of issues and returns during the year. Individual amounts totalling U 122,920 will have been debited to various expenditure accounts.

We must now consider the figure of U 294,360 shown as Balance c/d. It is (at this stage) nothing more than a balancing figure calculated from the other three figures. It does NOT represent the value of the goods in the store at 31 Dec. 19_6. It would only do so in a hypothetical situation of perfection which never exists in practice. To take an extreme example, suppose the stock was completely destroyed by fire on 31 Dec. 19_6. The control account would show the value to be U 294,360 - yet the actual value would be NIL.

The value of stocks and stores to be carried forward in the books and shown in the balance sheet must always be the value of the actual goods in the store, arrived at by stocktaking and stock valuation at the end of the financial period.

Stocktaking should be carried out by at least two competent and fairly senior officials, neither of whom is the storekeeper. In the authority of reasonable size the chief officer of the department controlling the stores will send to the chief financial officer a certified list of all items and quantities held in stores.

Municipal Accounting for Developing Countries

The finance department will compare the items on the stock lists with balances shown in the stores ledgers and price out the values of the stocks, usually at cost.

Let us suppose that the values of stocks for Kambale Municipal Council at 31 Dec. 19_6, as shown by the priced stocktaking lists is U 293,840, which is U 520 less than the book figure. This net deficiency will arise for a variety of reasons which will be dealt with later. As it is a reduction in the value of assets it is a loss (or expense) which must be debited to an expenditure account and credited to the control account. The simplest method would be to debit the loss to a "deficiency on stores" account in the accounts of the department concerned by a journal entry as follows:

19_6 Dec.31	Deficiency on Stores DR.
	  To Stores (Control)
	  Being net deficiency on
	  stocktaking at 31/12/_6
		520	520

Normally, writing off the deficiency will require the approval of the Finance Committee or Council.

Other methods of dealing with deficiencies will be shown later.

After the above journal entry has been posted to the ledger accounts the Stores (Control) Account will appear as follows:

Stores (Control)

To Balance b/f	310,460	By Issues (net)	122,920
To Purchases	106,820	By Deficiency (net)	520
		By Balance c/d	293,840
	417,280		417,280
	=======		=======
To Balance b/d	293,840		

The balance carried down, which will appear in the balance sheet as at 31 Dec. 19_6, now correctly represents the value of actual physical stocks in hand at that date, and is not merely a fictitious "book" figure.

In our example we have assumed a single store for all commodities. In practice even where there is central purchasing and storing, there will be a number of sub-stores for (say) housing, water, works, education and health departments.

Readers may have noted that the stores balance in hand approximates 3 years' usage. Clearly, this would be excessive for a local authority near its supply area, but may well be necessary for a remote developing country importing most of its needs.

Income and Expenditure Analysis

142. STORES LEDGER

In the previous section we dealt with the accounting for expenditure in detail, whereas the materials were accounted for in total. We shall now reverse the procedure, to show how the materials are accounted for in detail against the totals in the control account.

Reference to the control account on this page shows that purchases amounted to U 106,820 during the year, but this does not merely represent a vague quantity of goods. Different quantities of many different commodities have been purchased at various prices and all must be separately accounted for.

Similarly, the issues (net) totalling U 122,920 will include cement, pipes, stopcocks, bricks and many other commodities.

The net deficiency of U 520 is made up of a number of different surpluses and deficiences and the balance of U 293,840 represents a list of the various items in the stores, all individually priced out.

A separate account is opened in a stores ledger for every different type and size of commodity in the stores. For example, in the stores ledger of Kambale Municipal Council there will be separate accounts for cement, 1" pipes (cast iron), $1\frac{1}{2}$" pipes (cast iron), $\frac{1}{2}$" stopcocks, $\frac{1}{4}$" stopcocks, best quality bricks, second quality bricks, petrol, oil - SAE 20, oil - SAE 30, and so on.

To show how the stores ledger operates in practice we will take three specimen accounts as follows:

STORES LEDGER ACCOUNT											
Material: Stopcocks (CI) $1\frac{1}{2}$"										Folio: S/23	
Max: 20				Min: 10						Re-order: 14	
Date	Received				Issued				Balance		
	GR No	Qty	P	Amt	SR No	Qty	P	Amt	Qty	P	Amt
19_6			U	U			U	U		U	U
Jan. 1									15	80	1,200
Feb.18					1568	2	80	160	13	80	1,040
Mar. 7					1593	1	80	80	12	80	960
Apr.16					1621	1	80	80	11	80	880
23	431	10	80	800					21	80	1,680
Aug. 3					1847	3	80	240	18	80	1,440
Oct.18					1928	1	80	80	17	80	1,360

STORES LEDGER ACCOUNT

Material: Ferrules (CI) 1½" **Folio:** F/9

Max: 25 **Min:** 10 **Re-order:** 14

Date	Received				Issued				Balance		
	GR No	Qty	P	Amt	SR No	Qty	P	Amt	Qty	P	Amt
19_6			U	U			U	U		U	U
Jan. 1									18	60	1,080
Feb.18					1568	2	60	120	16	60	960
Mar. 7					1593	1	60	60	15	60	900
May 9					1656	1	60	60	14	60	840
Jun.23					1695	1	60	60	13	60	780
Jul. 1					1756	1	60	60	12	60	720
Nov. 9	546	10	71	710					22	65	1,430
Dec.31					Def	1	65	65	21	65	1,365

STORES LEDGER ACCOUNT

Material: Cover boxes (for stopcocks) **Folio:** C/32

Max: 180 **Min:** 100 **Re-order:** 130

Date	Received				Issued				Balance		
	GR No	Qty	P	Amt	SR No	Qty	P	Amt	Qty	P	Amt
19_6			U	U			U	U		U	U
Jan. 1									162	15	2,430
Feb.18					1568	2	15	30	160	15	2,400
Mar. 7					1593	1	15	15	159	15	2,385
(etc)								(etc)			(etc)
Aug.16					1859	4	15	60	126	15	1,890
Sept.3					(351)	(1)	(15)	(15)	127	15	1,905
(etc)								(etc)			
Dec.19					2046	1	15	15	108	15	1,620
Dec.31					(Sur)	(1)	(15)	(15)	109	15	1,635

Each page of the stores ledger is headed by the description and size of the item and is given a folio number. Following the normal rules of book-keeping, stores received (ie increases in assets) are recorded as debits and stores issued (ie decreases in assets) as credits. Because the stores accounts are real accounts (ie of assets) the balance must always be a debit.

Also shown in the headings are figures of maximum and minimum stocks and the re-ordering level. The quantity of stocks held in the store will normally be kept between the maximum and minimum levels, and new stock will be ordered when the quantity falls below the re-ordering level.

Income and Expenditure Analysis

Taking the account for "Stopcocks - 1½" we can see that the balance of stock in the store at 1 Jan. 19_6 was 15 items at a unit price of U 80 giving a total value of U 1,200. Various issues take place, and when, on 18 Feb., stocks fall below the re-ordering level (14) another 10 items are ordered. These are received on 23 April and entered on a "Goods Received Note" as follows:

	GOODS RECEIVED NOTE					No.431
From: United Metals Ltd					Date 23/4/_6	
Goods	Size	Pkgs	Order No	Qty	Rate	Amount
Stopcocks Cast Iron	1½"	2	58249	10	Units / 80	Units / 800
Carried	Received By		Inspected By			
E.A.R.	A. Kintu		B. Katoa			
Purchase Requisition	Bin	Ledger	Remarks		Inv No	Voucher
4856	85	S/23	Correct		4825	363

The note will be made out in triplicate by the storekeeper except for the "rate" and "amount" columns. Two copies will be sent to the expenditure section of the finance department where they will be compared with the invoice. The overall amount of the invoice, including carriage and less discounts, will be divided by the quantity to give a rate (ie price per unit). The rate and amount will be entered on the goods received note and one copy sent to the stores ledger keeper who will enter the details in the stores ledger as shown. The invoice will be passed for payment and posted to the stores ledger control account in the expenditure ledger.

The control account and the stores ledger are in agreement, because U 800 has been debited to each.

Now let us consider the issue of stores. Let us assume that on 7 March a 1½" inch pipe is to be connected to a water main. Among the materials required will be a stopcock, a ferrule and a cover-box. The engineer or foreman in charge of the job will send to the storekeeper a "Stores Requisition Note" in triplicate as follows (the "rate" and "amount" columns being left blank):

Municipal Accounting for Developing Countries

	STORES REQUISITION NOTE				No.1593
Department:	Works				
Charge to:	Water Connections			Date:	7/3/_6
Materials Required	Ref	Size	Qty	Rate	Amount
Stopcocks CI	S/23	1½"	1	80	80
Ferrules CI	F/9	1½"	1	60	60
Cover Box	C/32	-	1	15	15
					155 ===
Ordered By: A. Musoke	Issued By: A. Kintu			Expenditure Code	
Received By: B. Musa	Ledger FG	Exp NP		01/25/46	

The storekeeper will issue the goods from the stores and sign the requisition. He will retain one copy as his authority for the issue and pass the other two to the stores ledger clerk. The stores ledger clerk will put the rate and amount on each of the two copies and send one copy to the accountancy section for analysis in the store journal as expenditure. The other copy will be posted into the three separate accounts in the stores ledger as shown. The U 155 will be debited (through the stores journal) to the appropriate expenditure account, ie Water Connections - code 01/25/46. As part of the stores journal total, this U 155 will be credited to the stores control account. This credit will be equal to the individual amounts credited in the stores ledger, thus still keeping the books in balance.

Sometimes requisition notes are not used. Instead, "Stores Issued Notes" are made out in triplicate by the storekeeper and signed by the persons drawing the stores. The accounting procedures are the same as for a requisition note, which itself becomes an issue note as soon as stores are issued.

Let us now assume that on 3 Sept. a cover box, in good condition, is returned to the stores, having been issued for a job but not now required. Two accounting adjustments are necessary:

(a) the original charge against the job in the expenditure accounts must be reversed; and

(b) the original issue shown in the stores ledger must be reversed.

The storekeeper would prepare a "Stores Returned Note" in triplicate as follows (the "rate" and "amount" columns being left blank):

Income and Expenditure Analysis

	STORES RETURNED NOTE				No.351
Department: Works					
Credit to: Water Connections			Date: 3/9_6		
Materials Returned	Ref	Size	Qty	Rate	Amount
Cover Box	C/32	-	1	15	15
Returned By: B. Musa	Received By: A. Kintu		Expenditure Code		
Approved By: A. Musoke	Ledger FG	Exp NO	01/25/46 (CR)		

The note would probably be printed in red to emphasise its "credit" or "minus" nature. Sometimes it is called a "stores credit note" to indicate a credit in the expenditure accounts (but at least one standard text book refers to it as a "stores debit note" because it is debited in the stores ledger!)

Two copies will be passed to the stores ledger clerk who will put the rate and amount on each of the two copies and send one copy to the accountancy section for inclusion as a red-ink entry in the stores journal, so that the expenditure account is credited with the value of goods returned. The other copy will be posted, as shown, in the stores ledger but it is normal practice to post them as "minus credits" to emphasise that they are cancellations of issues rather than new stock. (The figures are shown in brackets in our example to show that they are red ink figures.)

The U 15 will be debited (actually as a minus credit) to the stores control account as part of the net total in the stores journal. As this sum is also debited (again as a minus credit) in the stores ledger the books are once again kept in balance.

We must now consider how the stores ledger is affected by stocktaking. Reference to the "Stores Control Account" on page 431 will show that the book value of stock (ie before stocktaking) on 31 Dec. 19_6 was U 294,360. Up to this point, as we have seen, the individual accounts in the stores ledger have been carefully kept in agreement with the control account. The individual book balances in the stores ledger will therefore total U 294,360.

Let us suppose that part of the stocktaking list reads as follows:

Municipal Accounting for Developing Countries

Ref	Material	Size	Quantity		Price	Value	Adjustments			
			Actual	Book			Deficit		Surplus	
							Q		Q	
A/1	Acid - Sulphuric	(pints)	55	53	1	55			2	2
A/2	Angles - Steel (etc)	2"	14	14	20	280 (etc)		(etc)		(etc)
C/32	Cover Boxes (etc)		109	108	15	1,635 (etc)		(etc)	1	15 (etc)
F/9	Ferrules (etc)	1½"	21	22	65	1,365 (etc)	1	65 (etc)		(etc)
S/23	Stopcocks (etc)	1½"	17	17	80	1,360 (etc)		(etc)		(etc)
						293,840 =======		1,425 =====		905 =====
						NET SURPLUS/ DEFICIT		520		

MAIN STORES STOCKTAKING 31/12/_6

The stores ledger clerk will prepare the list, giving the details of materials in the first three columns. The stocktakers will enter up the actual stock in column four and return the list to the stores ledger clerk. The stores ledger clerk will insert the "book" figures in column five and the prices in column six from the stores ledger. The values of the actual stock will then be calculated by multiplying the rate (or price) by the actual stock (NOT the book stock).

When the values have been inserted in column seven they will be totalled to give the value of all stocks held in the stores. This value of U 293,840 is the one which must be carried forward as a balance on the stores control account and included in the balance sheet. As shown on page 432 it is less than the book value of U 294,360 by U 520 which is written off as a deficiency.

However, if the U 520 is credited only in the stores control account the total balance carried forward (U 293,840) will no longer agree with individual balances in the stores ledger, which still total U 294,360. The next stage, therefore, is for the stores ledger clerk to compare actual values with book values and to calculate the surpluses and deficiencies on individual commodities, as shown under "adjustments". For example the actual stock of cover boxes was 109 but the stores ledger shows a balance of 108; thus there is a surplus of 1 item, which is valued at U 15. On the other hand 1½" ferrules show a deficiency of 1 item, valued at U 65.

When all the surpluses and deficiencies have been calculated they will be posted as adjustments in the stores ledger. For example the surplus on cover boxes has been posted as a debit (actually a minus credit) in folio C/32 of the stores ledger; the deficiency on 1½" ferrules has been posted as a credit in folio F/9 of the stores ledger.

When all adjustments have been posted in the stores ledger we shall have:

Income and Expenditure Analysis

		Units
	Deficiencies (credited)	1,425
Less	Surpluses (debited)	905
	Net Deficiency (credited)	520

The net deficiency agrees with the figure credited to the control account and the books are brought finally into agreement for preparation of final accounts.

This agreement of the stores ledger and the stores control account with the values of actual physical stocks is most important. Some authorities have been known to produce final accounts with stores shown as credit balances. This is of course completely incorrect because real (asset) accounts must always have debit balances.

In this chapter we have studied the basic book-keeping aspects of the stores ledger. We shall give further consideration to other aspects of stores accounting in Chapter 13.

143. EXPENDITURE LEDGER

Amounts accumulated in the various columns of the expenditure journal, wages journal, vehicles and plant journal, and stores journal may be totalled at the year end and individual totals posted direct to the main ledger.

However, it is more likely that the various journals will be totalled monthly, or even weekly, and posted to appropriate accounts in an expenditure ledger. There will be a separate folio in the expenditure ledger for each control account, revenue account or capital account against which expenditure is incurred or payment made. In other words, each page will correspond to a column of the various journals.

If we assume that Kambale Municipal Council posts monthly to its expenditure ledger the folio for "Clinics and Dispensaries - Repair and Maintenance of Buildings" might appear as follows:

EXPENDITURE ACCOUNT

Code   02/15/19   Estimate   U 3,000

Head   Health - Clinics and Dispensaries - Repair and Maintenance of Buildings

Date	Details	Ref	Debit	Credit	Cumulative Expenditure	Balance of Estimate
19 6	Source					
Feb.28	Exp Jnl	13	240		240	2,760
Apr.30	Exp Jnl	29	380		620	2,380
May 31	Stores Jnl	11	160		780	2,220
Jun.30	Wages Jnl	15	1,260		2,040	960
30	Trans Jnl	9	620		2,660	340
30	Stores Jnl	13	390		3,050	(50)
Jul.31	Main Jnl	53		120	2,930	70

Municipal Accounting for Developing Countries

The code number can be broken down as:

        02   = Health Committee
          15   = Clinics and Dispensaries
              19   = Repair and Maintenance.

The estimate of U 3,000 is from item 57 of the Clinics and Dispensaries estimates (page 294 of Chapter 9).

The expenditure ledger has been kept in the same form as that referred to in Section 51 of Chapter 4. In addition to providing an accumulating balance of expenditure an additional column headed "Balance of Estimate" shows how much of the estimate (or vote) remains unspent. It must be recognised, however, that unless commitment accounting is in operation this figure must be treated with care, as there may have been orders issued which have not yet been paid for.

Commitment accounting is a system whereby the expenditure account is debited at the time an order is placed. This enables the budget to be charged (encumbered) on the basis of a quoted or estimated price as soon as the commitment is made to expend the funds. When the goods are supplied, the invoiced price is substituted for the commitment, the entry for which is then reversed. In effect, the commitment is a temporary substitute in the expenditure ledger for the actual cost of the goods or services. If the goods or services are not provided by the end of the accounting period, the commitment must be reversed, because the rules of accounting provide for expenditure to be recorded only when goods and services are received. The system must be used with great care, otherwise muddle and confusion can arise through the use of information from two separate sources in a single account.

Postings from the subsidiary records have been made on the last day of each month. The account shows the source and reference of each posting and normally these postings come from the various special journals (or abstracts). The posting from the main journal arose because after the stores journal had been posted on 30 June the vote became overspent by (U 50) - the amount of budget overspending is enclosed in brackets. A check on the postings revealed that, in February, two replacement window frames were supplied at U 120 each and the invoice for U 240 was allocated to 02/15/19 (ie Clinics and Dispensaries - Repair and Maintenance of Buildings). One of the items was for the health administration office and should have been charged to code (say) 02/12/19 (ie Health Administration - Repair and Maintenance of Buildings).

An adjustment was therefore made as follows:

19_6 Jul.31	Health Administration - Repair and Maintenance DR. To Health - Clinics - Repairs and Maintenance Being correction of wrong posting on Voucher 298 dated 28/2/_6	02/12/19 02/15/19	120	120

When the final accounts are prepared, the accumulated totals of the various expenditure accounts will be posted as debits in the main ledger (as shown later). For example, the U 2,930 for Clinics and Dispensaries

Income and Expenditure Analysis

- Repair and Maintenance of Buildings will appear on the debit side of the main ledger as follows:

	Account Clinics and Dispensaries			Main Code	02/15	
Code	Details	Expenditure Analysis	Income Analysis	Transfers	Balances	Total
02.15.01	Salaries					
02	Wages (etc)					
19	Repair and Maintenance of Buildings (etc)	2,930				2,930

Within each objective classification (ie committee, service, division of service, sub-division of service) there should be fairly standard groupings for subjective analysis. The actual classifications will depend upon budgetary (and sometimes legal) requirements, but the form set out below may be useful as a guide. It is based upon recommendations of the CIPFA.

Employees

Salaries
Wages
Provident Fund Contributions
Gratuities
Leave Travel Provisions
Staff Housing

Running Expenses

Premises
  repair and maintenance of buildings
  alterations to buildings (not capitalised)
  maintenance of grounds
  fuel, light, cleaning materials and water
  furniture and fittings
  rent and rates
  contributions to repair and renewals funds (buildings)
  apportionment of expenses of operational buildings
Supplies and Services
  equipment, tools and materials
  provisions (food)
  clothing and uniform
  laundry
Transport and Plant
  use of transport and heavy plant (own transport)
  hire of transport and heavy plant
  car and cycle allowances
  petrol, oil, tyres and licences
  new vehicles and heavy plant (not capitalised)
  repairs to vehicles and heavy plant

contributions to repairs and renewals funds (transport and plant)
Establishment Expenses
  printing, stationery, advertising, postages, telephones and general
    offices expenses
  travelling, subsistence and conference expenses
  insurances
  apportionment of expenses of administrative buildings
  central (and/or departmental) establishment charges
  other establishment expenses re-allocated (detailed)
Miscellaneous Expenses
  consultants' fees
  other fees
  subscriptions
  grants to voluntary associations
  training of staff and study grants
  debt management expenses
  other expenses (detailed if necessary)

Debt Charges (also known as Loan Charges)

Revenue Contributions to Capital Outlay

144. **TRANSFERS AND ADJUSTMENTS**

In considering the analysis of income and expenditure we have seen that four main types of record are normally involved:

(a) prime records (eg receipts, invoices, muster rolls and stores notes);

(b) journals or subsidiary records (eg expenditure journal, wages abstract);

(c) subsidiary ledgers (eg income ledger, expenditure ledger); and

(d) main ledger (where final accounts are eventually drawn up).

In drawing up any system of analysis, an accountant should maintain a flexible attitude, remembering that the ultimate aim is to get the information on the prime records classified into a proper order in the main ledger. Indeed, if the main ledger were posted direct from prime records we should be carrying out book-keeping in the correct theoretical manner as explained in Chapters 1 to 5. Only the volume of transactions makes it necessary for the accounting work to be sectionalised, introducing the need for intermediate records. However, in certain circumstances, there is no reason why subsidiary ledgers should not be posted direct from prime documents, or the main ledger posted direct from journals or abstracts. As explained before, systems given as examples should be used only as a guide.

The way in which the systems are designed will largely determine how transfers and adjustments are made between accounts.

Sundry creditors, for example, at the year end, could be posted from the creditors list to the expenditure journal (or abstract). Alternatively they could be passed through a separate creditors journal (or abstract) and posted in total, direct to the appropriate accounts in the expenditure ledger. If few in number they might be posted individually direct to the expenditure ledger or even, in special circumstances, to the main ledger.

Adjustments must sometimes be made, transferring amounts between one account and another. In the above examples we have seen two such

Income and Expenditure Analysis

adjustments made through the journal, between different accounts in the income ledger and between various accounts in the expenditure ledger.

There is no practical reason why journal adjustments should not be made in the abstracts if required, but there might be theoretical objections to making journal adjustments to figures in another journal.

Alternatively, all journal adjustments could be made in the main ledger. However, if expenditure and income accounts are not adjusted during the year there will be defects in the system of budgetary control. Also, a large number of adjustments in the main ledger would make it cumbersome and untidy.

A sensible compromise would be to make day-to-day journal adjustments between accounts in the income ledger and in the expenditure ledger. Adjustments arising when final accounts are prepared can be made in the main ledger.

We have, so far, spoken of the journal as a bound book, but in certain circumstances it would be in a series of consecutively numbered "journal adjustment" slips containing the same information as a bound journal and kept in a journal file.

For example, the journal entry shown on page 440 might appear in loose leaf form as follows:

JOURNAL ADJUSTMENT NOTE

Date: 31 Jul. 19_6   Number: 53/6

Details of Debit			Details of Credit		
Account	Code	Amount	Account	Code	Amount
Health - Administration Repair and Maintenance of Buildings	02/12/19	120	Health - Clinics Repair and Maintenance of Buildings	02/15/19	120

Reason for Adjustment:
    Correction of posting error on voucher 298 (28/2/_6)

Authorised By: ABC   Posted By: PRT

It is most important for journal adjustments to have adequate references, otherwise tracing the entries at a later date is most difficult.

145. TABLES OF POSTINGS

The system of analysis of income and expenditure can be summarised in the following tables:

Municipal Accounting for Developing Countries

(a) **Analysis of Income**

Type of Income	Source	Debit	Credit
1. Cash Income	Copy Receipt	Cash	Income Accounts
2. Credit Income	Copy Invoice (analysed and summarised in personal account)	Debtors' Accounts	Income Accounts
3. Cash Receipts for Credit Income	Copy Receipt	Cash	Debtors' Accounts

(b) **Analysis of Expenditure**

Type of Expenditure	Source	Debit	Credit
1. Direct Payments	Paid Invoice	Expenditure Accounts	Cash
2. Accrued Expenditure	Unpaid Invoice (Creditors List)	Expenditure Accounts	Sundry Creditors
3. Settlement of Creditors	Paid Invoice	Sundry Creditors	Cash
4. Payment of Wages	Payroll	Wages (Control)	Cash
5. Allocation of Wages	Time Sheet (listed in wages journal)	Expenditure Accounts	Wages (Control)
6. Vehicle and Plant Expenditure	Paid Invoice Unpaid Invoice Time Sheet Stores Note	Transport and Plant (Control)	Cash Sundry Creditors Wages (Control) Stores (Control)
7. Use of Vehicles and Plant	Log Sheets (listed in transport journal)	Expenditure Accounts	Transport and Plant (Control)
8. Purchase of Stores	Paid Invoice Unpaid Invoice	Stores (Control)	Cash Sundry Creditors
9. Issue of Stores	Stores Requisition or Issue Note	Expenditure Accounts	Stores (Control)
10. Return of Stores	Stores Return Note	Stores (Control)	Expenditure Account

13. Stores and Costing

Section		Page
146.	Physical Control of Stores.	446
147.	Bin Cards and Stock Book.	447
148.	Maximum and Minimum Stocks.	448
149.	Re-Ordering Level.	449
150.	Issue Prices.	451
151.	Continuous Inventory.	455
152.	Surpluses and Deficiencies.	456
153.	Stock Valuation.	457
154.	Costing and Budgetary Control.	458
155.	Elements of Cost.	460
156.	Job Costing.	462
157.	Process Costing.	462
158.	Unit Costing.	463
159.	Standard Costing.	464
160.	Marginal Costing.	465
161.	Labour Overheads.	466
162.	Stores Overheads.	477
163.	Light Plant and Tools.	479
164.	Administrative Overheads.	481

146. PHYSICAL CONTROL OF STORES

The purchase of materials and goods by an authority will be either for immediate use on a job, or taken into stores and held until required.

Materials held in stores represent assets of the authority and should be strictly controlled and accounted for. In the last chapter some of the accounting procedures were explained in detail but these do not provide a proper safeguard of stores unless supported by an adequate system of physical controls. Although cash is controlled by accounting procedures, no one would leave the cash on the counter overnight or leave the strongroom unlocked - yet materials of huge monetary value, although carefully accounted for, are often subject to little or no physical control.

One important factor in stores control is the ability and integrity of the storekeeper. He should be carefully selected for his duties and paid an adequate salary. He should be capable of dealing with the necessary clerical work and have some technical knowledge of the uses of materials. He should have a personality which will enable him to resist unauthorised requests for stores from persons of all grades of seniority. He must be thoroughly trustworthy and must rigidly adhere to instructions given by the Chief Officer controlling the stores (who should preferably be the Chief Financial Officer).

Materials, where appropriate, should be stored in properly constructed buildings. The store should be in a fairly central position and should have adequate facilities for handling and transport. No unauthorised person must be allowed in the stores, and there must be strict control of keys. Issue of stores should be made at a window or counter, and should only be made on properly authorised stores requisitions or issue notes. Materials should be stored in clearly labelled bins, shelves and racks. Liquids should be stored in proper containers such as bottles, cans or drums. Some bulky items such as large pipes, sand and gravel may have to be stored outside the stores building, but should still be in an enclosed yard and given adequate protection from the weather (eg tarpaulin sheets).

The main risks to be guarded against are deterioration (due to weather or improper storage) and pilferage (theft) by employees and others. Many materials, such as large diameter pipes for water mains, will have little value to a potential thief. On the other hand there may be commodities which have a high risk of theft and which must be carefully controlled. These include portable and attractive items such as paint, cement, timber, light bulbs, petrol, lubricants, paraffin, vehicle

Stores and Costing

spares, tyres and items (such as stopcocks) which may contain valuable raw materials (such as brass). Petrol should be stored in underground tanks and issued through a properly controlled petrol pump.

Finally, the stores must be covered by adequate insurance against such risks as fire, theft, third-party liability and industrial injury.

147. BIN CARDS AND STOCK BOOK

Sometimes the stores ledger will be kept in the stores. However, as it is an accounting record, and an integral part of the costing system, it is far preferable for it to be kept in the finance department. This being so, the storekeeper will require some simple records to control the quantities of stocks. The most common of these are bin cards which will be attached to each bin, shelf or rack. There will be a separate card for each item of stock, corresponding with a folio in the stores ledger. A bin card for the 1½" stopcocks shown in the stores ledger folio on page 433 of Chapter 12 might appear as follows:

BIN CARD

Material: Stopcocks (CI) 1½"	Bin No: 125
Normal Quantity to order: 10	Code No: 586
	Max: 20
Stores Ledger Folio: S/23	Min: 10
	Re-order: 14

Receipts			Issues			Balance	Remarks
Date	G.R. No	Qty	Date	S.R. No	Qty	Qty	Goods Ordered and Audit Notes
						15	Balance 1/1/ 6
			18.2	1568	2	13	Re-ordered ($\overline{10}$)
			7.3	1593	1	12	
			16.4	1621	1	11	19/4 ST
23.4	431	10				21	
			3.8	1847	3	18	
			18.10	1928	1	17	

The bin card should be entered up by the storekeeper as he draws the materials from the bin, rack, shelf or other container and before they are issued. Sometimes the storekeeper will use slack periods between issues to enter up bin cards from issue notes, but experience shows that unless cards are entered up promptly the work is often forgotten, causing difficulties when stock is later checked.

The bin card is similar to a stores ledger, but with prices and values omitted. These do not concern the storekeeper, who is controlling only on quantities. When the quantity falls below the "re-order" level the storekeeper initiates the procedure for ordering new stocks, perhaps by sending a purchase requisition to the central purchasing section of the finance department. Notice that an internal auditor (ST) checked the stock on 19 April.

Although, in theory, bin cards should be kept in the place where materials are stored, a practical difficulty arises where bulky items are stored in the yard. A bin card can hardly be placed upon a pile of sand or upon a stack of 12 inch pipes. In these cases bin cards will be kept in a suitable tray or box in the storekeeper's office.

Sometimes a stock book will be kept in the storekeeper's office in addition to the bin cards on the containers. Sometimes the stock book will be used instead of bin cards. A stock book will be rather like a series of bin cards bound into a looseleaf binder, but unlike bin cards will probably be entered up from issue notes and returned notes, rather than at the time of issue.

The actual system chosen will be based upon the layout of stores, quantities and types of materials, numbers and calibre of the storekeeping staff and the standard of stock control. Where material control is highly developed, stock requirements are carefully planned in advance of the work to be done. In this case the stock book may have special columns to show stock reserved for jobs (but not yet issued) and stocks on order (but not yet received). Increasingly, well-organised stores will have their records computerised, with linkage to centralised accounting records.

148. MAXIMUM AND MINIMUM STOCKS

It is the duty of the officers controlling stocks to ensure that sufficient goods are retained in stores to meet all requirements without carrying unnecessarily large stocks.

To ensure that all requirements for materials can be met without delay a minimum stock level is fixed for each commodity. In our own homes, if we can avoid it, we do not allow ourselves to run completely out of food before we buy some more. Neither in business do we allow our stocks of materials to become exhausted before more are ordered.

The minimum stock level fixed for each commodity is a matter of judgement based on experience. Matters considered will include whether the material is easily and quickly obtainable; whether an emergency (such as a burst water main) could cause serious public inconvenience if stocks were not available; whether other materials could be substituted if stocks ran out; and the frequency with which the materials are used.

To avoid holding unnecessarily large quantities of materials in stores a maximum stock level is fixed for each commodity. As with minimum stock levels, skilled judement is involved in fixing levels of maximum stocks.

Whilst it is generally accepted that minimum stock levels are necessary to avoid running out of materials it is sometimes more difficult to appreciate the necessity for fixing maximum stock levels. It is sometimes argued that if enough materials are available to meet immediate requirements there is no need to worry if extra quantities are held because a few more will always be a useful reserve. This is not a valid argument and is refuted by the following important points:

(a) **Working Capital**

Money spent and held in the form of stores is no longer available as cash. For example the 1½" stopcocks shown in the stores ledger folio on page 433 of Chapter 12 have a maximum stock level of 20 items, thus tying up U 1,600 of cash which would otherwise be available. If maximum

Stores and Costing

stocks were allowed to rise to 40 items a further U 1,600 would not be available. If there were 500 different items in stock at an average value of U 20, the total cash tied up would be U 10,000. Allowing stocks to double would tie up a further U 10,000, which would have to be raised from the public in additional rates and taxes, or temporarily borrowed at current rates of interest.

(b) **Storage Space and Cost of Storage**

Increased quantities of materials also require increased storage space (perhaps involving capital expenditure) and will incur increased storage costs, such as storekeepers' wages, cleaning, lighting and stationery. If, as in the above example, maximum stocks were allowed to double, a new store might have to be built and additional staff employed. Tasks such as stocktaking, auditing and even cleaning the stores would take up to twice as long or would be done far less efficiently.

(c) **Risk of Loss**

If too much of a perishable commodity is held in stores it may perish before being used; volatile materials such as petrol may evaporate; materials may become out of date and have to be thrown away because new discoveries make them obsolete; and the authority may be unable to take advantage of a fall in price, if old stocks, purchased at higher prices, are still in the stores.

On the other hand, maximum stocks must not be set at too low a level for the following reasons:

(a) **Economic Ordering Quantities**

If maximum stocks are too low it will not be possible to order goods in bulk to take advantage of discounts and lower transport costs. To continue the example of the 1½" stopcocks, if it were not economical to order less than 10 at a time it would be wrong to fix the maximum stocks at (say) 15.

(b) **Delivery Periods**

If delivery periods are long, maximum stocks may have to be fixed at a higher point than if delivery periods are short.

149. **RE-ORDERING LEVELS**

Between the maximum and minimum stock levels of each commodity should be fixed a re-ordering level. When the stock level falls to this point, more materials should be ordered. The level will be fixed with reference to delivery periods and the rate of consumption of materials so that as far as possible the goods are delivered just before minimum stocks are reached. In the case of the 1½" stopcocks, new stocks were ordered after the issue on 18 Feb. when stocks fell below the re-order level of 14 to 13. They appear to have been supplied before minimum stocks were reached and when taken into stores the maximum was exceeded until the issue on 3 Aug. Although not serious in this case, consideration should be given to widening the margin between maximum and minimum stock levels to allow for fluctuating delivery periods.

Maximum stock, minimum stock and re-ordering levels should all be reviewed from time to time and adjusted to meet changing requirements. Queries might well be raised when stocktaking, particularly if a continuous inventory system is used (Section 151). Reference to the stores ledger folio for cover boxes on page 434 of Chapter 12 shows maximum stocks to be approximately three years' supply. This might be

STORES LEDGER ACCOUNT

Material: Indicator Plates - Stopcock   Folio: I/38

Max: 35   Min: 10   Re-order: 15

Date	G.R. No	Received Quantity U14	U15	U16	Amt U	S.R. No	Issued Quantity U14	U15	U16	Amt U	Balance Quantity U14	U15	U16	Amt U
19_6 Jan. 1	395	20			280						20			280
16						1511	3			42	17			238
23						1523	2			28	15			210
Feb. 3						1536	4			56	11			154
12	413		20		300						11	20		454
16						1547	3			42	8	20		412
27						1574	6			84	2	20		328
Mar. 6						1586	2			28	–	20		300
8						1602		3		45		17		255
9						1613		10		150		7		105
Apr. 8	425			20	320							7	20	425
16						1622		7	2	137			18	288

450

Stores and Costing

an indication of over-stocking but would not be so if, for example, a new housing estate of 100 houses were under construction and the houses would all be connected to the water main in the following year (19_7). However, because of the fluctuating nature of capital works it is arguable whether stocks should be built up in advance or whether they should be ordered as required. After all, the architect designing the houses would know about the connections well in advance and precise requirements could be ordered to arrive at the proper time. In certain circumstances, mathematical formulae can be used to assist in determining stock levels.

150. **ISSUE PRICES**

In Chapter 12 we referred briefly to the issue price of a unit of stores as being the cost price. There are three main methods of issuing stores at cost price and we shall consider each in turn.

(a) **First In First Out (FIFO)**

This method of pricing is based upon the assumption that materials are issued from stores in the order in which they are received into the stores. To illustrate how the system operates, let us examine a stores ledger folio for (say) stopcock indicator plates. An example appears on page 450.

On 1 Jan. 19_6 indicator plates were established as a stock item for the first time when 20 were received from suppliers. The invoice after allowing for carriage and discounts totalled U 280 and a unit price of issue was calculated as:

$$\frac{U\ 280}{20} = U\ 14\ each$$

On 16 Jan., 3 items were issued at U 14 per unit, the job being charged with U 42 leaving 17 units at U 14 still in stock, valued (at cost) at U 238. Further issues take place until on 3 Feb. there are 11 items in stock at U 14 per unit giving a value of U 154. On 12 Feb. another 20 items are received, but this time the net invoice totals U 300 giving a unit price of U 15 for the new items. The total in stock is now:

		Units
11 @ U 14	=	154
20 @ U 15	=	300
		454

On 16 Feb., more issues are required, and the issue price remains at U 14 per unit because there are still 11 items of the first delivery in stock. Issues continue to be made at U 14 per unit, until the last two items of the first delivery are issued on 6 March leaving a balance of the 20 units from the second delivery at U 15 per unit, a total value of U 300. On 8 March issues were made at U 15 per unit for the first time and after the further issue of 10 units on 9 March there were 7 units at U 15 in stock, giving a value of U 105.

On 8th April a further delivery of 20 items is received, the net amount of the invoice this time being U 320 giving a unit price for the new items of U 16. The stock is now:

	Units
7 @ U 15	105
20 @ U 16	320
	425

On 16 April a requisition (1622) is made for 9 items. There are only 7 in stock from the second delivery so the issues will be priced out as follows:

	Units
7 @ U 15	105
2 @ U 16	32
	137

18 items from the third delivery now remain in stock at a unit price of U 16 giving a value of U 288.

This method is straightforward and logical and it reflects the actual costs of material in the order in which they were incurred. However, if used for slow moving stocks, the charges made to jobs will bear little relationship to current costs.

(b) **Last in First Out (LIFO)**

This method of pricing is based upon the assumption that materials are

Stores and Costing

issued from stores in the reverse order to that in which they are received. In other words the last items received are the first to be issued. If the above method were applied to the example of the indicator plates, issues would be priced out in the same way as for FIFO until the second delivery. Immediately after this delivery the issues woud be charged out at U 15 per unit ie the unit price of the latest stock. After the third delivery the unit price of issue would immediately be changed to U 16 per unit.

The method is not a logical one and it is no longer accepted as an international accounting standard. However, it does result in charges to jobs being more or less related to current costs. Disadvantages are that balances on hand must be calculated at many different prices and also, where slow moving stocks are running down, charges to jobs will become more and more remote from current costs, to a much greater extent than under the FIFO method.

(c) **Average Price**

In theory, the FIFO and LIFO methods attempt to relate prices to individual deliveries. In practice all items of a single commodity in stock will be more or less the same as one another and no attempt will normally be made by the storekeeper to identify issues as coming from a particular batch of deliveries. Naturally, to avoid deterioration, he will try to issue earlier deliveries before later ones but when drawing items from bins or shelves he will probably take the one nearest to him or one on the top of the pile without much caring when it was delivered.

Because of this it would seem reasonable that all stock in the stores at a particular time should be issued at the same price, the prices of any new stocks being averaged with the prices of existing stocks.

Continuing the example of the indicator plates, the first lot of deliveries have an average price of U 14 as with the other methods. However, when the second delivery arrives the stocks are (as shown under FIFO).

		Units
11 @ U 14	=	154
20 @ U 15	=	300
31		454

The stocks are therefore 31 items with a total value of U 454. The new average unit price will therefore be:

$$\frac{454}{31} = U\ 14.65 \text{ approximately.}$$

New issues will therefore be made at the unit price of U 14.65 until further deliveries, when the average price will again be calculated.

In our example issues would be as follows:

					Units	Cents
	Balance	12/2 =		31 @ 14.65	454	00
Less	Issues	16/2 =	3			
		27/2 =	6			
		6/3 =	2			
		8/3 =	3			
		9/3 =	10			
			24 @ 14.65 =		351	60
	Balance	9/3 =		7 @ 14.63	102	40
Add	Receipts	8/4 =		20 @ 16.00	320	00
	Balance	8/4 =		27 @ 15.64	422	40

New average price = U $\frac{422.40}{27}$ = U 15.64 approximately.

The advantage of this method is that costs are recovered in a uniform manner and related to the average values of goods in stores at the time of issue. A disadvantage is that prices must be recalculated after every new delivery of materials.

Another example of this method is given in the stores ledger folios on pages 433-434 of Chapter 12.

A further method sometimes encountered is that of "most expensive out first", which is similar to LIFO but charges out the most expensive items (even if not the last deliveries) before the less expensive items. It is a somewhat crude method to ensure that highest costs are recovered at the earliest possible opportunity but it suffers from the same disadvantages as LIFO to an even greater extent. This method should not be confused with charging market price.

Other methods of charging out stores do not attempt to recover exact costs, but may have other advantages. They include the following:

(a) **Market Price**

With this method the amount charged to the job is the current market price per unit, irrespective of the original cost of the materials. It is based upon the assumption that stocks issued today must be replaced at current prices.

(b) **Standard Price**

This is a predetermined price, fixed in advance of a budget (financial) period and used throughout the period, usually without revision. Differences between actual prices and standard prices are dealt with as variances, and the reasons for fluctuations are investigated as part of the system of budgetary control. This method is mainly used in standard costing. Variances and standard costing will be explained later in this chapter.

(c) **Loaded Price**

This method attempts to recover from jobs not only the cost of actual materials but also overhead costs connected with stores, such as wages of the storekeeper and costs of providing and running the stores building. If stores running costs represented (say) five per cent of the value of materials issued during the year the issue prices would be cost prices plus five per cent (eg bolts costing U 1 would be issued out at U 1.05).

Where the stores accounting system is a fairly simple one, the issue prices will attempt to recover exact costs (ie FIFO, LIFO or average price).

The other methods form part of more complex costing systems and should not be used unless there is a proper system of accounts for controlling variances and overheads. A fault sometimes found is for stores receipts to be priced at cost whilst issues are made at current market prices. Where prices are fluctuating, the book values of stores will very soon bear no resemblance to actual values, and if prices are continually rising, credit balances will appear in the stores accounts - which is absurd.

151. CONTINUOUS INVENTORY

One of the drawbacks of an annual stocktaking is that it creates a bottleneck in the flow of work. Sometimes it is found necessary to close down the stores for a day (or longer) whilst stocks are checked. Another disadvantage is that because of the urgent nature of the work, inexperienced staff are often detailed to take stock but they may have no real interest in the task other than disposing of an irksome job as quickly as possible.

To avoid these difficulties, a system of continuous inventory should be established. Under this system, stock is taken continuously throughout the year. Officers from the internal audit section will visit the stores weekly, or even daily in a large authority, and will check the stock of a few items of stores selected at random. The stocktaking will be planned in advance to ensure that every item is checked at least twice during the financial year. The storekeeper will not be told in advance of these items. The plan to cover every item at least twice is necessary because experience shows that it cannot always be adhered to. Staff may be withdrawn from stocktaking occasionally to deal with more urgent work, and although they should catch up with the work later this is not always possible. Adjustment to the plan will ensure that every item is still counted at least once (which of course is the absolute minimum) and most will still be counted twice. The plan should provide for items of particular risk and those of greater value (referred to in Section 146) to be counted more frequently.

As each item of stock is checked it should be compared with the bin card. Surpluses and deficiencies should be noted on the bin card and the actual stock entered on the stocktaking list. The storekeeper's stock book should be similarly adjusted.

Attention should be given to maximum and minimum stock levels. Instances of overstocking or understocking should be taken up with the storekeeper, and if necessary reported to the Chief Financial Officer.

The stocktaking list must then be compared with the stores ledger. Any differences between the two records must be adjusted in the accounts. Where there is a deficiency, a stores issue note should be prepared for the number of items short and these will be priced out at normal issue prices. In the stores ledger and in the control account the issue note will be treated like any other. In the stores journal and expenditure accounts the issue will be charged to a "Difference on Stores" account. Where there is a surplus, this will be recorded on a stores returned note, priced and recorded in the normal way. The surplus will be credited through the stores journal to the "Difference on Stores" account.

Periodically, perhaps monthly or quarterly, a statement of surpluses and deficiencies will be presented to the Chief Financial Officer who will either allow the adjustments or require the internal audit section to make further enquiries. The Chief Financial Officer may need to seek formal approval to the writing off of deficiencies and acceptance of surpluses, perhaps from the Council's chief executive or a finance committee.

152. SURPLUSES AND DEFICIENCIES

In any stores system, certain surpluses and deficiencies are bound to arise from time to time. Some of these may be the result of carelessness but others arise because of the complex, yet somewhat inflexible, nature of stores accounting and because of the nature of the materials themselves, for example food and drink.

Some of the reasons for stores differences are set out below:

(a) Faulty Accounting Procedures

These include the issue of stocks without a requisition or issue note; not recording stocks returned on a stores returned note; making out issue notes after materials have left the store and forgetting quantities; and not amending requisition notes to exact quantities issued where different from quantities requisitioned. Sometimes, too, a works supervisor might issue duplicate requisition notes for the same issues, intending only to remind the storekeeper of his requirements. None of these should normally occur in a well-organised system.

(b) Faulty Issue Procedure

One problem arising is the estimating (or even guessing) of quantities issued, particularly of bulk items such as sand or gravel, where no weighing devices are available. Sometimes issues are made in excess of the quantities recorded, perhaps for "good measure". Another difficulty arises when materials normally issued in bulk are issued in smaller quantities. Two examples, one quite normal, the other more unusual, will illustrate the point.

(i) A request might be made to the storekeeper for a small quantity of cement (say a bucketful) for a trivial job. The storekeeper obtains a signature for the minimum quantity issuable (ie 50 kilo bag). During the storekeeper's absence from the store, his relief issues the almost complete bag for another job and records it again as an issue. Thus one bag of cement has been issued twice and stocktaking will reveal a surplus.

(ii) Roadworkers returning from their day's work with tar-covered shovels use a "tiny drop" of diesel fuel to clean them (again - quite a reasonable thing to do). As fuel issues are normally in gallons no record is made of the minute quantities used, as the storekeeper thinks it "will not be missed". The procedure, however, becomes a habit and before long, quite a large deficiency can occur.

Another frequent cause of difference is where there are items of similar type but different sizes. For example a $1\frac{1}{2}$" stopcock may be recorded when in fact a $1\frac{1}{4}$" stopcock has been issued (or returned). This will cause a surplus on one account which should cancel with a deficiency on another (a compensating error).

Certain surpluses and deficiencies due to faulty issue procedure must be accepted within reasonable limits: each case should be judged on its merits.

Stores and Costing

(c) Faulty Storage and Handling

Losses can occur through breakages, evaporation and deterioration. These can be minimised by proper storage containers and by careful handling but they can never be entirely eliminated. Storekeepers should not be allowed to dispose of breakages and deteriorated stocks without proper authority.

Differences can sometimes arise when items are returned to the wrong bins or shelves. Sometimes, goods booked out to jobs or purchased direct are left lying around in the stores and are counted as stock, thus causing a surplus and sometimes, too, a storekeeper will build up secret stocks of odds and end which have been returned to stores or "scrounged" without bringing them on charge in the accounts. Once again, differences within reasonable limits must be accepted.

(d) Fraud

This arises where goods are misappropriated by storekeepers or other staff. Apart from straightforward theft, which will reveal a deficiency, most frauds will be covered up by manipulating the accounts.

(e) Falsification of Records

This can sometimes occur where correct issues of stores are deliberately charged to incorrect jobs to cover up inefficiency or lack of budgetary control.

(f) Clerical Errors

These arise where issues are credited against incorrect stores ledger folios, and come to light through differences between the stores ledger and the bin cards or actual stock. For example a stores ledger may show a quantity of 25 whilst the bin card and actual stock shows a quantity of 24, because the ledger clerk has posted an issue to the wrong folio. In such a case a correcting entry must be made and if this means that the job has been charged with the wrong amount, adjusting entries should be passed through the nominal accounts.

One way of correcting such errors and to keep all accounts in line would be to make out a returned note for the incorrect entry and a fresh issue note for the correct one.

153. STOCK VALUATION

As already explained, stocks of materials in the stores are assets and should appear in the balance sheet. The quantities of stores to be included in the balance sheet will be the actual physical stocks as revealed by an annual stocktaking or by the continuous inventory. The basic rule for valuation of stocks in a balance sheet is that they should be valued at cost or market value whichever is lower.

Practical application of this rule usually means that stocks are valued at cost prices because these are readily available from the accounts and where stocks are turning over fairly regularly there should be little difference between costs and market values: in times of rising prices, market values tend to exceed costs.

Where issues are priced out on a cost basis (FIFO, LIFO or average price) the total stock valuations, after allowing for surpluses and deficiencies, should agree with the debit balance on the stores control account. Where this is the case, the balance on the control account will be the correct figure to use in the balance sheet.

However, as we have already seen, poor accounting procedures can sometimes result in a balance on the stores control account which differs widely from the valuations of actual stock. In all cases the figure shown in the balance sheet should be the values of actual stocks at cost (or market value). If book values shown in the balance sheet were different from actual values, the statutory auditor would be entitled to insist upon adjustments being made. It is not unknown for a local authority to show in its balance sheet (or equivalent) a negative (credit) balance for stores. The statutory auditor would be failing in his duty if he did not draw attention to this completely absurd situation.

Where periodical stocktaking (continuous inventory) and efficient pricing out is in force the balance on the Stores Control Account can be taken straight to the balance sheet without a special stocktaking being done.

A schedule of closing balances should, however, be extracted from individual item folios in the stores ledger to ensure that this ledger is in agreement with the Stores Control Account.
Some authorities are required by law to appoint committees (sometimes called "boards of survey") to check the stores at the end of the financial year. These bodies should be regarded as additions to (and not substitutions for) the detailed stocktaking procedures described above. Often the committees consist of laymen and their work cannot be accepted as the sole basis upon which accounts are to be prepared.

154. COSTING AND BUDGETARY CONTROL

During the last four chapters we have studied the procedures used by an authority in drawing up its budget, collecting budgeted income, incurring budgeted expenditure and accounting for its activities. We have seen how an authority may compare its actual income and expenditure against budgeted figures through a proper system of analysis.

Not unnaturally, we have concentrated upon the financial aspects of budgeting and accounting. We have regarded the budget as divided into various "votes" or "allocations" of money to be spent on various approved services. The Chief Financial Officer, working in close co-operation with other departmental heads, must account for these sums to the authority and ensure that the various items in the budget are not exceeded. This accountability of officials for public funds administered by them is fundamental to almost every type of public activity, whether administered by central government, local authorities or public boards.

However, this is only a part of the full story. Accountability is not the same as efficiency. Vote control, preventing the overspending of budgeted funds, falls considerably short of budgetary control, which is designed to promote the most efficient use of limited public funds.

An item in a budget for say "repairs and maintenance of buildings" may total U 1,000. If the actual amount spent during the period is U 950, there has been proper accountability or vote control. But if only one-third of the intended work, covered by the U 1,000 estimate, has been carried out, it indicates a lack of efficiency in spending the U 950.

If a businessman is less efficient than his competitors he may well be driven out of business. Their costs of production are lower than his and they can afford to sell at a lower price. A commercial organisation

Stores and Costing

must therefore keep a detailed watch upon its costs through some system of costing, however rudimentary.

A public authority is different from a commercial undertaking in two major respects:

(a) it normally has a monopoly of the services it provides; and

(b) it normally has power to raise funds from taxation.

Thus, the incentives to effiency through competition and profit-making do not exist. It is an unfortunate fact that inefficiency can so easily be passed on to the public in the form of higher charges, increased taxes and poorer services.

It is therefore most important for a public authority to attempt to set high standards of efficiency and to see that they are maintained, by keeping a watch over the detailed costs of carrying out its services.

A budget can be defined as: "The financial interpretation of a plan to give effect to the policies of management".

A budget is a plan of work, rather than a plan for spending money. The authority will lay down its policies, the officers will prepare plans to put them into operation and the Chief Financial officer will produce a budget expressing these plans in terms of money - the common measure of value.

Budgetary control can be defined as: "The establishment of a budget to relate the responsibilities of officials to the requirements of a policy. The continuous comparison of actual results with estimated results will ensure proper execution of policy decisions or provide a basis for their revision".

The budget expresses (in financial terms) what the authority requires to be done during a period of time. Budgetary control is necessary to make sure that as far as possible the instructions of policy-makers are carried out by the officials. Where it is not possible to adhere to budgeted plans the policy-makers must be informed and asked for revised instructions.

A good system of budgetary control should be effective as it would:

(a) define the objectives of the authority as a whole concerning services, charges and taxation;

(b) define the objectives to be achieved by various departments and services;

(c) show the extent to which actual results have exceeded or failed to reach the defined objectives;

(d) show the size of and the reasons for the variations from the budget to enable remedial action to be taken;

(e) assist in securing the most efficient use of the factors of production (labour, materials and equipment);

(f) assist in providing common standards of efficiency among the various activities of the authority;

(g) provide a basis for future policy and, if necessary, revision of current policy;

(h) facilitate centralised control over decentralised activities; and

(i) facilitate adjustment of the authority's activities as a result of changes in economic conditions. These may arise from seasonal or political factors or trade cycles.

The close comparison of actual results with budgeted results will require a detailed analysis and explanation of the financial accounts - in other words a costing system.

Comparison of actual costs with estimated costs will permit:

(a) corrective action affecting expenditure and income where the budget standard has not been achieved;

(b) investigation of cases where the budget has been exceeded by an appreciable margin; and

(c) adjustment of the budget to correct errors in its compilation and to allow for changing circumstances.

These requirements necessitate costs being kept with a high degree of detail.

155. ELEMENTS OF COST

The study of economics shows us that production is made up of three "factors of production" - labour, land (including raw materials) and capital. The economist defines the factors as they affect the community in general.

The accountant follows a somewhat similar pattern but defines his elements of cost as they relate to a particular activity. He includes within his definition of "materials" any manufactured goods purchased from another supplier. Even though they may be the product of earlier labour, capital and raw materials, they are (for a particular costed activity) merely materials. In the same way, for a particular activity, labour may be combined with capital and materials (eg driver, lorry and petrol) to perform "services".

The accountant therefore defines his elements of cost as:

                labour
                materials
                services.

These elements of cost are normally related to expenditure of money and are usually classified as follows:

Direct	**Indirect**
Wages	Wages
Materials	Materials
Expenses	Expenses

Direct costs are those which can easily be related to a particular activity. For example in a road repair job the direct costs would include the wages of the road-workers, the cost of materials such as tarmac or paving stones and the hire of transport and plant.

Indirect costs are those which, though necessary, cannot be easily related to a particular activity. Continuing the example of road

Stores and Costing

repairs, indirect costs would include the wages (or salaries) of the foreman, engineering staff, wages clerk, stores clerk and so on,

together with stationery for timesheets, payrolls and stores ledgers and expenses of the highways depot.

It is often the practice to refer to the direct expenses collectively as "prime cost" and indirect expenses as "overheads".

It is not always possible to distinguish clearly between direct and indirect costs. Indeed, the same item may be either direct or indirect depending upon the circumstances. For example the salary of the storekeeper is clearly an indirect cost of road repairs - but it is a direct cost when the costs of the stores depot are being considered.

Sometimes the scale of operations will determine whether costs are direct or indirect. For example, in a small authority, the salary of a works foreman would be an indirect cost. A large authority might have a separate foreman for each gang (or each service). Thus his salary could be a direct charge to the work upon which his gang is engaged, or to the service for which he is responsible.

Direct costs can normally be allocated through the expenditure analysis system to the appropriate jobs or services. Indirecto costs, on the other hand, are normally charged to holding accounts to be re-allocated, (often somewhat arbitrarily) to jobs or services.

Costs are incurred when the "factors of production" are used or used up - not as they are paid for. For example, if a workman is employed on a particular activity for 8 hours, costs have been incurred equal to 8 hours of his time at his gross hourly rate of pay, plus any appropriate overheads, even though he may not be paid his wages until the end of the month. Conversely materials purchased for stores do not become costs until they are issued to a job.

We have already seen in the chapter on "sundry creditors" that all direct materials and expenses must be reckoned as part of costs, even though payment takes place in a subsequent accounting period.

Costs can also be classified as follows:

>   variable costs
>   semi-variable costs
>   fixed costs.

Once again, the division is somewhat arbitrary but, in general, variable costs are those which vary directly with the volume of activity whereas fixed costs are not affected by such changes. Semi-variable costs tend to vary with the volume of activity but not in direct proportion.

Direct wages and materials are variable expenses, because for example, (at maximum efficiency) twice as many men and twice as much material will be needed for twice the quantity of work. At the other end of the scale the salary of the engineer or the rent of the offices are fixed expenses because they would not vary with different levels of activity in the works department.

Semi-variable expenses usually comprise a combination of fixed and variable expenses, such as in the operation of machinery, where up to a point, excess (unused) capacity may exist. For example if workmen were laying concrete, an increase of (say) 10% in the area to be laid would tend to require a 10% increase in direct labour and materials (ie variable expenses). If the mechanical concrete-mixer were capable of producing more concrete it would require more petrol, but the operator's wages and the standing charges (eg depreciation) would remain fixed. The operation of the mixer would therefore be a semi-variable expense.

Fixed and variable expenses can only be thus classified in what economists call the "short run", where there are limited variations in the volume of activity. In the "long run" all costs tend to be variable. For example, a doubling of output in laying concrete would probably require two mechanical mixers. Furthermore, if a local authority of a certain size required the services of a town engineer and a deputy it would not be unreasonable to expect a town of twice the size to require the services of a more highly paid town engineer and deputy together with perhaps two assistant town engineers, though there would tend to be certain "economies of scale".

The division of costs into "direct" and "indirect" draws attention to the fact that the "prime cost" of a job or service is only a part of the full cost. Administrative and other overheads may add a considerable amount to prime cost, before the full cost is arrived at.

The division into "fixed" and "variable" costs is important in marginal costing (see later).

156. JOB COSTING

Job costing is used where items of prime cost are traceable to specific jobs. A "job" may be regarded as a unit of work which can be clearly distinguished from another unit, whether of the same type of work or of a different type.

This form of costing can often be used for such work as house building, housing repairs, road repairs and rechargeable works. For example: "construction of three-bedroom house on plot 55 Tanu Drive";

"repairs to ceiling in kitchen of No 37 Church Road";

"reconstruction and resurfacing of Riverside Road from National Bank to the junction with Nakiwogo Lane"; and

"repair leaking water service to plot 345 High View (rechargeable to Mr B. Juma)"

can all be described as "jobs". The prime costs can be allocated to each job separately through the expenditure analysis system and the various overheads can also be apportioned.

Although some of the costs may be apportioned on an arbitrary basis it will be possible in each case to state a definite and final cost for each job. We can say "Job A cost X units".

157. PROCESS COSTING

Where the items of prime cost cannot be traced to specific jobs, process costing is used. This system is used where a continuous service is being performed (such as road sweeping or refuse collection) or a particular commodity is being continuously produced (such as water or electricity).

Process costing has little significance unless related to periods of time and volume of output. For example, the cost of a refuse collection service or a water undertaking could be related to a week, month or financial year. The costs of the refuse collection service could be further related to the number of premises served and those of the water

Stores and Costing

undertaking to the number of gallons supplied.

With job costing it is possible to say, for example, that the cost of connecting No 85 Elgon Avenue to the public water supply was U 485.35. Process costing will not tell us the cost of supplying a particular 300 gallons of water to No 85 Elgon Avenue because these costs are lost in the volume of general production and distribution.

Costs of providing continuous services can, however, be broken down to deal with separate processes. For example, we can distinguish the separate costs for refuse collection from those for refuse disposal or distinguish among the costs of (say) gathering and collection, storage, pumping, filtration, treatment and distribution of water.

158. UNIT COSTING

Unit costing is an extension of the system of process costing whereby the costs of an activity are related to units of production or other appropriate units to give an average cost per unit. For example unit costs could be calculated for a refuse collection service on the basis of "cost per bin emptied" or "cost per unit of premises". A water undertaking could be costed on the basis of "cost per thousand gallons pumped".

Sometimes a composite unit must be used. For example the costs of a hospital may be expressed in terms of a "patient/day", or the cost of a transport undertaking in terms of a "passenger/mile".

The calculation of a unit cost for any service is made according to the simple formula:

$$\frac{\text{Total cost of process or service}}{\text{Number of units}} = \text{Unit cost.}$$

Unit costs are important in fixing charges for services. It is easy to fix individual charges to consumers where the service can be job-costed (e.g. a water connection). Where the service is process-costed, the unit charge will be related to the unit cost of producing the service. The minimum unit charge to recover full costs will be equal to unit cost.

The calculation of unit costs enables comparisons to be made with:

(a) unit costs of budgeted performance;

(b) unit costs of past performances; and

(c) unit costs of similar services performed elsewhere (e.g. by another authority).

Each of these comparisons can provide a means of measuring relative efficiency but care must be taken to ensure that costs and cost units are strictly comparable or that allowance has been made for known differing circumstances. In particular, comparisons with other authorities should be made with caution, as circumstances of operating a service may be vastly different from place to place.

Care must be taken in selecting an appropriate unit, otherwise the value of unit costs is considerably diminished. The unit should be easily ascertainable with a high degree of accuracy, preferably from information in the authority's own records. It should also be strictly relevant. For example it would be absurd to express expenditure on road repairs as a unit cost per vehicle using the roads or per vehicle registered. In the first case, accurate information could not easily be defined or obtained and in the second case there is little relationship between the factors. Similarly in a water undertaking, care should be exercised in making direct comparisons between unit costs of water pumped and unit price per thousand gallons supplied because

this fails to allow for wastage of water between waterworks and consumer.

Unit costs prepared for publication and comparison with other authorities must cover full costs including overheads, which necessitates the full allocation of central administrative charges. However, when unit costs are used for purposes of internal financial control it is often useful to compare those based on prime costs only. This will direct attention to those items of cost which can be closely controlled (i.e. variable costs), without clouding the issue by the inclusion of overheads, which are usually apportioned arbitrarily.

159. **STANDARD COSTING**

As we have already seen, budgetary control is based upon:

(a) setting of standards;

(b) measurement of actual performance;

(c) ascertaining the amount and cause of variance; and

(d) taking corrective action where necessary.

In budgetary control these principles are applied to the authority as a whole or to its various departments. In standard costing they are applied to individual operations or processes. For example the budget for housing repairs may be analysed and controlled under headings of labour, materials, transport and various overheads. A system of standard costing will ensure that individual jobs (e.g. repairs to bathroom wall at 15 Church Road) and individual processes (e.g. painting a batch of houses) are controlled in detail.

A complete system of standard costing can be quite complicated to operate but its basic principles are simple. Actual costs of jobs or processes are compared with standard costs which are calculated in advance. The standard costs are estimated of what a job or process should cost and are calculated by relating a specification of labour and materials to given wages rates and prices. Overheads are then added to give full standard costs. Comparisons of actual costs and standard costs should be made in a way which will reveal not only the amount of variations but also the reasons for them.

Variations in material costs can arise principally through:

(a) usage variances - where different quantities of materials are used than were estimated for; and

(b) price variances - where prices paid for materials are different from those upon which estimates were based.

Variations in direct labour costs can also arise through:

(a) efficiency variances - where work is done at a different standard of efficiency than was allowed for; and

(b) wage rates variances - where wage rates are different from those upon which estimates were based.

Control over usage of materials and labour efficiency should be made the responsibility of foreman and supervisors, whereas variations in prices and wage rates can be regarded as being outside their control.

The calculation of standards of performance must, of course, be the duty of technical officers, not accountants. Co-operation between technical and finance departments is essential for it should result in improved standards of efficiency and economy.

Standard costs should be based upon realistic assessments of what is possible under normal working conditions. They should not be based on the ideal conditions of hypothetical maximum efficiency. If they were, no one would take them seriously and there would be considerable variation between standard costs and actual costs.

160. MARGINAL COSTING

Marginal cost can be said to be the cost of adding a single unit of activity to those already being performed, or the saving in cost of subtracting a single unit of activity from those already being performed.

Marginal costing is particularly concerned with the capacity of an authority to meet steadily increasing demands upon its services. Where a service is being operated below the full capacity of its capital equipment the marginal costs of additional activity will be much lower than unit costs (i.e. average costs). Unit costs cover fixed costs and variable costs, whereas marginal costs cover increases and decreases only in variable costs. This is because a small change in activity does not affect fixed costs which have already been incurred.

For example the unit costs of a refuse collection service would cover labour, operation and depreciation of vehicles and supervision. The marginal cost of emptying an additional bin along a route already covered by the vehicle would be the additional cost of labour only - the additional costs of stopping and starting the vehicle and of carrying the extra load would be negligible and the additional supervision costs would probably be nil.

However, where excess capacity is gradually being absorbed by expansion of the services there is eventually a saturation point in the use of existing capital equipment. Beyond this point, the marginal cost of further expansion of the service will exceed unit cost by a considerable amount.

In the above example of the refuse collection service, it will be seen that a point will eventually be reached where the vehicle can carry no more. At this point, the emptying of an additional bin will require the services of another vehicle, causing a heavy increase in fixed costs for operation and depreciation. Once the new vehicle is in operation it will require the services of a driver and a loading gang. As the service is further expanded within the new available capacity marginal costs will once more be lower than unit costs.

The massive increase in fixed costs which can arise as a result of a marginal increase in activity is a problem often faced by local and public authorities, particularly in developing countries, where demand for services is rapidly expanding but supply of capital finance is severely limited. One aspect of marginal costing concerns the additional costs to the authority of making decisions based upon alternative choices. Let us suppose that the hourly rate for running (say) a grader belonging to the authority's central transport and plant pool is U 27.50 whereas the charge made by an outside plant hire firm is U 25. Faced with these alternative charges against votes under his control, the highways superintendent might well be tempted to hire a grader from outside, rather than indent for one from the Council's plant pool. This must only be permitted if the plant in the pool is being fully utilised on other work. This is because fixed expenses (e.g. depreciation, garaging, wages of drivers, licence and insurance) are being incurred whether the Council's plant is being used or not.

In deciding whether or not to hire the plant from an outside contractor the rate for Council vehicles should be calculated on marginal costs (eg petrol, oil and general maintenance). This should then be compared with the all-inclusive rate for outside hire. Only in the unlikely event of the contractor's overall rate being less than the marginal rate for Council vehicles would it pay to hire from outside. From a purely practical viewpoint it would be foolish to use hired plant when the Council's own plant was standing idle.

However, comparison of the two rates might well be the cause of an investigation into the efficiency of the Council's plant pool. If the difference in costs persisted, it might be necessary to effect a re-organisation or even, perhaps, to close down the pool. A likely discovery might be that the pool had more plant than it required, and much idle time was pushing up the hourly rate of charge.

The above example illustrates that in the short run, decisions must be based upon comparison of marginal costs to the authority as a whole rather than upon comparison of total costs to individual jobs or departments.

In the long run, however, a comparison of total costs may reveal a need for greater centralisation or decentralisation of operations depending upon the circumstances. The relatively high overhead costs of operating a central department must be more than offset by eventual savings in the overhead costs of departments no longer performing the services. The efficiency of central departments depends upon what economists call "division of labour" (i.e. specialisation) and "economies of scale". Unless a central department is relatively large and its services are fully employed, these economies may not materialise. Indeed, if plant can be obtained from outside contractors at lower unit prices than those of council vehicles, it suggests strongly that the work should be done on contract by the private sector and not by council workers at all.

161. LABOUR OVERHEADS

We have so far assumed that all wages paid to workers can be allocated direct to particular jobs or processes. However, not all wages paid result in direct productive work, and there are also certain expenses which must be incurred beyond the amount of gross wages paid. These are known as labour overheads. Payments made to workers which are not directly related to work done include:

(a) sick pay;

(b) idle time (bad weather, travelling); and

(c) holiday pay.

Other expenses incurred which may relate to employment of labour included:

Stores and Costing

(a) personnel insurance;

(b) supervision (i.e. foremen);

(c) pension fund contributions;

(d) medical expenses; and

(e) housing subsidies (i.e. full economic cost, less rents).

Sick pay relates to the payment to a worker of all or part of his wages whilst he is unable to work through injury or illness. Idle time represents wages paid to workers whilst they are in the employment of the authority, but are prevented from working perhaps because it is raining or because the workers are travelling to or from the job. Holiday pay represents payments made to workers for public holidays and annual "holidays with pay". Personnel insurance represents premiums paid to cover personal accident and other employers' liabilities. Supervision covers the wages and other expenses (e.g. car allowances) of foreman and supervisors who may be responsible for a large number of jobs. Pension fund contributions have already been mentioned, but as well as the normal "employers' contribution" referred to in Section 130 of Chapter 11 an employing authority may sometimes have to pay a "deficiency contribution" into a pension fund. This is an amount paid into a superannuation (pension) fund to meet future deficiencies. A deficiency in this sense is not a book-keeping deficiency but is the estimated amount by which a pension fund will be unable to meet future calls upon its resources to pay pensions to contributors who have not yet started to draw them. These estimated deficiencies sometimes arise through changes in money values and in expectations of life. They are calculated, not by accountants, but by experts in life assurance statistics known as "actuaries". Medical benefits and housing subsidies arise as a result of special conditions of service: alternatively a housing allowance may be paid instead of a housing subsidy.

Sometimes the above expenses are charged direct to special heads in the accounts but where a single labour force is employed upon a number of jobs or processes, accurate costing is not possible by this method. Where a detailed costing system is in operation, the labour overheads will be charged initially to a "holding account" and re-allocated to jobs and processes by apportionment, usually as a percentage of direct wages.

Sick pay, idle time, holiday pay and supervisor's pay will be debited to the holding account and credited to the wages control account through the wages journal.

The other expenses will be debited to the holding account and credited to the cash book (or to the creditors' control account) through the expenditure journal (or creditors' list). The overheads will then be charged to the actual jobs or processes by applying a percentage to the direct wages charged to those activities. This is known as "overhead recovery". As with vehicle running expenses the overhead recovery must take place during the financial year, whereas actual overheads are not known until the year end. This necessitates overheads being recovered on an estimated basis and will almost certainly leave a debit or credit balance on the holding account at the year end. As with vehicles, this balance can be disposed of in several ways. The simplest and least accurate method is to debit (or credit) the difference to a single head in the revenue account. Making supplementary allocation involves extra work but will result in a more accurate recovery of all expenses incurred during the year. If the balance is carried forward it must be taken into account in fixing the rate of recovery for the following year recognising that accountancy is a continuous process and that the work

Municipal Accounting for Developing Countries

of an authority is not confined within individual financial years.

It is not unusual to have separate holding accounts for each department. The overheads are then recovered in proportion to the direct wages paid to workers of that department only.

To illustrate the above principles, let us assume that the works department of Kambale Municipal Council incurred the following labour expenses during 19_6.

	Estimate	Actual
Gross Wages		
Direct Labour	815,000	813,460
2 Foremen	18,000	18,320
Provident Fund		
Direct Labour	62,500	62,440
2 Foremen	1,000	920
TOTAL (Wages Control Account)	896,500	895,140
Other Expenses		
Personnel Insurance	6,000	5,880
Car Allowances (Foremen)	2,500	2,620
Pension Fund (Deficiency)	25,400	25,400
Medical Expenses	3,200	2,980
Housing Allowances	7,300	7,480
TOTAL (Cash and Creditors)	44,400	44,360
GRAND TOTAL	940,900	939,500

Let us assume that labour costs are required for the various jobs (or processes) carried out by the department during the year. We shall refer to these jobs (or processes) as A,B,C,D,E, etc. Direct wages and the Council's Provident (Pension) Fund contribution will be charged to various activities through the wages journal analysis. Other expenses will be charged out as overheads in proportion to the direct charges. The estimated allocation of wages might be calculated as follows:

Total Gross Pay and Provident Fund		896,500
Less Foremen:		
Gross Pay	18,000	
Provident Fund	1,000	19,000
		877,500
Less Holiday Pay (say 2 weeks annual leave plus 1 week public holiday)		
U 877,500 x 3/52	50,625	
Less Sick Pay (say 1 week per man)		
U 877,500 x 1/52	16,875	67,500
		810,000
Less Idle Time (say 10%)		81,000
Net Wages Charged Direct		729,000

A statement can now be prepared to relate total estimated payments to total estimated expenditure.

Stores and Costing

Expenditure	Amount	Payments	Amount
Direct Wages Charged to Jobs	729,000	Gross Pay	833,000
Overheads:		Council's Provident Fund Contributions	63,500
Foremen (W)	19,000	Personnel Insurance	6,000
Holiday Pay (W)	50,625	Car Allowances	2,500
Sick Pay (W)	16,875	Pension Fund Deficiency	25,400
Idle Time (W)	81,000	Medical Expenses	3,200
Personnel Insurance (E)	6,000	Housing Allowances	7,300
Car Allowances (E)	2,500		
Pension Fund Deficiency (E)	25,400		
Medical Expenses (E)	3,200		
Housing Allowances (E)	7,300		
	211,900		
TOTAL EXPENDITURE	940,900	TOTAL PAYMENTS	940,900

Of the estimated expenditure of U 940,900, only U 729,000 will be charged direct to jobs through the wages journal. The remaining U 211,900 will be charged to the Labour Overheads Holding Account through the wages journal (W) or expenditure journal (E).

However, the overhead expenses are just as much a part of the costs of jobs as the direct wages. They must be allocated from the holding account to the jobs in proportion to direct wages. The "labour overhead recovery rate", as it is called, is expressed as a percentage, calculated as follows:

Total Expenditure - Direct Expenditure = Overheads

$$\frac{Overheads}{Direct\ Expenditure} \times 100 = Recovery\ Rate$$

$$U\ \frac{211,900}{729,000} \times 100 = 29.06721\%$$

Because we are using estimates at this stage, the overheads can be recovered from jobs at the rate of 29% of direct wages. Recovery will take place continually during the year by debits to the individual expenditure accounts and credits to the holding account. At the end of the year a summary of the wages analysis might appear as follows:

Municipal Accounting for Developing Countries

Head	Direct Wages - Charged To Overheads	Direct Wages - Charged Direct	Overheads (Recovered at 29%)	Provisional Labour Costs of Jobs
Foremen	19,240			
Holiday Pay	54,360			
Sick Pay	16,280			
Idle Time	81,440			
Job A		6,200	1,798	7,998
Job B		18,420	5,342	23,762
Job C		6,020	1,746	7,766
Job D		440	128	568
Job E		11,360	3,294	14,654
(etc)		681,380	197,600	878,980
	171,320	723,820	209,908	933,728
	(U 895,140)			

The total wages allocated from the Wages Control Account is U 895,140 which agrees with the "actual" figure shown on page 468.

A summary of the expenditure journal (including sundry creditors) might appear as follows:

Head	Allocation - Wages Control	Allocation - Overhead Holding
Wages	831,780	
Provident Fund	63,360	
Personnel Insurance		5,880
Car Allowances		2,620
Pension Fund		25,400
Medical Expenses		2,980
Housing Allowances		7,480
	895,140	44,360
	(U 939,500)	

The U 939,500 represents the total expenditure incurred on labour during the year. A glance at the wages analysis shows that the labour cost charged to jobs totals only U 933,728 a difference of U 5,772 which arises as shown in the following table:

Stores and Costing

Expenditure	Amount	Payments	Amount
Direct Wages Charged to Jobs	723,820	Gross Pay	831,780
	-------	Council's Provident Fund Contributions	63,360
Overheads (recovered at the rate of 29%)	209,908	Personnel Insurance	5,880
		Car Allowances	2,620
Balance - (overheads under-recovered)	5,772	Pension Fund Deficiency	25,400
		Medical Expenses	2,980
		Housing Allowances	7,480
TOTAL EXPENDITURE	939,500	TOTAL PAYMENTS	939,500

Compare this with the estimated statement shown on page 365. The under recovery of U 5,772 arises because whereas a recovery rate of 29% was used the actual recovery rate should have been:

$$\frac{\text{Overheads}}{\text{Direct Expenditure}} \times 100$$

$$U \frac{215,680}{723,820} \times 100 = 29.79746\%$$

The U 5,772 therefore represents 0.79746% of U 723,820.

If this small balance is carried forward to 19_7 the provisional labour costs will become the final costs. If a supplementary allocation is made, the provisional costs will be adjusted as follows:

(a)	(b)	(c)	(d)	(e)	(f)
Job	Direct Wages	Overhead Recovery Provisional (29%)	Supplementary (0.79746%)	Labour Costs Provisional (b + c)	Final (e + d)
A	6,200	1,798	49	7,998	8,047
B	18,420	5,342	147	23,762	23,909
C	6,020	1,746	48	7,766	7,814
D	440	128	4	568	572
E	11,360	3,294	90	14,654	14,744
(etc)	681,380	197,600	5,434	878,980	884,414
	723,820	209,908	5,772	933,728	939,500

The final costs (i.e. expenditure charged to jobs) now total U 939,500 which is equal to total expenditure incurred in the financial accounts.

In theory the journal entries would appear as follows:

Date	Particulars		Folio	Dr.	Cr.
19_6 Dec.31	Wages (Control) To Cash and Creditors Being gross pay and Council's provident fund contributions	DR.	1 C	895,140	895,140
Dec.31	Labour Overhead (Holding) To Cash and Creditors Being sundry expenses relating to labour	DR.	2 C	44,360	44,360
Dec.31	Labour Overhead (Holding) To Wages (Control) Being allocation of Foremen, Holiday Time, Sick Pay and Idle Time	DR.	2 1	171,320	171,320
Dec.31	Job A B C D E (etc) To Wages (Control) Being allocation of direct wages	DR. DR. DR. DR. DR. DR.	3 4 5 6 7 8 1	6,200 18,420 6,020 440 11,360 681,380	723,820
Dec.31	Job A B C D E (etc) To Labour Overhead (Holding) Being provisional recovery of overheads at a rate of 29%	DR. DR. DR. DR. DR. DR.	3 4 5 6 7 8 2	1,798 5,342 1,746 128 3,294 197,600	209,908
Dec.31	Job A B C D E (etc) To Labour Overhead (Holding) Being supplementary recovery of overheads at a rate of 0.79746%	DR. DR. DR. DR. DR. DR.	3 4 5 6 7 8 2	49 147 48 4 90 5,434	5,772
Dec.31	Works Revenue Account To Job A B C D E (etc) Being final costs transferred to revenue account	DR.	9 3 4 5 6 7 8	939,500	8,047 23,909 7,814 572 14,744 884,414

In theory the ledger accounts will appear as follows, (cash and creditors transactions are grouped together for simplicity - the actual division does not affect the issue):

Stores and Costing

Cash and Creditors C

19_6				19_6			
Dec.31	To Balance	c/d	939,500	Dec.31	By Wages (Control)	J	895,140
					By Labour Overhead (Holding)	J	44,360
			939,500				939,500
				Dec.31	By Balance	b/d	939,500

Wages (Control) 1

19_6				19_6			
Dec.31	To Cash and Creditors	J	895,140	Dec.31	By Labour Overhead (Holding)	J	171,320
					By Sundry Jobs	J	723,820
			895,140				895,140

Labour Overhead (Holding) 2

19_6				19_6			
Dec.31	To Cash and Creditors	J	44,360	Dec.31	By Sundry Jobs	J	209,908
	To Wages (Control)	J	171,320		By Sundry Jobs	J	5,772
			215,680				215,680

Job A (Labour) 3

19_6				19_6			
Dec.31	To Wages (Control)	J	6,200	Dec.31	By Revenue Account	J	8,047
	To Labour Overhead (Holding)	J	1,798				
	To Labour Overhead (Holding)	J	49				
			8,047				8,047

			Job B (Labour)			4
19_6 Dec.31	To Wages (Control) To Labour Overhead (Holding) To Labour Overhead (Holding)	J J	18,420 5,342 147 23,909	19_6 Dec.31 By Revenue Account	J	23,909 23,909

			Job C (Labour)			5
19_6 Dec.31	To Wages (Control) To Labour Overhead (Holding) To Labour Overhead (Holding)	J J J	6,020 1,746 48 7,814	19_6 Dec.31 By Revenue Account	J	7,814 7,814

			Job D (Labour)			6
19_6 Dec.31	To Wages (Control) To Labour Overhead (Holding) To Labour Overhead (Holding)	J J J	440 128 4 572	19_6 Dec.31 By Revenue Account	J	572 572

Stores and Costing

Job E (Labour) — 7

19_6				19_6			
Dec.31	To Wages (Control)	J	11,360	Dec.31	By Revenue Account	J	14,744
	To Labour Overhead (Holding)	J	3,294				
	To Labour Overhead (Holding)	J	90				
			14,744				14,744

Remaining Jobs (Labour) — 8

19_6				19_6			
Dec.31	To Wages (Control)	J	681,380	Dec.31	By Revenue Account	J	884,414
	To Labour Overhead (Holding)	J	197,600				
	To Labour Overhead (Holding)	J	5,434				
			884,414				884,414

Works Revenue Account — 9

19_6				19_6			
Dec.31	To Job A	J	8,047	Dec.31	By Balance	c/d	939,500
	B	J	23,909				
	C	J	7,814				
	D	J	572				
	E	J	14,744				
	(etc)	J	884,414				
			939,500				939,500
Dec.31	To Balance	b/d	939,500				

Treating the above exercise in isolation from the remainder of the authority's activities will give a balance sheet as follows:

475

Municipal Accounting for Developing Countries

Balance Sheet as at 31 Dec. 19_6

	Units		Units
Current Liabilities		**Deficiency**	
Sundry Creditors)	939,500	Works Revenue Account	939,500
Cash Overdrawn)			
	939,500		939,500

In practice of course the above transactions would form a part only of the comprehensive system of accounts.

It would not be unreasonable to question the necessity for having two separate allocations of overheads. Why not make a single allocation at the end of the year? The answer to this question is the key to costing and budgetary control.

If supervisors are able to exercise cost control, the costing information (though approximate) must be presented to them promptly. Costs presented to supervisors within 24 hours (even if slightly inaccurate) can form the basis of remedial action where necessary. On the other hand, costs which are accurate to the last cent are relatively useless if they take weeks to produce. In practice periodical adjustments of the percentage are made during the year.

In the above example the provisional cost of (say) Job A was U 7,998 whereas final cost was U 8,047, an error of U 49. Expressed as a percentage the margin of error on all jobs is:

$$U \frac{5,772}{939,500} \times 100 = 0.61\%$$

which is quite an acceptable margin for day-to-day control.

Had the estimates been slightly different, a recovery rate of 30% might have been used. This would have resulted in an over-recovery, but with a smaller margin of error.

A cost statement would show:

(a)	(b)	(c)	(d)	(e)	(f)
Job	Direct Wages	Overhead Recovery		Labour Costs	
		Provisional (30%)	Supplementary (0.20254%)	Provisional (b + c)	Final (e - d)
A	6,200	1,860	13(-)	8,060	8,047
B	18,420	5,526	37(-)	23,946	23,909
C	6,020	1,806	12(-)	7,826	7,814
D	440	132	1(-)	572	571
E	11,360	3,408	23(-)	14,768	14,745
(etc)	681,380	204,414	1,380(-)	885,794	884,414
	723,820	217,146	1,466(-)	940,966	939,500

The final costs are the same as under the previous rate of recovery (differences of U 1 arise through rounding-off). The margin of error is 0.16%.

Stores and Costing

Some accountants may question the logic of basing overhead recovery in proportion to direct wages paid. It might be suggested for example that recovery should be based upon man-hours, or that the foremen's car allowances should be recovered on a mileage basis. These are, in theory, valid arguments and it is not asserted that the method used in this section is necessarily the most logical. However, it is found from experience to be the most convenient and straightforward method in the absence of special factors, requiring different treatment. When making comparisons with the sometimes more sophisticated methods used in industry and commerce it must be remembered that the cost heads over which apportionment is made are far more numerous in public authorities than in many commercial concerns.

162. STORES OVERHEADS

We have seen earlier that materials passing through the stores are charged to jobs at cost or at prices closely related to cost (e.g. standard prices). This, however, ignores the cost to the authority of storing and issuing the materials. Such costs will include:

(a) capital charges on stores buildings (e.g. depreciation or loan charges);

(b) wages of storekeepers (including labour overheads);

(c) costs of heating, ventilating, lighting and cleaning the stores;

(d) stationery;

(e) repairs to the buildings;

(f) rates;

(g) furniture and fittings;

(h) protective clothing;

(i) insurance (i.e. fire, burglary etc); and

(j) deficiencies on stocktaking (less surpluses).

In order to make sure that the individual jobs or processes bear a proportion of overhead costs relating to stores, these costs will be initially debited to a stores overhead holding account, and recovered from cost heads in proportion to the value of stores issued to each job.

A complete statement of stores expenses might appear as follows:

Employees	
Wages	6,200
Other Employees Expenses	1,847
Running Expenses	
Repairs to Buildings	860
Fuel, Light, Cleaning Materials and Water	2,346
Furniture and Fittings	433
Rates	1,850
Protective Clothing	132
Printing and Stationery	249
Insurance	2,150
Net Deficiency (See Section 142, Chapter 12)	520
Loan Charges	3,540
	20,127

Municipal Accounting for Developing Countries

The net value of stores issues shown in Section 141 of Chapter 12 is U 122,920. The stores overhead recovery rate will therefore be:

$$\frac{\text{Stores Overheads}}{\text{Net Issues}} \times 100$$

$$= \frac{20,127}{122,920} \times 100 = 16.3741\%$$

The stores requisition note appearing on page 436 of Chapter 12 shows that U 155 has been charged to "water connections". In addition to the direct charge, a sum of U 25.38 will be debited to water connections for stores overheads (U 155 x 16.3741%).

In theory the journal entries for the total stores overheads would appear as follows:

19_6			
Dec.31	Stores Overhead (Holding) DR. To Wages (Control) Being direct wages and overheads relating to stores	8,047	8,047
Dec.31	Stores Overhead (Holding) DR. To Cash and Creditors Being sundry expenses relating to stores	11,560	11,560
Dec.31	Stores Overhead (Holding) DR. To Stores Overhead (Holding) To Stores (Control) Being deficiencies and surpluses on stocktaking (see pages 433 and 439 of Chapter 12)	1,425	905 520
Dec.31	Sundry Accounts DR. To Stores Overhead (Holding) Being recovery of stores overheads at a rate of 16.3741%	20,127	20,127

The Stores Overhead (Holding) Account would appear as follows:

Stores Overhead (Holding)								
19_6 Dec.31	To Wages (Control) To Cash and Creditors To Stores (Control)	J J J	8,047 11,560 1,425 ——— 21,032 ======	19_6 Dec.31	By Stores (Control) By Sundry Accounts	J J	905 20,127 ——— 21,032 ======

For simplicity, the recovery has been shown as having been made at the end of the year. In practice, it might well be made on an estimated

Stores and Costing

basis (say 16%) during the year, any balance being carried forward or dealt with as a supplementary allocation in the same way as for wages overheads.

As with wages, recovery of overheads in proportion to prime cost is the most convenient rather than the most logical method. In theory, a case could be made out for recovering overheads in proportion to weight, number of units, number of requisition notes and so on, but in practice this could involve a great deal of extra clerical work.

163. LIGHT PLANT AND TOOLS

In Chapter 12 we studied how to deal with the expenses of operation of vehicles and other mechanical plant. In addition to these, the employees of an authority will use different types of tools and equipment which cannot be charged out on a mileage or time basis. Such equipment ranges from hand-mowers and wheelbarrows to shovels and pick-axes.

In theory, the cost of using such equipment during a period is the amount by which the stock has deteriorated or worn out, after allowing for new purchases and scrap-values. If the stock of tools were counted and valued at the end of each year a statement of depreciation (or deterioration through use) could be prepared rather on the lines of a commercial trading account. For example:

			Units
	Opening Stock		8,468
Add	Purchases during year		3,824
			12,292
Less	Sales of Scrapped Equipment	156	
	Closing Stock	8,340	8,496
	Net Depreciation		3,796

One difficulty with the above method is how to value the closing stock. To value the equipment at cost would be wrong in principle, because most of it would be partly worn out.

Two methods are possible:

(a) obtain an estimated valuation from a technical officer; and

(b) value unused equipment (if any) at cost, and used equipment at (say) 50% of cost, thus roughly equating the value of equipment which is almost new with the value of that which is almost worn out.

Either of these methods is somewhat arbitrary and there is a great deal to be said for treating the annual cost of light plant and tools as the annual replacement cost. In other words the cost of light plant and tools charged in the accounts for a particular year is the net cost of purchases of new equipment less sales of scrapped equipment (if any).

The use of tools is an expense connected with labour and the cost of light plant and tools can be recovered from cost heads in proportion to direct wages. Many accountants would regard the cost as a part of labour overheads, but there are sometimes good reasons for recording them separately.

Municipal Accounting for Developing Countries

Let us suppose that Kambale Municipal Council costs its light plant and tools for the works department on a replacement basis and that the figures are as follows:

	Purchase of new equipment during the year	14,865
Less	Sale of worn-out equipment for scrap during the year (eg old mowing machines)	245
	Net cost of equipment	14,620

The overhead recovery rate, based on the direct wages will be:

$$\frac{\text{Net Cost of Light Plant and Tools}}{\text{Direct Wages}} \times 100$$

$$= \frac{14,620}{723,820} \times 100 = 2.02\%$$

In theory, journal entries will appear as follows:

19_6				
Dec.31	Light Plant and Tools (Holding) DR. To Cash and Creditors Being purchases of equipment during year		14,865	14,865
Dec.31	Cash DR. To Light Plant and Tools (Holding) Being sales of scrapped equipment during year		245	245
Dec.31	Sundry Accounts DR. To Light Plant and Tools (Holding) Being recovery of overheads at a rate of 2.02% of direct labour		14,620	14,620

The Light Plant and Tools (Holding) Account might appear as follows:

Light Plant and Tools (Holding)							
19_6 Dec.31	To Cash and Creditors	J	14,865	19_6 Dec.31	By Cash By Sundry Accounts	J J	245 14,620
			14,865				14,865

Once again, provisional recovery could be made during the year on an estimated basis (say 2%), the balance being adjusted, carried forward or written off.

Stores and Costing

164. ADMINISTRATIVE OVERHEADS

One important group of costs incurred in running a service is that of administrative overheads. These expenses include salaries, office accommodation, printing, stationery, postages, telephones, insurance, subscriptions, staff training and general office expenses. Where they are incurred in running particular services or departments they are known as departmental establishment charges. Where they cannot be charged against a particular service but relate to the authority as a whole they are known as central establishment charges.

Thus, the salary and office expenses of a Chief Education Officer are departmental establishment charges, relating to the education service, whereas similar expenses of the Chief Financial Officer are central establishment charges because finance is common to all services. The most usual sources of central establishment charges are the so-called "Central Departments" of the Chief Executive Officer, Chief Financial Officer, Chief Engineer and Chief Architect. Staff in these departments provide the administrative, professional and technical skills required by all the other departments of the authority.

Sometimes there are other central departments dealing with such matters as planning, property valuation, purchasing, stores, establishment, organisation and methods, printing and transport. The extent of centralisation depends upon the size and administrative structure of the authority concerned. In a very large authority, each centralised function may warrant a separate department with its own chief officer. In authorities of more moderate size, the functions may still be centralised but without separate departments. For example, property valuation, purchasing, stores and establishment may be under the control of the Chief Financial Officer; or establishment, O & M and printing under the Chief Executive Officer; or yet again, planning, stores and transport under the engineer.

How are administrative overheads to be charged in the accounts? It is usual for all expenses relating to a particular service to be charged under the appropriate service, division of service or sub-division of service head. For example, the salary of the market superintendant will be charged under "markets", and the salary of the chief of police under "police". Sometimes a department may be responsible for several services and in these cases the general salaries and expenses will be charged against a department without being allocated to services. For example, the works department may be responsible for highways, water, sewerage; housing repairs and so on. The salaries and office expenses of the chief engineer (or works superintendant) and his staff will be charged to a separate division of service "works department". Similarly the health department may be responsible for inspection, clinics, markets, ambulances and so on. The salaries and office expenses of the chief medical officer (or medical superintendant) and his staff will be charged to a separate division of service "health department".

The extent to which central establishment charges are allocated to services and the extent to which departmental establishment charges (including a share of central establishment charges) are allocated to specific jobs or processes will depend upon the purpose for which costs are required. It is often found that not nearly enough attention is given to the effect of overheads on the full costs of services. However, it must be admitted that the more detailed the allocation of overheads over jobs and services, the more arbitrary it is likely to be.

Where the full cost of a service is required, for the purpose of fixing charges or for making grant claims, it is essential that these costs include both departmental and central establishment charges. Even where charges are not fixed on an economic basis, the presentation of full inclusive costs will draw proper attention to the extent to which the service is subsidised.

Where costs of a service are being produced for the purpose of comparison with other authorities, perhaps through unit costs, central establishment charges are often omitted. This is to avoid fluctuations caused by different systems of apportionment as between one authority and another. There is often sound argument for producing costs on this basis, provided it is recognised that the costs are not full costs, because of the exclusion of central establishment charges. Another problem which must be watched is that one authority may have centralised services (thus omitted from costs) which another performs at departmental level (thus included in costs). A good example might be where the health service of one authority is housed in separate offices, whereas that of another authority shares (say) the town hall with other departments.

When calculating individual job costs for rechargeable works, it is essential that a share of overhead expenses is included in the costs. Sometimes it is possible to make apportionments on a fairly scientific basis. At other times we find that we are restricted to adding "a reasonable percentage" (often 5%) to prime costs and works overheads to allow for administrative overheads.

Where costs are being calculated for the purposes of budgetary control over individual services or jobs there is often a case for omitting administrative overheads altogether. There will probably be easier comparison between prime costs and prime cost estimates (with or without works overheads) than between total costs and total cost estimates. In the latter case the issue can often be clouded by the arbitrary nature of apportionment of administrative overheads.

Detailed methods of apportionment of administrative overheads (including central establishment charges) vary greatly. However we should recognise them as just as much an integral part of the costs of services as prime costs and works overheads. Where administrative overheads are recovered by an arbitrary percentage, for rechargeable works or otherwise, the percentage is normally applied to the grand total of all other costs (i.e. wages, materials, transport, labour overheads, stores overheads etc).

The accountant must maintain a flexible attitude towards administrative overheads, dealing with them as the circumstances require. It is sometimes difficult to decide whether a particular expense is "operational" or "administrative". For example the chief medical officer will almost certainly be working in an administrative capacity and he will have clerical staff to assist him. But what happens when (say) assistant medical officers attend clinics to deal with patients, as well as carrying out administrative work?

One item of expenditure which requires particular mention is that of loan charges. These form just as much a part of the cost of running a service as do salaries. Yet often we find, where accounting techniques are not fully developed, that loan charges are grouped together in a single lump sum in the accounts, as though they were a separate service. Loan charges should always be charged in the revenue account of the service to which they relate, otherwise an important element of cost is permanently overlooked. The same applies to renewals fund contributions and other capital recovery costs.

14. Capital Expenditure

Section		Page
165.	Capital Expenditure.	484
166.	Capital Receipts and Payments.	484
167.	Suspense Account System.	490
168.	Capital Accounts - Introduction.	494
169.	Capital Finance - Capital Receipts.	494
170.	Capital Finance - Loans.	503
171.	Capital Finance - Fund Contributions.	521

165. CAPITAL EXPENDITURE

We have already dealt with the distinctions between capital and revenue expenditure. In this chapter we shall study in detail the procedures used in accounting for capital expenditure, which (for accounting purposes) can be defined as:

"All expenditure incurred in the provision of fixed assets which give a future flow of benefit and which it would be reasonable to finance over a number of years".

This is substantially the same definition as used in other parts of this book but a proviso has been added to include only those items which it would be reasonable to finance over a period of years. Thus a typewriter, and small items of works equipment would normally be excluded from our working definition because, although they are (strictly speaking) fixed assets, they would normally be financed in a single year. Their purchase would be treated as revenue expenditure and not shown in the balance sheet. On the other hand, a vehicle, even if financed from revenue, would normally be treated as capital expenditure. This is because "it would be reasonable" for its cost to be financed over a number of years, even if in individual cases it may not be. The vehicle would be shown in the balance sheet, and the charge to the revenue account would be treated as "Revenue contribution to capital outlay".

Before proceeding with this chapter you should reread Chapters 7 and 8 and refer to the capital programmes and budgets in Chapter 9.

166. CAPITAL RECEIPTS AND PAYMENTS

The sources from which finance is obtained to make capital payments can, for accounting purposes, be divided into three main groups:

(a) capital receipts;

(b) loans; and

(c) fund contributions.

Examples of receipts from the various sources can be shown by the following table:

Capital Expenditure

Source	Examples
1. Capital Receipts	a) Specific government grants
	b) Donations
	c) Receipts from sales of fixed assets
	d) Land premia
	e) Commodity bonuses (1)
	f) Receipts from insurance claims for assets damaged or destroyed
	g) Voluntary labour
2. Loans	a) Instalment loans from central agencies and other sources
	b) Maturity mortgages
	c) Stock issues
	d) Bank overdrafts and temporary loans
	e) Internal loans
3. Fund Contributions	Contributions from:
	a) Revenue account
	b) Reserves
	c) Renewals funds
	d) Capital funds
	e) Internal insurance fund (claims for assets damaged or destroyed)

Capital payments are sometimes made for the direct purchase of existing assets such as land, buildings, vehicles or equipment. Often, however, capital payments result from the construction of building and permanent works by contractors or by the authority's own direct labour force.

Examples of the various capital payments which may arise can be shown as follows:

(1.) Commodity bonuses include government receipts from the marketing of cash crops and (particularly) petroleum, some of which may be distributed to local authorities for development purposes.

Municipal Accounting for Developing Countries

Type of Payment	Examples of Payments
1. Purchase of Existing Assets (e.g. land, buildings, vehicles and equipment)	a) Purchase prices to vendors or suppliers b) Legal fees (e.g. on land transfers) c) Transport of assets to the place where they are to be used d) Charges for initial installation e) Incidental expenses (car allowances, insurances, stationery etc) f) Administrative overheads g) Interest on purchase money (sometimes payable where a compulsory purchase is delayed)
2. Construction of New Assets in the Form of Buildings and Permanent Works	a) Payments to contractors b) Wages of authority's staff engaged on construction work c) Purchase of direct materials used in construction work d) Issue from stores of materials used in construction work e) Hire of vehicles and plant used in construction work f) Use of authority's own plant in construction work g) Payments for production e.g. printing of plans, specifications and contract documents h) Legal fees incurred in drawing-up contracts and raising loans i) Professional fees (e.g. to "outside" architects, engineers and quantity surveyors) j) Salaries of the authority's own technical staff (e.g. architects, engineers and quantity surveyors) engaged in planning and supervising construction work k) Salaries of clerks of works and site engineers l) Incidental expenses (e.g. car allowances, insurances, stationery) m) Administrative overheads relating to capital works

Capital Expenditure

Often, of course, a capital project will involve both purchase and construction of assets. An existing building may be purchased and alterations and additions may then require construction work. Alternatively when a new building has been constructed it will be necessary to purchase furniture and equipment.

You will notice that in Section 165 we have referred in general terms to "capital expenditure". We are now using the terms "capital receipts" and "capital payments". This draws attention to two important facts:

(a) capital payments bring about the acquisition of fixed assets and therefore, in the strict book-keeping sense, they are not expenditure (because expenditure results in a loss); and

(b) the rules of income and expenditure accounting, strictly adhered to in dealing with revenue transactions, are somewhat relaxed when dealing with capital transactions, in relation to sundry creditors (payables).

The theoretical reason for the different terms will be obvious from earlier chapters. The relaxation of the rules dealing with sundry creditors is entirely a matter of practical convenience. In strict theory, invoices relating to capital expenditure, which are unpaid at the end of a financial period, should be brought into the books as "sundry creditors". This is not difficult with ordinary invoices for supplies of materials and equipment, but the exercise becomes somewhat meaningless unless quantity surveyors or other technical staff can give estimates of the value of all construction work in progress on the last day of the financial period, so that amounts due to contractors can be calculated. This must, of course, be ruled out on the grounds of expense and technical difficulty.

For this purely practical reason, it has become customary to treat capital expenditure on a "receipts and payments basis" whilst a scheme is in progress. When a scheme is completed, the total expenditure incurred will be equal to the total cash outlay and the capital accounts will again be on a strict "income and expenditure" basis.

It has already been demonstrated that any departure from the strict principles of income and expenditure accounting when dealing with revenue transactions can result in serious mis-statement of the authority's financial position.

Fortunately, with capital transactions, the effects are not serious. This is because the "double-account" system tends to isolate the capital transactions, and to prevent them from affecting the revenue account.

A balance sheet will, of course, understate the precise up-to-date costs of assets under construction and consequently will understate liabilities to creditors. However, these figures are only of an interim nature. The important figures are the total estimated cost of each scheme and the total estimated liabilities to contractors under currently proceeding contracts. These can be calculated by relating the balance sheet information to the capital programme.

This is another example of how the strict theory of book-keeping is modified to meet practical circumstances.

When cash is received on capital account it will initially be dealt with in the same way as other cash receipts. An official receipt will be issued for it and the details will eventually be recorded through the income analysis system. The amount will eventually appear as a credit in an account in the "capital" section of the income ledger (see Chapter 10).

Similarly, when cash is paid out on capital account the payment will normally be made by cheque, in the same way as other payments. A voucher will have been used to support the payment, and the details will be recorded through the expenditure analysis system. There will eventually be a debit in an account in the "capital" section of the expenditure ledger (see Chapter 11).

Before going on to the more complex aspects of capital accounting, let us consider this relatively straightforward matter of the receipt and payment of cash.

If you will refer to the "Capital Expenditure Programme 19_6/19_0 Summary" on page 288 of Chapter 9 you will see that a sum of U 57,000 has been provided in the programme in 19_6 for "Vacuum Tanker Service". Let us suppose that this is to enable Kambale Municipal Council to purchase a "Vacuum Tanker Lorry" during the year.

For simplicity, we shall consider the "capital cash" transactions relating only to this item, as though a separate cash account were kept for them.

As we have already seen, cash to finance the purchase may come from several different sources. However, the "capital cash" transactions will be recorded in more or less the same way for any of the sources.

Let us assume that the purchase is to be financed by a grant from the central government equal to the sum shown in the programme U 57,000.

If the grant were received on (say) 23 April 19_6 a receipt would be issued and the amount banked. The cash book (in theory) would then show:

Cash							
19_6 Apr.23	To Capital Grant	85	57,000				

If the vehicle were purchased for U 57,000 on 16 May 19_6 a cheque would be sent to the supplier. The cash book (in theory) would then show:

Cash							
19_6 Apr.23	To Capital Grant	85	57,000	19_6 May 16	By Vacuum Tanker Lorry	96	57,000

The capital payment has been exactly equal to the capital receipt, so of course there is no remaining cash balance.

Capital Expenditure

If the vehicle had cost U 53,465 the cash book would have shown:

	Cash
19_6 Apr.23	To Capital Grant	85	57,000	19_6 May 16	By Vacuum Tanker Lorry By Balance	96 c/d	53,465 3,535
			57,000 ======				57,000 ======
May 17	To Balance	b/d	3,535				

This time there would be an unspent cash balance of U 3,535 which would have to be repaid to the central government or disposed of in accordance with its instructions.

If the vehicle had cost U 59,330 the cash book would have shown:

	Cash
19_6 Apr.23 May 16	To Capital Grant To Balance	85 c/d	57,000 2,330	19_6 May 16	By Vacuum Tanker Lorry	96	59,330
			59,330 ======				59,330 ======
				May 17	By Balance	b/d	2,330

Here, there would be an overdrawn cash balance of U 2,330 which would have to be made good from a further government grant or from another source altogether (e.g. a loan or fund contribution). When this further cash had been paid into the cash account, the overdrawn balance would be eliminated.

To prevent surplus cash balances arising, it would be preferable for the capital receipt to be raised after the payment has been made.

Let us return to the example where the vehicle cost U 53,465. If the vehicle had been purchased (with approval) before the receipt of the grant, the cash position would be:

Municipal Accounting for Developing Countries

Cash								
19_6 May 16	To Balance	c/d	53,465	19_6 May 16	By Vacuum Tanker Lorry	96	53,465
			53,465 ======				53,465 ======
				May 17	By Balance	b/d	53,465

There would now be an overdrawn cash balance of U 53,465 in relation to this particular project. In practice, this would mean that the overall cash balances of the authority would be reduced by this sum, pending reimbursement from capital receipts.

A grant claim would now be made for the exact amount of the expenditure. If the grant of U 53,465 was received on (say) 9 June 19_6 the cash position would then be:

Cash								
19_6 May 16	To Balance	c/d	53,465	19_6 May 16	By Vacuum Tanker Lorry	96	53,465
			53,465 ======				53,465 ======
Jun. 9	To Capital Grant	85	53,465	May 17	By Balance	b/d	53,465
			53,465 ======				53,465 ======

The overdrawn cash balance has now been eliminated, or to put it another way the U 53,465 which was used from the authority's other cash balances has now been replaced.

It should be stressed that, up to this point in the example, the source of capital finance does not affect the issue. The cash transactions will all be substantially the same, whatever the sources of finance.

167. SUSPENSE ACCOUNT SYSTEM

So far we have only considered the "receipts and payments" or "single entry" aspect of the transactions. The principles of double-entry show that the debits and credits in the cash book must be balanced by complementary entries elsewhere in the ledger system.

A simple (though somewhat incomplete) system of double-entry can be brought about by the following procedure, which was amplified for the Vacuum Tanker Lorry shown on page 488 as being purchased for U 53,465 out of a grant of U 57,000.

Capital Expenditure

The receipt of the grant U 57,000 would have been debited in the cash book as shown and through the income analysis system would eventually be credited to an account called "Capital Receipts (Suspense) Account".

The payment for the vehicle, on the other hand, would have been credited in the cash book as shown and through the expenditure analysis system would eventually be debited to an account called "Capital Expenditure - Vacuum Tanker Lorry (No.UBC 789)".

The accounts will then appear in the ledger (in theory) as:

Cash

19_6				19_6			
Apr.23	To Capital Grant	85	57,000	May 16	By Vacuum Tanker Lorry	96	53,465
				16	By Balance	c/d	3,535
			57,000				57,000
May 17	To Balance	b/d	3,535				

Capital Receipts (Suspense)   85

				19_6			
				Apr.23	By Cash	C.B.	57,000

Capital Expenditure - Vacuum Tanker Lorry (UBC 789)   96

19_6			
May 16	To Cash	C.B.	53,465

Capital receipts will now be transferred to the extent to which they are required to finance the capital expenditure. This will be done by a journal entry as follows:

19_6				
Jun.30	Capital Receipts (Suspense) DR.	85	53,465	
	To Capital Expenditure (Vacuum Tanker Lorry)	96		53,465
	Being cost of purchase of Lorry UBC 789 during the last quarter, now financed from capital receipts			

After this entry has been made the books will appear as follows:

Municipal Accounting for Developing Countries

Cash							
19_6 Apr.23	To Capital Grant	85	57,000	19_6 May 16	By Vacuum Tanker Lorry	96	53,465
				16	By Balance	c/d	3,535
			57,000 ======				57,000 ======
May 17	To Balance	b/d	3,535				

Capital Receipts (Suspense)							85
19_6 Jun.30	To Capital Expenditure	J	53,465	19_6 Apr.23	By Cash	C.B.	57,000
	To Balance	c/d	3,535				
			57,000 ======				57,000 ======
				Jul.1	By Balance	b/d	3,535

Capital Expenditure - Vacuum Tanker Lorry (UBC 789)							96
19_6 May 16	To Cash	C.B.	53,465	19_6 Jun.30	By Capital Receipts	J	53,465

The balance on the capital expenditure account has now been eliminated, leaving the unspent cash balanced by a credit entry in the "suspense" account.

If the unspent balance of the grant were returned to the government on (say) 27 July the payment would be credited in the cash book and debited to the suspense account. These accounts would then appear as follows:

Capital Expenditure

Cash									
19_6 Apr.23	To Capital Grant	85	57,000	19_6 May 16	By Vacuum Tanker Lorry	96	53,465
					By Balance	c/d	3,535
			57,000				57,000
May 17	To Balance	b/d	3,535	Jul.27	By Capital Receipts (Suspense)	85	3,535
			3,535				3,535

Capital Receipts (Suspense) 85									
19_6 Jun.30	To Capital Expenditure	J	53,465	19_6 Apr.23	By Cash	C.B.	57,000
	To Balance	c/d	3,535				
			57,000				57,000
Jul.27	By Cash	C.B.	3,535	Jul.1	By Balance	b/d	3,535

The accounting entries have now been completed, all balances in the books having been eliminated.

Suppose the lorry had been financed by the raising of a loan from (say) the government instead of by a grant. Had the loan been raised on 23 April 19_6 with the unspent balance repaid on 27 July 19_6 the entries in the "capital accounts" would have been exactly as shown above. If we assume that the loan was to be repaid by half-yearly annuities over 5 years at 10%, a cash payment of U 6923.96 would have to be made upon each of 10 occasions. The first might be made on 27 Jan. 19_7 (six months after the net amount of the loan was determined) and thereafter, payments would be made at half-yearly intervals until 27 July 19_1.

The half-yearly annuity would be calculated as shown in Chapter 8 page 257 namely .12950458 x U 53,465 = U 6923.96

In addition to this annuity, interest would become payable on 27 July 19_6 for the use of the unspent U 3,535 from 23 April 19_6 until 27 July 19_6, (95 days) calculated as follows:

$$\frac{U\ 3,535 \times 95 \times 10}{100 \times 365} = U\ 92.01$$

This interest is a good example of "idle loan charges". They could have been avoided by deferring the borrowing until after the payment had been made. Only the net amount of U 53,465 would then have been borrowed.

The payment of the interest and the subsequent half-yearly annuities will not affect the capital accounts in any way. Each payment will be a credit in the cash book and a debit to an account for "Loan Charges" in the revenue section of the expenditure ledger. Indeed, under this system, it is not necessary to divide the annuity payments into their "principal" and "interest" elements.

The above system has the merit of simplicity. It is, perhaps, a suitable system for a local authority in its early stages of development. There may be very few trained finance staff, making it necessary to concentrate upon strict vote control rather than upon developing a comprehensive professional accounting system.

However, the system falls somewhat short of the professionally accepted principles of capital accounting (outlined in Chapter 7) for it has the following main defects:

(a) the fixed assets of the authority are not retained in the books and not included in the balance sheet;

(b) no permanent record is kept of the extent to which fixed assets have been fully financed; and

(c) no permanent record is kept, as part of the double-entry system, of the amounts owing in respect of loans - consequently these long-term liabilities are omitted from the balance sheet.

The omission from the accounts of loan liabilities is a particularly serious fault of the system, especially as extremely large sums are usually involved.

Where an authority wishes to record and publish comprehensive information about its capital expenditure transactions, full professional accounting principles must be observed. These will be explained in subsequent sections.

However, the principle of keeping a suspense account has a useful application, even in a complete set of accounts: this will be dealt with later.

168. CAPITAL ACCOUNTS - INTRODUCTION

For each of the main sources of capital receipts shown on page 485 there is a different set of accounting procedures. These are best understood if they are broken down into a series of logical steps.

Each step in the accounting procedures can be demonstrated by a theoretical journal entry, though not all of the journal entries illustrated will be made in practice. For instance, book-keeping entries involving cash will normally be made by direct postings from copy receipts and payment vouchers.

In demonstrating the various accounting procedures, examples will be taken from the capital expenditure programme on page 289 of Chapter 9.

169. CAPITAL FINANCE - CAPITAL RECEIPTS

Where capital expenditure is to be financed from capital receipts there are three logical steps to be recorded:

Capital Expenditure

(a) record the capital receipt;

(b) record the capital payments; and

(c) apply the capital receipt to the discharge of the capital expenditure.

Let us examine the above steps as they would affect the Land Drainage for Swamp Area, which is being financed by a grant. For simplicity we shall use the exact figure of U 140,000 shown in the capital programme and assume that the work is completed in 19_6.

The steps will be as follows:

(a) Record the Capital Receipt

| 19_6 Oct.1 | Cash (Capital)   DR. To Capital Receipts (Unapplied) - Grant Being receipt of capital grant for Land Drainage - Swamp Area | C.B. 1 | 140,000 | 140,000 |

Although we know the purpose for which the grant will be applied, it has not at this stage been applied to finance the capital expenditure - hence it is credited (through the income analysis) to a "Capital Receipts Unapplied" account.

The procedure would be precisely the same where cash of a capital nature is received and held pending a decision about its application to finance a particular scheme. Most of the capital receipts shown in the table on page 485 would, in fact, fall into this latter category (e.g. receipts from sales of assets, commodity bonuses).

(b) Record the Capital Payments

| 19_6 Dec.31 | Capital Expenditure (Swamp Area)   DR. To Cash (Capital) Being capital payments made during the year | 2 C.B. | 140,000 | 140,000 |

In practice, of course, many different payments of the type shown in the table on page 486 will be made. Eventually, however, there will have been total payments of U 140,000 which will have been credited in the cash book and debited (through expenditure analysis) in the capital section of the expenditure ledger.

(c) Apply the Capital Receipt

| 19_6 Dec.31 | Capital Receipts (Unapplied) DR. To Capital Discharged - Grant Applied Being application of capital grant to discharge of capital expenditure on Land Drainage - Swamp Area | 1 3 | 140,000 | 140,000 |

Municipal Accounting for Developing Countries

This entry is the only one of the three which will actually be made through the journal in practice. The grant has now been applied to finance the capital expenditure and the ledger accounts will appear as follows:

	Cash (Capital)						C.B.
19_6 Oct.1	To Capital Grant	1	140,000	19_6 Dec.31	By Capital Expenditure	3	140,000
			140,000 ======				140,000 ======

	Capital Receipts Unapplied (Government Grant)						1
19_6 Dec.31	To Capital Discharged	J	140,000	19_6 Oct.1	By Cash	C.B.	140,000
			140,000 ======				140,000 ======

	Capital Expenditure (Land Drainage - Swamp Area)						2
19_6 Dec.31	To Cash	C.B.	140,000 ======	19_6 Dec.31	By Balance	c/d	140,000 ======
19_7 Jan.1	To Balance	b/d	140,000				

	Capital Discharged (Government Grant Applied)						3
19_6 Dec.31	To Balance	c/d	140,000	19_6 Dec.31	By Capital Receipts Unapplied	J	140,000
			140,000 ======				140,000 ======
				19_7 Jan.1	By Balance	b/d	140,000

The balance sheet for this scheme (in isolation) would appear as follows:

Capital Expenditure

Balance Sheet as at 31 Dec. 19_6

Surplus	Units	Fixed Assets	Units
Capital Discharged Government Grant Applied	140,000	Land Drainage - Swamp Area	140,000
	140,000		140,000
	======		======

To illustrate the principles we have assumed that everything works out in a neat and tidy fashion. This would rarely happen in practice. A glance at the capital programme shows that only U 110,000 is estimated to be spent during 19_6, the remainder being spent in 19_7. Let us now suppose that the grant of U 140,000 was received as before, but that only U 103,360 has been spent on the scheme by 31 Dec. 19_6.

The journal entries (in theory) would then be:

19_6					
Oct.1	Cash (Capital) DR. To Capital Receipts (Unapplied) - Grant Being receipt of capital grant for Land Drainage - Swamp Area	C.B. 1	140,000		140,000
Dec.31	Capital Expenditure (Swamp Area) DR. To Cash (Capital) Being capital payments made during the year	2 C.B.	103,360		103,360
Dec.31	Capital Receipts (Unapplied) DR. To Capital Discharged - Grant Applied Being application of capital grant to discharge of capital expenditure to date on Land Drainage - Swamp Area	1 3	103,360		103,360

The ledger accounts and (isolated) balance sheet would appear as follows:

Municipal Accounting for Developing Countries

		Cash (Capital)					C.B.
19_6 Oct.1	To Capital Grant	1	140,000	19_6 Dec.31	By Capital Expenditure By Balance	3 c/d	103,360 36,640
			140,000 =======				140,000 =======
19_7 Jan.1	To Balance	b/d	36,640				

		Capital Receipts Unapplied (Government Grant)					1
19_6 Dec.31	To Capital Discharged To Balance	J c/d	103,360 36,640	19_6 Oct.1	By Cash	C.B.	140,000
			140,000 =======				140,000 =======
				19_7 Jan.1	By Balance	b/d	36,640

		Capital Expenditure (Land Drainage - Swamp Area)					2
19_6 Dec.31	To Cash	C.B.	103,360 =======	19_6 Dec.31	By Balance	c/d	103,360 =======
19_7 Jan.1	To Balance	b/d	103,360				

		Capital Discharged (Government Grant Applied)					3
19_6 Dec.31	To Balance	c/d	103,360	19_6 Dec.31	By Capital Receipts Unapplied	J	103,360
			103,360 =======				103,360 =======
				19_7 Jan.1	By Balance	b/d	103,360

Capital Expenditure

Balance Sheet as at 31 Dec. 19_6

	Units		Units
Surplus		**Fixed Assets**	
Capital Discharged -		Land Drainage - Swamp	
Government Grant	103,360	Area	103,360
Capital Receipts		**Current Assets**	
Unapplied	36,640	Cash at Bank	36,640
	140,000		140,000
	======		======

In this case, the grant has been applied only to the extent of capital expenditure already incurred. The balance remains as "Unapplied" and is held in the form of a cash balance.

Let us now take the matter a stage further and assume that the grant is paid in two instalments. An instalment of (say) 50% of the estimated cost is paid on 1 Oct. 19_6 (ie U 70,000), the balance to be paid in 19_7 when the actual cost of completed work is known.

The journal entries (in theory) would then be:

19_6
Oct.1
	Cash (Capital) DR.
	  To Capital Receipts (Unapplied
	    Grant)
	Being receipt of first
	instalment of capital grant for
	Land Drainage - Swamp Area
			C.B.
			
			1
				70,000		70,000

Dec.31	Capital Expenditure (Swamp
	  Area) DR.
	  To Cash (Capital)
	Being capital payments made
	during the year
			2
			C.B.
				103,360		103,360

Dec.31	Capital Receipts (Unapplied) DR.
	  To Capital Discharged - Grant
	    Applied
	Being application of first
	instalment of capital grant
	towards partial discharge of
	capital expenditure to date on
	Land Drainage - Swamp Area
			1
			
			3
				70,000		70,000

The ledger accounts and (isolated) balance sheet would appear as follows:

Cash (Capital)   C.B.

19_6
Oct.1
Dec.31
	To Capital
	  Grant
	To Balance
		2
		c/d
			70,000
			33,360
			———
			103,360
			======
				19_6
				Dec.31
				
				19_7
				Jan.1
					By Capital
					  Expendi-
					  ture
					
					By Balance
						2
						
						b/d
							103,360
							
							———
							103,360
							======
							
							33,360

Capital Receipts Unapplied (Government Grant)   1

19_6
Dec.31
	To Capital
	  Dischar-
	  ged
		J	70,000
			———
			70,000
			======
				19_6
				Dec.31
					By Cash	C.B.	70,000
							———
							70,000
							======

Capital Expenditure

Capital Expenditure (Land Drainage - Swamp Area)								2
19_6 Dec.31	To Cash	C.B.	103,360	19_6 Dec.31	By Balance	c/d	103,360	
			=======				=======	
19_7 Jan.1	To Balance	c/d	103,360					

Capital Discharged (Government Grant Applied)								3
19_6 Dec.31	To Balance	c/d	70,000	19_6 Dec.31	By Capital Receipts Unapplied	J	70,000	
			70,000				70,000	
			======				======	
				19_7 Jan.1	By Balance	c/d	70,000	

Balance Sheet as at 31 Dec. 19_6

	Units		Units
Current Liabilities		**Fixed Assets**	
Cash Overdrawn	33,360	Land Drainage - Swamp Area	103,360
Surplus			
Capital Discharged - Government Grant	70,000		
	103,360		103,360
	=======		=======

In this case the whole of the grant so far received has been applied towards the discharge of the capital expenditure, yet there is insufficient grant money to cover the total payments made to date. Because of this, the capital cash account is overdrawn. Cash belonging to other funds of the authority has been temporarily used to meet the capital payments.

In 19_7 the amount of "cash overdrawn" will continue to increase, as further capital payments are made.

When the final cost of the scheme is known, a grant claim will be made for the balance of the grant. For example, a claim might be made as follows on (say) 30 April 19_7:

		Units
	Total Cost of Scheme	142,460
Less	Payment of Grant on account	70,000
	Balance of Grant now due	72,460
		=======

Municipal Accounting for Developing Countries

At this point the (isolated) balance sheet would show:

Balance Sheet as at 31 April 19_7

Current Liabilities	Units	Fixed Assets	Units
Cash Overdrawn	72,460	Land Drainage - Swamp Area	142,460
Surplus			
Capital Discharged - Government Grant	70,000		
	142,460		142,460
	=======		=======

If the balance of the grant were paid over on 31 May 19_7 the journal entry (in theory) would be:

19_7 May 31	Cash (Capital) DR. C.B.	72,460	
	To Capital Discharged - Government Grant 3		72,460
	Being balance of capital grant for Land Drainage - Swamp Area		

After this the (isolated) balance sheet would show:

Balance Sheet as at 31 May 19_7

Surplus		Fixed Assets	
Capital Discharged - Government Grant	142,460	Land Drainage - Swamp Area	142,460
	142,460		142,460
	=======		=======

The preparation (or visualisation) of small balance sheets, isolating the transactions of a particular scheme, is a very useful technique in dealing with capital accounts.

Sometimes a capital receipt can arise in the form of a fixed asset instead of in cash. For example:

(a) a public building or other asset (e.g. an ambulance) may be presented to the authority by a private person, a local company or as overseas aid;

(b) assets may be taken over from the central government by a local authority as a result of transferred services (e.g. dispensaries may be taken over as a result of health functions being transferred);

(c) assets may be developed and constructed by (say) an area

Capital Expenditure

development authority and then handed over to a municipality to operate and maintain; and

(d) a building or other asset may be constructed by voluntary labour. In each case the asset should be valued as at the date of its take-over by the authority. It should then be written into the books.

For example, let us suppose that on 1 Jan. 19_6 the central government hands over responsibility for local health services to Kambale Municipal Council. There are three dispensaries valued in total at U 190,000 taken over from the central government. A medical store, constructed by local voluntary labour, is completed just prior to 1 Jan. 19_6 and handed over to the authority on that date. The Council's valuer estimates its capital value at U 27,000. On the same date an ambulance is presented to the authority by the United Nations Childrens Fund (UNICEF). The all-in cost of purchasing a similar ambulance at the date of presentation was U 43,300.

The assets would be brought into the books as follows:

19_6				
Jan.1	Capital Expenditure (Dispensaries) DR. To Capital Discharged (Takeover Values) Being 3 dispensaries taken over from Central Government at agreed valuation	1 1	190,000	190,000
Jan.1	Capital Expenditure (Medical Store) DR. To Capital Discharged (Gifts) Being medical store constructed by voluntary labour now taken over by the authority at Valuer's valuation	2 5	27,000	27,000
Jan.1	Capital Expenditure (Ambulance) DR. To Capital Discharged (Gifts) Being ambulance presented by UNICEF now brought into books at current market price	3 6	43,300	43,300

The ledger accounts and balance sheet will be completely straightforward.

170. **CAPITAL FINANCE - LOANS**

Where capital expenditure is to be financed by the raising of loans, the logical steps to be followed are:

(a) record the loan receipt;

(b) record the capital payments;

(c) record the annual or half-yearly repayments of loan principal;

(d) record the annual or half-yearly payments of interest on the outstanding loan; and

(e) apply the repayments of principal to the discharge of the capital expenditure.

Let us consider the construction of the Central Car Park for U 118,000 to be financed by a loan. For the moment we shall assume that all the payments are made in 19_6 and the total cost of the work is the same as the sum in the capital programme.

The steps will be as follows:

(a) **Record the Loan Receipt**

| 19_6 Feb.1 | Cash (Capital)   DR.
  To Loans Outstanding
    (National Government)
  Being loan raised to construct
  Central Car Park | C.C.

1 | 118,000 | 118,000 |

At this stage we are recording an increase in assets (cash) and a corresponding increase in liabilities (to the National Government). We have credited the loan to the account of a particular lender to draw attention to the fact that there is a specific liability to repay the loan. In practice the individual loans would probably be recorded in a subsidiary loans ledger (or register) with a control account for "Loans Outstanding" in the main ledger, which would be posted through the expenditure analysis system.

(b) **Record the Capital Payments**

| 19_6 Dec.31 | Capital Expenditure (Central
  Car Park)   DR.
  To Cash (Capital)
  Being capital payments made
  during the year | 2
C.C. | 118,000 | 118,000 |

This represents an accumulation of many different payments posted to the expenditure ledger through the expenditure analysis system.

Before we can consider the next steps in the exercise we must draw up a table to show how the loan is to be repaid with interest over the loan period. Even if the full table were not prepared at this stage, it would be necessary to prepare the calculations for the current year.

Let us assume that the loan of U 118,000 was raised from the National Government on 1 Feb. 19_6. It is repayable over 20 years in equal half-yearly instalments to include principal and interest at the rate of 6.25%

The first instalment is due six months after the receipt of the loan, in this case on 1 Aug. 19_6. Thereafter, instalments will fall due on 1 Feb. and 1 Aug. in each year, the last one being paid on 1 Feb. 19_6.

The half-yearly annuity required to repay the loan will be calculated

Capital Expenditure

as shown in Chapter 8 page 257 namely .044140878 x U 118,000 = U 5,208.65.

The loan repayment table will now be calculated as shown in Section 86 of Chapter 8.

The complete repayment table will appear as shown on page 506. Each half-yearly payment, except the last, is U 5208.65. The last payment (U 5206.65) is slightly less than the others because of earlier "rounding up" to the nearest 5 cents. Although the annuity remains constant, the interest proportion steadily decreases, whilst the principal proportion steadily increases by equivalent amounts. This is because each instalment of interest is based upon the current balance of principal outstanding and this is constantly being reduced by principal repayments.

We are now in a position to carry out the remaining steps in the exercise.

(c) **Record the Half-Yearly Repayment of Principal**

19_6 Aug.1	Loans Outstanding (National Government) DR. To Cash (Revenue) Being repayment of first instalment of Government Loan as shown by repayment table	1 C.R.	U 1,521	Cts 15	U 1,521	Cts 15

The amount of the instalment is obtained from the repayment table. The repayment has been made from "revenue" cash and not "capital" cash. This point will be referred to later.

(d) **Record the Half-Yearly Payment of Interest**

19_6 Aug.1	Loans Charges (Interest) DR. To Cash (Revenue) Being half-yearly interest on loan from Government as shown by repayment table	3 C.R.	U 3,687	Cts 50	U 3,687	Cts 50

As explained earlier this payment is made from "revenue" cash and is treated as normal revenue expenditure.

Municipal Accounting for Developing Countries

Loan Repayment Table

Loan of U 118,000 at 6½% to be repaid by half-yearly annuities over 20 years

Instal-ment Number	Annuity Units	Annuity Cents	Interest Units	Interest Cents	Principal Units	Principal Cents	Principal Outstanding Units	Principal Outstanding Cents
	-		-		-		118,000	00
1	5,208	65	3,687	50	1,521	15	116,478	85
2	5,208	65	3,639	95	1,568	70	114,910	15
3	5,208	65	3,590	95	1,617	70	113,292	45
4	5,208	65	3,540	40	1,668	25	111,624	20
5	5,208	65	3,488	25	1,720	40	109,903	80
6	5,208	65	3,434	50	1,774	15	108,129	65
7	5,208	65	3,379	05	1,829	60	106,300	05
8	5,208	65	3,321	90	1,886	75	104,413	30
9	5,208	65	3,262	90	1,945	75	102,467	55
10	5,208	65	3,202	10	2,006	55	100,461	00
11	5,208	65	3,139	40	2,069	25	98,391	75
12	5,208	65	3,074	75	2,133	90	96,257	85
13	5,208	65	3,008	05	2,200	60	94,057	25
14	5,208	65	2,939	30	2,269	35	91,787	90
15	5,208	65	2,868	35	2,340	30	89,447	60
16	5,208	65	2,795	25	2,413	40	87,034	20
17	5,208	65	2,719	80	2,488	85	84,545	35
18	5,208	65	2,642	05	2,566	60	81,978	75
19	5,208	65	2,561	85	2,646	80	79,331	85
20	5,208	65	2,479	10	2,729	55	76,602	40
21	5,208	65	2,393	85	2,814	80	73,787	60
22	5,208	65	2,305	85	2,902	80	70,884	80
23	5,208	65	2,215	15	2,993	50	67,891	30
24	5,208	65	2,121	60	3,087	05	64,804	25
25	5,208	65	2,025	15	3,183	50	61,620	75
26	5,208	65	1,925	65	3,283	00	58,337	75
27	5,208	65	1,823	05	3,385	60	54,952	15
28	5,208	65	1,717	25	3,491	40	51,460	75
29	5,208	65	1,608	15	3,600	50	47,860	25
30	5,208	65	1,495	65	3,713	00	44,147	25
31	5,208	65	1,379	60	3,829	05	40,318	20
32	5,208	65	1,259	95	3,948	70	36,369	50
33	5,208	65	1,136	55	4,072	10	32,297	40
34	5,208	65	1,009	30	4,199	35	28,098	05
35	5,208	65	878	05	4,330	60	23,767	45
36	5,208	65	742	75	4,465	90	19,301	55
37	5,208	65	603	15	4,605	50	14,696	05
38	5,208	65	459	25	4,749	40	9,946	65
39	5,208	65	310	85	4,897	80	5,048	85
40	5,206	65	157	80	5,048	85	-	-

Capital Expenditure

At this point the accounts will appear as follows:

Cash (Capital)   C.C.

19_6					19_6				
Feb.1	To Loans Outstanding	1	118,000		Dec.31	By Capital Expenditure (Central Car Park)	1	118,000	00

Cash (Revenue)   C.R.

					19_6				
					Aug.1	By Loans Outstanding (Government)	1	1,521	15
						By Loan Charges (Interest)	3	3,687	50

Loans Outstanding (Government)   1

19_6					19_6				
Aug.1	To Cash	CR	1,521	15	Feb.1	By Cash	CC	118,000	00

Capital Expenditure (Central Car Park)   2

19_6									
Dec.31	To Cash	CC	118,000	00					

Loan Charges - Interest   3

19_6									
Aug.1	To Cash	CR	3,687	50					

Municipal Accounting for Developing Countries

A trial balance will show the books to be in balance as follows:

	DR		CR	
	Units	Cents	Units	Cents
Cash (Revenue)			5,208	65
Loans Outstanding	1,521	15	118,000	00
Capital Expenditure	118,000	00		
Loan Charges Interest	3,687	50		
	123,208	65	123,208	65

However, if an (isolated) balance sheet were drawn up on the "double account" system the two sections (capital and revenue) would each be out of balance as follows:

Balance Sheet as at 31 Dec. 19_6
Capital

	Units	Cents		Units	Cents
Long-Term Liabilities			**Fixed Assets**		
			Capital Expenditure		
Loans Outstanding	116,478	85	Central Car Park	118,000	00
	116,478	85		118,000	00

Revenue

	Units	Cents		Units	Cents
Current Liabilities			**Deficiency**		
Cash Overdrawn	5,208	65	Revenue Account Deficiency (Loan Charges - Interest)	3,687	50
	5,208	65		3,687	50
	121,687	50		121,687	50

This has occurred because a "capital" liability (loans outstanding) has been discharged by a "revenue" asset (revenue cash).

The balance in each section will be restored by the final step:

(e) **Apply the Principal Repayment to Discharge the Capital Expenditure**

19_6						
Dec.31	Loan Charges (Principal) DR.	4	1,521	15		
	To Capital Discharged (Loan Repaid)	5			1,521	15
	Being charge to revenue account for discharge of capital expenditure by repayment of loan principal					

Capital Expenditure

The final ledger accounts and (isolated) double account balance sheet will appear as follows:

		Cash (Capital)							C.C.	
19_6 Feb.1	To Loans Outstanding	1	118,000	00	19_6 Dec.31	By Capital Expenditure (Central Car Park)	2	118,000	00
			118,000 =======	00 ==				118,000 =======	00 ==

		Cash (Revenue)							C.R.	
19_6 Dec.31	To Balance	c/d	5,208	65	19_6 Aug.1	By Loans Outstanding (Government)	1	1,521	15
						By Loan Charges (Interest)	3	3,687	50
			5,208 =====	65 ===				5,208 =====	65 ===
					19_7 Jan.1	By Balance	b/d	5,208	65

		Loans Outstanding							1	
19_6 Aug.1	To Cash	CR	1,521	15	19_6 Feb.1	By Cash	CC	118,000	00
Dec.31	To Balance	c/d	116,478	85					
			118,000 =======	00 ===				118,000 =======	00 ===
					19_7 Jan.1	By Balance	b/d	116,478	85

Municipal Accounting for Developing Countries

Capital Expenditure (Central Car Park) 2

19_6 Dec.31	To Cash	CC	118,000	00	19_6 Dec.31	By Balance	c/d	118,000	00
19_7 Jan.1	To Balance	b/d	118,000	00					

Loan Charges - Interest 3

19_6 Aug.1	To Cash	CR	3,687	50	19_6 Dec.31	By Revenue Account	6	3,687	50
			3,687	50				3,687	50

Loan Charges - Principal 4

19_6 Dec.31	To Capital Discharged	J	1,521	15	19_6 Dec.31	By Revenue Account	J	1,521	15
			1,521	15				1,521	15

Capital Discharged - Loan Repaid 5

19_6 Dec.31	To Balance	c/d	1,521	15	19_6 Dec.31	By Loan Charges (Principal)	J	1,521	15
			1,521	15				1,521	15
					19_7 Jan.1	By Balance	b/d	1,521	15

Capital Expenditure

		Revenue Account							6
19_6 Dec.31	To Loan Charges Interest Principal	3 4	3,687 1,521	50 15	19_6 Dec.31	By Balance	c/d	5,208	65
			5,208 =====	65 ===				5,208 =====	65 ===
19_7 Jan.1	To Balance	b/d	5,208	65					

Balance Sheet as at 31 Dec. 19_6
Capital

	Units	Cents		Units	Cents
Long-Term Liabilities			**Fixed Assets**		
Loans Outstanding	116,478	85	Capital Expenditure Central Car Park	118,000	00
Surplus					
Capital Discharged	1,521	15			
	118,000	00		118,000	00

Revenue

	Units	Cents		Units	Cents
Current Liabilities			**Deficiency**		
Cash Overdrawn	5,208	65	Revenue Account Deficiency	5,208	65
	5,208	65		5,208	65
	123,208	65		123,208	65

The balance sheet now shows the facts in their proper form. In particular:

(a) a capital surplus is held in the form of fixed assets to the extent that they are debt-free; and

(b) a revenue deficiency is represented by a bank overdraft. When income is raised to clear the deficiency (eg rates, taxes) the cash overdraft will be wiped out.

To illustrate principles, we have assumed that everything has neatly worked out. However, in practice the position will be more complicated, for several reasons.

In the first place, the capital payments will be spread over the whole period during which the scheme is in progress, perhaps covering several financial years. In our example the capital programme shows that work on the Central Car Park is due to begin during the last quarter of 19_5 and to continue during 19_6.

Secondly, as we have already seen, the total actual expenditure will differ from the estimated amount shown in the programme. It will also differ from the amount of the loan.

Thirdly, a shrewd Chief Financial Officer will not time the loan-raising operation merely with reference to the particular scheme to which the loan relates. Having obtained a loan sanction (i.e. Government authority to borrow) he will tend to delay the actual raising of the loan for as long as possible, in order to save idle loan charges. If the Chief Financial Officer is preparing periodical cash forecasts he should be able to judge the time at which his cash balances are likely to fall below their safe level. He will then select a suitable loan sanction from among those he holds (if there are several schemes proceeding simultaneously) and exercise it by raising the loan. He will arrange for the money to be received no earlier than is required to stabilise the cash position.

Finally, a local authority may have many different loans outstanding from the Government. When this happens, it is sensible for all repayments to take place on the same dates, either half-yearly or quarterly. This considerably reduces clerical work.

In UK the Public Works Loans Board send out half-yearly schedules to local authorities, each containing details for repayment of hundreds of different loans. Many other countries have established local government loans funds, which work (or could be made to work) in similar fashion. An advantage of borrowing from government sources is that government shares the developmental responsibility with the local authority and is thus more likely to allow mutually convenient administrative practices.

Let us now assume that the car park actually cost U 115,260 of which U 19,380 was paid out in 19_5. Let us assume that the loan of U 118,000 was received on 15 April 19_6 and that the authority pays its half-yearly instalments to the Government on 30 June and 31 December.

The payments made during 19_5 can be journalised as follows:

| 19_6 Dec.31 | Capital Expenditure (Central Car Park) DR. To Cash (Capital) Being capital payments made during the year | 2 C.C. | 19,380 | 00 | 19,380 | 00 |

At the end of 19_5 the (isolated) balance sheet will show:

Balance Sheet as at 31 Dec. 19_5
Capital

	Units	Cents		Units	Cents
Current Liabilities			**Fixed Assets**		
Cash Overdrawn	19,380	00	Capital Expenditure Central Car Park	19,380	00
	19,380	00		19,380	00

Capital Expenditure

The capital transactions during 19_6 can be journalised as follows:

19_6						

Apr.15	Cash (Capital) DR.
	  To Loans Outstanding
	  Being loan raised to
	  construct Central Car Park
		C.C.
		1
			118,000	00	118,000	00

Dec.31	Capital Expenditure
	  (Central Car Park) DR.
	  To Cash (Capital)
	  Being capital payments
	  made during year
		2
		C.C.
			95,880	00	95,880	00

If we ignore, for the moment, the effect of loan repayments during 19_6 the ledger accounts and (isolated) balance sheet at 31 Dec. 19_6 would appear as follows:

Cash (Capital)   C.C.

19_6					19_6				
Apr.15	To Loans Outstanding	1	118,000	00	Jan.1	By Balance b/f By Capital Expenditure (Central Car Park)		19,380	00
							2	95,880	00
								115,260	00

Loans Outstanding (Government)   1

					19_6				
					Apr.15	By Cash	CC	118,000	00

Capital Expenditure (Central Car Park)   2

19_6				
Jan.1	To Balance b/f		19,380	00
Dec.31	To Cash	CC	95,880	00
			115,260	00

Municipal Accounting for Developing Countries

Balance Sheet as at 31 Dec. 19_6
Capital

	Units	Cents		Units	Cents
Long-Term Liabilities			**Fixed Assets**		
Loans Outstanding	118,000	00	Capital Expenditure		
			Central Car Park	115,260	00
			Current Assets		
			Cash in Hand	2,740	00
	118,000	00		118,000	00
	==========			==========	

Although a loan was raised for U 118,000 the completed scheme cost only U 115,260. There is therefore a balance of capital cash in hand, representing the amount overborrowed, amounting to U 2,740.

This cash should not be used for revenue expenditure but will normally be disposed of in one of two ways.

In the first place it may be returned to the lender. This is only possible if the lender agrees to accept premature repayment. The loan repayment table will then be calculated on the net amount borrowed.

Instead of the balance being repaid to the lender it might be applied to assist in the financing of a further capital scheme. This would usually require the approval of the Government.

If the loan charges on the further scheme were chargeable in the same section of the revenue account as those relating to the original scheme there would be no accounting difficulties. This would happen, for example, if the unspent balance was applied towards the construction of another car park. However, if the new scheme related to an entirely different section of the revenue account (for example - Health) the loan repayment table figures would have to be apportioned.

In our example we have deliberately drawn attention to certain accounting difficulties which may arise concerning unspent cash balances. However, these problems could be reduced or eliminated by using one of several devices.

The loan (or the final instalment where appropriate) could be raised for the exact final cost of the scheme, after the work had been completed.

Alternatively, a loan could be raised for a lesser amount than the full cost of the scheme. The "odd sum" would then be financed by a "revenue contribution to capital outlay".

Later in this book we shall see how these problems can be eliminated by using a "loans pool".

Let us now return to the question of the payment of the loan instalments. As shown on page 512 instalment No.1 is payable on 30 June and instalment No.2 on 31 December.

A glance at the loan repayment table on page 506 shows the first instalment to be U 5,208.65. However, this includes interest for a complete half-year, whereas the loan was raised only on 15 April. The first instalment is therefore reduced by an interest rebate as follows:

Capital Expenditure

	Units	Cents	Units	Cents
Principal			1,521	15
Interest:				
Full Period 1/1 to 30/6	3,687	50		
Less Rebate for 104 days from 1/1				
to 14/4	2,118	80	1,568	70
Total Instalment			3,089	85

The rebate is calculated as:

$$U \frac{3,687.50 \times 104}{181} = U\ 2,118.80$$

(181 days being the period from 1/1 to 30/6).

If the journal entries for the June instalments followed the correct theoretical pattern they would appear as follows:

19_6						
Jun.30	Loans Outstanding (Government) DR. To Cash (Revenue) Being first instalment of principal repaid to lender	1 C.R.	1,521	15	1,521	15
Jun.30	Loan Charges (Interest) DR. To Cash (Revenue) Being first instalment of interest paid on Government Loan	3 C.R.	1,568	70	1,568	70
Jun.30	Loan Charges (Principal) DR. To Capital Discharged (Loan Repaid) Being repayment of principal now charged to revenue account	4 5	1,521	15	1,521	15

However, in practice, when loan charges are paid the principal and interest payments are combined. Also it is sometimes more convenient to debit both payments (through the expenditure analysis) to nominal accounts (i.e. for loan charges) than to post the principal repayment in the correct theoretical manner.

The payment of loan charges can therefore be represented as follows:

19_6						
Jun.30	Loan Charges (Interest) DR. Loan Charges (Principal) DR. To Cash (Revenue) Being first instalment of loan charges on Government loan	3 4 C.R.	1,568 1,521	70 15	3,089	85

Municipal Accounting for Developing Countries

The revenue accounts are thus correctly adjusted and are in balance.

However, the principal repayment has not been recorded in the capital accounts. The account for "Loans Outstanding" still shows a balance of U 118,000 even though a repayment has been made.

The position is adjusted as follows:

19_6 Jun.30	Loans Outstanding (Government) DR. To Capital Discharged (Loan Repaid) Being adjustment for first repayment of principal on loan	1 5	1,521 15	1,521 15

Comparison of the two sets of journal entries will show that in each case the same accounts are respectively debited and credited:

Debits
Loans Outstanding
Loan Charges (Interest)
Loan Charges (Principal)

Credits
Cash
Cash
Capital Discharged (Loan Repaid)

In practice the cash payments would be recorded in a loans ledger (a subsidiary creditors' ledger) and then debited to the appropriate nominal accounts.

The adjustment in the capital accounts would probably be made by a single journal entry at the year end, using totals of information in the loans ledger. In our example, therefore, the full position regarding loan charges during 19_6 can be journalised as follows:

Capital Expenditure

19_6 Jun.30	Loan Charges (Interest) DR. Loan Charges (Principal) DR. To Cash (Revenue) Being first instalment of loan charges on Government loan	3 4 C.R.	1,568 1,521	70 15			3,089	85
Dec.31	Loan Charges (Interest) DR. Loan Charges (Principal) DR. To Cash (Revenue) Being second instalment of loan charges on Government loan	3 4 C.R.	3,639 1,568	95 70			5,208	65
Dec.31	Loans Outstanding DR. To Capital Discharged (Loan Repaid) Being adjustment for first and second repayment of principal on Government loan: Units Cents 1. 1,521 15 2. 1,568 70 3,089 85	1 5	3,089	85			3,089	85

(By a most extraordinary coincidence in our example the first instalment of interest is the same as the second instalment of principal. This has no significance whatever.)

The ledger accounts and (isolated) balance sheet will now appear as follows:

Cash (Capital)   C.C.

19_6 Apr.15	To Loans Outstanding	1	118,000	00	19_6 Jan.1 Dec.31	By Balance b/f By Capital Expenditure (Central Car Park) By Balance c/d	2	19,380 95,880 2,740	00 00 00
			118,000 =======	00 ===				118,000 =======	00 ===
19_7 Jan.1	To Balance b/d		2,740	00					

517

Municipal Accounting for Developing Countries

		Cash (Revenue)					C.R.
19_6 Dec.31	To Balance c/d	8,298	50	19_6 Jun.30	By Loan Charges Interest	3	1,568 70
					Principal	4	1,521 15
				Dec.31	By Loan Charges Interest	3	3,639 95
					Principal	4	1,568 70
		8,298	50				8,298 50
		=====	===				===== ===
				19_7 Jan.1	By Balance b/d		8,298 50

		Loans Outstanding (Government)					1
19_6 Dec.31	To Capital Discharged (Loan Repaid) J	3,089	85	19_6 Apr.15	By Cash CC		118,000 00
	To Balance c/d	114,910	15				
		118,000	00				118,000 00
		=======	===				======= ===
				19_7 Jan.1	By Balance b/d		114,910 15

		Capital Expenditure (Central Car Park)					2
19_6 Jan.1	To Balance b/f	19,380	00	19_6 Dec.31	By Balance c/d		115,260 00
Dec.31	To Cash CC	95,880	00				
		115,260	00				115,260 00
		=======	===				======= ===
19_7 Jan.1	To Balance b/d	115,260	00				

Capital Expenditure

Loan Charges - Interest 3

19_6					19_6				
Jun.30	To Cash	CR	1,568	70	Dec.31	By Revenue Account	6	5,208	65
Dec.31	To Cash	CR	3,639	95					
			5,208	65				5,208	65
			=====	===				=====	===

Loan Charges - Principal 4

19_6					19_6				
Jun.30	To Cash	CR	1,521	15	Dec.31	By Revenue Account	6	3,089	85
Dec.31	To Cash	CR	1,568	70					
			3,089	85				3,089	85
			=====	===				=====	===

Capital Discharged - Loan Repaid 5

19_6					19_6				
Dec.31	To Balance	c/d	3,089	85	Dec.31	By Loans Outstanding	J	3,089	85
			3,089	85				3,089	85
			=====	===	19_7			=====	===
					Jan.1	By Balance	b/d	3,089	85

Revenue Account 6

19_6					19_6				
Dec.31	To Loan Charges Interest	3	5,208	65	Dec.31	By Balance	c/d	8,298	50
	Principal		3,089	85					
			8,298	50				8,298	50
			=====	===				=====	===
19_7									
Jan.1	To Balance	b/d	8,298	50					

Municipal Accounting for Developing Countries

Balance Sheet as at 31 Dec. 19_6
Capital

	Units	Cents		Units	Cents
Long-Term Liabilities			**Fixed Assets**		
			Capital Expenditure		
Loans Outstanding	114,910	15	Central Car Park	115,260	00
Surplus			**Current Assets**		
Capital Discharged	3,089	85	Cash	2,740	00
	118,000	00		118,000	00

Revenue

	Units	Cents		Units	Cents
Current Liabilities			**Deficiency**		
Cash Overdrawn	8,298	50	Revenue Account Deficiency	8,298	50
	8,298	50		8,298	50
	126,298	50		126,298	50

Earlier in this chapter we considered the case where assets were taken over from Central Government or acquired as gifts. Sometimes an asset may be taken over on which there is outstanding loan debt.

Let us suppose that in Kambale there is a sports stadium which is owned and managed by the National Sports Council. It cost the Sports Council U 91,000 in 19_0 and was financed by a 20-year loan from the National Government Treasury. It is decided that as from 1 July 19_6 the stadium will be vested in Kambale Municipal Council, which will take over all management responsibilities and be responsible to this Government for all outstanding loan debt.

The stadium is estimated on 1 July 19_6 to have a capital value of U 136,000 (due to increasing urban land values) and the outstanding loan debt on that date is U 74,100.

A statement of affairs concerning the take-over would show:

Statement of Affairs as at 1 July 19_6

	Units		Units
Long-Term Liabilities		**Fixed Assets**	
Loans Outstanding	74,100	Sports Stadium (at valuation)	136,000
Surplus			
Capital Discharged (Take-Over Values)	61,900		
	136,000		136,000

The asset will be brought into the books as follows:

Capital Expenditure

19_6				
Jul.1	Capital Expenditure (Sports Stadium) DR.	1	136,000	
	To Loans Outstanding	2		74,100
	Capital Discharged (Take-Over Value)	3		61,900
	Being take-over of stadium and outstanding loan debt from the National Sports Council at agreed valuation			

The ledger accounts are quite straightforward. Kambale Municipal Council will pay all future half-yearly loan instalments to the Treasury of the National Government. The future repayments of principal will be credited to a "Capital Discharged - Loan Repaid" Account in the normal way.

Although the stadium originally cost U 91,000 in 19_0 it has been brought into the books of Kambale Municipal Council at current capital value U 136,000 to reflect this in the accounts. The "Capital Discharged" figure of U 61,900 consists partly of loan already repaid by the National Sports Council U 16,900 and partly of appreciation (increase) in the capital value U 45,000. Nevertheless, the Kambale Municipal Council treats the whole sum as "Capital Discharged - Take-Over Values" because the earlier transactions are of no concern to Kambale Municipal Council.

171. CAPITAL FINANCE - FUND CONTRIBUTIONS

Where capital expenditure is to be financed by fund contributions the logical steps are as follows:

(a) record the capital payments; and

(b) record the contribution from the revenue account or special fund.

Special funds, such as renewals funds and capital funds, will have been built up by earlier contributions from the revenue account.

Capital receipts, such as land premia and commodity bonus may also be paid into a capital fund as an alternative to holding them as "capital receipts unapplied".

The accounting entries necessary to build up special funds are given in Chapter 8.

Referring once more to the capital programme we see that it was intended in 19_7 to replace the refuse vehicle which was purchased in 19_2. The purchase was to be financed from the vehicle renewals fund.

Let us suppose that the existing vehicle becomes so unserviceable during 19_6 that a decision is made to accelerate its replacement and to purchase the new vehicle in October 19_6.

The balance sheet on page 285 of Chapter 9 shows that renewals funds total U 85,000. Let us suppose that U 62,500 is in the "Vehicle Renewals Fund", the remaining U 22,500 relating to office equipment.

Municipal Accounting for Developing Countries

The position could be represented (in isolation) by the following balance sheet:

Balance Sheet as at 1 Jan. 19_6
Revenue

Provisions		**Current Assets**	
Vehicle Renewals Fund	62,500	Investments	62,500
	62,500		62,500
	======		======

If the vehicle were purchased on (say) 9 Oct. 19_6 for (say) U 50,380 the transaction could be journalised as follows:

19_6 Oct.9	Capital Expenditure (Refuse Vehicle - URT 495) DR. To Cash (Revenue) C.R. Being purchase of refuse vehicle	1	50,380	50,380

Each section of the "double account" balance sheet would now be out of balance as follows:

Balance Sheet as at 9 Oct. 19_6
Capital

	Units		Units
		Fixed Assets	
		Refuse Vehicle	50,380

Revenue

	Units		Units
Current Liabilities		**Current Assets**	
Cash Overdrawn	50,380	Investments	62,500
Provisions			
Vehicles Renewals Fund	62,500		
	-------		-------
	112,880		62,500
	-------		-------
	112,880		112,880
	=======		=======

The balance can be restored by making a contribution from the Renewals Fund to finance the purchase as follows:

19_6 Oct.9	Vehicle Renewals Fund DR. To Capital Discharged (Renewals Fund) Being purchase of Refuse Vehicle (URT 495) now charged to Renewals Fund	2 3	50,380	50,380

Capital Expenditure

The individual sections of the "double account" balance sheet are now in balance as follows:

Balance Sheet as at 9 Oct. 19_6
Capital

	Units		Units
Surplus		**Fixed Assets**	
Capital Discharged (Renewals Fund)	50,380	Refuse Vehicle	50,380
	50,380		50,380

Revenue

	Units		Units
Current Liabilities		**Current Assets**	
Cash Overdrawn	50,380	Investments	62,500
Provisions			
Vehicles Renewals Fund	12,120		
	62,500		62,500
	112,880		112,880

Although the capital and revenue sections of the balance sheet are now separately in balance there is an overdrawn cash balance on the Revenue Account. This is because the Vehicle Renewals Fund is now heavily over-invested. The sum of U 50,380 must be withdrawn from investments to wipe out the cash overdrawn, as follows:

19_6						
Oct.9	Cash (Revenue) DR.			C.R.	50,380	
	To Investments (Renewals Fund)			4		50,380
	Being realisation of Renewals Fund Investments to finance purchase of Refuse Vehicle (URT 495)					

The complete ledger accounts and (isolated) balance sheet would appear as follows:

		Cash (Revenue)						C.R.
19_6 Oct.9	To Investments	4	50,380	19_6 Oct.9	By Capital Expenditure (Refuse Vehicle)		1	50,380
			50,380					50,380

Capital Expenditure (Refuse Vehicle - URT 495)								1
19_6 Oct.9	To Cash	C.R.	50,380	19_6 Dec.31	By Balance	c/d	50,380
19_7 Jan.1	To Balance	b/d	50,380				

Vehicle Renewals Fund								2
19_6 Oct.9	To Capital Discharged	J	50,380	19_6 Jan.1	By Balance	b/f	62,500
Dec.31	To Balance	c/d	12,120				
			62,500				62,500
				19_7 Jan.1	By Balance	b/d	12,120

Capital Discharged (Renewals Fund)								3
19_6 Dec.31	To Balance	c/d	50,380	19_6 Oct.9	By Vehicle Renewals Fund	J	50,380
			50,380				50,380
				19_7 Jan.1	By Balance	b/d	50,380

Investments (Renewals Fund)								4
19_6 Jan.1	To Balance	b/f	62,500	19_6 Oct.9	By Cash	C.R.	50,380
				Dec.31	By Balance	c/d	12,120
			62,500				62,500
19-7 Jan.1	To Balance	b/d	12,120				

Capital Expenditure

Balance Sheet as at 31 Dec. 19_6
Capital

	Units		Units
Surplus		**Fixed Assets**	
Capital Discharged		Refuse Vehicles	50,380
(Renewals Fund)	50,380		
	------		------
	50,380		50,380
	------		------

Revenue

	Units		Units
Provisions		**Current Assets**	
Vehicles Renewals Fund	12,120	Investments	12,120
	------		------
	12,120		12,120
	------		------
	62,500		62,500
	======		======

There is now a capital surplus held in the form of a fixed asset, together with the unapplied balance of the renewals fund held in the form of investments. In practice, the adjustments affecting the renewals fund and the investments will probably be made at the end of the financial year.

In dealing with the investments, it is likely that a net sum would be realised (or invested) after taking account of the contributions to the fund for 19_6. Let us suppose that the Vehicle Renewals Fund is invested in a 5% deposit account at Commercial Bank.

The balance sheet at 1 Jan. 19_6 would be as shown on page 523.

There appear to be two vehicles being financed by the fund. Each is estimated to have a replacement cost of U 51,000 and a life of 5 years.

The annual contribution for each vehicle might well be:

$$\frac{51,000}{5} = U\ 10,200$$

The transactions of the fund during 19_6 would then be as follows:

		Units
	Balance at 1 Jan.	62,500
Add	Contributions for 19_6	
	(2 x U 10,200)	20,400
		82,900
Add	Investment Interest	
	(5% x U 62,500)	3,125
		86,025
Less	Contribution towards purchase of new vehicle	50,380
	Balance of fund 31 Dec. 19_6	35,645
		======

Municipal Accounting for Developing Countries

The balance sheet for the Renewals Fund in isolation before adjusting the investments would show:

Revenue

	Units		Units
Current Liabilities		**Current Assets**	
Cash Overdrawn	26,855	Investments	62,500
Provision			
Vehicle Renewals Fund	35,645		
	62,500		62,500
	======		======

U 26,855 of the investment is now realised (ie withdrawn) to clear the cash overdraft. The amount is calculated as follows:

	Units	Units
Purchase of New Vehicle		50,380
Less Contributions	20,400	
Interest	3,125	23,525
Cash Withdrawn		26,855
		======

Let us now consider the schemes for levelling the refuse disposal tip, (Stages I and II) which took place mainly in 19_5, and which was to be financed by "Revenue Contributions to Capital Outlay".

We shall assume that the costs worked out as follows:

Stage I	19_4	920
	19_5	48,140
		49,060
		======
Stage II	19_5	45,380
		======

The balance sheet at 1 Jan. 19_5 would show:

Balance Sheet as at 1 Jan. 19_5
Capital

	Units		Units
Surplus		**Fixed Assets**	
Capital Discharged		Capital Expenditure	
(Revenue Contributions)	920	Refuse Tip (Stage I)	920
	920		920
	===		===

Capital Expenditure

The transactions during 19_5 could be journalised as follows:

19_5					
Dec.31	Capital Expenditure (Refuse Tip - Stage I) To Cash (Revenue) Being payments during year for remainder of levelling work on Stage I	DR. C.R.	1	48,140	48,140
Dec.31	Capital Expenditure (Refuse Tip - Stage II) To Cash (Revenue) Being payments made during year for levelling work on Stage II	DR. C.R.	2	45,380	45,380
Dec.31	Revenue Account (Refuse Disposal) To Capital Discharged (RCCO) Being revenue contributions to capital outlay for levelling work on refuse tip: Stage 1 (bal) 48,140 Stage 2 45,380 93,520 ======	DR.	4 3	93,520	93,520

The ledger accounts and balance sheet would appear as follows:

Cash (Revenue)								C.R.
19_5 Dec.31	To Balance	c/d	93,520	19_5 Dec.31	By Capital Expenditure Refuse Tip Stage I Stage II	1	48,140 45,380 93,520 ======	
				19_6 Jan.1	By Balance	b/d	93,520	

527

Municipal Accounting for Developing Countries

Capital Expenditure (Refuse Tip - Levelling - Stage I)								1
19_5				19_5				
Jan.1	To Balance	b/f	920	Dec.31	By Balance	c/d		49,060
Dec.31	To Cash	C.R.	48,140					
			49,060					49,060
			======					======
19_6								
Jan.1	To Balance	b/d	49,060					

Capital Expenditure (Refuse Tip - Levelling - Stage II)								1
19_5				19_5				
Dec.31	To Cash	C.R.	45,380	Dec.31	By Balance	c/d		45,380
			======					======
19_6								
Jan.1	To Balance	b/d	45,380					

Capital Discharged (Revenue Contributions to Capital Outlay)								3
19_5				19_5				
Dec.31	To Balance	c/d	94,440	Jan.1	By Balance	b/f		920
				Dec.31	By Revenue Account	J		93,520
			94,440					94,440
			======					======
				19_6				
				Jan.1	By Balance	b/d		94,440

Revenue Account - Refuse Disposal (Revenue Contributions to Capital Outlay)								4
19_5				19_5				
Dec.31	To Capital Dis-charged	J	93,520	Dec.31	By Revenue Account (Summary)	5		93,520
			93,520					93,520
			======					======

Capital Expenditure

Revenue Account (Summary) Refuse Disposal — 5

19_5 Dec.31	To Revenue Contributions to Capital Outlay	4	93,520	19_5 Dec.31	By Balance	c/d	93,520
			93,520 ======				93,520 ======
19_6 Jan.1	To Balance	b/d	93,520				

Balance Sheet as at 31 Dec. 19_5

Capital

	Units		Units
Surplus		**Fixed Assets**	
Capital Discharged (Revenue Contributions)	94,440	Capital Expenditure Refuse Tip (Stage I) Refuse Tip (Stage II)	49,060 45,380
	94,440		94,440

Revenue

Current Liabilities Cash Overdrawn	93,520	**Deficiency** Revenue Account Deficiency	93,520
	187,960 =======		187,960 =======

In practice, income would be raised (rates, taxes, etc) during the year to meet the deficiency, thus eliminating the overdrawn cash balance.

Sometimes an authority will set up a "Capital Fund", with which to finance capital expenditure. Capital receipts, such as land premiums, commodity bonus, and receipts from sales of assets, will be paid into the fund. In effect, this is an advance revenue contribution to capital.

For example, on 13 August 19_6, Kambale Municipal Council might receive a land premium for a lease of building land amounting to U 266,500. The Council may decide to use the money to set up a capital fund. The transaction could be journalised as follows:

19_6 Aug.13	Cash (Capital) DR. To Capital Fund Being premium on lease of land @ plots 4-7 Kitani Road now credited to capital fund	C.C. 2	266,500	266,500

Municipal Accounting for Developing Countries

By definition, the cash in this fund must be regarded as "capital" cash and should only be used for capital purposes. The position would be as follows:

Balance Sheet as at 13 Aug. 19_6
Capital

	Units		Units
Surplus		**Current Assets**	
Capital Fund	266,500	Cash in Hand	266,500
	=======		=======

If the cash were not immediately required for capital purposes it might be invested as follows:

19_6					
Sept.1	Investments (Capital Fund)　DR.	4	266,500		
	To Cash (Capital)	C.C.		266,500	
	Being investment of capital fund				

The balance sheet would then show:

Balance Sheet as at 1 Sept. 19_6
Capital

	Units		Units
Surplus		**Current Assets**	
Capital Fund	266,500	Investments	266,500
	=======		=======

Let us now suppose that the cash is not immediately invested, but held to finance a capital scheme during 19_6. A glance at the capital programme summary on page 288 of Chapter 9 will show U 180,000 provided in 19_6 under "Clinics and Dispensaries". We shall assume that this relates to a new clinic which eventually cost U 183,360, all payments being made during 19_6, and financed entirely from the Capital Fund. The various transactions could be journalised as follows:

Capital Expenditure

19_6				

Dec.31	Capital Expenditure (Clinic) DR.
	   To Cash (Capital)
	     Being capital payments during
	     year
		1
		C.C.
			183,360	183,360

Dec.31	Capital Fund
	   To Capital Discharged (Capital
	     Fund)
	     Being finance of capital
	     expenditure on clinic
		2
		3
			183,360	183,360

Dec.31	Investments (Capital Fund) DR.
	   To Cash (Capital)
	     Being surplus cash of capital
	     fund now invested
		4
		C.C.
			83,140	83,140

The ledger accounts and (isolated) balance sheet would appear as follows:

Cash (Capital)   C.C.

19_6				19_6			
Aug.13	To Capital Fund	2	266,500	Dec.31	By Capital Expenditure (Clinic) By Investments	1 4	183,360 83,140
			266,500 =======				266,500 =======

Capital Expenditure - Clinic   1

19_6				19_6			
Dec.31	To Cash	C.C.	183,360 =======	Dec.31	By Balance	c/d	183,360 =======
19_7							
Jan.1	To Balance	b/d	183,360				

Municipal Accounting for Developing Countries

			Capital Fund			2
19_6 Dec.31	To Capital Dis- charged To Balance	J c/d	183,360 83,140 ———— 266,500 ======	19_6 Aug.13 By Cash 19_7 Jan.1 By Balance	C.C. b/d	266,500 ———— 266,500 ====== 83,140

			Capital Discharged - Capital Fund			3
19_6 Dec.31	To Balance	c/d	183,360 ———— 183,360 ======	19_6 Dec.31 By Capital Fund 19_7 Jan.1 By Balance	J b/d	183,360 ———— 183,360 ====== 183,360

			Investments - Capital Fund			4
19_6 Dec.31 19_7 Jan.1	To Cash To Balance	C.C. b/d	83,140 ====== 83,140	19_6 Dec.31 By Balance	c/d	83,140 ======

Balance Sheet as at 31 Dec. 19_6
Capital

	Units		Units
Surplus		**Fixed Assets**	
Capital Discharged		Capital Expenditure -	
(Capital Fund)	183,360	Clinic	183,360
Capital Fund	83,140	**Current Assets**	
		Investments	83,140
	————		————
	266,500		266,500
	======		======

In this example the revenue accounts are not affected in any way.

However, it is possible for the Fund to be increased by contributions from the Revenue Account.

Capital Expenditure

Suppose Kambale Municipal Council had decided, (in addition to placing capital receipts in the fund), to make an annual contribution from Revenue of U 40,000. The journal entry would be:

| 19_6 Dec.31 | Revenue Account (Capital Fund Contributions) DR.
To Capital Fund
Being annual contribution to capital fund for 19_6 | 6
2 | 40,000 | 40,000 |

The two sections of the double-account balance sheet would then be out of balance as follows:

Balance Sheet as at 31 Dec. 19_6
Capital

	Units		Units
Surplus		**Fixed Assets**	
Capital Discharged		Capital Expenditure	
(Capital Fund)	183,360	Clinic	183,360
Capital Fund	123,140	**Current Assets**	
		Investments	83,140
	-------		-------
	306,500		266,500
	-------		-------

Revenue

		Deficiency	
		Revenue Account Deficiency	40,000

			40,000

	306,500		306,500
	=======		=======

This would be corrected by appropriating an equivalent amount of "revenue" cash as "capital" cash journalised as follows:

| 19_6 Dec.31 | Cash (Capital) DR.
To Cash (Revenue)
Being appropriation of cash relating to capital fund contribution | C.C.
C.R. | 40,000 | 40,000 |

The balance sheet would then show:

Municipal Accounting for Developing Countries

Balance Sheet as at 31 Dec. 19_6
Capital

	Units		Units
Surplus		**Fixed Assets**	
Capital Discharged		Capital Expenditure	
(Capital Fund)	183,360	Clinic	183,360
Capital Fund	123,140	**Current Assets**	
		Investments	83,140
		Cash in Hand	40,000
	-------		-------
	306,500		306,500
	-------		-------

Revenue

	Units		Units
Current Liability		**Deficiency**	
Cash Overdrawn	40,000	Revenue Account	
		Deficiency	40,000
	-------		-------
	40,000		40,000
	-------		-------
	346,500		346,500
	=======		=======

Alternatively, if the contribution to the capital fund is to be immediately invested, an equivalent amount of "revenue" cash must be appropriated for the investment, journalised as follows:

19_6						
Dec.31	Investments (Capital Fund)	DR.	4	40,000		
	To Cash (Revenue)		C.R.		40,000	
	Being investment of cash					
	relating to capital fund					
	contribution					

The balance sheet would then show:

Balance Sheet as at 31 Dec 19_6
Capital

	Units		Units
Surplus		**Fixed Assets**	
Capital Discharged		Capital Expenditure	
(Capital Fund)	183,360	Clinic	183,360
Capital Fund	123,140	**Current Assets**	
		Investments	123,140
	-------		-------
	306,500		306,500
	-------		-------

Revenue

	Units		Units
Current Liabilities		**Deficiency**	
Cash Overdrawn	40,000	Revenue Account	
		Deficiency	40,000
	-------		-------
	40,000		40,000
	-------		-------
	346,500		346,500
	=======		=======

15. Capital Expenditure (continued)

Section		Page
172.	Deferred Charges.	536
173.	Alienation of Fixed Assets.	541
174.	Capital Register.	552
175.	Loans Register.	560
176.	Earmarked and Pooled Loans.	566
177.	Instalment and Annuity Loans.	569
178.	Maturity Loans.	570
179.	Sinking Funds - Introduction.	571
180.	Sinking Funds - Application.	573
181.	Capital Cash.	586
182.	Deferred Payment of Land Premiums.	593
183.	Advance Payment of Deferred Premiums.	603

172. DEFERRED CHARGES

A deferred charge, as defined in Section 89 of Chapter 8, is an accumulated loss. It can arise in the books in two main ways:

(a) where a loan is raised to meet expenditure which does not result in the creation of fixed assets; and

(b) where fixed assets are disposed of, leaving outstanding loan debt.

The first case arises where expenditure is incurred which would normally be treated as revenue expenditure. However, for various reasons, the expenditure is too great to be financed from the revenue account of a single year and a loan is raised to spread the cost over a number of years.

An example which sometimes arises in the United Kingdom is where a local authority promotes a "Local Act of Parliament". Such an Act gives a particular authority certain powers which it may exercise within its own jurisdiction and which are not available to other authorities under the general law. In promoting a "Local Act" the authority concerned will have to pay out thousands of pounds in legal and parliamentary fees; normally these are covered by raising a loan.

Deferred charges could also arise as a result of widespread damage to roads and bridges by bad weather, loans being raised to finance the cost of repairs. In a rural area, a famine relief scheme might be financed out of loan moneys.

In none of the above examples are any fixed assets created, even though there may be a future flow of benefit.

The accounting procedures for raising the loans and making the payments are similar to those for capital expenditure. However, instead of the expenditure being retained in the books at cost, it is written down gradually as the loan is repaid.

Let us assume that a large bridge in Kambale collapses on 15 May 19_6 as a result of floods. It costs U 400,000 to repair the damage and there is no insurance cover. No new asset is to be created. The existing asset (the damaged bridge) is merely to be repaired, restoring it to its former state. However, the Kambale Municipal Council is unable to finance the whole of the cost of repairs during 19_6 so it is authorised to raise a loan. The loan is raised for a period of 5 years from the National Development Corporation at 5% repayable in 5 equal annual instalments.

Capital Expenditure

The logical steps to be followed are:

(a) record the loan receipt;

(b) record the payments as a deferred charge;

(c) record the annual repayments of loan principal;

(d) record the annual payments of interest on the outstanding loan; and

(e) apply the repayments of principal towards the elimination of the deferred charge.

(a) Record the Loan Receipts

19_6				
May 31	Cash (Capital) DR. To Loans Outstanding (NDC) Being loan raised to finance repairs to bridge at Great River	C.C. 1	400,000	400,000

(b) Record the Payments as a Deferred Charge

19_6				
Dec.31	Deferred Charge (Bridge Repairs) DR. To Cash (Capital) Being payments for repairs to bridge at Great River damaged by floods	2 C.C.	400,000	400,000

It is customary to deal with these receipts and payments through the "Capital" cash account even though (strictly speaking) they are not "capital" transactions.

Similarly, the deferred charge customarily appears in the "capital" section of the double-account balance sheet, in order to balance the loan.

At the end of 19_6 the balance sheet would show:

Balance Sheet as at 31 Dec. 19_6
Capital

	Units		Units
Long-Term Liabilities		**Deficiency**	
Loans Outstanding	400,000	Deferred Charge	400,000
	-------		-------
	400,000		400,000
	=======		=======

Municipal Accounting for Developing Countries

(c) **Record the First Annual Repayment of Loan Principal**

| 19_7 May 31 | Loans Outstanding (NDC)   DR.
    To Cash (Revenue)   C.R.
    Being repayment of first
    instalment of NDC loan | 1 | 80,000 | 80,000 |

(d) **Record the First Payment of Interest**

| 19_7 May 31 | Loan Charges (Interest)   DR.
    To Cash (Revenue)   C.R.
    Being annual interest on loan
    from NDC (5% on U 400,000) | 3 | 20,000 | 20,000 |

At this point the two sections of the double-account balance sheet will be out of balance as follows:

Balance Sheet as at 31 May 19_7
Capital

	Units		Units
Long-Term Liability		**Deficiency**	
Loans Outstanding	320,000	Deferred Charge	400,000
	-------		-------

Revenue

Current Liability		**Deficiency**	
Cash Overdrawn	100,000	Revenue Account	
		Deficiency (Loan	
		Charges - Interest)	20,000
	-------		-------
	100,000		20,000
	-------		-------
	420,000		420,000
	=======		=======

The balance is restored by the following entry:

(e) **Apply the Principal Repayment Towards the Elimination of the Deferred Charge**

| 19_7 May 31 | Loan Charges (Principal)   DR.
    To Deferred Charge
    Being application of loan
    repayment towards elimination
    of deferred charge | 4
2 | 80,000 | 80,000 |

The complete ledger accounts and (isolated) balance sheet will appear as follows:

Capital Expenditure

			Cash (Capital)				C.C.
19_6 May 31	To Loans Outs- tanding		400,000	19_6 Dec.31	By Deferred Charge	2	400,000
			400,000 ======				400,000 ======

			Cash (Revenue)				C.R.
19_7 Dec.31	To Balance	c/d	100,000	19_7 May 31	By Loan Charges: Princ- ipal Inter- est	1	80,000 20,000
			100,000 ======				100,000 ======
				19_8 Jan.1	By Balance	b/d	100,000

			Loans Outstanding (NDC)				1
19_6 Dec.31	To Balance	c/d	400,000 ======	19_6 May 31	By Cash	C.C.	400,000 ======
19_7 May 31 Dec.31	To Cash To Balance	C.R. c/d	80,000 320,000	19_7 Jan.1	By Balance	b/d	400,000
			400,000 ======				400,000 ======
				19_8 Jan.1	By Balance	b/d	320,000

Municipal Accounting for Developing Countries

Deferred Charge - Bridge Repairs - Great River · 2

19_6 Dec.31	To Cash	C.C.	400,000	19_6 Dec.31	By Balance	c/d	400,000
			=======				=======
19_7 Jan.1	To Balance	b/d	400,000	19_7 May 31	By Loan Charges Principal	J	80,000
					By Balance	c/d	320,000
			400,000				400,000
			=======				=======
19_8 Jan.1	To Balance	b/d	320,000				

Loan Charges - Interest · 3

19_7 May 31	To Cash	C.R.	20,000	19_7 Dec.31	By Revenue Account	5	20,000
			20,000				20,000
			======				======

Loan Charges - Principal · 4

19_7 May 31	To Deferred Charge	J	80,000	19_7 Dec.31	By Revenue Account	5	80,000
			80,000				80,000
			======				======

Revenue Account · 5

19_7 Dec.31	To Loan Charges Principal	4	80,000	19_7 Dec.31	By Balance	c/d	100,000
	Interest	3	20,000				
			100,000				100,000
			=======				=======
19_8 Jan.1	To Balance	b/d	100,000				

Capital Expenditure

Balance Sheet as at 31 Dec. 19_7
Capital

	Units		Units
Long-Term Liability		**Deficiency**	
Loans Outstanding	320,000	Deferred Charge	320,000

Revenue

	Units		Units
Current Liability		**Deficiency**	
Cash Overdrawn	100,000	Revenue Account Deficiency Loan Charges	100,000
	100,000		100,000
	420,000		420,000

There is a liability and a deficiency in both the "capital" section and the "revenue" section. However, the deferred charge and the outstanding loan are being carried forward, whereas the revenue account deficiency will be covered by revenue income, thus eliminating the overdrawn cash balance.

Deferred charges arising as a result of the disposal of fixed assets will be dealt with later.

173. ALIENATION OF FIXED ASSETS

In the previous chapter we dealt with the various accounting procedures involved in acquiring fixed assets, dealing with the various methods by which capital expenditure is financed.

We must now consider how capital expenditure is retained in the books and how it is written out of the books when assets are disposed of. The technical term used to describe the process whereby fixed assets are taken (or deemed to be taken) out of use is called "alienation of assets".

Reference to Sections 85 and 86 of Chapter 8 shows that it is not normal for a local authority to depreciate its assets but to retain them in the books at cost. We have seen how the costs of the assets in the books are offset by "loans outstanding" or "capital discharged" accounts.

How long should assets remain in the accounts (at cost) before they are written off?

The logical rule would be to retain them in the books (at cost) until they are disposed of. With land, buildings and equipment, application of this rule is straightforward. However with certain other permanent works it is sometimes difficult to say precisely when an asset falls out of use.

In its publication, "The Form of Published Accounts of Local Authorities" the Institute of Municipal Treasurers and Accountants (UK) (now the Chartered Institute of Public Finance and Accountancy (UK)) made the following recommendations:

Municipal Accounting for Developing Countries

"Classification of Capital Expenditure"

"Two kind of capital expenditure should be distinguished:
(a) Capital Outlay (all land, and buildings and plant, etc);

(b) Other Long Term Outlay (such as roads, sewers, sea defence works, and dredging works).

"This (latter) class is exceedingly difficult to define, but is intended for those partly intangible, unsaleable items of capital outlay which are common in local authorities but rare in other concerns. They are the assets for which there is no precise day of alienation or falling out of use. For this reason alone all items of plant and furniture will be classified under (a).

"Retention of Capital Expenditure in the Accounts

"Capital expenditure falling under (a) should be retained at cost in the accounts until the asset is disposed of.

"Expenditure classified under (b) is of a peculiar kind. As explained above its distinguishing characteristics are that it does not represent saleable assets nor does it represent assets which fall out of use upon a specifiable date. A new road is made and in due course reconstructed and re-made. Is the original expenditure to remain in the accounts indefinitely? If so, is the expenditure of reconstruction to be "capitalised"? If on the other hand the expenditure is to be written out when should this be done?

"Clearly, there is no completely logical answer to these questions; some rule of thumb method must be sought.

"The easiest method of dealing with this class of expenditure is to segregate it in the accounts and write it out at the end of the loan period, or of the hypothetical loan period in cases where the expenditure is met from revenue. There is then no suggestion that the "life" of the asset necessarily coincides with that of the loan: the expiration of the loan is merely used as a rough and ready method of establishing a date for writing out assets which are best not retained indefinitely in the books."

An alternative method sometimes adopted is to treat class (b) expenditure as deferred charges, dealt with as shown above.

Assets which are retained in the books at cost will be written off either when disposed of or at the expiry of a hypothetical loan period depending upon their nature.

The simplest case arises where an asset has been fully financed. In other words, the whole cost of the asset is covered by a "capital discharged" account and there is no outstanding loan debt.

In Chapter 14 Section 171 we considered the case where Kambale Municipal Council purchased a refuse vehicle in 19_6 to replace the one purchased in 19_2. Let us assume that the vehicle purchased in 19_2 cost U 39,100 and was financed from the renewals fund. At 1 Jan. 19_6 it would have stood in the books as follows:

Capital Expenditure

Balance Sheet as at 1 Jan 19_6
Capital

Surplus	Units	Fixed Assets	Units
Capital Discharged		Refuse Vehicle (at Cost)	
(Renewals Fund)	39,100	(Purchased 19_2)	39,100
	39,100		39,100
	======		======

The vehicle became unserviceable during 19_6 and was replaced in October.

Had the old vehicle been written off for a NIL value on 30 September the journal entry would have been:

19_6 Sept.30	Capital Discharged (Renewals Fund) DR. To Capital Expenditure Refuse Vehicle (No.......) Being vehicle purchased in 19_2 now written off as unserviceable	39,100	39,100

Although we have assumed that the vehicle was originally financed from the renewals fund, it would have made little difference to the accounting entries shown above had it been been financed in some other way. There would still be a "Capital Discharged" account but the parenthesis would show:

> "(Loans Repaid)"
> "(Capital Fund)"
> "Revenue Contributions"
> or other source of finance as the case might be.

When income arises from the disposal of assets we must follow three logical steps:

(a) write off the asset;

(b) record the capital receipt; and

(c) apply the capital receipt to a new capital purpose.

Let us assume that instead of the above vehicle being written off at a NIL value it had been sold (as scrap) for U 1,000. The logical steps would be:

(a) **Write Off the Asset**

19_6 Sept.30	Capital Discharged (Renewals Fund) DR. To Capital Expenditure Refuse Vehicle (No......) Being vehicle purchased in 19_2 now disposed of as scrap	39,100	39,100

(b) **Record the Capital Receipts**

19_6 Sept.30	Cash (Capital) DR. To Capital Receipts (Unapplied) Being proceeds of sale of Refuse Vehicle (No.....) for scrap	1,000	1,000

The balance sheet would then show:

Balance sheet as at 30 Sept. 19_6
Capital

	Units		Units
Surplus		**Current Assets**	
Capital Receipts (Unapplied)	1,000	Cash in Hand	1,000
	1,000		1,000
	======		======

Revenue

Provisions		**Current Assets**	
Vehicle Renewals Fund	62,500	Investments	62,500
	======		======

(c) **Apply the Capital Receipts**

The proceeds of the sale should normally be applied to another capital purpose, as described in Chapter 14. It would seem that in this case they should be applied towards the purchase of the replacement vehicle (referred to in Section 171 of Chapter 14), the complete transaction being journalised as follows:

Capital Expenditure

19_6			

Oct. 9	Capital Expenditure - Refuse Vehicle - (URT 495) DR.
	    To Cash (Revenue)
	    To Cash (Capital)
	    Being purchase of refuse vehicle
		50,380	49,380
			1,000

Oct. 9	Vehicle Renewals Fund DR.
	    To Capital Discharged (Renewals Fund)
	    Being part of cost of purchase of Refuse Vehicle (URT 495) now charged to Renewals Fund
		49,380	49,380

Oct. 9	Capital Receipts (Unapplied) DR.
	    To Capital Discharged (Capital Receipts)
	    Being part of cost of purchase of Refuse Vehicle (URT 495) now financed by Capital Receipts from sale of old vehicle
		1,000	1,000

Oct. 9	Cash (Revenue) DR.
	    To Investments (Renewals Fund)
	    Being realisation of Renewals Fund Investments to finance part cost of purchase of Refuse Vehicle (URT 495)
		49,380	49,380

The (isolated) balance sheet at 31 Dec. 19_6 would appear as follows:

Balance sheet as at 31 Dec. 19_6
Capital

	Units		Units
Surplus		**Fixed Assets**	
Capital Discharged		Capital Expenditure	
(Renewals Fund)	49,380	Refuse Vehicle	50,380
(Capital Receipts)	1,000		
	50,380		50,380

Revenue

	Units		Units
Provisions		**Current Assets**	
Vehicles Renewals Fund	13,120	Investments	13,120
	13,120		13,120
	63,500		63,500

Had the old vehicle been traded in part exchange for the new one at a price of U 1,000 there would be no need to open a "Capital Receipts unapplied)" account. The transaction could be journalised as follows:

| 19_6 Oct. 9 | Capital Expenditure (Refuse Vehicle - URT 495) DR.
   To Cash (Revenue)
   To Capital Discharged (Capital Receipt)
Being purchase of refuse vehicle and allowance on old vehicle traded in part-exchange | 50,380 | 49,380

1,000 |

The balance sheet would be unchanged.

If the balance sheet is compared with that shown on page 524 of Chapter 14, it will be seen that the Renewals Fund now contains an additional U 1,000: the capital receipt being used partly to finance the new vehicle, the Renewals Fund contributed U 1,000 less.

The same position would have been achieved by paying the capital receipt direct into the renewals fund as follows:

| 19_6 Sept.30 | Cash (Revenue) DR.
   To Renewals Fund
Being sale proceeds of old refuse vehicle now paid into renewals fund | 1,000 | 1,000 |

Where capital expenditure on permanent works (e.g. roads, sewers and lake defences) is written out at the end of the hypothetical loan period, the entries are quite straightforward:

        DR. Capital Discharged (Loan Repaid)*
        CR. Capital Expenditure (i.e. Fixed Asset)

* or other source of finance as the case may be.

These assets cannot be sold and no income arises to be dealt with as capital recepts.

Sometimes an asset will be disposed of before the loan debt on it has been fully repaid. For example, let us assume that when the clinic referred to on page 531 of Chapter 14 comes into operation it becomes no longer necessary to use an existing (unsatisfactory) building as a clinic. This building, which is of no further use to the Kambale Municipal Council, is sold on 18 Oct. 19_6 for U 210,000.

It was originally purchased in 19_3 for U 365,000 and the loan debt outstanding on the date of sale is U 188,700.

Immediately before the sale, it would appear in a balance sheet as follows:

Capital Expenditure

Balance sheet as at 31 Oct. 19_6
Capital

	Units		Units
Long-Term Liability		**Fixed Asset**	
Loans Outstanding	188,700	Capital Expenditure Clinic	365,000
Surplus			
Capital Discharged (Loan Repaid)	176,300		
	365,000		365,000
	======		======

When the asset is disposed of on 18 Oct. it must be written out of the books.

However, we cannot in this case merely write off the debit balances against the credit balances. To do so, would eliminate the balance of U 188,700 for loans outstanding which would be wrong, because the loan does not cease to be repayable just because the asset is disposed of.

Alternatively, to write off the asset only to the extent of capital discharged would leave a debit balance on the account of an asset no longer owned by the authority. This would be equally wrong.

If we apply the accounting equation:

Assets minus Liabilities = Surpluses minus Deficiencies

to the above balance sheet we shall get:

Assets minus Liabilities   = Surplus
(Clinic) minus (Loan)   = (Capital Discharged)
U 365,000 - U 188,700   = U 176,300.

After the asset is disposed of the equation will be:

Assets minus Liabilities   = Surplus minus Deficiency
(Clinic) minus (Loan)   = (Capital Discharged) minus (?)
NIL - U 188,700   = NIL - U 188,700.

There are now NO assets but the liabilities remain. Therefore, there is a deficiency. This deficiency is another form of deferred charge.

The accounting entries necessary to bring about this position can be journalised as follows:

19_6 Oct.18	Capital Discharged
	Deferred Charge
	  To Clinic
	    Being clinic at .... now
	    written out on sale
		DR.
		DR.
			1
			2
			3
				176,300
				188,700
					365,000

Municipal Accounting for Developing Countries

It is now necessary to record the capital receipt resulting from the sale of the building, journalised as follows:

19_6				

Oct.18	Cash DR.
	  To Capital Receipts (Unapplied)
	  Being receipts from sale of
	  building formerly used as clinic
	  at ....
		C.C.
		4
			210,000	210,000

At this point the balance sheet will show:

Balance sheet as at 18 Oct. 19_6
Capital

	Units		Units
Long-Term Liability		**Current Assets**	
Loans Outstanding	188,700	Cash in Hand	210,000
Surplus		**Deficiency**	
Capital Receipts (Unapplied)	210,000	Deferred Charge	188,700
	398,700		398,700
	======		======

It is now necessary to consider how the capital receipt can be applied. A glance at the above balance sheet draws attention to an obvious application of the capital receipt. If U 188,700 of cash is used to repay the loan outstanding, the equivalent amount of capital receipts will have been applied to wipe out the deferred charge, journalised as follows:

19_6				

Oct.18	Loans Outstanding DR.
	  To Cash
	  Being repayment of outstanding
	  loan debt
		5
		C.C.
			188,700	188,700

Oct.18	Capital Receipts (Unapplied) DR.
	  To Deferred Charge
	  Being application of capital
	  receipts to elimination of
	  deferred charge
		4
		2
			188,700	188,700

The ledger accounts and (isolated) balance sheet would appear as follows:

Capital Expenditure

Cash (Capital) — C.C.

19_6				19_6			
Oct.18	To Capital Receipts (Unapplied)	4	210,000	Oct.18	By Loans Outstanding	5	188,700
				Dec.31	By Balance c/d		21,300
			210,000				210,000
19_7							
Jan.1	To Balance b/d		21,300				

Capital Discharged (Loan Repaid) — 1

19_6				19_6			
Oct.18	To Capital Expenditure (Clinic)	J	176,300	Jan.1	By Balance b/f		176,300
			176,300				176,300

Deferred Charge — 2

19_6				19_6			
Oct.18	To Capital Expenditure (Clinic)	J	188,700	Oct.18	By Capital Receipts (Unapplied)	J	188,700
			188,700				188,700

Capital Expenditure – Clinic — 3

19_6				19_6			
Jan.1	To Balance b/f		365,000	Oct.18	By Deferred Charge	J	188,700
				Oct.18	By Capital Discharged (Loan Repaid)	J	176,300
			365,000				365,000

	Capital Receipts (Unapplied)						4
19_6				19_6			
Oct.18	To Deferred Charge	J	188,700	Oct.18	By Cash	C.C.	210,000
Dec.31	To Balance	c/d	21,300				
			210,000				210,000
			======				======
				19_7			
				Jan.1	By Balance	b/d	21,300

	Loans Outstanding						5
19_6				19_6			
Oct.18	To Cash	C.C.	188,700	Jan.1	By Balance	b/f	188,700
			======				======

Balance sheet as at 31 Dec. 19_6
Capital

Surplus	Units	Current Assets	Units
Capital Receipts (Unapplied)	21,300	Cash in Hand	21,300
	21,300		21,300
	======		======

The balance of capital receipts will be applied in due course to finance another capital project.

It is not always possible or desirable to use the capital receipts to repay the outstanding loan debt.

In the first place, the lender may not agree to accept the premature repayment of the loan. For example, interest rates may have fallen since the loan was made. The lender would therefore tend to receive a lower return by having to invest elsewhere the prematurely repaid loan moneys. Because of this he might insist upon the loan running its full course with the local authority.

In the second place it may not be in the interest of the authority to repay the loan. For example, if interest rates have risen since the loan was made, the interest on a new loan raised to finance capital expenditure will be greater than the interest saved by repayment of the old loan. It will therefore be advantageous to retain the existing loan and to use the capital receipt to finance new capital expenditure.

The position will remain as shown in the balance sheet on page 548. The balance sheet can be regarded as being split into two sub-sections. One sub-section will show the loan balanced against the deferred charge and the other will shown the capital receipt balanced against cash in

Capital Expenditure

hand. The deferred charge will be dealt with as shown in Section 172 and the capital receipt will eventually be applied to a new capital purpose as demonstrated in Section 169 of Chapter 14.

Where the capital receipt is insufficient to repay the whole loan, any remaining loan balance will be carried forward and offset by a deferred charge of equivalent amount.

An unusual case may sometimes arise where the asset and responsibility for the balance of the loan debt is taken over by another authority.

Such would have been the case with the National Sports Council in connection with the sports stadium taken over by Kambale Municipal Council (see Section 170 of Chapter 14 page 520).

Prior to the take-over, the position as shown in the books of the National Sports Council could be expressed in balance sheet form as follows:

Balance sheet as at 30 June 19_6
Capital

	Units		Units
Long-Term Liabilities		**Fixed Assets**	
Loans Outstanding	74,100	Sports Stadium (at cost)	91,000
Surplus			
Capital Discharged (Loan Repaid)	16,900		
	91,000		91,000

The above balance sheet differs from the statement of affairs shown on page 502 of Chapter 14. This is because the stadium is recorded in the books of the National Sports Council at cost, whereas it was taken into the books of Kambale Municipal Council at the current valuation.

Had the loan debt been completely taken over by Kambale Municipal Council on 1 July the stadium would have been written out of the books of the National Sports Council as follows:

19_6 Jul.1	Loans Outstanding DR.	74,100	
	Capital Discharged DR.	16,900	
	To Capital Expenditure (Sports Stadium)		91,000
	Being property and outstanding loan debt now taken over by Kambale Municipal Council		

An alternative would have been for the loan to remain in the books of the National Sports Council. The Kambale Municipal Council would then reimburse the half-yearly loan charges to the National Sports Council as they were incurred. In this case the stadium would have been written out of the books as follows:

19_6					
Jul.1	Deferred Debtor (Kambale Municipal Council) DR.	74,100			
	Capital Discharged DR.	16,900			
	To Capital Expenditure (Sports Stadium)		91,000		
	Being property taken over by Kambale Municipal Council together with liability to reimburse future loan charges				

The balance sheet would show:

Balance sheet as at 1 July 19_6
Capital

Long-Term Liability	Units	**Current Assets**	Units
Loans Outstanding	74,100	Deferred Debtor	74,100

Subsequent payment and reimbursement of loan charges (using assumed figures) would be dealt with as follows:

19_6				
Dec.31	Loans Outstanding DR.	3,540		
	Kambale Municipal Council (Interest) DR.	2,360		
	To Cash		5,900	
	Being payment of half-yearly loan charges on loan raised to finance Sports Stadium			
Dec.31	Cash DR.	5,900		
	To Kambale Municipal Council (Deferred Debtor)		3,540	
	(Interest)		2,360	
	Being reimbursement of half-yearly loan charges by Kambale Municipal Council			

174. CAPITAL REGISTER

Up to this point we have dealt separately with the cash aspect of each scheme, rather as though there was a separate cash account for each one.

In practice, all the cash transactions would pass through a single cash book, probably being dealt with in total. Furthermore, the entries in the cash book are unlikely to be analysed into "revenue" and "capital" aspects.

However, the capital cash position of each scheme can be separately shown by the application of the "suspense account" principles referred to in Section 167 of Chapter 14.

Capital Expenditure

This is done by using a capital register, which can be entered up periodically (often annually) from individual accounts in the income and expenditure ledgers.

A separate page of the register can be used for each capital scheme, giving an analysis of receipts and payments together with the cash position, relating to the individual project.

The register follows a similar pattern to a "suspense account" but it is not an account and does not form part of the ledger system. It would, however, be reasonable to use the detailed information in the register as a basis for making total entries in the main ledger.

An example of a page in such a capital register is given on page 554. The "Capital Expenditure Programme 19_6/_0 - Summary" shown on page 288 of Chapter 9, includes a sum of U 2,203,500 for "Sewage Disposal". We have assumed that the amount shown as spent up to 31 Dec. 19_4 was U 1,125,740 and the amount likely to be spent during 19_5 was U 569,800 both relating to the construction of a new sewage disposal works.

It will be useful to trace the detailed progress of the scheme, to see how this is reflected through the accounts to the capital register:

CONSTRUCTION OF SEWAGE DISPOSAL WORKS

Progress	Accountancy and Finance
19_1 1. Works Committee resolution (MIN 124/_1), subsequently agreed to by the Finance Committee and approved by the Council, authorises the preparation of a capital scheme for a Sewage Disposal Works	1. Now or subsequently, separate folios will be opened for the scheme in the capital section of the expenditure ledger as follows: a) contract payments; b) professional fees: c) plans and printing; d) capital salaries; and e) other.

CAPITAL REGISTER

Service: Sewage Disposal

Scheme: Sewage Disposal Works

Authority: Works Committee 124/_1 and 116/_3

Remarks: Contribution from Bunyoni Municipality U 240,000 Loan U 860,000
Government Grant U 500,000

Estimate: U 1,700,000

Details of Capital Expenditure

Date	Contract Payments	Professional Fees	Plans and Printing	Capital Salaries	Other	Total
	Units	Units	Units	Units	Units	Units
31.12._2	-	-	-	8,460	4,280	12,740
31.12._3	212,380	15,440	10,460	21,280	860	260,420
To date 31.12._4	212,380	15,440	10,460	29,740	5,140	273,160
	811,500	-	680	38,220	2,180	852,580
To date 31.12._5	1,023,880	15,440	11,140	67,960	7,320	1,125,740
	529,000	21,540	-	20,420	360	571,320
To date 31.12._6	1,552,880	36,980	11,140	88,380	7,680	1,697,060
	-	-	-	-	-	-
TOTAL	1,552,880	36,980	11,140	88,380	7,680	1,697,060

Details of Capital Finance

Govt Grant	Loan	Capital Receipts	Revenue	Total	Capital In Hand	Cash Over-Drawn
Units	Units	Units	Units	Units	Units	Units
-	-	-	8,460	8,460	-	4,280
500,000	-	-	21,280	521,280	260,860	-
500,000	-	-	29,740	529,740	256,580	-
-	-	240,000	38,220	278,220	-	574,360
500,000	860,000	240,000	67,960	807,960	-	317,780
-	-	-	20,420	880,420	309,100	-
500,000	860,000	240,000	88,380	1,688,380	-	8,680
-	-	-	8,680	8,680	8,680	-
500,000	860,000	240,000	97,060	1,697,060	-	-

Capital Expenditure

Progress	Accountancy and Finance

19_2
 2. Works department engineering staff prepare outline plans and cost estimates are produced as follows:
 	
                                   Units
   Construction   1,540,000
   QS Fees   40,000
   Plans and Printing   10,000
   Other Expenses   10,000
                            1,600,000
   Capital Salaries   100,000
                            1,700,000
 	
 The engineers state that the scheme is designed to deal with sewage from certain premises within the area of Bunyoni Municipality in addition to the premises in Kambale.
	2. After consultation with the Ministry and Bunyoni Municipality, the Chief Financial Officer of Kambale Municipal Council recommends finance as follows:
	
	                                    Units
	 Government Grant 500,000
	 Contribution from
	   Bunyoni
	   Municipality 240,000
	 Loan 860,000
	                                1,600,000
	 Capital Salaries
	   to be financed
	   by revenue
	   contributions 100,000
	                                1,700,000

3. Committees, Council and Government approve the outline scheme, and financial recommendations. Engineers proceed with preparation of detailed plans. Work begins on clearing the site.	3. a) Salaries of engineering staff (U 8,460) and expenses of clearing the site (U 4,280) are debited in the expenditure ledger. Totals at the end of the year are entered in the capital register. b) Revenue cash (U 8,460) is appropriated to meet capital salaries in accordance with the Council resolution. No finance is yet available to meet other expenses, so cash is overdrawn (U 4,280) at end of 19_2.
19_3 4. Engineers continue planning and supervision of the work. Quantity surveyors prepare bills of quantities. Plans and contract documents are printed. Tenders are invited from contractors.	4. a) Salaries of engineering staff (U 21,280), fees to quantity surveyors (U 15,440), expenses of printing plans and contract documents (U 10,460) and legal expenses (U 860) are debited in the expenditure ledger. Totals at the end of the year are entered in the capital register. b) Revenue cash (U 21,280) is appropriated to meet capital salaries.

Municipal Accounting for Developing Countries

Progress	Accountancy and Finance
5. Works Committee resolution (MIN 116/_3) subsequently agreed to by the Finance Committee and approved by the Council, accepts the most favourable tender. The selected contractor begins work. The government grant is received. Quantity surveyors begin to measure the progress of work so that payments on interim certificates may be made to the contractor.	5. a) Contract payments (U 212,380) are debited in the expenditure ledger. The total at the end of the year is entered in the capital register. b) The government grant (U 500,000) is credited in the income ledger. The total at the end of the year entered in the capital register. c) Cash receipts during the year (U 521,280) exceed cash payments during the year (U 260,420) by U 260,860. d) Receipts and payments for the year are added to earlier figures to give cumulative figures. These show that total receipts to date (U 529,740) have exceeded total payments to date (U 273,160) leaving a cash balance in hand of U 256,580.
19_4 6. The contractor continues the work. Additional printing costs are incurred. Engineering staff continue to supervise the work. Other miscellaneous payments are made. Quantity surveyors continue to measure the progress of work for the issue of interim certificates. The contribution is received from Bunyoni Municipality.	6. a) Contract payments (U 811,500), printing expenses (U 680), salaries of engineering staff (U 38,220) and other expenses (U 2,180) are debited in the expenditure ledger. Totals at the end of the year are entered in the capital register. b) Revenue cash (U 38,220) is appropriated to meet capital salaries. c) The Bunyoni Municipality (U 240,000) contribution is credited in the income ledger. The total at the end of the year is entered in the capital register. d) Cash payments during the year (U 852,580) exceed cash receipts during the year (U 278,220) by U 574,360.

Capital Expenditure

Progress	Accountancy and Finance
	e) Receipts and payments for the year are added to earlier figures to give cumulative figures. These show that total payments to date (U 1,125,740) have exceeded total receipts to date (U 807,960) leaving an overdrawn cash balance of U 317,780.
	f) No claim was received during the year for the professional fees of the quantity surveyors.
19_5 7. The construction work is completed early in the year. After the maintenance (defects liability) period expires the contractor receives final settlement. Engineering staff continue to supervise the work. Quantity surveyors continue to measure the work for interim certificates and they prepare the final account. Further miscellaneous payments are made. The loan is received.	7. a) Contract payments (U 529,000) quantity surveyors' fees (U 21,540), salaries of engineering staff (U 20,420) and other expenses (U 360) are debited in the expenditure ledger. Totals at the end of the year are entered in the capital register.
	b) Revenue cash (U 20,420) is appropriated to meet capital salaries.
	c) The U 860,000 loan is credited in the income ledger. The total at the end of the year is entered in the capital register.
	d) Cash receipts during the year (U 880,420) exceed cash payments during the year (U 571,320) by U 309,100.
	e) Receipts and payments for the year are added to earlier figures to give cumulative figures. These show that total payments to date (U 1,697,060) have exceeded total receipts to date (U 1,688,380) leaving an overdrawn cash balance of U 8,680.

Municipal Accounting for Developing Countries

Progress	Accountancy and Finance
19_6 8. No further expenditure is incurred. On the recommendations of the Chief Financial Officer, the Finance Committee and the Council resolve to meet the balance of the cost by a revenue contribution to capital outlay.	8. a) Revenue cash (U 8,680) is appropriated to meet the overdrawn cash balance. b) The capital register is finally totalled, balanced and ruled off.

Reference in the above table to the expenditure ledger and income ledger draw attention to the fact that there will be some form of analysis system to which individual receipts and payments will be posted during the year as shown in Chapters 10, 11 and 12. For each column in the capital register there will be a separate analysis (code) in the detailed income and expenditure records. This could mean separate ledger folios, separate abstract columns or some other system depending upon detailed accounting arrangements in force.

The capital register gives a complete history of the progress of each scheme, showing clearly how it is financed.

NOTE:

Do not confuse the "capital register" with the "contracts register" referred to in Chapter 11. The contracts register is used for controlling in detail the payments made to individual contractors, whereas the capital register controls, in total, the entire capital scheme.

In the above example, reference has been made to "revenue" cash being "appropriated" to meet certain capital expenditure.

The method of financing capital expenditure from revenue was explained in Section 171 of Chapter 14.

Because there was no "capital cash" we assumed that the payments were made from "revenue cash", demonstrated in the journal entries at the top of page 527.

Another way of looking at this type of transaction is to assume that payments are made initially from "capital cash". Because (in theory) there is no "capital cash" to start with, the payment would cause the "capital cash" account to be overdrawn. The contribution from revenue to the "capital discharged (RCCO)" account would then be matched by a transfer of "revenue cash" to eliminate the cash overdrawn on capital account.

Looked at in this way, the financing of the expenditure in (say) 19_2 on the Sewage Disposal Works could be journalised as follows:

Capital Expenditure

19_2 Dec.31	Capital Expenditure (Sewage Works): Capital Salaries DR. Other DR. To Cash (Capital) Being capital payments made during year	8,460 4,280	12,740

At this point the balance sheet would show:

Balance Sheet as at 31 Dec. 19_2
Capital

Current Liability	Units	**Fixed Assets**	Units
Cash Overdrawn	12,740	Sewage Works	12,740
	======		======

Capital salaries are then financed by a revenue contribution as follows:

19_2 Dec.31	Revenue Account (Sewage Disposal) DR. To Capital Discharged (RCCO) Being capital salaries now financed by a Revenue Contribution to Capital Outlay	8,460	8,460
Dec.31	Cash (Capital) DR. To Cash (Revenue) Being appropriation of cash to meet Revenue Contribution to Capital Outlay	8,460	8,460

Municipal Accounting for Developing Countries

The balance sheet would then show:

Balance Sheet as at 31 Dec. 19_2
Capital

	Units		Units
Current Liabilities		**Fixed Assets**	
Cash Overdrawn	4,280	Sewage Works	12,740
Surplus			
Capital Discharged	8,460		
	------		------
	12,740		12,740
	------		------

Revenue

	Units		Units
Current Liabilities		**Deficiency**	
Cash Overdrawn	8,460	Revenue Account	8,460
	------		------
	8,460		8,460
	------		------
	21,200		21,200
	======		======

There is still an overdrawn cash balance (U 4,280) on capital account because no cash has yet been received or appropriated to meet "other" expenditure. The Council has authorised revenue contributions to meet only capital salaries and (for the time being at least) it is assumed that "other" expenditure will be met from other capital receipts not yet to hand. The "cash overdrawn" figure agrees with the figure in the capital register.

The overdrawn cash balance in the revenue section (U 8,460) will be eliminated by income raised to clear the revenue account deficiency (e.g. rates and taxes).

175. LOANS REGISTER

It is often found convenient to record the details of individual loans in a specially designed loose-leaf record known as a loans ledger or loans register.

One form of record uses a separate page for each loan. Full details of the loan would appear at the head of each page and the entries of loans raised and repaid would appear in a similar form to the loan repayment table on page 506 of Chapter 14. There would be additional columns for dates.

An alternative form of record is illustrated on page 561. This type of record uses one horizontal line for each loan. Details of the loan appear on the left-hand side and the accounting entries appear in the section marked _____ A _____ . Further sheets printed like this can be inserted to provide for entries for future years. The use of these "narrow" or "short" leaves obviates the necessity to rewrite the details each year.

The loans can be entered in chronological order of borrowing or in

LOANS REGISTER

Service: Market

_____ A _____

Loans Sanctioned		Loans Raised						Balance 1st Jan		New Loans			Financial Year 19 6						
Purpose	Years	Amount	Date	Lender	Amount Borrowed	Rate %	Repayment Method	Dates	U	Cts	FO	Amount U	Cts	Total U	Cts	Interest U	Cts	Principal U	Cts
		U			U											Repayments			
Construction of Market at Kibule	20	100,000	13/9/_4	Govt	95,000	6¼	A	M/S	61,671	40				4,193	40	1,927	25	2,266	15
Construction of Market at Kitoro	20	150,000	19/2/_1	Govt	141,000	6¼	A	A/O	122,440	-				4,193	40	1,856	40	2,337	00
														6,223	90	3,826	25	2,397	65
														6,223	90	3,751	30	2,472	60
Extensions to Market at Busira	5	50,000	2/11/_3	Private	50,000	5	I	J/J	30,000	-				6,500	-	1,500	-	5,000	-
											C/8	163,000	-	6,250	-	1,250	-	5,000	-
Extensions to Market at Kibule	20	230,000	3/3/_6	Govt	230,000	6¼	A	M/S	-	-	C/8	67,000	-	7,194	95	5,093	75	2,101	20
									214,111	40		230,000	-	40,779	55	19,204	95	21,574	60

561

Municipal Accounting for Developing Countries

alphabetical order of lender. Alternatively separate pages can be used for each service. This is the method which has been followed in our example. It enables the loan charges to be posted in total from the loans register to the appropriate section of the revenue account. The first loan in the example was a 20 year loan sanctioned for U 100,000 for the construction of Kibule Market. A loan of U 95,000 was raised on 13 Sept. 19_4, the full sanctioned amount not being required. The rate of interest was $6\frac{1}{4}$% and repayment was to be by the annuity method (A) in March and September (M/S). At 1 Jan. 19_6 there was a balance of U 61,671.40 outstanding and during the year two further sums of U 4,193.40 were paid to the Government, entered in the register one below the other. The two separate items of principal (U 2,266.15 and U 2,337.00) when added together (U 4,603.15) and deducted from the balance at 1 Jan. (U 61,671.40) would give a new principal outstanding of U 57,068.25 which would be entered in the first column of the 19_7 sheet.

The second loan raised in 19_1 follows a similar pattern, repayments being due in April and October (A/O).

The third loan, of U 50,000, borrowed from a private lender at 5% is repayable by the equal instalment method (I). Under this method an equal instalment of principal U 5,000 is repaid for each of ten half-years, interest being calculated on the outstanding balance at the beginning of each half-year.

The fourth loan was raised in two instalments during 19_6. U 163,000 was raised in March upon which the first annuity (U 7,194.95) became payable in September. The balance of U 67,000 was raised in September, no repayment falling due until 19_7.

The total loan charges of U 40,779.55 agrees approximately with the estimate U 40,800 shown on page 295 of Chapter 9.

When, as in our example, a separate page of the loans register is used for each service, the book-keeping procedures can be shortened as follows:

(a) all loan charges payable during the year are debited to a single "Loan Charges (Control) Account" in the expenditure ledger;

(b) individual loan repayments are entered in the loans register;

(c) a single total of loan charges for each service is debited to the revenue account and credited to the "Loan Charges (Control) Account"; and

(d) a single total of principal repayment for each service is debited to the "Loans Outstanding" account and credited to the "Capital Discharged - Loans Repaid" account.

The "Loan Charges (Control) Account" is a "holding" account similar to that for "wages" shown in Chapter 12.

The position of the market undertaking (relevant to these loans) might have been on 1 Jan. 19_6 as follows:

Capital Expenditure

Balance Sheet as at 1 Jan. 19_6
Capital

	Units	Cents		Units	Cents
Long-Term Liabilities			**Fixed Assets**		
Loans Outstanding	214,111	40	Kibule Market	95,000	00
Surplus			Kitoro Market	141,000	00
Capital Discharged			Busira Market		
Loans Repaid	71,888	60	(Extns)	50,000	00
	286,000	00		286,000	00

The transactions during 19_6 can be journalised as follows:

19_6						
Dec.31	Cash (Capital) DR. To Loans Outstanding Being new loans raised during year as shown by loans register	230,000	–	230,000	–
Dec.31	Capital Expenditure - Kibule Market (Extns) DR. To Cash (Capital) Being capital payments during year as shown by expenditure ledger	230,000	–	230,000	–
Dec.31	Loan Charges (Control) DR. To Cash (Revenue) Being payment of loan charges during year (included in the total payment of loan charges by Kambale Municipal Council for all services - all of which would be debited to the control account)	40,779	55	40,779	55
Dec.31	Markets Revenue Account: Loan Charges DR. To Loan Charges (Control) Being allocation of loan charges to appropriate service as shown by loans register (debits for loan charges would also be made in the revenue accounts of other services - a single total being credited to the control account)	40,779	55	40,779	55
Dec.31	Loans Outstanding DR. To Capital Discharged Being total principal repaid during the year on Markets loans as shown by loans register	21,574	60	21,574	60

Municipal Accounting for Developing Countries

The ledger accounts and (isolated) balance sheet would appear as follows:

		Cash (Capital)					C.C.
19_6 Dec.31	To Loans Outstanding	5	230,000 00	19_6 Dec.31	By Capital Expenditure (Kibule Market Extensions)	4	230,000 00
			230,000 00 ======= ===				230,000 00 ======= ===

		Cash (Revenue)					C.R.
19_6 Dec.31	To Balance	c/d	40,779 55	19_6 Dec.31	By Loan Charges (Control)	7	40,779 55
			40,779 55 ======= ===	19_7 Jan.1	By Balance	b/d	40,779 55 ======= === 40,779 55

		Capital Expenditure (Kibule Market)					1
19_6 Jan.1	To Balance	b/f	95,000 00 ====== ===	19_6 Dec.31	By Balance	c/d	95,000 00 ====== ===
19_7 Jan.1	To Balance	b/d	95,000 00				

		Capital Expenditure (Kitoro Market)					2
19_6 Jan.1	To Balance	b/f	141,000 00 ======= ===	19_6 Dec.31	By Balance	c/d	141,000 00 ======= ===
19_7 Jan.1	To Balance	b/d	141,000 00				

Capital Expenditure

Capital Expenditure (Busira Market Extensions) — 3

19_6					19_6				
Jan.1	To Balance	b/f	50,000	00	Dec.31	By Balance	c/d	50,000	00
19_7									
Jan.1	To Balance	b/d	50,000	00					

Capital Expenditure (Kibule Market Extensions) — 4

19_6					19_6				
Dec.31	To Cash	CC	230,000	00	Dec.31	By Balance	c/d	230,000	00
19_7									
Jan.1	To Balance	b/d	230,000	00					

Loans Outstanding — 5

19_6					19_6				
Dec.31	To Capital Dis-charged (Loans Repaid)	J	21,574	60	Jan.1	By Balance	b/f	214,111	40
	To Balance	c/d	422,536	80	Dec.31	By Cash	CC	230,000	00
			444,111	40				444,111	40
					19_7				
					Jan.1	By Balance	b/d	422,536	80

Capital Discharged - Loans Repaid — 6

19_6					19_6				
Dec.31	To Balance	c/d	93,463	20	Jan.1	By Balance	b/f	71,888	60
					Dec.31	By Loans Outs-tanding	J	21,574	60
			93,463	20				93,463	20
					19_7				
					Jan.1	By Balance	b/d	93,463	20

	Loan Charges (Control) (Market Loans Only)								7
19_6 Dec.31	To Cash	CR	40,779	55	19_6 Dec.31	By Market Revenue	J	40,779	55
			40,779	55				40,779	55
			======	===				======	===

	Markets Revenue Account								8
19_6 Dec.31	To Loan Charges	J	40,779	55	19_6 Dec.31	By Balance	c/d	40,779	55
			40,779	55				40,779	55
			======	===				======	===
19_7 Jan.1	To Balance	b/d	40,779	55					

Balance Sheet as at 31 Dec. 19_6
Capital

	Units	Cents		Units	Cents
Long-Term Liabilities			**Fixed Assets**		
Loans Outstanding	422,536	80	Kibule Market (Incl Extns)	325,000	00
Surplus			Kitoro Market	141,000	00
Capital Discharged Loans Repaid	93,463	20	Busira Market (Extns)	50,000	00
	516,000	00		516,000	00

Revenue

Current Liabilities			**Deficiency**		
Cash Overdrawn	40,779	55	Market Revenue Account	40,779	55
	40,779	55		40,779	55
	556,779	55		556,779	55

The deficiency on the Market Revenue Account represents part of the annual expenditure. This will be met from market fees and charges, thus eliminating the overdrawn cash balance.

176. EARMARKED AND POOLED LOANS

A loan which is raised and wholly applied to the purpose for which it is sanctioned is sometimes known as an "earmarked" loan. This is the

Capital Expenditure

type of loan which has so far been demonstrated in our examples. Each loan has been separately raised and accounted for, any unspent balances being repaid to the lender or used on another scheme after approval by the sanctioning authority.

An alternative to this system is for all loans raised to be "pooled". They are raised and accounted for all together in a "loans pool" or "consolidated loans fund". A special set of accounts (usually with a separate cash book and bank account) is kept to record the activities of the loans pool. Loan sanctions for individual capital schemes are exercised by borrowing from the loans pool instead of direct from a lender.

The loans pool acts as an intermediate stage between the outside lender and the accounts of a particular capital scheme. It becomes advantageous to use such a pool when loans cannot be raised for the exact period or the exact amount of each sanction, and where borrowers will not accept repayment by instalments. For example a local authority might have obtained loan sanctions for two separate schemes as follows:

$$\text{Scheme A U 400,000 (20 years)}$$
$$\text{Scheme B U 200,000 (5 years)}$$

Assuming for the moment that the authority was authorised to borrow elsewhere than from the Government, it might find that the only loans it could raise were:

Lender x U 300,000 (repayable in a single lump sum after 7 years)
Lender y U 300,000 (repayable by equal instalments over 15 years).

Neither of these loans could be earmarked to a particular scheme but with a loans pool they could be raised and paid into the pool, the balance sheet of the pool then being:

Loans Pool
Balance Sheet as at 1 Jan. 19_6

	Units		Units
Long-Term Liabilities		**Current Assets**	
Loans Outstanding		Cash	600,000
Lender x	300,000		
Lender y	300,000		
	600,000		600,000

The pool would then lend U 400,000 for scheme A and U 200,000 for scheme B, after which its balance sheet would show:

Loans Pool
Balance Sheet as at 1 Jan. 19_6

Long-Term Liabilities	Units	Current Assets	Units
Loans Outstanding		Advances:	
Lender x	300,000	Scheme A	400,000
Lender y	300,000	Scheme B	200,000
	600,000		600,000
	======		======

Let us assume for simplicity that the scheme "A" advance is to be repaid to the pool in 20 equal annual instalments of U 20,000 and the scheme "B" advance is to be repaid to the pool in 5 equal annual instalments of U 40,000. The calculation of the instalments to be repaid to the pool in respect of each scheme must be related to the loan sanction for that scheme. By 31 Dec. 19-0, the advance for Scheme A would have repaid 5 instalments of U 20,000, a total of U 100,000, leaving U 300,000 outstanding. The advance for scheme B would have been completely repaid. In addition, 5 instalments of U 20,000 would have been repaid to lender y, a total of U 100,000, leaving U 200,000 outstanding. The loan from lender x is still fully outstanding. The balance sheet will show:

Loans Pool
Balance Sheet as at 31 Dec. 19_0

Long-Term Liabilities	Units	Current Assets	Units
Loans Outstanding		Advances:	
Lender x	300,000	Scheme A	300,000
Lender y	200,000	Cash in Hand	200,000
	500,000		500,000
	======		======

The cash balance of U 200,000 can either be invested or used to make another advance.

On 31 December 19_2 the loan to Lender x must be repaid. By this time a further 2 instalments of the scheme "A" advance will have been repaid leaving U 260,000 outstanding. A further 2 instalments will have been repaid to lender y leaving U 160,000 outstanding.

Immediately before the loan to Lender x is repaid the balance sheet will show:

Capital Expenditure

Loans Pool
Balance Sheet as at 31 Dec. 19_2

Long-Term Liabilities	Units	Current Assets	Units
Loans Outstanding		Advances:	
Lender x	300,000	Scheme A	260,000
Lender y	160,000	Cash in Hand	200,000
	460,000		460,000
	=======		=======

The loan to be repaid is U 300,000 but the cash in the pool is only U 200,000. To deal with this, the pool merely raises another loan. In theory it would try to raise a loan of U 100,000 for a period of 13 years (the remainder of the 20 year period for Scheme A) but in practice it will raise whichever loans will produce a minimum of U 100,000 on the most advantageous terms available at the time.

And so it will continue. The pool will borrow whenever it is short of cash, using its surplus cash to make further advances and to repay earlier loans.

Control is still exercised by the Government through the loan sanction procedure. No advance may be made from the pool for any capital scheme unless proper loan sanction has been granted. Furthermore, every advance made by the pool must be repaid to it by instalments within the maximum period specified by the sanction.

The pool, in turn, will raise only sufficient loans from outside lenders to meet the necessary advances covered by loan sanctions. Any surplus cash balances will be of purely temporary duration and will be applied as quickly as possible towards further advances or loan repayment.

Control is therefore exercised in total over outside borrowing and in detail over individual schemes.

Loans pools will be dealt with in greater detail in a later chapter. The above explanation and example are merely to give a general outline of the subject.

177. INSTALMENT AND ANNUITY LOANS

A loan which is repaid to the lender in instalments over the period during which it is outstanding can be either an "instalment" loan or an "annuity" loan, depending upon the precise method of repayment.

Instalment loans are repaid by equal annual or half-yearly instalments of principal. Each time a repayment of principal is made there is also a payment of interest. This is calculated on the principal sum outstanding during the year or half-year since the last repayment was made.

Annuity loans are repaid by equal annual or half-yearly sums called annuities. These annuities, calculated from loan tables (or by a financial calculator) are a combined payment of principal and interest. The interest included in an annuity is calculated on the principal sum outstanding during the year or half year since the last repayment was made. The balance of the annuity is a repayment of principal.

The annuity method calculations have been demonstrated in Section 170 of of Chapter 14.

An example of an instalment loan is that shown in the loans register (Section 175) as borrowed from a private lender for "Extensions to Market at Busira".

A comparison of the two methods of repayment can be made if we consider a loan of U 10,000 borrowed for 4 years at 10% and repaid by annual instalments.

(a) Repaid by Equal Instalments of Principal

Instalment Number	Total Payment Units	Interest Units	Principal Instalment Units	Principal Outstanding Units
				10,000
1	3,500	1,000	2,500	7,500
2	3,250	750	2,500	5,000
3	3,000	500	2,500	2,500
4	2,750	250	2,500	-
TOTAL	12,500	2,500	10,000	

(b) Repaid by Annuity Method

Instalment Number	Total Instalment Units	Interest Units	Principal Units	Principal Outstanding Units
				10,000
1	3,155	1,000	2,155	7,845
2	3,155	785	2,370	5,475
3	3,155	548	2,607	2,868
4	3,155	287	2,868	-
TOTAL	12,620	2,620	10,000	

Comparison of the two methods reveals that the instalment method has a lower total cost (U 12,500) than the annuity method (U 12,620). However, whereas the annuity method results in an equal annual charge, (U 3,155), the instalment method involves a variable annual charge, ranging from U 3,500 in the first year to U 2,750 in the last year. Under the instalment method the principal repayment remains the same, whilst the interest and the total amount payable gradually decrease. The annuity method has a fixed total amount but the principal sum gradually increases, offset by the gradual fall in interest.

The annuity method is often preferred to the instalment method because it gives an equal annual charge to the revenue account.

178. MATURITY LOANS

A loan which is repaid to the lender in a single lump sum at the end of the period for which it was borrowed is known as a "maturity" loan. Such loans include stock (bond) issues and mortgages. When a maturity loan is raised, the annual interest is the same for each year of the loan period, because none of the principal is being repaid during the life of the loan. Had the above loan been a maturity loan the

Capital Expenditure

repayment table would have appeared as follows:

Instalment Number	Total Instalment Units	Interest Units	Principal Units	Principal Outstanding Units
			-	10,000
1	1,000	1,000	-	10,000
2	1,000	1,000	-	10,000
3	1,000	1,000	-	10,000
4	11,000	1,000	10,000	-
TOTAL	14,000	4,000	10,000	

The total cost (U 14,000) appears to be much greater than under either of the other two methods. However, this is because the authority has the use of the whole of the principal sum for the whole of the loan period. This can often be a distinct advantage, as explained later.

179. SINKING FUNDS - INTRODUCTION

Before considering the operation of sinking funds it is necessary to clearly understand the difference between "repayment of loans" and "redemption of debt".

This can best be illustrated by some very simple examples.
Suppose you wished to buy (say) an electric sewing machine for U 1,200. Let us assume that you borrowed the money at 6% per annum from "Lender P", and agreed to repay it by equal instalments over twelve months with interest paid monthly. Your loan repayment table, assuming you borrowed the sum on 1 Jan. 19_6 would appear as follows:

Date	Total Payment		Interest ($\frac{1}{2}$% per month)		Principal Instalment		Principal Outstanding	
19_6	Units	Cents	Units	Cents	Units	Cents	Units	Cents
Jan. 1	-		-		-		1,200	00
31	106	00	6	00	100	00	1,100	00
Feb.28	105	50	5	50	100	00	1,000	00
Mar.31	105	00	5	00	100	00	900	00
Apr.30	104	50	4	50	100	00	800	00
May 31	104	00	4	00	100	00	700	00
Jun.30	103	50	3	50	100	00	600	00
Jul.31	103	00	3	00	100	00	500	00
Aug.31	102	50	2	50	100	00	400	00
Sep.30	102	00	2	00	100	00	300	00
Oct.31	101	50	1	50	100	00	200	00
Nov.30	101	00	1	00	100	00	100	00
Dec.31	100	50	-	50	100	00	-	-
	1,239	00	39	00	1,200	00		

Month by month during 19_6 you will be "repaying the loan" by instalments to the lender and "redeeming the debt" out of your monthly salary. Because it is an instalment loan, the gradual repayment of it automatically redeems the debt.

Now consider that your loan from "Lender P" was a maturity loan, and

Municipal Accounting for Developing Countries

that he required repayment in a single lump sum on 31 Dec. 19_6. Your loan repayment table would then appear as follows:

Date	Total Payment		Interest (½% per month)		Principal Repayment		Principal Outstanding	
19_6	Units	Cents	Units	Cents	Units	Cents	Units	Cents
Jan. 1	-		-		-		1,200	00
31	6	00	6	00	-		1,200	00
Feb.28	6	00	6	00	-		1,200	00
Mar.31	6	00	6	00	-		1,200	00
Apr.30	6	00	6	00	-		1,200	00
May 31	6	00	6	00	-		1,200	00
Jun.30	6	00	6	00	-		1,200	00
Jul.31	6	00	6	00	-		1,200	00
Aug.31	6	00	6	00	-		1,200	00
Sep.30	6	00	6	00	-		1,200	00
Oct.31	6	00	6	00	-		1,200	00
Nov.30	6	00	6	00	-		1,200	00
Dec.31	1,206	00	6	00	1,200	00	-	-
	1,272	00	72	00	1,200	00		

If you merely dealt with the payments as they fell due, you would find it very easy to meet the monthly payments of interest (U 6 per month) but you might find it extremely difficult to repay the principal sum in December, particularly if your salary was only (say) U 1,000 per month. This difficulty would arise because, although you were not required to make "loan repayments" during the first eleven months of the year, you have made no provision for "debt redemption". In other words, you did not ensure that U 100 per month was set aside from your salary each month to repay the loan at the year end.

Let us now assume that you prudently paid U 100 each month out of your salary into a deposit account at your bank. At the end of the year the deposit account will have a "credit" balance of U 1,200 sufficient to repay the whole loan.

On 31 Dec. 19_6 you will repay the loan: but you will have redeemed the debt by the monthly charges against your salary. What you will have done is to set up the equivalent of a sinking fund, your deposit account at the bank being (technically) a sinking fund investment.

One further point to note is that your bank deposit (i.e. sinking fund investment) will have earned interest on the accumulating balance, let us say at 3% per annum on the accumulated balance at the end of each month. This interest, assuming it were paid into your current account, would partially offset the monthly interest payable to the lender.

The complete position could be shown by the following table:

Capital Expenditure

Date Jan.31	Interest Paid		Interest Received		Net Interest		Sinking Fund Contribution		Sinking Fund Accumulation		Debt Unredeemed	
	U	Cts	U	Cts	U	Cts	U	Cts	U	Cts	U	Cts
19_6 Jan. 1	-		-		-		-		-		1,200	00
31	6	00	-		6	00	100	00	100	00	1,100	00
Feb.28	6	00		25	5	75	100	00	200	00	1,000	00
Mar.31	6	00		50	5	50	100	00	300	00	900	00
Apr.30	6	00		75	5	25	100	00	400	00	800	00
May 31	6	00	1	00	5	00	100	00	500	00	700	00
Jun.30	6	00	1	25	4	75	100	00	600	00	600	00
Jul.31	6	00	1	50	4	50	100	00	700	00	500	00
Aug.31	6	00	1	75	4	25	100	00	800	00	400	00
Sep.30	6	00	2	00	4	00	100	00	900	00	300	00
Oct.31	6	00	2	25	3	75	100	00	1,000	00	200	00
Nov.30	6	00	2	50	3	50	100	00	1,100	00	100	00
Dec.31	6	00	2	75	3	25	100	00	1,200	00	-	-
	72	00	16	50	55	50	1,200	00				

The three columns marked * are very similar to the instalment table shown on page 571. In fact, in the unlikely event of the interest on the sinking fund investment being the same as the loan interest (6%) the effect of the two methods would be precisely the same, demonstrated in the following table:

Date	Instalment Loan				Total Monthly Charge (Either Loan)		Maturity Loan							
	Interest Payment		Principal Instalment				Interest Payment		Interest Received		Net Interest		Sinking Fund Contributions	
	U	Cts	U	Cts	U	Cts	U	Cts	U	Cts	U	Cts	U	Cts
19_6 Jan.31	6	00	100	00	106	00	6	00	-		6	00	100	00
Feb.28	5	50	100	00	105	50	6	00		50	5	50	100	00
Mar.31	5	00	100	00	105	00	6	00	1	00	5	00	100	00
Apr.30	4	50	100	00	104	50	6	00	1	50	4	50	100	00
May 31	4	00	100	00	104	00	6	00	2	00	4	00	100	00
Jun.30	3	50	100	00	103	50	6	00	2	50	3	50	100	00
Jul.31	3	00	100	00	103	00	6	00	3	00	3	00	100	00
Aug.31	2	50	100	00	102	50	6	00	3	50	2	50	100	00
Sep.30	2	00	100	00	102	00	6	00	4	00	2	00	100	00
Oct.31	1	50	100	00	101	50	6	00	4	50	1	50	100	00
Nov.30	1	00	100	00	101	00	6	00	5	00	1	00	100	00
Dec.31		50	100	00	100	50	6	00	5	50		50	100	00
	39	00	1,200	00	1,239	00	72	00	33	00	39	00	1,200	00

180. SINKING FUNDS - APPLICATION

Let us now consider how the sinking fund principle can be applied to deal with a maturity loan raised by a local authority. Let us assume that the maturity loan referred to in Section 182 had been raised on 1 Jan. 19_6 by Kambale Municipal Council to purchase an accounting machine for the finance department on (say) 9 Jan. 19_6. These transactions are recorded exactly as if the loan had been an annuity or instalment loan, journalised as follows:

19_6 Jan.1	Cash (Capital) DR.
	  To Loans Outstanding
	  Being 5-year maturity loan
	  raised to purchase accounting
	  machine
		C.C.
		1
			10,000	10,000

Jan.9	Capital Expenditure
	  (Accounting Machine) DR.
	  To Cash (Capital)
	  Being purchase of accounting
	  machine for finance department
		2
		C.C.
			10,000	10,000

On 31 Dec. 19_6 the first instalment of interest would become due, payment being journalised as follows:

19_6 Dec.31	Loan Charges - Interest DR.
	  To Cash (Revenue)
	  Being payment of annual
	  interest on 10% loan
		3
		C.R.
			1,000	1,000

Provision must now be made for the first instalment of the principal sum to be set aside in a sinking fund. The annual provision should be the same as the annual repayment would be on an instalment loan. Thus in this example the annual provision to repay the loan at the end of 5 years would be:

$$U \frac{10,000}{5} = U\ 2,000$$

The provision will be set aside by the following journal entry:

19_6 Dec.31	Loan Charges - Principal DR.
	  To Sinking Fund
	  Being first contribution to
	  sinking fund for 5-year
	  maturity loan
		4
		5
			2,000	2,000

Instead of revenue cash being paid out in the form of a repayment of principal, an amount equal to the annual provision will be invested in (say) a 3% bank deposit, journalised as follows:

Capital Expenditure

19_6 Dec.31	Sinking Fund Investment DR. To Cash (Revenue) Being investment of first sinking fund contribution in (say) 3% bank deposit	6 C.R.	2,000	2,000

The ledger accounts and (isolated) balance sheet for 19_6 would appear as follows:

Cash (Capital)   C.C.

19_6 Jan.1	To Loans Outstanding	1	10,000 ======	19_6 Jan.9	By Capital Expenditure	2	10,000 ======

Cash (Revenue)   C.R.

19_6 Dec.31	To Balance	c/d	3,000 3,000 =====	19_6 Dec.31 19_7 Jan.1	By Loan Charges- Interest Sinking Fund Investment By Balance	3 6 b/d	1,000 2,000 3,000 ===== 3,000

Loans Outstanding   1

19_6 Dec.31	To Balance	c/d	10,000 ======	19_6 Jan.1 19_7 Jan.1	By Cash By Balance	C.C. b/d	10,000 ====== 10,000

575

Capital Expenditure (Accounting Machine)								2
19_6 Jan.9	To Cash	C.C.	10,000	19_6 Dec.31	By Balance	c/d	10,000	
			======				======	
19_7 Jan.1	To Balance	b/d	10,000					

Loan Charges - Interest								3
19_6 Dec.31	To Cash	C.R.	1,000	19_6 Dec.31	By Revenue Account	7	1,000	
			1,000				1,000	
			=====				=====	

Loan Charges - Principal								4
19_6 Dec.31	To Sinking Fund	J	2,000	19_6 Dec.31	By Revenue Account	7	2,000	
			=====				=====	

Sinking Fund								5
19_6 Dec.31	To Balance	c/d	2,000	19_6 Dec.31	By Loan Charges Principal	J	2,000	
			2,000				2,000	
			=====				=====	
				19_7 Jan.1	By Balance	b/d	2,000	

Sinking Fund Investment								6
19_6 Dec.31	To Cash	C.R.	2,000	19_6 Dec.31	By Balance	c/d	2,000	
			=====				=====	
19_7 Jan.1	To Balance	b/d	2,000					

Capital Expenditure

Finance Department Revenue Account — 7

19_6				19_6			
Dec.31	To Loan Charges			Dec.31	By Balance	c/d	3,000
	Interest	3	1,000				
	Principal	4	2,000				
			3,000				3,000
			=====				=====
19_7							
Jan.1	To Balance	b/d	3,000				

Balance Sheet as at 31 Dec. 19_6

Capital

	Units		Units
Long-Term Liabilities		**Fixed Assets**	
Loans Outstanding	10,000	Capital Expenditure Accounting Machine	10,000
Surplus			
Sinking Fund	2,000	**Current Assets** Investments	2,000
	12,000		12,000
	======		======

Revenue

	Units		Units
Current Liabilities		**Deficiency**	
Cash Overdrawn	3,000	Revenue Account Deficiency	3,000
	------		------
	3,000		3,000
	------		------
	15,000		15,000
	======		======

As in previous examples, income will be raised from rates, taxes etc to meet the revenue account deficiency. The overdrawn cash balance will then be eliminated.

In certain circumstances the sinking fund may remain uninvested. When this happens an equivalent amount of revenue cash is appropriated as capital cash, the journal entry for making the investment being replaced by the following:

19_6					
Dec.31	Cash (Capital) DR. To Cash (Revenue) Being appropriation of cash to meet sinking fund contribution	C.C.	2,000		2,000

Municipal Accounting for Developing Countries

During each of the years 19_7 to 19_0 a further contribution will be made to the sinking fund and an equivalent amount of cash will be invested or appropriated, journalised as before.

The "loans outstanding" account will remain unaffected during this period, as will the "capital expenditure" account, unless the machine is disposed of. At 31 Dec. 19_0, immediately before the loan is repaid, the complete ledger accounts of the sinking fund and the sinking fund investment will appear as follows:

			Sinking Fund				5
19_6 Dec.31	To Balance	c/d	2,000	19_6 Dec.31	By Loan Charges Principal	J	2,000
			2,000				2,000
19_7 Dec.31	To Balance	c/d	4,000	19_7 Jan. 1 Dec.31	By Balance b/d By Loan Charges Principal	J	2,000 2,000
			4,000				4,000
19_8 Dec.31	To Balance	c/d	6,000	19_8 Jan. 1 Dec.31	By Balance b/d By Loan Charges Principal	J	4,000 2,000
			6,000				6,000
19_9 Dec.31	To Balance	c/d	8,000	19_9 Jan. 1 Dec.31	By Balance b/d By Loan Charges Principal	J	6,000 2,000
			8,000				8,000
				19_0 Jan. 1 Dec.31	By Balance b/d By Loan Charges Principal	J	8,000 2,000
							10,000

Capital Expenditure

Sinking Fund Investment								6
19_6 Dec.31	To Cash	C.R.	2,000 =====	19_6 Dec.31	By Balance	c/d	2,000 =====	
19_7 Jan. 1 Dec.31	To Balance To Cash	b/d C.R.	2,000 2,000 ⎯⎯⎯⎯ 4,000 =====	19_7 Dec.31	By Balance	c/d	4,000 ⎯⎯⎯⎯ 4,000 =====	
19_8 Jan. 1 Dec.31	To Balance To Cash	b/d C.R.	4,000 2,000 ⎯⎯⎯⎯ 6,000 =====	19_8 Dec.31	By Balance	c/d	6,000 ⎯⎯⎯⎯ 6,000 =====	
19_9 Jan. 1 Dec.31	To Balance To Cash	b/d C.R.	6,000 2,000 ⎯⎯⎯⎯ 8,000 =====	19_9 Dec.31	By Balance	c/d	8,000 ⎯⎯⎯⎯ 8,000 =====	
19_0 Jan. 1 Dec.31	To Balance To Cash	b/d C.R.	8,000 2,000 ⎯⎯⎯⎯ 10,000					

The capital section of the balance sheet would appear as follows:

Balance Sheet as at 31 Dec. 19_0
Capital

	Units		Units
Long-Term Liabilities		**Fixed Assets**	
Loans Outstanding	10,000	Capital Expenditure	
Surplus		Accounting Machine	10,000
Sinking Fund	10,000	**Current Assets**	
	------	Investments	10,000
	20,000		------
	------		20,000

The investment will then be realised, the resulting cash being used to repay the loan on 31 Dec. 19_0. The sinking fund, having served its purpose, is no longer required, the balance being transferred to a "Capital Discharged - Loans Repaid" account. These final transactions can be journalised as follows:

19_0
Dec.31
	Cash (Capital) DR.
	   To Sinking Fund Investment
	   Being realisation of investment
		C.C.
		6
			10,000	10,000

Dec.31	Loans Outstanding DR.
	   To Cash (Capital)
	   Being repayment of loan on
	   maturity
		1	10,000	10,000

Dec.31	Sinking Fund DR.
	   To Capital Discharged -
	     Loan Repaid
	   Being application of sinking
	   fund to discharge of loan debt
		5	10,000	10,000

After these transactions the balance sheet will show:

Balance Sheet as at 31 Dec. 19_0
Capital

Surplus	Units	Fixed Assets	Units
Capital Discharged		Capital Expenditure	
Loan Repaid	10,000	Accounting Machine	10,000
	------		------
	10,000		10,000
	------		------

Having dealt with the capital aspects of the sinking fund we must now consider how the revenue accounts for the years 19_7 to 19_0 are affected. This will be as follows:

(a) each year, provision for repayment, in the form of the sinking fund contribution (U 2,000) will be debited to the revenue account as "Loan Charges - Principal";

(b) each year, interest will be paid on the outstanding loan at 10% (U 1,000) and debited to the revenue account as "Loan Charges - Interest"; and

(c) each year, interest will be earned at 3% on the sinking fund investment and credited to the revenue account as "Loan Charges - Interest".

Each year the ledger account for "Loan Charges - Principal" will appear as follows:

		Loan Charges - Principal				4

19
Dec.31
	To Sinking
	   Fund
		J	2,000
			=====
				19
				Dec.31
					By Revenue
					   Account 7
						2,000
						=====

Capital Expenditure

The successive revenue accounts for "Loan Charges - Interest" will appear as follows:

			Loan Charges - Interest			3
19_6 Dec.31	To Cash	C.R.	1,000	19_6 Dec.31 By Revenue Account	7	1,000
			1,000			1,000

			Loan Charges - Interest			3
19_7 Dec.31	To Cash	C.R.	1,000	19_7 Dec.31 By Cash	C.R.	60
				By Revenue Account	7	940
			1,000			1,000

			Loan Charges - Interest			3
19_8 Dec.31	To Cash	C.R.	1,000	19_8 Dec.31 By Cash	C.R.	120
				By Revenue Account	7	880
			1,000			1,000

			Loan Charges - Interest			3
19_9 Dec.31	To Cash	C.R.	1,000	19_9 Dec.31 By Cash	C.R.	180
				By Revenue Account	7	820
			1,000			1,000

			Loan Charges - Interest			3
19_0 Dec.31	To Cash	C.R.	1,000	19_0 Dec.31 By Cash	C.R.	240
				Revenue Account	7	760
			1,000			1,000

Municipal Accounting for Developing Countries

The complete position could be shown by the following table:

Date	Interest	Interest Received	Net Interest	Sinking Fund Contribution	Sinking Fund Accumulation	Debt Unredeemed
1. 1._6	-	-	-	-	-	10,000
31.12._6	1,000	-	1,000	2,000	2,000	8,000
31.12._7	1,000	60	940	2,000	4,000	6,000
31.12._8	1,000	120	880	2,000	6,000	4,000
31.12._9	1,000	180	820	2,000	8,000	2,000
31.12._0	1,000	240	760	2,000	10,000	-
	5,000	600	4,400	10,000		

What we have just examined is known as a "non-accumulating" sinking fund. Interest earned on the investment of the fund is not accumulated in the fund but is credited direct to the revenue account. This type of sinking fund suffers from the same disadvantage as an instalment loan: it results in an unequal annual charge for loan charges in the successive revenue accounts. In the above example the loan charges for 19_6 were:

```
        Principal      2,000
        Interest       1,000
                       -----
                       3,000
                       =====
```

The loan charges for 19_0 were:

```
        Principal       2,000
        Interest (net)    760
                        -----
                        2,760
                        =====
```

To avoid this difficulty, an "accumulating" sinking fund can be used. In this type of fund the interest earned on the investment is credited to the fund. The annual contribution from the revenue account is calculated from loan tables. It ensures that the total of contributions, plus accumulated interest, will amount to the required sum at the end of the loan period.

Continuing the earlier example, let us assume that the 3% interest on the bank deposit is to be accumulated in the sinking fund, instead of being credited to the revenue account. The annual contribution is calculated from Sinking Fund Tables as follows:

- Annual contribution to accumulate an amount of 1 at the end of 5 years @ 3% = 0.18835465

∴ Annual contribution to accumulate an amount of 10,000 = 0.18835465 x 10,000 = 1883.5465

∴ Annual contribution to accumulate U 10,000 = U 1883.55

Capital Expenditure

The sinking fund and sinking fund investment would accumulate as follows:

			Units	Cents
19_6	Annual Contribution		1,883	55
19_7	Interest (3% on 1,883.55)		56	50
	Annual Contribution		1,883	55
		Balance 31.12._7	3,823	60
19_8	Interest (3% on 3,823.60)		114	70
	Annual Contribution		1,883	55
		Balance 31.12._8	5,821	85
19_9	Interest (3% on 5,821.85)		174	65
	Annual Contribution		1,883	55
		Balance 31.12._9	7,880	05
19_0	Interest (3% on 7,880.05)		236	40
	Annual Contribution		1,883	55
		Balance 31.12._0	10,000	00

At the end of the loan period the fund holds the exact sum necessary to repay the loan, ie U 10,000.

The ledger accounts will be similar to those shown above, except that the interest earned on the investment will be credited to the sinking fund account and will be debited to the sinking fund investment account when reinvested.

These transactions for 19_7 would be journalised as follows:

19_7 Dec.31	Cash (Capital) DR. To Sinking Fund Being interest earned on investment (3% on U 1,883.55)	C.C. 5	56	50		56	50
Dec.31	Sinking Fund Investment DR. To Cash (Capital) Being reinvestment of interest	6 C.C.	56	50		56	50

If interest is automatically reinvested by the body with whom the investment is made there will be no cash changing hands, the entry being journalised as follows:

19_7 Dec.31	Sinking Fund Investment DR. To Sinking Fund Being interest earned on investment (3% on U 1,883.55) now reinvested		56	50		56	50

One important practical difficulty which arises with accumulating sinking funds is that the actual rate of interest to be earned on investments is not usually known in advance when the contribution is to be calculated from the tables. Because of this it is normal to make the calculation on the basis of what is called a "notional" interest rate which is really a conservative estimate of the average rate of interest to be earned over the whole period.

Sometimes (as in the UK) the Government prescribes a maximum (notional) interest rate which can be credited to an accumulating sinking fund. This does not limit the amount of interest which can be earned on a sinking fund investment in any one year. Clearly, an authority will seek to maximise its earnings, depending on market rates. The limit is imposed to ensure the adequacy of the annual contribution, so that the necessary sum is accumulated at the end of the loan period. The loan can then be fully repaid.

The actual interest earned on the investment is thus credited to the revenue account under "Loan Charges - Interest" whilst the annual sinking fund contribution is annually increased by the notional rate of interest. If in our example 3% had been the notional rate of interest and the actual rate of interest for that year had been 4%, the transactions for 19_7 would have been journalised as follows:

19_7						

Dec.31	Loan Charges - Interest DR.
	  To Cash (Revenue)
	  Being interest payable on
	  10% loan of U 10,000
		3
		C.R.
			1,000	00	1,000	00

Dec.31	Cash (Revenue) DR.
	  To Loan Charges - Interest
	  Being actual interest
	  earned on sinking fund
	  investment (4% on
	  U 1,883.55)
		C.R.
		3
			75	34	75	34

Dec.31	Loan Charges - Principal DR.
	  To Sinking Fund
	  Being second contribution
	  to the sinking fund as
	  shown by table
		6
		5
			1,940	05	1,940	05

Dec.31	Sinking Fund Investment DR.
	  To Cash (Revenue)
	  Being investment of second
	  contribution to sinking
	  fund
		6
		C.R.
			1,940	05	1,940	05

Set out below are two tables. The first (A) shows the effect where notional interest and actual interest are the same (3%).

The second table (B) shows the effect where the sinking fund is invested at an initial rate of 4%, but where interest changes to 2½% on 1 July 19_8 and to 3½% on 1 Jan. 19-0.

Capital Expenditure

TABLE "A"

Date (a)	Interest Paid (b)		Interest Received (c)		Net Interest (d)		Sinking Fund Contribution (e)		Sinking Fund Accumulation (f)		Net Loan Charges (d)+(e) (g)	
	U	Cts	U	Cts	U	Cts	U	Cts	U	Cts	U	Cts
31.12._6	1,000	00	-	-	1,000	00	1,883	55	1,883	55	2,883	55
31.12._7	1,000	00	56	50	943	50	1,940	05	3,823	60	2,883	55
31.12._8	1,000	00	114	70	885	30	1,998	25	5,821	85	2,883	55
31.12._9	1,000	00	174	65	825	35	2,058	20	7,880	05	2,883	55
31.12._0	1,000	00	236	40	763	60	2,119	95	10,000	00	2,883	55
	5,000	00	582	25	4,417	75	10,000	00				

TABLE "B"

Date (a)	Interest Paid (b)		Interest Received (c)		Net Interest (d)		Sinking Fund Contribution (e)		Sinking Fund Accumulation (f)		Net Loan Charges (d)+(e) (g)	
	U	Cts	U	Cts	U	Cts	U	Cts	U	Cts	U	Cts
31.12._6	1,000	00	-		1,000	00	1,883	55	1,883	55	2,883	55
31.12._7	1,000	00	75	34	924	65	1,940	05	3,823	60	2,864	70
31.12._8	1,000	00	124	27	875	75	1,998	25	5,821	85	2,874	00
31.12._9	1,000	00	145	55	854	45	2,058	20	7,880	05	2,912	65
31.12_0	1,000	00	275	80	724	20	2,119	95	10,000	00	2,844	15
	5,000	00	620	96	4,379	05	10,000	00				

"Interest Received" in table "B" was calculated as follows:

$$
\begin{array}{llll}
19\_7 & 4\% \times U\ 1,883.55 & = & 75.34 \\
19\_8 & 4\% \times U\ 3,823.60 \times \tfrac{1}{2} & = & 76.47 \\
     & 2\tfrac{1}{2}\% \times U\ 3,823.60 \times \tfrac{1}{2} & = & 47.80 \\
     & & & \overline{124.27} \\
19\_9 & 2\tfrac{1}{2}\% \times U\ 5,821.85 & = & 145.55 \\
19\_0 & 3\tfrac{1}{2}\% \times U\ 7,880.05 & = & 275.80 \\
\end{array}
$$

In each case the increasing annual contribution was calculated as follows:

	Units	Cents
1st Instalment (from tables)	1,883	55
add 3% Notional Interest	56	50
2nd Instalment	1,940	05
add 3% Notional Interest	58	20
3rd Instalment	1,998	25
add 3% Notional Interest	59	95
4th Instalment	2,058	20
add 3% Notional Interest	61	75
5th Instalment	2,119	95

The first table (A) has a constant annual charge to the consecutive revenue accounts because it is based upon a somewhat hypothetical situation where the two rates of interest coincide.

The second table shows slight variations in the consecutive annual charges because of fluctuations in the actual rate of interest on investments. However, the contributions to the sinking fund are stabilised to produce the required sum U 10,000 at the end of the period. Furthermore, the fluctuations in the annual charge are much less severe than with the non-accumulating sinking fund.

So far, we have considered sinking funds set up only for the repayment of single maturity loans, the fund being invested to earn interest.

In a later chapter we shall consider the situation where a sinking fund is set up for the full period of the loan sanction but where maturity loans are raised for shorter periods. Each scheme is financed by a series of "short-term mortgages", raised in succession. Earlier loans are repaid out of the proceeds of later loans, the sinking fund providing the money to repay the final loan at the end of the sanction period.

A further development we shall consider is where the money in a sinking fund is prematurely appropriated for new capital purposes, as an alternative to raising an additional loan.

181. CAPITAL CASH

We have so far been dealing with the receipt and payment of cash as it affects individual capital schemes. We have also drawn up balance sheets for each scheme, considered in isolation from the rest of the transactions of the authority. In practice it is likely that all receipts and payments will be dealt with through a single cash account, with a capital register being used to show the cash position of individual schemes.

The balance sheets illustrated in recent examples have been prepared in double-account form. However, it is not customary to use this form for publication and the published balance sheet is likely to show single cash and bank balances for the authority without distinguishing between "revenue" and "capital" cash.

As well as having a record of the cash position of individual schemes the Chief Financial Officer will wish to know the overall position with

Capital Expenditure

regard to "capital" cash. This is important from a management point of view, because "capital" cash balances must be regarded in a different way from "revenue" cash balances. This is because "capital" cash balances are likely to fluctuate much more widely than "revenue" cash balances.

There are three main methods by which the cash position can be analysed into its "capital" and "revenue" aspects:

These methods are complementary rather than alternatives and we shall consider each in turn. They are:

(a) preparation of a double-account balance sheet;

(b) preparation of a receipts and payments account for capital transactions; and

(c) listing the balances relating to individual capital schemes together with unapplied capital receipts and capital funds.

(a) **Double-Account Balance Sheet**

To illustrate this method let us consider the balance sheet of Kambale Municipal Council shown on page 285 of Chapter 9 together with one or two variations.

The original balance sheet, in somewhat simplified form appears as follows:

Balance Sheet as at 31 Dec. 19_5

	Units		Units
Long-Term Liabilities		**Fixed Assets**	
Loans Outstanding	15,009,300	Buildings	10,093,740
Current Liabilities		Permanent Works	9,686,520
Creditors	491,340	Equipment	512,900
Provisions		**Current Assets**	
Repairs Fund	63,000	Stocks and Stores	310,460
Renewals Funds	85,000	Debtors	115,160
Surplus		Investments	148,000
Capital Discharged	5,283,860	Cash	414,440
General Fund Surplus	348,720		
	21,281,220		21,281,220
	==========		==========

There is a modest cash balance in hand of U 414,440.

If the "revenue" and "capital" balances are separated, a double-account balance sheet would show:

Municipal Accounting for Developing Countries

Balance Sheet as at 31 Dec. 19_6

Capital

	Units		Units
Long-Term Liabilities		**Fixed Assets**	
Loans Outstanding	15,009,300	Buildings	10,093,740
Surplus		Permanent Works	9,686,520
Capital Discharged	5,283,860	Equipment	512,900
	20,293,160		20,293,160

Revenue

	Units		Units
Current Liabilities		**Current Assets**	
Creditors	491,340	Stocks and Stores	310,460
Provisions		Debtors	115,160
Repairs Funds	63,000	Investments	148,000
Renewals Funds	85,000	Cash	414,440
Surplus			
General Fund Surplus	348,720		
	988,060		988,060
	21,281,220		21,281,220

It will be seen that the two sections separately balance with the whole of the cash balance treated as "revenue" cash.

Now let us consider a variation from the original balance sheet as follows:

Balance Sheet as at 31 Dec. 19_5

	Units		Units
Long-Term Liabilities		**Fixed Assets**	
Loans Outstanding	15,129,300	Buildings	10,093,740
Current Liabilities		Permanent Works	9,686,520
Creditors	291,340	Equipment	512,900
Provisions		**Current Assets**	
Repairs Funds	63,000	Stocks and Stores	510,460
Renewals Funds	85,000	Debtors	215,160
Surplus		Investments	1,858,000
Capital Discharged	5,283,860	Cash	1,014,440
Capital Receipts Unapplied	980,000		
Capital Fund	1,710,000		
General Fund Surplus	348,720		
	23,891,220		23,891,220

Certain figures have been changed and new balances introduced. The cash balance, at U 1,014,440, is more than double the amount shown in

Capital Expenditure

the earlier balance sheet and appears at first sight to be quite satisfactory.

However, preparation of a double-account balance sheet will disclose the following situation:

Balance Sheet as at 31 Dec. 19_5
Capital

	Units		Units
Long-Term Liabilities		**Fixed Assets**	
Loans Outstanding	15,129,300	Buildings	10,093,740
Surplus		Permanent Works	9,686,520
Capital Discharged	5,283,860	Equipment	512,900
Capital Receipts		**Current Assets**	
Unapplied	980,000	+ Investments	1,710,000
Capital Fund	1,710,000	* Cash	1,100,000
	23,103,160		23,103,160

Revenue

	Units		Units
Current Liabilities		**Current Assets**	
Creditors	291,340	Stocks and Stores	510,460
* Cash Overdrawn	85,560	Debtors	215,160
Provisions		+ Investments	148,000
Repairs Funds	63,000		
Renewals Funds	85,000		
Surplus			
General Fund Surplus	348,720		
	873,620		873,620
	23,976,780		23,976,780

We now see that the overall cash balance of U 1,014,440 was more than covered by "capital" cash in hand of U 1,100,000 (*) representing unexpended loans and unapplied capital receipts. This left an overdrawn balance of "revenue" cash amounting to U 85,560 (*) which in normal circumstances would not be satisfactory.

The instability of the capital cash balance can be appreciated if we visualise, for example, that on the day following the balance sheet (1 Jan. 19_6), the capital receipt was used to purchase property for U 980,000 and the unexpended loan was used to make an instalment payment to a contractor of U 120,000. The "capital" cash balance would be entirely eliminated and the authority would then actually be overdrawn at the bank.

Investments (+) total U 1,858,000. We have assumed that these are related to the capital fund (U 1,710,000) and to repairs and renewals funds (U 148,000).

Finally, let us consider another alternative position as shown by the following balance sheet:

Municipal Accounting for Developing Countries

Balance Sheet as at 31 Dec. 19_5

	Units		Units
Long-Term Liabilities		**Fixed Assets**	
Loans Outstanding	13,609,300	Buildings	10,093,740
Current Liabilities		Permanent Works	9,686,520
Creditors	491,340	Equipment	512,900
Cash Overdrawn	585,560	**Current Assets**	
Provisions		Stocks and Stores	310,460
Repairs Funds	63,000	Debtors	115,160
Renewals Funds	85,000	Investments	1,858,000
Surplus			
Capital Discharged	5,283,860		
Capital Fund	1,710,000		
General Fund Surplus	748,720		
	22,576,780		22,576,780
	==========		==========

In this case there is an overdrawn cash balance of U 585,560 which appears at first sight to be a very unsatisfactory state of affairs.

However, preparation of a double-account balance sheet will disclose the following situation:

Balance Sheet as at 31 Dec. 19_5
Capital

	Units		Units
Long-Term Liabilities		**Fixed Assets**	
Loans Outstanding	13,609,300	Buildings	10,093,740
Current Liabilities		Permanent Works	9,686,520
Cash Overdrawn	1,400,000	Equipment	512,900
Surplus		**Current Assets**	
Capital Discharged	5,283,860	Investments	1,710,000
Capital Fund	1,710,000		
	22,003,160		22,003,160
	----------		----------

Revenue

	Units		Units
Current Liabilities		**Current Assets**	
Creditors	491,340	Stocks and Stores	310,460
Provisions		Debtors	115,160
Repairs Funds	63,000	Investments	148,000
Renewals Fund	85,000	Cash	814,440
Surplus			
General Fund Surplus	748,720		
	1,388,060		1,388,060
	----------		----------
	23,391,220		23,391,220
	==========		==========

We can now see that the revenue account position is most satisfactory. There is a cash balance in hand of U 814,440, which is almost double

Capital Expenditure

that shown in the balance sheet on page 588.

This situation arises because the net overdrawn cash balance U 585,560 was considerably more than covered by the overdrawn balance on capital account U 1,400,000.

Although the "capital" cash is overdrawn, this by no means represents the same unsatisfactory position as an overdrawn "revenue" cash balance. It can be assumed that the capital expenditure shown under "fixed assets" has all been properly authorised and that (where no other finance is available) loan sanctions have been granted. All the authority is doing is to exercise the loan sanctions by borrowing temporarily from the bank, instead of from another lender.

This is perfectly proper and is in complete accordance with the usual provisions of local government law. This provides that where an authority has lawfully incurred expenditure, frequently pending the raising of a loan to which the Government has consented, the authority may obtain advances of money capital by way of temporary loan or overdraft for the purpose of meeting such capital expenditure.

What has actually happened in our case is that the cash balances on revenue account have been temporarily appropriated for capital purposes, thus keeping the actual bank overdraft to a minimum and permitting a delay in the raising of a more permanent loan. This procedure results in a saving of interest charges, even if the bank overdraft rate of interest is higher than the interest on a longer term loan.

In our example $6\frac{1}{4}$% on a permanent loan of U 1,400,000 would result in a greater payment of interest than (say) 7% on a day-to-day balance which (all other things being equal) might fluctuate around U 600,000 (i.e. U 585,560).

This practice of temporarily using "revenue" cash balances to meet capital expenditure and of raising the "marginal" loan by way of bank overdraft is widely practised in the United Kingdom. It does, however, require discipline and control.

(b) **Receipts and Payments Account**

The preparation of a double-account balance sheet will show the cash balance at a particular point in time, but will give no indication of the flow of capital cash over a period of time. This can be shown by the preparation of a statement of receipts and payments in a form similar to the following:

Municipal Accounting for Developing Countries

CAPITAL CASH ACCOUNT FOR THE YEAR ENDED 31 DEC 19			

RECEIPTS
 Loans Raised
   (Details)
 Capital Receipts
   Grants
   Donations
   Sales of Fixed Assets
   Land Premiums
   Commodity Bonuses
   Insurance Claims
   (etc)
 	
 Fund Contributions
   Contributions towards
     Capital Expenditure
     from:
       Revenue Account
       Reserve Funds
       Renewals Funds
   Contributions from
     Revenue Account
     into:
       Capital Funds
       Sinking Funds
 Investments Sold
   (Details)
	Units	**PAYMENTS**
		 Capital Expenditure
		   (Details)
		 Repayments
		   Unexpended Loans
		   Unapplied Capital
		     Receipts
		   Premature Repayment of
		     Loans out of Capital
		     Receipts
		   Repayment of Loans out
		     of Sinking Funds
		 Investments Bought
		   (Details)
			Units

Cash in Hand at
   1 Jan. 19 brought
   forward
 Cash Overdrawn at
   31 Dec. 19 carried
   forward
		Cash Overdrawn at
		   1 Jan. 19 brought
		   forward
		 Cash in Hand at
		   31 Dec. 19 carried
		   forward	

	=======		=======

NOTES:

1. Fund contributions are appropriations of revenue cash for:

   (a) capital expenditure financed from revenue funds; and

   (b) contributions into capital funds and sinking funds from revenue accounts.

2. The purchase and sale of investments relates to the investment of surplus "capital" cash such as capital funds, sinking funds and capital receipts unapplied. Revenue investments are excluded.

3. Repayments exclude normal repayments of instalment and annuity loans, which are made from "revenue" cash.

Capital Expenditure

4. The balance brought forward (in hand or over-drawn) will agree with that shown in the "capital" section of the double-account balance sheet at the beginning of the year.

5. The balance carried forward (in hand or overdrawn) will agree with that shown in the "capital" section of the double-account balance sheet at the end of the year.

(c) List of Balances

As explained in Section 178 the cash position of each scheme will be shown at the end of each year in the capital register. If the balances are listed, together with other "capital" cash balances, the net balance will agree with that shown in the double-account balance sheet.

The balances could be listed in a statement along the following lines.

CAPITAL CASH BALANCES AS AT 31 DEC. 19				
Details			Cash Balances	
			In Hand	Overdrawn
Capital Schemes in Progress (listed in details from the capital register)			Units	Units
SUB-TOTALS					
Other Capital Funds				
Fund or Account	Total Balance	Invested		
	Units	Units		
Capital Fund Capital Receipts Unapplied Sinking Funds (Details)				
SUB-TOTALS					
Balance in hand (*) or overdrawn (μ)			μ	*
TOTALS			==========	==========

As with all cash accounts, balances in hand are carried forward from the credit side, overdrawn balances being carried forward from the debit side.

182. DEFERRED PAYMENT OF LAND PRICES OR PREMIUMS

Sometimes, local authorities will dispose of land by way of sale or on the basis of a long lease. This may, for example, be to a potential developer, to encourage commercial and/or residential development which will benefit the community. As part of these arrangements, the local

Municipal Accounting for Developing Countries

authority may wish to encourage the involvement of small contractors or developers who may be unlikely to have sufficient capital to invest in the land purchase (or lease) until construction is completed and the property disposed of.

This is not the place to discuss the complex and sometimes controversial questions of land pricing and marketing. However, if land is to be disposed of otherwise than on the basis of a straight sale, the accounting complexities increase and must be properly dealt with.

Some authorities may, for example, make provision for the payment of land sale prices or lease premiums to be deferred for a period of grace. They may also permit the premiums to be paid by annual instalments, with interest, for a further period after the end of the grace period. This raises several accountancy problems which have not yet been considered. These arise because:

(a) a record is required of the debt due from the developer during the periods of grace and credit;

(b) although the premiums due from developers represent capital income to the authority they cannot be appropriated for capital purposes until received in cash; and

(c) interest transactions cause certain complications.

Reference to Sections 169 and 171 of Chapter 14 will indicate that a normal capital receipt may be treated as either a "capital receipt unapplied" or paid into a "capital fund". Apart from terminology, the accounting procedures for these two methods are the same. They are:

(a) Upon receipt of the capital moneys:

DR Cash (Capital)
CR Capital Fund (or Capital Receipts Unapplied).

(b) Upon appropriation of the capital moneys for a specific capital purpose:

DR Capital Fund (or Capital Receipts Unapplied)
CR Capital Discharged (Capital Fund or Capital Receipts Unapplied).

(c) Upon acquisition or construction of the fixed asset:

DR Capital Expenditure (appropriately designated)
CR Cash (Capital).

Should the cash for a premium not be received immediately it has been assessed, item (a) above should, strictly, be split into two stages:

i) Upon fixing the premium due from the developer:

DR Developer (personal account)
CR Capital Fund (or Capital Receipts Unapplied).

ii) Upon receiving cash from the developer:

DR Cash
CR Developer (personal account).

The above procedures can apply only where a payment becomes due

Capital Expenditure

immediately upon demand and where there is only a slight delay in the actual receipt of the cash. In the case of a premium, the developer would, presumably, not be allowed to exercise any rights over the land until the premium had been paid.

Where a premium is not due to be paid until after a definite period of grace, the developer will presumably be given legal rights over the land and be required to begin development of the site within a reasonable time. At the time the premium is fixed, the amount due will have to be treated as a "deferred premium", only to be appropriated for capital purposes when the money is actually received. Clearly, if a premium or sale price is to be deferred, it will have a higher future value than if received at once, because the future price will include (expressly or implicitly) the accumulated interest foregone by the authority in permitting all or part of the sale price or lease premium to be deferred. The relationship between future and present values is explained in Section 183, dealing with advance payments.

Let us assume an example where on 1 July 19_8 a developer is granted a lease of land with a premium of U 15,000, with a period of grace of 3 years, followed by a further period of 5 years, during which instalments may be paid. During the period of deferred payment, interest is to be charged at 2% above bank rate. Let us assume that the interest rate will be 10% and the premiums are to be paid into a "capital fund".

There are three main ways in which the developer could discharge his debt of U 15,000.

(a) pay it in full when assessed;

(b) pay it in full at the end of the grace period; and

(c) begin to pay it by instalments at the end of the grace period.

The accounting treatment for case (a) will be that already explained above, and in Chapter 14.

In case (b) the entry necessary when the premium is assessed can be journalised as follows:

19_8 July 1	Developer DR.
	   To Deferred Premium
	   Being assessment of premium
	   due from developer at the end
	   of 3 years
		1
		2
			15,000	15,000

An (isolated) balance sheet would show:

Balance Sheet as at 1 July 19_8
Capital

	Units		Units
Provisions		**Current Assets**	
Deferred Premiums	15,000	Deferred Debtors	15,000
	======		======

Municipal Accounting for Developing Countries

When, on 1 July 19_1, the developer pays his premium, the entries can be journalised as follows:

19_1 July 1	Cash DR.	C.B. 1	15,000	
	To Developer	1		15,000
	Being receipt of deferred premium in cash			
July 1	Deferred Premium DR.	2	15,000	
	To Capital Fund	3		15,000
	Being appropriation of deferred premium to Capital Fund arising from full settlement in cash			

The appropriate ledger accounts would appear as follows:

Developer 1

19_8 Jul. 1	To Deferred Premium	J	15,000	19_8 Dec.31	By Balance	c/d	15,000
			15,000				15,000
19_9 Jan. 1	To Balance	b/d	15,000	19_9 Dec.31	By Balance	c/d	15,000
19_0 Jan. 1	To Balance	b/d	15,000	19_0 Dec.31	By Balance	c/d	15,000
19_1 Jan. 1	To Balance	b/d	15,000	19_1 Jul. 1	By Cash	J	15,000

Deferred Premium 2

19_8 Dec.31	To Balance	c/d	15,000	19_8 Jul. 1	By Developer	J	15,000
19_9 Dec.31	To Balance	c/d	15,000	19_9 Jan. 1	By Balance	b/d	15,000
19_0 Dec.31	To Balance	c/d	15,000	19_0 Jan. 1	By Balance	b/d	15,000
19_1 Jul. 1	To Capital Fund	J	15,000	19_1 Jan. 1	By Balance	b/d	15,000
			15,000				15,000

Capital Expenditure

				Capital Fund			3
				19_1 Jul. 1	By Deferred Premium	J	15,000

				Cash			C.B.
19_1 Jul. 1	To Developer	J	15,000				

An (isolated) balance sheet would show:

Balance Sheet as at 31 Dec. 19_1
Capital

Surplus	Units	Current Assets	Units
Capital Fund	15,000	Cash	15,000
	======		======

Except for the figures, this is the same position as that shown at the top of page 530 in Chapter 14. Subsequent investments and appropriations of the Capital Fund will be as described in that chapter.

In case (c) the entry necessary when the premium is assessed will be the same as that for case (b).

On 1 July 19_1, the payments will become due over a period of 5 years according to the following table:

Date	Total Payment	Interest	Principal Sum	Principal Sum Outstanding
1.7._1	2,500	-	2,500	12,500
1.7._2	3,750	1,250	2,500	10,000
1.7._3	3,500	1,000	2,500	7,500
1.7._4	3,250	750	2,500	5,000
1.7._5	3,000	500	2,500	2,500
1.7._6	2,750	250	2,500	-

Note that there will be six payments over five years.

The accounting entries on 1 July 19_1 can be journalised as follows:

19_1 July 1	Cash DR.	C.B. 1	2,500	
	To Developer			2,500
	Being receipt of first instalment of deferred premium in cash			
July 1	Deferred Premium DR.	2	2,500	
	To Capital Fund	3		2,500
	Being appropriation of deferred premium to Capital Fund arising from partial cash settlement			

At this stage an (isolated) balance sheet would show:

Balance Sheet as at 1 July 19_1

Capital

	Units		Units
Provisions		**Current Assets**	
Deferred Premiums	12,500	Deferred Debtors	12,500
Surplus		Cash	2,500
Capital Fund	2,500		
	15,000		15,000
	======		======

On 1 July 19_2 the second instalment will become due, together with a year's interest. The interest will be debited to the developer who will then be required to pay the total sum of U 3,750. This can be journalised as follows:

19_2 July 1	Developer DR.	1	1,250	
	To Deferred Premium	2		1,250
	Being interest @ 10% on U 12,500 for the year			
July 1	Cash DR.	C.B. 1	3,750	
	To Developer			3,750
	Being receipt of second instalment of deferred premium and interest in cash			
July 1	Deferred Premium DR.	2	3,750	
	To Capital Fund	3		3,750
	Being appropriation of deferred premium to Capital Fund arising from partial cash settlement with interest			

An (isolated) balance sheet would then show:

Capital Expenditure

Balance Sheet as at 1 July 19_2
Capital

	Units		Units
Provisions		**Current Assets**	
Deferred Premiums	10,000	Deferred Debtors	10,000
Surplus		Cash	6,250
Capital Fund	6,250		
	16,250		16,250

The journal entries for subsequent payments until 19_6 would follow exactly the same pattern using the figures in the table. After all payments had been made, appropriate ledger accounts (excluding the cash account) would appear as follows:

			Developer				1
19_8				19_8			
Jul. 1	To Deferred Premium	J	15,000	Dec.31	By Balance	c/d	15,000
			15,000				15,000
			======				======
19_9				19_9			
Jan. 1	To Balance	b/d	15,000	Dec.31	By Balance	c/d	15,000
			======				======
19_0				19_0			
Jan. 1	To Balance	b/d	15,000	Dec.31	By Balance	c/d	15,000
			======				======
19_1				19_1			
Jan. 1	To Balance	b/d	15,000	Jul. 1	By Cash	J	2,500
				Dec.31	By Balance	c/d	12,500
			15,000				15,000
			======				======
19_2				19_2			
Jan. 1	To Balance	b/d	12,500	Jul. 1	By Cash	J	3,750
Jul. 1	To Deferred Premium (Interest)	J	1,250	Dec.31	By Balance	c/d	10,000
			13,750				13,750
			======				======
19_3				19_3			
Jan. 1	To Balance	b/d	10,000	Jul. 1	By Cash	J	3,500
Jul. 1	To Deferred Premium (Interest)	J	1,000	Dec.31	By Balance	c/d	7,500
			11,000				11,000
			======				======
19_4				19_4			
Jan. 1	To Balance	b/d	7,500	Jul. 1	By Cash	J	3,250
Jul. 1	To Deferred Premium (Interest)	J	750	Dec.31	By Balance	c/d	5,000
			8,250				8,250
			======				======
19_5				19_5			
Jan. 1	To Balance	b/d	5,000	Jul. 1	By Cash	J	3,000
Jul. 1	To Deferred Premium (Interest)	J	500	Dec.31	By Balance	c/d	2,500
			5,500				5,500
			======				======
19_6				19_6			
Jan. 1	To Balance	b/d	2,500	Jul. 1	By Cash	J	2,750
Jul. 1	To Deferred Premium (Interest)	J	250				
			2,750				2,750
			======				======

Capital Expenditure

		Deferred Premium					2
19_8 Dec.31	To Balance	c/d	15,000 ======	19_8 Jul. 1	By Developer	J	15,000 ======
19_9 Dec.31	To Balance	c/d	15,000 ======	19_9 Jan. 1	By Balance	b/d	15,000 ======
19_0 Dec.31	To Balance	c/d	15,000 ======	19_0 Jan. 1	By Balance	b/d	15,000 ======
19_1 Jul. 1 Dec.31	To Capital Fund To Balance	J c/d	2,500 12,500 ——— 15,000 ======	19_1 Jan. 1	By Balance	b/d	15,000 ——— 15,000 ======
19_2 Jul. 1 Dec.31	To Capital Fund To Balance	J c/d	3,750 10,000 ——— 13,750 ======	19_2 Jan. 1 Jul. 1	By Balance By Developer (Interest)	b/d J	12,500 1,250 ——— 13,750 ======
19_3 Jul. 1 Dec.31	To Capital Fund To Balance	J c/d	3,500 7,500 ——— 11,000 ======	19_3 Jan. 1 Jul. 1	By Balance By Developer (Interest)	b/d J	10,000 1,000 ——— 11,000 ======
19_4 Jul. 1 Dec.31	To Capital Fund To Balance	J c/d	3,250 5,000 ——— 8,250 ======	19_4 Jan. 1 Jul. 1	By Balance By Developer (Interest)	b/d J	7,500 750 ——— 8,250 ======
19_5 Jul. 1 Dec.31	To Capital Fund To Balance	J c/d	3,000 2,500 ——— 5,500 ======	19_5 Jan. 1 Jul. 1	By Balance By Developer (Interest)	b/d J	5,000 500 ——— 5,500 ======
19_6 Jul. 1	To Capital Fund	J	2,750 ——— 2,750 ======	19_6 Jan. 1 Jul. 1	By Balance By Developer (Interest)	b/d J	2,500 250 ——— 2,750 ======

Municipal Accounting for Developing Countries

			Capital Fund					3
19_1 Dec.31	To Balance	c/d	2,500	19_1 Jul. 1	By Deferred Premium		J	2,500
			2,500 ======					2,500 ======
19_2 Dec.31	To Balance	c/d	6,250	19_2 Jan. 1 Jul. 1	By Balance By Deferred Premium		b/d J	2,500 3,750
			6,250 ======					6,250 ======
19_3 Dec.31	To Balance	c/d	9,750	19_3 Jan. 1 Jul. 1	By Balance By Deferred Premium		b/d J	6,250 3,500
			9,750 ======					9,750 ======
19_4 Dec.31	To Balance	c/d	13,000	19_4 Jan. 1 Jul. 1	By Balance By Deferred Premium		b/d J	9,750 3,250
			13,000 ======					13,000 ======
19_5 Dec.31	To Balance	c/d	16,000	19_5 Jan. 1 Jul. 1	By Balance By Deferred Premium		b/d J	13,000 3,000
			16,000 ======					16,000 ======
19_6 Dec.31	To Balance	c/d	18,750	19_6 Jan. 1 Jul. 1	By Balance By Deferred Premium		b/d J	16,000 2,750
			18,750 ======	19_7 Jan. 1	By Balance		b/d	18,750 ====== 18,750

The final (isolated) balance sheet would show:

Balance Sheet as at 1 July 19_6
Capital

	Units		Units
Surplus		**Current Assets**	
Capital Fund	18,750 ======	Cash	18,750 ======

Capital Expenditure

In practice, the above entries could well be made annually, in total for all developers. The "Deferred Premium" and "Developer" accounts would be treated as control accounts. Transactons relating to individual developers could be recorded in a tabular register along similar lines to that suggested for motor advances on page 389 of Chapter 11. The first few columns could appear as follows:

REGISTER OF DEFERRED LAND PREMIUMS

Name of Developer	Location and Description of Plot	Dates - Lease Granted	Dates - Interest Begins	Balance 1.1._8	Premium Interest	Payments (Including Interest)	(etc)

The register would be kept as described in Section 132 of Chapter 11. It would be balanced off and totalled annually to provide the information necessary for the accounting adjustments.

183. ADVANCE PAYMENT OF DEFERRED PREMIUMS

It will be seen above that the deferment of premium payments will delay receipt by the local authority of scarce capital finance at the very time when this finance is required for development of initial services. This means that the authority will have to finance the development of initial services from other resources, probably by borrowing.

The problem could possibly be eased to a certain extent by giving discounts to developers who pay their premiums before the end of the grace period. Such a scheme could require Government approval. The developer could be allowed to settle his premium in full by paying immediately to the authority a sum of money known as the "present value" of the full premium due in several years time.

To understand the concept of a "present value", let us assume that a developer with ample capital knows that he has to pay a premium of U 10,000 in 3 years time. He goes to a bank or other institution which offers a rate of compound interest on deposits of (say) 6% and asks the following question of the manager:

"How much do I have to deposit now, so that my deposit, if undisturbed and earning compound interest at 6%, will amount to exactly U 10,000 at the end of 3 years?"

The manager will calculate from loan tables that the necessary sum is U 8,396.20. The deposit will build up as follows:

Municipal Accounting for Developing Countries

Date	Details	Withdrawn		Deposited		Balance	
		Units	Cts	Units	Cts	Units	Cts
19_8 Jul. 1	Deposit	-		8,396	20	8,396	20
19_9 Jun.30	Interest @ 6% on U 8,396.20	-		503	75	8,899	95
19_0 Jun.30	Interest @ 6% on U 8,899.95	-		534	00	9,433	95
19_1 Jun.30	Interest @ 6% on U 9,433.95			566	05	10,000	00
Jul. 1	Withdrawn	10,000	00	-		-	

The bank is thus borrowing the sum of U 8,396.20 at compound interest of 6% for 3 years. Total interest payable amounts to U 1,603.80 so that a total of U 10,000 is repaid at the end of the period. In technical terms we say:

"The present value of U 10,000 due in 3 years time, discounted at 6%, amounts to U 8,396.20".

Looking at the matter another way it means that a creditor who was due to receive U 10,000 in 3 years time would be prepared to accept only U 8,396.20 immediately if he could either invest that money at 6%, or avoid borrowing at 6% - which amounts to the same thing.

A local authority, granting periods of grace for land premiums is precisely such a creditor. Indeed, if its only alternative source of capital finance is to borrow at (say) 6½% from the Government, it would be a definite financial advantage to accept present values of premiums discounted at 6%. Even if there were no interest advantage it would still be a means of generating a flow of capital finance for development work. This is particularly important in developing countries, where capital funds are usually in very short supply.

Let us suppose, therefore, that the above developer had agreed to pay U 8,396.20 to the local authority immediately in full discharge of a U 10,000 premium due after a three year period of grace.

When the premium was assessed, the book-keeping entries would be as follows:

19_8 July 1	Developer DR. To Deferred Premiums Being assessment of premium due from Developer at the end of 3 years	1 2	10,000	10,000

Upon immediate payment of the present value the journalised entries would be:

604

Capital Expenditure

19_8							

July 1	Cash DR.
	   To Developer
	   Being full settlement of
	   premium of U 10,000 due
	   after 3 years by payment
	   of present value
		C.B.
		1
			8,396	20	8,396	20	

July 1	Deferred Premium DR.
	   To Developer
	   Being discount granted on
	   immediate settlement of
	   premium U 10,000 due after
	   3 years
		2
		1
			1,603	80	1,603	80	

July 1	Deferred Premium DR.
	   To Capital Fund
	   Being present value of
	   U 10,000 due after 3 years
	   now appropriated after
	   cash settlement
		2	8,396	20	8,396	20	

The appropriate ledger accounts would appear as follows:

Developer   1

19_8					19_8				
Jul. 1	To Deferred Premium	J	10,000	00	Jul. 1	By Cash By Deferred Premium	J J	8,396 1,603	20 80
			10,000	00				10,000	00

Deferred Premium   2

19_8					19_8				
Jul. 1	To Developer To Capital Fund	J J	1,603 8,396	80 20	Jul. 1	By Developer	J	10,000	00
			10,000	00				10,000	00

Municipal Accounting for Developing Countries

					Capital Fund				3
19_8 Dec.31	To Balance	c/d	8,396	20	19_8 Jul. 1	By Deferred Premium	J	8,396	20
			8,396 ======	20 ===				8,396 ======	20 ===
					19_9 Jan. 1	By Balance	b/d	8,396	20

					Cash				C.B.
19_8 Jul. 1	To Developer	J	8,396	20					

The (isolated) balance sheet would show:

Balance Sheet as at 1 July 19_8

	Units	Cents		Units	Cents
Surplus			**Current Assets**		
Capital Fund	8,396	20	Cash	8,396	20
	=========			=========	

The sum appropriated to the Capital Fund would be only U 8,396.20 instead of the full premium of U 10,000. This is justified because, if the sum were immediately invested by the authority at 6%, it would amount to U 10,000 by 1 July 19_1, the date the premium becomes legally payable.

As explained at Section 182 (page 593), the details of individual premiums can be recorded in a tabular register, leaving the main accounting entries to be dealt with in total only. Discounts could be entered in red ink in the register in the places where interest would otherwise be shown.

Where premiums are held separately, pending appropriation, instead of being paid into a Capital Fund the above book-keeping entries should show "Capital Receipts Unapplied" instead of "Capital Fund" wherever it occurs. In all other respects they will be the same.

Shown below is a table of "present value" coefficients for interest rates from 5% to 10%.

Thus, in the example used above, the calculation of the present value for a premium of U 10,000 for 3 years, using a rate of interest of 6% would be as follows:

Present Value of 1 Due in a Number of Years

Number of Years	Rate of Interest					
	5	6	7	8	9	10
1	0.952380952	0.9433962226	0.9345794439	0.9259259259	0.9174311192	0.9090909090
2	0.9070294784	0.8899964440	0.8734438728	0.8573383820	0.8416799993	0.8264462814
3	0.8638375984	0.8396192483	0.8162978760	0.7938323041	0.7721834802	0.7513148008
4	0.8227024740	0.7920936360	0.7628952123	0.7350298524	0.7084252116	0.6830134553
5	0.7835261660	0.7472581723	0.7129861795	0.6805831966	0.6580519974	0.6209213231
6	0.7462153964	0.7049605400	0.6663422230	0.6301696260	0.5962673264	0.5644739300
7	0.7106813300	0.6650571136	0.6227497411	0.5834903951	0.5470342440	0.5131581180
8	0.6768393624	0.6274123715	0.5820091043	0.5402688843	0.5018662790	0.4665073805
9	0.6446089164	0.5918984636	0.5439337424	0.5002489672	0.4604277730	0.4240976180
10	0.6139132537	0.5583947766	0.5083492920	0.4631934881	0.4224108063	0.3855432890

Municipal Accounting for Developing Countries

Amount of Premium	=	U 10,000
Period of Grace	=	3 years
Rate of Interest	=	6%
Figure from Loan Tables for an amount of 1	=	0.8396192830
Present Value	=	U 0.8396192830 x 10,000
	=	U 8396.192830
	=	U 8396.20 (to nearest 5 cents)

Should a developer wish to settle his premium part of the way through the period of grace, the present value would be calculated for the number of years of grace remaining. For example, a premium of U 25,000 may be due after a grace period of 5 years and the developer may offer to settle it after three years by which time the interest rate is (say) 5%. The amount due would be calculated as follows:

Amount of Premium	=	U 25,000
Period of Grace remaining Unexpired	=	2 years
Rate of Interest	=	5%
Figure from Loan Tables for an amount of 1	=	0.9070294785
Present Value	=	U 0.9070294785 x 25,000
	=	U 22675.7369625
	=	U 22675.75 (to nearest 5 cents)

These calculations, done in reverse, will indicate how to fix the amount of a deferred premium relative to its present value. For example if the premium were valued at U 8,396 and current interest rates were 6%, the deferred premium after 3 years should be valued at U 10,000. For a premium of U 22,675 deferred for 2 years, with interest at 5%, the value should be set at U 25,000. This links back to the explanation at the beginning of Section 182.

LOAN TABLES

Repayment of a Loan by Way of Annuity

(Half-yearly payment to include Principal and Interest)

Number of Half-Years	\multicolumn{5}{c}{Half-Yearly Payment to Repay a Loan of U 1}
	3%	3½%	4%	4½%	5%
10	.10843418	.10987534	.11132653	.11278768	.11425876
20	.05824574	.05969122	.06115672	.06264207	.06414713
30	.04163919	.04312975	.04464992	.04619934	.04777764
40	.03342710	.03497209	.03655575	.03817738	.03983623
50	.02857168	.03017391	.03182321	.03351836	.03525806
60	.02539343	.02705336	.02876797	.03053533	.03235340
70	.02317235	.02488930	.02666765	.02850458	.03039712
80	.02154832	.02332093	.02516071	.02706376	.02902605
90	.02032113	.02214760	.02404602	.02601126	.02803809
100	.01937057	.02124880	.02320274	.02522594	.02731188

Capital Expenditure

Number of Half-Years	Half-Yearly Payment to Repay a Loan of U 1				
	5½%	6%	6½%	7%	7½%
10	.11573972	.11723051	.11873107	.12024137	.12176134
20	.06567173	.06721571	.06877888	.07036108	.07196210
30	.04938442	.05101926	.05268172	.05437133	.05608762
40	.04153151	.04326238	.04502794	.04682728	.04865946
50	.03704092	.03886549	.04073027	.04263371	.04457422
60	.03422002	.03613296	.03808993	.04008862	.04212670
70	.03234218	.03433663	.03637727	.03846095	.04058456
80	.03104342	.03311175	.03522690	.03738489	.03958184
90	.03012125	.03225556	.03443601	.03665781	.03891646
100	.02945418	.03164667	.03388351	.03615927	.03846895

Number of Half-Years	Half-Yearly Payment to Repay a Loan of U 1				
	8%	8½%	9%	9½%	10%
10	.12329094	.12483012	.12637882	.12793699	.12950458
20	.07358175	.07521983	.07687614	.07855047	.08024259
30	.05783010	.05959825	.06139154	.06320945	.06505144
40	.05052349	.05241839	.05434315	.05629675	.05827816
50	.04655620	.04856005	.05060215	.05267490	.05477674
60	.04420185	.04631178	.04845426	.05062710	.05282818
70	.04274506	.04493952	.04716511	.04941917	.05169915
80	.04181408	.04407811	.04637069	.04868879	.05102962
90	.04120775	.04352783	.04587316	.04824054	.05062711
100	.04080800	.04317236	.04555839	.04796292	.05038314

Number of Half-Years	Half-Yearly Payment to Repay a Loan of U 1				
	10½%	11%	11½%	12%	12½%
10	.13108152	.13266777	.13426327	.13586796	.13748179
20	.08195228	.08367933	.08542350	.08718456	.08896227
30	.06691693	.06880539	.07071624	.07264891	.07460284
40	.06028673	.06232034	.06437907	.06646154	.06856675
50	.05690609	.05906145	.06124133	.06344429	.06566893
60	.05505549	.05730707	.05958107	.06187572	.06418938
70	.05400269	.05632754	.05867166	.06103313	.06341019
80	.05339063	.05576948	.05816409	.06057678	.06299315
90	.05303032	.05544788	.05787781	.06031836	.06276799
100	.05281664	.05526132	.05771540	.06017736	.06264588

16. Final Accounts

Section		Page
184.	Final Accounts - Introduction.	611
185.	The Trial Balance.	612
186.	The Main Ledger.	613
187.	The Main Journal.	614
188.	Working Papers.	614
189.	Explanation of Final Adjustments.	615
190.	Published Final Accounts.	617
191.	Capital Statements Supporting Final Accounts.	618
192.	Final Accounts - Conclusion.	619
	Appendices	620
	Appendix A. Trial Balance.	622
	B. Ledger Accounts (Detailed).	631
	C. Ledger Accounts (Outline).	655
	D. Main Journal.	666
	E. Published Final Accounts.	673
	F. Capital Statements.	678
	G. Working Papers.	684

184. FINAL ACCOUNTS - INTRODUCTION

In Section 92 of Chapter 9 on this subject we referred to a balance sheet of Kambale Municipal Council as at 31 Dec. 19_5, as follows:

"We shall show, in due course, how each of the balances is brought into the accounts; how it is dealt with in detail; how the activities of the Council are recorded in the accounts for 19_6 and how the final accounts for the year ended Dec. 19_6 can be prepared".

In Chapters 9-15 we did, in fact, consider a variety of transactions affecting Kambale Municipal Council, basing these transactions on the balance sheet and estimates appearing on pages 285-295 of Chapter 9.

We now show how the transactions explained in Chapters 9-15 can be integrated into a full set of final accounts. Wherever possible, the information contained in the records shown in earlier chapters will be the same as that used in the final accounts. Where certain information is incomplete, valid assumptions will be made. The purpose of this chapter is to link the final accounts directly to the earlier examples of day-to-day transactions.

It would be impossible to show how to prepare a "model" set of accounts for local authorities in general. It is not even possible to give instructions, except of a very general nature, as to how local authorities should prepare their accounts. What we shall try to do in this chapter is to take the particular (though imaginary) authority of Kambale and prepare its accounts. We shall then have produced a model, not to be arbitrarily imposed in detail upon every authority - but as a basis from which to draw experience in planning the accounts of other individual authorities.

It must be admitted that the process of completing a full set of final accounts is somewhat lengthy and complex. There is, however, no need to become fearful of the task, provided we work with cool heads and clear thinking, taking each step logically.

In dealing with this chapter it would be advisable to read it through several times, just to get the general outline, before proceeding to study matters of detail. The key to the whole process is to start with a properly balanced set of prime records and thereafter to make each adjustment to affect the debit and credit aspects equally.
In our example it has been assumed that during the year no entries are made in the main ledger, which therefore shows only opening balances, even at the year end. Transactions during the year are entered in

subsidiary ledger accounts. These accounts may be in the form of cash analysis columns, abstracts, ledger pages, machine cards or tabulations from a computer system. Whatever the system employed, the purpose will be to produce a detailed analysis of income and expenditure during the year as explained in Chapter 12. The cash book serves, of course, as a "main ledger account" "subsidiary ledger account" and "prime record" all in one.

It has also been assumed that the minimum of adjustments have been made during the year, leaving most to be made during the process of "closing down" the accounts. This is done to demonstrate the accounting procedures in a comprehensive way, but there may well be instances where the adjustments could have been made during the year, to save time at the year-end. Indeed, with the increasing use of computers, it has become easier to produce comprehensive financial statements at much shorter intervals, such as monthly or quarterly. The principles are the same as illustrated here.

In our example, the allocation of stores, wages, labour overheads, vehicle expenses and the majority of sundry creditors has been assumed to have already taken place, because these processes have been explained in detail elsewhere.

As an alternative to the method shown here, some authorities bring the opening balances straight into the subsidiary accounts (e.g. computer cards) and merge them with later transactions. This means that the ledger is self-contained and continuous and this is found to be particularly useful for personal accounts. Opening balances can still be identified at the year-end. This system, to be really efficient, requires full utilisation of management aids, particularly computers.

The accounts and other documents are shown in a series of appendices to this chapter. Accounts will be posted to the nearest five cents. This has been demonstrated in the Markets Revenue Account. Elsewhere, to avoid unnecessary detail, odd cents are ignored, and postings made only in units.

185. **THE TRIAL BALANCE**

The trial balance, shown in appendix "A" has two main functions. Firstly, it is an indication that the accounts are balanced: this is not the same as being correct, for as we shall see, it contains certain errors. Secondly, it is a list of all balances on the individual subsidiary accounts.

Many of the entries in the trial balance are shown in the greatest possible detail (e.g. Finance Department, Markets) but to avoid unnecessary duplication, only totals are given for some services (e.g. Education, Works). Where only totals are given, it may be assumed that in practice the detailed amounts comprising these totals would be shown in the accounts and in the trial balance.

Each entry in the trial balance shows an appropriate reference to the page number of the earlier chapter from which the figure is taken, or in which an estimated figure appears (estimates are indicated by an asterisk *) together with the ledger folio or other references.

We know that a bank balance shown in the accounts cannot be considered as final until a reconciliation statement has been prepared. The figure of U 408,420 shown in the trial balance (page 629) has been amended as shown by the footnotes. The appropriate income and expenditure analyses are also adjusted before posting to the main ledger can begin. The balance sheet on page 285 of Chapter 9 shows that the special

Final Accounts

funds for repairs and renewals were at that time wholly invested. During the year these funds were increased by income and contributions. They were also decreased by the financing of expenditure. In addition, certain new funds were created. At the end of the year we might expect to see the net balances of all funds held as investments. Unfortunately, this is not quite as simple as it sounds. For investments to be correctly shown in a balance sheet, any adjustments will have to be made before the end of the financial year: yet the exact balances of funds will not usually be known until the final accounts have been completed, some time after the end of the financial year. A rough calculation is therefore made of the amount to be adjusted as shown by W.P.2 (page 686) and the sum of U 120,000 added to investments by a transfer of cash to a deposit account.

The adjusted items of the trial balance are now ready for posting to the main ledger.

186. THE MAIN LEDGER

Each folio of the main ledger can be assumed to be drawn up in the form shown by appendix "B".

The debit side and the credit side each have five columns. The balances from 19_5 will be (or will already have been) inserted in the columns headed "balances". Each balance brought forward will be indicated by the letter (b) and each balance carried forward by the letter (c). The remaining debit entries in the trial balance will normally be posted to the column headed "expenditure analysis" on the debit side of the main ledger and the remaining credit entries to the column headed "income analysis" on the credit side. Exceptionally, debit entries will be posted as "minus" entries on the credit side. This happens, as in the case of "Finance Department - Sale of Publications (refund)" page 634 where the item U 80 represents a reduction of income rather than an increase in expenditure. In the same way, a few credit items will be posted as "minuses" on the debit side, as in the case of "Health - Markets - Insurance Premium (refund)" U 60 which represents a reduction of expenditure rather than an increase in income. Page 639 minus entries might, in practice, be made in red ink but we have shown them in parenthesis - e.g. (60.00).

Although the figures to be posted will be those shown in the trial balance, the actual postings will be made directly from the appropriate folios or columns in the expenditure and income analysis system.

To avoid needless repetition only a selection of the ledger accounts have been shown in complete detail in appendix "B" page 631. The remainder are shown in outline only in appendix "C" page 655. The accounts shown in appendix "C" are not, therefore, intended as models but merely to show how the books are kept in balance.

The item for "Miscellaneous Licences" U 5,540 has been shown as being posted direct to the revenue account summary, page 632. An alternative would have been to post it to its own income account in the ledger and transfer it from there to the summary.

The cash accounts (L.127-129) pages 665 are not shown in detail because, for our purposes, only the balances are required.

Because we are concerned mainly with the accountancy aspects of the work we have shown each balance transferred as the "net" income or expenditure. For publication and certain other purposes it might well be better to show "gross" expenditure and "gross" income separately, but this practice has been ignored in our examples. Only one example is given of a capital account (Markets L.6 page 640) but others will be on similar lines. Details of capital transactions will be clearly seen in the statements in appendix "F" page 678.

When all the items in the expenditure and income analyses have been posted to the main ledger they can, if required, be proved in total against the totals of the prime records. As already explained these may range from abstract columns to computer tabulations. By the use of separate columns, the "expenditure" and "income" sources may be proved separately. By bringing in the cash balances the ledger system can then be balanced as a whole before proceeding further.

The next stage is to take final adjustments, principally through the Main Journal.

187. THE MAIN JOURNAL

The Main Journal is shown in appendix "D" page 666. It is used to record the explanations of final adjustments and to show clearly the effect of these adjustments on the debit and credit aspects of the accounts. It is common practice for many of these entries to be in outline only and we have followed this practice here. The greater part of the detail will usually be recorded in a set of "working papers" and individual postings may sometimes be made from these working papers rather than direct from the journal.

Every adjustment will appear in a column of the ledger headed "transfers". The "details" column will be entered with the journal entry number or journal folio. The postings will be made in the normal debit and credit fashion, though exceptionally a posting will appear as a "minus" entry on the "wrong" side. An example of the latter appears in folio L.4A page under "Drugs and Medical Supplies", U 840.

In Chapter 12 we saw that "journal adjustment notes" could be used to make adjustments during the year. However, the final adjustments referred to in this chapter will probably be made in a conventional bound journal and this practice has much to recommend it. When all journal entries have been correctly made, the total debits in the "transfers" columns will balance with total credits.

The ledger is designed in such a way as to make the main journal not strictly necessary. Direct transfers could be made between ledger accounts using ledger folios as references but this practice is not, generally speaking, recomended. In our model this method has been used only to make straightforward transfers of balances from one account to another. For example the net expenditure of the Finance Department - U 472,180 (ledger folio L.2B) has been transferred direct to the General Revenue (Summary) (ledger folio L.1).

188. WORKING PAPERS

Many of the final adjustments are of a somewhat complex nature, so that full details could not easily be entered in the Main Journal. The detailed workings are therefore set out in a set of "working papers" as shown in appendix "G" page 684.

These working papers follow no set pattern, being drawn up as circumstances require. They must not, however, be regarded as "rough notes" to be thrown away. They are an integral part of the final accounts and will be available for future reference and for production to the auditor.

Final Accounts

189. EXPLANATION OF FINAL ADJUSTMENTS

The various adjustments can now be briefly commented upon.

Entry No.1

U 2,500 cash received for rates has apparently, during the year, been posted by mistake to "Finance Department - Miscellaneous".

Entry No.2

When this account for U 840 was paid early in 19_6 the clerk concerned ignored the fact that it related to 19_5 and charged it to the current year's expenditure instead of to "Sundry Creditors (Control)" as explained in Chapter 11.

Entry No.3

Although most outstanding invoices for 19_6 have been brought into the accounts, a few came to hand late or had to be estimated for. These were summarised on a list drawn up in ink (see W.P.3 page 687) and posted from this to the ledger. The total is, of course, credited as an additional item to "Sundry Creditors (Control)".

Entry No.4

Investments held during the year have yielded a total of U 10,280 in interest which has initially been credited as general income. Interest charged against motor advances must also be taken credit for. However, some of the interest is not "General Income" but has been earned by the investment of special funds. This interest is appropriated to the funds concerned.

Entry No.5

This is explained in the letter (W.P.7 page 692). Although the balance of the grant will not be paid until 19_7 it related to 19_6 and must therefore be accrued.

Entry No.6

This is explained in Section 142 of Chapter 12 page 433 and the stocktaking list is reproduced as W.P.6 page 691.

Entry No.7

Explained in Chapter 13 Sections 152 and 162.

Entry No.8

It is assumed that the vehicles are garaged in a common building with the stores. An arbitrary apportionment of costs is therefore made to cover the various expenses incurred (e.g. cleaning, rates) in using part of the building as a garage.

Entry No.9

Explained in Chapter 13 Section 163.

Entry No.10

Self-explanatory.

Municipal Accounting for Developing Countries

Entry No.11

Refer to the second paragraph on page 428 of Chapter 12.

Entry No.12

This item assumes that provision is being made to replace office equipment, likely to cost U 20,000 after a life of four years.

Entry No.13

Self Explanatory.

Entries No.14-16

Explained in Chapter 10 Section 107.

Entries 17 and 18

Explained in Chapter 10 Section 113, page 322.

Entries No.19-23

Explained in Chapter 10 Section 120.

Entry No.24

Certain assumptions have been made regarding income analysis, otherwise this entry is explained in Chapter 10 Section 115.

Entry No.25

This entry merely clears out of the way certain credit income not referred to in detail elsewhere, after making certain assumptions. It should, perhaps, be fully appreciated that the term "Sundry Debtors" is used in two different contexts. For balance sheet purposes the term can be said to include all debts owed to the Council not otherwise separately shown. They will include arrears of rates, water charges, licences and other credit income. When dealing with individual types of credit income we find that after each specific type has been eliminated there are still a number of items left over, not easily classified. These we also refer to as "Sundry Debtors" and will be recorded (as explained in Section 111 of Chapter 10) in a composite account.

Entry No.26

These items were paid in 19_5 but related to expenditure for 19_6. They were therefore held "in suspense" at the end of 19_5 and are now charged against 19_6 expenditure, as explained in principle in Chapter 11 Section 131.

Entries No.27-28

Certain capital payments have been made for legal fees relating to the clinic. Also, at the end of 19_5, there was an overspent cash balance relating to the Sewage Disposal Works as shown on page 554 of Chapter 15. Each of these items is to be met by a Revenue Contribution to Capital Outlay.

Entries No.29-34

Explained in detail in Chapters 14 and 15 as indicated.

Final Accounts

Entry No.35

It is assumed that these assets, though recorded elsewhere, were not brought into the accounts until the end of the year. This is explained in Chapter 14 pages 503 and 521.

Entry No.36

It is assumed that actual loan charges, including principal repayments, have been debited directly to various revenue accounts. An adjustment is therefore necessary as explained in principle on pages 515-18 of Chapter 14. U 80,000 of the loan repayments are used to write down a deferred charge, instead of to discharge capital expenditure, as explained in Chapter 15 Section 172.

Entry No.37

It is assumed that the old vehicle is not written out of the accounts until the end of the year. This is explained in detail in Chapter 15 page 541.

Entry No.38

Only one example has been shown, in complete detail, of an investment account, that of the Vehicles Renewals Fund page 654. There will, of course, be an investment account for each of the funds listed on W.P.14.

Since the total value of the funds exceeds investments by U 3,000 this sum has been taken, quite arbitrarily, to be the uninvested cash of the Housing Repairs Fund: this fund is probably the most appropriate, as it has a more continuous turnover. As the balance in the Vehicle Renewals Fund falls by U 24,755 to U 37,755 at 31.12.19_6, the Vehicles Renewals Fund investments are reduced to this amount by Journal transfer.

Finance - Other Travelling Allowances

This figure of U 720 shown on folio L.2A refers to two return air passages to London for a conference to take place in January 19_7. Although the payment was made in 19_6 the expenditure will not be incurred until 19_7. The sum is therefore carried forward as a balance and shown in the balance sheet as "Payments in Advance". By this method we are using a nominal account as a personal account, following the well-known commercial procedure described in Section 131 of Chapter 11.

190. PUBLISHED FINAL ACCOUNTS

Included in appendix "E" pages 673-677 are two alternative forms of Revenue Account. These merely reproduce the information from ledger folios L.1 and L.106 in ways which will appeal to the eye and illustrate certain points.

The first alternative (F.1) is in conventional form and the second (F.2) is in more of a narrative form. In the second statement the figures are comparable with the budget summary on page 290 of Chapter 9.

Also included in appendix "E" are two alternative forms of balance sheet. The various balances have, of course, been taken from the ledger accounts, though certain "capital" balances are more fully explained in appendix "F".

The first alternative (F.3) is in double-account form and the second

Municipal Accounting for Developing Countries

(F.4) is in the more modern form for the layout has been slightly "streamlined" to admit comparison with the earlier balance sheet shown on page 285 of Chapter 9.

The balance sheet could, of course, also have been published in "narrative" form if required.

191. CAPITAL STATEMENTS SUPPORTING FINAL ACCOUNTS

Included in appendix "F" is a series of statements dealing with capital transactions.

The first statement, (S.1) dealing with capital expenditure would, in practice, show projects in some detail. It shows the book value of fixed assets as at 31 Dec. 19_5; capital expenditure during 19_6; the book value of assets disposed of (written off) during 19_6; leaving the book value of assets shown in the balance sheet as at 31 Dec. 19_6.

As explained in Chapter 13 the book values of assets will normally be cost or takeover valuations.

The second statement (S.2) shows how much of the capital expenditure has been fully financed, leaving it debt-free. It shows how much of the capital expenditure had been discharged (or financed) up to the 31 Dec. 19_5; how much, in addition, was discharged during 19_6; how much related to the value of assets written off during 19_6; leaving the amount discharged as shown in the balance sheet as at 31 Dec. 19_6.

The third statement (S.3) shows the "deferred charge" expenditure incurred during the year 19_6; how much has been financed during 19_6 and how much remains to be financed in future years as shown by the balance sheet as at 31 Dec. 19_6.

The fourth statement (S.4) shows the expenditure on current capital projects in greater detail than elsewhere. The figures in this statement are used to build up totals for Statement S.1. Certain projects appear to have been completed, whilst others (marked *) appear to be still under construction.

The next statement (S.5) is a Capital Cash Account which merely records the incoming and outgoing movements of "capital" cash. This does not, of course, give the complete picture of all capital transactions because, as shown in W.P.13, there are certain assets which have been financed and acquired without actual cash being involved. The use of this statement and also the Statement of Capital Cash Balances (S.6) is explained in Section 185 of Chapter 15.

The Statement of Outstanding Loan Debt (S.7 page 683) shows how the loan debt has been built up and repaid.

None of the above statements is a ledger account and they do not form part of the double-entry system. Their purpose is to explain and to exemplify the figures in the balance sheet or to assist in its preparation. Certain of the statements, particularly S.1 - S.4 could quite well be published as appendices to the balance sheet. Others, such as S.5 - S.7 would be more likely to be used for internal management purposes.

192. FINAL ACCOUNTS – CONCLUSION

In presenting these final accounts of Kambale Municipal Council we have tried to make our approach as realistic as possible, whilst at the same time trying to avoid laborious repetition. Realism can only be achieved if we try to visualize the Kambale example not as a mere exercise but as a real town. We have tried to show as many as possible of the real systems and techniques which might be employed by this particular local authority in solving its own particular problems. Other authorities, it must be appreciated, will have different problems and employ different techniques to those we have studied here. However, it is to be hoped that our intensive study of one particular case will give us sufficient insight into the problems involved to enable us to apply the experience gained to the solution of many other problems.

Municipal Accounting for Developing Countries

APPENDICES

KAMBALE MUNICIPAL COUNCIL

FINAL ACCOUNTS 19_6

Appendix A

Trial balance as at 31.12._6 (excluding certain final adjustments)

Appendix B

Selected ledger accounts in detail.

L. 1.	General Revenue (Summary)
L. 2A.	Finance Department Revenue (debit side)
L. 2B.	Finance Department Revenue (credit side)
L. 3.	Health Revenue (Summary)
L. 4A.	Clinics and Dispensaries Revenue (debit side)
L. 4B.	Clinics and Dispensaries Revenue (credit side)
L. 5A.	Markets Revenue (debit side)
L. 5B.	Markets Revenue (credit side)
L. 6.	Markets Capital
L. 7.	Sundry Creditors (Control)
L. 8.	Stores (Control)
L. 9.	Stores Overhead (Holding)
L.10.	Vehicles and Plant (Control)
L.11.	Ratepayers - Rates (Control)
L.12.	Rate Income
L.13.	Market Tenants (Control)
L.14.	Market Rent Income
L.15.	Sundry Taxpayers (Control)
L.16.	Tax Income
L.17.	Tax Income Appropriation
L.18.	Sundry Debtors (Control)
L.19.	Vehicles and Plant Renewals Fund
L.20.	Renewals Fund Investment (VRF)

Appendix C

Remaining ledger accounts in outline only.

L.101.	Loans Outstanding
L.102.	National Government
L.103.	Housing Repairs Fund
L.104.	Office Equipment Renewals Fund
L.105.	Capital Discharged
L.106.	General Fund
L.107.	Capital Expenditure
L.108.	Deferred Charges
L.109.	Payments in Advance
L.110.	Investments (Control)
L.111.	Sundry Debtors (Main Control)
L.112.	Education Revenue
L.113.	General Purposes Revenue
L.114.	Health - Administration Revenue
L.115.	Health - Abattoir Revenue
L.116.	Health - Ambulances Revenue
L.117.	Health - Parks Revenue

Final Accounts

L.118.	Housing Revenue
L.119.	Land Control Revenue
L.120.	Works Revenue
L.121.	Light Plant and Tools Revenue
L.122.	Wages and Labour Overheads (Control)
L.123.	Capital Fund
L.124.	Capital Receipts Unapplied
L.125.	Provision for Bad and Doubtful Debts
L.126.	Sinking Fund
L.127.	Cash (Bank)
L.128.	Cash (Cashiers)
L.129.	Petty Cash

Appendix D

Main Journal.

Appendix E

Published Final Accounts 19_6.

F. 1.	General Fund Revenue Account
F. 2.	General Fund Revenue Account (Alternative)
F. 3.	Consolidated Balance Sheet (Double Account)
F. 4.	Consolidated Balance Sheet (Single Account)

Appendix F

Capital Statements Supporting Final Accounts.

S. 1.	Details of Capital Expenditure
S. 2.	Details of Capital Expenditure Discharged
S. 3.	Details of Deferred Charges
S. 4.	Details of Capital Projects in Progress
S. 5.	Capital Cash Account
S. 6.	Statement of Capital Cash Balances
S. 7.	Statement of Outstanding Loan Debt

Appendix G

Detailed Working Papers.

W.P. 1.	Bank Reconciliation Statement
W.P. 2.	Investments (Rough Calculation)
W.P. 3.	Sundry Creditors (Pen List)
W.P. 4.	Sundry Debtors Summary
W.P. 5.	Investment Interest Allocation
W.P. 6.	Stocktaking List - Main Stores (See Ch.12/P412)
W.P. 7.	General Grant - Ministry Letter
W.P. 8.	Joint Stores/Garage/Workshop Building - Apportionment
W.P. 9.	Stores Overheads Apportionment
W.P.10.	Allocation of Light Plant and Tools
W.P.11.	Sundry Debtors - Analysis of Net Income
W.P.12.	Credit Income - Analysis
W.P.13.	Capital Expenditure - Assets Acquired otherwise than by Cash
W.P.14.	Investments (Final Apportionment)

APPENDIX A

Trial Balance

Final Accounts

KAMBALE MUNICIPAL COUNCIL

Trial Balance as at 31 Dec. 19_6
(Excluding certain final adjustments)

Item	Ledger Folio	Reference	DR U	Cts	CR U	Cts
Opening Balances 1.1._6						
Loans Outstanding	101	C.9/P.285			15,009,300	00
Sundry Creditors	7	C.9/P. "			316,460	00
Receipts in Advance (WP4)	11, 111	C.9/P. "			30,720	00
Government (Graduated Tax)	102	C.9/P. "			144,160	00
Housing Repairs Fund	103	C.9/P. "			63,000	00
Renewals Fund	19, 104	C.9/P. "			85,000	00
Capital Discharged:						
Grants	105	C.9/P. "			1,008,400	00
Takeover Values	105	C.9/P. "			3,000,000	00
Loans Repaid	105	C.9/P. "			1,032,460	00
Revenue Contributions	105	C.9/P. "			243,000	00
General Fund Surplus	106	C.9/P. "			348,720	00
Buildings	107	C.9/P. "	10,093,740	00		
Permanent Works	107	C.9/P. "	9,686,520	00		
Equipment	107	C.9/P. "	512,900	00		
Stocks and Stores	8	C.9/P. "	310,460	00		
Sundry Debtors (WP4)	11, 13, 18, 15	C.9/P. "	110,320	00		
Payments in Advance	109	C.9/P. "	4,840	00		
Investments	20, 110	C.9/P. "	148,000	00		
Revenue Expenditure 19_6						
Education (various items totalling)	112	(note "d" page 630)	1,884,620	00		
Finance Department						
Salaries	2A	C.9/P.292	369,460	00		
Provident Fund	2A	C.9/P. "	31,820	00		
Housing	2A	C.9/P. "	41,200	00		
Wages	2A	C.9/P. "	7,740	00		
Furniture and Fittings	2A	C.9/P. "	6,820	00		
Books and Journals	2A	C.9/P. "	1,860	00		
Sale of Publications (refund)	2A	C.9/P. "	80	00		
Equipment	2A	C.9/P. "	4,180	00		
Vehicle Expenses	2A	C.9/P. "	9,160	00		
Car and Cycle Allowances	2A	C.9/P. "	7,220	00		
		c/fwd	23,230,940	00	21,281,220	00

Municipal Accounting for Developing Countries

Item	Ledger Folio	Reference	DR U	Cts	CR U	Cts
		b/fwd	23,230,940	00	21,281,220	00
Revenue Expenditure 19_6 (cont)						
Other Travelling Allowances	2A	C.9/P.292	720	00		
Printing and Stationery	2A	C.9/P. "	30,720	00		
Advertising	2A	C.9/P. "	2,720	00		
Postages	2A	C.9/P. "	2,100	00		
Telephones	2A	C.9/P. "	6,620	00		
Insurance	2A	C.9/P. "	560	00		
Audit Fee	2A	C.9/P. "	8,780	00		
Study Grants	2A	C.9/P. "	4,220	00		
Cash Security	2A	C.9/P. "	160	00		
Bank Charges (See note "a" + WP1)	2A	C.9/P. "	680	00		
Loan Interest	2A	C.15/P.573	500	00		
General Purposes (various items totalling)	113	(note "d" page 630)	738,760	00		
Health - Administration (various items totalling)	114	(note "e" page 630)	330,200	00		
Health - Abattoir (various items totalling)	115	(note "e" page 630)	83,910	00		
Health - Ambulance (various items totalling)	116	(note "e" page 630)	37,080	00		
Health - Clinics and Dispensaries						
Salaries	4A	C.9/P.294	322,700	00		
Provident Fund	4A	C.9/P. "	22,840	00		
Housing	4A	C.9/P. "	5,120	00		
Wages	4A	C.9/P. "	49,900	00		
Repair and Maintenance of Buildings	4A	C.12/P.439	2,930	00		
Electricity	4A	C.9/P.294	7,880	00		
Water	4A	C.9/P. "	5,160	00		
Cleaning Materials	4A	C.9/P. "	2,240	00		
Rates	4A	C.9/P. "	1,820	00		
Equipment	4A	C.9/P. "	26,180	00		
Drugs and Medical Supplies	4A	C.9/P.294	257,260	00		
		c/fwd	25,182,700	00	21,281,220	00

Final Accounts

Item	Ledger Folio	Reference	DR U	Cts	CR U	Cts
		b/fwd	25,182,700	00	21,281,220	00
Revenue Expenditure 19_6 (cont)						
Uniform	4A	C.9/P.294	5,160	00		
Printing and Stationery	4A	C.9/P. "	3,240	00		
Telephones	4A	C.9/P. "	1,280	00		
Insurance	4A	C.9/P. "	520	00		
Loan Interest	4A	C.9/P. "	16,960	00		
Loan Repayment	4A	C.9/P. "	11,420	00		
Health - Markets						
Salaries	5A	C.9/P.295	66,406	15		
Provident Fund	5A	C.9/P. "	2,605	25		
Wages	5A	C.9/P. "	87,423	90		
Repair and Maintenance of Buildings	5A	C.9/P. "	7,773	45		
Electricity	5A	C.9/P. "	950	20		
Water	5A	C.9/P. "	20,433	80		
Cleaning Materials	5A	C.9/P. "	4,940	45		
Rates	5A	C.9/P. "	35,115	00		
Equipment Maintenance	5A	C.9/P. "	1,946	30		
Uniform	5A	C.9/P. "	2,965	75		
Use of Transport	5A	C.9/P. "	1,015	15		
Printing and Stationery	5A	C.9/P. "	3,315	05		
Insurance	5A	C.9/P. "	990	00		
Loan Interest	5A	C.15/P.561	19,204	95		
Loan Repayment	5A	C.15/P.561	21,574	60		
Health - Parks (various items totalling)	117	(note "e", 630)	424,620	00		
Housing (various items totalling)	118	(note "d", 630)	708,000	00		
Housing Repairs Fund (various items totalling)	103	-	69,415	00		
Land Control (various items totalling)	119	(note "d, page 630)	16,420	00		
Works (various items totalling)	120	(note "d", page 630)	3,025,653	00		
		c/fwd	29,742,048	00	21,281,220	00

Municipal Accounting for Developing Countries

Item	Ledger Folio	Reference	DR U	Cts	CR U	Cts
		b/fwd	29,742,048	00	21,281,220	00
Capital Payments 19_6						
Vacuum Tanker Lorry (S5)	107	C.14/P.491	53,465	00		
Swamp Drainage (S5)	107	C.14/P.497	103,360	00		
Central Car Park (S5)	107	C.14/P.512	95,880	00		
Refuse Vehicle (S5)	107	C.14/P.525	50,380	00		
Clinic (S5)	107	C.14/P.532	183,360	00		
Clinic (Legal Fees) (RCCO) (S5)	107	C.9/P.294	4,120	00		
Bridge Repairs (deferred charge) (S5)	108	C.15/P.537	400,000	00		
Market Extensions - Kibule (S5)	6	C.15/P.563	230,000	00		
Accounting Machine (S5)	107	C.15/P.573	10,000	00		
Capital Fund Investment	110	C.14/P.531	83,140	00		
Premature Loan Repayment (out of Capital Receipts)	101	C.15/P.548	188,700	00		
Roads (S5) (various items totalling)	107	C.9/P.286	940,000	00		
Estates (S5 (various items totalling)	107	C.9/P.286	85,000	00		
Control and Holding Accounts						
Sundry Creditors (Control)	7	-	315,620	00		
National Government	102	C.10/P.355	344,160	00		
Stores (Control)	8	C.12/P.431	106,820	00		
Rate Refunds	11	C.10/P.319	4,860	00		
Water Refunds (WP4)	111	-	420	00		
Motor Advances (Control) (WP4)	111	C.11/P.402	90,000	00		
Personal Advances (Control) (WP4)	111	-	2,140	00		
Renewals Fund (Office Equipment)	104	-	2,480	00		
		c/fwd	33,035,953	00	21,281,220	00

Final Accounts

Item	Ledger Folio	Reference	DR U	Cts	CR U	Cts
		b/fwd	33,035,953	00	21,281,220	00
Control and Holding Accounts (cont)						
Vehicle Running Expenses (pool)						
Wages	10	(note "f" page 630)	66,640	00		
Other Employees Expenses	10	(note "f")	18,980	00		
Petrol	10	(note "f")	67,020	00		
Oil	10	(note "f")	8,540	00		
Tyres	10	(note "f")	28,360	00		
Licences	10	(note "f")	13,240	00		
Repairs	10	(note "f")	61,320	00		
Insurance	10	(note "f")	27,520	00		
Loan Charges	10	(note "f")	122,460	00		
Stores Overhead Expenses						
Wages	9	(note "g", page 630)	6,890	00		
Other Employees Expenses	9	(note "g")	1,847	00		
Repairs to Buildings	9	(note "g")	2,150	00		
Fuel, Light, Cleaning and Water	9	(note "g")	3,336	00		
Furniture and Fittings	9	(note "g")	433	00		
Rates	9	(note "g")	4,625	00		
Protective Clothing	9	(note "g")	132	00		
Printing and Stationery	9	(note "g")	249	00		
Insurance	9	(note "g")	5,375	00		
Loan Charges	9	(note "g")	8,850	00		
Wages and Employees Expenses						
Gross Pay	122	C.13/P.470	831,780	00		
Councils Provident Fund Contributions	122	C.13/P.470	63,360	00		
Personnel Insurance	122	C.13/P. "	5,880	00		
Car Allowances	122	C.13/P. "	2,620	00		
Pension Fund Deficiency	122	C.13/P. "	25,400	00		
Medical Expenses	122	C.13/P. "	2,980	00		
Housing Allowances	122	C.13/P. "	7,480	00		
Light Plant and Tools Purchases	121	C.13/P.480	14,865	00		
		c/fwd	34,438,285	00	21,281,220	00

Municipal Accounting for Developing Countries

Item	Ledger Folio	Reference	DR U	Cts	CR U	Cts
		b/fwd	34,438,285	00	21,281,220	00
Revenue Income 19_6						
Education (various items totalling)	112	(note "d", page 630)			288,200	00
Finance						
Sales of Publications	2B	C.9/P.292			540	00
Miscellaneous	2B	C.9/P.292			2,560	00
General Purpose (various items totalling)	113	(note "d", page 630)			5,860	00
Health - Abattoir (various items totalling)	115	(note "e", page 630)			58,940	00
Health - Markets						
Dues	5B	C.12/P.415			168,320	00
Insurance Premium (Refund)	5A	-			60	00
Health - Parks (various items totalling)	117	(note "e", page 630)			9,420	00
Land Control (various items totalling)	119	(note "d", page 630)			346,040	00
Works (various items totalling)	121	(note "d")			283,140	00
Licences - Miscellaneous	1	C.9/P.291			5,540	00
Investment Income (see note "b") (WP1)	1	C.9/P.291			5,140	00
Grants	1	C.9/P.291			3,000,000	00
Graduated Tax (cash income)	16	C.10/P.354			60,600	00
		c/fwd	34,438,285	00	25,515,580	00

Final Accounts

Item	Ledger Folio	Reference	DR U	Cts	CR U	Cts
		b/fwd	34,438,285	00	25,515,580	00
Capital Receipts 19_6						
Grant - Vacuum Tanker	105	C.14/P.490			53,465	00
Grant - Swamp Drainage	105	C.14/P.498			70,000	00
Loan - Car Park (S7)	101	C.14/P.512			118,000	00
Loan Bridge Repairs (S7)	101	C.15/P.537			400,000	00
Loan - Market Extensions (S7)	101	C.15/P.564			230,000	00
Loan - Accounting Machine (S7)	101	C.15/P.573			10,000	00
Capital Receipt - Sale of old Clinic Building	124	C.15/P.548			210,000	00
Capital Fund - Land Premium	123	C.14/P.531			266,500	00
Loans - Roads and Estates (S7) (various items totalling)	101	C.9/P.287			996,940	00
Control and Holding Accounts						
Ratepayers (Rates) (Control)	11	C.10/P.319			3,850,520	00
Water Consumers (Control) (WP4)	111	-			95,500	00
Housing Tenants (Control) WP4	111	-			482,500	00
Market Tenants (Control)	13	C.10/P.336			118,620	00
Sundry Debtors (Control)	18	C.10/P.330			123,500	00
Trading Licences (Control) (WP4)	111	C.9/P.290			176,400	00
Liquor Licences (Control) (WP4)	111	C.9/P.290			52,620	00
Motor Advances (Control) (WP4)	111	C.11/P.402			36,040	00
Personal Advances (Control) (WP4)	111	-			2,520	00
Sundry Taxpayers (Control)	15	C.10/P.355			313,200	00
Stores (Control)	8	C.12/P.432			122,920	00
Wages (Control)	122	C.13/P.471			723,820	00
Labour Overhead (Holding)	122	C.13/P.471			215,680	00
Vehicles and Plant (Holding)	10	C.12/P.427			456,920	00
Vehicles Renewals Fund - Sales	19	C.15/P.544			1,000	00
Office Equipment Renewals Fund - Sales	104	-			475	00
Sundry Creditors (Control)	7	-			327,980	00
Light Plant and Tools Sales of Scrap	121	C.13/P.480			245	00
Cash on Deposit	110	-	120,000	00		
Cash at Bank (See note "c")	127		408,420	00		
Cash in Hand:						
Cashiers	128	-	3,740	00		
Petty Cash	129	-	500	00		
		c/fwd	34,970,945	00	34,970,945	00

Municipal Accounting for Developing Countries

NOTES:

(a) Increased by further U 740 to U 1,420 after bank reconciliation. (See W.P.1 page 685.)

(b) Increased by further U 5,140 to U 10,280 after bank reconciliation. (See W.P.1.)

(c) Increased by U 5,140 (interest) and reduced by U 740 (bank charges) to give a final figure of U 412,820 after bank reconciliation (See W.P.1.)

(d) Expenditure and income is shown "gross". If appropriate expenditure and income figures are "netted" they will approximate to estimates shown on page 290 of Chapter 9.

(e) Expenditure and income is shown "gross". If appropriate expenditure and income figures are "netted" they will approximate to estimates shown on page 292 of Chapter 9.

(f) After adjustment these figures will total exactly to the expenditure of U 456,920 shown on page 427 of Chapter 12. (See Ledger folio L.10.)

(g) After adjustment these figures will individually equal those shown on page 478 of Chapter 13. (See Ledger folio L.9.)

All references are by chapter and page numbers (eg C.9/P.2 refers to Chapter 9, Page 2).

APPENDIX B

Ledger Accounts (Detailed)

ACCOUNT. General Revenue (Summary)　　　MAIN CODE　　　Folio L.1.

DR

Code	Details	Expenditure Analysis U cts	Income Analysis U cts	Transfers Details	Transfers Amount U cts	Balances (b) or (c) U cts	Total U cts
	Net Expenditure of Committees						
	Education			L.112	1,569,420 00		1,569,420 00
	Finance			L.2B	472,189 00		472,189 00
	General Purposes			L.113	739,960 00		739,960 00
	Health			L.3	1,552,420 00		1,552,420 00
	Housing			L.118	401,280 00		401,280 00
	Works			L.120	2,645,420 00		2,645,420 00
	Contribution to Capital Fund			J.31	40,000 00		40,000 00
	Net Surplus transferred to General Fund			L.106	143,791 00		143,791 00
					7,564,480 00		7,564,480 00

CR

Code	Details	Income Analysis U cts	Expenditure Analysis U cts	Transfers Details	Transfers Amount U cts	Balances (b) or (c) U cts	Total U cts
	Net Income of Committee						
	Land Control			L.119	365,240 00		365,240 00
	General Income Trading						
	Licences			J.25	176,360 00		176,360 00
	Liquor Licences			J.25	52,600 00		52,600 00
	Miscellaneous	5,540 00		J.4	(1,960 00)		5,540 00
	Investment Income	10,280 00		J.5	107,220 00		8,320 00
	Government Grants	3,000,000 00					3,107,220 00
	Rates			J.16	3,849,200 00		3,849,200 00
		3,015,820 00			4,548,660 00		7,564,480 00

ACCOUNT. Finance Department Revenue   MAIN CODE   Folio L.2A.

Code	EXPENDITURE Details	Expenditure Analysis U cts	Income Analysis U cts	Transfers Details	Transfers Amount U cts	Balances (b) or (c) U cts	Total U cts
	EMPLOYEES						
	Salaries	369,460 00					369,460 00
	Provident Fund and Gratuities	31,820 00					31,820 00
	Housing	41,200 00					41,200 00
	Wages	7,740 00					7,740 00
	PREMISES						
	Furniture and Fittings	6,820 00					6,820 00
	SUPPLIES AND SERVICES						
	Books and Journals	1,860 00					1,860 00
	Equipment	4,180 00					4,180 00
	TRANSPORT						
	Vehicle Expenses	9,160 00					9,160 00
	Car and Cycle Allowances	7,220 00					7,220 00
	Other Travelling Allowances	720 00				(c)(720 00)	
	ESTABLISHMENT EXPENSES						
	Printing and Stationery	30,720 00		J.3	560 00		31,280 00
	Advertising	2,720 00		J.3	120 00		2,840 00
	Postages	2,100 00					2,100 00
	Telephones	6,620 00					6,620 00
	Insurance	560 00					560 00
	MISCELLANEOUS EXPENSES						
	Audit Fee	8,780 00					8,780 00
	Study Grants	4,220 00					4,220 00
	Cash Security	160 00					160 00
	Bank Changes (see note (a) page)	1,420 00					1,420 00
	LOAN CHARGES						
	Interest	500 00					500 00
	Principal			J.29	2,000 00		2,000 00
		537,980 00			2,680 00	(c) (720 00)	539,940 00

Folio L.2B.

ACCOUNT. Finance Department Revenue   MAIN CODE

CR

Code	INCOME Details	Income Analysis U cts	Expenditure Analysis U cts	Transfers Details	Transfers Amount U cts	Balances (b) or (c) U cts	Total U cts
	Graduated Tax - Agency Fees	540 00		J.23	67,231 00		67,231 00
	Sales of Publications	2,560 00	(80 00)	J.1	(2,500 00)		460 00
	Miscellaneous						60 00
	Net Expenditure transferred to Summary			L.1	472,189 00		472,189 00
		3,100 00	(80 00)		536,920 00		539,940 00

Folio L.3.

ACCOUNT. Health Revenue (Summary)   MAIN CODE

Code	Details	Expenditure Analysis U cts	Income Analysis U cts	Transfers Details	Transfers Amount U cts	Balances (b) or (c) U cts	Total U cts
	Net Expenditure on Services:						
	Administration			L.114	330,860 00		330,860 00
	Abattoir			L.115	26,440 00		26,440 00
	Ambulances			L.116	38,680 00		38,680 00
	Clinics and Dispensaries			L.4B	746,100 00		746,100 00
	Parks			L.117	418,060 00		418,060 00
					1,560,140 00		1,560,140 00

CR

Code	Details	Income Analysis U cts	Expenditure Analysis U cts	Transfers Details	Transfers Amount U cts	Balances (b) or (c) U cts	Total U cts
	Net Income on Services Markets			L.5A	7,720 00		7,720 00
	Net Expenditure transferred to Summary			L.1	1,552,420 00		1,552,420 00
					1,560,140 00		1,560,140 00

Folio L.4A.

ACCOUNT. Clinics and Dispensaries Revenue

MAIN CODE _____

DR Code	EXPENDITURE Details	Expenditure Analysis U	cts	Income Analysis U	cts	Transfers Details	Amount U	cts	Balances (b) or (c) U	cts	Total U	cts
	EMPLOYEES											
	Salaries	322,700	00								322,700	00
	Provident Fund	22,840	00								22,840	00
	Housing	5,120	00								5,120	00
	Wages	49,900	00								49,900	00
	PREMISES											
	Repair and Maintenance of Buildings	2,930	00			J.3	50	00			2,980	00
	Electricity	7,880	00								7,880	00
	Water	5,160	00								5,160	00
	Cleaning Materials	2,240	00			J.8	160	00			2,400	00
	Rates	1,820	00								1,820	00
	SUPPLIES AND SERVICES											
	Equipment	26,180	00								26,180	00
	Drugs and Medical Supplies	257,260	00			J.2	(840	00)			256,420	00
	Uniform	5,160	00								5,160	00
	ESTABLISHMENT EXPENSES											
	Printing and Stationery	3,240	00								3,240	00
	Telephones	1,280	00								1,280	00
	Insurance	520	00								520	00
	LOAN CHARGES											
	Interest	16,960	00								16,960	00
	Principal	11,420	00								11,420	00
	REVENUE CONTRIBUTIONS TO CAPITAL OUTLAY					J.27	4,120	00			4,120	00
		742,610	00				3,490	00			746,100	00

Folio 4B

Code	Details	Income Analysis		Expenditure Analysis		Transfers			Balances (b) or (c)		Total		CR
		U	cts	U	cts	Details	Amount U	cts	U	cts	U	cts	
	Net Expenditure transferred to Summary					L.3	746,100	00			746,100	00	
		=========	===	=========	===	=========	746,100	00	=========	===	746,100	00	

Folio L.5A.

ACCOUNT. Market Revenue   MAIN CODE

DR Code	EXPENDITURE Details	Expenditure Analysis U cts	Income Analysis U cts	Transfers Details	Transfers Amount U cts	Balances (b) or (c) U cts	Total U cts
	EMPLOYEES						
	Salaries	66,406 15					66,406 15
	Provident Fund	2,605 25					2,605 25
	Wages	87,423 90					87,423 90
	PREMISES						
	Repair and Maintenance of Buildings	7,773 45		J.8	2,360 00)		10,493 45
	Electricity	950 20					950 20
	Water	20,433 80		J.3	2,360 00)		20,433 80
	Cleaning Materials	4,940 45		J.8	420 00		5,360 45
	Rates	35,115 00					35,115 00
	SUPPLIES AND SERVICES						
	Equipment Maintenance	1,946 30					1,946 30
	Uniform	2,965 75					2,965 75
	TRANSPORT						
	Use of Transport	1,015 15					1,015 15
	ESTABLISHMENT EXPENSES						
	Printing and Stationery	3,315 05					3,315 05
	Insurance	990 00	(60 00)				930 00
	LOAN CHARGES						
	Interest	19,204 95					19,204 95
	Principal	21,574 60					21,574 60
	Net Income transferred to Summary			L.3	7,720 00		7,720 00
		276,660 00	(60 00)		10,860 00		287,460 00

638

Folio L.5B.

ACCOUNT. Markets Revenue   MAIN CODE

CR

INCOME		Income Analysis		Expenditure Analysis		Transfers			Balances (b) or (c)		Total	
Code	Details	U	cts	U	cts	Details	U	cts	U	cts	U	cts
	Rents										119,140	00
	Dues	168,320	00			J.18	119,140	00			168,320	00
		168,320	00				119,140	00			287,460	00

639

Folio L.6.

ACCOUNT. Markets Capital MAIN CODE

DR

Code	Details	Expenditure Analysis U cts	Income Analysis U cts	Transfers Details	Transfers Amount U cts	Balances (b) or (c) U cts	Total U cts
	Kibule Market	230,000 00				(b) 95,000 00	325,000 00
	Kitoro Market					(b) 141,000 00	141,000 00
	Busira Market					(b) 135,000 00	135,000 00
		230,000 00				371,000 00	601,000 00

CR

Code	Details	Income Analysis U cts	Expenditure Analysis U cts	Transfers Details	Transfers Amount U cts	Balances (b) or (c) U cts	Total U cts
	Kibule Market					(c) 325,000 00	325,000 00
	Kitoro Market					(c) 141,000 00	141,000 00
	Busira Market					(c) 135,000 00	135,000 00
						601,000 00	601,000 00

N.B. This is an example of the many detailed accounts which are represented in the summary shown as folio L.107 in appendix "C" page

Folio L.7.

ACCOUNT. Sundry Creditors (Control)

MAIN CODE

DR

Code	Details	Expenditure Analysis U / cts	Income Analysis U / cts	Transfers Details	Transfers Amount U / cts	Balances (b) or (c) U / cts	Total U / cts
	Cash and Adjustments	315,620 00		J.2	840 00		316,460 00
	Balance Carried Forward					(c) 367,240 00	367,240 00
		315,620 00			840 00	(c) 367,240 00	683,700 00

CR

Code	Details	Income Analysis U / cts	Expenditure Analysis U / cts	Transfers Details	Transfers Amount U / cts	Balances (b) or (c) U / cts	Total U / cts
	Balance Brought Forward					(b) 316,460 00	316,460 00
	Sundry Accounts Invoices paid Jan. 19_7	243,880 00					243,880 00
	Invoices accrued Jan. 19_7 Pen List	84,100 00		J.3	39,260 00		84,100 00 / 39,260 00
		327,980 00			39,260 00	(b) 316,460 00	683,700 00

641

Folio L.8.

ACCOUNT. Stores (Control)   MAIN CODE

DR

Code	Details	Expenditure Analysis U	cts	Income Analysis U	cts	Transfers Details	Amount U	cts	Balances (b) or (c) U	cts	Total U	cts
	Balance Brought Forward								(b) 310,460	00	310,460	00
	Purchases	106,820	00								106,820	00
		106,820	00						(b) 310,460	00	417,280	00

CR

Code	Details	Income Analysis U	cts	Expenditure Analysis U	cts	Transfers Details	Amount U	cts	Balances (b) or (c) U	cts	Total U	cts
	Issues (Net)	122,920	00								122,920	00
	Deficiency (Net)					J.6	520	00			520	00
	Balance Carried Forward								(c) 293,840	00	293,840	00
		122,920	00				520	00	(c) 293,840	00	417,280	00

Folio L.9.

ACCOUNT. Stores Overhead (Holding)　　　　**MAIN CODE**

DR

Code	Details	Expenditure Analysis U cts	Income Analysis U cts	Transfers Details	Transfers Amount U cts	Balances (b) or (c) U cts	Total U cts
	EMPLOYEES						
	Wages	6,890 00					6,200 00
	Other Employees Expenses	1,847 00					1,847 00
	RUNNING EXPENSES						
	Repairs to Buildings	2,150 00		J.7	(690) 00		
	Fuel Light Cleaning and Water	3,336 00		J.7	(1,290) 00		860 00
	Furniture and Fittings	433 00					2,346 00
	Rates	4,625 00		J.7	(990) 00		433 00
	Protective Clothing	132 00					1,850 00
	Printing and Stationery	249 00					132 00
	Insurance	5,375 00		J.7	(3,225) 00		249 00
	Deficiency			J.6	1,425 00		2,150 00
	LOAN CHARGES	8,850 00		J.7	(5,310) 00		1,425 00
							3,540 00
		33,887 00			(12,855) 00		21,032 00

CR

Code	Details	Income Analysis U cts	Expenditure Analysis U cts	Transfers Details	Transfers Amount U cts	Balances (b) or (c) U cts	Total U cts
	Surplus			J.6	905 00		905 00
	Recharges to Services			J.8	20,127 00		20,127 00
					21,032 00		21,032 00

643

Folio L.10.

ACCOUNT. Vehicles and Plant (Control)

MAIN CODE

DR

Code	Details	Expenditure Analysis U cts	Income Analysis U cts	Transfers Details	Transfers Amount U cts	Balances (b) or (c) U cts	Total U cts
	EMPLOYEES						
	Wages	66,640 00					66,640 00
	Other Employees Expenses	18,980 00					18,980 00
	PREMISES						
	Apportionment of Garage			J.7	14,280 00		14,280 00
	OTHER RUNNING EXPENSES						
	Petrol	67,020 00		J.3	4,240 00		71,260 00
	Oil	8,540 00					8,540 00
	Tyres	28,360 00		J.3	2,820 00		31,180 00
	Licences	13,240 00					13,240 00
	Repairs	61,320 00					61,320 00
	Contribution to Renewals Fund			J.11	1,100 00)		21,500 00
				J.10	20,400 00)		
	ESTABLISHMENT EXPENSES						
	Insurance	27,520 00					27,520 00
	LOAN CHARGES	122,460 00					122,460 00
		414,080 00			42,840 00		456,920 00

CR

Code	Details	Income Analysis U cts	Expenditure Analysis U cts	Transfers Details	Transfers Amount U cts	Balances (b) or (c) U cts	Total U cts
	Recharges to Services	456,920 00					456,920 00
		456,920 00					456,920 00

Folio L.11.

ACCOUNT. Ratepayers Rates (Control)   MAIN CODE

DR

Code	Details	Expenditure Analysis U	cts	Income Analysis U	cts	Transfers Details	Transfers Amount U	cts	Balances (b) or (c) U	cts	Total U	cts
	Balance Brought Forward								(b) 23,220	00	23,220	00
	Rate Income: Site Rates					J.14	2,699,580	00			2,699,580	00
	Improvement Rates					J.14	1,165,700	00			1,165,700	00
	Penalties					J.14	4,940	00			4,940	00
	Balance Carried Forward								(c) 8,380	00	8,380	00
							3,870,220	00	(b) 23,220 (c) 8,380	00 00	3,901,820	00

CR

Code	Details	Income Analysis U	cts	Expenditure Analysis U	cts	Transfers Details	Transfers Amount U	cts	Balances (b) or (c) U	cts	Total U	cts
	Balance Brought Forward								(b) 13,540	00	13,540	00
	Cash	3,850,520	00			J.1	2,500	00			3,848,160	00
	Allowances			(4,860	00)	J.15	21,020	00			21,020	00
	Balance Carried Forward								(c) 19,100	00	19,100	00
		3,850,520	00	(4,860	00)		23,520	00	(b) 13,540 (c) 19,100	00 00	3,901,820	00

645

Folio L.12.

ACCOUNT. Rate Income

MAIN CODE

DR

Code	Details	Expenditure Analysis U	cts	Income Analysis U	cts	Transfers Details	Transfers Amount U	cts	Balances (b) or (c) U	cts	Total U	cts
	Allowances					J.15	7,240	00			7,240	00
	Appeals					J.15	11,880	00			11,880	00
	Voids					J.15	1,900	00			1,900	00
	Other											
	Net Rate Income transferred to General Revenue Account					J.16	3,849,200	00			3,849,200	00
							3,870,220	00			3,870,220	00

CR

Code	Details	Income Analysis U	cts	Expenditure Analysis U	cts	Transfers Details	Transfers Amount U	cts	Balances (b) or (c) U	cts	Total U	cts
	Gross Rate Income					J.14	2,699,580	00			2,699,580	00
	Site Rates											
	Improvements Rates					J.14	1,165,700	00			1,165,700	00
	Penalties					J.14	4,940	00			4,940	00
							3,870,220	00			3,870,220	00

Folio L.13.

ACCOUNT. Market Tenants (Control)   MAIN CODE

DR

Code	Details	Expenditure Analysis U cts	Income Analysis U cts	Transfers Details	Transfers Amount U cts	Balances (b) or (c) U cts	Total U cts
	Balance Brought Forward					(b) 3,020 00	3,020 00
	Rent Due			J.17	120,000 00		120,000 00
					120,000 00	(b) 3,020 00	123,020 00

CR

Code	Details	Income Analysis U cts	Expenditure Analysis U cts	Transfers Details	Transfers Amount U cts	Balances (b) or (c) U cts	Total U cts
	Cash	118,620 00					118,620 00
	Allowances			J.17	860 00		860 00
	Balance Carried Forward					(c) 3,540 00	3,540 00
		118,620 00			860 00	3,540 00	123,020 00

647

Folio L.14.

ACCOUNT. Market Rent Income   MAIN CODE

DR

Code	Details	Expenditure Analysis U | cts	Income Analysis U | cts	Transfers Details	Transfers Amount U | cts	Balances (b) or (c) U | cts	Total U | cts
	Allowances - Voids			J.17	860 00		860 00
	Markets Revenue Account - Net Rent			J.18	119,140 00		119,140 00
					120,000 00		120,000 00

CR

Code	Details	Income Analysis U | cts	Expenditure Analysis U | cts	Transfers Details	Transfers Amount U | cts	Balances (b) or (c) U | cts	Total U | cts
	Gross Rent Income			J.17	120,000 00		120,000 00
					120,000 00		120,000 00

Folio L.15.

ACCOUNT. Summary Taxpayers (Control)   MAIN CODE

DR

Code	Details	Expenditure Analysis U cts	Income Analysis U cts	Transfers Details	Transfers Amount U cts	Balances (b) or (c) U cts	Total U cts
	Basic Assessments			J.19	284,500 00		284,500 00
	Additional Assessments			J.19	63,300 00		63,300 00
					347,800 00		347,800 00

CR

Code	Details	Income Analysis U cts	Expenditure Analysis U cts	Transfers Details	Transfers Amount U cts	Balances (b) or (c) U cts	Total U cts
	Cash						
	Basic	266,700 00					266,700 00
	Additional	46,500 00					46,500 00
	Allowances						
	Basic			J.20	3,600 00		3,600 00
	Additional			J.20	400 00		400 00
	Balance Carried Forward						
	Basic					(c) 14,200 00	14,200 00
	Additional					(c) 16,400 00	16,400 00
		313,200 00			4,000 00	(c) 30,600 00	347,800 00

Folio L.16.

ACCOUNT. Tax Income   MAIN CODE

DR

Code	Details	Expenditure Analysis U cts	Income Analysis U cts	Transfers Details	Transfers Amount U cts	Balances (b) or (c) U cts	Total U cts
	Sundry Taxpayers – Allowances Basic Additional			J.20 J.20	3,600 00 400 00		3,600 00 400 00
	Provision for Bad and Doubtful Debts Basic Additional			J.21 J.21	7,100 00 13,120 00		7,100 00 13,120 00
	Tax Income Appropriation			J.22	384,180 00		384,180 00
					408,400 00		408,400 00

CR

Code	Details	Income Analysis U cts	Expenditure Analysis U cts	Transfers Details	Transfers Amount U cts	Balances (b) or (c) U cts	Total U cts
	Sundry Taxpayers Basic Additional Cash	60,600 00		J.19 J.19	284,500 00 63,300 00		284,500 00 63,300 00 60,600 00
		60,600 00			347,800 00		408,400 00

650

Folio L.17.

ACCOUNT. Tax Income Appropriation   MAIN CODE

DR

Code	Details	Expenditure Analysis U cts	Income Analysis U cts	Transfers Details	Transfers Amount U cts	Balances (b) or (c) U cts	Total U cts
	National Government Finance Department Revenue Account			J.23	316,949 00		316,949 00
				J.23	67,231 00		67,231 00
					384,180 00		384,180 00

CR

Code	Details	Income Analysis U cts	Expenditure Analysis U cts	Transfers Details	Transfers Amount U cts	Balances (b) or (c) U cts	Total U cts
	Tax Income			J.22	384,180 00		384,180 00
					384,180 00		384,180 00

651

Folio L.18.

ACCOUNT. Sundry Debtors (Control) MAIN CODE _____

DR

Code	Details	Expenditure Analysis U | cts	Income Analysis U | cts	Transfers Details	Transfers Amount U | cts	Balances (b) or (c) U | cts	Total U | cts
	Balance Brought Forward					(b) 23,040 | 00	23,040 | 00
	Sundry Income Due			J.24	126,360 | 00		126,360 | 00
					126,360 | 00	(b) 23,040 | 00	149,400 | 00

CR

Code	Details	Income Analysis U | cts	Expenditure Analysis U | cts	Transfers Details	Transfers Amount U | cts	Balances (b) or (c) U | cts	Total U | cts
	Cash	123,500 | 00					123,500 | 00
	Allowances			J.24	1,580 | 00		1,580 | 00
	Balance Carried Forward					(c) 24,320 | 00	24,320 | 00
		123,500 | 00			1,580 | 00	(c) 24,320 | 00	149,400 | 00

Folio L.19.

ACCOUNT. Vehicles and Plant Renewals Fund

MAIN CODE

DR

Code	Details	Expenditure Analysis U	cts	Income Analysis U	cts	Transfers Details	Amount U	cts	Balances (b) or (c) U	cts	Total U	cts
	Finance of Purchases					J.30	50,380	00			50,380	00
	Balance Carried Forward								(c) 37,745	00	37,745	00
							50,380	00	(c) 37,745	00	88,125	00

CR

Code	Details	Income Analysis U	cts	Expenditure Analysis U	cts	Transfers Details	Amount U	cts	Balances (b) or (c) U	cts	Total U	cts
	Balance Brought Forward								(b) 62,500	00	62,500	00
	Contributions					J.11	1,100	00			1,100	00
	Interest					J.10	20,400	00			20,400	00
						J.4	3,125	00			3,125	00
	Sales of Assets	1,000	00								1,000	00
		1,000	00				24,625	00	(b) 62,500	00	88,125	00

653

Folio L.20.

ACCOUNT. Renewals Fund Investment (VRF)   MAIN CODE

DR

Code	Details	Expenditure Analysis U cts	Income Analysis U cts	Transfers Details	Transfers Amount U cts	Balances (b) or (c) U	Total U cts
	Balance Brought Forward					(b) 62,500 00	62,500 00
						(b) 62,500 00	62,500 00

CR

Code	Details	Income Analysis U cts	Expenditure Analysis U cts	Transfers Details	Transfers Amount U cts	Balances (b) or (c) U	Total U cts
	Net Withdrawal Balance Carried Forward			J.38	24,755 00	(c) 37,745 00	24,755 00 37,745 00
					24,755 00	(c) 37,745 00	62,500 00

APPENDIX C

Ledger Accounts (Outline Only)

Municipal Accounting for Developing Countries

Loans Outstanding — 101

19_6				19_6			
Dec.31	To Expenditure Analysis		188,700	Jan. 1	By Balance	b/f	15,009,300
	To Sundry Accounts	J.36	1,158,160	Dec.31	By Income Analysis*		1,754,940
	To Balance	c/f	15,491,480		By Capital Expenditure	J.35	74,100
			16,838,340				16,838,340

* Details shown in appendix "F" statement S.7.

National Government — 102

19_6				19_6			
Dec.31	To Expenditure Analysis		344,160	Jan. 1	By Balance	b/f	144,160
	To Balance	c/f	116,949	Dec.31	By Tax Income Appropriation	J.23	316,949
			461,109				461,109

Housing Repairs Fund — 103

19_6				19_6			
Dec.31	To Expenditure Analysis		69,415	Jan. 1	By Balance	b/f	63,000
	To Sundry Creditors	J.3	8,240	Dec.31	By Investment Interest	J.4	3,150
	To Stores Overheads	J.8	860		By Housing Revenue	J.13	177,000
	To Balance	c/f	164,635				
			243,150				243,150

Final Accounts

Office Equipment Renewals Fund — 104

19_6				19_6			
Dec.31	To Expenditure Analysis		2,480	Jan. 1	By Balance	b/f	22,500
	To Balance	c/f	26,620	Dec.31	By Income Analysis		475
					By Investment Interest	J.4	1,125
					By Contribution	J.12	5,000
			29,100				29,100

Capital Discharged (S2) — 105

19_6				19_6			
Dec.31	To Capital Expenditure	J.33	176,300	Jan. 1	By Balance	b/f	5,283,860
	To Capital Expenditure	J.37	39,100	Dec.31	By Income Analysis Grants*		123,465
	To Balance	c/f	6,838,825		By Revenue Contribution	J.27	4,120
					By Revenue Contribution	J.28	8,680
*Vacuum Tanker 53,465					By Contribution from VRF	J.30	50,380
Swamp Drainage 70,000					By Contribution from Capital Fund	J.32	183,360
123,465					By Capital Expenditure	J.35	322,200
					By Loans Repaid	J.35	1,078,160
			7,054,225				7,054,225

General Fund 106

19_6 Dec.31	To Balance	c/f	492,511	19_6 Jan. 1	By Balance	b/f	348,720
				Dec.31	By Net Surplus Transferred from General Revenue Account	L.106	143,791
			492,511				492,511

Capital Expenditure (S1) 107

19_6 Jan. 1	To Balance (S1)	b/f	20,293,160	19_6 Dec.31	By Sundry Accounts (S1)	J.33	365,000
Dec.31	To Expenditure Analysis* (S4)		1,755,565		By Capital Discharged (S1)	J.37	39,100
	To Sundry Accounts (S4)	J.35	396,300		By Balance (S1)	c/f	22,040,925
			22,445,025				22,445,025

```
* Details                    U
  shown in
  appendix "F"
  Statement
  S.5:
     Total Payments    2,155,565
Less Deferred Charge     400,000
                       ─────────
                       1,755,565
                       =========
```

Deferred Charges (S3) 108

19_6 Dec.31	To Expenditure Analysis		400,000	19_6 Dec.31	By Capital Receipts	J.34	188,700
	To Capital Expenditure	J.33	188,700		By Loans Repaid	J.36	80,000
					By Balance	c/f	320,000
			588,700				588,700

Final Accounts

Payments in Advance — 109

Date	Particulars	Folio	Amount	Date	Particulars	Folio	Amount
19_6 Jan. 1	To Balance	b/f	4,840	19_6 Dec. 31	By Sundry Accounts	J.26	4,840
			4,840				4,840

Investments (Control) (Items Not Included Elsewhere) — 110

Date	Particulars	Folio	Amount	Date	Particulars	Folio	Amount
19_6 Jan. 1	To Balance	b/f	85,500	19_6 Dec. 31	By Balance	c/f	313,395
Dec. 31	To Expenditure Analysis		83,140				
	To Expenditure Analysis		120,000				
	To Vehicle Renewals Fund	J.38	24,755				
			313,395				313,395

Sundry Debtors (Main Control) (Items Not Included Elsewhere) — 111

Date	Particulars	Folio	Amount	Date	Particulars	Folio	Amount
19_6 Jan. 1	To Balance	b/f	61,040	19_6 Jan. 1	By Balance	b/f	17,180
Dec. 31	To Expenditure Analysis*		92,560	Dec. 31	By Income Analysis*		845,580
	To Motor Advances Interest	J.4	5,440		By Sundry Accounts	J.25	2,400
	To Government Grant	J.5	107,220		By Balance	c/f	227,580
	To Sundry Accounts	J.25	808,700				
	To Balance	c/f	17,780				
			1,092,740				1,092,740

* Details shown in appendix "G" statement W.P.4.

Education Revenue — 112

19_6 Dec.31				19_6 Dec.31			
	To Expenditure Analysis		1,884,620		By Income Analysis		288,200
	To Sundry Creditors	J.3	4,380		By Sundry Debtors	J.24	32,220
	To Stores Overheads	J.8	840		By Net Expenditure Transferred to Summary	L.1	1,569,420
			1,889,840				1,889,840

General Purposes Revenue — 113

19_6 Dec.31				19_6 Dec.31			
	To Expenditure Analysis		738,760		By Income Analysis		5,860
	To Sundry Creditors	J.3	6,540		By Sundry Debtors	J.24	8,480
	To Office Equipment Renewals Fund	J.12	5,000		By Net Expenditure Transferred to Summary	L.1	739,960
	To Payment in Advance	J.26	4,000				
			754,300				754,300

Health - Administration Revenue — 114

19_6 Dec.31				19_6 Dec.31			
	To Expenditure Analysis		330,200		By Net Expenditure Transferred to Summary	L.3	330,860
	To Sundry Creditors	J.3	660				
			330,860				330,860

Final Accounts

		Health - Abattoir Revenue						115
19_6 Dec.31	To Expenditure Analysis			83,910	19_6 Dec.31	By Income Analysis By Net Expenditure Transferred to Summary		58,940
	To Sundry Creditors	J.3		840				
	To Stores Overheads	J.8		630			L.3	26,440
				85,380				85,380

		Health - Ambulances Revenue						116
19_6 Dec.31	To Expenditure Analysis			37,080	19_6 Dec.31	By Net Expenditure Transferred to Summary		
	To Sundry Creditors	J.3		1,320			L.3	38,680
	To Stores Overheads	J.8		280				
				38,680				38,680

		Health - Parks Revenue						117
19_6 Dec.31	To Expenditure Analysis			424,620	19_6 Dec.31	By Income Analysis By Net Expenditure Transferred to Summary		9,420
	To Stores Overheads	J.8		2,020				
	To Payments in Advance	J.26		840			L.3	418,060
				427,480				427,480

		Housing Revenue				118
19_6 Dec.31	To Expenditure Analysis		708,000	19_6 Dec.31	By Rent Income	J.25	483,720
	To Housing Repairs Fund	J.13	177,000		By Net Expenditure Transferred to Summary	L.1	401,280
			885,000				885,000

		Land Control Revenue				119
19_6 Dec.31	To Expenditure Analysis		16,420	19_6 Dec.31	By Income Analysis		346,040
	To Net Income Transferred to Summary	L.1	365,240		By Sundry Debtors	J.24	35,620
			381,660				381,660

		Works Revenue				120
19_6 Dec.31	To Expenditure Analysis		3,025,653	19_6 Dec.31	By Income Analysis		283,140
	To Sundry Creditors	J.3	7,130		By Sundry Debtors	J.24	48,460
	To Stores Overheads	J.8	14,557		By Water Consumers	J.25	93,620
	To Light Plant and Tools	J.9	14,620		By Net Expenditure Transferred to Summary	L.1	2,645,420
	To Revenue Contribution	J.28	8,680				
			3,070,640				3,070,640

Final Accounts

Light Plant and Tools (Holding) — 121

19_6				19_6			
Dec.31	To Expenditure Analysis		14,865	Dec.31	By Income Analysis		245
					By Recharges to Services	J.9	14,620
			14,865				14,865

Wages and Labour Overheads (Control) — 122

19_6				19_6			
Dec.31	To Expenditure Analysis*		939,500	Dec.31	By Recharges to Services		723,820
					By Recharges to Services		215,680
			939,500				939,500

```
* Gross Pay                831,780
  Provident Fund            63,360
  Personnel Insurance        5,880
  Car Allowances             2,620
  Pension Fund
    Deficiency              25,400
  Medical Expenses           2,980
  Housing Allowances         7,480
                           939,500
```

Capital Fund — 123

19_6				19_6			
Dec.31	To Capital Discharged	J.32	183,360	Dec.31	By Income Analysis		266,500
	To Balance	c/f	123,140		By General Revenue	J.31	40,000
			306,500				306,500

Municipal Accounting for Developing Countries

		Capital Receipts Unapplied				124
19_6 Dec.31	To Deferred Charges	J.34	188,700	19_6 Dec.31	By Income Analysis	210,000
	To Balance	c/f	21,300			
			210,000			210,000
			======			======

		Provision for Bad and Doubtful Debts				125
19_6 Dec.31	To Balance	c/f	20,220	19_6 Dec.31	By Tax Income J.21	20,220
			20,220			20,220
			======			======

		Sinking Fund				126
19_6 Dec.31	To Balance	c/f	2,000	19_6 Dec.31	By Finance Department Revenue J.29	2,000
			2,000			2,000
			=====			=====

Final Accounts

Cash (Bank) — 127

Date	Description			Amount	Date	Description			Amount
19_6 Jan. 1	To Balance	b/f		410,780	19_6 Jan.–Dec.	By Various Cheque and Direct Payments during year in the form shown on page 363 of Chapter 11			13,989,280
Jan.–Dec.	To Various Deposits during year in the form shown on page 347 of Chapter 10		128	13,986,420	Dec. 31	By Balance	c/d		407,920
				14,397,200					14,397,200
Dec. 31	To Balance	b/d		407,920	Dec. 31	By Bank Charges			740
	To Deposit Account Interest			5,140		By Balance	c/f		412,320
				413,060					413,060

Cash (Cashiers) — 128

Date	Description			Amount	Date	Description			Amount
19_6 Jan. 1	To Balance	b/f		3,160	19_6 Jan.–Dec.	By Various Deposits (as shown in C & D book of type illustrated on page 345 of Chapter 10)	127		13,986,420
Jan.–Dec.	To Various Collections (as shown in C & D book of type illustrated on page 345 of Chapter 10)			13,987,000	Dec. 31	By Balance	c/f		3,740
				13,990,160					13,990,160

Petty Cash — 129

Date	Description			Amount	Date	Description			Amount
19_6 Jan. 1	To Balance	b/f		500	19_6 Dec. 31	By Balance	c/f		500

APPENDIX D
Main Journal

Final Accounts

JOURNAL

Date	Particulars	Folio	U	Cts	U	Cts

19_6 Dec.31	**Entry No.1**
	Finance Department
	   Revenue DR.
	     To Ratepayers Rates
	        (Control)
	Being adjustment of misal-
	location in income analysis
	- disagreement with rate-
	book summary on W.P.4 page
	688.
		L.2B
		
		L.11
			2,500	-	2,500	-

Dec.31	**Entry No.2**
	Sundry Creditors
	   (Control) DR.
	     To Clinics and Dispensary
	        Revenue
	Being adjustment of mis-
	allocation in expenditure
	analysis - disagreement
	with creditors list 19_5
		L.7
		
		L.4A
			840	-	840	-

Dec.31	**Entry No.3**
	Sundry Accounts DR.
	     To Sundry Creditors
	        (Control)
	Being allocation of addi-
	tional creditors from pen
	list as shown in W.P.3
	page 687.
		V
		
		L.7
			39,260	-	39,160	-

Dec.31	**Entry No.4**
	Motor Advances DR.
	General Revenue DR.
	     To Housing Repairs Fund
	     To Vehicles Renewals Fund
	     To Office Equipment
	        Renewals Fund
	Being allocation of
	investment interest as
	shown by W.P.5
		L.111
		L.1
		L.103
		L.19
		
		J.104
			5,440
			1,960
				-
				-
					
					3,150
					3,125
					
					1,125
						-
						-
						-

Dec.31	**Entry No.5**
	Ministry of Local
	   Government DR.
	     To Government Grants
	Being balance of grant due
	for financial year as shown
	by Ministry letter dated
	14/1/_7 (file G.123)
	(copy W.P.7)
		L.111
		L.1
			107,220	-	107,220	-

Dec.31	**Entry No.6**
	Stores Overhead (Holding) DR.
	     To Stores Overhead
	        (Holding)
	     To Stores (Control)
	Being transfer of surplus
	and deficiencies as shown
	by stocktaking list (W.P.6)
		L.9
		
		L.9
		L.8
			1,425	-	
					
					905
					520
						-
						-

Date	Particulars		Folio	Dr.		Cr.	

19_6 Dec.31	**Entry No.7**
	Vehicles and Plant
	  (Control) DR.
	  To Stores Overhead
	    (Holding)
	Being apportionment of costs for garaging of vehicles as shown by W.P.8
			L.10
			
			L.9
				14,280	−	
						
						14,280
							
							−

Dec.31	**Entry No.8**
	Sundry Accounts DR.
	  To Stores Overhead
	    (Holding)
	Being apportionment of net stores overheads as shown by W.P.9
			V
			
			L.9
				20,127	−	
						
						20,127
							
							−

Dec.31	**Entry No.9**
	Works Revenue
	  Sundry Accounts DR.
	  To Light Plant and Tools
	Being allocation of net expenditure on light plant and tools as shown by W.P.10
			L.120
			L.121
				14,620	−	
						14,620
							
							−

Dec.31	**Entry No.10**
	Vehicles and Plant
	  (Control) DR.
	  To Vehicles and Plant
	    Renewals Fund
	Being annual contribution to provide replacement cost of U 51,000 in respect of each of two refuse vehicles over a life of 5 years (see Chapter 14 page 525)
			L.10
			
			L.19
				20,400	−	
						
						20,400
							
							−

Dec.31	**Entry No.11**
	Vehicles and Plant
	  (Control) DR.
	  To Vehicles and Plant
	    Renewals Fund
	Being vehicle expenses over-recovered, now transferred to Renewals Fund
			L.10
			
			L.19
				1,100	−	
						
						1,100
							
							−

Dec.31	**Entry No.12** General Purposes Revenue DR. To Office Equipment Renewals Fund Being annual contributions for replacement cost of U 20,000 over 4 years		L.113 L.104	5,000	−	 5,000	 −
Dec.31	**Entry No.13** Housing Revenue DR. To Housing Repairs Fund Being annual contribution for 295 houses at U 600 per house		L.118 L.103	177,000	−	 177,000	 −

Final Accounts

19_6						
Dec.31	**Entry No.14** Ratepayers Rates (Control) DR. To Rate Income Being gross income transferred as shown in detail in rate book summary. (See Chapter 10 page 320)	L.11 L.12	3,870,220	-	3,870,220	-

Dec.31	**Entry No.15**
	Rate Income DR.
	  To Ratepayers Rates
	    (Control)
	Being allowances transferred as shown in detail in rate book summary. (See Chapter 10 page 320)
		L.12
		L.11
			21,020	-	21,020	-

Dec.31	**Entry No.16** Rate Income DR. To General Fund Revenue Being net income transferred	L.12 L.1	3,849,200	-	3,849,200	--

Dec.31	**Entry No.17**
	Market Tenants (Control) DR.
	Market Rent Income DR.
	  To Market Rent Income
	  To Market Tenants (Control)
	Being gross rent and allowances transferred as shown in detail in market rental (See Chapter 10 page 335)
		L.13
		L.14
		L.14
		L.13
			120,000
			860
				-
				-
					120,000
					860
						-
						-

Dec.31	**Entry No.18** Market Rent Income DR. To Markets Revenue Being net income transferred	L.14 L.5B	119,140	-	119,140	-
Dec.31	**Entry No.19** Sundry Taxpayers (Control) DR. To Tax Income Being gross income transferred as shown in detail in tax register summaries. (See Chapter 10 page 354)	L.15 L.16	347,800	-	347,800	-

Dec.31	**Entry No.20**
	Tax Income DR.
	  To Sundry Taxpayers
	    (Control)
	Being allowances transferred as shown in detail in tax register summaries. (See Chapter 10 page 354)
		L.16
		L.15
			4,000	-	4,000	-

Date	Entry	Ref	Dr		Cr	

19_6 Dec.31	**Entry No.21**
	Tax Income DR.
	  To Provision for Bad and
	    Doubtful Debts
	Being 50% of arrears on basic assessments U 14,200 and 80% of arrears on additional assessments U 16,400 now set aside as provision against non-settlement
		L.16
		L.125
			20,220	-	20,220	-

Dec.31	**Entry No.22** Tax Income DR. To Tax Income Appropriation Being net income transferred	L.16 L.17	384,180	-	384,180	-

Dec.31	**Entry No.23**
	Tax Income Appropriation DR.
	  To National Government
	  To Finance Department
	    Revenue Account
	Being appropriation of net income in the ratio prescribed by the Minister
	  National Government 82½%
	  Kambale Municipal
	    Council 17½%
		L.17
		L.102
		
		L.2B
			84,180	-	316,949
					67,231
						-

Dec.31	**Entry No.24**
	Sundry Debtors (Control) DR.
	  To Sundry Debtors (Control)
	  To Sundry Accounts
	Being allocation of net income as shown by W.P.11
		L.18
		L.18
			126,360	-	1,580
					124,780
						-
						-

Dec.31	**Entry No.25**
	Sundry Debtors (Main
	  Control) DR.
	  To Sundry Debtors (Main
	    Control)
	  To Sundry Accounts
	Being allocation of net income as shown by W.P.12
		L.111
		
		L.111
			808,700	-	2,400
					806,300
						-
						-

Dec.31	**Entry No.26** General Purposes Revenue DR. Parks Revenue DR. To Payments in Advance Being 19_6 expenditure paid in 19_5 now charged to revenue	L.113 L.117 L.109	4,000 840	-	4,840	-

Dec.31	**Entry No.27**
	Clinics and Dispensaries
	  Revenue DR.
	  To Capital Discharged (RCCO)
	Being Revenue Contribution to Capital Outlay to meet legal fees on Clinic (see estimate on page 293 of Chapter 9 - remaining expenditure met from Capital Fund - See Chapter 14 page 531)
		L.4A
		L.105
			4,120	-	4,120	-

Final Accounts

Date	Particulars	Folio	Dr.		Cr.	
19_6 Dec.31	**Entry No.28** Works Revenue　　　　　DR. 　To Capital Discharged (RCCO) 　Being Revenue Contribution 　to Capital Outlay to meet 　overspending on Sewage 　Disposal Works as shown by 　Capital Register (See 　Chapter 15 page 554) 　Finance Committee resolution 　No........... refers 　(See Chapter 15 page 558)	L.120 L.105	8,680	-	8,680	-
Dec.31	**Entry No.29** Finance Department Revenue DR. 　To Sinking Fund 　Being first annual contrib- 　ution to repay 5-year 　maturity loan of U 10,000 　for purchase of accounting 　machine (See Chapter 15 　page 574)	L.2A L.126	2,000	-	2,000	-
Dec.31	**Entry No.30** Vehicles and Plant Renewals Fund　　　　　　　　　DR. 　To Capital Discharged 　　(V.R.F.) 　Being contribution to 　finance purchase of refuse 　vehicle (URT 495) (See 　Chapter 14 page 417)	L.19 L.105	50,380	-	50,380	-
Dec.31	**Entry No.31** General Fund Revenue　　DR. 　To Capital Fund 　Being annual contribution 　for 19_6 (See Chapter 14 　page 532)	L.1 L.123	40,000	-	40,000	-
Dec.31	**Entry No.32** Capital Fund　　　　　　DR. 　To Capital Discharged 　　(Capital Fund) 　Being construction of Clinic 　now financed from Capital 　Fund (See Chapter 14 page 　531)	L.123 L.105	183,360	-	183,360	-
Dec.31	**Entry No.33** Capital Discharged (Loan 　Repaid)　　　　　　　DR. Deferred Charge　　　　DR. 　To Capital Expenditure 　Being Clinic at .... 　disposed of on 18/10/_6 and 　now written out 　(See Chapter 15 page 548)	L.105 L.108 L.107	176,300 188,700	- -	365,000	-

19_6
Dec.31
	Entry No.34
	Capital Receipts
	  (Unapplied) DR.
	  To Deferred Charge
	Being application of capital receipts to elimination of deferred charge
	(See Chapter 15 page 531)
		L.124
		L.108
			188,700	–	188,700	–

Dec.31	**Entry No.35**
	Capital Expenditure DR.
	  To Capital Discharged
	  To Loans Outstanding
	Being assets acquired otherwise than by cash now written into the books together with loan debt taken over as shown by W.P.13
		L.107
		L.105
		L.101
			396,300	–	322,200
					74,100
						–
						–

Dec.31	**Entry No.36**
	Loan Outstanding DR.
	  To Capital Discharged
	    (Loans Repaid)
	  To Deferred Charges
	Being appropriation of principal repayments of loan charges to discharge of capital expenditure and writing off deferred charges
		L.101
		
		L.105
		L.108
			1,158,160	–	1,078,160
					80,000
						–
						–

Dec.31	**Entry No.37** Capital Discharged (Loan Repaid) DR. To Capital Expenditure Being refuse vehicle (No...) purchased in 19_2 disposed of for scrap on 30/9/_6 (See Chapter 15 page 546)	J.105 J.107	39,100	–	39,100	–
Dec.31	**Entry No.38** Investments (Control) DR. To Renewals Fund Investment (VRF) Being adjustment of investments as shown by W.P.14	L.110 L.20	24,755	–	24,755	–

NOTE

Where the symbol "V" appears, it indicates that various accounts (folios) have been posted, from the working papers.

APPENDIX E

Published Final Accounts 19_6

F.1.

KAMBALE MUNICIPAL COUNCIL

General Fund Revenue Account for Year Ended 31 Dec. 19_6

Expenditure	Units	Income	Units
Net Expenditure of Committees (L1)		Net Income of Committees (L1)	
Education	1,569,420	Land Control	365,240
Finance	472,189		
General Purposes	739,960		
Health	1,552,420		
Housing	401,280		
Works	2,645,420		
Contribution to Capital Fund (L1)	40,000	General Income (L1)	
		Trading Licences	176,360
		Liquor Licences	52,600
		Miscellaneous Licences	5,540
		Investment Income	8,320
		Government Grants	3,107,220
		Rates	3,849,200
Balance - being surplus of income over expenditure carried to general fund (L1)	143,791		
	7,564,480		7,564,480
	=========		=========

General Fund (L106)

Balance carried forward	492,511	Balance brought forward	348,720
		Surplus for year	143,791
	492,511		492,511
	=========		=========

Final Accounts

F.2.

KAMBALE MUNICIPAL COUNCIL

General Fund Revenue Account for Year Ended 31 Dec. 19_6

	Gross Expenditure Units	Income Units	Net Expenditure Units
Committee			
Education	1,889,840	320,420	1,569,420
Finance	539,940	67,751	472,189
General Purposes	754,300	14,340	739,960
Health	1,560,140	7,720	1,552,420
Housing	885,000	483,720	401,280
Land Control	16,420	381,660	(365,240)
Works	3,070,640	425,220	2,645,420
	8,716,280	1,700,831	7,015,449
Add			
Contribution to Capital Fund			40,000
			7,055,449
Less			
General Income:			
Trading Licences		176,360	
Liquor Licences		52,600	
Miscellaneous Licences		5,540	
Investment Income		8,320	
Grants		3,107,220	
Rates		3,849,200	7,199,240
Net Surplus for year			143,791
Add			
Accumulated Surplus Brought Forward			348,720
Accumulated Surplus Carried Forward		U	492,511

F.3.

KAMBALE MUNICIPAL COUNCIL

Balance Sheet as at 31 Dec. 19_6

Capital

	Units		Units
Long Term Liabilities		Fixed Assets (L107)	
Loans Outstanding (L101)	15,491,480	Buildings	10,584,220
Current Liabilities		Permanent Works	10,825,760
Cash Overdrawn (L127)	9,320	Equipment	630,945
Capital Discharged (L105)		Current Assets	
Grants	1,131,865	Investments	
Takeover Values	3,251,900	Capital Fund (L110)	123,140
Loans Repaid	1,895,220	Sinking Fund (L110)	2,000
Revenue Contributions	255,800	Deferred Charges (L108)	320,000
Renewals Funds	50,380		
Capital Fund	183,360		
Gifts	70,300		
Capital Fund (L123)	123,140		
Capital Receipts Unapplied			
(L124)	21,300		
Sinking Fund (L126)	2,000		
	----------		----------
	22,486,065		22,486,065
	----------		----------

Revenue

	Units		Units
Current Liabilities		Current Assets	
Creditors (L7)	367,240	Stocks and Stores (L8)	293,840
Receipts in Advance		Debtors (L11,13,14,	
(L11, 111)	26,160	18,111) 305,140	
National Government (L102)	116,949	Less Provisions	
Provisions		for Bad	
Housing Repairs Fund (L103)	164,635	Debts (L125) 20,220	
Vehicles Renewals Fund (L19)	37,745		284,920
Office Equipment Renewals		Payments in Advance (L2A)	720
Fund (L104)	26,620	Investments	
General Revenue Surplus		Housing Repairs Fund	
(L106)	492,511	(L110)	161,635
		Vehicles Renewals Fund	
		(L20)	37,745
		Office Equipment Renewals	
		Fund (L110)	26,620
		Cash	
		At Bank (L127) (WP1)	422,140
		In Hand (L128 + 129)	4,240
	----------		----------
	1,231,860		1,231,860
	----------		----------
	23,717,925		23,717,925
	==========		==========

F.4.

KAMBALE COUNCIL

Balance Sheet as at 31 Dec. 19_6_

	Units	Units		Units	Units
Long Term Liabilities			**Fixed Assets**		
Loans Outstanding		15,491,480	Buildings	10,584,220	
			Permanent Works	10,825,760	
			Equipment	630,945	22,040,925
Current Liabilities					
Creditors*	367,240		**Current Assets**		
Sundry Creditors	26,160		Stocks and Stores	293,840	
Receipts in Advance	116,949		Debtors*		
Government		510,349	Sundry Debtors	284,920	
			Payments in Advance	720	
			Investments*	351,140	
			Cash in Hand*	417,060	1,347,680
Provisions					
Repairs Funds	164,635		**Other Balances**		
Renewals Funds	64,365	229,000	Deferred Charges		320,000
Other Balances					
Capital Discharged	6,838,825		*Statement showing division of		
Capital Fund	123,140		items between Capital and Revenue		
Capital Receipts Unapplied	21,300				
Sinking Fund	2,000				
Revenue Account Surplus	492,511	7,477,776			
		23,708,605			23,708,605
		==========			==========

	Capital	Revenue
	Units	Units
Cash	(9,320)	426,380
Debtors	-	285,640
Creditors	-	510,349
Investments	125,140	226,000

677

APPENDIX F

Capital Statements Supporting Final Accounts

Final Accounts

S.1.

DETAILS OF CAPITAL EXPENDITURE

At 31 Dec. 19_5		Expenditure during year	Written-off during year	Total at 31 Dec. _6
10,093,740	Buildings (various items totalling)	855,480	365,000	10,584,220
9,686,520	Permanent Works (various items totalling)	1,139,240	-	10,825,760
512,900	Equipment (various items totalling)	157,145	39,100	630,945
20,293,160	(See L107 page 658)	2,151,865	404,100	22,040,925

S.2.

DETAILS OF CAPITAL EXPENDITURE DISCHARGED

At 31 Dec. 19_5		Expenditure discharged during year	Written-off during year	Total at 31 Dec. _6
1,032,460	Loans Repaid	1,078,160	215,400	1,895,220
1,008,400	Grants Applied	123,465	-	1,131,865
3,000,000	Takeover Values	251,900	-	3,251,900
-	Capital Funds Applied	183,360	-	183,360
-	Renewals Funds Applied	50,380	-	50,380
-	Gifts	70,300	-	70,300
243,000	Revenue Contributions to Capital Outlay	12,800	-	255,800
5,283,860	(See L105 Page 657)	1,770,365	215,400	6,838,825

S.3.

DETAILS OF DEFERRED CHARGES

At 31 Dec. 19_5		Expenditure during year	Written-off during year	Total at 31 Dec. _6
-	Repairs expenditure met from loans	400,000	80,000	320,000
-	Unexpired loan debt on assets disposed of	188,700	188,700	-
-	(See L108 page 658)	588,700	268,700	320,000

Municipal Accounting for Developing Countries

S.4.

DETAILS OF CAPITAL PROJECTS IN PROGRESS

	Expenditure during year	Total Expenditure at 31 Dec. 19_6
Buildings		
Market Extensions	230,000	230,000
Housing Estates - Staff	85,000	85,000*
Clinic	187,480	187,480
Dispensaries	190,000	190,000
Medical Store	27,000	27,000
Sports Stadium	136,000	136,000
	855,480	855,480
Permanent Works (e.g. page 288)		
Car Park	95,880	115,260*
Roads - Church Road Re-alignment	50,000	448,000
- North Street/Park Road - New Road	890,000	890,000*
Swamp Drainage	103,360	103,360*
	1,139,240	1,556,620
Equipment		
Accounting Machine	10,000	10,000
Vacuum Tanker Lorry	53,465	53,465
Refuse Vehicle	50,380	50,380
Ambulance	43,300	43,300
	157,145	157,145
	2,151,865	2,569,245

* Final cost of the project has not yet been charged in the accounts

Reconciliation

Total Payments (S5) excluding deferred charge	1,755,565	
Add Property at Valuation	353,000	
Ambulance at Valuation	43,300	
	2,151,865	2,151,865
Add Car Park Balances Overspent 31.12.19_5 (S5)		19,380
Church Road Expenditure to 31.12.19_5 (e.g. page 279)		398,000
		2,569,245

S.5.

Final Accounts

CAPITAL CASH ACCOUNT FOR YEAR ENDED 31 DEC. 19_6

RECEIPTS		PAYMENTS	
Loans Raised		**Capital Expenditure**	
Car Park	118,000	Car Park	95,880
Bridge Repairs	400,000	Bridge Repairs	400,000
Market Extensions	230,000	Market Extensions	230,000
Account Machine	10,000	Accounting Machines	10,000
Roads and Estates		Roads and Estates	
(various items totalling)	996,940	(various items totalling)	1,025,000
	---------	Vacuum Tanker Lorry	53,465
	1,754,940	Swamp Drainage	103,360
	---------	Refuse Vehicle	50,380
Capital Receipts		Clinic	183,360
Grants	123,465	Clinic (legal fees)	4,120
Sales of Fixed Assets	210,000		---------
Land Premi	266,500		2,155,565
	---------		---------
	599,965		

Fund Contributions		**Repayments**	
Contributions towards		Premature repayment of	
Capital Expenditure		loans out of capital	
from:		receipts	188,700
Revenue Account	12,800		---------
Renewals Fund	50,380	**Investments Bought**	
Contributions from Revenue		Capital Fund	123,140
Account into:		Sinking Fund	2,000
Capital Funds	40,000		---------
Sinking Funds	2,000		125,140
	---------		---------
	105,180		

	2,460,085		2,469,405
Cash overdrawn at 31 Dec.			
19_6 carried forward	9,320		
	2,469,405		2,469,405

NOTE:

Although there was no net cash balance brought forward on 1 Jan. 19_6 the position of individual capital accounts was as follows:

Balances Overspent:	
Car Park (Chapter 14 page 512)	19,380
Sewage Works (Chapter 15 page 558)	8,680
	28,060
Less Balances Underspent:	
Roads and Estates	28,060
Net Balance	NIL

S.6.

STATEMENT OF CAPITAL CASH BALANCES
AS AT 31 DEC. 19_6

Details	Cash Balances	
	In Hand	Overdrawn
Capital Schemes in Progress		
Car Park*	2,740	-
Bridge Repairs	-	-
Market Extensions	-	-
Accounting Machine	-	-
Roads and Estates (various items totalling)	-	-
Vacuum Tanker Lorry	-	-
Swamp Drainage (Chapter 14 page 494)	-	33,360
Sewage Works	-	-
Refuse Vehicle	-	-
Clinic	-	-
Sports Stadium	-	-
Dispensaries	-	-
Medical Store	-	-
Ambulance	-	-
SUB TOTALS	2,740	33,360

Other Capital Funds

Fund or Account	Total Balance	Invested		
Capital Fund	123,140	123,140	-	-
Capital Receipts Unapplied (L124)	21,300	-	21,300	-
Sinking Fund	2,000	2,000	-	-
SUB TOTALS			24,040	33,360
Balance Overdrawn (S5)			9,320	-
TOTALS			33,360	33,360

```
* CAR PARK
    Balance Overspent 31.12.19_5 (S5)      19,380
    Capital Payments (S5)                  95,880
                                          -------
                                          115,260
    Loans Raised (S7)                     118,000
                                          -------
                    Capital Cash in Hand    2,740
                                          =======
```

Final Accounts

S.7.

STATEMENT OF OUTSTANDING LOAN DEBT

	Loans Outstanding as at 1.1._6		15,009,300
Add	Loans Raised:		
	Car Park	118,000	
	Bridge Repairs	400,000	
	Market Extensions	230,000	
	Accounting Machine	10,000	
	Roads and Estates	996,940	1,754,940
			16,764,240
Add	Loan Debt Taken Over:		
	Stadium		74,100
			16,838,340
Less	Loans Repaid:		
	Premature Repayment		
	(out of capital receipts)	188,700	
	Annual Loan Charges		
	(principal repayments)	1,158,160	1,346,860
	Loans Outstanding as at 31.12_6		15,491,480

APPENDIX G

Working Papers

Final Accounts

W.P.1.

BANK RECONCILIATION

PRELIMINARY STATEMENT

Bank Balance (in hand) as per statement			420,360
Add Deposits not yet cleared		920	
Add Payments not in Cash Book:			
Bank Charges (2nd half year)		740	1,660
			422,020
Less Unpresented Cheques (list attached)		8,460	
Less Receipts not in Cash Book:			
Deposit Account Interest (2nd half year)		5,140	13,600
Bank Balance (in hand) as per Cash Book			408,420

FINAL STATEMENT

Bank Balance (in hand) as per statement		420,360
Add Deposits not yet cleared		920
		421,280
Less Unpresented Cheques		8,460
Bank Balance (in hand) as per Cash Book		412,820
Revenue Cash	422,140	
Less Capital Cash (Overdrawn)	9,320	
Net Cash	412,820	

W.P.2.

INVESTMENTS (ROUGH CALCULATION)

	Housing Repairs Fund	Vehicles Renewals Fund	Office Equipment Renewals Fund	Capital Fund	Sinking Fund	Total
	Units	Units	Units	Units	Units	Units
Balance 1.1._6	63,000	62,500	22,500	-	-	148,000
Contributions	177,000	20,400	5,000	40,000	2,000	244,400
Interest @ 5%	3,150	3,125	1,125	-	-	7,400
Sales	-	1,000	475	-	-	1,475
Other Income	-	-	-	266,500	-	266,500
	243,150	87,025	29,100	306,500	2,000	667,775
Less Expenditure	80,000*	50,380	2,480	183,360	-	316,220
Estimated Fund Balances 31.12_6	163,150	36,645	26,620	123,140	2,000	351,555
Less Investments already held:						
Opening Balances	63,000	62,500	22,500	-	-	148,000
Made during year	-	-	-	83,140	-	83,140
Net Additional Investment Required	100,150	25,855*	4,120	40,000	2,000	120,415
	(L.110)	(L.20)	(L.110)	(L.110)	(L.110)	

* Estimate

Transfer sum of (say) U 120,000 (L.110) to deposit account on 23/12/_6.

Final Accounts

W.P.3.

\multicolumn{8}{c}{KAMBALE MUNICIPAL COUNCIL Estimated Creditors 19_6}
Date	Name	Details	Account to be Debited	Amount	Ledger Folio	Date Paid
				Units		
(Various)	(Various)	(Various)	Education (Various totalling)	4,380	112	
13.11._6	Kambale Printers	Account Forms	Finance - Printing and Stationery	560	2A	
8.12._6	Kambale Argus	Advertisement - Accounts Clerk	Finance - Advertising	120	2A	
(Various)	(Various)	(Various)	General Purposes (Various totalling)	6,540	113	
(Various)	(Various)	(Various)	Health - Admin (Various totalling)	660	114	
(Various)	(Various)	(Various)	Health - Abattoir (Various totalling)	840	115	
(Various)	(Various)	(Various)	Health - Ambulance (Various totalling)	1,320	116	
13.12._6	Builders Ltd	Window Fitting	Health - Clinics Repair and Maintenance of Buildings	50	4A	
11.10._6	Constructors Ltd	Rendering Wall at Kitoro Market	Health - Markets Repair and Maintenance of Buildings	2,360	5A	
(Various)	(Various)	(Various)	Housing Repairs Fund (Various totalling)	8,240	103	
(Various)	(Various)	(Various)	Works (Various totalling)	7,130	120	
31.12._6	National Oils Ltd	Petrol for Vehicles	Vehicles - Petrol	4,240	10	
14.11._6	Kambale Tyres Ltd	Tyres for Vehicles	Vehicles - Tyres	2,820	10	
				39,260		

W.P.14.

INVESTMENTS FINAL APPORTIONMENT

	Total	Housing Repairs Fund	Vehicle Renewals Fund	Office Equipment Renewals Fund	Capital Fund	Sinking Fund
	Units	Units	Units	Units	Units	Units
Balance 1/1/_6 (Fund Balances wholly invested)	148,000	63,000	62,500	22,500	-	-
Add Net Increases in Fund Balances	230,895	101,635	-	4,120	123,140	2,000
	378,895	164,635	62,500	26,620	123,140	2,000
Less Net Decreases in Fund Balances	24,755	-	24,755	-	-	-
Fund Balances 31/12/_6	354,140	164,635	37,745	26,620	123,140	2,000
Investments at 31/12/_6 reallocated over Funds	351,140	161,635	37,745	26,620	123,140	2,000
Balance Uninvested (allocated to Housing Repairs Fund)	3,000	3,000	-	-	-	-

Revenue	226,000
Capital	125,140
	351,140

688

Final Accounts

W.P.5.

Investment Interest

	Cash Credited to Current Account		10,280
Add	Transfer from Motor Advances (W.P.4)		5,440
			15,720
Less	Transfers to other funds*		
	Housing Repairs	3,150	
	Vehicles Renewals	3,125	
	Office Equipment Renewals	1,125	7,400
	Balance to General Revenue		8,320

*At rate of 5% on balances at 1/1/_6.

Transfer

	Balance in General Revenue	10,280
Less	Correct Allocation (as above)	8,320
	Net Transfer to other Accounts	1,960

(Transferred by J.4)

W.P.6.

MAIN STORES STOCKTAKING 31/12._6									
Ref	Material	Size	Quantity		Price	Value	Adjustments		
			Actual	Book			Deficit		Surplus
					U	U	Q	U	Q	U
A/1	Acid - Sulphuric	(pints)	55	53	1	55			2	2
A/2	Angles - Steel	2"	14	14	20	280				
	(etc)					(etc)		(etc)		(etc)
C/32	Cover Boxes		109	108	15	1,635			1	15
	(etc)					(etc)		(etc)		(etc)
F/9	Ferrules	1½"	21	22	65	1,365	1	65		
	(etc)					(etc)		(etc)		(etc)
S/23	Stopcocks	1½"	17	17	80	1,360				
	(etc)					(etc)		(etc)		(etc)
						U 293,840		U 1,425		U 905
						NET DEFICIT		U 520		

Municipal Accounting for Developing Countries

W.P.7.

Ref G/895/A.6　　　　　　　　　　Ministry of Local Government
　　　　　　　　　　　　　　　　　PO Box 4037
　　　　　　　　　　　　　　　　　(capital city)

　　　　　　　　　　　　　　　　　　　　　14 January 19_7

The Chief Executive Officer,
Kambale Municipal Council,
PO Box 165,
Kambale.

Dear Sir,

　　　　　　　　　　　General Grant

I am directed by the Minister to inform you that the general grants due to local authorities for the financial year 19_6 have now been finally determined.

The amount due to your Council has been calculated as U 3,107,220.

According to my records, the sum of U 3,000,000 has been paid to your Council by instalments during 19_6 on account. If you will be kind enough to confirm your agreement of the above figures I will arrange for the final balance of U 107,220 to be paid to your Council without delay.

Two copies of this letter are enclosed for the use of the Chief Financial Officer.

　　　　　　　　　　　　　　　　　Yours faithfully,

　　　　　　　　　　　　　　　　　M. Musoke

　　　　　　　　　　　　　　　　　(M. Musoke)
　　　　　　　　　　　　　　　　　for PERMANENT SECRETARY.

Journalise U 107,220 (J.5).

Final Accounts

W.P.8.

JOINT STORES/GARAGE/WORKSHOP BUILDING

APPORTIONMENT OF COSTS

Expenditure	Basis of Charge for Vehicles	Total Cost	Vehicles (Garage)	Stores (Overheads)
		Units	Units	Units
Wages	10%	6,890	690	6,200
Other Employees Expenses	-	1,847	-	1,847
Repairs to Buildings	60%	2,150	1,290	860
Fuel Light etc	Meter	3,336	990	2,346
Furniture and Fittings	-	433	-	433
Rates	60%	4,625	2,775	1,850
Protective Clothing	-	132	-	132
Printing and Stationery	-	249	-	249
Insurance	60%	5,375	3,225	2,150
Deficiency (NET)	-	520	-	520
Loan Charges	60%	8,850	5,310	3,540
		34,407	14,280	20,127

W.P.9.

STORES OVERHEADS

APPORTIONMENT

Service	Stores Issues Expenditure	Overhead at 16.3741%	Folio
Education (Various totalling)	5,130	840	L.112
Abattoir (Various totalling)	3,848	630	L.115
Ambulances (Various totalling)	1,710	280	L.116
Clinics and Dispensaries			
Cleaning Materials	977	160	L. 4A
Markets			
Repair and Maintenance of Buildings	2,199	360	L. 5A
Cleaning Materials	2,565	420	L. 5A
Parks (Various totalling)	12,337	2,020	L.117
Housing (Various totalling)	5,252	860	L.103
Works (Various totalling)	88,902	14,557	L.120
	122,920	20,127	

Municipal Accounting for Developing Countries

W.P.10.

WORKS COMMITTEE

Allocation of Expenditure on Light Plant and Tools

Service	Direct Wages	L.P. & T. @ 2.02%
Land Drainage	41,587	840
Refuse Disposal	119,812	2,420
Roads	120,307	2,430
Sewage Disposal	75,749	1,530
Sewerage	141,595	2,860
Street Lighting	52,975	1,070
Surface Water Drainage	75,253	1,520
Water Supply	96,542	1,950
	723,820	14,620

W.P.11.

SUNDRY DEBTORS

ANALYSIS OF NET INCOME

Income Head	Gross Income	Allow-ances	Net Income	Folio
Education (Various items totalling)	33,000	780	32,220	L.112
General Purposes (Various items totalling)	8,480	–	8,480	L.113
Land Control (Various items totalling)	35,940	320	35,620	L.119
Works (Various items totalling)	48,940	480	48,460	L.120
	126,360	1,580	124,780	

W.P.14.

INVESTMENTS FINAL APPORTIONMENT

	Total	Housing Repairs Fund	Vehicle Renewals Fund	Office Equipment Renewals Fund	Capital Fund	Sinking Fund
	Units	Units	Units	Units	Units	Units
Balance 1/1/_6 (Fund Balances wholly invested)	148,000	63,000	62,500	22,500	-	-
Add Net Increases in Fund Balances	230,895	101,635	-	4,120	123,140	2,000
	378,895	164,635	62,500	26,620	123,140	2,000
Less Net Decreases in Fund Balances	24,755	-	24,755	-	-	-
Fund Balances 31/12/_6	354,140	164,635	37,745	26,620	123,140	2,000
Investments at 31/12/_6 reallocated over Funds	351,140	161,635	37,745	26,620	123,140	2,000
Balance Uninvested (allocated to Housing Repairs Fund)	3,000	3,000	-	-	-	-
Revenue	226,000					
Capital	125,140					
	351,140					

693

W.P.12.

CREDIT INCOME

ANALYSIS OF CREDIT INCOME NOT INCLUDED ELSEWHERE

Type of Income	Account	Gross Income	Allow-ances	Net Income	Folio
Water Consumers	Works Revenue	94,360	740	93,620	L.120
Housing Rents	Housing Revenue	485,380	1,660	483,720	L.118
Trading Licences	General Revenue	176,360	-	176,360	L.1
Liquor Licences	General Revenue	52,600	-	52,600	L.1
		808,700	2,400	806,300	

W.P.13.

CAPITAL EXPENDITURE

Statement of Assets Acquired Otherwise than by Cash

Asset	Amount	Source of Finance	Amount
1. Dispensaries	190,000	1. Takeover from Central Government	190,000
2. Medical Store	27,000	2. Voluntary Labour	27,000
3. Ambulance	43,300	3. Gift from UNICEF	43,300
4. Sports Stadium	136,000	4. (a) Takeover from National Sports Council	61,900
		(b) Loan Debt Taken Over	74,100
	396,300		396,300

These transactions are fully explained in Chapter 14, see page 503 for items 1 - 3 and page 523 for item 4.

17. Internal Borrowing

Section		Page
193.	Internal Borrowing - Introduction.	696
194.	Application of Internal Borrowing to Local Authorities.	698
195.	Availability of Funds.	698
196.	Use of Reserves for New Capital Project.	699
197.	Raising of Internal Loan.	700
198.	Repayment of Internal Loan.	704
199.	Integration of Accounting Procedures.	706
200.	Internal Borrowing - Conclusion.	714

193. INTERNAL BORROWING - INTRODUCTION

Most public authorities find it necessary to raise loans for capital expenditure. Some authorities will have surplus balances on special funds, such as repairs and renewals funds. A large part of the surplus balances may have been invested to earn interest, until required for their intended purpose. An authority might well be investing (i.e. lending) at the same time that it is borrowing. Furthermore, the rate of interest earned on its investments may be lower than that paid for its loans.

The position of such an authority would be like a small trader who has a special business reserve fund of U 10,000 set aside for future business expansion and also to meet certain unforeseen expenditure. It is held as a bank deposit earning interest at 4%. He then raises a loan for U 10,000 from a building society at 6% to buy himself a house. Why does he not use his bank deposit to finance the purchase of his house? Although losing 4% investment interest he would save 6% loan interest, a net saving of 2% per annum. The answer is in his need for liquidity. If he uses his bank deposit to buy the house, the whole of the reserve fund is tied up in bricks and mortar. The balance sheet of the fund would be, in effect:

	Units		Units
Reserve Fund	10,000	House	10,000

By raising the loan he is able to obtain the house and still retain his bank balance from which to meet those items of unforeseen business expenditure which the reserve fund is intended to finance. The balance sheet, in this case would show:

	Units		Units
Loan Debt	10,000	House	10,000
Reserve Fund	10,000	Bank Deposit	10,000
	20,000		20,000

Assume that the building society loan is for 10 years, repayable by equal quarterly instalments of principal (U 250) from business earnings. Let us further suppose that pending business expansion, the man expects the average annual disbursements from his reserve fund, for the time being, to be no more than (say) U 1,000. How could he arrange his affairs differently, so as to save the 2% interest and at the same time always have sufficient liquidity in his reserve fund to meet his

Internal Borrowing

disbursements? The answer lies in what is called internal borrowing. Instead of using his business bank deposit for buying his house he merely borrows it. This means that the U 10,000 bank deposit is spent on the purchase of the house, but that the man commits himself to rebuilding the bank deposit by (say) equal quarterly instalments of U 250 out of his business earnings. If the bank deposit had not been appropriated for the purchase of the house it would have earned interest for the business at the rate of 4%. To build up the bank deposit, at least to the figure it would have reached had it been left undisturbed, a sum equivalent to interest on the outstanding "loan" must be paid into the deposit account. This is in addition to the U 250 quarterly repayments of the principal sum. As the bank deposit builds up, it will earn interest from the bank in the usual way, but nothing like the amount it would have earned had it been left undisturbed. It is to compensate for this that the man must increase his deposits to represent "interest" on the money he has "borrowed" from his own business - in effect from himself. During the first year, he will have paid U 1,000 into the deposit account as repayment of principal. In addition, he would have further increased the deposit by "interest" at (say) 4% per annum (ie 1% per quarter). This would be U 385 calculated as follows:

```
         1st Quarter  1% on U 10,000  =   100.00
         2nd Quarter  1% on U  9,750  =    97.50
         3rd Quarter  1% on U  9,500  =    95.00
         4th Quarter  1% on U  9,250  =    92.50
                                      U  385.00
                                         ======
```

The bank will also pay interest at (say) 4%. If, for simplicity, the "compound" aspect is ignored, this will amount to U 15 as follows:

```
         2nd Quarter  1% on U 250  =   2.50
         3rd Quarter  1% on U 500  =   5.00
         4th Quarter  1% on U 750  =   7.50
                                   U  15.00
                                      =====
```

Thus the interest equivalent paid by the man (U 385) plus the interest paid by the bank (U 15) equals U 400, which is 4% on the U 10,000 "borrowed". This compensates exactly for the loss of bank deposit interest.

At the end of the first year his bank deposit would have reached U 1,400, which would be adequate to cover his estimated disbursements (U 1,000). The rate of interest he chose to set aside upon his "internal loan" logically should be between 4% and 6%. Choosing 4% (as shown above) would exactly compensate his business for the loss of interest on the full original amount of the deposit and "save" him (personally) 2% when compared with the loan from the building society. Choosing 6% would cost the same amount from his annual earnings as the building society loan but would enable his "internal investment" to earn 2% more interest for the business than could be earned on a bank deposit. Choosing a rate between the two limits would give greater or lesser effect to each of these objectives. He must decide upon a single rate of interest, after considering his position, both as the proprietor of his business and as the private borrower from it. Whatever rate of interest he decides to pay (as borrower) his business will receive (as lender). Since, in law, the private financial transactions of a sole proprietor cannot usually be divorced from those of his business, he is, in effect, merely transferring money from one pocket to another.

The overall financial position of the man (i.e. his surplus of assets over liabilities) remains unchanged as a result of the various manipulations of figures. His "reserve fund" remains at **U** 10,000. The only difference is that as a result of "internal borrowing" it is held partially in the form of a house instead of in the form of a bank deposit.

194. APPLICATION OF INTERNAL BORROWING TO LOCAL AUTHORITIES

Let us now consider how the basic principles of internal borrowing can be applied to a local authority. On page 287 of Chapter 9 the 19_6/_0 capital programme for Kambale Municipal Council is set out. It was intended to build an abattoir estimated to cost **U** 90,000 during 19_7. Assume that this intention remains unchanged in the 19_7/_1 capital programme, where the abattoir again appears. However, by this time, because of increased costs and more detailed plans, the abattoir is estimated to cost **U** 96,000.

Having received permission to borrow **U** 96,000 for a maximum of (say) 10 years, the chief financial officer of Kambale Municipal Council knows that a loan from the National Government will cost $6\frac{1}{4}$% pa. He also realises, from a study of the latest balance sheet (Chapter 16 - Appendix E), that the Housing Repairs Fund stands at **U** 164,635. All but **U** 3,000 of this sum is invested, earning interest at 5% p.a.

If **U** 96,000 were borrowed from the Housing Repairs Fund to finance the building of the abattoir it would save the Council $1\frac{1}{4}$% pa interest. Moreover, whilst it would "tie up" **U** 96,000 of the Repairs Fund in the form of a building, there would still be a considerable balance available in cash or readily realisable investments to meet current repairs expenditure. Subsequent repayment of the internal loan will gradually release more and more of the repairs fund in the form of liquid assets. At the end of the ten year loan period, assuming that no further internal borrowing took place, the fund would once again be held wholly in the form of cash or easily realisable investments.

195. AVAILABILITY OF FUNDS

Let us suppose, therefore, that the Kambale Municipal Council resolves to finance the building of the abattoir by an internal loan from the Housing Repairs Fund.

The (isolated) balance sheet of the repairs fund (ignoring sundry creditors) as at 31 Dec. 19_6 would appear as follows:

Housing Repairs Fund
Balance Sheet as at 31 Dec. 19_6

	Units		Units
FUND SURPLUS		CURRENT ASSETS	
Repairs Fund	164,635	Investments	161,635
		Cash in Hand	3,000
	164,635		164,635
	=======		=======

Assume that repairs expenditure charged against the fund during the following year (19_7) is **U** 97,842. At 31 Dec. 19_7 there are (say) 329 completed houses, which at **U** 600 per house gives a total contribution from the Housing Revenue Account of **U** 197,400. Interest earned at 5%

Internal Borrowing

on investments of U 161,635 will be U 8,082.

The Housing Repairs Fund Account for 19_7 might therefore appear (in outline) as follows:

Housing Repairs Fund for year ended 31 Dec. 19_7

	Units		Units
Repairs Expenditure	97,842	Balance brought forward	164,635
Balance carried forward	272,275	Contributions	197,400
		Investment Interest	8,082
	370,117		370,117

Before any adjustment had been made in investments, the (isolated) balance sheet at the end of the year would appear as follows:

Housing Repairs Fund
Balance Sheet as at 31 Dec. 19_7

	Units		Units
FUND SURPLUS		CURRENT ASSETS	
Repairs Fund	272,275	Investments (unchanged)	161,635
		Cash in Hand	110,640
	272,275		272,275

196. USE OF RESERVES FOR NEW CAPITAL PROJECT

Let us now assume that work began in April 19_7 and finished in November 19_7. We shall assume the position at 31 Dec. 19_7 to be:

	Units
Construction Costs:	
(a) payments to contractor during 19_7	78,180*
(b) retention - to be released in May 19_8	
(subject to audit)	8,680
Technical Salaries:	
(a) paid during 19_7	4,820*
(b) estimate for 19_8	1,900
Quantity Surveyors Fees:	
(a) paid during 19_7	1,360*
(c) estimate for 19_8	900
Legal and Other Expenses:	
(a) paid during 19_7	1,580*
	97,420

(payments made to 31/12/_7 total U 85,940*)

An (isolated) balance sheet of the situation at the end of the year would appear as follows:

Municipal Accounting for Developing Countries

Abattoir
Capital Balance Sheet as at 31 Dec. 19_7

	Units		Units
CURRENT LIABILITY		FIXED ASSET	
Cash Overdrawn	85,940	Abattoir (under construction)	85,940
	85,940		85,940

Because no external loan (or other form of finance) has been raised during 19_7, the capital payments have resulted in capital cash (on this account) becoming overdrawn. The latest estimates show that the capital finance required for the scheme is likely to total approximately U 97,500. Since the Kambale Municipal Council has already resolved to finance the scheme by an internal loan from the Housing Repairs Fund, the Chief Financial Officer can make the necessary adjustments in the accounts. However, only U 96,000 can be borrowed from the Housing Repairs Fund, because this is the maximum amount authorised by the Government in its loan sanction. Unless a further loan sanction is granted, the excess expenditure in 19_8 (likely to be about U 1,500) will have to be met from another source (e.g. by a revenue contribution to capital outlay).

197. RAISING OF INTERNAL LOAN

In theory, the adjustments in the accounts to deal with the internal loan will be as follows:

Housing Accounts

19_7 Dec.31	Repairs Fund Investments (Internal Loan) DR. To Cash (Housing) Being internal loan made at 6% for construction of abattoir	96,000	96,000

Abattoir Accounts

19_7 Dec.31	Cash (Abattoir) DR. To Loans Outstanding (Internal Loan) Being internal loan at 6% raised from Housing Repairs Fund	96,000	96,000

Internal Borrowing

After these adjustments the (isolated) balance sheets will present the following situation:

Housing Repairs Fund
Balance Sheet as at 31 Dec. 19_7

	Units		Units
FUND SURPLUS		CURRENT ASSETS	
Repairs Fund	272,275	Investments (external)	161,635
		Investments (internal)	96,000
		Cash in Hand	14,640
	272,275		272,275

Abattoir
Balance Sheet as at 31 Dec. 19_7

	Units		Units
LONG-TERM LIABILITY		FIXED ASSET	
Loan Outstanding		Abattoir	85,940
(internal)	96,000	Cash in Hand	10,060
	96,000		96,000

The Repairs Fund has now "invested" all but U 14,640 of its cash, whilst the Abattoir has a loan, which has not only covered its payments to date, but also leaves U 10,060 in hand to meet further payments in 19_8.

Of course, the actual cash in hand of the Repairs Fund would depend upon the adjustment of all the Council's investments at the end of 19_7 calculated as shown by W.P.2 and W.P.14 of Chapter 16. In making these adjustments the Chief Financial Officer would take the proposed internal loan into account. His rough calculation for the Repairs Fund might have been:

```
    Balance 1/1/_7                                      164,635
    Contributions                                       197,400
    Interest @ 5%                                         8,082
                                                        -------
                                                        370,117
Less Expenditure (estimate)                             100,000
                                                        -------
                                                        270,117
Less Investments already held                           161,635
                                                        -------
     Amount available for investment                    108,482
Less Internal Investment (proposed)                      96,000
                                                        -------
     Uninvested Cash 31/12/_7                            12,482*
```

(*available for external investment if required)

Having considered the position of other funds (e.g. renewals, capital) and adjusted the overall investments in round figures, the final calculation (using actual figures) might have been:

Municipal Accounting for Developing Countries

	Balance 1/1/_7	164,635
Add	Net Increase in Fund Balance	107,640
		272,275
Less	Internal Investment	96,000
		176,275
Less	Reallocated share of Council's external investments generally	174,000
		2,275

The (isolated) balance sheet of the Repairs Fund would then show:

Housing Repairs Fund
Balance Sheet as at 31 Dec. 19_7

	Units		Units
FUND SURPLUS		CURRENT ASSETS	
Repairs Fund	272,275	Investments (external)	174,000
		Investments (internal)	96,000
		Cash in Hand	2,275
	272,275		272,275

If the (isolated) balance sheets of the Repairs Fund and Abattoir were aggregated the position would appear as follows:

Housing Repairs Fund and Abattoir
Aggregate Balance Sheet as at 31 Dec. 19_7

	Units		Units
LONG-TERM LIABILITIES		FIXED ASSETS	
Loans Outstanding	96,000	Abattoir	85,940
FUND SURPLUS		CURRENT ASSETS	
Repairs Fund	272,275	Investments (external)	174,000
		Investments (internal)	96,000
		Cash in Hand	12,335
	368,275		368,275

Such a balance sheet does not truly represent the Council's position in relation to the outside world. The figures for the loan and the internal investment are "book" entries representing the indebtedness of one of the Council's funds to another of its funds. Looked at as a whole, it is merely an indebtedness of the Council to itself. The internal transactions merely cancel out each other.

The position can be stated more realistically by a consolidated balance sheet, which eliminates internal liabilities between funds, as follows:

Internal Borrowing

Housing Repairs Fund and Abattoir
Consolidated Balance Sheet as at 31 Dec. 19_7

	Units		Units
FUND SURPLUS		FIXED ASSET	
Repairs Fund	272,275	Abattoir	85,940
		CURRENT ASSETS	
		Investments	174,000
		Cash in Hand	12,335
	272,275		272,275
	=======		=======

This form of balance sheet also gives a better picture of the liquidity position. It shows that the Repairs Fund totals U 272,275. Of this, U 85,940 is "invested" in bricks and mortar (abattoir) and U 174,000 in easily realisable investments. A total of U 12,335 is held in cash but as further payments take place during 19_8 an additional (estimated) U 10,060 will be converted into bricks and mortar. Notice that the actual balance of the Repairs Fund is unaffected by the internal loan.

Changes occur only in the type of assets in which the fund balance is held.

Incidentally, our example assumed that by 31 Dec. 19_7 there was sufficient uninvested cash in the Repairs Fund from which to make the internal loan. Had the cash balance been insufficient, some of the existing investments would have been converted into cash before making the internal loan. For example, had the estimated repairs expenditure been U 150,000 instead of U 100,000 the rough calculation of the investment position would have been:

Balance 1/1/_7	164,635
Contributions	197,400
Interest @ 5%	8,082
	370,117
Less Expenditure (estimate)	150,000
	220,117
Less Investments already held	161,635
Amount available for investment	58,482
Less Internal Investment (proposed)	96,000
Cash Shortage 31/12/_7	37,518
	=======

This would mean that (say) about U 40,000 worth of external investments would have to be realised, to cover the internal loan and leave a small reserve of cash, the journal entry (in theory) being:

19_7			
Dec.27	Cash DR.	40,000	
	To Repairs Fund Investments		40,000
	Being realisation of investments		

In practice a decision upon whether a net addition to, or withdrawal from the Council's investments was required would be taken in relation to the whole of its invested funds, with the Housing Repairs Fund position taken into account. In our example the other investments of the Council have been ignored.

Why was 6% chosen as the rate of interest for the internal loan? Clearly it was right to set it between 5% and $6\frac{1}{4}$%. If it were less than 5% it would be preferable to invest the Repairs Fund externally. If it were more than $6\frac{1}{4}$% it would be preferable to borrow for the abattoir externally. At 6% the Housing Repairs Fund earns 1% more on its investments and the Abattoir account pays $\frac{1}{4}$% less on its loan. The rate chosen is, of course, a matter of judgement for the Chief Financial Officer, looking at the matter both as custodian of the Council's investments and as manager of its capital finance. In a developing country with scarce capital finance, the rate chosen might approximate more closely to the higher limit rather than to the lower limit. In this way, marginally more is taken from the public in the form of rates and taxes and the authority's reserves are built up to a higher level. In economic terms, the public is being forced to save a little more.

198. REPAYMENT OF INTERNAL LOAN

Having dealt with the raising of the internal loan, arrangements must be made for the payment of the interest and the annual repayments to the fund from which it was raised. In our example, interest must be charged against the revenue account of the Abattoir and credited to the Repairs Fund. Principal repayments must also be charged in the revenue account of the Abattoir and treated as realisation of investments from the point of view of the Repairs Fund. Cash adjustments must also be made between the two accounts, but there is a short cut method for adjusting cash balances, as explained later.

An important point arises when an internal loan is compared with an external loan. The latter is raised from a particular lender and its terms are specifically laid down in the loan agreement (e.g. mortgage document, deposit receipt, stock certificate). The terms must be exactly adhered to, ensuring that neither the authority nor the lender suffers at the expense of the other party. With internal loans, any slight losses or gains to one fund are exactly offset in the other fund, the authority as a whole neither gaining nor losing. Highly sophisticated loan repayment tables are therefore, with internal loans, not quite so necessary and in the interests of simplicity, round figures are often used.

The repayment table for the loan in our example could therefore be drawn up as follows. The "odd" sum of U 6,000 has been added to the first repayment, leaving subsequent instalments in round amounts of U 10,000.

Internal Borrowing

Loan Repayment Table
Internal Loan of U 96,000 @ 6% to be repaid by Annual Instalments over 10 years

Instalment Number	Total Payment	Interest	Principal	Principal Outstanding
1	2,880	2,880	-	96,000
2	21,760	5,760	16,000	80,000
3	14,800	4,800	10,000	70,000
4	14,200	4,200	10,000	60,000
5	13,600	3,600	10,000	50,000
6	13,000	3,000	10,000	40,000
7	12,400	2,400	10,000	30,000
8	11,800	1,800	10,000	20,000
9	11,200	1,200	10,000	10,000
10	10,600	600	10,000	-

The accounting entries relation to the internal loan were made on 31 Dec. 19_7. However, this was only for administrative convenience. The capital payments for the abattoir began to be made around April 19_7, and by 31 Dec. the majority of payments had been made. Because the abattoir capital account had no cash of its own, the capital payments must have been made from cash belonging to those other funds of the Council with cash balances in hand, including of course, the Housing Repairs Fund which, technically, is financing the project. The abattoir accounts should therefore pay for using cash balances of other funds, because had they not existed, a bank overdraft would have been required. We have therefore followed a common practice and assumed that the loan was "deemed to have been made" half way through the year 19_7. It is therefore reasonable to charge half a year's interest (U 2,880) on the loan for 19_7. No adjustment is made in 19_7 for a repayment of principal, because it is felt to be somewhat illogical to show the first repayment on the same day as the book entry for raising the loan. (However, the odd U 6,000 might have been treated as repaid in 19_7 - not done in our example). The interest adjustment will therefore be journalised as follows:

Abattoir Accounts

Dec.31	Loan Charges - Interest DR. To Cash (Abattoir) Being payment of half-year's interest @ 6% on internal loan of U 96,000 from Housing Repairs Fund	2,880	2,880

Housing Accounts

Dec.31	Cash (Housing) DR. To Housing Repairs Fund Being receipt of half-year's interest @ 6% on internal loan of U 96,000 for construction of Abattoir	2,880	2,880

Municipal Accounting for Developing Countries

199. INTEGRATION OF ACCOUNTING PROCEDURE

In accounting for the internal loan transactions above, each fund has been shown separately, with cash adjustments made between them. However, since the Council is a single entity, a payment of cash by one fund is a receipt of cash by another. The overall cash position does not alter, because the cash transactions exactly cancel out. In practice, therefore, direct adjustments can be made between the accounts of the funds, completely ignoring the cash aspect. The journal entries and accounts for 19_7 will therefore appear as follows:

Date	Particulars	Folio	Dr.	Cr.

Dec.31	Housing Repairs Fund Investments (Internal Investment) DR.
	  To Loans Outstanding
	    (Abattoir - Internal Loan)
	Being internal loan @ 6% from Housing Repairs Fund for erection of Abattoir
		3
		
		5
			96,000	96,000

Dec.31	Housing Repairs Fund Investments (External Investment) DR. To Cash* Being further investment in 5% bank deposit	2 C.B.	12,365	12,365
Dec.31	Cash DR. To Housing Repairs Fund Being interest @ 5% on external investment of U 161,635	C.B. 1	8,082	8,082

Dec.31	Abattoir Revenue
	  (Loan Charges - Interest) DR.
	  To Housing Repairs Fund
	Being interest @ 6% on internal loan of U 96,000 deemed to have been made on 1/7/_7
		6
		1
			2,880	2,880

*This ignores the other investments of the Council. In practice there would be a reallocation of investments over funds, only the net addition to, or withdrawal from investments being dealt with by a payment or receipt of cash.

Internal Borrowing

Housing Repairs Fund   1

19_7				19_7			
Dec.31	To Cash (and Creditors) - Repairs Expenditure	C	97,842	Jan. 1	By Balance	b/f	164,635
	To Balance	c/d	275,155		By Housing Revenue Contributions	J	197,400
					By Cash - Investment Interest (External)	C	8,082
					By Abattoir Revenue - Investment Interest (Internal)	J	2,880
			372,997				372,997
				19_8 Jan. 1	By Balance	b/d	275,155

Housing Repairs Fund Investments (External)   2

19_7				19_7			
Jan. 1	To Balance	b/f	161,635	Dec.31	By Balance	c/d	174,000
Dec.31	To Cash	C	12,365				
			174,000				174,000
19_8 Jan. 1	To Balance	b/d	174,000				

Housing Repairs Fund Investments (Internal)   3

19_7				19_7			
Dec.31	To Loans Outstanding (Abattoir)	J	96,000	Dec.31	By Balance	c/d	96,000
			96,000				96,000
19_8 Jan. 1	To Balance	b/d	96,000				

Capital Expenditure - Abattoir   4

19_7				19_7			
Dec.31	To Cash	C	85,940	Dec.31	By Balance	c/d	85,940
19_8 Dec.31	To Balance	b/d	85,940				

Municipal Accounting for Developing Countries

Loans Outstanding (Internal)							5
19_7 Dec.31	To Balance	c/d	96,000	19_7 Dec.31	By Housing Repairs Fund Investments (Internal)	J	96,000
			96,000 ======				96,000 ======
				19_8 Jan. 1	By Balance	b/d	96,000

Abattoir Revenue Account							6
19_7 Dec.31	To (Various Items of Revenue Expenditure) To Loan Charges - Interest	J	? 2,880 =====	19_7 Dec.31	By (Various Items of Revenue Income)		? =====

(Balance transferred to General Revenue Account)

Note that cash is still involved when dealing with the external transactions.

It is unlikely that balance sheets of the two funds would be prepared, because the relevant transactions would be merged into the overall financial position of the authority. However, if for any reason, the balance sheets were required, the figures could appear as follows:

Housing Repairs Fund
Balance Sheet as at 31 Dec. 19_7

	Units		Units
FUND SURPLUS		CURRENT ASSETS	
Repairs Fund	275,155	Investments (internal)	96,000
		Investments (external)	174,000
		Cash in Hand	?
	275,155 =======		275,155 =======

Internal Borrowing

Abattoir
Balance Sheet as at 31 Dec. 19_7

	Units		Units
LONG-TERM LIABILITIES		FIXED ASSET	
Loans Outstanding		Abattoir (under	
(Internal)	96,000	construction)	85,940
		CURRENT ASSET	
		Cash in Hand	?
	96,000		96,000

Because the cash transactions relating to the internal loan are not separately recorded, the cash balances cannot be entered in the balance sheets directly from the accounts.

However, since all other balances are known, the cash balances can be calculated - from the remaining figures - to give the following:

Housing Repairs Fund
Balance Sheet as at 31 Dec. 19_7

	Units		Units
FUND SURPLUS		CURRENT ASSETS	
Repairs Fund	275,155	Investments (internal)	96,000
		Investments (external)	174,000
		Cash in Hand	5,155
	275,155		275,155

Abattoir
Balance Sheet as at 31 Dec. 19_7

	Units		Units
LONG-TERM LIABILITIES		FIXED ASSET	
Loans Outstanding		Abattoir (under	
(internal)	96,000	construction)	85,940
		CURRENT ASSET	
		Cash in Hand	10,060
	96,000		96,000

The calculation of cash balances from the remaining figures in the accounts is sometimes known as "forcing" the cash balances. Of course, if all cash balances on various funds (in hand or overdrawn) are totalled, with credit balances offset against debit balances, the resulting figure will be equal to the overall net cash balance (in hand or overdrawn) of the authority.

For the first repayment of principal we shall have to look at the financial year, 19_8. Assume the following:

Municipal Accounting for Developing Countries

Opening Balances as at 1 Jan. 19_8

Repairs Fund	275,155
Repairs Fund Investments (external)	174,000
Internal Loan	96,000
Abattoir (under construction)	85,940

Transactions during 19_8

Repairs Fund Contributions from Housing Revenue Account (343 @ U 600)	205,800
Repairs Fund Expenditure	143,840
Interest @ 5% on Repairs Fund Investments (external) of (U 174,000)	8,700
Capital Expenditure on Abattoir (Balance not covered by loan sanction to be met from revenue)	11,480
*Repayment of Internal Loan	16,000
*Interest @ 6% on Internal Loan	5,760
Additional Investments (external) of Housing Repairs Fund	92,000

(*from table on page 705)

Ignoring sundry creditors and cash adjustments relating to internal transactions, the transactions during 19_8 could be journalised as follows:

19_8 Dec.31	Housing Revenue Account DR. To Housing Repairs Fund Being annual contribution for 343 houses at U 600 per house.	1 2	205,800	205,800
Dec.31	Housing Repairs Fund DR. To Cash (or Creditors, Wages, Stores etc) Being repairs expenditure during year	2 C	143,840	143,840
19_8 Dec.31	Cash DR. To Housing Repairs Fund Being interest @ 5% on external investments	C 2	8,700	8,700
Dec.31	Capital Expenditure (Abattoir) DR. To Cash Being capital payments during year	3 C	11,480	11,480
Dec.31	Abattoir Revenue (Revenue Contribution to Capital) DR. To Capital Discharged (Revenue Contributions to Capital) Being finance from revenue of capital expenditure in excess of loan sanction	4 5	1,420	1,420

Internal Borrowing

Dec.31	Abattoir Revenue -
	    (Loan Charges - Interest) DR.
	  To Housing Repairs Fund
	  Being annual loan interest @
	  6% on internal loan of U 96,000
		4
		2
			5,760	5,760

Dec.31	Loans Outstanding DR.
	  To Housing Repairs Fund
	    Investments (Internal)
	  Being repayment of first
	  instalment of principal on
	  internal loan
		7
		8
			16,000	16,000

Dec.31	Abattoir Revenue -
	    (Loan Charges - Principal) DR.
	  To Capital Discharged (Loans
	    Repaid)
	  Being repayment of principal
	  now charged to revenue account
		4
		5
			16,000	16,000

Dec.31	Housing Repairs Fund
	    Investments (External) DR.
	  To Cash
	  Being additional investments
	  in 5% bank deposit
		9
		C
			92,000	92,000

The ledger accounts would appear as follows:

	Housing Revenue						1

19_8
Dec.31
	To (Various
	  Items of
	  Revenue
	  Expendi-
	  ture)
	To Repairs
	  Contrib-
	  ution
		
		J
			?
			
			205,800
			=======
				19_8
				Dec.31
					By (Various
					  Items of
					  Revenue
					  Income)
							?
							
							=======

(Balance carried forward or transferred to General Revenue Account)

	Housing Repairs Fund							2
19_8 Dec.31	To Cash (and Creditors) - Repairs Expenditure	J	143,840	19_8 Jan. 1	By Balance By Housing Revenue - Contributions	b/f J	275,155 205,800	
	To Balance	c/d	351,575		By Cash - Investment Interest (External)	J	8,700	
					By Abattoir Revenue - Investment Interest (Internal)	J	5,760	
			495,415				495,415	
			======	19_9 Jan. 1	By Balance		351,575	

	Capital Expenditure - Abattoir							3
19_8 Jan. 1 Dec.31	To Balance To Cash	b/f J	85,940 11,480	19_8 Dec.31	By Balance	c/d	97,420	
			97,420				97,420	
19_9 Jan. 1	To Balance	b/d	97,420					

	Abattoir Revenue							4
19_8 Dec.31	To (Various Items of Revenue Expenditure)		?	19_8 Dec.31	By (Various Items of Revenue Income)		?	
	To Loan Charges Interest Principal	J	5,760 16,000					
	To Revenue Contributions to Capital Outlay	J	1,420					
			======				======	

(Balance transferred to General Revenue Account)

Internal Borrowing

Capital Discharged (Revenue Contributions to Capital Outlay) 5

19_8				19_8			
Dec.31	To Balance	c/d	1,420	Dec.31	By Revenue Account	J	1,420
			1,420				1,420
				19_9 Jan. 1	By Balance		1,420

Capital Discharged (Loans Repaid) 6

19_8				19_8			
Dec.31	To Balance	c/d	16,000	Dec.31	By Revenue Account	J	16,000
			16,000				16,000
				19_9 Jan. 1	By Balance		16,000

Loans Outstanding 7

19_8				19_8			
Dec.31	To Housing Repairs Fund Investments (Internal)	J	16,000	Jan. 1	By Balance	b/f	96,000
	To Balance	c/d	80,000				
			96,000				96,000
				19_9 Jan. 1	By Balance	b/d	80,000

Housing Repairs Fund Investment (External) 9

19_8				19_8			
Jan. 1	To Balance	b/f	174,000	Dec.31	By Balance	c/d	266,000
Dec.31	To Cash		92,000				
			266,000				266,000
19_9 Jan. 1	To Balance	b/d	266,000				

If required, balance sheets can be shown as follows, with cash balances "forced" from other figures:

Housing Repairs Fund
Balance Sheet as at 31 Dec. 19_8

	Units		Units
FUND SURPLUS		CURRENT ASSETS	
Repairs Fund	351,575	Investments (internal)	80,000
		Investments (external)	266,000
		Cash in Hand	5,575
	351,575		351,575

Abattoir
Capital Balance Sheet as at 31 Dec. 19_8

	Units		Units
LONG TERM LIABILITY		FIXED ASSET	
Loans Outstanding	80,000	Abattoir	97,420
CAPITAL DISCHARGED			
Loans Repaid	16,000		
Revenue Contributions			
to Capital Outlay	1,420		
	97,420		97,420

In planning the additional investments of the Repairs Fund for 19_8, account would have been taken of the U 16,000 cash released as a result of the repayment of the internal loan. The rough calculation might have been as follows:

Balance 1/1/_8	275,155
Contributions	205,800
Interest	14,460
	495,415
Less Expenditure (estimate)	145,000
	350,415
Less Investments already held	270,000
	80,415
Add Repayment due on Internal Loan	16,000
Uninvested Cash 31/12/_8	96,415*

*Invest a further round sum of (say) U 92,000

200. INTERNAL BORROWING - CONCLUSION

Experience seems to show that the Housing Repairs Fund of Kambale Municipal Council is at present growing from year to year. Because the houses are relatively new and because more and more new houses are being constructed, this is only to be expected, if contributions are adequate. More use might therefore be made of internal borrowing from this fund, provided it is realised that the time will ultimately come when expenditure from the fund begins to exceed income. Planned internal borrowing must ensure adequate liquidity, not only at present, but also in the future. As repayments of internal loans are made, decisions will have to be taken as to whether they can be re-lent

Internal Borrowing

internally for other capital works or whether they should be invested externally to increase liquidity.

18. Temporary Borrowing

Section		Page
201.	Temporary Borrowing - Introduction.	717
202.	Temporary Borrowing - Revenue Purposes.	717
203.	Temporary Borrowing - Capital Purposes.	720
204.	Provision for Debt Redemption.	723
205.	Raising of Long-Term Loan.	725
206.	Accounting Procedures.	726
207.	Calculation of Interest.	731

201. TEMPORARY BORROWING - INTRODUCTION

A local or public authority may raise temporary loans or overdrafts:

(a) to meet normal revenue payments, pending the receipt of revenue income; and

(b) to meet capital payments, pending the raising of a long-term loan.

202. TEMPORARY BORROWING - REVENUE PURPOSES

Although an authority may have budgeted for sufficient revenue income to meet its revenue expenditure during a particular financial year, the receipts and payments will not flow evenly during that year. If the authority maintains an adequate working balance, there should always be sufficient cash on hand to meet outgoings at any time during the year. However, if the working balance is low, there will be certain times during the year when cash is being paid out faster than it is coming in, creating a temporary cash shortage. For example, rates and taxes legally become payable on the first day of a financial year but many people will refrain from paying them for as long as possible, taking full advantage of the period of grace allowed before the authority takes legal proceedings. In the meantime, the authority must make payments for salaries, services and supplies to carry out its functions. The cash shortage may be covered by raising a temporary loan or incurring a bank overdraft.

The book-keeping entries are simple. If, for example on 13 Jan. 19_7 the Kambale Municipal Council raised a temporary loan for U 100,000 at (say) 6% from Kambale Industrial Provident Fund, the loan would be debited in the cash book when received and credited to the personal account of the lender. If, instead, a bank overdraft were incurred, no book-keeping entries would be required. It would merely mean that the cash book would no longer always have a debit (i.e. cash in hand) balance. It would from time to time have a credit balance, fluctuating up to a maximum credit (i.e. overdrawn) balance of U 100,000 or whatever other limit was agreed with the bank.

If the temporary loan had been repaid on (say) 3 June 19_7, interest at the rate of 6% would be payable for the period from 13 Jan. to 3 June, a period of 141 days, calculated as follows:

$$I = \frac{PRT}{100} = U \frac{100,000 \times 6 \times 141}{100 \times 365} = U\ 2,317.80$$

Municipal Accounting for Developing Countries

The repayment of the loan with interest could (in theory) be journalised as follows:

19_7 June 3	Kambale Industrial Provident Fund DR.	100,000	00		
	Interest - Temporary Borrowing DR.	2,317	80		
	To Cash			102,317	80
	Being repayment of temporary loan with accrued interest				

If the above loan had not been repaid until after 30 June, interest would have been paid on this date for the period of 169 days from 13 Jan. to 30 June. Thereafter, interest would be payable half-yearly on 31 Dec. and 30 June, until the loan was finally repaid with any interest remaining since the last payment. In practice, of course, a temporary loan pending receipt of revenues would not last for longer than a few months but the same principles apply to temporary loans raised for capital purposes, which might well be for a longer period.

If a bank overdraft had been used, instead of a temporary loan, interest would have been calculated on the average daily balance. The relevant sum would be entered in the bank statement by the bank and probably "picked up" when preparing the reconciliation statement. It would (after checking) be credited in the cash book and debited to the "Interest on overdraft" account.

It would be reasonable, when preparing final accounts, to offset temporary loan or overdraft interest against interest earned on the Council's general investments (if any), but not normally against interest earned from investment of special funds (e.g. repairs, renewals).

Any temporary loans or bank overdrafts at the date of a balance sheet will be included on the left-hand side under "CURRENT LIABILITIES" as follows:

CURRENT LIABILITIES
    Creditors
    Temporary Loans
    Cash Overdrawn

The loan document issued to the lender would be a simple deposit receipt along the following lines, of which a duplicate copy would be kept by the authority:

Temporary Borrowing

```
                KAMBALE MUNCIPAL COUNCIL                        43

                                      Finance Department
                                      PO Box 165,
                                      Kambale.

Received this ...thirteenth...day of ...January.....19_7......

from ...Kambale Industrial Provident Fund...................

the sum of ...One hundred thousand units....................

as a temporary loan under Section 101 of the Local Government

Act 19_2, repayable on or after ...20 January 19_7...........

on seven days notice being given by either party to the other,

such loan to bear interest at a rate of ...six...... per centum

per annum, payable half-yearly on 30 June and 31 December.


                                              ┌──────────┐
                                              │  STAMP   │
                                              │          │
                                              │  DUTY    │
                                              └──────────┘

 U 100,000..... @ ..6..%         (Signed) Chief Financial Officer.
```

Sometimes a second paragraph is added to the wording on the receipt as follows:

"I hereby undertake that if called upon to do so the Council will execute a mortgage deed securing the above loan and interest or will, alternatively, immediately repay the loan".

These words may sometimes be requested by a lender, as giving apparent added security. Clearly there is no real intention of issuing a mortgage and if one were called for the loan would be repaid, being replaced by a further loan if necessary.

It is quite common, in many countries, for legal documents involving financial transactions to be taxed by governments, using stamp duty, which may vary according to the transaction size.

Where the "mortage" clause is included on the receipt it would legally become an "agreement" and would often bear stamp duty at the prescribed rate, (if any). Where the "mortgage" clause was omitted the stamp duty payable would depend upon the law and the precise wording of the document. It might be deemed to be a "receipt" bearing stamp duty, (if any). The document might require adjudication by the appropriate taxing authority.

For an occasional temporary loan, the deposit receipt would be in the form of a typed letter. However, where temporary borrowing was effected fairly frequently it would be sensible to have specially printed and numbered receipts. These would be in a bound book and subject to the same systems of internal check as other receipt forms.

Municipal Accounting for Developing Countries

The loan referred to above is on a simple seven days notice, repayable at any time. Some loans have an initial fixed period of (say) one, three or six months, being allowed to run on at seven days notice thereafter. For example, had the above loan been for what, in financial jargon is called "three months firm and seven days", the deposit receipt would show it as "repayable on or after 13 April 19_7 on seven days notice....." Sometimes a loan will be for a definite fixed period, repayable on a certain date. For example, had the above loan been for "four months fixed" the deposit receipt would show it as "repayable on 13 May 19_7". The words "or after" and "on seven days notice........the other" would, in this case, be deleted.

203. TEMPORARY BORROWING - CAPITAL PURPOSES

The procedure for raising temporary loans or overdrafts, pending the receipt of a long-term loan, is the same as for those pending the receipt of revenue, as described above. However, there are differences in accountancy treatment, best illustrated by an example.

In the capital programme (page 287 - Chapter 9) there is provision for U 264,000 for sewerage in 19_7. Assume that the latest estimates now put the figure at U 292,000, which is to be financed as part of a loan from the United Kingdom under an aid programme. The loan is to be channelled through the Ministry of Local Government.

Let us imagine that on 9 Jan. 19_7 the Kambale Municipal Council receives the following letter from the Ministry of Local Government:

>> Ministry of Local Government,
>> PO Box 4037,
>> Kambale.
>>
>> 9 January 19_7

The Chief Executive Officer,
Kambale Municipal Council,
PO Box 165,
Kambale.

Sir,

<u>Relief Sewer - Kisali</u>

I am directed to inform you that the above scheme has been approved as a loan project and a formal offer of a U 292,000 loan from the Ministry for a period of 30 years will be made in due course. As you know, the scheme is to be financed as part of an aid programme from the United Kingdom Government. Therefore the formal offer of a loan from the Ministry cannot be made until the necessary funds have been received from overseas. I understand from the Ministry of Planning that this is unlikely to be before the end of 19_7.

The Minister is aware that your Council's scheme is in an advanced stage of preparation. Furthermore, the government is anxious that the work should start at the earliest possible date. Therefore, the Minister is prepared to sanction the raising of a temporary loan under Section 102 of the Local Government Act, pending the issue of a more permanent loan from the Ministry. If satisfactory arrangements can be made by your Council for raising such a loan, permission will be given for the work to proceed.

Temporary Borrowing

A copy of this letter is enclosed for the Chief Financial Officer.

                                          A.B. MUSOKE
                                          for Permanent Secretary
                                          Ministry of Local Government.

Assume that the Chief Financial Officer forecasts the cash requirements for the scheme as follows:

	Units
Payments prior to 1 Jan. 19_7	22,000
February)	8,000
March)	10,000
April)	20,000
May) 19_7	60,000
June)	60,000
July)	20,000
August)	40,000
September)	12,000
During 19_8	40,000
	292,000

From his overall cash forecast he decides that payments until the end of May can be borne from the Council's working balances but that a loan will be required in June. He receives a firm promise of such a loan from the National Development Corporation at a rate of interest of 5½% for a fixed term of six months and thereafter at seven days notice. He is assured by the Corporation that the loan will be allowed to run on at notice until the Ministry loan is forthcoming. The arrangements are accepted by the Ministry and the work is allowed to commence.

By 31 May the position might be as follows:

Kisali Relief Sewer
Capital Balance Sheet as at 31 May 19_7

CURRENT LIABILITES	Units	FIXED ASSET	Units
Cash Overdrawn	116,800	Relief Sewer - Kisali (under construction)	116,800
	116,800		116,800

The raising of the temporary loan on (say) 1 June 19_7 can be journalised as follows:

| 19_7 June 1 | Cash
    To Temporary Loan - National
        Development Corporation
    Being temporary loan raised to
    finance construction of Kasali
    Relief Sewer | C.B.

1 | 292,000 |

292,000 |

Municipal Accounting for Developing Countries

The position is now as follows:

Balance Sheet as at 1 June 19_7

	Units		Units
CURRENT LIABILITIES		FIXED ASSET	
Temporary Loan	292,000	Relief Sewer - Kisali	116,800
		CURRENT ASSET	
		Cash in Hand	175,200
	292,000		292,000

Of course, interest is being paid on the full U 292,000, whereas only U 116,800 has so far been spent. However, the cash forecast suggests that the loan had become esential by the time it was raised and the implication is that a bank overdraft would otherwise have been necessary. Therefore although not earning interest, part of the unspent cash balance might be saving overdraft interest from being incurred by other funds of the Council. Even so, in certain circumstances, it might have been preferable for the Council to incur a bank overdraft up to the maximum permitted limit, thus further delaying the raising of the loan. Although bank interest might have been at the rate of (say) 7%, this rate of interest would have been payable only on the average daily balance overdrawn and not on the overall limit. The amount of interest payable would almost certainly be less than at $5\frac{1}{2}$% on the full temporary loan. Interest could perhaps have been saved by raising the temporary loan in instalments of (say) U 40,000 - 50,000 as required, probably from different lenders. In the United Kingdom, for example, this would certainly be done, because in the highly organised London Money Market there is rarely any shortage of temporary loans, provided the interest rate offered is high enough. In other countries temporary loans may be much harder to obtain, whatever the rate of interest and it is perhaps of greatest importance to secure whatever reasonable loans are on offer as soon as they become available. However, where circumstances permit, there is much to be said for raising the marginal temporary loan as a bank overdraft, as a matter of general policy.

On 30 June, interest for the period from 1 - 30 June would become payable as follows:

$$I = \frac{PRT}{100} = \frac{U\ 292,000 \times 5\frac{1}{2}\% \times 30}{100 \times 365} = U\ 1,320$$

Let us now assume that at 31 Dec. 19_7 the loan is still running on at seven days notice, the permanent loan not yet having been raised from the Ministry. Interest payable for the half year would be calculated as follows:

$$I = \frac{PRT}{100} = \frac{U\ 292,000 \times 5\frac{1}{2}\% \times 184}{100 \times 365} = U\ 8,096$$

Because the loan has been raised for capital purposes, the interest must be treated as "loan charges" and debited to the sewerage revenue account as follows:

Temporary Borrowing

19_7				

Jun.30	Sewerage Revenue -
	   Loan Charges - Interest DR.
	     To Cash
	   Being interest on temporary loan
	   @ 5½% from 1/6/_7 - 30/6/_7
		5	1,320	1,320

Dec.31	Sewerage Revenue -
	   Loan Charges - Interest DR.
	     To Cash
	   Being interest on temporary loan
	   @ 5½% from 1/7/_7 - 31/12/_7
			8,096	8,096

204. PROVISION FOR DEBT REDEMPTION

Because no part of the loan is repaid, there is no entry for "Loan Charges - Principal". However, this is, strictly speaking, incorrect. The loan sanction has, in theory, been exercised by the raising of the temporary loan. The more permanent loan, when raised, will only be in the nature of a replacement for the temporary loan. Strictly, the loan debt on the sewer should be wholly repaid within 30 years from the date that the loan sanction is first exercised. In other words, if the temporary loan is held for one year, the more permanent loan should be raised for 29 years only, to comply with the conditions of the loan sanction. Furthermore, provision would have to be made for the loan repayment during the first year, even though no instalments were actually repaid. In the United Kingdom, for example, this would be strictly insisted upon and might well require a 30 year sinking fund, running alongside a 29 year instalment or annuity loan.

Some other government might allow the permanent loan, when raised, to be for the original intended period of 30 years, thus effectively extending the sanctioned repayment period to 31 (or even perhaps 32 or 33) years. Since the choice of 30 years is, in any case, quite arbitrary there can be no objection to a slight extension of the period, in the interests of simplicity.

The only problem which arises is that during the period of the temporary loan, no provision is made for repayment. This is not very sound finance, because the revenue account will become distorted. This may affect calculations of charges, rates or taxes to be levied. Furthermore, if left unchecked, an authority could continually put off its obligations to redeem the debt by raising one temporary loan after another.

The problem can quite easily be resolved by making a notional charge in the revenue account for each half-yearly principal repayment during the period of the temporary loan. This would be credited to a temporary sinking fund. When the temporary loan was subsequently replaced out of the proceeds of a more permanent loan the amount in the sinking fund would be deducted from the full amount of the loan. The temporary loan would be repaid in full but the more permanent loan raised only for the balance of requirements, after taking into account the repayment provisions already made.

In our example, let us assume that the permanent loan is taken up from the Ministry on 17 Feb. 19_8. The first half-yearly repayment on this loan will be due on 17 Aug. 19_8 and will be the only instalment to fall in this financial year. It would therefore seem reasonable to make one half-yearly provision for repayment of the temporary loan in 19_7 and another in 19_8. The simplest method of calculating the repayment provision would be to divide the loan by the number of half-years in the sanction period, as follows:

$$\frac{292,000}{60} = U\ 4,867 \text{ (to nearest unit)}$$

However, it could be argued that this method treats the loan as an instalment loan, whereas the permanent loan, when raised, will be an annuity loan. As we have discovered from earlier chapters an instalment loan gives a much heavier charge to revenue in the earlier years than an annuity loan. There would, in our example, be much to be said for using the instalment calculation because it would bring about accelerated redemption of debt. However, the instalment calculation, when added to the interest on the full loan already charged in the revenue account, might represent too much of a burden. It could therefore be replaced by an annuity repayment, calculated on the basis of a hypothetical 5½% annuity loan as follows:

Amount of Loan	=	U 292,000
Period of Loan	=	30 years (60 half years)
Rate of Interest	=	5½%
Figure from Loan Tables for a Loan of 1	=	0.03422002
Half-Yearly Annuity	=	0.03422002 x 292,000
	=	9,992.25
Half-Yearly Annuity	=	9,992.25
Less Half-Yearly Interest (½ x 5½% x 292,000)	=	8,030.00
Principal Element		1,962.25

The repayment provision for the first half year might therefore be U 1,960 (to the nearest U 20). Subsequent repayment provisions would increase at the rate of 2¾% each half year (i.e. one-half of 5½% per annum) as follows:

Instalment Number	Repayment Provision (nearest U 20)
1	1,960
2	2,020
3	2,080
4	2,140
5	2,200
6	2,260

Because we are dealing only with a purely hypothetical annuity, no greater accuracy than to the nearest U 20 is required. In fact the calculation might well be rounded off to the nearest one hundred units, particularly in the case of a larger loan. In any case a suitable adjustment will be made to ensure that the permanent loan is ultimately raised for a convenient round sum.

It is stressed that these short cut methods can only be used where the temporary loan is intended to bridge the gap between making the capital payments and raising the long-term loan. Sometimes (as in the United

Temporary Borrowing

Kingdom for example) capital schemes are financed by continually raising and repaying temporary loans over the periods of the loan sanctions. When this happens, proper sinking funds or loans pooling arrangements are necessary. Returning to the Kambale Municipal Council temporary loan, the first repayment provision would be made on 31 Dec. 19_7 as follows:

19_7 Dec.31	Sewerage Revenue - Loan Charges - Principal DR. To Temporary Sinking Fund Being half-yearly provision for repayment of loan debt on relief sewer at Kisali	5 4	1,960	1,960

The position at 31 Dec. 19_7 might appear as shown in the following (isolated) balance sheet.

Kisali - Relief Sewer
Capital Balance Sheet as at 31 Dec. 19_7

	Units		Units
CURRENT LIABILITY		FIXED ASSET	
Temporary Loan	292,000	Relief Sewer - Kisali	
OTHER BALANCES		(under construction)	257,520
Temporary Sinking Fund	1,960	CURRENT ASSET	
		Cash in Hand	36,440
	293,960		293,960

The cash in hand represents the unspent balance of the loan (U 34,480) to be paid out during 19_8 and the uninvested temporary sinking fund (U 1,960).

205. RAISING OF LONG-TERM LOAN

The loan debt position would be unchanged until immediately prior to raising the more permanent loan on 17 Feb. 19_8. The amount to be raised would be calculated as follows:

	Units	Units
Full Amount of Loan		292,000
Less Provision for Repayment:		
1st Instalment	1,960	
2nd Instalment (proposed)	2,020	3,980
		288,020
Less Additional Repayment Provision to round off odd sum		20
Long-Term Loan from Ministry		288,000

The second repayment provision will therefore be adjusted to U 2,040 (i.e. 2,020 + 20) to round off the odd sum.

In addition to the repayment of the temporary loan of U 292,000 to the lender, interest will be payable for the odd period from 1 Jan. to 17 Feb. calculated as follows:

$$I = \frac{PRT}{100} = \frac{292{,}000 \times 5\tfrac{1}{2}\% \times 47}{100 \times 365} = U\ 2{,}068$$

Let us assume that the final capital payments on the Relief Sewer are made during 19_8 and that the position is as follows:

Payments made up to 31 Dec. 19_7	257,520
Payments made during 19_8	36,840
Final Cost of Scheme	294,360
Less Covered by Loan Sanction	292,000
Balance - Financed from Revenue	2,360

On 17 Aug. 19_8, the first instalment of the long-term loan would become payable to the Ministry, calculated as follows:

Amount of Loan	=	U 288,000
Period of Loan	=	30 years (60 half years)
Rate of Interest	=	$6\tfrac{1}{4}\%$
Figure from Loan Tables for a Loan of 1	=	0.03710609
Half-Yearly Annuity	=	0.03710609 x 288,000
	=	10,686.55
Half-Yearly Annuity	=	10,686.55
Less Half-Yearly Interest ($\tfrac{1}{2}$ x $6\tfrac{1}{4}\%$ x 288,000)	=	9,000.00
Principal Element		1,686.55

206. ACCOUNTING PROCEDURE

The various transactions during 19_8 could be journalised as follows:

19_8						
Feb. 17	Sewerage Revenue - Loan Charges - Principal DR. To Temporary Sinking Fund Being half-yearly provision for repayment of loan debt on Relief Sewer at Kisali. (Date advanced to meet raising of permanent loan)	6 4	2,040	00	2,040	00

Temporary Borrowing

Date	Particulars	Folio	Dr.		Cr.	
Feb.17	Cash DR. To Loans Outstanding (National Government) Being receipt of 30 year loan for Kisali Relief Sewer from Ministry of Local Government	C.B. 2	288,000	00	288,000	00
Feb.17	National Development Corporation DR. Sewerage Revenue - Loan Charges - Interest DR. To Cash Being repayment of temporary loan, together with accrued interest from 1/1/_8 - 17/2/_8 (47 days)	1 6 C.B.	292,000 2,068	00 00	294,068	00
Feb.17	Temporary Sinking Fund DR. To Capital Discharged (Loans Repaid) Being sinking fund applied in redemption of loan debt. Page 1st 1,960 + 2nd 2,040	4 8	4,000	00	4,000	00
Aug.17	Loans Outstanding (National Government) DR. To Cash Being repayment of first instalment of principal	2 C.B.	1,686	55	1,686	55
Aug.17	Sewerage Revenue - Loan Charges - Interest DR. To Cash Being half-year's interest @ 6¼% on U 288,000	6 C.B.	9,000	00	9,000	00
Aug.17	Sewerage Revenue - Loan Charges - Principal DR. To Capital Discharged (Loans Repaid) Being first repayment of principal now charged to revenue account	6	1,686	55	1,686	55
Dec.31	Capital Expenditure - Kisali Relief Sewer DR. To Cash Being further capital payments during year	3 C.B.	36,840	00	36,840	00

Dec.31	Sewerage Revenue - Revenue Contributions to Capital DR. To Capital Discharged (RCCO) Being excess capital payments on Kisali Relief Sewer not covered by loan sanction and now financed by a contribution from revenue	6 8	2,360	00		
					2,360	00

The ledger accounts, including entries made in 19_7, will appear as follows:

Temporary Loan Development Corporation 1

19_7 Dec.31	To Balance	c/d	292,000	00	19_7 Jun. 1	By Cash	C.B	292,000	00
19_8 Feb.17	To Cash	C.B	292,000	00	19_8 Jan. 1	By Balance	b/d	292,000	00

Loans Outstanding (MLG) 2

19_8 Aug.17 Dec.31	To Cash To Balance	C.B c/d	1,686 286,313	55 45	19_8 Feb.17	By Cash	C.B	288,000	00
			288,000	00				288,000	00
					19_9 Jan. 1	By Balance	b/d	286,313	45

Capital Expenditure - Kisale - Relief Sewer 3

19_7 Dec.31	To Cash	C.B	257,520	00	19_7 Dec.31	By Balance	c/d	257,520	00
19_8 Jun. 1 Dec.31	To Balance To Cash	b/d C.B	257,520 36,840	00 00	19_8 Dec.31	By Balance	c/d	294,360	00
			294,360	00				294,360	00
19_9 Jan. 1	To Balance	b/d	294,360	00					

Temporary Borrowing

Temporary Sinking Fund — 4

Date	Particulars	F	£		Date	Particulars	F	£	
19_7 Dec.31	To Balance c/d		1,960	00	19_7 Dec.31	By Sewerage Revenue - Loan Charges Principal	J	1,960	00
			1,960	00				1,960	00
19_8 Feb.17	To Capital Discharged (Loans Repaid)	J	4,000	00	19_8 Jan. 1 Feb.17	By Balance b/d By Sewerage Revenue Loan Charges Principal	J	1,960 2,040	00 00
			4,000	00				4,000	00

Sewerage Revenue Account (19_7) — 5

Date	Particulars	F	£		Date	Particulars	F	£	
19_7	(Various Items of Revenue Expenditure including:)		?		19_7 Dec.31	(Various Items of Revenue Income)		?	
Jun.30	To Cash - Loan Charges Interest	C.B	1,320	00					
Dec.31	To Cash - Loan Charges Interest	C.B	8,096	00					
	To Temporary Sinking Fund - Loan Charges Principal	J	1,960	00					

(Balance transferred to General Revenue Account)

Municipal Accounting for Developing Countries

	Sewerage Revenue Account (19_8)								6
19_8	(Various Items of Revenue Expenditure including:)				19_8 Dec.31	(Various Items of Revenue Income)		?	
Feb.17	To Temporary Sinking Fund - Loan Charges Principal	J	2,040	00					
	To Cash - Loan Charges Interest	C.B	2,068	00					
Aug.17	To Cash - Loan Charges Interest	C.B	9,000	00					
	To Capital Discharged Loan Charges Principal	J	1,686	55					
Dec.31	To Capital Discharged Revenue Contribution to Capital Outlay	J	2,360	00					
			=====	==				=====	==

(Balance transferred to General Revenue Account)

Temporary Borrowing

Capital Discharged (Loans Repaid)									
19_8 Dec.31	To Balance	c/d	5,686	55	19_8 Feb.17	By Temporary Sinking Fund	J	4,000	00
					Aug.17	By Sewerage Revenue	J	1,686	55
			5,686	55				5,686	55
					19_9 Jan. 1	By Balance	b/d	5,686	55

Capital Discharged (Revenue Contribution)									8
19_8 Dec.31	To Balance	c/d	2,360	00	19_8 Dec.31	By Sewerage Revenue	J	2,360	00
					19_9 Dec.31	By Balance	b/d	2,360	00

The (isolated) Capital Balance Sheet as at 31 Dec. 19_8 will appear as follows:

Kisali - Relief Sewer
Capital Balance Sheet as at 31 Dec. 19_8

	U	Cts		U	Cts
LONG-TERM LIABILITES			FIXED ASSET		
Loans Outstanding	286,313	45	Kisali - Relief Sewer (at cost)	294,360	00
OTHER BALANCES					
Capital Discharged:					
Loans Repaid	5,686	55			
Revenue Contributions	2,360	00			
	294,360	00		294,360	00

207. CALCULATION OF INTEREST

When calculating a half-yearly payment of interest on a long-term loan it is customary to take one half of a full year's interest. This is often done by applying half the interest rate to the full principal sum. For example a half year's interest on a 6% loan may be found by multiplication of the principal by 3%.

Municipal Accounting for Developing Countries

Strictly speaking, this is not completely accurate, because the number of days in each half year is not normally the same. For example, in a calendar year (January to December) there are 181 days in the first half year and 184 days in the second half year. (Exceptionally a financial year running from April to March or from December to November will have the same number of days in each half year - during a leap year only).

With long-term loans, bearing regular interest, these technicalities are ignored, each half-yearly payment being regarded as an instalment of the annual sum.

However, with temporary loans, it is usual to calculate interest on a strict daily basis as shown in our examples. Confusion sometimes arises as to the exact number of days to be counted. The following is a useful rule which covers all circumstances:

"Interest is payable for every day upon which the loan is held at the close of business".

One or two examples will illustrate the point.

(a) A loan raised on 14 April and repaid on 15 April is held at the close of business only on 14 April, because by the close of business on 15 April it has been repaid. Therefore one day's interest is payable.

(b) A loan raised on 14 April and repaid on 19 June is held at the close of business on 14 April and on every subsequent day up to and including 18 June. By the close of business on 19 June it has been repaid, so that day does not count. Interest is payable from 14 April to 18 June inclusive, a total of 60 days.

(c) A loan raised on 14 April and still in hand on 30 June, (when half-yearly interest is due) is held at the close of business on 14 April and on every subsequent day up to and including 30 June. At the close of business on 30 June the loan is still in hand, not having been repaid. Interest is payable for 14 April to 30 June inclusive, a total of 78 days.

(d) A loan raised on 14 April and repaid on 30 June incurs interest for one day less than in (c) above, a total of 77 days, because by the close of business on 30 June the loan has been repaid.

Practice varies on the exact method of calculating interest during leap years. Feb. 29 must, of course, be counted as an additional day but professional opinions differ upon whether to divide by 366 days or 365 days. Of course, for a loan both raised and repaid during a leap year it is more accurate to use 366 days. However, a loan may be raised during a non leap year and repaid during a leap year (or vice versa). Here, strictly speaking, the calculation should be made in two parts, dividing by 365 for the non leap year and by 366 for the leap year. Few would go to such lengths, however, unless the loan was very large. Most people would use 365 days. In practice, many use 365 days without exception, leap year or not, as in our example.

Although the percentage variation between the two methods is only just over 0.18% it could make a noticeable difference on a large loan. For example, a loan of U 1,000,000 held for a substantial proportion of the year at a rate of interest around 6% would incur about U 100 additional interest by using 365 days than by using 366 days.

Temporary Borrowing

An alternative practice, often followed in the United States, assumes that the year contains 12 months of 30 days each, giving a 360-day year. Under this system, each complete month counts as 1/12 of a year and odd days as 1/30 of a month.

19. Replacement Borrowing and Sinking Funds

Synopsis		Page
208.	Replacement Borrowing - Introduction.	735
209.	Raising Short-Term Maturity Loans.	736
210.	Payment of Interest.	737
211.	Establishment of Sinking Fund.	738
212.	Repayment of Loans at Maturity.	740
213.	New Loans and Sinking Fund Appropriations.	742
214.	Adjustment of Loan Charges.	744
215.	Further Loan Repayments.	745
216.	Internal Borrowing from Sinking Fund.	748

208. REPLACEMENT BORROWING - INTRODUCTION

Discussion of borrowing procedures has so far centred mainly upon loans raised from a central authority for the full period of a loan sanction and repaid by annual instalments of principal and interest. This type of loan we have referred to as an earmarked loan. We have also seen how to make provision for the redemption of a maturity loan, raised for the full period of the sanction, by the use of a sinking fund.

In many developing countries scarce capital resources and the need for tight central control over borrowing operations, makes it likely that earmarked loans from a central authority will remain the main source of borrowing for some time to come.

However, as the nation's economy grows, internal sources of capital will increase, and some of this capital might well be available in the form of loans to local authorities. Furthermore, given the budgetary constraints upon national governments, innovative local authorities, if so authorised, may wish to seek for alternative capital funds from local private sources, to supplement what is available from public borrowings. For example, the mayor of a city or town may build up a good mutual relationship with commercial and industrial enterprises. There may then be readily perceived mutual advantage in such enterprises making loans to the municipal government whereas the incentive to lend to a higher level of government may be much less.

Unfortunately, the earmarked instalment loan, which has to be for the exact amount and period of a particular capital scheme, is not really a suitable type of investment for commercial and industrial capital. To attract this form of investment, a public authority must be prepared to accept maturity loans in relatively small sums for relatively shorter periods, even though the bulk of its capital schemes will require loan finance involving large sums for long periods.

A suitable form of investment to offer might well be maturity mortgages. Loans of (say) U 5,000 and upwards might be raised by local authorities for periods of up to 10 years. Borrowing would take place gradually and continuously, repayments being made from the proceeds of new loans. A single capital scheme might therefore be financed by a number of individual loans which will be replaced several times during the sanction period.

These same principles would also apply to municipal stock (bond) issues, but these introduce some additional complications which will not be considered here. Municipal stock (bond) issues are relatively uncommon in developing countries.

We have already seen in Chapter 18, how a temporary loan may be subsequently replaced by a more permanent loan. We must now extend our consideration of replacement borrowing, to cover all those types of loans which are not earmarked to either the amount or the period of a loan sanction.

209. RAISING SHORT-TERM MATURITY LOANS

Referring once again to the Capital Programme of Kambale Municipal Council, on page 287 of Chapter 9, we find a provision of U 180,000 in 19_7 under "Clinics and Dispensaries". We shall assume that this is for a Maternity and Child Welfare Clinic, constructed during 19_7. We shall further assume that the Ministry of Local Government grants a 20-year loan sanction for U 180,000 to be raised by maturity mortgages.

Kambale Municipal Council now issues a public advertisement for (say) 6% mortgage loans maturing (at the option of the lender) in 5, 7 or 10 years. The advertisement might well attempt to raise loans for several schemes together and we shall consider this point further when dealing with loans pools. For the moment we shall limit our consideration to a single scheme.

If the response to the advertisement is poor, insufficient loans will be raised, and further efforts will have to be made to seek loan finance elsewhere. If the response is exceptionally good, more loans will be offered than are required. In this case, the authority will be limited to raising loans only up to the total amount specified in the sanction, and some applications will have to be refused.

Assuming the response to be satisfactory, scores of different loans might be raised, with the total position being as follows:

Maturity (Yrs)	Total Loans Raised Units
5	110,000
7	30,000
10	40,000
	180,000

Included in the loan offers might be one of one of (say) U 1,000 for 5 years from Mr Mukasa, a farmer of Bukalasa; one of (say) U 9,000 for 7 years from Mr Kyeyune, a businessman who is investing for his retirement; one of (say) U 30,000 for 10 years from Food Products Pension Fund; and so on.

A personal record will be required for each lender, which might well be in the form of the register shown on page 561 of Chapter 15. Interest will be payable half-yearly on (say) 30 June and 31 December and will be entered in the register against the name of each lender as already explained in that chapter. Computerisation would be very appropriate.

We are here concerned mainly with the overall effect of the operation and will consider the accounting entries in total, rather than for individual loans.

Replacement Borrowing and Sinking Funds

Assume that the mortgage loan moneys are received on the following dates:

Date	Years	Amount
		Units
17/1/_7	5	10,000
22/1/_7	5	4,000
	10	30,000
23/1/_7	5	46,000
25/1/_7	7	16,000
	10	6,000
26/1/_7	5	32,000
30/1/_7	7	14,000
	10	4,000
2/2/_7	5	18,000
		180,000

The receipt of the loans could be journalised as follows:

19_7 (Various)	Cash DR. To Loans Outstanding Being receipt of various short-term maturity mortgage loans for construction of Maternity and Child Welfare Clinic	180,000	180,000

210. PAYMENT OF INTEREST

On 30 June 19_7, interest will be paid to individual lenders for the broken periods from the dates of raising the loans. Because interest is payable in equal half-yearly sums, the calculations will be based upon the number of days in the first half year (181). The total sum payable can be calculated as follows:

Date	Amount	No of Days	Product
	Units		'000
17/1/_7	10,000	165	1,650
22/1/_7	34,000	160	5,440
23/1/_7	46,000	159	7,314
25/1/_7	22,000	157	3,454
26/1/_7	32,000	156	4,992
30/1/_7	18,000	152	2,736
2/2/_7	18,000	149	2,682
	180,000		28,268

The payment of all interest on the last day of each half year ensures that the correct interest is charged in the accounts of each financial period without further adjustment.

$$\text{Interest} = \frac{28{,}268{,}000}{181} \times \frac{6}{100} \times \frac{1}{2}$$

$$= \text{U } 4{,}685 \text{ (to nearest unit)}$$

This figure would be used as a control total against which to prove the individual payments of interest to lenders, which will be recorded in their respective personal records.

The total payment of interest can be journalised as follows:

19_7 Jun.30	Clinics and Dispensaries (Revenue Account) Loan Charges - Interest DR. To Cash Being loan interest @ 6% on various short-term maturity mortgages as shown by loans ledger	4,685	4,685

At 31 Dec. 19_7, another instalment of interest will be payable, this time for the complete half year, journalised as follows:

19_7 Dec.31	Clinics and Dispensaries (Revenue Account) Loan Charges - Interest DR. To Cash Being loan interest @ 6% on various short-term maturity mortgages as shown by loans ledger	5,400	5,400

211. ESTABLISHMENT OF SINKING FUND

In order to provide funds to enable the whole of the loan debt to be redeemed over the period of the loan sanction (20 years) the authority must begin to make annual contributions to a sinking fund. Assuming an accumulated sinking fund with a notional interest rate of 3% the initial sinking fund contribution will be calculated as follows:

Amount of Loan	=	U 180,000
Period of Loan Sanction	=	20 years
Rate of Interest	=	3%
Figure from Loan Tables for a Loan of 1	=	0.03721571
Annual Contribution	=	U 0.03721571 x 180,000
	=	U 6,698.8278

The sinking fund contribution for 19_7 will therefore be U 6,699 (to the nearest unit).

In 19_8 and in each subsequent year until 19_6, the annual contribution will be 3% more than that of the immediately preceding year, as follows:

Replacement Borrowing and Sinking Funds

Instalment 2 (19_8)
U 6,698.8278 x 103% = 6,899.7926

Instalment 3 (19_9)
U 6,899,7926 x 103% = 7,106,7864

(and so on)

As shown in the following table, the contributions will be calculated to a high degree of accuracy (perhaps by a calculating machine or computer) and the figures afterwards rounded off to the nearest unit. (The figures marked (*) have been rounded downwards instead of upwards, so that the total contributions will come to exactly U 180,000.)

The complete sinking fund table will appear as follows:

ACCUMULATING SINKING FUND TABLE
To Provide a Sum of U 180,000 over 20 years with Contributions Accumulating at a Notional Rate of 3%

Instalment No	Year	Sinking Fund Contribution To Four Decimal Places	Sinking Fund Contribution To Nearest Unit	Sinking Fund Accumulation
1	19_7	6,698.8278	6,699	6,699
2	19_8	6,899.7926	6,900	13,599
3	19_9	7,106.7864	7,107	20,706
4	19_0	7,319.9900	7,320	28,026
5	19_1	7,539.5897	7,540	35,566
6	19_2	7,765.7774	7,766	43,332
7	19_3	7,998.7507	7,999	51,331
8	19_4	8,238.7132	8,239	59,570
9	19_5	8,485.8746	8,486	68,056
10	19_6	8,740.4508	8,740	76,796
11	19_7	9,002.6643	9,003	85,799
12	19_8	9,272.7442	9,273	95,072
13	19_9	9,550.9265	9,551	104,623
14	19_0	9,837.4543	9,837	114,460
15	19_1	10,132.5779	10,132*	124,592
16	19_2	10,436.5552	10,436*	135,028
17	19_3	10,749.6519	10,750	145,778
18	19_4	11,072.1415	11,072	156,850
19	19_5	11,404.3057	11,404	168,254
20	19_6	11,746.4349	11,746	180,000
		180,000.0096	180,000	

The sinking fund contribution for 19_7 can be journalised as follows:

19_7 Dec.31	Clinics and Dispensaries Loan Charges - Principal DR. To Sinking Fund Being contribution for year as shown by sinking fund table	6,699	6,699

The contribution should be invested in easily realisable investments. Assuming this to be a fixed 4% bank deposit the transaction can be journalised as follows:

| 19_7 Dec.31 | Sinking Fund Investment (4% Bank Deposit) DR. To Cash Being investment of sinking fund contribution | 6,699 | 6,699 |

Each sinking fund contribution, apart from the first, includes an element of notional interest. Actual interest received on the investment of the sinking fund will be credited to the Clinics and Dispensaries Revenue Account to be offset against loan interest paid. Loan charges for the first years (assuming the investment interest rate remains unchanged) can be shown by the following table, which shows how the use of an accumulating sinking fund keeps the annual loan charges reasonably constant.

Year	Interest Paid 6%	Interest Received 4%	Net Interest	Sinking Fund Contribution	Total Loan Charges
	Units	Units	Units	Units	Units
19_7	10,085	-	10,085	6,699	16,784
19_8	10,800	268	10,532	6,900	17,432
19_9	10,800	544	10,256	7,107	17,363
19_0	10,800	828	9,972	7,320	17,292
19_1	10,800	1,121	9,679	7,540	17,219

212. REPAYMENT OF LOANS AT MATURITY

We shall assume that the Maternity and Child Welfare Clinic finally cost U 183,240, the excess cost being financed from revenue. If all payments had been made by 31 Dec. 19_7 the (isolated) Capital Balance Sheet would appear as follows:

Maternity and Child Welfare Clinic
Capital Balance Sheet as at 31 Dec. 19_7

	Units		Units
LONG-TERM LIABILITY		FIXED ASSET	
Loans Outstanding	180,000	Buildings	183,240
OTHER BALANCES		CURRENT ASSET	
Capital Discharged		Investments	6,699
(RCCO)	3,240		
Sinking Fund	6,699		
	189,939		189,939

Four years later, by 31 Dec. 19_1, (had no loan repayments been pending) the position would have been as follows:

Replacement Borrowing and Sinking Funds

Maternity and Child Welfare Clinic
Capital Balance Sheet as at 31 Dec. 19_1

	Units		Units
LONG-TERM LIABILITIES		FIXED ASSET	
Loans Outstanding	180,000	Buildings	183,240
OTHER BALANCES		CURRENT ASSETS	
Capital Discharged		Investments	35,566
(RCCO)	3,240		
Sinking Fund	35,566		
	218,806		218,806

However, referring to the table on page 737 it can be seen that loans totalling **U** 110,000 have a maturity of five years. They are therefore due to be repaid on various dates early in 19_2 as follows:

Date	Amount
	Units
17/1/_2	10,000
22/1/_2	4,000
23/1/_2	46,000
26/1/_2	32,000
2/2/_2	18,000
	110,000

The total cash required to repay these loans will be **U** 110,000. However, the sinking fund has so far accumulated only **U** 35,566, which is obviously insufficient. It will therefore be necessary to raise some additional short-term mortgages for the balance, as follows:

Loan Repayments Due	110,000	
Less Sinking Fund in Hand	35,000	(round figures)
Replacement Borrowing	75,000	

On 31 Dec. 19_1, all sinking fund investments will be realised, only the odd **U** 566 remaining invested (or being reinvested). The amount actually held in the deposit account at this date, before the 19_1 contribution had been made would be **U** 28,026, because it would be quite pointless to invest the 19_1 contribution if it was intended to withdraw it on the same date. The withdrawal could be journalised as follows:

19_1 Dec.31	Cash DR.	27,460	
	To Sinking Fund Investment		
	(4% Bank Deposit)		27,460
	Being realisation of investment, pending repayment of short-term mortgage loans		

At this point, before the 19_1 contribution, the position will be as follows:

Maternity and Child Welfare Clinic
Capital Balance Sheet as at 31 Dec. 19_1

	Units		Units
LONG-TERM LIABILITIES		FIXED ASSET	
Loans Outstanding	180,000	Buildings	183,240
OTHER BALANCES		CURRENT ASSETS	
Capital Discharged		Investments	566
(RCCO)	3,240	Cash	27,460
Sinking Fund	28,026		
	211,266		211,266

After the 19_1 contribution of U 7,540 the position will be as follows:

Maternity and Child Welfare Clinic
Capital Balance Sheet as at 31 Dec. 19_1

	Units		Units
LONG-TERM LIABILITIES		FIXED ASSET	
Loans Outstanding	180,000	Buildings	183,240
OTHER BALANCES		CURRENT ASSETS	
Capital Discharged		Investments	566
(RCCO)	3,240	Cash	35,000
Sinking Fund	35,566		
	218,806		218,806

(The additional capital cash has been appropriated from revenue cash.)

213. NEW LOANS AND SINKING FUND APPROPRIATIONS

During Jan. 19_2, the replacement loans, totalling U 75,000, will be raised. There might well be a number of mortgages with various maturities as originally raised in 19_7. However, for simplicity, we shall assume that on 15 Jan. 19_2 a single 10-year $6\frac{1}{2}$% maturity mortgage is raised for the full sum, journalised as follows:

19_2 Jan.15	Cash DR.	75,000	
	To Loans Outstanding		75,000
	Being receipt of short-term maturity mortgage as replacement for earlier loans now to be repaid		

The position will be as follows:

Replacement Borrowing and Sinking Funds

Maternity and Child Welfare Clinic
Capital Balance Sheet as at 15 Jan. 19_2

	Units		Units
LONG-TERM LIABILITIES		FIXED ASSET	
Loans Outstanding	255,000	Buildings	183,240
OTHER BALANCES		CURRENT ASSETS	
Capital Discharged		Investments	566
(RCCO)	3,240	Cash	110,000
Sinking Fund	35,566		
	293,806		293,806

There is now sufficient cash to begin paying off the earlier loans on 17 Jan.

Legally, of course, for a few days, loans would be held in excess of sanction figure of U 180,000, but this is a technicality which can be safely accepted. The alternative would be to pay off the earlier loans first, borrowing to meet the resulting overdraft. This would keep strictly to the letter of the law but might well create practical difficulties, especially if the Council's working balances were low.

The Chief Financial Officer must try to avoid, as far as possible, the payment of "idle" interest on the double loan burden or the payment of "penal" interest on a bank overdraft. He can do this by arranging the raising of new loans to be synchronized with the repayment of the old. It would, however, be too much to expect that this could always be done exactly and a few days' overlap can reasonably be accepted.

By 2 Feb., all the old loans will have been repaid, journalised as follows:

19_2 (Various)	Loans Outstanding DR.
	  To Cash
	  Being repayment of various
	  short-term maturity loans
		110,000	110,000

The sinking fund has been used to discharge loan debt of U 35,000 and the following adjustment is therefore required:

19_2
Feb. 2
	Sinking Fund DR.
	  To Capital Discharged
	    (Loans Repaid)
	  Being application of sinking
	  fund in redemption of loan
	  debt
		35,000	35,000

After this, the balance sheet will appear as follows:

Maternity and Child Welfare Clinic
Capital Balance Sheet as at 2 Feb. 19_2

	Units		Units
LONG-TERM LIABILITIES		FIXED ASSETS	
Loans Outstanding	145,000	Buildings	183,240
OTHER BALANCES		CURRENT ASSET	
Capital Discharged:		Investments	566
RCCO	3,240		
Loans Repaid	35,000		
Sinking Fund	566		
	183,806		183,806

214. ADJUSTMENT OF LOAN CHARGES

The balance of interest due on the loans repaid would be calculated as followed:

Date	Amount	No of Days	Product '000
17/1/_2	10,000	16	160
22/1/_2	4,000	21	84
23/1/_2	46,000	22	1,012
26/1/_2	32,000	25	800
2/2/_2	18,000	32	576
	110,000		2,632

$$\text{Interest} = \frac{2,632,000}{181} \times \frac{6}{100} \times \frac{1}{2}$$

$$= \text{U } 436 \text{ (to nearest unit)}$$

The payment of interest could be journalised as follows:

19_2 (Various)	Clinics and Dispensaries Loan Charges - Interest DR.
	  To Cash
	    Being loan interest @ 6% on various short-term maturity mortgages as shown by loans ledger
		436	436

The net total of loan charges payable during 19_2 will be as follows:

Replacement Borrowing and Sinking Funds

Interest

Interest at 6% for broken periods on loans (U 110,000) 17 Jan. to 2 Feb.	436	
Interest at 6½% on new loan (U 75,000) raised on 15 Jan:		
First half year (167 days)	2,249	
Second half year (full)	2,438	
Interest at 6% on remaining loans (U 70,000) for full year	4,200	
	9,323	
Less Interest at 4% on sinking fund investment (U 566)	23	9,300

Principal

Sinking Fund Contribution for year		7,766
Total Loan Charges		17,066

The annual sinking fund contributions will continue to be made in accordance with the table on page 739, even though some of the Fund has been applied. This is because it is based on the full amount and period of the loan sanction. However, from 19_2 onwards the accumulations will be U 35,000 less than those shown in the table.

Loan charges for 19_3 will consist of:

Interest

6% on original loans remaining (U 70,000)	4,200	
6½% on replacement loan (U 75,000)	4,875	
	9,075	
Less Interest at 4% on sinking fund investment of U 8,332 (U 43,332 − 35,000)	332	8,743

Principal

Sinking Fund Contribution for year		7,999
Total Loan Charges		16,742

215. FURTHER LOAN REPAYMENTS

During 19_4 the seven-year loans totalling U 30,000 require repayment, and a replacement loan (or loans) will be required as follows:

Loan Repayments Due	30,000
Less Sinking Fund in Hand (Dec. 19_3)	16,000 (round figures)
Replacement Borrowing	14,000

The procedure will be exactly the same as before and will be repeated again and again during the sanction period until the final loans are repaid. The complete pattern might well be as shown in the table on page 725.

The table shows how the sinking fund is gradually appropriated for the

KAMBALE MUNICIPAL COUNCIL

Maternity and Child Welfare Centre - Replacement Borrowing

(a)	(b)	(c)	(d)	(e)		(f)		(g)		(h)	(i)	(j)	(k)
Year	Transactions During Year			Various Blocks of Maturity Loans						Position after the Transactions			
	Loans Repaid	Financed From		Block 1		Block 2		Block 3		Loan Debt		Sinking Fund	
		Sinking Fund Appropriations	Replacement Loans	Amount	Period to Run	Amount	Period to Run	Amount	Period to Run	Out-standing	Repaid from Sinking Fund	Gross Contributions to end of Previous Year	Net Balance after Appropriations
				Units	Yrs	Units	Yrs	Units	Yrs	Units	Units	Units	Units
19_7			180,000										
	ORIGINAL LOAN			110,000	5	30,000	7	40,000	10	180,000	-	-	-
19_8	-	-	-	110,000	4	30,000	6	40,000	9	180,000	-	6,699	6,699
19_9	-	-	-	110,000	3	30,000	5	40,000	8	180,000	-	13,599	13,599
19_0	-	-	-	110,000	2	30,000	4	40,000	7	180,000	-	20,706	20,706
19_1	-	-	-	110,000	1	30,000	3	40,000	6	180,000	-	28,026	28,026
19_2	110,000	35,000	75,000	75,000	10	30,000	2	40,000	5	145,000	35,000	35,566	566
19_3	-	-	-	75,000	9	30,000	1	40,000	4	145,000	35,000	43,332	8,332
19_4	30,000	16,000	14,000	75,000	8	14,000	5	40,000	3	129,000	51,000	51,331	331
19_5	-	-	-	75,000	7	14,000	4	40,000	2	129,000	51,000	59,570	8,570
19_6	-	-	-	75,000	6	14,000	3	40,000	1	129,000	51,000	68,056	17,056
19_7	40,000	25,000	15,000	75,000	5	14,000	2	15,000	7	104,000	76,000	76,796	796
19_8	-	-	-	75,000	4	14,000	1	15,000	6	104,000	76,000	85,799	9,799
19_9	14,000	14,000	-	75,000	3			15,000	5	90,000	90,000	95,072	5,072
19_0	-	-	-	75,000	2			15,000	4	90,000	90,000	104,623	14,623
19_1	-	-	-	75,000	1			15,000	3	90,000	90,000	114,460	24,460
19_2	75,000	34,000	41,000	41,000	5			15,000	2	56,000	124,000	124,592	592
19_3	-	15,000	-	41,000	4			15,000	1	56,000	124,000	135,028	11,028
19_4	15,000	-	-	41,000	3					41,000	139,000	145,778	6,778
19_5	-	-	-	41,000	2					41,000	139,000	156,850	17,850
19_6	-	-	-	41,000	1					41,000	139,000	168,254	29,254
19_7	41,000	41,000	-							-	180,000	180,000	-

Replacement Borrowing and Sinking Funds

repayment of various maturity loans as and when they fall due. Replacement borrowing is made only for net requirements, after appropriation of sinking fund balances in hand at the repayment date of particular loans.

Column (a) shows the years covered by the loan sanction, beginning with the year in which it is first exercised and ending with the year in which the loan debt is finally redeemed.

Columns (b) to (d) show the replacement borrowing transactions taking place during appropriate years. Column (b) shows the amount of loans to be repaid and column (c) shows the amount appropriated from the sinking fund to finance the repayment. The difference is met by replacement borrowing as shown by column (d).

Columns (e) to (g) show the original "blocks" of short-term mortgage loans raised, grouped according to maturity. Each column indicates how many years the loans have to run and show what loans, if any, are raised to finance repayments. Column (e) shows that the original loans of U 110,000 were replaced after 5 years by others totalling U 75,000 with maturities of 10 years, the balance being repaid from the sinking fund. After this further 10-year period expired, loans totalling U 41,000 were raised for a 5-year period. Column (f) shows that loans totalling U 30,000 were replaced after 7 years by others totalling U 14,000 for 5 years. These, in turn, could be repaid wholly out of the sinking fund and no further loans were required. Column (g) shows that loans totalling U 40,000 were replaced after 10 years by others totalling U 15,000 for 7 years. Once again, these were repaid wholly out of the sinking fund.

Columns (h) and (i) show how much of the loan debt remains outstanding and how much has been repaid from the sinking fund. The two columns together always total to the amount of the original loan (U 180,000). Column (h) is the total of columns (e) (f) and (g) whereas column (i) is built up by the items shown in column (c).

Column (j) shows the total sinking fund contributions made up to the end of the previous year and is a repeat of the figures shown in the tables on page 739. Column (k) shows how much of the sinking fund remains after the appropriations shown in column (i) have been deducted.

To show how the table operates we shall examine the transactions in 19_7. Column (e) shows loans of U 75,000 with 5 years to run and column (f) shows loans of U 14,000 with 2 years to run. Column (g) shows that in 19_6 there were loans of U 40,000 with only 1 year to run, indicating that they must be repaid during 19_7. Sinking fund contributions available total U 76,796 less the sum of U 51,000 already appropriated by the end of 19_6. The net amount available to meet further loan repayments is therefore U 76,796 - 51,000 = U 25,796. The odd sum of U 796 is allowed to remain in the fund and U 25,000 appropriated as shown in column (c). New loans totalling U 15,000 are raised for the balance not covered by the sinking fund as shown by column (d). The U 25,000 now appropriated is added to the U 51,000 already appropriated, to give a total of U 76,000 as shown in column (i) and leaving a balance of U 796 in hand.

In 19_9 it can be seen that the U 14,000 in column (f) is due for repayment. The sinking fund contributions have totalled U 95,072 of which U 76,000 has been appropriated, leaving a balance of U 19,072. This is more than enough to repay the U 14,000 loan, so that on this occasion no replacement borrowing is required. The U 14,000 is appropriated from the sinking fund, leaving a balance of U 5,072 in hand.

The table should be regarded as flexible. For example, let us now assume that the loan of **U** 40,000 in column (g) is from a single lender, who in 19_7 is prepared to renew his loan at a favourable interest rate for a further period of 10 years. At the same time, replacement loans of **U** 15,000 might be difficult to obtain. It might then be of advantage to the authority to retain the original loan. In this case nothing further will be appropriated from the sinking fund, which will thus stand at **U** 25,796 instead of **U** 796. Each subsequent balance of the sinking fund shown in column (k) will be increased by **U** 25,000 until 19_3 and then by **U** 40,000 until the loan is finally repaid in 19_7. In this case columns (a) and (k) will appear as follows:

(a)	(k)
19_7	25,796
19_8	34,799
19_9	30,072
19_0	39,623
19_1	49,460
19_2	25,592
19_3	36,028
19_4	46,778
19_5	57,850
19_6	69,254
19_7	-

216. INTERNAL BORROWING FROM SINKING FUND

Amongst the advantages of raising loans by short-term mortgages is that, by the use of skilful debt management techniques, the sinking fund provided for repayment of mortgages can often be used temporarily for new capital purposes.

In the example just given, this advantage could materialise by raising in 19_7 an internal loan of (say) **U** 25,000 from the sinking fund for a maximum period of 10 years and for a completely different capital scheme. The accounting procedures would be exactly the same as those explained in Chapter 17. The sinking fund would, of course, be substituted for the repairs fund illustrated in that chapter. It is important to note the contrast between the external loan and the internal loan regarding provision for repayment. The external loan is a maturity loan, with repayments covered by the sinking fund. However, the internal loan is an instalment loan. The borrowing account must make provision for annual debt service to the sinking fund, as if it had raised an external, earmarked, instalment loan.

20. Loans Pooling

Section		Page
217.	Loans Pooling - Introduction.	750
218.	Internal Borrowing by the Pool.	751
219.	External Borrowing by the Pool.	754
220.	Records of the Pool.	755
221.	Appropriation of Existing Sinking Fund.	756
222.	Internal Investment of Capital Fund Monies.	758
223.	Advances from Loans Pool for Capital Expenditure.	759
224.	Further Advances Financed from Internal Sources.	761
225.	Advances from External Maturity Mortgages.	763
226.	Repayments of Principal to the Loans Pool.	768
227.	Ledger Accounts - Capital Transactions.	772
228.	Revenue Transactions - Interest.	785
229.	Revenue Transactions - Debt Management Expenses.	790
230.	Ledger Accounts - Revenue Transactions.	793
231.	Loans Pool Transactions - Subsequent Years.	805
232.	Loans Pooling - Conclusion.	818

217. LOANS POOLING - INTRODUCTION

We have seen how the use of maturity mortgages with sinking funds can create a more flexible system of borrowing than is possible with earmarked instalment loans. However, where there are a number of schemes to be financed, the calculation and operation of separate sinking funds can become somewhat complex. This is particularly so if one scheme is financed by an internal loan from the sinking fund relating to another scheme.

For even greater flexibility, a system has been devised whereby all borrowing from external sources is pooled, money being re-lent from the pool to finance various capital schemes. This system, called loans pooling, has already been briefly referred to in Section 176 of Chapter 15.

A loans pool may be set up to include only the loans of a particular class (e.g. all maturity mortgages). On the other hand it may include all the loans of the authority, including stock issues, instalment loans, maturity mortgages and bonds. The former type is sometimes known as a mortgage pool whilst the latter type is usually referred to as a consolidated loans fund.

There is little advantage to be gained from the pooling of earmarked instalment loans, unless they can be pooled with a reasonable proportion of loans of other types. Thus, in countries where most local authority borrowing is from government sources, using instalment repayments, loans pooling is inappropriate. However, the system, which is infinitely flexible, can provide additional opportunities for municipalities to attract capital finance from local private sources. Borrowing instruments suitable to commercial lenders can be reconciled with the requirements of municipalities for long-term finance.

A word of warning is appropriate. As with maturity loans and sinking funds, loans pools can only be operated successfully where there is a reasonably efficient market, in which loans can be "rolled over" (as the Americans say), to provide for replacement of loans repayable prior to maturity of the repayment provisions. There is, indeed, an element of "borrowing short and lending long", with the consequent mismatching of maturities.

The system would be very suitable for operation with a government guarantee. Also, it could be used jointly by several authorities or by (say) a metropolitan development authority servicing several municipalities.

Loans Pooling

The accounting procedures are almost the same as would be used for a local authorities loans fund operated under the supervision of a national, state or provincial government. The principal difference is that a national fund would recover its costs through fixed or variable interest rates, rather than by the process of apportionment.

We shall not deal in detail with a consolidated loans fund but confine our attention to a pool for maturity mortgages. With this type of loan, pooling is often unavoidable. The general principles and accounting arrangements are, however, applicable to any system of loans pooling and they can be extended to cover the requirements of a wider range of pooled loans.

Referring to the Capital Programme on page 287 of Chapter 9, let us assume the following details about selected schemes to be financed from a loans pool. The pool, in turn, is to be financed mainly by the raising of short-term maturity mortgages.

		Loan Sanction		Actual Capital Expenditure			
Year	Scheme	Period Yrs	Amount	Total	19_7	19_8	19_9
19_7	Administrative Buildings	40	420,000	421,580	120,420	301,160	-
19_7	Ambulance	5	46,000	45,660	45,660	-	-
19_7	Sewerage Disposal Works	30	510,000	508,920	241,360	173,880	93,680
19_8	Ambulance	5	47,000	46,220	-	46,220	-
19_8	Sewerage Diwali Road	30	192,000	191,700	-	191,700	-
19_9	Ambulance	5	48,000	48,740	-	-	48,740
19_9	Clinic - Bugoma	40	200,000	196,320	-	-	196,320
19_9	Street Lighting	20	180,000	182,360	-	-	182,360
	TOTALS		1,643,000	1,641,500	407,440	712,960	521,100

A capital financing forecast might have been prepared as shown on page 752. The timing of loan-raising operations will depend upon the detailed arrangements under which the pooling system operates. A common system is for advances to be made from the loans pool quarterly, in arrears. These advances cover, in round figures, the various capital payments made during the preceding quarter. If this practice were followed in our case, we should estimate that U 46,000 will be advanced from the pool at the end of the first quarter of 19_7, that is, on 31 March. An estimated U 40,000 will be advanced on 30 June, U 150,000 on 30 September and so on.

218. **INTERNAL BORROWING BY THE POOL**

Of course, the loans pool cannot advance money which it does not have. Therefore, sufficient loans must be raised to put the pool in funds by the time the advances are due.

Before searching for outside loans, the Chief Financial Officer will consider what internal funds are available for lending to the pool. In the case of Kambale Municipal Council some proportion of the following

CAPITAL FINANCING FORECAST

Capital Expenditure to be Financed from Loans Pool

Scheme	Total Estimated Cost	19 7 1st Qtr	19 7 2nd Qtr	19 7 3rd Qtr	19 7 4th Qtr	19 8 1st Qtr	19 8 2nd Qtr	19 8 3rd Qtr	19 8 4th Qtr	19 9 1st Qtr	19 9 2nd Qtr	19 9 3rd Qtr	19 9 4th Qtr
Administrative Buildings	420,000	-	-	50,000	65,000	150,000	150,000	5,000	-	-	-	-	-
Ambulance	46,000	46,000	-	-	-	-	-	-	-	-	-	-	-
Sewage Disposal Works	510,000	-	40,000	100,000	100,000	60,000	60,000	30,000	30,000	30,000	30,000	30,000	-
Ambulance	47,000	-	-	-	-	-	47,000	-	-	-	-	-	-
Sewerage - Diwali Road	192,000	-	-	-	-	20,000	140,000	-	-	-	-	-	-
Ambulance	48,000	-	-	-	-	-	-	-	32,000	-	48,000	-	-
Clinic - Bugoma	200,000	-	-	-	-	-	-	-	-	60,000	130,000	10,000	-
Street Lighting	180,000	-	-	-	-	-	-	-	-	10,000	60,000	80,000	30,000
	1,643,000	46,000	40,000	150,000	165,000	230,000	397,000	35,000	62,000	100,000	268,000	120,000	30,000

Loans Pooling

funds would be considered as possible sources of internal investment:

> Capital Fund
> Capital Receipts Unapplied
> Sinking Fund
> Housing Repairs Fund
> Vehicle Renewals Fund
> Office Equipment Renewals Fund

Not all of these funds could be invested internally. Consideration would have to be given to the existing form of investments, cash requirements, forthcoming commitments etc. In order to show how the position might be dealt with in practice, let us consider each fund in detail.

(a) **General**

The whole of the investments are in the form of 5% bank deposits, easily realised at short notice. There will, therefore, be no loss or difficulty in changing any investment to an internal one with the pool. The position might have been different had some of the investments been held, in (say) securities currently valued at below cost or earning a higher rate of interest than the current rate for borrowing. In the first case the authority would incur a capital loss by realising the investments. In the second case, it would suffer a loss in interest earnings.

(b) **Capital Fund**

The total value of the fund is U 123,140. At 31 Dec. 19_6 it was held in easily realisable investments earning 5% interest. Let us assume that U 70,000 is being earmarked to finance, by an outright contribution, an expected overspending on the scheme for the North Street/Park Road new road. This means that U 53,140 is likely to be available for investment in the loans pool. This is more than sufficient to meet the expected advance of U 46,000 on 31 March. The Chief Financial Officer, therefore, arranges to withdraw U 46,000 from external investments and invest the money in the loans pool on 31 March 19_7.

(c) **Capital Receipts Unapplied**

Since these funds were not invested at all on 31 Dec. 19_6 there is an implication that they are shortly to be used to meet capital payments. We shall, therefore, assume that they are not available for investment in the loans pool. However, in appropriate circumstances such funds could well be invested in the pool.

(d) **Sinking Fund**

One important purpose of a pool is to enable sinking funds to be made available for future borrowing, instead of being separately invested. It would, therefore, be quite in order for both the existing and future sinking fund contributions to be invested in the pool. In practice, however, separate sinking funds would be abolished when a pool was established. The contributions would be made to the pool as repayments. We shall later demonstrate how this is done.

(e) **Housing Repairs Fund**

It might not only be permissible but prudent to invest in the loans pool any balance of the Housing Repairs Fund not immediately required for day-to-day purposes. However, in Chapter 17 we used the Housing Repairs Fund to demonstrate internal borrowing for the construction of an abattoir. In practice, when the loans pool was established, it might well be sensible to handle all internal borrowing through the pool. Nevertheless, for the purpose only of avoiding undue complication in this book, we shall leave the transactions of the Housing Repairs Fund undisturbed.

(f) Vehicle Renewals Fund

The total value of the fund is U 37,745, held at 31 Dec. 19_6 in easily realisable investments earning 5% interest. We shall assume that U 16,000 is being earmarked for the purchase of a new staff car in 19_7. This means that U 21,745 is likely to be available for investment in the loans pool, provided other future commitments are safeguarded.

(g) Office Equipment Renewals Fund

The total value of the fund is U 26,620, held at 31 Dec. 19_6 in easily realisable investments earning 5% interest. We shall assume that U 6,000 is being earmarked for the purchase of office equipment during 19_7. This means that U 20,620 is likely to be available for investment in the loans pool, provided other future commitments are safeguarded.

The pool's loan requirements for March 31 are to be met from the capital fund. Its requirements for 30 June 19_7 can be met by the investment in the pool of U 20,000 from each of the renewals funds, making U 40,000.

By thus making maximum use of all available internal funds, the need to raise loans externally is delayed until the third quarter of 19_7.

219. EXTERNAL BORROWING BY THE POOL

All available internal funds have been used to finance the activities of the pool for the first and second quarters of 19_7. Until further internal funds or repayments of advances become available, subsequent advances will have to be financed by external loans, in the form of short-term maturity mortgages. U 150,000 is likely to be required by 30 September and a further U 165,000 by 31 December.

We have seen in Section 209 that when short-term mortgages are raised, there may be a large number of loans of varying amounts, raised on different dates for different periods. Section 210 illustrates how interest is calculated for the odd number of days until the end of the particular half year in which the loans are first raised. These principles are precisely the same when short-term mortgages are raised for a loans pool. However, to avoid repeating earlier explanations and introducing unnecessary complications, we shall assume that the whole of the required sum for a particular quarter's advances is raised as if on one particular day from a single lender. For example, actual loans for (say) the last quarter of 19_7 might be raised as follows:

Date	Amount	Number of Days	Product
	Units	to end of Period	
11.12._7	40,000	21	840,000
13.12._7	31,000	19	589,000
14.12._7	28,000	18	504,000
15.12._7	18,000	17	306,000
16.12._7	12,000	16	192,000
18.12._7	26,000	14	364,000
31.12._7	10,000	1	10,000
	165,000		2,805,000

Loans Pooling

The product of 2,805,000 is exactly as it would have been for a single loan raised on 15 Dec. 19_7 for the full amount of U 165,000 and running for 17 days until the end of the year. (Note that this is not a short-cut method of calculating interest - merely a means of simplifying the explanation.)

220. RECORDS OF THE POOL

Because the loans pool is deemed to act as an intermediate stage between borrowing and lending, it is appropriate to treat it as a separate fund, with a separate set of accounts including a separate cash account. A separate bank account might well provide an additional element of financial control but it is not essential, in principle. The subsidiary records of the pool lend themselves readily to computerisation. They will include the following:

(a) Cash Account - preferably as special columns in the main cash book of the authority. (A separate cash account does not necessarily imply a separate bank account.)

(b) Lenders Personal Accounts - giving details of names and addresses of lenders, the amount and terms of loans and the rates and amounts of periodical interest payable.

(c) Diary of Loans - giving details of the dates when various loans fall due for repayments.

(d) Loans Sanction Register - giving full details of the various approvals to borrow, granted by the Government or other authorising body. The register will have columns for:

   Consecutive No.
   File No.
   Official reference number of sanction
   Name of sanctioning authority
   Borrowing account
   Purpose of loan
   Period for which loan is sanctioned
   Amount

Additional columns can be added to give details of the exercise of the sanction. This may not always be for the maximum approved amount and period, as shown later. Details may also be entered about sanctions which have been cancelled or not exercised for any reason.

(e) Register of Advances - giving details of all advances made from the pool against loan sanctions. Details will include the amount and date of the advances to borrowing accounts and the details and amounts of instalments to be repaid to the pool.

(f) Register of Investments - giving details of investment of surplus cash in the pool. In normal circumstances pool investments will be few. The object of the loans pool is to raise funds to invest internally for capital purposes, not to invest externally. However, there may be times when the pool has borrowed in advance of its lending requirements; alternatively it may have received repayments from borrowing accounts before repayments of external loans are due. These circumstances will create temporary cash surpluses, which can be invested externally for short periods.

An additional note of caution is necessary regarding pool investments. With a flourishing and efficient money market these will largely be unnecessary. However, in circumstances where re-borrowing opportunities are expected to be difficult or limited in amount, it would be prudent to make monetary investments to assure funds availability for future loan repayments. A loans pool is not, after all, an additional source of funds - merely an accounting device and fund-raising facilitator.

221. APPROPRIATION OF EXISTING SINKING FUNDS

The only separate sinking fund at 31 Dec. 19_6 relates to the purchase of an accounting machine as described in Section 180 of Chapter 15. As shown on page 576 of that chapter the Capital Balance Sheet would appear as follows:

Balance Sheet as at 31 Dec. 19_6
(Capital)

	Units		Units
LONG-TERM LIABILITES		FIXED ASSETS	
Loans Outstanding	10,000	Accounting Machine	10,000
OTHER BALANCES		CURRENT ASSETS	
Sinking Fund	2,000	Investments	2,000
	12,000		12,000

On 1 Jan. 19_7, the pool will take over responsibility for repayment of the external loan. In return for this, the accounts of the finance department (known as the borrowing accounts) will hand over to the pool all provisions made to date for debt redemption. The accounts of the borrowing fund or department will be treated as having actually repaid part of its loan debt instead of merely having made provision for repayment. The journal entries affecting the borrowing account will be as follows:

19_7					
Jan. 1	Loans Outstanding DR. To Investments Being the handing over of sinking fund investments to the Council's Loans Pool - to be treated as a loan repayment	1 4	2,000	2,000
Jan. 1	Sinking Fund DR. To Capital Discharged (Loans Repaid) Being appropriation of sinking fund towards redemption of loan debt	2 5	2,000	2,000

Loans Pooling

The Capital Balance Sheet will now appear as follows:

Accounting Machine
Balance Sheet as at 1 Jan. 19_7
(Capital)

	Units		Units
LONG-TERM LIABILITIES		FIXED ASSET	
Loans Outstanding	8,000	Accounting Machine	10,000
OTHER BALANCES			
Capital Discharged:			
Loans Repaid	2,000		
	10,000		10,000

The position as it affects the borrowing account is now precisely the same as if an instalment of the loan had been repaid to an outside lender. In fact, to a borrowing account, this is exactly what the loans pool represents.

Now let us consider the accounts of the loans pool. The journal entries for taking over the external loan debt and the repayment provisions will be as follows:

19_7					
Jan. 1	Advances to Borrowing Accounts (Finance) DR.	P.1	8,000		
	Investments DR.	P.2	2,000		
	To Loans Outstanding	P.3			10,000
	Being assumption of responsibility for external loan debt on accounting machine				

The balance sheet of the pool will appear as follows:

Loans Pool
Balance Sheet as at 1 Jan. 19_7

	Units		Units
LOANS OUTSTANDING		ADVANCES TO BORROWING	
External Mortgages	10,000	ACCOUNTS	
		Finance Department	8,000
		INVESTMENTS	2,000
	10,000		10,000

The left-hand side of the balance sheet reflects the Council's liability to repay the external loan of U 10,000. The right-hand side shows that U 8,000 is still advanced by the pool to a borrowing account. The amount already repaid by the borrowing account is held as an investment.

Because the loans pool will not make any advances or repayments until 31 March 19_7, the investment is taken over undisturbed. Had cash been immediately required by the pool, the investment would have been realised, before being handed over. We can understand this alternative by assuming that the sinking fund was appropriated on 31 March 19_7 instead of on 1 Jan. 19_7. In this case, cash would have been required immediately. The journal entries would be as follows:

(a) **Borrowing Accounts (Finance)**

19_7				
Mar.31	Cash DR.		2,000	
	To Investments			2,000
	Being realisation of investments			
Mar.31	Loans Outstanding DR.		2,000	
	To Cash (General)			2,000
	Being the handing over of sinking fund cash to the Council's Loans Pool - to be treated as a loan repayment			
Mar.31	Sinking Fund DR.		2,000	
	To Capital Discharged (Loans Repaid)			2,000
	Being appropriation of sinking fund towards redemption of loan debt			

(b) **Loans Pool Accounts**

19_7				
Mar.31	Advances to Borrowing Accounts (Finance) DR.		8,000	
	Cash (Pool) DR.		2,000	
	To Loans Outstanding			10,000
	Being assumption of responsibility for external loan debt on accounting machine			

We shall now return to where the investment (as opposed to cash) was taken over by the pool. In this case the pool (as opposed to the borrowing account) will realise the investment, journalised as follows:

Loans Pool Account

19_7					
Mar.31	Cash (Pool) DR.	C.P. P.2	2,000		
	To Investments			2,000	
	Being realisation of investments				

222. **INTERNAL INVESTMENT OF CAPITAL FUND MONIES**

On 31 March 19_7 it is planned to realise U 46,000 of investments relating to the Capital Fund, investing the proceeds in the loans pool. The journal entries will be as follows:

Loans Pooling

(a) **Capital Fund Accounts**

19_7				
Mar.31	Cash DR. To Capital Fund Investments (External) Being realisation of investments	C.G. 7	46,000	46,000
Mar.31	Capital Fund Investments (Pool) DR. To Cash Being internal investment surplus funds in Council's Loans Pool	8 C.G.	46,000	46,000

(b) **Loans Pool Accounts**

19_7				
Mar.31	Cash (Pool) DR. To Loans Outstanding Being internal loan raised from the Capital Fund	C.P. P.4	46,000	46,000

The Loans Pool Balance Sheet now becomes:

Loans Pool
Balance Sheet as at 31 March 19_7

	Units		Units
LOANS OUTSTANDING		ADVANCES TO BORROWING	
External Mortgage	10,000	ACCOUNTS	
Internal Funds	46,000	Finance Department	8,000
		CASH IN HAND	48,000
	56,000		56,000

223. ADVANCE FROM LOANS POOL FOR CAPITAL EXPENDITURE

On 31 March 19_7 the pool is due to make an advance of U 46,000 for the purchase of an ambulance. However, examination of the table on page 752 shows the actual final cost of the ambulance to be U 45,660. Since this is within the amount of the loan sanction, it will be the sum actually advanced by the pool. The transactions can be journalised as follows:

(a) **Borrowing Accounts (Ambulances)**

19_7				
Mar.31	Capital Expenditure (Ambulance) DR. To Cash Being purchase of ambulance	9 C.G.	45,660	45,660

Municipal Accounting for Developing Countries

Mar.31	Cash DR.	C.G.	45,660	
	To Loans Outstanding	10		45,660
	Being loan raised from Loans			
	Pool to finance purchase of			
	ambulance			

(b) **Loans Pool Accounts**

19_7 Mar.31	Advances to Borrowing Accounts (Ambulances) DR.	P.5	45,660	
	To Cash Being advance for the purchase of an ambulance			45,660

Once again, the ambulance accounts are no different from what they would have been had the loan been an external one. The position will be as illustrated by the following (isolated) balance sheet:

Ambulances
Capital Balance Sheet as at 31 Mar. 19_7

	Units		Units
LONG-TERM LIABILITY		FIXED ASSET	
Loans Outstanding	45,660	Ambulance	45,660
	45,660		45,660

The Loans Pool Balance Sheet will now show:

Loans Pool
Balance Sheet as at 31 Mar. 19_7

	Units		Units
LOANS OUTSTANDING		ADVANCES TO BORROWING	
External Mortgages	10,000	ACCOUNTS	
Internal Funds	46,000	Ambulances	45,660
		Finance	8,000
		CASH IN HAND	2,340
	56,000		56,000

It will be seen that there is a slight cash balance remaining in the loans pool. This could be invested. In fact, it might not really have been necessary to realise the U 2,000 investment held by the pool, until some later date. However, whether or not this small balance would be invested would depend upon the overall cash position of the authority.

The capital financing programme indicates that payments will begin to be made during the second quarter of 19_7, for the sewage disposal works. Although, strictly speaking, no further advances will be made from the loans pool until 30 June 19_7 the cash still has to be found to make

Loans Pooling

these payments, prior to funds being formally made available from the loans pool. If the authority's general working balances are adequate, then the spare cash of the loans pool might be placed on deposit. On the other hand, it would be most imprudent for example, to be running an overall bank overdraft at (say) 8% whilst at the same time earning (say) 4% on loans pool investments. We shall assume in our case that no investments are made.

224. FURTHER ADVANCES FINANCED FROM INTERNAL SOURCES

On 30 June 19_7 the pool is estimated to make advances of U 40,000. These advances are to be financed by the investment, in the pool, of renewals fund moneys, as explained in Section 218. The advance is to be made for capital expenditure on a Sewage Disposal Works. Although payments to 30 June might not be exactly as estimated, the advance can be for a convenient round sum, because payments are to continue during the following quarter. Assuming the actual payments to have amounted to U 39,120 the transactions could be journalised as follows:

(a) **Renewals Fund Accounts**

19_7				
Jun.30	Cash DR.	C.G.	40,000	
	To Renewals Fund Investments (External)			
	Vehicles	13		20,000
	Office Equipment	13		20,000
	Being realisation of investments			
Jun.30	Renewals Fund Investments (Pool) -			
	Vehicles DR.	14	20,000	
	Office Equipment DR.	14	20,000	
	To Cash	C.G.		40,000
	Being internal investment of surplus funds in Council's Loans Pool			

(b) **Loans Pool Accounts**

19_7				
Jun.30	Cash (Pool) DR.	C.P.	40,000	
	To Loans Outstanding	P.4		40,000
	Being internal loans raised from the Renewals Funds			
Jun.30	Advances to Borrowing Accounts (Sewage Disposal) DR.	P.6	40,000	
	To Cash (Pool)	C.P.		40,000
	Being advance for capital expenditure on sewage disposal works			

(c) **Borrowing Accounts (Sewage Disposal)**

19_7 Jun.30	Capital Expenditure (Sewage Disposal Works) DR. To Cash Being payments for construction of sewage disposal works	15 C.G.	39,120	39,120
19_7 Jun.30	Cash DR. To Loans Outstanding Being instalment of loan raised from Loans Pool to finance payments made to date on sewage disposal works	C.G. 16	40,000	40,000

Assuming the Renewals Fund balances to have remained unchanged since 31 Dec. 19_6, the various (isolated) balance sheets as at 30 Jun. 19_7 resulting from the above transactions will appear as follows:

Renewals Funds
Balance Sheet as at 30 Jun. 19_7

	Units		Units
PROVISIONS		CURRENT ASSETS	
Renewals Funds:		Investments:	
Vehicles	37,745	External	24,365
Office Equipment	26,620	Internal (Loans Pool)	40,000
	64,365		64,365

Sewage Disposal Works
Capital Balance Sheet as at 30 Jun. 19_7

	Units		Units
LONG-TERM LIABILITIES		FIXED ASSET	
Loans Outstanding	40,000	Sewage Disposal Works (Under Construction)	39,120
		CURRENT ASSET	
		Cash in Hand	880
	40,000		40,000

Loans Pool
Balance Sheet as at 30 Jun. 19_7

	Units		Units
LOANS OUTSTANDING		ADVANCES TO BORROWING ACCOUNTS	
External Mortgages	10,000	Ambulances	45,660
Internal Funds	86,000	Finance	8,000
		Sewage Disposal	40,000
		CASH IN HAND	2,340
	96,000		96,000

Loans Pooling

225. ADVANCES FROM EXTERNAL MATURITY MORTGAGES

To make advances from the loans pool on 30 Sept. 19_7, it is necessary to raise external maturity mortgages. The capital financing forecast shows us that approximately U 150,000 will be required. We shall assume that during the third quarter of 19_7, various 6% maturity mortgages are raised, equivalent to a single loan of U 150,000 raised on 9 Sept. 19_7. On 30 Sept., advances are to be made for Administrative Buildings and the Sewage Disposal Works. Let us also assume, that U 43,260 has been paid on the Administrative Buildings during the quarter, and U 108,840 on the Sewage Disposal Works. An advance of (say) U 45,000 will, therefore, be made for the former and (say) U 110,000 for the latter, a total of U 155,000. The various transactions can be journalised as follows:

(a) **Loans Pool Accounts**

19_7				

Sept. 9	Cash (Pool) DR.
	   To Loans Outstanding
	   Being 6% maturity mortgages
	   raised from external sources
		C.P.
		P.3
			150,000	150,000

Sept.30	Advances to Borrowing Accounts
	   Administrative Buildings DR.
	   Sewage Disposal DR.
	   To Cash
	   Being advances for capital
	   expenditure
		P.7
		P.6
		C.P.
			45,000
			110,000
				155,000

(b) **Borrowing Accounts (Administrative Buildings)**

19_7				

Sept.30	Capital Expenditure
	  (Administrative Buildings) DR.
	   To Cash
	   Being payments for construction
	   of administrative buildings
		17
		C.G.
			43,260	43,260

Sept.30	Cash DR.
	   To Loans Outstanding
	   Being instalment of loan raised
	   from Loans Pool to finance
	   capital payments to date
		C.G.
		18
			45,000	45,000

(c) **Borrowing Accounts (Sewage Disposal)**

19_7				

Sept.30	Capital Expenditure
	  (Sewage Disposal Works) DR.
	   To Cash
	   Being payments for construction
	   of sewage disposal works
		15
		C.G.
			108,840	108,840

Sept.30	Cash DR.
	   To Loans Outstanding
	   Being instalment of loan raised
	   from Loans Pool to finance
	   capital payments to date
		C.G.
		16
			110,000	110,000

Municipal Accounting for Developing Countries

The various (isolated) balance sheets as at 30 Sept. 19_7 resulting from the the above transactions will appear as follows:

Loans Pool
Capital Balance Sheet as at 30 Sept. 19_7

	Units		Units
LOANS OUTSTANDING		ADVANCES TO BORROWING	
External Mortgages	160,000	ACCOUNTS	
Internal Funds	86,000	Administrative Buildings	45,000
		Ambulances	45,660
CASH OVERDRAWN	2,660	Finance	8,000
		Sewage Disposal	150,000
	248,660		248,660

Administrative Buildings
Capital Balance Sheet as at 30 Sept. 19_7

	Units		Units
LONG-TERM LIABILITIES		FIXED ASSET	
Loan Outstanding	45,000	Administrative Buildings	
		(Under Construction)	43,260
		CURRENT ASSET	
		Cash in Hand	1,740
	45,000		45,000

Sewage Disposal Works
Capital Balance Sheet as at 30 Sept. 19_7

	Units		Units
LONG-TERM LIABILITIES		FIXED ASSET	
Loans Outstanding	150,000	Sewage Disposal Works	
		(Under Construction)	147,960
		CURRENT ASSET	
		Cash in Hand	2,040
	150,000		150,000

The balance sheet of the loans pool now shows an overdrawn cash balance, indicating that it has lent out more cash than it has borrowed. However, the overdraft represents just another form of borrowing. If the loans pool has a separate bank account, then this will actually be overdrawn. If the pool shares the common bank account of the authority it will be temporarily using other cash resources belonging to the authority as a whole. The overdraft will be eliminated as additional mortgage loans are raised. Interest on the overdraft will either be paid to the bank or calculated as a charge against the loans pool accounts for the credit of the general revenue account.

Each of the borrowing accounts has a balance of cash in hand but this will quickly be eliminated as further payments take place during the following quarter.

Loans Pooling

The Capital Financing Forecast page 731 shows that U 165,000 was estimated as likely to be required during the last quarter of 19_7. However, the loans pool is already overdrawn and we shall assume that latest estimates show that up to U 80,000 will be paid on the Administrtive Buildings and up to U 95,000 on the Sewage Disposal Works, during the last quarter. It would, therefore, appear that about U 180,000 will be required to be raised in loan moneys during the final quarter.

This could come from four sources:

(a) external mortgages;

(b) bank overdraft (or cash overdrawn against other funds of the Council);

(c) additional internal funds available for investment as a result of 19_7 contributions; and

(d) repayments to the loans pool by borrowing accounts.

As explained in Section 185 of Chapter 16, a rough calculation would be made towards the end of December to determine the additional investments (if any) to be made on behalf of the various special funds. Instead of being invested externally, the available funds could well be invested in the loans pool, particularly in view of the usually unsatisfactory margin between interest rates on investments and those on borrowings. Of course, as with straightforward internal borrowing, attention must be paid to the liquidity position. Internal funds lent to the loans pool will be re-lent for capital works, thus being held in the form of fixed assets, not liquid assets. However, the pooling system has greater flexibility than ordinary internal borrowing. If internal funds are required to be repaid by the loans pool to be used for their intended purpose, they will be replaced by raising other loans externally, provided these can be readily obtained. The greater the scarcity of external loans, the more conservative must be the internal borrowing policy and the general cash management of the pool.

Since internal borrowing by the loans pool has already been explained, we shall assume that no further internal borrowing takes place during 19_7.

Because the end of the financial year (in this case, December) is likely to be a time when cash balances are low, it might not be sound financial practice to place too much reliance upon drawing against other cash resources of the Council. An overdraft raised from the bank could help to make the system more flexible. With a consolidated bank account, interest would be paid only on the net overdrawn balance of the Council as a whole. This would make full use of whatever limited cash resources were available.

However, we shall assume that the loans pool does not intend to rely upon a bank overdraft. This means that the December advances must be met from additional external mortgages and repayments of earlier advances by borrowing accounts. In round figures the estimated repayments are U 15,000 (see later). If this sum is deducted from the total required sum of U 180,000 it leaves U 165,000 to be raised from external mortgages. We shall assume that this sum is raised as if on 15 Dec. 19_7 as explained earlier.

On 31 Dec. 19_7 an advance of U 80,000 will be made for Administrative Buildings and U 95,000 for the Sewage Disposal Works. Expenditure on the former will be U 77,160 and on the latter U 93,400. However, advances can still be made in round figures because capital payments are to continue in 19_8.

Municipal Accounting for Developing Countries

The transactions can be journalised as follows:

(a) **Loans Pool Account**

19_7					
Dec.15	Cash (Pool) DR. To Loans Outstanding Being 6½% maturity mortgages raised from external sources		C.P. P.3	165,000	165,000
Dec.31	Advances to Borrowing Accounts: Administrative Buildings DR. Sewage Disposal DR. To Cash (Pool) Being advances for capital expenditure		P.7 P.6 C.P.	80,000 95,000	175,000

(b) **Borrowing Accounts (Administrative Buildings)**

19_7					
Dec.31	Capital Expenditure (Administrative Buildings) DR. To Cash Being payments for construction of administrative buildings		17 C.G.	77,160	77,160
Dec.31	Cash DR. To Loans Outstanding Being instalment of loan raised from Loans Pool to finance capital payments to date		C.G. 18	80,000	80,000

(c) **Borrowing Accounts (Sewage Disposal Works)**

19_7					
Dec.31	Capital Expenditure (Sewage Disposal Works) DR. To Cash Being payments for construction of sewage disposal works		15 C.G.	93,400	93,400
Dec.31	Cash DR. To Loans Outstanding Being instalment of loan raised from Loans Pool to finance capital payments to date		C.G. 16	95,000	95,000

At this stage the balance sheet of the loans pool appears as follows:

Loans Pooling

Loans Pool
Balance Sheet as at 31 Dec. 19_7

	Units		Units
LOANS OUTSTANDING		ADVANCES TO BORROWING	
External Mortgages	325,000	ACCOUNTS	
Internal Funds	86,000	Administrative Buildings	125,000
		Ambulances	45,660
CASH OVERDRAWN	12,660	Finance	8,000
		Sewage Disposal	245,000
	423,660		423,660

The (isolated) balance sheet of all the borrowing accounts will appear as follows:

Administrative Buildings
Capital Balance Sheet as at 31 Dec. 19_7

	Units		Units
LONG-TERM LIABILITIES		FIXED ASSET	
Loans Outstanding	125,000	Administrative Buildings	
		(Under Construction)	120,420
		CURRENT ASSET	
		Cash in Hand	4,580
	125,000		125,000

Ambulance
Capital Balance Sheet as at 31 Dec. 19_7

	Units		Units
LONG-TERM LIABILITIES		FIXED ASSET	
Loans Outstanding	45,660	Ambulance	45,660
	45,660		45,660

Finance
Accounting Machine
Capital Balance Sheet as at 31 Dec. 19_7

	Units		Units
LONG-TERM LIABILITIES		FIXED ASSET	
Loans Outstanding	8,000	Accounting Machine	10,000
OTHER BALANCES			
Capital Discharged:			
Loan Repaid	2,000		
	10,000		10,000

Municipal Accounting for Developing Countries

Sewage Disposal Works
Capital Balance Sheet as at 31 Dec. 19_7

LONG-TERM LIABILITIES	Units		Units
Loans Outstanding	245,000	FIXED ASSET	
		Sewage Disposal Works	
		(Under Construction)	241,360
		CURRENT ASSET	
		Cash in Hand	3,640
	245,000		245,000

All the advances from the loans pool for 19_7 have now been made. At this stage the loans pool shows an overdrawn cash balance of U 12,660. This is because each of the borrowing accounts still has to repay to the loans pool an annual instalment in repayment of its advance.

226. REPAYMENTS OF PRINCIPAL TO THE LOANS POOL

Each of the borrowing accounts must now make provision to repay an instalment of principal to the loans pool in exactly the same way as if it had raised an external loan. Chapter 15, Section 177 shows that loan repayments may be made either by equal instalments of principal or by the annuity method. The latter method, by combining principal and interest into equal annual sums (annuities) is slightly more complicated to calculate, but gives a constant annual charge to the revenue account.

With loans raised from a loans pool, the same considerations apply. Quite obviously, the annual charges to revenue for loan charges should be as even as possible. However, exact annuity tables cannot be calculated for loans pool advances because, as we shall see, the precise rate of interest charged by the loans pool differs from year to year.

The problem is solved in the same way as for sinking funds - by using a notional rate of interest. The repayment instalments will be calculated in the same way as the sinking fund contributions shown in Section 211 of Chapter 19. Using a notional interest rate of 3% we can demonstrate the repayment calculations as follows:

(a) **Ambulance**

Amount of Advance	=	U 45,660
Period of Loan	=	5 years
Annual Contribution to accumulate an amount of 1 at the end of 5 years @ 3%	=	0.18835457
Annual Contribution to accumulate an amount of 45,660	=	0.18835457 x 45,660
	=	8,600.2697
Annual Contribution to accumulate U 45,660 (to nearest unit)	=	U 8,600

The loan repayment table can then be calculated by increasing the initial instalment annually by 3% as follows:

Loans Pooling

Instalment Number	Annual Instalment	Loan Outstanding
0	-	45,660
1	8,600	37,060
2	8,858	28,202
3	9,124	19,078
4	9,398	9,680
5	9,680	-

Instalment No 2 U 8,858 represents instalment No 1 U 8,600 multiplied by 103%; instalment No 3 U 9,124 represents instalment No 2 U 8,858 multiplied by 103%; and so on.

(b) **Administrative Buildings**

Amount of Total Advances during year	=	U 125,000
Period of Loan	=	40 years
Annual Contribution to accumulate an amount of 1 at the end of 40 years @ 3%	=	0.01326238
Annual Contribution to accumulate an amount of 125,000	=	0.01326238 x 125,000
	=	1,657.7975
Annual Contribution to accumulate U 125,000 (to nearest unit)	=	U 1,658

The first five instalments of the loan repayment table will appear as follows:

Instalment Number	Annual Instalment	Loan Outstanding
0	-	125,000
1	1,658	123,342
2	1,708	121,634
3	1,759	119,875
4	1,812	118,063
5	1,866	116,197
	.....	....

(c) **Finance - Accounting Machine**

Amount of Advance	=	U 10,000 (U 2,000 already repaid - leaving U 8,000 outstanding)
Period of Loan	=	5 years
Annual Repayment to redeem the Loan over 5 years by the straight-line method (i.e. equal instalments of principal)	=	U 2,000

In this case, redemption of the original loan was being provided for by a non-accumulating sinking fund. It is logical to replace this by a repayment schedule giving equal instalments of principal, as follows:

Municipal Accounting for Developing Countries

Instalment Number	Annual Instalment	Loan Outstanding
0	-	10,000
1	2,000	8,000
2	2,000	6,000
3	2,000	4,000
4	2,000	2,000
5	2,000	-

Repayment No 1 was, of course, deemed to have been made in 19_6. In the 19_7 accounts, currently being considered, we shall deal with repayment No 2.

(d) **Sewage Disposal Works**

Amount of Total Advances during year	=	U 245,000
Period of Loan	=	30 years
Annual Contribution to accumulate an amount of 1 at the end of 30 years @ 3%	=	0.02101926
Annual Contribution to accumulate an amount of 245,000	=	0.02101926 x 245,000
	=	5,149.7187
Annual Contribution to accumulate U 245,000 (to nearest unit)	=	U 5,150

The loan repayment table, showing the first five instalments and the last five instalments will appear as follows:

Instalment Number	Annual Instalment	Loan Outstanding
0	-	245,000
1	5,150	239,850
2	5,305	234,545
3	5,464	229,081
4	5,628	223,453
5	5,797	217,656
...	...	...
...	...	...
...	...	57,211
26	10,784	46,427
27	11,108	35,319
28	11,441	23,878
29	11,784	12,094
30	12,094	-

For simplicity, the annual instalments have been rounded off to the nearest unit. We have already seen that even the slightest degree of approximation will result in a repayment table becoming distorted over a long period. In our case, because the transactions are internal, we can be quite liberal with approximations. In the case of the Sewage Disposal Works we have included the last instalments of the loan table to show how distorted the table can become after a period of 30 years. The last instalment but one amounts to U 11,748. If this is increased by 3%, the resultant figure is U 12,137. But only U 12,094 remains to be repaid, so this will be the amount of the final instalment. It differs from the calculated figure by U 43.

Loans Pooling

In this case, the use of approximation has resulted in the loan being redeemed at a slightly faster rate than would otherwise have been the case. Rounding up to the next 10 units (or even 100 units) would result in still faster redemption of the debt even, perhaps, to the extent of shortening the repayment period by a year or two.

The repayment of advances can be journalised as follows:

(a) **Loans Pool Accounts**

19_7				
Dec.31	Cash DR.	C.P.	17,408	
	To Advances to Borrowing Accounts:			
	Administrative Buildings	P.7		1,658
	Ambulances	P.5		8,600
	Finance	P.1		2,000
	Sewage Disposal Works	P.6		5,150
	Being loan repayments by borrowing accounts			

(b) **Borrowing Accounts (Administrative Buildings)**

19_7				
Dec.31	Loans Outstanding DR.	18	1,658	
	To Cash	C.G.		1,658
	Being repayment to Loans Pool of first instalment of loan for Adminstrative Buildings			
Dec.31	Revenue Account - Loan Charges - Principal DR.	19	1,658	
	To Capital Discharged (Loans Repaid)	20		1,658
	Being first instalment of loan repayment now charged to revenue account			

(c) **Borrowing Accounts (Ambulances)**

19_7				
Dec.31	Loans Outstanding DR.	10	8,600	
	To Cash	C.G.		8,600
	Being repayment to Loans Pool of first instalment of loan for ambulance			
Dec.31	Revenue Account - Loan Charges - Principal DR.	21	8,600	
	To Capital Discharged (Loan Repaid)	22		8,600
	Being first instalment of loan repayment now charged to revenue account			

Municipal Accounting for Developing Countries

(d) **Borrowing Accounts (Finance)**

19_7					
Dec.31	Loans Outstanding　　　　　DR. 　To Cash 　Being repayment to Loans Pool 　of second instalment of loan 　for accounting machine	1 C.G.	2,000		2,000
Dec.31	Revenue Account 　Loan Charges - Principal　　DR. 　To Capital Discharged 　　(Loans Repaid) 　Being second instalment of loan 　repayment now charged to 　revenue account	23 5	2,000		2,000

(e) **Borrowing Accounts (Sewage Disposal)**

19_7					
Dec.31	Loans Outstanding　　　　　DR. 　To Cash 　Being repayment to Loans Pool 　of first instalment of loan 　for sewage disposal works	16 C.G.	5,150		5,150
Dec.31	Revenue Account 　Loan Charges - Principal 　To Capital Discharged 　　(Loan Repaid) 　Being first instalment of loan 　repayment now charged to 　revenue account	24 25	5,150		5,150

227. LEDGER ACCOUNTS - CAPITAL TRANSACTIONS

The year's capital transactions are now complete. The relevant ledger accounts will appear as follows:

(a) **Loans Pool Accounts**

	Advances to Borrowing Accounts (Finance)						P.1
19_7 Jan. 1	To Loans 　Outstand- 　ing	J	8,000 ――― 8,000 =====	19_7 Dec.31	By Cash By Balance	J c/d	2,000 6,000 ――― 8,000 =====
19_8 Jan. 1	To Balance	b/d	6,000				

Loans Pooling

Investments — P.2

19_7				19_7			
Jan. 1	To Loans Outstanding	J	2,000	Mar.31	By Cash	J	2,000
			2,000				2,000

Loans Outstanding (External Maturity Mortgages) — P.3

19_7				19_7			
Dec.31	To Balance	c/d	325,000	Jan. 1	By Sundry Accounts	J	10,000
				Sep. 9	By Cash	J	150,000
				Dec.15	By Cash	J	165,000
			325,000				325,000
				19_8			
				Jan. 1	By Balance		325,000

Loans Outstanding (Internal) — P.4

19_7				19_7			
Dec.31	To Balance	c/d	86,000	Mar.31	By Cash	J	46,000
				Jun.30	By Cash	J	40,000
			86,000				86,000
				19_8			
				Jan. 1	By Balance	b/d	86,000

Advances to Borrowing Accounts (Ambulances) — P.5

19_7				19_7			
Mar.31	To Cash	J	45,660	Dec.31	By Cash	J	8,600
					By Balance	c/d	37,060
			45,660				45,660
19_8							
Jan. 1	To Balance	b/d	37,060				

	Advances to Borrowing Accounts (Sewage Disposal)						P.6
19_7				19_7			
Jun.30	To Cash	J	40,000	Dec.31	By Cash	J	5,150
Sep.30	To Cash	J	110,000		By Balance	c/d	239,850
Dec.31	To Cash	J	95,000				
			245,000				245,000
			=======				=======
19_8							
Jan. 1	To Balance	b/d	239,850				

	Advances to Borrowing Accounts (Administrative Buildings)						P.7
19_7				19_7			
Sep.30	To Cash	J	45,000	Dec.31	By Cash	J	1,658
Dec.31	To Cash	J	80,000		By Balance		123,342
			125,000				125,000
			=======				=======
19_8							
Jan. 1	To Balance	b/d	123,342				

	Cash (Loans Pool)						C.P.
19_7				19_7			
Mar.31	To Investment	J	2,000	Mar.31	By Advances	J	45,660
	To Loans Outstanding		46,000	Jun.30	By Advances	J	40,000
				Sep.30	By Advances	J	155,000
				Dec.31	By Advances	J	175,000
Jun.30	To Loans Outstanding	J	40,000				415,660*
Sep. 9	To Loans Outstanding	J	150,000				
Dec.15	To Loans Outstanding	J	165,000				
21	To Advances Repaid	J	17,408				
			420,408*				

Loans Pooling

(b) General Accounts (including borrowing accounts and special funds)

Loans Outstanding (Accounting Machine)								1
19_7 Jan. 1	To Investments	J	2,000	19_7 Jan. 1	By Balance	b/f	10,000	
Dec.31	To Cash	J	2,000					
	To Balance	c/d	6,000					
			10,000				10,000	
				19_8 Jan. 1	By Balance	b/d	6,000	

Sinking Fund (Accounting Machine)								2
19_7 Jan. 1	To Capital Discharged	J	2,000	19_7 Jan. 1	By Balance	b/f	2,000	
			2,000				2,000	

Capital Expenditure - Accounting Machine								3
19_7 Jan. 1	To Balance	b/f	10,000	19_7 Dec.31	By Balance	c/d	10,000	
19_8 Jan. 1	To Balance	b/d	10,000					

Sinking Fund Investments								4
19_7 Jan. 1	To Balance	b/f	2,000	19_7 Jan. 1	By Loans Outstanding	J	2,000	
			2,000				2,000	

Municipal Accounting for Developing Countries

Capital Discharged - Loans Repaid (Accounting Machine)								5
19_7 Dec.31	To Balance	c/d	4,000	19_7 Jan. 1	By Sinking Fund	J		2,000
				Dec.31	By Revenue Account	J		2,000
			4,000					4,000
				19_8 Jan. 1	By Balance			4,000

Capital Fund								6
				19_7 Jan. 1	By Balance	b/f		123,140*

Capital Fund Investments (External)								7
19_7 Jan. 1	To Balance	b/f	123,140	19_7 Mar.31	By Cash	J		46,000
				Dec.31	By Balance	c/d		77,140
			123,140					123,140
19_8 Jan. 1	To Balance	b/d	77,140					

Capital Fund Investments (Pool)								8
19_7 Mar.31	To Cash	J	46,000	19_7 Dec.31	By Balance	c/d		46,000
19_8 Jan. 1	To Balance	b/d	46,000					

*NOTE: Accounts No 6, 7 and 8 ignore contributions to and withdrawals from the Capital Fund during 19_7. These are irrelevant for the purposes of this exemplification.)

Loans Pooling

Capital Expenditure (Ambulance) 9

19_7				19_7			
Mar.31	To Cash	J	45,660	Dec.31	By Balance	c/d	45,660
19_8							
Jan. 1	To Balance	b/d	45,660				

Loans Outstanding (Ambulance) 10

19_7				19_7			
Dec.31	To Cash	J	8,600	Mar.31	By Cash	J	45,660
	To Balance	c/d	37,660				
			45,660				45,660
				19_8			
				Jan. 1	By Balance	b/d	37,060

Renewals Fund (Vehicles) 11

				19_7			
				Jan. 1	By Balance	b/f	37,745*

Renewals Fund (Office Equipment) 12

				19_7			
				Jan. 1	By Balance	b/f	26,620*

Renewals Fund Investments (External) (Vehicles and Office Equipment) 13

19_7				19_7			
Jan. 1	To Balance	b/f	64,365	Jun.30	By Cash	J	40,000
				Dec.31	By Balance	c/d	24,365
			64,365				64,365
19_8							
Jan. 1	To Balance	b/d	24,365				

Municipal Accounting for Developing Countries

Renewals Fund Investments (Pool) (Vehicles and Office Equipment)							14
19_7 Jun.30	To Cash	J	40,000	19_7 Dec.31	By Balance	c/d	40,000
19_8 Jan. 1	To Balance	b/d	40,000				

*NOTE: Accounts No 11,12,13 and 14, ignore contributions to and withdrawals from the Renewals Funds during 19_7. These are irrelevant for the purposes of this exemplification.)

Capital Expenditure (Sewage Disposal Works)							15
19_7 Jun.30	To Cash	J	39,120	19_7 Dec.31	By Balance	c/d	241,360
Sep.30	To Cash	J	108,840				
Dec.31	To Cash	J	93,400				
			241,360				241,360
19_8 Jan. 1	To Balance	b/d	241,360				

Loans Outstanding (Sewage Disposal Works)							16
19_7 Dec.31	To Cash	J	5,150	19_7 Jun.30	By Cash	J	40,000
	To Balance	c/d	239,850	Sep.30	By Cash	J	110,000
				Dec.31	By Cash	J	95,000
			245,000				245,000
				19_8 Jan. 1	By Balance	b/d	239,850

Capital Expenditure (Administrative Buildings)							17
19_7 Sep.30	To Cash	J	43,260	19_7 Dec.31	By Balance	c/d	120,420
Dec.31	To Cash	J	77,160				
			120,420				120,420
19_8 Jan.1	To Balance	b/d	120,420				

Loans Pooling

Loans Outstanding (Administrative Buildings) — 18

19_7				19_7			
Dec.31	To Cash	J	1,658	Sep.30	By Cash	J	45,000
	To Balance	c/d	123,342	Dec.31	By Cash	J	80,000
			125,000				125,000
			======				======
				19_8			
				Jan. 1	By Balance	b/d	123,342

Revenue Account (Administrative Buildings) — 19

19_7			
Dec.31	To Capital Discharged (Loan Charges Principal)	J	1,658
			1,658*

Capital Discharged – Loans Repaid (Administrative Buildings) — 20

19_7				19_7			
Dec.31	To Balance	c/d	1,658	Dec.31	By Revenue Account	J	1,658
			1,658				1,658
			=====				=====
				19_8			
				Jan. 1	By Balance	b/d	1,658

Revenue Account (Ambulances) — 21

19_7			
Dec.31	To Capital Discharged (Loan Charges Principal)	J	8,600
			8,600*

Capital Discharged - Loans Repaid (Ambulances) — 22

19_7				19_7			
Dec.31	To Balance	c/d	8,600	Dec.31	By Revenue Account	J	8,600
			8,600				8,600
				19_8 Jan. 1	By Balance	b/d	8,600

Revenue Account (Finance) — 23

19_7			
Dec.31	To Capital Discharged (Loan Charges Principal)	J	2,000
			2,000*

Revenue Account (Sewage Disposal) — 24

19_7			
Dec.31	To Capital Discharged (Loan Charges Principal)	J	5,150
			5,150*

Capital Discharged - Loans Repaid (Sewage Disposal) — 25

19_7				19_7			
Dec.31	To Balance	c/d	5,150	Dec.31	By Revenue Account	J	5,150
			5,150				5,150
				19_8 Jan. 1	By Balance	b/d	5,150

Loans Pooling

			Cash (General)			C.G.
19_7			19_7			
Mar.31	To Capital Fund Investments (External)	J 46,000	Mar.31	By Capital Fund Investments (Pool)	J	46,000
	To Loans Outstanding	J 45,660		By Capital Expenditure (Ambulance)	J	45,660
Jun.30	To Renewals Fund Investments (External)	J 40,000	Jun.30	By Renewals Fund Investments (Pool)	J	40,000
	To Loans Outstanding	J 40,000		By Capital Expenditure (Sewage Disposal Works)	J	39,120
Sep.30	To Loans Outstanding	J 45,000	Sep.30	By Capital Expenditure (Administrative Buildings)	J	43,260
	To Loans Outstanding	J 110,000		By Capital Expenditure (Sewage Disposal Works)	J	108,840
Dec.31	To Loans Outstanding	J 80,000	Dec.31	By Capital Expenditure (Administrative Buildings)	J	77,160
	To Loans Outstanding	J 95,000		By Capital Expenditure (Sewage Disposal Works)	J	93,400
		501,660*		By Loans Outstanding: Administrative Buildings	J	1,658
				Ambulances	J	8,600
				Finance	J	2,000
				Sewage Disposal	J	5,150
						510,848*

781

Municipal Accounting for Developing Countries

Trial balances can now be extracted. The trial balance for the loans pool accounts can be separate from that for the general accounts, each section being self-balancing. Most of the ledger accounts have been closed off and balances carried down, because the year's entries have been finalised. However, on a few of the accounts, totals have been marked * indicating that, on these accounts, there are to be further entries relating to the revenue transactions of the loans pool.

The general accounts are very little different from those which would be used where ordinary external borrowing took place. One is impressed, however, by the simplicity of the accounts of the loans pool. This is a particular feaure of loans pooling and it reflects the main purpose behind such arrangements. Channelling all borrowing through the pool eliminates any need for complex transfers between accounts and also eliminates the need for separate sinking funds.

The trial balances will appear as follows:

(a) **Loans Pool Accounts**

Trial Balance

Accounts	Folio	DR	CR
Advances - Finance	P.1	6,000	
Loans Outstanding - External	P.3		325,000
Loans Outstanding - Internal	P.4		86,000
Advances - Ambulances	P.5	37,060	
Advances - Sewage Disposal	P.6	239,850	
Advances - Administrative Buildings	P.7	123,342	
Cash	C.P.	420,408*	415,660*
		826,660	826,660

* Net balance in hand = 4,748

Loans Pooling

(b) **General Accounts**

Trial Balance

Accounts	Folio	DR	CR
Loans Outstanding (Accounting Machine)	1		6,000
Capital Expenditure (Accounting Machine)	3	10,000	
Capital Discharged - Loans Repaid (Accounting Machine)	5		4,000
Capital Fund	6		123,140
Capital Fund Investments (External)	7	77,140	
Capital Fund Investments (Pool)	8	46,000	
Capital Expenditure (Ambulance)	9	45,660	
Loans Outstanding (Ambulance)	10		37,060
Renewals Fund (Vehicles)	11		37,745
Renewals Fund (Office Equipment)	12		26,620
Renewals Fund Investments (External)	13	24,365	
Renewals Fund Investments (Pool)	14	40,000	
Capital Expenditure (Sewage Works)	15	241,360	
Loans Outstanding (Sewage Works)	16		239,850
Capital Expenditure (Administrative Buildings)	17	120,420	
Loans Outstanding (Administrative Buildings)	18		123,342
Revenue Account (Administrative Buildings)	19	1,658	
Capital Discharged - Loans Repaid (Administrative Buildings)	20		1,658
Revenue Account (Ambulances)	21	8,600	
Capital Discharged - Loans Repaid (Ambulances)	22		8,600
Revenue Account (Finance)	23	2,000	
Revenue Account (Sewage Disposal)	24	5,150	
Capital Discharged - Loans Repaid (Sewage Disposal)	25		5,150
Cash	C.G.	501,660*	510,848*
		1,124,013	1,124,013

* Net balance overdrawn = 9,188

The balance sheet of the loans pool will now appear as follows:

Loans Pool
Balance Sheet as at 31 Dec. 19_7

	Units		Units
LOANS OUTSTANDING		ADVANCES TO BORROWING ACCOUNTS	
External Mortgages	325,000	Administrative Buildings	123,342
Internal Funds	86,000	Ambulances	37,060
		Finance	6,000
		Sewage Disposal	239,850
		CASH IN HAND	4,748
	411,000		411,000

Municipal Accounting for Developing Countries

An aggregate balance sheet for the appropriate general accounts will appear as follows:

General Accounts
Aggregate Balance Sheet as at 31 Dec. 19_7

Capital

	Units		Units
LONG-TERM LIABILITIES		FIXED ASSETS	
Loans Outstanding		Administrative Buildings	120,420
Loans Pool	406,252	Ambulance	45,660
		Accounting Machine	10,000
OTHER BALANCES		Sewage Disposal Works	241,360
Capital Fund	123,140		
Capital Discharged		CURRENT ASSETS	
Loans Repaid	19,408	Investments	
		External	77,140
		Internal	46,000
		Cash in Hand	8,220
	548,800		548,800

Revenue

	Units		Units
CURRENT LIABILITIES		CURRENT ASSETS	
Cash Overdrawn	17,408	Investments	
		External	24,365
		Internal	40,000
PROVISIONS		OTHER BALANCES	
Renewals Fund Vehicles	37,745	Revenue Account	
Office Equipment	26,620	Deficiency	17,408
	81,77		81,773
	630,573		630,573

Working Notes

Account	Capital Cash	Loans Out-standing	Loans Repaid	Revenue Deficiency
Administrative Buildings	4,580	123,342	1,658	1,658
Ambulances	-	37,060	8,600	8,600
Finance (Accounting Machine)	-	6,000	4,000	2,000
Sewage Disposal	3,640	239,850	5,150	5,150
	8,220	406,252	19,408	17,408
Less Revenue Cash Overdrawn	17,408			
Net Cash Overdrawn	9,188			

Loans Pooling

In practice, of course, income would be raised during the year in the form of rates, taxes, etc. to meet the Revenue Account Deficiency, thus eliminating the overdrawn cash balance.

228. **REVENUE TRANSACTIONS - INTEREST**

Interest on all loans is paid initially by the loans pool. This is then recharged to borrowing accounts in proportion to outstanding advances. Appropriate adjustments are made to take account of advances which are outstanding for only part of a year.

An external loan bearing 5% interest was taken over by the loans pool on 1 Jan. and the pool must pay to the lender a full year's interest for 19_7. In addition, mortgage loans raised as if on 9 Sept. bear 6% interest and those raised as if on 15 Dec. bear $6\frac{1}{2}$% interest. In both cases, the pool will be responsible for paying interest for the periods from the dates of raising the loans until 31 Dec. 19_7.

We shall assume that the loans pool will pay interest on its internal borrowings from the Capital Fund and Renewals Fund at the current rate of $6\frac{1}{4}$%, calculated for the appropriate periods.

After the advances were made on 30 Sept. 19_7 the balance sheet of the loans pool on page 764 showed an overdrawn cash balance of **U** 2,660. This balance would have remained overdrawn until the loan of **U** 40,000 was raised on 11 Dec. 19_7 as shown by the table on page 754. Interest on the overdraft would, therefore, be paid to the bank, if there were a separate overdrawn bank account. If there were no separate bank account the equivalent interest would be appropriated to the general funds of the authority. There may be a slight air of artificiality here, because the general funds of the authority might be carrying a large cash balance in hand, actually incurring no overdraft interest. However, looking at the loans pool transactions in isolation, it can be argued that, if cash had not been available from general funds, bank overdraft would have been unavoidable.

A reverse argument could, of course, be put forward. During the periods when the loans pool held a cash balance in hand it was investing this balance for use by the general funds, thus earning hypothetical interest payable by the general funds to the loans pool. This argument is not quite so strong as that for charging interest against the loans pool because:

(a) whilst the loans pool would be obliged to raise an overdraft to meet a cash shortage, there would be no absolute necessity for it to invest a cash surplus; and

(b) whilst the loans pool cash might assist the liquidity position of the general funds, it might, just as easily, merely add to the idle cash balances.

In our example we shall ignore any hypothetical interest earned by the loans pool on idle cash balances but we shall take into account overdraft interest. However, it should be noted that differences of opinion can arise and each case should be treated on its merits.

The loans pool does, in actual fact, earn interest on the external investment. This relates to the sinking fund which it took over on 1 Jan. Interest is earned up to the time the investment is realised on 31 Mar.

The total net interest borne by the loans pool during 19_7 can, therefore, be summarised as follows:

Municipal Accounting for Developing Countries

Type of Loan	Principal Sum	Dates From	Dates To	Number of Days	Rate of Interest	Amount of Interest
		19_7	19_7		%	U
External - Maturity Mortgage	10,000	1 Jan.	31 Dec.	365	5	500
External - Maturity Mortgages	150,000	9 Sep.	31 Dec.	114	6	2,811
External - Maturity Mortgages	165,000	15 Dec.	31 Dec.	17	$6\frac{1}{2}$	500
Internal - Capital Fund	46,000	31 Mar.	31 Dec.	276	$6\frac{1}{4}$%	2,174
Internal - Renewals Funds	40,000	30 Jun.	31 Dec.	185	$6\frac{1}{4}$%	1,267
Overdraft - General Funds	2,660	30 Sep.	11 Dec.	72+	7	37
						7,289
Less External Investment	2,000	1 Jan.	31 Mar.	89+	4	20
NET INTEREST BORNE BY LOANS POOL						7,269

(+ the day of repayment is not counted for interest)

The interest borne by the pool must be recovered from the various borrowing accounts. The most practical way of making the apportionment is to take each separate advance and to adjust it to an equivalent annual sum. This is done after taking into account the date from which each advance was made. Because advances from the Loans Pool are wholly internal transactions, the calculations are approximated to a quarterly basis, rather than worked out on an exact number of days.

For example, the advance for the ambulance amounting to U 45,660 was made on 31 Mar. It was, therefore, outstanding for three-quarters of the full year. Interest on the full sum of U 45,660 for three-quarters of the year is the same as that on three-quarters of U 45,660 (i.e. U 34,245) for a full year.

Using the above principle, the various advances can be summarised as follows:

Loans Pooling

Purpose of Advance	Date of Advance	Amount of Advance	Number of Quarters Outstanding	Annual Equivalent
Accounting Machine	1 Jan.	8,000	4	8,000
Ambulance	31 Mar.	45,660	3	34,245
Sewage Disposal Works	30 June	40,000	2	20,000
	30 Sep.	110,000	1	27,500
	31 Dec.	95,000	0	-
		245,000		47,500
Administrative Buildings	30 Sep.	45,000	1	11,250
	31 Dec.	80,000	0	-
		125,000		11,250
TOTALS		423,660		100,995

Although a total of U 423,660 was advanced during the year, interest will be charged only upon the annual equivalents, (sometimes called equated sums) totalling U 100,995.

Interest of U 7,269 must now be apportioned over the equated principal sums by the calculation of an average rate of interest, known as the "Pool Rate". This is done, quite simply, as follows:

$$\frac{7,269}{100,995} = 7.197\%$$

It will be noted that the "Pool Rate" of 7.197% is higher than any of the individual rates payable by the loans pool. This occurs not only because loans raised by the pool were for slightly larger sums than those advanced to borrowing accounts but also because they were raised on slightly earlier dates than the dates of the advances. In any case, these factors are only prominent because the loans pool is in its early stages of operation, with very few advances. As its activities expand, these "idle interest charges" of the pool will be insignificant in proportion to the total interest transactions.

Interest will be charged to borrowing accounts as follows:

Borrowing Account	Equated Advances	Interest at 7.197%
Finance	8,000	576
Ambulances	34,245	2,465
Sewage Disposal	47,500	3,418
Administrative Buildings	11,250	810
	100,995	7,269

Municipal Accounting for Developing Countries

Payment and receipt of interest by the loans pool could be journalised as follows:

19_7					

Dec.31	Revenue Account - Interest DR.
	   To Cash (Pool)
	   Being payment of interest on
	   external maturity mortgages
		P.8
		C.P.
			3,811		3,811

Dec.31	Revenue Account - Interest DR.
	   To Cash (Pool)
	   Being payment of interest on
	   internal loans
		P.9
		C.P.
			3,441		3,441

Dec.31	Revenue Account - Interest DR.
	   To Cash (Pool)
	   Being payment of interest on
	   overdraft
		P.10
		C.P.
			37		37

Dec.31	Cash DR.
	   To Revenue Account - Interest
	   Being receipt of investment
	   interest
		C.P.
		P.11
			20		20

These transactions leave the pool with a Revenue Account Deficiency of U 7,269. Since this is to be made good by income from borrowing accounts, their indebtedness could be journalised as follows:

19_7			

Dec.31	Borrowing Accounts:
	  Finance DR.
	  Ambulances DR.
	  Sewage Disposal DR.
	  Administrative Buildings DR.
	     To Revenue Account - Interest
	  Being interest due to Loans Pool
	  from borrowing accounts at
	  7.197% on equated advances
		576
		2,465
		3,418
		810
			7,269

Loans Pooling

At this stage, the balance sheet of the loans pool will appear as follows:

Loans Pool
Balance Sheet as at 31 Dec. 19_7

Capital

	Units		Units
LOANS OUTSTANDING		ADVANCES TO BORROWING ACCOUNTS	
External Mortgages	325,000	Administrative Buildings	123,342
Internal Funds	86,000	Ambulances	37,060
		Finance	6,000
		Sewage Disposal	239,850
		CASH IN HAND	4,748
	411,000		411,000

Revenue

	Units		Units
CASH OVERDRAWN	7,269	DEBTORS	7,269
	418,269		418,269

Reimbursement of the interest could be journalised as follows:

19_7 Dec.31	Cash DR.		7,269	
	To Borrowing Accounts:			
	Finance			576
	Ambulances			2,465
	Sewage Disposal			3,418
	Administrative Buildings			810
	Being reimbursement of interest due from borrowing accounts			

The last two journal entries are somewhat theoretical. It might be simpler to assume a straightforward cash adjustment between the loans pool and the borrowing accounts, as follows:

19_7 Dec.31	Cash DR.	C.P. P.14	7,269	
	To Revenue Account - Interest			7,269
	Being reimbursement of interest due to Loans Pool from borrowing accounts at 7.197% on equated advances			

The transactions affecting the borrowing accounts can be journalised as follows:

19_7				
Dec.31	Revenue Accounts - Loan Charges (Interest):			
	Finance	DR.	23	576
	Ambulances	DR.	21	2,465
	Sewage Disposal	DR.	24	3,418
	Administrative Buildings	DR.	19	810
	To Cash	C.G.		7,269
	Being loan interest payable to Loans Pool at 7.197% on equated advances			

Interest received by the Capital Fund and Renewals Fund on internal loans could be journalised as follows:

19_7				
Dec.31	Cash	DR.	C.G.	3,441
	To Capital Fund		6	2,174
	To Renewals Fund (Vehicles)		11	634
	To Renewals Fund (Office Equipment)		12	633
	Being interest paid by Loans Pool on internal loans			

229. REVENUE TRANSACTIONS - DEBT MANAGEMENT EXPENSES

Apart from interest charges, there are many other costs which can arise as a result of the raising and repayment of loans.

Among the more important costs incurred are those for the following:

(a) **Salaries**

Staff of the finance department are involved in negotiating and making arrangements for the raising and repayment of loans; calculating repayment and sinking fund schedules; issuing receipts for loans; drawing cheques for repayments and interest; and keeping appropriate records.

Staff of the chief executive officer (town clerk or administrative secretary) or of the legal department, might be involved in negotiations or correspondence with the Ministry of Local Government (e.g. about loan sanctions); drafting finance committee resolutions for loan-raising operations; preparation of mortgage deeds; and sealing and stamping formal documents.

(b) **Printing and Stationery**

Documents such as mortgage deeds, stock certificates, deposit receipts and borrowers registers all cost money to print or to prepare and, therefore, represent part of the costs of borrowing.

(c) **Travelling Expenses**

Expenses might be incurred by senior staff in travelling to (say) large

Loans Pooling

international organisations, government departments and industrial or commercial organisations, to negotiate loans.

(d) **Advertisements**

Fees must be paid to newspapers and periodicals for advertisements for mortgage loans, stock etc.

(e) **Stamp Duty**

Loan documents may bear revenue stamps. Deposit receipts and deeds may bear stamp duty at a flat rate or "ad valorum" (based on the principal sum).

(f) **Fees and Commission**

Fees and commission may have to be paid to brokers and other agents for assisting in loan-raising operations. Legal fees may also be incurred, if lawyers in private practice assist in drawing up any of the loan documents.

(g) **Bank charges**

These may arise as a result of the operation of a separate Bank Account for the loans pool or by an apportionment of general bank charges. They are fees charged for services rendered and should not be confused with bank interest charged on overdrafts.

Some of the above expenses (e.g. stamp duty) can be directly allocated to the expenses of debt management. Others (e.g. salaries) are more likely to be charged to debt management as part of an allocation of central establishment charges.

In our example, because of the small size of the operations, we shall assume Central Establishment Charges to be negligible, confining our attention to direct expenses as follows:

		Units
Stamp Duty (say U 2.50 per U 1,000 on external mortgage loans of U 315,000)		788
Printing and Stationery:		
Paid during year	136	
Outstanding at 31 Dec.	62	198
		986

These expenses could be journalised in the loans pool accounts as follows:

19_7				
Dec.31	Revenue Account - Expenses DR. To Cash Being payment of stamp duty on mortgage deeds	P.12 C.P.	788	788
Dec.31	Revenue Account - Expenses DR. To Cash Being payment for printing and stationery relating to loans	P.13 C.P.	136	136

| Dec.31 | Revenue Account - Expenses   DR.
   To Sundry Creditors
   Being outstanding accounts for
   printing and stationery relating
   to loans | 13
P.16 | 62 | 62 |

The total expenses incurred by the loans pool, amounting to **U** 986 must now be recovered from the borrowing accounts in a similar manner to interest. It could be argued that recovery based on "equated" principal sums is inappropriate for expenses because these are related largely to the actual raising of the loans rather than to the periods during which they are outstanding. Some opinions, therefore, suggest that recovery should be made by calculating an average percentage rate based on total advances made or on total advances outstanding. However, we shall follow the practice of "equated" principal sums, in exactly the same way as for interest. The percentage rate of recovery will, therefore, be calculated as follows:

$$\frac{986}{100,995} = 0.976\%$$

Recovery will be effected as follows:

Borrowing Account	Equated Advances	Expenses at 0.976%
Finance	8,000	78
Ambulances	34,245	334
Sewage Disposal	47,500	464
Administrative Buildings	11,250	110
	100,995	986

Cash transfers to effect the recoveries of expenses from borrowing accounts could be journalised as follows:

(a) **Loans Pool Accounts**

| 19_7
Dec.31 | Cash   DR.
   To Revenue Account - Expenses
   Being reimbursement of expenses
   due to Loans Pool from borrowing
   accounts at 0.976% on equated
   advances | C.P.
P.15 | 986 | 986 |

Loans Pooling

(b) **Borrowing Accounts**

19_7 Dec.31	Revenue Accounts Debt Management Expenses:			
	Finance	DR.	23	78
	Ambulances	DR.	21	334
	Sewage Disposal	DR.	24	464
	Administrative Buildings	DR.	19	110
	To Cash	C.G.		986
	Being expenses payable to Loans Pool at 0.976% on equated advances			

230. LEDGER ACCOUNTS - REVENUE TRANSACTIONS

All the capital and revenue account transactions of the Loans Pool for the year 19_7 are now complete. The relevant ledger accounts for revenue transactions will appear as follows:

(a) **Loans Pool Accounts**

Revenue Account - Interest (External Mortgages)							P.8
19_7 Dec.31	To Cash	J	3,811	19_7 Dec.31	By Revenue Account	P.17	3,811
			3,811				3,811

Revenue Account - Interest (Internal Loans)							P.9
19_7 Dec.31	To Cash	J	3,441	19_7 Dec.31	By Revenue Account	P.17	3,441
			3,441				3,441

Revenue Account - Interest (Bank)							P.10
19_7 Dec.31	To Cash	J	37	19_7 Dec.31	By Revenue Account	P.17	37
			37				37

Municipal Accounting for Developing Countries

		Investment Interest				P.11
19_7 Dec.31	To Revenue Account	P.17	20	19_7 Dec.31	By Cash	J	20
			$\overline{20}$ ==				$\overline{20}$ ==

	Revenue Account - Expenses (Stamp Duty)					P.12
19_7 Dec.31	To Cash	J	788	19_7 Dec.31	By Revenue Account	P.17	788
			$\overline{788}$ ===				$\overline{788}$ ===

	Revenue Account - Expenses (Printing and Stationery)					P.13
19_7 Dec.31	To Cash To Creditors	J J	136 62	19_7 Dec.31	By Revenue Account	P.17	198
			$\overline{198}$ ===				$\overline{198}$ ===

	Interest Recharged to Borrowing Accounts					P.14
19_7 Dec.31	To Revenue Account	P.17	7,269	19_7 Dec.31	By Cash	J	7,269
			$\overline{7,269}$ =====				$\overline{7,269}$ =====

	Expenses Recharged to Borrowing Accounts					P.15
19_7 Dec.31	To Revenue Account	P.17	986	19_7 Dec.31	By Cash	J	986
			$\overline{986}$ ===				$\overline{986}$ ===

Loans Pooling

Sundry Creditors　　　　　　　　　　　　　　　P.16

19_7					19_7			
Dec.31	To Balance	c/d		62	Dec.31	By Expenses (Printing and Stationery)	J	62
				62				62
					19_8 Jan. 1	By Balance	b/d	62

Cash (Loans Pool)　　　　　　　　　　　　　　　C.P.

19_7					19_7			
Mar.31	To Investments	J	2,000		Mar.31	By Advances	J	45,660
	To Loans Outstanding	J	46,000		Jun.30	By Advances	J	40,000
Jun.30	To Loans Outstanding	J	40,000		Sep.30	By Advances	J	155,000
Sep. 9	To Loans Outstanding	J	150,000		Dec.31	By Advances	J	175,000
Dec.15	To Loans Outstanding	J	165,000			By Interest-External	J	3,811
Dec.31	To Advances Repaid	J	17,408			By Interest-Internal	J	3,441
	To Investment Interest	J	20			By Interest-Bank	J	37
	To Interest Recharged	J	7,269			By Expenses-Stamp Duty	J	788
	To Expenses Recharged	J	986			By Expenses-Printing	J	136
						By Balance	c/d	4,810
			428,683					428,683
19_8 Jan. 1	To Balance	b/d	4,810					

(b) Borrowing Accounts and Other General Accounts

\multicolumn{8}{c}{Capital Fund}	6
19_7 Dec.31	To Balance	c/d	125,314	19_7 Jan. 1 Dec.31	By Balance By Cash	b/f J	123,140 2,174	
			125,314 ======				125,314 ======	
				19_7 Jan. 1	By Balance	b/d	125,314	

\multicolumn{8}{c}{Renewals Fund (Vehicles)}	11
19_7 Dec.31	To Balance	c/d	38,379	19_7 Jan. 1 Dec.31	By Balance By Cash	b/d J	37,745 634	
			38,379 ======				38,379 ======	
				19_7 Jan. 1	By Balance	b/d	38,379	

\multicolumn{8}{c}{Renewals Fund (Office Equipment)}	12
19_7 Dec.31	To Balance	c/d	27,253	19_7 Jan. 1 Dec.31	By Balance By Cash	b/f J	26,620 633	
			27,253 ======				27,253 ======	
				19_8 Jan. 1	By Balance	b/d	27,253	

(NOTE: Accounts No. 6,11 and 12 ignore interest on external investments. This is irrelevant for the purposes of this explanation.)

Loans Pooling

Revenue Account (Administrative Buildings) — 19

19_7				19_7			
Dec.31	To Capital Discharged (Loan Charges Principal)	J	1,658	Dec.31	By General Revenue	25	2,578
	To Cash Loan Charges Interest	J	810				
	To Debt Management Expenses	J	110				
			2,578				2,578
			=====				=====

Revenue Account (Ambulances) — 21

19_7				19_7			
Dec.31	To Capital Discharged (Loan Charges Principal)	J	8,600	Dec.31	By General Revenue	25	11,399
	To Cash Loan Charges Interest	J	2,465				
	To Debt Management Expenses	J	334				
			11,399				11,399
			======				======

Revenue Account (Finance) — 23

19_7				19_7			
Dec.31	To Capital Discharged (Loan Charges Principal)	J	2,000	Dec.31	By General Revenue	25	2,654
	To Cash Loan Charges - Interest	J	576				
	To Debt Management Expenses	J	78				
			2,654				2,654
			=====				=====

Municipal Accounting for Developing Countries

		Revenue Account (Sewage Disposal)					24
19_7 Dec.31	To Capital Discharged (Loan Charges Principal)	J	5,150	19_7 Dec.31	By General Revenue	25	9,032
	To Cash Loan Charges - Interest	J	3,418				
	To Debt Management Expenses	J	464				
			9,032				9,032
			=====				=====

		General Revenue Account (Loan Transactions only)					25
19_7 Dec.31	To Administrative Buildings	19	2,578	19_7 Dec.31	By Various Items of Revenue Income (as part of other activity of the General Revenue Account)		25,663
	To Ambulances	21	11,399				
	To Finance	23	2,654				
	To Sewage Disposal	24	9,032				
			25,663				25,663
			======				======

Loans Pooling

Cash (General)   C.G.

19_7				19_7			
Mar.31	To Capital Fund Investments (External)	J	46,000	Mar.31	By Capital Fund Investments (Pool)	J	46,000
	To Loans Outstanding	J	45,660		By Capital Expenditure (Ambulances)	J	45,660
Jun.30	To Renewals Fund Investments (External)	J	40,000	Jun.30	By Renewals Fund Investments (Pool)	J	40,000
	To Loans Outstanding	J	40,000		By Capital Expenditure (Sewage Disposal Works)	J	39,120
Sep.30	To Loans Outstanding	J	45,000	Sep.30	By Capital Expenditure (Administrative Buildings)	J	43,260
	To Loans Outstanding	J	110,000		By Capital Expenditure (Sewage Disposal Works)	J	108,840
Dec.31	To Loans Outstanding	J	80,000	Dec.31	By Capital Expenditure (Administrative Buildings)	J	77,160
	To Loans Outstanding	J	95,000		By Capital Expenditure (Sewage Disposal Works)	J	93,400
	To Sundry Funds (Internal Loan Interest)	J	3,441		By Loans Outstanding: Administrative Buildings	J	1,658
	To Balance	c/d	14,002		Ambulances	J	8,600
					Finance	J	2,000
					Sewage Disposal	J	5,150
					By Loan Charges - Interest: Administrative		

Municipal Accounting for Developing Countries

						Buildings	J	810
						Ambulances	J	2,465
						Finance	J	576
						Sewage Disposal	J	3,418
					By Debt Management Expenses:			
						Administrative Buildings	J	110
						Ambulances	J	334
						Finance	J	78
						Sewage Disposal	J	464
			519,103					519,103
				19_8 Jan. 1	By Balance	b/d		14,002

The final balance sheet of the loans pool will appear as follows:

Loans Pool
Balance Sheet as at 31 Dec. 19_7

Capital

	Units		Units
LOANS OUTSTANDING		ADVANCES TO BORROWING ACCOUNTS	
External Mortgages	325,000	Administrative Buildings	123,342
Internal Funds	86,000	Ambulances	37,060
		Finance	6,000
		Sewage Disposal	239,850
		CASH IN HAND	4,748*
	411,000		411,000

Revenue

CREDITORS	62	CASH IN HAND	62*
	411,062		411,062

(*Net balance in hand = 4,810)

Loans Pooling

The Aggregate Balance Sheet for the appropriate General Accounts will now appear as follows:

General Accounts
Aggregate Balance Sheet as at 31 Dec. 19_7

Capital

	Units		Units
LONG-TERM LIABILITIES		**FIXED ASSETS**	
Loans Outstanding		Administrative Buildings	120,420
Loans Pool	406,252	Ambulance	45,660
		Accounting Machine	10,000
OTHER BALANCES		Sewage Disposal Works	241,360
Capital Fund	125,314		
Capital Discharged		**CURRENT ASSETS**	
Loans Repaid	19,408	Investments	
		External	77,140
		Internal	46,000
		Cash in Hand	10,394*
	550,974		550,974

Revenue

	Units		Units
CURRENT LIABILITES		**CURRENT ASSETS**	
Cash Overdrawn	24,396*	Investments	
		External	24,365
PROVISIONS		Internal	40,000
Renewals Funds			
Vehicles	38,379	**OTHER BALANCES**	
Office Equipment	27,253	Revenue Account	
		Deficiency	25,663
	90,028		90,028
	641,002		641,002

(*Net balance overdrawn = 14,002)

In practice, of course, income would be raised during the year in the form of rates, taxes etc. to meet the Revenue Account Deficiency, thus eliminating the overdrawn cash balance.

The Chartered Institute of Public Finance and Accountancy (UK) recommends that the final accounts of a Loans Pool be published in the form shown on pages 802-804. For the sake of completeness, the entire recommended forms are shown, with figures from our example inserted where appropriate. In practice, of course, headings would only be included where there are figures to support them.

LOANS POOL

Revenue Transactions for the year ended 31 Dec. 19_7

INTEREST TRANSACTIONS

Interest paid to External Mortgages ...	3,811	
Interest paid to Internal Funds ...	3,441	
Bank Interest ...	37	
		7,289

OTHER FINANCING TRANSACTIONS

Stamp Duty and Other Expenses of Raising Loans	788	
Expenses of Making and Selling Investments	–	
Bank Charges ...	–	
Loss of Realisation of Investments ...	–	
Central and Departmental Establishment Charges	198	
Other Expenses ...	–	
		986
		8,275
		=====

INTEREST TRANSACTIONS

Interest on Investments		20
Bank Interest ...		–
Interest Charged to Borrowing Accounts:		
Administrative Buildings ...	810	
Ambulances ...	2,465	
Finance ...	576	
Sewage Disposal ...	3,418	
Etc ...	–	
	7,269	7,289

OTHER FINANCING TRANSACTIONS

Fees and Fines		–
Profit on Sale of Investments		–
Amounts charged to Borrowing Accounts:		
Administrative Buildings	110	
Ambulances	334	
Finance	78	
Sewage Disposal	464	
Etc	–	
	986	986
		8,275
		=====

LOANS POOL

Capital Cash Account for the year ended 31 Dec. 19_7

	Units		Units
LOANS RAISED		LOANS REPAID	
External Mortgages	325,000	External Mortgages	-
Internal Funds	86,000	Internal Funds	-
	411,000		
REPAYMENT BY BORROWING ACCOUNTS		ADVANCES TO BORROWING ACCOUNTS	
Administrative Buildings	1,658	Administrative Buildings	125,000
Ambulances	8,600	Ambulances	45,660
Finance	2,000	Finance	8,000
Sewage Disposal	5,150	Sewage Disposal	245,000
Etc	-	Etc	-
	17,408		423,660
INVESTMENTS SOLD		INVESTMENTS BOUGHT	
Sinking Fund	2,000	Sinking Fund	2,000
Etc	-	Etc	-
	2,000		425,660
Cash in hand at 1 Jan. 19_7 brought forward	-	Cash overdrawn at 1 Jan. 19_7 brought forward	-
Cash overdrawn at 31 Dec. 19_7 carried forward	-	Cash in hand at 31 Dec. 19_7 carried forward	4,748
	430,408		430,408
	=======		=======

LOANS POOL

Balance Sheet as at 31 Dec. 19_7

	Capital	Units		Capital		Units
LOANS OUTSTANDING			ADVANCES TO BORROWING ACCOUNTS			
External Mortgages	325,000		Administrative	123,342		
Internal Funds	86,000	411,000	Buildings	37,060		
			Ambulances	6,000		
CASH OVERDRAWN		–	Finance	239,850		
			Sewage Disposal	–		
			Etc		406,252	
			ADVANCES TO OTHER AUTHORITIES			
			Details		–	
			INVESTMENTS		–	
			CASH IN HAND		4,748	411,000
		411,000				411,000

	Revenue			Revenue	
CREDITORS	62		DEBTORS	–	
CASH OVERDRAWN	–	62	CASH IN HAND	62	62
		411,062			411,062
		========			========

Loans Pooling

231. LOANS POOL TRANSACTIONS IN SUBSEQUENT YEARS

We shall now briefly examine the loans pool transactions for 19_8 and 19_9. This is done to study one or two aspects not readily apparent from the transactions of a single year. We shall assume that during 19_8 the internal loan of U 46,000 from the Capital Fund is repaid. During 19_9, U 75,000 of mortgage loans are repaid upon reaching their maturity after (say) two years and U 20,000 is repaid to the Vehicle Renewals Fund.

During 19_9, the sum of U 35,000 is borrowed from the Housing Repairs Fund.

The transactions for 19_8 and 19_9 can perhaps best be considered by an examination of the various statements shown on pages 806-815. Each shows a particular aspect of loans pooling and some of the statements would be of value even where a formal loans pool was not in operation.

Municipal Accounting for Developing Countries

LOANS POOL

FORECAST OF APPROXIMATE LOAN REQUIREMENTS FOR 19_8

1. Balance overdrawn on Loans Pool
   at beginning of year

2. Estimated capital expenditure during year:

   (i) Schemes in hand
       (a) Administrative Buildings   300,000
       (b) Sewage Disposal Works   175,000

   (ii) Schemes not yet started
       (a) Ambulance   47,000
       (b) Sewerage - Diwali Road   192,000

3. Loans falling due for repayment to lenders during year:

Month	External	Internal
Jan.	-	-
Feb.	-	-
Mar.	-	-
Apr.	-	46,000
May	-	-
June	-	-
July	-	-
Aug.	-	-
Sep.	-	-
Oct.	-	-
Nov.	-	-
Dec.	-	-
U	-	46,000

    46,000

4.   TOTAL OUTGOINGS   760,000

5. Balance in hand in Loans Pool at beginning of year   4,000

6. Instalments to be repaid by borrowing accounts   36,000

7. Investments available from other funds of the authority   -

8. Other capital receipts   -

9.   TOTAL INCOMINGS   40,000

10.   LOAN REQUIREMENTS   720,000

Memo: Loans falling due for replacement in next 2 years:

    19_9   1st half   20,000
                      2nd half   75,000   95,000

                      2nd half   35,000   60,000

Loans Pooling

LOANS POOL

FORECAST OF APPROXIMATE LOAN REQUIREMENTS FOR 19_9

1.	Balance overdrawn on Loans Pool at beginning of year	1,000
2.	Estimated capital expenditure during year:	
	(i) Schemes in hand	
	(a) Sewage Disposal Works	95,000
	(ii) Schemes not yet started	
	(a) Ambulance	48,000
	(b) Clinic - Bugoma	200,000
	(c) Street Lighting	180,000

3. Loans falling due for repayment to lenders during year:

Month	External	Internal
Jan.	-	-
Feb.	-	-
Mar.	-	-
Apr.	-	20,000
May	-	-
June	-	-
July	-	-
Aug.	-	-
Sep.	45,000	-
Oct.	-	-
Nov.	-	-
Dec.	30,000	-
U	75,000	20,000

                                                                                                        95,000

4.	TOTAL OUTGOINGS	619,000
5.	Balance in hand in Loans Pool at beginning of year	-
6.	Instalments to be repaid by borrowing accounts	60,000
7.	Investments available from other funds of the authority	35,000
8.	Other capital receipts	-
9.	TOTAL INCOMINGS	95,000
10.	LOAN REQUIREMENTS	524,000

Memo: Loans falling due for replacement in next 2 years:

	19_0	1st half	25,000	
		2nd half	35,000	60,000
	19_1	1st half	15,000	
		2nd half	85,000	100,000

CAPITAL SCHEMES FINANCED FROM LOANS POOL
APPLICATION OF LOAN SANCTIONS

Scheme	Amount of Loan Sanction	Gross Capital Expenditure	Loan Sanctions Under-spent	Loan Sanctions Over-spent	Remarks
1. Administrative Buildings	420,000	421,580		1,580	Balance financed by RCCO
2. Ambulance (19_7)	46,000	45,660	340		Balance remains unexercised
3. Sewage Disposal Works	510,000	508,920	1,080		Balance remains unexercised
4. Ambulance (19_8)	47,000	46,220	780		U 740 applied towards over-spending on item 6 (below) Balance (40) remains unexercised
5. Sewerage - Diwali Road	192,000	191,700	300		Balance remains unexercised
6. Ambulance (19_9)	48,000	48,740		740	Balance financed from item 4 (above)
7. Clinic - Bugoma	200,000	196,320	3,680		Balance remains unexercised
8. Street Lighting	180,000	182,360		2,360	Balance financed by additional loan sanction
TOTALS	1,643,000	1,641,500	6,180	4,680	

Loans Pooling

LOANS POOL

Revenue Transactions for the year ended 31 Dec. 19_8

INTEREST TRANSACTIONS		INTEREST TRANSACTIONS	
Interest paid to		Interest charged to	
External Mortgages	47,173	Borrowing Accounts:	
Interest paid on		Administrative	
Internal Funds	3,450	Buildings	21,100
Bank Interest	1,832	Ambulances	3,327
		Finance	410
		Sewage Disposal	21,802
		Sewerage	5,816
	52,455		52,455
OTHER FINANCING TRANSACTIONS		OTHER FINANCING TRANSACTIONS	
Stamp Duty	1,775	Expenses charged to	
Other Expenses	5,055	Borrowing Accounts:	
		Administrative	
		Buildings	2,747
		Ambulances	433
		Finance	54
		Sewage Disposal	2,839
		Sewerage	757
	6,830		6,830
	59,285		59,285

Capital Cash Account for Year Ended 31 Dec. 19_8

LOANS RAISED		LOANS REPAID	
External Mortgages	710,000	Internal Funds	46,000
REPAYMENT BY BORROWING ACCOUNTS		ADVANCES TO BORROWING ACCOUNTS	
Administrative Buildings	5,620	Administrative Buildings	295,000
Ambulances	17,564	Ambulances	46,220
Finance	2,000	Sewage Disposal	175,000
Sewage Disposal	8,983	Sewerage	191,700
Sewerage	4,029		
	38,196		707,920
	748,196		753,920
Cash in hand 1 Jan. b/fwd	4,748		
Cash overdrawn 31 Dec. c/fwd	976		
	753,920		753,920

CASH RECEIPTS AND PAYMENTS

Year Ended 31 Dec. 19_8

Scheme	Capital Cash in Hand B/fwd	Quarterly Payments					Quarterly Receipts					Capital Cash In Hand B/fwd
		March	June	September	December	Total	March	June	September	December	Total	
Administrative Buildings	4,580	153,260	147,900	—	—	301,160	150,000	145,000	1,580*	—	296,580	—
Ambulance (19_8)	—	—	—	46,220	—	46,220	—	—	46,220	—	46,220	—
Sewage Disposal Works	3,640	61,340	49,880	34,680	27,980	173,880	60,000	50,000	35,000	30,000	175,000	4,760
Sewerage – Diwali Road	—	18,320	139,620	520	33,240	191,700	20,000	140,000	—	31,700	191,700	—
	8,220	232,920	337,400	81,420	61,220	712,960	230,000	335,000	82,800	61,700	709,500	4,760

* Revenue Contribution

Year Ended 31 Dec. 19_9

Scheme	Capital Cash in Hand B/fwd	Quarterly Payments					Quarterly Receipts					Capital Cash In Hand B/fwd
		March	June	September	December	Total	March	June	September	December	Total	
Sewage Disposal Works	4,760	42,300	21,880	29,500	—	93,680	40,000	25,000	23,920	—	88,920	—
Ambulance (19_9)	—	—	48,740	—	—	48,740	—	48,740	—	—	48,740	—
Clinic – Bugoma	—	61,560	122,320	12,440	—	196,320	65,000	120,000	11,320	—	196,320	—
Street Lighting	—	8,180	79,720	94,460	—	182,360	10,000	80,000	90,000	2,360	182,360	—
	4,760	112,040	272,660	136,400	—	521,100	115,000	273,740	125,240	2,360	516,340	—

STATEMENT OF ADVANCES AND REPAYMENTS 19_7 - 19_9_

Borrowing Account and Scheme	19_7_ Additions During Year	19_7_ Reductions During Year	19_7_ Outstanding At Year End	19_8_ Additions During Year	19_8_ Reductions During Year	19_8_ Outstanding At Year End	19_9_ Additions During Year	19_9_ Reductions During Year	19_9_ Outstanding At Year End
Administrative Buildings	125,000	1,658	123,342	295,000	5,620	412,722	-	5,788	406,934
Ambulances Ambulance (19_7_)	45,660	8,600	37,060	-	8,858	28,202	-	9,124	19,078
Ambulance (19_8_)	-	-	-	46,220	8,706	37,514	-	8,967	28,547
Ambulance (19_9_)	-	-	-	-	-	-	48,740	9,180	39,560
Clinics and Centres Clinic - Bugoma	-	-	-	-	-	-	196,320	2,604	193,716
Finance Accounting Machine	8,000	2,000	6,000	-	2,000	4,000	-	2,000	2,000
Sewage Disposal Sewage Disposal Works	245,000	5,150	239,850	175,000	8,983	405,867	88,920	11,121	483,666
Sewerage Sewer - Diwali Road	-	-	-	191,700	4,029	187,671	-	4,150	183,521
Street Lighting	-	-	-	-	-	-	182,360	6,787	175,573
TOTALS	423,660	17,408	406,252	707,920	38,196	1,075,976	516,340	59,721	1,532,595
Add Loans Pool Cash Unapplied			4,748			-			2,405
Loans Outstanding (Real)			411,000			1,075,976			1,535,000

LOAN REPAYMENT SCHEDULES

Borrowing Account and Scheme	19_7 Repayments First Advance	19_7 Repayments Second Advance	19_7 Repayments Third Advance	19_7 Repayments Total	19_8 Repayments First Advance	19_8 Repayments Second Advance	19_8 Repayments Third Advance	19_8 Repayments Total	19_9 Repayments First Advance	19_9 Repayments Second Advance	19_9 Repayments Third Advance	19_9 Repayments Total
Administrative Buildings	1,658	-	-	1,658	1,708	3,912	-	5,620	1,759	4,029	-	5,788
Ambulances Ambulance (19_7)	8,600	-	-	8,600	8,858	-	-	8,858	9,124	-	-	9,124
Ambulance (19_8)	-	-	-	-	8,706	-	-	8,706	8,967	-	-	8,967
Ambulance (19_9)	-	-	-	-	-	-	-	-	9,180	-	-	9,180
Clinics and Centres Clinic - Bugoma	-	-	-	-	-	-	-	-	2,604	-	-	2,604
Finance Accounting Machine	2,000	-	-	2,000	2,000	-	-	2,000	2,000	-	-	2,000
Sewage Disposal Sewage Disposal Works	5,150	-	-	5,150	5,305	3,678	-	8,983	5,464	3,788	1,869	11,121
Sewerage Sewer - Diwali Road	-	-	-	-	4,029	-	-	4,029	4,150	-	-	4,150
Street Lighting	-	-	-	-	-	-	-	-	6,787	-	-	6,787
TOTALS	17,408	-	-	17,408	30,606	7,590	-	38,196	50,035	7,817	1,869	59,721

812

LOANS POOL
ADVANCES AND APPORTIONMENT OF INTEREST AND EXPENSES
Year Ended 31 Dec. 19_8_

Borrowing Account	March	June	September	December	Annual Equivalent	Advances Outstanding for Full Year	Basis of Allocation	Interest @ 6.843%	Expenses @ 0.891%
Administrative Buildings	150,000	145,000	-	-	185,000	123,342	308,342	21,100	2,747
Ambulances	-	-	46,220	-	11,555	37,060	48,615	3,327	433
Finance	-	-	-	-	-	6,000	6,000	410	54
Sewage Disposal	60,000	50,000	35,000	30,000	78,750	239,850	318,600	21,802	2,839
Sewerage	20,000	140,000	-	31,700	85,000	-	85,000	5,816	757
TOTAL	230,000	335,000	81,220	61,700	360,305	406,252	766,557	52,455	6,830

Year Ended 31 Dec. 19_9_

Borrowing Account	March	June	September	December	Annual Equivalent	Advances Outstanding for Full Year	Basis of Allocation	Interest @ 7.236%	Expenses @ 1.017%
Administrative Buildings	-	-	-	-	-	412,722	412,722	29,864	4,197
Ambulances	-	48,740	-	-	24,370	65,716	90,086	6,519	916
Clinics and Centres	65,000	120,000	11,320	-	111,580	-	111,580	8,074	1,135
Finance	-	-	-	-	-	4,000	4,000	289	41
Sewage Disposal	40,000	25,000	23,920	-	48,480	405,867	454,347	32,877	4,621
Sewerage	-	-	-	-	-	187,671	187,671	13,580	1,908
Street Lighting	10,000	80,000	90,000	2,360	70,000	-	70,000	5,065	712
TOTAL	115,000	273,740	125,240	2,360	254,430	1,075,976	1,330,406	96,268	13,530

Municipal Accounting for Developing Countries

Balance Sheet as at 31 Dec. 19_8

Capital

LOANS OUTSTANDING		ADVANCES TO BORROWING ACCOUNTS	
External Mortgages	1,035,000	Administrative Buildings	412,722
Internal Funds	40,000	Ambulance	65,716
Cash Overdrawn	976	Finance	4,000
		Sewage Disposal	405,867
		Sewerage	187,671
	1,075,976		1,075,976

Revenue

CREDITORS	133	CASH IN HAND	133
	1,076,109		1,076,109

LOANS POOL

Revenue Transactions for the year ended 31 Dec. 19_9

INTEREST TRANSACTIONS		INTEREST TRANSACTIONS	
Interest paid to		Interest charged to	
External Mortgages	89,603	Borrowing Accounts:	
Interest paid on		Administrative Buildings	29,864
Internal Funds	2,820	Ambulances	6,519
Bank Interest	3,845	Clinics and Centres	8,074
		Finance	289
		Sewage Disposal	32,877
		Sewerage	13,580
		Street Lighting	5,065
	96,268		96,268
OTHER FINANCING TRANSACTIONS		OTHER FINANCING TRANSACTIONS	
Stamp Duty	1,300	Expenses charged to	
Other Expenses	12,230	Borrowing Accounts:	
		Administrative Buildings	4,197
		Ambulances	916
		Clinics and Centres	1,135
		Finance	41
		Sewage Disposal	4,621
		Sewerage	1,908
		Street Lighting	712
	13,530		13,530
	109,798		109,798

Loans Pooling

Capital Cash Account for year ended 31 Dec. 19_9

LOANS RAISED		LOANS REPAID	
External Mortgages	520,000	External Mortgages	75,000
Internal Funds	35,000	Internal Funds	20,000
	555,000		95,000
REPAYMENTS		ADVANCES TO BORROWING ACCOUNTS	
Administrative Buildings	5,788	Ambulances	48,740
Ambulances	27,271	Clinics and Centres	196,320
Clinics and Centres	2,604	Sewage Disposal	88,920
Finance	2,000	Street Lighting	182,360
Sewage Disposal	11,121		
Sewerage	4,150		
Street Lighting	6,787		
	59,721		516,340
	614,721		611,340
		Cash overdrawn 1 Jan. b/fwd	976
		Cash in hand 31 Dec. c/fwd	2,405
	614,721		614,721

Balance Sheet as at 31 Dec. 19_9

Capital

LOANS OUTSTANDING		ADVANCES TO BORROWING ACCOUNTS	
External Mortgages	1,480,000	Administrative Buildings	406,934
Internal Funds	55,000	Ambulances	87,185
		Clinics and Centres	193,716
		Finance	2,000
		Sewage Disposal	483,666
		Sewerage	183,521
		Street Lighting	175,573
		CASH IN HAND	2,405
	1,535,000		1,535,000

Revenue

CREDITORS	561	CASH IN HAND	561
	1,535,561		1,535,561

Municipal Accounting for Developing Countries

(a) **Forecasts of Approximate Loan Requirements for 19_8 and 19_9** (pages 806 and 807).

These statements would be drawn up at the beginning of each year, to determine approximately how much loan finance would be required from external sources. Funds will be required to finance new capital expenditure and to repay existing loans and overdrafts. Some of this money will be available from cash already in hand, repayments by borrowing accounts and new internal borrowing. The balance will have to be raised from external mortgages.

A useful addition to the statement is the memo showing loans falling due for repayment during the next two years. This, taken together with planned capital expenditure, gives a broad indication of future loan requirements, for advance planning.

(b) **Application of Loan Sanctions** (page 808)

No funds can be advanced from the loans pool unless covered by loan sanctions. This applies even where adequate moneys are available in the pool. Where the capital expenditure is less than the amount of the loan sanction, only sufficient is advanced to cover it. The balance of the sanction remains unexercised and is regarded as cancelled. This has happened in the majority of cases in our example.

The final cost of administrative buildings is U 1,580 in excess of the sanction. Only the approved sum of U 420,000 can be advanced from the loans pool. The balance, assumed not to be covered by an additional sanction, is met from revenue.

The underspending on the 19_8 ambulance has been partially used to offset an overspending on the 19_9 ambulance. This would require the approval of the sanctioning authority (e.g. the Ministry of Local Government) but would appear to be a reasonable decision because the two items are for the same service.

The overspending on the street lighting scheme has been covered by an additional loan sanction. Without this further approval, another source would be needed to finance the excess of U 2,360.

(c) **Capital Receipts and Payments** (page 809)

This statement shows the payments made on capital schemes in progress during 19_8 and 19_9, together with the capital receipts from which they were financed. With the exception of the revenue contribution of U 1,580 marked (*) all capital receipts represent advances from the loans pool. Advances in excess of expenditure are shown as cash balances in hand at the beginning and end of each year. For example, advances in respect of the Sewage Disposal Works had exceeded expenditure by U 3,640 at the end of 19_7, leaving this sum as a cash balance in the hands of the borrowing account at the beginning of 19_8. During 19_8 further advances of 175,000 were made. Payments on the scheme totalled U 173,880 leaving a balance of U 4,760 to carry forward at the end of 19_8. The exact cash position of each borrowing account can, if necessary, be calculated at the end of each quarter. For example, the position relating to Administrative Buildings at the end of June is as follows:

Loans Pooling

Cash in hand brought forward				4,580
Add New advances	March	150,000		
	June	145,000		295,000
				299,580
Less Payments	March	153,260		
	June	147,900		301,160
Cash overdrawn 30 June				1,580

The loans pool has advanced funds to the maximum limit permitted by the sanction. This has left the borrowing account with an overspent cash balance, afterwards corrected by a revenue contribution.

(d) **Advances and Repayments 19_7 - 19_9** (page 810)

This statement shows details of advances made to borrowing accounts, repayments made by borrowing accounts and balances outstanding. The statement will agree exactly with the successive balance sheets of the loans pool on pages 814 and 815. At the end of 19_8 the loans pool has no cash balance in hand. U 1,075,000 is outstanding on external and internal loans and U 976 has been raised by a bank overdraft.

(e) **Loan Repayment Schedules** (page 811)

This statement shows how the various repayments have been calculated. A separate repayment table, along the lines of those on pages 768 to 770 will be calculated from sinking fund tables for each separate loan. Where advances are spread over more than one year, the total advances in each year are treated as a separate loan from the pool. In the case of the Sewage Disposal Works, for example, three separate repayment tables will be worked out to cover advances for 19_7 (U 245,000) 19_8 (U 175,000) and 19_9 (U 88,920). The two separate repayments for 19_8 and also the three for 19_9 will be added together for inclusion in the table of advances and repayments.

(f) **Advances and Apportionment of Interest**

The table shows the way in which interest and debt management expenses are apportioned over advances outstanding at the beginning of a year and advances made during a year. Continuing our example of the Sewage Disposal Works the basis of apportionment for 19_8 is worked out as follows:

$$60,000 \times \tfrac{3}{4} = 45,000$$
$$50,000 \times \tfrac{1}{2} = 25,000$$
$$35,000 \times \tfrac{1}{4} = 8,750$$
$$30,000 \text{ (advanced 31/12)} = -$$

Annual Equivalent		78,750
Add Balance Outstanding at 1 Jan. 19_8		239,850
Basis of Apportionment		318,600

Interest during 19_8 totalled U 52,455 representing 6.843% of the total basis of apportionment of U 766,557. Expenses of U 6,830 represented 0.891% of the total. In 19_9 the average rates for interest (7.236%) and for expenses (1.017%) have both increased, indicating that market rates of interest are generally higher than hitherto and that debt management is becoming more expensive.

Municipal Accounting for Developing Countries

(g) Final Published Accounts

The final published accounts for 19_8 and 19_9 are reproduced in full. Notice how the figures in these accounts are related to those in the other statements, referred to above. It will be seen from the Capital Cash Account that loans actually raised differ slightly from those forecast.

232. LOANS POOLING - CONCLUSION

In this chapter we have attempted a case study of a particular loans pool. There are many variations in arrangements for loans pools although the basic principles of operation are the same as those explained above.

The system is based upon the assumption that most local authority expenditure is financed by borrowing. The explanations also make the assumption that local authority borrowing is subject to some form of legal approval by a supervising government department, here referred to as a loan sanction. The supervisory department would typically be a Ministry of Local Government, Ministry of Finance or Ministry of Planning. Although the law and practice will vary from one country to another, such supervision over borrowing, in one form or another, is very typical. Often it is a specific provision in local government law.

21. Depreciation and Capital Funds

SECTION		PAGE
233	Capital Accounts - Commercial Practices.	820
234	Capital Fund.	822
235	Appropriation of Balances by the Capital Fund.	823
236	Valuation of Fixed Assets.	824
237	Financing New Capital Expenditure.	835
238	Review of Half-Yearly Balances.	844
239	Interest Apportionment and Recovery.	847
240	Chargeable Interest Rate.	848
241	Capital Fund Management Expenses.	849
242	Depreciation Charges.	850
243	Interest Charges Amortisation and Capital Fund Accounts.	851
244	Capital Fund Investments.	869
245	Renewals Provisions.	870
246	Capital Fund Transactions in Subsequent Years.	876
247	Capital Fund Cash Transactions.	881
248	External Loans.	881
249	Capital Fund Revenue Account.	882
250	Capital Discharged.	882
251	Capital Fund Balance Sheets for Subsequent Years.	883
252	Capital Expenditure.	884
253	Depreciation.	888
254	Interest and Management Expenses.	889
255	Grants and Contributions.	889
256	Municipal Banks and Loans Funds.	892
257	Electronic Data Processing.	892

233 CAPITAL ACCOUNTS - COMMERCIAL PRACTICES

In this final chapter, we shall depart somewhat from the usual conventions of municipal accounting to deal comprehensively with the application of depreciation concepts to the accounts of non-revenue-earning services, largely financed from local and national taxes. The need for the introduction of such a practice has long been asserted by many in the accountancy profession.

It is not unreasonable, after all, to ask that costs of public services, however financed, should be ascertained by following the same accounting principles as are used in the commercial sector. If reinforcement of this claim were needed, it is becoming increasingly evident that public community assets (roads, sewers, drains, etc.) in many countries, have seriously deteriorated, yet no consistent financial provision has usually been made for their renewal or replacement. Legislators and governmental authorities may not be readily prepared to authorize current tax reveneues to be earmarked for depreciation charges, as such, because these are non-cash expenditures. However, this misses the point. It seems reasonable always to provide, from recurrent income, for revenue contributions to capital outlay (to finance new assets or to redeem existing debt) at least equal to the total chargeable depreciation. Only in this way will a community be faced with a total recognition of, and become fully responsible for, the costs of its public services. Also, funds would be provided to ensure that community capital is sustained, at least at cost prices.

There is another important reason for putting forward a change of approach in this chapter. Most of this book has been based on specific assumptions regarding the separate financing of capital and recurrent expenditure. A basic assumption is that most capital expenditure would be financed by loans, with relatively small proportions of the capital finance coming from other sources. Experience in many developing countries suggests that this pattern is not necessarily a standard one. A great deal of capital expenditure is financed by government grants, rather than by loans. Also, many local authorities often have to provide for the financing of relatively high proportions of capital expenditures out of annual revenue sources.

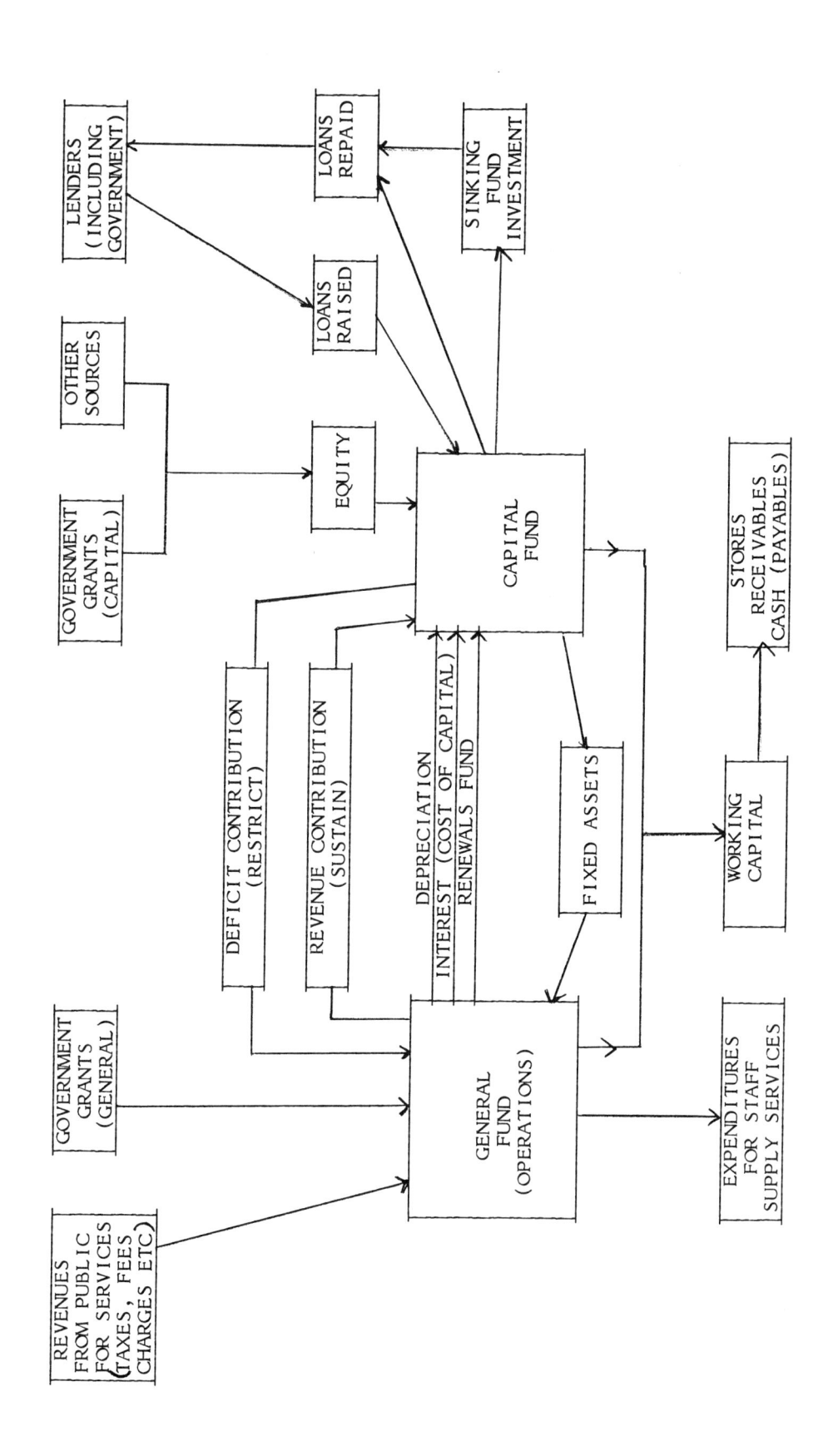

These factors would, if uncontrolled, allow a variety of arbitrary charges against revenue accounts, which might bear little relationship to costs. Thus, in order to have a closer ascertainment of costs, whilst continuing to recognize the distinctions between capital and revenue funds, the accounting system could be somewhat restructured. This could be done by extending the concept of the "loans pool" to cover all capital financing, from whatever source. The result would be a Capital Fund. This type of capital fund differs markedly from the one described in Chapter 14 since it would be all-embracing. Indeed, it goes beyond, and incorporates, loans pooling, capital funds, renewals funds and grant financing.

The proposed system is illustrated by the diagram on page 821. The two focal points of the system are the General Fund (for operations) and the Capital Fund. As at present, the General Fund would be funded from revenue income in the form of general taxes, fees and user charges.

General government grants (including the proceeds of revenue-sharing systems) also represent income. This income would be used, as at present, for revenue expenditures on staff, supplies and services. It would also be used to transfer funds to the Capital Fund. This would be done in two principal ways. First, transfers would be made in respect of depreciation charges and interest. Second, there might be lump-sum transfers representing those portions of revenue account surpluses not required to be retained for increased working capital.

The Capital Fund would receive all funds for capital expenditure, including loans, specific capital grants and other contributions, from which would be disbursed all capital payments. These fixed asset costs would be regarded as a charge against the appropriate section of the revenue accounts comprising the General Fund, to be discharged by annual depreciation, together with interest. There would also be matching funds transfers from the General Fund to the Capital Fund. The Capital Fund would be responsible for discharging all debt service obligations. This would include the establishment of sinking fund investments, if considered necessary. In contrast to loans pooling, the capital fund system would be appropriate whether there were instalment loans or maturity loans.

234 CAPITAL FUND

Let us suppose that the Kambale Council operates such a system instead of a loans pool. We shall assume that its capital programme is that shown in the table in Section 217 of Chapter 20. The loan sanction periods shown in the table will be regarded as the reasonable asset life of each scheme for depreciation purposes.

Assume that the ambulances and Bugoma Clinic are being financed by a 50-year loan from the International Aid Administration (IAA) with interest at 2% (well below market rates) and with repayments to begin, after a 5-year grace period, in 19_0. The Sewage Disposal Works is to be financed by a government grant of U 200,000, with the balance of U 310,000 to be borrowed from the Local Government Loans Fund (LGLF). The loan is to be repaid over 25 years at 10% interest. The Sewerage for Diwali Road is to be financed by a government grant of U 50,000 with a further U 50,000 to be collected as one-time plot charges from new sites to be served. These charges may also be referred to as betterment charges, hook-up fees or frontage charges, depending on the manner of assessment. The remaining U 92,000 will be raised by a loan from LGLF for 25 years at 10%. Administrative Buildings and Street Lighting will be financed by the general borrowing of the

Depreciation and Capital Funds

Capital Fund, assumed to be maturity mortgages. For simplicity, all calculations and book-keeping entries will be rounded to the nearest unit.

235 APPROPRIATION OF BALANCES BY THE CAPITAL FUND

In Section 218, prior to the operation of a loans pool for Kambale, a review was made of various funds which could be considered as possible sources of finance for the loans pool. In the case of the system using a Capital Fund and depreciation, all the other funds for capital expenditure would be abolished and their assets would form part of the new Capital Fund. Thus, the following balances would be used as initial balances of the Capital Fund:

	U
Capital Fund	123,140
Capital Receipts Unapplied	21,300
Vehicle Renewals Fund	37,745
Office Equipment Renewals fund	26,620
Sinking Fund	2,000
	210,805

The Housing Repairs Fund, not considered a source of funding for capital expenditure, would not be incorporated in the Capital Fund. However, as indicated in Section 218, the Housing Repairs Fund could be considered as a possible source of internal borrowing by the newly-established Capital Fund.

It might, of course, be pointed out that the introduction of depreciation concepts would bring the accounting procedures of Kambale Council very close to those of commercial systems. In such circumstances, the concept of a Housing Repairs Fund might also be out of place, in which case it would also be abolished. Its balance would then form part of the general revenue surplus. For the purpose of this example, however, we shall assume it to have been retained separately, but that it will not make internal loans to the Capital Fund.

The winding up of the (old) capital fund and renewals funds and the transfer of their assets to the (new) Capital Fund, together with the balances of capital receipts unapplied and the sinking fund, would be journalised as follows:

Municipal Accounting for Developing Countries

		General Fund				
19-7 Jan.1		Capital Fund	DR	3	123,140	
		Capital Receipts Unapplied	DR	4	21,300	
		Vehicles Renewals Fund	DR	6	37,745	
		Office Equipment Renewals Fund	DR	7	26,620	
		Sinking Fund	DR	5	2,000	
		To Investments		8		189,505
		Cash		CB		21,300
		Being transfer of balances to Capital Fund				
		Capital Fund				
Jan.1		Investments	DR	1	189,505	
		Cash	DR	CB	21,300	
		To Capital Discharged (RCCO)				210,805
		Being balances taken over by the Capital Fund on initial establishment				

It should be noted that the opening balances of the Capital Fund are defined as Capital Discharged (Revenue Contributions to Capital Outlay). This is because, under this, system there are no separate funds with balances. Since the various special funds are wound up, it is just as if lump-sum transfers had been made directly from the General Fund to the Capital Fund.

236 VALUATION OF FIXED ASSETS

In the setting up of a Capital Fund, the next step is both simple in concept but difficult in practice. It is necessary for Kambale Council to change from a "gross fixed assets" position to a "gross fixed assets less depreciation" position. To do this in detail, it will be necessary to establish detailed fixed asset records for each major asset or group of assets. These records will show:

(a)   description and location of fixed asset;

(b)   source of finance;

(c)   balances brought forward (at cost);

(d)   additions during year;

(e)   disposals during year;

(f)   balances carried forward (at cost);

(g)   depreciation rate and method;

(h)   accumulated depreciation brought foward;

(i)   annual depreciation charge;

Depreciation and Capital Funds

- (j) accumulated depreciation on asset disposals during year (written out of books);

- (k) accumulated depreciation carried forward; and

- (l) net balance of fixed assets _less_ accumulated depreciation.

These records may take a variety of forms. However, it is recommended that the gross balances of fixed asset cost and accumulated depreciation be carried forward separately from year to year. They should not be offset against each other at the end of each year, except for purposes of presentation in balance sheets.

For Kambale Council, there should already be adequate records of gross fixed asset costs, available from its existing system. It is suggested that each class of asset would be assigned an arbitrary asset life. Then, using dates of acquisition, accumulated depreciation would be calculated for each asset or group.

As with commercial fixed assets, there is a choice as to methods of depreciation which can be used. Kambale Council will need to choose a suitable method. Some of the possibilities are indicated in Chapter 8 Section 85. The most obvious choice is to use the straight-line method, the one most commonly used in commercial accounting. This has the advantage of being straightforward and simple. However, where, as in municipalities, a large proportion of capital expenditure is financed from loans, it will be necessary to apportion interest charges to the various accounts of the General Fund, as under the loans pooling system. Interest on instalment loans is higher in earlier years. Straight line depreciation would not counterbalance this.

Neither would the reducing balance method of depreciation, discussed on page 254 of section 85. This is further considered in section 242.

Let us now suppose that, by whatever method used, accumulated depreciation is assessed against the fixed assets of Kambale Council as follows:

	Gross Value Cost	Accumulated Depreciation	Net Value
Buildings	10,584,220	2,318,520	8,265,700
Permanent Works	10,825,760	2,005,640	8,820,120
Equipment	630,945	350,820	280,125
	22,040,925	4,674,980	17,365,945

Municipal Accounting for Developing Countries

The depreciation provision is less than the accumulated figure for capital discharged, as shown by the following table:

Capital Discharged	U
Grants	1,131,865
Takeover values	3,251,900
Loans repaid	1,895,220
Revenue contribution	255,800
Renewals fund	50,380
Capital fund	183,360
Gifts	70,300
	6,838,825
Less Accumulated depreciation	4,674,980
Balance of capital discharged	2,163,845

The resulting net balance should be no surprise. Under the funding principle, the capital cost of all assets not financed by loans is regarded as being financed (or discharged) immediately upon acquisition. In effect, there has been "accelerated depreciation", which is inconsistent with the actual depreciation based upon asset life. For the purpose of setting up the new Capital Fund, the excess capital discharged balance will be transferred to the Capital Fund as an additional revenue contribution to capital outlay.

The journal entries in the General Fund would be as follows:

		General Fund				
19-7 Jan.1		Capital Discharged:				
		Grants	DR	2	1,131,865	
		Takeover values	DR	2	3,251,900	
		Loans repaid	DR	2	1,895,220	
		Revenue contributions	DR	2	255,800	
		Renewals fund	DR	2	50,380	
		Capital fund	DR	2	183,360	
		Gifts	DR	2	70,300	
		To Accumulated Depreciation		11		4,674,980
		Capital Fund		12		2,163,845
		Being establishment of accumulated depreciation balances on fixed assets and transfer of capital discharged balance to the Capital Fund				

Depreciation and Capital Funds

The main principles behind the establishment of the Capital Fund are as follows:

(a) all fixed asset financing is made by the Capital Fund by way of an advance to the appropriate account in the General Fund, irrespective of the actual source of funding;

(b) annual depreciation charges on fixed assets are deemed to be repayments of advances to the Capital Fund; and

(c) interest and other costs paid (or deemed to be paid) by the Capital Fund are recharged to the appropriate accounts of the General Fund.

Thus, the Capital Fund will operate on the "advances" side, very similarly to a loans pool. On the "funding" side there will be some differences, however, as explained below. Following these principles, the net value of fixed assets will be regarded as outstanding advances from the Capital Fund to the General Fund, with the accumulated depreciation regarded as advances repaid.

Also, the Capital Fund will take over all outstanding loan balances, together with capital cash balances (overdrawn or in hand) of the General Fund. Removing these from the General Fund would be journalised as follows:

	General Fund				
19-7 Jan.1	Loans outstanding DR		1	15,491,480	
	Cash (overdrawn) DR		C	9,320	
	To Capital Fund		13		15,500,800
	Being takeover of outstanding loan debt and overdrawn cash balances by the Capital Fund				
Jan.1	Capital Fund DR		12	17,365,945	
	To Advances from Capital Fund		13		17,365,945
	Being advances from Capital Fund for capital expenditures, equivalent to fixed assets less accumulated depreciation				

It will also be necessary for an additional advance to be made from the Capital Fund to cover outstanding (i.e. unamortized) deferred charges, journalised as follows:

	19-7 Jan.1	General Fund Capital Fund DR To advances from Capital Fund Being advances to cover unamortized deferred charges	12 13	320,000	320,000

The final entry is really a "dummy" adjustment to eliminate the cash balance against the balance on the Capital Fund. The effect is as if, after all other transactions have been made, there is a net balance due from the Capital Fund to the General Fund, journalised as follows:

	19-7 Jan.1	General Fund Cash DR To Capital Fund Being clearance of offsetting balances	CB 12	21,300	21,300

In fact, the adjustment represents the <u>implied</u> cash balance, appropriated by the Capital Fund for "capital receipts unapplied" for which no actual cash was available.

The ledger accounts of the General Fund will now appear as follows:

			Cash				CB
19-7 Jan.1	To Balance To Capital Fund	J J	9,320 21,300 30,620	19-7 Jan.1 1	By Balance By Capital Receipts Unapp- lied	b/f J	9,320 21,300 30,620

			Loans Outstanding				1
19-7 Jan.1	To Capital Fund	J	15,491,480	19-7 Jan.1	By Balance	b/f	15,491,480

Depreciation and Capital Funds

			Capital Discharged (Various Accounts Separately)				2
19-7 Jan.1	To Accumulated Depreciation	J	4,674,980	19-7 Jan.1	By Balance b/f		6,838,825
	To Capital Fund (new)	J	2,163,845				
			6,838,825				6,838,825

			Capital Fund (old)				3
19-7 Jan.1	To Investments	J	123,140	19-7 Jan.1	By Balance b/f		123,140

			Capital Receipts (Unapplied)				4
19-7 Jan.1	To Cash	J	21,300	19-7 Jan.1	By Balance b/f		21,300

			Sinking Fund				5
19-7 Jan.1	To Investments	J	2,000	19-7 Jan.1	By Balance b/f		2,000

			Vehicle Renewals Fund				6
19-7 Jan.1	To Investments	J	37,745	19-7 Jan.1	By Balance b/f		37,745

			Office Equipment Renewals Fund				7
19-7 Jan.1	To Investments	J	26,620	19-7 Jan.1	By Balance b/f		26,620

Investments
(Various Accounts Separately) — 8

19-7				19-7			
Jan.1	To Balance	b/f	189,505	Jan.1	By Various a/cs	J	189,505

Fixed Assets
(Various Accounts Separately) — 9

19-7							
Jan.1	To Balance	b/f	22,040,925				

Deferred Charges
(Various Accounts Separately) — 10

19-7							
Jan.1	To Balance	b/f	320,000				

Accumulated Depreciation
(Various Accounts Separately) — 11

				19-7			
				Jan.1	By Capital Discharged	J	4,674,980

Capital Fund (New) — 12

19-7				19-7			
Jan.1	To Advances	J	17,365,945	Jan.1	By Capital Discharged	J	2,163,845
Jan.1	To Advances	J	320,000	Jan.1	By Loans Outstanding	J	15,491,480
				Jan.1	By Cash	J	9,320
				Jan.1	By Cash	J	21,300
			17,685,945				17,685,945

NOTE: This is just a temporary or suspense account within which to clear offsetting balances. It is not a substantive account.

Depreciation and Capital Funds

						Advances from Capital Fund			13
					19-7 Jan.1	By Capital Fund	J	17,365,945	
					Jan.1	By Capital Fund	J	320,000	
								17,685,945	

The remaining opening entries for the Capital Fund would be journalized as follows:-

19-7 Jan.1	Advances to General Fund for:				
	Capital Expenditure	DR.	3	17,365,945	
	Deferred Charges	DR.	3	320,000	
	To General Fund		4		17,685,945
	Being advances deemed outstanding to General Fund for net fixed assets and unamortized deferred charges.				
Jan.1	General Fund	DR.	4	15,500,800	
	To Loans Outstanding	DR.	5		15,491,480
	Cash (overdrawn)		C		9,320
	Being the assumption of external debt and overdrawn cash balance by the Capital Fund from the General Fund.				
Jan.1	General Fund	DR.	4	2,163,845	
	To Capital Discharged		2		2,163,845
	Being the assumption of capital discharged balances by the Capital Fund from the General Fund.				
Jan.1	General Fund	Dr.	4	21,300	
	To Cash		C		21,300
	Being clearance of off-setting balances.				
Jan.1	Cash		C	21,300	
	To Capital Discharged (RCCO)		2		21,300
	Being clearance of off-setting balances.				
Jan.1	Investments		1	189,505	
	To Capital Discharged (RCCO)		2		189,505
	Being transfer of General Fund investments to Capital Fund				

The ledger accounts of the new Capital Funds would appear as follows:

Cash   C

19-7				19-7			
Jan.1	To Capital Disch.	J	21,300	Jan.1	By General Fund	J	9,320
Jan.1	To Balance	c/d	9,320	Jan.1	By General Fund	J	21,300
			30,620				30,620
				Jan.1	By Balance	b/d	9,320

Investments   1

19-7							
Jan.1	To Capital Disch.	J	189,505				

Capital Discharged (RCCO)   2

19-7				19-7			
Jan.	To Balance	c/d	2,374,650	Jan.1	By Cash	J	21,300
				Jan.1	By Investments	J	189,505
				Jan.1	By General Fund	J	2,163,845
			2,374,650				2,374,650
				Jan.1	By Balance	b/d	2,374,650

Advances for Capital Expenditure   3

19-7							
Jan.1	To General Fund	J	17,685,945				

General Fund   4

19-7				19-7			
Jan.1	To Loans outstanding	J	15,491,480	Jan.1	By Advances	J	17,685,945
Jan.1	To Cash	J	9,320				
Jan.	To Capital Disch.	J	2,163,845				
Jan.1	To Cash	J	21,300				
			17,685,945				17,685,945

Depreciation and Capital Funds

NOTE: This is just a temporary or suspense account within which to clear offsetting balances. It is **not** a substantive account.

			Loans Outstanding			5
			19-7 Jan.1	By General Fund	J	15,491,480

Following these transactions, the balance sheets would appear as follows:

KAMBALE COUNCIL

General Fund Balance Sheet as at 1 January 19-7

Long-Term Liabilities	U.		Fixed Assets		U.
Advances from Capital Fund	17,685,945		Buildings Permanent Works Equipment		10,584,220 10,825,760 630,945
Current Liabilities					22,040,925
Creditors	367,240				
Receipts in Advance	26,160		Less Accumulated		
National Govenment	116,949		Depreciation		4,674,980
	510,349				
			Net Fixed Assets		17,365,945
Provisions			Current Assets		
Housing Repairs Fund	164,635		Stocks & Stores		293,840
			Debtors	305,140	
Other Balances			Less Bad Debt Provision	20,220	284,920
General Revenue Surplus	492,511		Payments in Advance		720
			Investments (HRF)		161,635
			Cash		
			At Bank	422,140	
			In Hand	4,240	426,380
					1,167,495
			Other Balances		
			Unamortized Deferred Charges		320,000
	18,853,440				18,853,440

Municipal Accounting for Developing Countries

Capital Fund Balance Sheet
as at 1 January 19-7

Fund Equity		Long Term Assets	
Capital Discharged (from RCCO)	2,374,650	Advances for Capital Expenditure	17,685,945
Long-Term Liabilities		Current Assets	
Loans Outstanding	15,491,480	Monetary Investments	189,505
Current Liabilities			
Cash Overdrawn	9,320		
	17,875,450		17,875,450

The two balance sheets can very easily be consolidated. The offsetting advances from the Capital Fund would be eliminated and the net cash balance would be (U 426,380 - U 9,320) = U 417,060. Monetary investments would be (U 161,635 + U 189,505) = U 351,140. All other balances would simply be aggregated. Thus, the consolidated balance sheet would have a very definite commercial appearance, as follows:

KAMBALE COUNCIL
Consolidated Balance Sheet
as at 1 January 19-7

Equity			Fixed Assets		
Accumulated Fund Surpluses:			Buildings		10,584,220
Capital Fund	2,374,650		Permanent Works		10,825,760
General Fund	492,511	2,867,161	Equipment		630,945
					22,040,925
Long-Term Liabilities			Less Accumulated Depreciation		4,674,980
Loans Outstanding		15,491,480	Net Fixed Assets		17,365,945
			Current Assets		
Current Liabilities			Stocks & Stores		293,840
			Debtors	305,140	
Creditors	367,240		Less Bad Debt Provision	20,220	284,920
Receipts in Advance	26,160		Payments in Advance		720
National Government	116,949	510,349	Monetary Investments		351,140
Provisions			Cash		
			At Bank	412,820	
Housing Repairs Fund		164,635	In Hand	4,240	417,060
					1,347,680
			Other Balances		
			Unamortized Deferred Charges		320,000
		19,033,625			19,033,625

Depreciation and Capital Funds

237 FINANCING NEW CAPITAL EXPENDITURE

Before considering the transactions of the Capital Fund for 19-7 it should be pointed out that the management of the Fund will entail detailed record-keeping, as in the case of a loans pool. Thus the loans pool records described in Section 220 will apply also to the Capital Fund. However, although all <u>external</u> borrowing would have to be made against government loan approvals, capital expenditure advances will be made for <u>all</u> items, however financed externally. This procedure will be described below.

Let us continue to assume that the capital expenditure forecast is the same as that used for the loans pool. In the interest of further simplification, we shall also assume, unless otherwise stated, that actual transactions will be the same as those estimated. It will be clear that the Capital Fund has enough funds, in the form of monetary investments, not to require a draw-down on its loan or grant options until the third quarter of 19-7. However, if the investments were earning (say) 8%, it would be financially prudent to draw upon the 2% foreign loan and upon available government grants as alternatives to realizing the investments.

For simplicity, let us assume that all transactions take place on the last day of each quarter. The way to make allowances for transactions on other dates has already been explained in Chapter 20. Thus, we shall assume the following:

1. The ambulance is purchased on 31 March 19-7 from abroad by IAA, which makes a direct foreign exchange payment covering all c.i.f. charges, amounting to U. 43,500 (Chapter 11 Section 133). Local delivery and miscellaneous costs, amounting to U. 2,500 are paid in cash on 30 June 19-7 and claimed from IAA. Reimbursement is received on 30 September.

2. The sewage disposal works payments on 30 June are financed by drawing upon investments, assumed to be U. 50,000, which will wipe out the bank overdraft (U. 9,320). The government notifies Kambale Council that no more than U. 50,000 of grant funds will be available until the next financial year and that only U. 50,000 may be borrowed from LGLF, during the current year.

3. The administrative buildings will be financed by maturity mortgage loans to the extent necessary, after taking account of other financing in the Capital Fund. The market rate for such loans is 12%.

4. Investments continue to earn 8%, p.a. payable half-yearly. Outstanding loan debt on 31 December 19-6 had an average interest rate of 8.75%.

The purchase of the ambulance and its financing could be journalized as follows:

	General Fund			
19-7				

Mar.31	Fixed Asset (Ambulance) DR
	   To Advances (C.F.)
	   Being payment of c.i.f.
	   charges on ambulance,
	   by IAA.
		9A
		13
			43,500	43,500

Municipal Accounting for Developing Countries

	Capital Fund			

Mar.31	Advances (G.F.) DR
	  To Loans Outstanding
	    (IAA)
	Being loan raised from
	IAA for ambulance
		3
		5
			43,500	43,500

The transactions taking place on 30 June are assumed to include:

(a) payment of instalment on sewage disposal works (U 40,000);

(b) payment of delivery charges on ambulance (U 2,500);

(c) withdrawal of investments (U 50,000);

(d) receipt of investment interest (U 7,580);

(e) payment of half-yearly debt service assumed to amount to (say) principal repayments totalling U 149,138 and interest (8.75% x $\frac{1}{2}$ on U. 15,491,480) totalling U 677,752;

(f) transfer of cash from the General Fund representing half-yearly depreciation charges (U 186,120) and deferred charge amortization (U 40,000), a total of U 226,120; and

(g) apportionment of half-yearly interest charges to General Fund, together with the appropriate cash adjustment.

In addition to the interest payable on existing loans, there will be one-quarter's accrued interest due to IAA for the ambulance purchase. We shall asume that this interest is being capitalised by the lender during the grace period, as is common with international loans. However, although not immediately payable in cash, it must still be accounted for. Thus, provision must be made for an interest charge of U 43,500 x 2% x $\frac{1}{4}$ = U 218. This amount will be added to the loan.

On the depreciation side, there is another complication. Although interest charges have been incurred by the Capital Fund for the ambulance from 30 March 19-7, it does not arrive, and become available for use, until 30 June. In these circumstances, it might be appropriate to charge an apportionment of interest to the capital cost of the ambulance. Depreciation charges would then be made on cost plus capitalized interest, beginning when the ambulance comes into use, assumed to be 1 July.

There are two different kinds of capitalized interest being considered here which do not necessarily have any direct relationship. The first is contractual whereby a lender agrees to add certain early interest charges to the loan, to be recovered later as part of loan instalments. The other kind is an accounting arrangement to ensure that depreciation costs are not charged to the revenue account until the asset comes into use. Actually, the ambulance is not a very good example. A better one, as we shall see, concerns civil works construction, such as the sewage disposal works.

The various transactions of the General Fund could be journalized as follows:

Depreciation and Capital Funds

General Fund

19-7					

June 30	Fixed Assets (Sewage Disposal Works)
	   To Cash
	     Being instalment for construction
		DR
		CB
			9B	40,000	40,000

June 30	Fixed Assets (Ambulance)
	   To Cash
	     Being local delivery charges on ambulance
		DR
		CB
			9A	2,500	2,500

June 30	Depreciation (various)
	Interest (various)
	   To Accumulated Depreciation
	      Capital Fund (Int.)
	     Being allocation to various accounts of half-yearly charges for depreciation and interest
		DR
		DR
			14
			16
			
			11
			17
				186,120
				677,137
					
					186,120
					677,137

June 30	Cash
	   To Advances (C.F.)
	     Being advances from Capital Fund for capital expenditure
		DR	CB
			13
				42,500	42,500

June 30	Advances
	Capital Fund (Interest)
	   To Cash
	     Being repayment of advances in respect of depreciation and amortization of deferred charges together with half-yearly recovery of interest charges.
		DR
		DR
			13
			17
			CB
				226,120
				677,137
					
					903,257

June 30	Fixed Asset (Ambulance)
	   To Advances
	     Being capitalization of interest charges due to the Capital Fund (3.83% × 43,500 × ½) pending utilization of the ambulance.
		DR	9A
			13
				833	833

June 30	Deferred Charge Amortization
	   To Deferred Charges
	     Being half-yearly amortization now charged to revenue account
		DR	15
			10
				40,000	40,000

June 30	General Revenue Account
	  To Revenue Accounts
	    (Depreciation)
	  To Revenue Accounts
	    (Deferred Charge
	    Amortization)
	  To Revenue Accounts
	    (Interest)
	Being transfers to General
	Revenue Account (Summary)
		DR	18
			
			14
			
			15
			
			16
				903,257	
					186,120
					
					40,000
					
					677,137

Notice that under the generalized system of interest apportionment, the ambulance accounts bear an interest cost of **U 833**, compared with the **U 218** actually incurred. As already indicated, this is the subject of further discussion below, where the method of calculation is also explained. The remaining interest to be charged to various accounts would (under present arrangements) be **U 677,752 + 218 - 833 = U 677,137**.

The various transactions of the Capital Fund could be journalized as follows:

Capital Fund

19-7 June 30	Cash To Investments Being withdrawal of investments	DR	C.B. 1	50,000	50,000
June 30	Cash To Investment Interest Being receipt of interest on Capital Fund investments (8% x ½ on 189,505)	DR	C.B. 6	7,580	7,580
June 30	Loans Outstanding Interest To Cash Being payment of half- yearly debt charges	DR DR	5 7 C.B.	149,138 677,752	826,890

June 30	Cash
	  To Advances (GF)
	    Interest
	Being recovery of funds
	for half-yearly depreciation,
	deferred charge amortization,
	and interest from General
	Fund
		DR	C.B
			3
			7
				903,257	
					226,120
					677,137

June 30	Advances (GF) To Cash Being advances for new capital expenditure	DR	3 C.B.	42,500	42,500

Depreciation and Capital Funds

June 30	Interest 　To Loans Outstanding 　　Being accrued interest on loan from IAA for ambulance purchase, capitalized by the lender (43,500 x 2% x ¼)		DR	7 5	218	218
June 30	Advances 　To Interest 　　Being interest on ambulance capitalized prior to use of asset		DR	3 7	833	833
June 30	Investment Interest 　To Revenue Account 　　Being appropriation of investment interest as revenue of the Capital Fund		DR	6 12	7,580	7,580

The ledger accounts of the General Fund (if balanced off at 30 June 19-7) would appear as follows:

Cash　　　　　　　　　　　　　　　　　　　　　CB

19-7				19-7			
Jan. 1	To Balance	b/f	422,140	Jun.30	By Sewage Disp.Works	J	40,000
Jun.30	To Advances	J	42,500		By Ambulances	J	2,500
Jun.30	To Balance	c/d	481,117		By Advances & Interest	J	903,257
			945,757				945,757
Jun.30	To General Revenue Account	J	900,000	Jun.30	By Balance	b/d	481,117
				Jun.30	By Balance	c/d	418,883
			900,000				900,000
Jul. 1	To Balance	b/d	418,883				

Fixed Assets　　　　　　　　　　　　　　　　　9
(Various Accounts Separately)

19-7				19-7			
Jan. 1	To Balance	b/f	22,040,925	Jun.30	By Balance	c/d	22,040,925
Jul. 1	To Balance	b/d	22,040,925				

			Fixed Assets (Ambulances)					9A
19-7				19-7				
Mar.31	To Advances	J	43,500	Jun.30	By Balance	c/d		46,833
Jun.30	To Cash	J	2,500					
Jun.30	To Advances	J	833					
			46,833					46,833
Jul. 1	To Balance	b/d	46,833					

			Fixed Assets (Sewage Disposal Works)					9B
19-7				19-7				
Jun.30	To Cash	J	40,000	Jun.30	By Balance	c/d		40,000
Jul. 1	To Balance	b/d	40,000					

			Deferred Charges (Various Accounts Separately)					10
19-7				19-7				
Jan. 1	To Balance	b/f	320,000	Jun.30	By Advances	J		40,000
				Jun.30	By Balance	c/d		280,000
			320,000					320,000
JUL. 1	To Balance	b/d	280,000					

			Accumulated Depreciation (Various Accounts Separately)					11
19-7				19-7				
Jun.30	To Balance	c/d	4,861,100	Jan. 1	By Capital Discharged	J		4,674,980
					By Depreciation	J		186,120
			4,861,100					4,861,100
				Jul. 1	By Balance	b/d		4,861,100

Depreciation and Capital Funds

Advances From Capital Fund — 13

19-7				19-7			
Jun.30	To Cash	J	226,120	Jan. 1	By Capital Fund	J	17,365,945
Jun.30	To Balance	c/d	17,546,658	Jan. 1	By Capital Fund	J	320,000
				Mar.31	By Ambulances	J	43,500
				Jun.30	By Cash	J	42,500
				Jun.30	By Ambulances	J	833
			17,772,778				17,772,778
				Jul. 1	By Balance	b/d	17,546,658

Revenue Account (Depreciation) (Various Accounts Separately) — 14

19-7				19-7			
Jun.30	To Acc. Depn.	J	186,120	Jun.30	By Gen.Rev. Account	18	186,120

Revenue Account (Deferred Charge Amortization) (Various Accounts Separately) — 15

19-7				19-7			
Jun.30	To Deferred Charges	J	40,000	Jun.30	By Gen.Rev. Account	18	40,000

Revenue Account (Interest) (Various Accounts Separately) — 16

19-7				19-7			
Jun.30	To Cap. Fund	J	677,137	Jun.30	By Gen.Rev. Account	18	677,137

Capital Fund (Interest) — 17

19-7				19-7			
Jun.30	To Cash	J	677,137	Jun.30	By Rev.Acct (Int.)	J	677,137

Municipal Accounting for Developing Countries

General Revenue Account (Relevant Transactions Only)								18
19-7 Jun.30	To Depre- ciation Deferred Charge Amorti- zation Interest	J J J	186,120 40,000 677,137 903,257	19-7 Jun.30	By Balance	c/d	903,257 903,257
Jun.30	To Balance	b/d	903,257 903,257	Jun.30	By Cash By Balance	J c/d	900,000 3,257 903,257
Jul. 1	To Balance	b/d	3,257				

The General Revenue Account would, in practice, contain a summary of all revenue transactions during the half-year, arranged by service, in the standard form, as explained in Chapter 16. The term "Loan Charges" would be changed to "Capital Charges" with sub-headings of "Depreciation (or Deferred Charge Amortization)" and "Interest".

In practice also it is obvious that expenditures would be incurred other than those shown here, with income being accrued approximately to balance the expenditures after allowing for minor fluctuations in working capital. Thus, the overdrawn cash balance would, in practice, be eliminated. To facilitate a more realistic presentation of the balance sheet, we have assumed that "Cash" and "General Revenue Account" balances have been adjusted by an offsetting U 900,000, journalized as follows:

19-7 June 30	Cash To Gen.Revenue Account Being assumed revenues (net of other expenditures) accrued in cash during the half-year.	DR	CB	900,000	900,000

The ledger accounts of the Capital Fund (if balanced off at 30 June 19-7), would appear as follows:-

Cash								CB
19-7 Jun.30 Jun.30 Jun.30 Jun.30	To Invest- ments To Invest- ment Int To Advances (G.F.) To Interest	 J J J J	 50,000 7,580 226,120 677,137 960,837	19-7 Jan. 1 Jun.30 Jun.30 Jun.30 Jun.30	By Balance By loans o/s By Interest By Advances By Balance	b/f J J J c/d	9,320 149,138 677,752 42,500 82,127 960,837
Jul. 1	To Balance	b/d	82,127				

842

Depreciation and Capital Funds

Investments | 1

19-7				19-7			
Jan. 1	To Cap. Disch.	J	189,505	Jun.30	By Cash	J	50,000
			_____	Jun.30	By Balance	c/d	139,505
			189,505				189,505
Jul. 1	To Balance	b/d	139,505				

Advances for Capital Expenditure | 3

19-7				19-7			
Jan. 1	To General Fund	J	17,685,945	Jun.30	By Cash	J	226,120
Mar.31	To Loans Outstanding	J	43,500	Jun.30	By Balance	c/d	17,546,658
Jun.30	To Cash	J	42,500				
Jun.30	To Interest	J	833				
			17,772,778				17,772,778
Jul. 1	To Balance	b/d	17,546,658				

Loans Outstanding | 5

19-7				19-7			
Jun.30	To Cash	J	149,138	Jan. 1	By General Fund	J	15,491,480
Jun.30	To Balance	c/d	15,386,060	Mar.31	By Advances	J	43,500
				Jun.30	By Interest	J	218
			15,535,198				15,535,198
				Jul. 1	By Balance	b/d	15,386,060

Investment Interest | 6

19-7				19-7			
Jun.30	To Rev. Account	J	7,580	Jun.30	By Cash	J	7,580

Interest | 7

19-7				19-7			
Jun.30	To Cash	J	677,752	Jun.30	By Cash	J	677,137
Jun.30	To Loans o/s	J	218	Jun.30	By Advances		833
			677,970				677,970

Capital Fund Revenue Account								12
19-7 Jun.30	To Balance	c/d	7,580 ——— 7,580	19-7 Jun.30 Jul. 1	By Investment Interest By Balance	J b/d	7,580 ——— 7,580 7,580

In presenting balance sheets of the General Fund and the Capital Fund it will be assumed that balances unaffected by the Capital Fund transactions will remain as at 1 January 19-7. In practice, of course, this would not be so, but the assumption is necessary in the interest of simplicity. On this basis, the balance sheets would appear as on pages 845 - 846.

A consolidated balance sheet could easily be prepared from the following fund balance sheets, as explained in Section 236 page 834.

238   REVIEW OF HALF-YEARLY BALANCES

A review of the half-yearly balances focuses attention on a number of features of Capital Fund operation and also poses a number of questions for resolution. Each will be considered in turn, later in this Chapter.

It will be noticed that, for illustrative purposes, the precise theoretical bookkeeping entries have been shown in the examples. Some of the entries, which affect both the General Fund and the Capital Fund are virtually "mirror images" of one another. In practice, the entries would be unlikely to be journalized and entered in the ledger accounts exactly as shown here. Instead, there would be registers for the detailed transactions, from which totals would be extracted for the various ledger accounts. However, if the theoretical principles are illustrated and kept in mind, adaptation of records to specific circumstances is made easier.

The amount shown as "Advances" from the Capital Fund to the General Fund (U 17,546,658) represents a liability of the General Fund and an asset of the Capital Fund. In a consolidated balance sheet, the two balances would offset one another and thus be eliminated. It should also be noticed that the "Advances" figure is equal to the written-down value of fixed assets (U 17,266,658) plus the amortized deferred charges (U 280,000). This is a continuous feature of the capital fund system.

It should also be noticed that the cash (bank) balance of the Capital Fund has improved, from U 9,320 overdrawn to U 82,127 in hand. This has come about as shown on page 847.

Capital Fund Balance Sheet
as at 30 June 19-7

Fund Equity

Capital Discharged from RCCO	2,374,650	
Revenue Account Surplus	7,580	
		2,382,230

Long-Term Liabilities

Loans Outstanding		15,386,060
		17,768,290

Long-Term Assets

Advances for Capital Expenditure		17,546,658

Current Assets

Monetary Investments	139,505	
Cash	82,127	
		221,632
		17,768,290

KAMBALE COUNCIL

General Fund Balance Sheet as at 30 June 19-7

	U				U
Long-Term Liabilities			**Fixed Assets**		
Advances from Capital Fund	17,546,658		Buildings	10,584,220	
			Permanent Works	10,865,760	
			Equipment	677,778	
				22,127,758	
Current Liabilities			Less Accumulated Depreciation	4,861,100	
Creditors	367,240		Net Fixed Assets		17,266,658
Receipts in Advance	26,160				
National Government	116,949	510,349	**Current Assets**		
			Stocks & Stores		293,840
Provisions			Debtors	305,140	
Housing Repairs Fund		164,635	Less Bad Debt Provision	20,220	284,920
			Payments in Advance		720
Other Balances			Investments (HRF)		161,635
General Revenue Surplus*		489,254	Cash		
			At Bank	418,883	
*(U.492,511-3,257)			In Hand	4,240	423,123
			Other Balances		
			Unamortized Deferred Charges		280,000
		18,710,896			18,710,896

Depreciation and Capital Funds

				U
	Opening balance (overdrawn)			(9,320)
ADD	Realization of investments			50,000
	Earnings from investments			7,580
				48,260
ADD	Depreciation			186,120
	Deferred Charge Amortization			40,000
				274,380
LESS	Capital Expenditure	42,500		
	Debt Amortization	149,138		191,638
				82,742
ADD	Interest recovered from general fund			677,137
				759,879
LESS	Interest paid			677,752
				82,127

The largest increase in cash balances resulted from the realization of (and earnings on) investments, (U 57,580) and from the difference between depreciation charges and debt repayment (U 36,982). On the other hand, the difference between the interest paid and that recovered from the General Fund caused the cash balance to change by only U 615, representing the difference between capitalized interest charged to the Capital Fund (U 218) and that charged to the General Fund (U 833). This is because of the assumption that only interest actually charged to and payable by the Capital Fund can be recovered from the General Fund. This concept will now be further examined.

239 **INTEREST APPORTIONMENT AND RECOVERY**

The system used for interest apportionment was very similar to that used for a loans pool, using the system of equated advances explained in Section 228 of Chapter 20. On a half-yearly basis, this would be as follows:

Purpose of Advance	Date of Advance	Amount of Advance	Number of Quarters Outstanding	Half-yearly Equivalent
Various (listed as appropriate)	1 Jan. (b/fwd)	17,685,945	2	17,685,945
Ambulance	31 Mar.	43,500	1	21,750
Totals		17,729,445		17,707,695

The interest payable was the amount paid (U. 677,752) plus the amount capitalized by IAA (U. 218) totalling U.677,970. The rate of apportionment, assumed to apply equally to all general fund accounts, in proportion to their depreciated fixed asset values (equivalent to advances outstanding) would be:

$$\frac{677,970 \times 100}{17,707,695} = 3.8287\%$$

As we saw from the accounts, U 677,137 was recovered immediately from the General Fund accounts, with U 833 being allowed to be capitalized against the ambulance. The use of a generalized interest rate follows an important and sensible principle - that the Kambale Council is a single corporate entity which seeks to apportion fairly, among all services, the costs of its borrowing operations. This principle disregards the fact that individual loans have been contracted for specific purposes and is consistent with the basic idea of an integrated Capital Fund.

However, it might be argued that the different rates of interest for different kinds of "earmarked" loans should be applied specifically to the assets to which they relate. There might, indeed, be legal requirements that this be so. If this were the case, only the general loans raised by the Capital Fund would be considered as "pooled" for interest purposes. This would tend to destroy one of the basic principles for operating a generalized Capital Fund. Furthermore, if asset lives and loan periods were not matched and, still further, if arbitrary grace periods were involved, the record-keeping for this combination of "earmarked" and "pooled" loan interest would become exceedingly complicated. If, for example, a decision were made (or there was a legal requirement) that the IAA loan interest be seen to be related specifically to the ambulance, the calculations would be as follows:

  A. Rate of interest applicable to the ambulance:

  $$= \frac{218 \times 100}{21,750} = 1.00\% \text{ (i.e. half of 2\% p.a.)}$$

  B. Rate of interest applicable to other municipal services:

  $$= \frac{677,752 \times 100}{17,685,945} = 3.8322\%$$

Indeed, if different ambulances had been financed by different kinds of loans, there would be different interest rates charged within the same service. However, despite these complications, the accounting convenience of charging a generalized interest rate could be undermined by political pressure or legal requirements if, for example, costs were being recovered by charges to (say) disadvantaged social groups (e.g. charitable hospitals).

We will assume that Kambale Council will use a generalized rate. We now must consider whether this rate must relate to the recovery of interest only on debt finance, or to capital funding generally.

240 CHARGEABLE INTEREST RATE

Whether or not all loans are pooled for interest rate purposes, it should be recognised that the system used in the present examples charges the General Fund only for actual interest expense incurred on the Capital Fund's outstanding debt. This is consistent with the prevalent view of the accountancy profession that only expenses explicitly incurred should be charged as costs in a cost-accounting system.

Depreciation and Capital Funds

However, the Capital Fund balance sheet shows that, in addition to outstanding loans, there is equity in the Fund which is also being used to finance capital expenditure, or is available to do so in the form of monetary investments and cash. These additional funds, from an ecomomic viewpoint, have an opportunity cost, viewed from at least three angles:

  (a) funds not invested in fixed assets can earn (indeed are earning) interest;

  (b) funds invested in one choice of fixed assets become unavailable for investment in others; and

  (c) somewhere in the economy, interest has been foregone to make these apparently costless funds available to Kambale Council.

To the extent that the funds have come as central government grants, they have either been borrowed (at an interest cost to the central goverment) or raised by taxes (depriving national taxpayers of interest earnings). To the extent that the surplus funds have been raised as local taxes, the interest loss has been borne directly by the taxpayers of Kambale Municipality.

Thus, it can be asserted that there is an implicit interest cost relating to all financing raised by the Capital Fund, which should be charged to the General Fund, to be included in the costs of various services. This would be consistent with the procedure used in many public utility organizations of setting financial objectives to earn a "rate of return on fixed assets". It is not necessarily consistent with recommended cost-accounting practice.

If such an implied "cost-of-capital" approach is to be used, the question arises as to how it would be determined. One possibility would be to apply the weighted average interest rate on debt to all sources of capital financing. This has the advantage of simplicity, precision of calculation and close consistency with accounting practices. A disadvantage would be that such an average would reflect all debt, including loans below market interest rates from government and international aid agencies. Being subsidized they contain an implicit "grant" element. Thus, including these loans in the calculation of the average interest rate would tend to contradict the purpose of implicit recognition of the cost of "grant" money. So, the rate might be calculated only after eliminating the sub-optimal interest rates. Another method might be to fix a rate prescribed (or used) by government for general public works loans or to link the rate to a specific and stable financial indicator. This could either be done by a policy decision of the local authority or perhaps be prescribed by law or regulation, depending on the circumstances.

241 CAPITAL FUND MANAGEMENT EXPENSES

As with the loans pooling system, a Capital Fund will incur a variety of management expenses, including direct charges and an apportionment of central administrative expenses. They would be very similar to the debt management expenses explained in section 229 of Chapter 20 and need not be again considered in detail. However, for the Capital Fund, management expenses would include those relating to all capital funding and not only to debt. For simplicity, the examples of the capital fund operations for Kambale Council have, so far, not included management expenses. They must be presumed to have been incurred, however, and it is appropriate for their costs to be recovered from the General Fund.

One way of recovering the management expenses would be to make a separate charge, as for a loans pool. However, it might be more convenient to include their costs in a generalized interest rate. This will be further examined later.

242 DEPRECIATION CHARGES

As indicated earlier, the calculation of depreciation charges for individual assets could be done by the straight line method. However, this would result in total annual charges, inclusive of interest, which were higher in the earlier years of operation. Thus, an alternative would be to use the sinking fund or annuity method of depreciation as explained in Chapter 8, Section 85 page 249.

An example of a comparison of the two methods could be shown in the case of the ambulance, by comparing the straight-line method, on a half-yearly basis, with that of an 8% p.a. sinking fund as follows. We shall assume that the interest is actually charged out at 8.75% p.a.

Date	Instalment Number	Total Half-Yearly Charge	Interest	Depreciation	Balance Outstanding
a. Straight Line Method					
30. 6.-7	0	-	-	-	46,833
31.12.-7	1	6,732	2,049	4,683	42,150
30. 6.-8	2	6,527	1,844	4,683	37,467
31.12.-8	3	6,322	1,639	4,683	32,784
30. 6.-9	4	6,117	1,434	4,683	28,101
31.12.-9	5	5,912	1,229	4,683	23,418
30. 6.-0	6	5,708	1,025	4,683	18,735
31.12.-0	7	5,503	820	4,683	14,052
30. 6.-1	8	5,299	615	4,684	9,368
31.12.-1	9	5,094	410	4,684	4,684
30. 6.-2	10	4,889	205	4,684	-
b. Sinking Fund Method					
30. 6.-7	0	-	-	-	46,833
31.12.-7	1	5,950	2,049	3,901	42,932
30. 6.-8	2	5,935	1,878	4,057	38,875
31.12.-8	3	5,920	1,701	4,219	34,656
30. 6.-9	4	5,904	1,516	4,388	30,268
31.12.-9	5	5,887	1,324	4,563	25,705
30. 6.-0	6	5,871	1,125	4,746	20,959
31.12.-0	7	5,853	917	4,936	16,023
30. 6.-1	8	5,834	701	5,133	10,890
31.12.-1	9	5,814	476	5,338	5,552
30. 6.-2	10	5,795	243	5,552	-

Depreciation and Capital Funds

Using the staight-line method, the half-yearly charge varies by U 1843 between the first and last periods, whereas the sinking fund method gives a range of only U 155. Of course, as explained in Section 228 of Chapter 20, the exact interest to be charged cannot be predicted in advance and may well vary from period to period. However, the depreciation charges will be those fixed in advance.

Half-yearly depreciation periods have been used, to be consistent with the usual practice of having half-yearly debt service.

243. **INTEREST CHARGES**

In preparing for the Capital Fund transactions for the second half of 19-7, let us assume that Kambale Council decides to charge out interest from the Capital Fund to the General Fund at the same rate as the weighted average rate of interest on its borrowings. Thus, a charge would be made to the General Fund for the implicit cost of capital. In addition, we shall assume that account will be taken of debt management expenses. These will be charged out by a proportionate adjustment to the interest rate charged to the General Fund.

Continuing with the assumptions in Section 237, let us further assume a financing plan for the second half-year as follows. However, we shall assume that because of delay in claiming reimbursement, the IAA loan balance of U 2,500, to cover the local costs of the ambulance, is not received until 31 December, 19-7.

	3rd Qtr.	4th. Qtr.	Total
Capital Expenditure			
Administrative Buildings	50,000	65,000	115,000
Sewage Disposal Works	100,000	100,000	200,000
Total	150,000	165,000	315,000
Sources of Finance			
I.A.A. Loan Balance	-	2,500	2,500
Government Grant	50,000	-	50,000
Local Govt. Loans Fund	-	50,000	50,000
Realisation of Investments	-	35,000	35,000
Maturity Mortgages	50,000	50,000	100,000
Reduction of Cash	50,000	27,500	77,500
Total	150,000	165,000	315,000

The timing of the financing arrangements needs explanation. Clearly, if the government grant is available in the third quarter, it should be drawn upon, postponing the raising of more costly financing. Also, it makes sense to use as much as possible of the Capital Fund's surplus cash balances. However, this should not be carried too far. The residual financing for Kambale Council is by loans raised in the market. There is thus a risk that market conditions will not be favourable for the raising of any or all of Kambale's loan requirements at a particular time. Also, there may be definite limits as to how much financing can be raised during a particular period.

Municipal Accounting for Developing Countries

For example, from a purely interest-rate cost point of view, there would have been no need to raise mortgage loans at all during 19-7. There were none raised during the first half-year and the second half-year's capital financing could have been met from available cash and investments (U 221,632) together with the government grant, LGLF loan (U 50,000 each) and the IAA reimbursement (U 2,500). However, this would have depleted cash reserves to virtually nil. Looking ahead this might not have been a good policy, because funds required for the first half of 19-8 would be over U 600,000, about twice the requirements for the second half of 19-7. Thus, it is probably wise to use the Capital Fund's cash resources as a "cushion" to lower the risk of later market saturation by Kambale Council's loans.

Let us suppose that the principal repayments on 31 December 19-7 are U. 155,663. This would relate entirely to the loans brought forward from 19-6, because there are no repayments due on the LGLF loan and the maturity mortgages. Also the IAA loan has a 5-year grace period.

Interest payments for the half-year would be as follows:

Loan	Amount	Quarters Out-standing	Equivalent	Rate %	Amount
Original	15,342,342	2	15,342,342	4.375	671,227
IAA (b/fwd)	43,718	2	43,718	1	437
(Dec.31)	2,500	0	-	1	-
LGLF	50,000	1	25,000	6	1,500
			15,411,060		673,164

The average rate, to be used for charging out to the General Fund would be $\frac{673,164 \times 100\%}{15,411,060} = 4.368\%$

The position with regard to advances would be as follows:

Purpose	Amount U	Quarters Outstanding	Equivalent U
Balance b/fwd	17,546,658	2	17,546,658
Sewage Disposal Works	100,000	1	50,000
Administrative Buildings	50,000	1	25,000
			17,621,658

The application of a rate of 4.368% to the equivalent total of U 17,621,658 would provide for the recovery of U 769,714 in interest. To this should be added the management expenses of the Capital Fund. Without going into detail, let us suppose these to be as follows:

	U
Cash expenses (stamp duty, postage, stationery, commissions, etc.)	1,465
Central administrative charges	3,685
	5,150

Depreciation and Capital Funds

The total to be charged to the General Fund would be U. 769,714 + 5,150 = U. 774,864. If applied to an equated balance of U. 17,621,658, would give a charge-out rate of 4.397%. Since the administrative buildings and sewage disposal works are under construction, the interest relating to these will be capitalised. However, since the ambulance is deemed to have come into service on 1 July 19-7, the interest relating to it would be charged to the General Fund revenue account (ambulances). This would be done even though the interest on the loan for the ambulance continues to be capitalised by IAA as part of the loan contract.

The charging out of interest and management expenses would therefore be as follows:

Advance	Amount	Equivalent	Charge at 4.397%
Balance b/f:			
General	17,179,825	17,179,825	755,397
Ambulance	46,833	46,833	2,059
Sewage Works	40,000	40,000	1,759 *
Deferred Charges	280,000	280,000	12,312
Sewage Disposal Works	100,000	50,000	2,199 *
Administrative Buildings	50,000	25,000	1,099 *
		17,621,658	774,825

By rounding the charge-out rate to 3 decimal places, the interest charged out differs from the original calculation by. U 40, which is of no particular importance. The items marked * will be capitalised. The amount charged to ambulances is U 2,059, compared to the U 2,049 shown in the sinking fund on table on page 850.

The deferred charge will continue to be amortised at U 40,000 per half-year. Depreciation charges on new assets (including the ambulance) are assumed to be based on a 4% (8% p.a.) sinking fund basis. Thus, depreciation and amortisation recoveries would be assumed as follows:

General	193,440
Ambulance	3,901
Deferred charges	40,000
	237,341

The journal entries for the general fund would be as follows:

General Fund

19-7 Sept.30	Fixed Assets (Sewage Disposal Works) DR	9B	100,000	
	Fixed Assets (Admin. Bldgs.) DR	9C	50,000	
	To Cash	C.B.		150,000
	Being instalments for construction			

Date	Particulars		Ref	Dr	Cr
Sept.30	Capital Fund (Suspense) To Advances (CF) Being Advances from Capital Fund for capital expenditure	DR	19 13	150,000	150,000
Dec.31	Fixed Assets (Sewage Disposal Works) Fixed Assets (Admin.Bldgs.) To Cash Being instalments for construction	DR DR	9B 9C C.B.	100,000 65,000	165,000
Dec.31	Capital Fund (Suspense) To Advances (CF) Being advances from Capital Fund for capital expenditure	DR	19 13	165,000	165,000
Dec.31	Depreciation (various) Deferred Charges Amortization To Accumulated Depreciation To Deferred Charges Being half-yearly charges for depreciation and deferred charge amortization.	DR DR	14 15 11 10	197,341 40,000	197,341 40,000
Dec.31	Advances To Capital Fund (Suspense) Being repayment of advances in respect of half-yearly depreciation and amortization.	DR	13 19	237,341	237,341
Dec.31	Interest (various) Fixed Assets (Sewage Disposal Works) Fixed Assets (Admin.Bldgs.) To Capital Fund (Suspense) To Advances Being half-yearly allocation of interest charges to revenue accounts and as capitalised.	DR DR DR	16 9B 9C 19 13	769,768 3,958 1,099	769,768 5,057
Dec.31	Capital Fund (Suspense) To Revenue Account (Admin. Expenses) Being allocation to Capital Fund of central administrative charges.	DR	19 16A	3,685	3,685

Depreciation and Capital Funds

As in the first half-year, we shall assume the preparation of a general fund revenue account, with a cash income to balance the revenue account. However, to illustrate a further point, we shall assume that the income for the year provides a revenue account surplus, sufficient to transfer some of it to the Capital Fund. Thus, we shall assume a journal entry as follows:

| Dec.31 | Cash   DR
    To Gen.Revenue Account
    Being assumed revenues
(net of other expenditures)
accrued in cash during the
half-year. | CB
18 | 1,035,000 | 1,035,000 |

The various income and expenses would be transferred to the general revenue account by journalising as follows:

| Dec.31 | General Fund Rev. a/c   DR
    To Depreciation
    Deferred Charge
      Amortization
    Interest
Administrative Expenses   DR
    To General Fund
      Revenue Account
Being transfer of
expenditures and income to
the general fund revenue
account. | 18
14

15
16
16A

18 | 1,007,109

3,685 | 197,341

40,000
769,768

3,685 |

Let us now assume that it is decided to transfer U 25,000 of the General Fund surplus to the Capital Fund. This would be journalised as follows:

| Dec.31 | General Revenue Account   DR
    To Capital Fund (Suspense)
    Being allocation of funds
from general revenue surplus
to Capital Fund | 18
19 | 25,000 | 25,000 |
| Dec.31 | Capital Fund (Suspense)   DR
    To Cash
    Being settlement of net
cash balance due to Capital
Fund. | 19
C.B. | 713,424 | 713,424 |

The journal entries for the Capital Fund would be as follows:

| 19-7
Sept.30 | Cash   DR
    To Government Grant
    Being receipt of capital
grant. | C.B.
8 | 50,000 | 50,000 |

Sept.30	Cash
	  To Loans Outstanding
	  Being raising of 12%
	maturity mortgage loans.
		DR	C.B.
			5
				50,000		50,000

Sept.30	Advances (G.F.)
	  To General Fund (Suspense)
	  Being advances for new
	capital expenditure
		DR	3
			9
				150,000		150,000

Dec.31	Cash
	  To Loans Outstanding
	  Being loan raised from
	LGLF.
		DR	C.B.
			5
				50,000		50,000

Dec.31	Cash
	  To Investments
	  Being withdrawal of
	investments
		DR	C.B.
			1
				35,000		35,000

Dec.31	Cash
	  To Investment Interest
	  Being receipt of interest
	on capital fund investments
	(8% x ½ on 139,505)
		DR	C.B.
			6
				5,580		5,580

Dec.31	Cash
	  To Loans Outstanding
	  Being receipt of loan from
	IAA in reimbursement of
	local costs relating to
	ambulance purchase, paid on
	30 June.
		DR	C.B.
			5
				2,500		2,500

Dec.31	Loans Outstanding
	Interest Payable
	  To Cash
	  Being payment of
	half-yearly debt charges.
		DR
		DR
			5
			7
			C.B.
				155,663
				672,727
						828,390

Dec.31	Interest Payable
	  To Loans Outstanding
	  Being half-yearly interest
	capitalised by IAA.
		DR	7
			5
				437		437

Dec.31	Management Expenses
	  To Cash
	  To General Fund (Suspense)
	  Being capital fund
	management expenses paid in
	cash and also allocated from
	the general fund as central
	administrative charges.
		DR	10
			C.B.
			9
				5,150		1,465
						3,685

Depreciation and Capital Funds

Dec.31	Advances (G.F.) DR
	  To General Fund (Suspense)
	  Being advances for new
	  capital expenditure.
			3
			9
				165,000	165,000

Dec.31	General Fund (Suspense) DR
	  To Advances
	  Being repayment of advances
	  in respect of half-yearly
	  depreciation and amortization.
			9
			3
				237,341	237,341

Dec.31	General Fund (Suspense) DR
	Advances DR
	  To Interest Receivable
	  Being half-yearly charge
	  to general fund for recovery
	  of interest and management
	  expenses.
			9
			3
			11
				769,768
				5,057
					774,825

Dec.31	Capital Fund Revenue Account DR
	  To Interest Payable
	  To Management Expenses
	  Being transfer of expenses
			12
			7
			10
				678,314	673,164
					5,150

Dec.31	Investment Interest DR
	Interest Receivable DR
	  To Capital Fund Revenue
	    Account DR
	  Being transfer of capital
	  fund earnings.
			6
			11
			
			12
				5,580
				774,825
					780,405

The government grant would be transferred directly to the capital discharged account as a capital receipt. It is treated here as if it were like a contribution to the equity of the Capital Fund. This matter will, however, be further considered below (Section 250). The journal entry would be:

19-7
Dec.31
	Government Grants DR
	  To Capital Discharged
	  Being government grants
	  now appropriated as (equity)
	  capital of the capital fund.
			8
			2
				50,000	50,000

The transfer of the U 25,000 to the Capital Fund from surplus balances of the General Fund would be journalised as follows:

Dec.31	General Fund (Suspense) DR
	  To Capital Fund
	    Revenue Account
	  Being transfer to capital
	  fund of part of general fund
	  surplus for year.
			9
			
			12
				25,000	25,000

Municipal Accounting for Developing Countries

The net cash settlement with the General Fund would be journalised as follows:

Dec.31	Cash DR	CB	713,424	
	To General Fund (Suspense)	9		713,424
	Being settlement of net			
	cash due from general fund.			

These journal entries have been made on a slightly different basis than those for the first half-year. Transactions between the Capital Fund and the General Fund have been placed in a special suspense account in each of the two sets of accounts. These suspense accounts are really short-term debtor and creditor accounts between the Capital Fund and the General Fund. After and other transactions have been entered, there will be a single cash transfer settling the net balances between the two funds. The journal entries have already been given.

On this basis, the ledger accounts of the General Fund will be as follows:

Cash   CB

19-7 Jul. 1	To Balance	b/f	418,883	19-7 Sep.30	By Sewage Disposal Works	J	100,000
Dec.31	To General Revenue Acct.	J	1,035,000	Sep.30	By Admin. Bldgs.	J	50,000
				Dec.31	By Sewage Disposal Works	J	100,000
				Dec.31	By Admin. Bldgs.	J	65,000
				Dec.31	By Cap. Fund (Suspense)	J	713,424
				Dec.31	By Balance	c/d	425,459
			1,453,883				1,453,883
19-8 Jan. 1	To Balance	b/d	425,459				

Fixed Assets (Various Accounts Separately)   9

19-7 Jul. 1	To Balance	b/f	22,040,925	19-7 Dec.31	By Balance	c/d	22,040,925
19-8 Jan. 1	To Balance	b/d	22,040,925				

Depreciation and Capital Funds

Fixed Assets (Ambulances) — 9A

19-7				19-7			
Jul. 1	To Balance	b/f	46,833	Dec.31	By Balance	c/d	46,833
19-8							
Jan. 1	To Balance	b/d	46,833				

Fixed Assets (Sewage Disposal Works) — 9B

19-7				19-7			
Jul. 1	To Balance	b/f	40,000	Dec.31	By Balance	c/d	243,958
Sep.30	To Cash	J	100,000				
Dec.31	To Cash	J	100,000				
Dec.31	To Cash	J	3,958				
			243,958				
19-8							
Jan. 1	To Balance	b/d	243,958				

Fixed Assets (Administrative Buidings) — 9C

19-7				19-7			
Sep.30	To Cash	J	50,000	Dec.31	By Balance	c/d	116,099
Dec.31	To Cash	J	65,000				
Dec.31	To Advances	J	1,099				
			116,099				
19-8							
Jan. 1	To Balance	b/d	116,099				116,099

Deferred Charges (Various Accounts Separately) — 10

19-7				19-7			
Jul. 1	To Balance	b/f	280,000	Dec.31	By Def. Charges Amortization	J	40,000
				Dec.31	By Balance	c/d	240,000
			280,000				280,000
19-8							
Jan. 1	To Balance	b/d	240,000				

Municipal Accounting for Developing Countries

\multicolumn{7}{c	}{Accumulated Depreciation (Various Accounts Separately)}	11
19-7 Dec.31	To Balance	c/d	5,058,441	19-7 Jul. 1	By Balance	b/f	4,861,100
				Dec.31	By Deprecia- tion	J	197,341
			5,058,441				5,058,441
				19-8 Jan. 1	By Balance	b/d	5,058,441

\multicolumn{7}{c	}{Advances From Capital Fund}	13
19-7 Dec.31	To Cap. Fund (Suspense)	J	237,341	19-7 Jul. 1	By Balance	b/f	17,546,658
Dec.31	To Balance	c/d	17,629,374	Sep.30	By Cap. Fund (Suspense)	J	150,000
				Dec.31	By Cap. Fund (Suspense)	J	165,000
				Dec.31	By Sew. Disp. Works	J	3,958
				Dec.31	By Admin.Bldgs	J	1,099
			17,866,715				17,866,715
				19-8 Jan. 1	By Balance	b/d	17,629,374

\multicolumn{7}{c	}{Revenue Account (Depreciation) (Various Accounts Separately)}	14
19-7 Dec.31	To Accumu- lated Deprec.	J	197,341	19-7 Dec.31	By Gen. Fund Revenue Acc.	J	197,341
			197,341				197,341

\multicolumn{7}{c	}{Revenue Account (Deferred Charge Amortization) (Various Accounts Separately)}	15
19-7 Dec.31	To Deferred Charges	J	40,000	19-7 Dec.31	By Gen. Fund Rev. Acc.	J	40,000

Depreciation and Capital Funds

Revenue Account (Interest) (Various Accounts Separately)								16
19-7 Dec.31	To Cap. Fund (Suspense)	J	769,768	19-7 Dec.31	By Gen. Fund Rev. Acc.	J	769,768	

Revenue Account (Admin. Expenses) (Allocation of Central Administrative Charges)								16A
19-7 Dec.31	To Gen. Fund Rev. Acc.	J	3,685	19-7 Dec.31	By Cap. Fund (Suspense)	J	3,685	

General Revenue Account (Relevant Transactions Only)								18
19-7 Jul. 1	To Balance	b/f	3,257	19-7 Dec.31	By Cash	J	1,035,000	
Dec.31	To Deprec.	J	197,341	Dec.31	By Admin. Exp.	J	3,685	
Dec.31	To Deferred Charge Amort'n	J	40,000					
Dec.31	To Interest	J	769,768					
Dec.31	To Balance	c/d	28,319					
			1,038,685				1,038,685	
Dec.31	To Cap. Fund (Suspense)		25,000	Dec.31	By Balance	b/d	28,319	
Dec.31	To Balance	c/d	3,319					
			28,319				28,319	
				Dec.31	By Balance	b/d	3,319	

Capital Fund (Suspense)								CB
19-7 Sep.30	To Advances	J	150,000	19-7 Dec.31	By Advances	J	237,341	
Dec.31	To Advances	J	165,000	Dec.31	By Interest	J	769,768	
Dec.31	To Rev. Acc (Admin. Exp.)	J	3,685	Dec.31	By Gen. Rev. Acc.	J	25,000	
Dec.31	To Cash	J	713,424					
			1,032,109				1,032,109	

Municipal Accounting for Developing Countries

The ledger accounts of the Capital Fund will be as follows:

				Cash				CB
19-7 Jul. 1	To Balance	b/f	82,127	19-7 Dec.31	By Loans Outst'ing	J	155,663
Sep.30	To Govt. Grant	J	50,000	Dec.31	By Int. P'ble	J	672,727
Sep.30	To Loans Outst'ing	J	50,000	Dec.31	By Debt Management	J	1,465
Dec.31	To Loans Outst'ing	J	50,000	Dec.31	By Balance	c/d	158,776
Dec.31	To Loans Outst'ing	J	2,500				
Dec.31	To Investm'ts	J	35,000				
Dec.31	To Investm't Interest	J	5,580				
Dec.31	To Gen. Fund (Suspense)	J	713,424				
			988,631				988,631
19-8 Jan. 1	To Balance	b/d	158,776				

			Investments				1
19-7 Jul. 1	To Balance	b/f	139,505	19-7 Dec.31	By Cash	J	35,000
				Dec.31	By Balance	c/d	104,505
			139,505				139,505
19-8 Jan. 1	To Balance	b/d	104,505				

			Capital Discharged				2
19-7 Dec.31	To Balance	c/d	2,424,650	19-7 Jul. 1	By Balance	b/f	2,374,650
				Dec. 1	By Gov't Grant	J	50,000
			2,424,650				2,424,650
				19-8 Jan. 1	By Balance	b/d	2,424,650

Depreciation and Capital Funds

Advances For Capital Expenditure 3

19-7				19-7			
Jul. 1	To Balance	b/f	17,546,658	Dec.31	By Gen. Fund (Suspense)	J	237,341
Sep.30	To Gen. Fund (Suspense)	J	150,000	Dec.31	By Balance	c/d	17,629,374
Dec.31	To Gen. Fund (Suspense)	J	165,000				
Dec.31	To Interest Rec'ble	J	5,057				
			17,866,715				17,866,715
19-8							
Jan. 1	To Balance	b/d	17,629,374				

Loans Outstanding 5

19-7				19-7			
Dec.31	To Cash	J	155,663	Jul. 1	By Balance	b/f	15,386,060
Dec.31	To Balance	c/d	15,333,334	Sep.30	By Cash	J	50,000
				Dec.31	By Cash	J	50,000
				Dec.31	By Cash	J	2,500
				Dec.31	By Interest Payable	J	437
			15,488,997				15,488,997
				19-8			
				Jan. 1	By Balance	b/d	15,333,334

Investment Interest 6

19-7				19-7			
Dec.31	To Cap. Fund Rev. Acc.	J	5,580	Dec.31	By Cash	J	5,580
			5,580				5,580

Interest Payable 7

19-7				19-7			
Dec.31	To Cash	J	672,727	Dec.31	By Cap. Fund Rev. Acc.	J	673,164
Dec.31	To Loans Outst'ing	J	437				
			673,164				673,164

Municipal Accounting for Developing Countries

Government Grant							8
19-7 Dec.31	To Capital Disch'd	J	50,000 / 50,000	19-7 Sep.30	By Cash	J	50,000 / 50,000

General Fund (Suspense)							9
19-7 Dec.31	To Advances	J	237,341	19-7 Sep.30	By Advances	J	150,000
Dec.31	To Interest Rec'ble	J	769,768	Dec.31	By Debt Managem't	J	3,685
Dec.31	To Cap. Fund Rev. Acc.	J	25,000	Dec.31	By Advances	J	165,000
			1,032,109	Dec.31	By Cash	J	713,424 / 1,032,109

Management Expenses							10
19-7 Dec.31	To Cash	C.B.	1,465	19-7 Dec.31	By Cap. Fund Rev. Acc.	J	5,150
Dec.31	To Gen. Fund (Suspense)	J	3,685 / 5,150				5,150

Interest Receivable							11
19-7 Dec.31	To Cap. Fund Rev. Acc.	J	774,825 / 774,825	19-7 Dec.31	By Gen. Fund	J	769,768
				Dec.31	By Advances for Cap. Exp.	J	5,057 / 774,825

Depreciation and Capital Funds

\multicolumn{9}{	c	}{Capital Fund Revenue Account 12}

19-7				19-7				
Dec.31	To Interest Payable	J	673,164	Jul. 1	By Balance	b/f		7,580
Dec.31	To Management Expenses	J	5,150	Dec.31	By Investment Interest	J		5,580
				Dec.31	By Interest Receivable	J		774,825
Dec.31	To Balance	c/d	134,671	Dec.31	By General Fund Transfer	J		25,000
			812,985					812,985
				19-8 Jan. 1	By Balance	b/d		134,671

In presenting the final 19-7 balance sheets we shall make the same simplistic (if somewhat unrealistic) assumptions regarding balances unaffected by the Capital Fund transactions. On this basis, the balance sheets would be as follows:

KAMBALE COUNCIL

General Fund Balance Sheet as at 31 December 19-7

	U			U
Long-Term Liabilities			**Fixed Assets**	
Advances from Capital Fund	17,629,374		Buildings	10,700,319
			Permanent Works	11,069,718
			Equipment	677,778
				22,447,815
Current Liabilities			Less Accumulated Depreciation	5,058,441
Creditors	367,240		Net Fixed Assets	17,389,374
Receipts in Advance	26,160			
National Government	116,949		**Current Assets**	
		510,349	Stocks & Stores	293,840
Provisions			Debtors	305,140
Housing Repairs Fund		164,635	Less Bad Debt Provision	20,220
				284,920
Other Balances			Payments in Advance	720
General Revenue Surplus*		495,830	Investments (HRF)	161,635
			Cash	
			At Bank	425,459
			In Hand	4,240
				429,699
				1,170,814
			Other Balances	
			Unamortized Deferred Charges	240,000
		18,800,188		18,800,188

*(U.492,511+3,319)

Capital Fund Balance Sheet
as at 31 December 19-7

Fund Equity

Capital Discharged	2,424,650	Long-Term Assets	
Revenue Account Surplus	134,671		
	2,559,321	Advances for Capital Expenditure	17,629,374
Long-Term Liabilities			
Loans Outstanding	15,333,334	Current Assets	
	17,892,655	Monetary Investments	104,505
		Cash	158,776
			17,892,655

By following the procedures explained in Section 236 page 834, the Consolidated Balance Sheet would appear as follows:

KAMBALE COUNCIL

Consolidated Balance Sheet as at 31 December 19-7

	U			U
Equity			Fixed Assets	
Accumulated Fund			Buildings	10,700,319
Surpluses:			Permanent Works	11,069,718
Capital Fund	2,559,321		Equipment	677,778
General Fund	495,830	3,055,151		22,447,815
			Less Accumulated Depreciation	5,058,441
Long-Term Liabilities				
Loans Outstanding		15,333,334	Net Fixed Assets	17,389,374
Current Liabilities			Current Assets	
Creditors	367,240		Stocks & Stores	293,840
Receipts in Advance	26,160		Debtors 305,140	
National Government	116,949	510,349	Less Bad Debt Provision 20,220	284,920
			Payments in Advance	720
Provisions			Monetary Investments	266,140
Housing Repairs Fund		164,635	Cash	
			At Bank 584,235	
			In Hand 4,240	588,475
				1,434,095
			Other Balances	
			Unamortized Deferred Charges	240,000
		19,063,469		19,063,469

868

Depreciation and Capital Funds

244 **CAPITAL FUND INVESTMENTS**

No provision has been made in the Capital Fund for the repayment of the maturity mortgages raised in the second half-year. Let us suppose that their maturities are 10 years. In principle, in common with all maturity loans, provision for repayment should be made by the establishment of sinking funds. However, as with a loans pool, the Capital Fund is, in effect, itself a sinking fund. Also, like a sinking fund, it holds a proportion of its assets in monetary investments.

A question to be considered is whether and to what extent, funds should be specifically invested to provide for the eventual redemption of the maturity loans. This is the same question that was argued extensively in Section 221 of Chapter 20. The basic conclusion was that if a loans pool is established, individual sinking funds are not required. The same conclusion would apply to a Capital Fund.

However, a word of caution is in order. As with a loans pool, a Capital Fund would only operate in the most flexible way where capital market conditions allowed for loans to be raised whenever needed, either to finance new capital expenditure or to "roll over" existing debt. Such circumstances are unlikely in many countries. Thus, it will be necessary to plan capital expenditure and related debt management for several years ahead to ensure that there will be a satisfactory equilibrium among the following:

(a) debt service obligations;

(b) capital expenditure requirements;

(c) availability of capital funds; and

(d) adequate margins of safety.

These are principles applicable to any prudently managed capital financing institution. Thus, a likely consequence would be the maintenance of adequate cash balances and monetary investments to ensure that all obligations could be met. Whether investments would need to be earmarked to specific loan obligations would be a matter of judgment. The principal advantage of such arrangements would be an absolute assurance of funds being available for debt redemption at maturity. The disadvantages, as discussed earlier, are lack of flexibility and loss of interest.

Sometimes, the influence of the government may be felt in these matters. For example, the law might require the establishment of earmarked sinking fund investments, in which case the local authority has no option but to comply. By contrast, specific sinking funds would be far less necessary or desirable if, for example, the government stood ready as a "lender of last resort" to meet all reasonable local authority borrowing requirements, including those necessary to re-finance existing debt. One purpose of a Capital Fund is to provide for flexibility. If cash-flow problems, however, appear likely, it is preferable to err on the side of conservatism. The underlying safeguard, which must be unfailingly maintained at all times, is for funds representing depreciation and interest to be periodically transferred from the General Fund to the Capital Fund, out of revenue income, as a priority charge on the revenue expenditure budget.

245 RENEWALS PROVISIONS

One of the principal features of the capital fund system is to facilitate the allocation of proper annual depreciation charges to general fund accounts. This ensures that costs of capital assets are fully allowed for as part of the total costs of operating various services. It also provides for funds to be raised from charges, taxes and other municipal income to ensure that fixed asset values can be maintained, if only on the basis of historical costs.

Unfortunately, in common with many traditional accountancy systems, inflation is not provided for. This applies as much to enterprise (commercial) accounting as to the fund accounting systems more appropriate to municipalities. The subject of "inflation accounting" has been under active discussion by the world's principal accountancy bodies for well over a decade. Whilst there is substantial acknowledgment that accounting systems should, in principle, recognize the effects of inflation, there is, as yet, no substantial international agreement on the details as to how this should be done.

Municipal accounting, as currently practised for non-revenue-earning activities, does not commonly recognize depreciation, even on the basis of historical costs. Indeed, the purpose of this Chapter is to offer some suggestions as to how this might be done. Thus, in the present state of uncertainty, it is somewhat pointless to put forward a system of "inflation accounting" for general municipal purposes.*

Inflation is a fact of life. In many countries, at different times, it has been a significant factor in the distortion of historically-based financial information. Furthermore, the calculation of depreciation based on historical costs does not allow for the generation of adequate cash-flows to provide for the eventual replacement of the fixed assets concerned. This is especially serious with assets of relatively short working lives, such as vehicles and plant.

A good example, in the case of Kambale Council, would be the ambulances. These are initially to be financed by a loan, with a highly-subsidized interest rate and a repayment period quite unrelated to working life. Yet, for example, the ambulance purchased in 19-7 will need to be replaced at the end of about 5 years (perhaps even before the loan which financed it starts to be repaid), with not necessarily any prospect of the replacement being financed on the same basis as the original.

This problem can be dealt with by a renewals fund system. This has been explained in principle in Chapter 8 (Section 87) but such a system can be incorporated within the Capital Fund. Let us examine its application to the ambulance which came into service on 30 June 19-7. The depreciation schedule (sinking fund method) shows that with a half-yearly depreciation charge starting at U 3,901 and rising to U 5,552 the Capital Fund would receive back the total cost, amounting to U 46,833, at the end of 5 years (10 half-years). If there were no inflation during that period, this would be enough to replace the original ambulance.

However, an inflation-free situation is unlikely. More probable would be a varying rate of inflation during the working life of the ambulance. Since inflation cannot be accurately forecast, adjustments will be necessary as time goes on.

---
*This is a pragmatic approach. The author believes that accountancy relating to depreciation should, in principle, reflect inflation as well.

Depreciation and Capital Funds

When dealing with depreciation, based on original cost, it has already been demonstrated that appropriate interest is charged for the use of the capital fund money by the ambulance accounts in the General Fund. By contrast, renewals fund contributions, where used, would be made to the Capital Fund in advance of the replacement purchase. It would thus be appropriate to allow for payment of interest by the Capital Fund to the General Fund. This would best be achieved by providing for renewals fund contributions based on the accumulating sinking fund principle, whereby contributions from the General Fund would be deemed to be earning interest within the Capital Fund until required for the purchase of a new vehicle.

The journal entries and accountancy are very simple. However, the calculation of half-yearly contributions is a little more complex. The situation is somewhat analagous to a person making deposits in a bank account so that by a certain date, with accrued interest, a specific sum will have been saved for a particular purpose. Unfortunately, however, the saver sees the price of the replacement continuously changing, usually upward. Thus, at the end of each period, the saver must:

(a) assess the amount already saved;

(b) calculate how much this sum will amount to, including the interest on it, by the deadline;

(c) identify the latest cost of what is to be purchased; and

(d) calculate a new periodic contribution which will cover the difference.

This practice could be followed with the ambulance, as shown in the following table. Although provision could be made for variable interest on contributions, we shall assume a fixed 8% per annum (4% per half-year).

Before considering the calculation process, it is important to note that the renewals fund arrangements here apply only to the excess of the replacement cost over the historical cost. The latter is already provided for by the depreciation process. This contrasts with earlier explanations, relating to situations where depreciation is not charged.

The calculation process is as follows. At the end of the first period, there has been inflation at 4.3%. So the replacement cost of the ambulance has increased by this percentage to U 48,847. This means that provision must be made, over 10 half-years at 4% interest, for an additional U 2,014. Reference will be made to the sinking fund tables to find out what must be invested in each of 10 periods, with interest at 4%, to accumulate U 2,014. The answer is U 0.083290944 x 2014 = U 167.75, rounded to U 168. (There is no need for greater accuracy, because the future can only be estimated). Thus, if there were no further inflation during the remaining working life of the ambulance, there would be enough in the Capital Fund to replace it.

However, this does not happen. By the end of the second period there has been a further 6.1% of inflation, raising the replacement cost to U 51,826. This is now U 4,993 above the purchase price. The U 168 already contributed to the Capital Fund will, if there are no further contributions, earn interest compounded at 4% for the remaining 9 periods, accumulating to U 239.12 by the time of replacement.

KAMBALE COUNCIL
Renewals Fund - Ambulance

Period	Inflation Rate	Replacement Cost	Additional Provision	Balance to Provide	Contribution	Periods Remaining	Interest Earned	Total Provided for	Cumulative Total Provided for
0	-	46,833	-	-	-	-	-	-	-
1	4.3	48,847	2,014	2,014	168	9	71	239	239
2	6.1	51,826	4,993	4,754	449	8	166	615	854
3	2.1	52,915	6,082	5,228	567	7	180	747	1,601
4	1.5	53,709	6,876	5,275	668	6	177	845	2,446
5	1.4	54,460	7,627	5,181	781	5	169	950	3,396
6	2.3	55,713	8,880	5,484	1,012	4	172	1,184	4,580
7	2.5	57,106	10,273	5,693	1,341	3	167	1,508	6,088
8	3.4	59,047	12,214	6,126	1,962	2	161	2,123	8,211
9	3.8	61,291	14,458	6,247	3,062	1	123	3,185	11,396
10	3.5	63,436	16,603	5,207	5,207	0	-	5,207	16,603

Depreciation and Capital Funds

Provision must therefore be made as follows:

	U
Replacement cost	51,826
Less Purchase price	46,833
Balance to provide for	4,993
Amount to be accumulated from contribution of U.168	239
	4,754

The amount to be contributed in each of the remaining 9 half-years would be U 0.094492993 x 4754 = U 449. This would be the contribution for the second period. It would also be the revised contribution for all subsequent periods if there were no further inflation. However, since we assume that inflation continues, the half-yearly calculation must be revised each time, using the same procedure as before.

The figures in the table show much higher contributions in later periods than in earlier ones. This is because, like the hypothetical saver, contributions are each time calculated on an assumption of no further inflation. Actually, the differences are not quite as dramatic as they appear. Given that the 5-year period has an overall inflation rate of about 35% (calculated by compounding the half-yearly rates) the last contribution (U 5,207) would be equivalent to U 3,844 at price levels of the first period. An alternative would be to assume that the rate of inflation will continue. In such a case the calculation at the end of the first period would be based upon a replacement cost calculated by compounding the purchase price at 4.3% over 10 periods. This would give a replacement cost of U 1.523502195 x 46833 = U 7,1350. It can readily be seen that this is considerably more than the replacement will eventually cost, but this is not known at the time of the calculation. Such a calculation might well represent a more prudent method, under which the first periodical contribution would be U (71,350 - 46,833) x 0.083290944 = U 2042.

Unfortunately, conventional wisdom is always to assume that the inflation is temporary and can be expected not to continue. Governments, in particular, are especially sensitive to assumptions of continued inflation. Furthermore, it can be argued that an automatic assumption of inflation becomes a self-fulfilling prophecy. Apart from these somewhat philosophical considerations, it is unlikely that the alternative method, though more prudent, would necessarily be acceptable as an accounting standard. As earlier indicated, the various accountancy bodies have not yet reached a full consensus on accounting for past inflation, let alone estimated future inflation.

If the latter method were used, however, the table would be revised to appear as follows:

KAMBALE COUNCIL
Renewals Fund - Ambulance

Period	Inflation Rate	Replacement Cost	Additional Provision	Balance to Provide	Contri-bution	Periods Remaining	Interest Earned	Total Provided for	Cumulative Total Provided for
0	-	46,833	-	-	-	-	-	-	-
1	4.3	71,350	24,517	24,517	2,042	9	864	2,906	2,906
2	6.1	83,229	36,396	33,490	3,165	8	1,166	4,331	7,237
3	2.1	61,201	14,368	7,131	774	7	244	1,018	8,255
4	1.5	58,727	11,894	3,639	461	6	122	583	8,838
5	1.4	58,381	11,548	2,710	409	5	88	497	9,335
6	2.3	61,018	14,185	4,850	895	4	153	1,048	10,383
7	2.5	61,497	14,664	4,281	1,008	3	126	1,134	11,517
8	3.4	63,131	16,298	4,781	1,532	2	125	1,657	13,174
9	3.8	63,620	16,787	3,613	1,771	1	71	1,842	15,016
10	3.5	63,436	16,603	1,587	1,587	0	-	1,587	16,603

Depreciation and Capital Funds

The only significant difference between the two tables would be the calculation of the replacement costs. For example, at the end of period 6 the first table shows a replacement cost of U 55,713, calculated by increasing the original U 46,833 by the successive rates of inflation. By contrast, the second table takes this figure of U 55,713 and assumes that the latest inflation rate (2.3%) will continue to the end of period 10, giving U 61,018.

The journal entries are simple and straightforward. For the first half-year, they would be as follows:

General Fund

19-7 Dec.31	Ambulances Revenue DR
	  To Capital Fund
	    (Suspense)
	  Being half-yearly
	  renewals contributions
			168	168

Capital Fund

19-7 Dec.31	General Fund (Suspense) DR
	  To Renewals
	    Contributions
	  Being half-yearly
	  renewals contributions
			168	168

The offsetting suspense account balances will be cleared, along with other transactions, by a cash transfer between the General Fund and the Capital Fund.

There is no need to make specific entries relative to accrued interest. This will be merely implied. If the interest were actually recorded in the General Fund, this would be correct also. However, it would introduce unnecessary complications, which the capital fund system is intended to prevent. The eventual purchase of the new (replacement) ambulance would be funded from the Capital Fund in exactly the same way as the original.

In the Ambulances Revenue Account of the General Fund, the accounts would be summarized as follows:

        Employees (etc.)

        Supplies and Services (etc.)

        Depreciation

        Interest

        Renewals Contributions

Municipal Accounting for Developing Countries

Looked at from another perspective, the charges in the General Fund revenue accounts for renewals could be regarded as allocations of the sum which might otherwise be transferred to the Capital Fund out of general revenue surpluses. However, the latter is discretionary, whereas the renewals contributions purport to cover actual costs arising from inflation. In other words, revenue account surpluses are "reserves" but renewals fund contributions are "provisions" (see Section 88).

The practices illustrated for the operation of a renewals fund system are intended primarily to show the various matters which must be taken into account in making provision for asset renewal, especially in relation to inflation. Whilst the methods shown can comfortably be used as accounting practices, their application will depend upon a variety of individual legal, administrative, political, financial, professional and other circumstances. It can be strongly asserted, however, that in the absence of strong capital markets there is a need to make adequate provision to sustain and renew the working assets of a community, to ensure that services are adequately maintained. Hence the need for what is, in effect, "life insurance" on the fixed assets. The shorter the expected working life, the more important it is to provide specifically for replacement. Thus, renewals funds systems are especially appropriate for vehicles and mechanical plant.

246 CAPITAL FUND TRANSACTIONS IN SUBSEQUENT YEARS

We shall now briefly examine the capital fund transactions for the next two years, 19-8 and 19-9. We shall do this in summary form, using tables rather than accounts, similar to that which was done in Chapter 20. For simplicity, we shall assume that the capital expenditure is exactly as planned and that transactions take place on the last day of each quarter. We shall also assume that the payments for the other two ambulances are each made by a single lump sum, ignoring the distinction between purchase and shipping costs. These ambulances will be financed from the same foreign loan (IAA) as the first one.

We shall make an assumption that maturity mortgages are raised as part of the capital financing. We shall also assume that at the end of each year U 100,000 is to be repaid on maturity mortgages raised before the establishment of the Capital Fund. General Fund transfers of U 10,000 for 19-8 and U 15,000 for 19-9 will be assumed.

After the first two quarters, cash begins to build up in the Capital Fund. Thus, we shall assume that U 50,000 is invested on 31 December 19-8 and a further U 100,000 on 30 June 19-9. The management expenses will all be assumed to be paid in cash, although in practice there would continue to be allocations of central administrative expenses.

We shall assume that for the administrative buildings, sewage disposal works and clinic, interest will be capitalised on advances from the Capital Fund until these assets, constructed over several periods, come into operation. The sewers (Diwali Road), ambulances, and street lighting will be assumed to come into operation as soon as the purchase or construction for each period is completed.

Although the question of renewals contributions has been extensively discussed above, we shall assume that Kambale Council has not yet decided to operate such a system.

KAMBALE COUNCIL

Capital Fund - Cash Flow Statement

Period Ended

Advances For Capital Expenditure	Mar. 19-8 U.	Jun. 19-8 U.	Sept. 19-8 U.	Dec. 19-8 U.	Mar. 19-9 U.	Jun. 19-9 U.	Sept. 19-9 U.	Dec. 19-9 U.
Admin. Buildings	150,000	150,000	5,000	-	-	-	-	-
Ambulances	-	47,000	-	-	-	48,000	-	-
Sewage Works	60,000	60,000	30,000	30,000	30,000	30,000	30,000	-
Sewerage (Diwali Road)	20,000	140,000	-	32,000	-	-	-	-
Clinic (Bugoma)	-	-	-	-	60,000	130,000	10,000	-
Street Lighting	-	-	-	-	10,000	60,000	80,000	30,000
Total	230,000	397,000	35,000	62,000	100,000	268,000	120,000	30,000

Sources of Funds

Loan - IAA	-	47,000	-	-	60,000	178,000	10,000	-
Loan - LGLF	30,000	90,000	10,000	42,000	10,000	15,000	15,000	-
Maturity Mortgages	50,000	50,000	-	-	-	-	-	-
Grants (Sewage Works)	30,000	30,000	20,000	20,000	20,000	15,000	15,000	-
Grants (Sewers)	20,000	30,000	-	-	-	-	-	-
Contributions (Sewers)	-	50,000	-	-	-	-	-	-
Total	130,000	297,000	30,000	62,000	90,000	208,000	40,000	-
Increase (Decrease) in Cash	(100,000)	(100,000)	(5,000)	-	(10,000)	(60,000)	(80,000)	(30,000)

continued on page 878

Other Transactions						
Payments						
Investments	–	–	–	–	100,000	–	100,000
Loans Repaid	–	162,712	–	270,405	178,115	–	286,033
Interest	–	672,167	–	675,047	665,812	–	659,387
Management Expenses	–	5,360	–	5,693	5,879	–	6,028
Total	–	840,239	–	1,001,145	949,806	–	951,448
Receipts						
Investment Interest	–	4,180	–	4,180	6,180	–	10,180
Depreciation	–	205,277	–	218,432	227,771	–	243,382
Deferred Charge Amt.	–	40,000	–	40,000	40,000	–	40,000
Interest Re-charged	–	761,242	–	769,146	768,653	–	772,363
General Fund Transfer	–	–	–	10,000	–	–	15,000
Total	–	1,010,699	–	1,041,758	1,042,604	–	1,080,925
Net Increase (Decrease) in Cash	(100,000)	70,460	(5,000)	40,613	32,798	(80,000)	99,477
Cum. Cash (B/F 158,776)	58,776	129,236	124,236	164,849	187,647	107,647	207,124

KAMBALE COUNCIL

Capital Fund
Debt Statement

For periods ended

	Dec. 19-7	Mar. 19-8	Jun. 19-8	Sep. 19-8	Dec. 19-8	Mar. 19-9	Jun. 19-9	Sep. 19-9	Dec. 19-9
Loans Raised									
Original	-	-	-	-	-	-	-	-	-
IAA(M)	-	-	47,000	-	-	60,000	178,000	10,000	-
IA/A(I)	-	233	234	471	473	475	778	1,672	1,730
LGLF	-	30,000	90,000	10,000	42,000	10,000	15,000	15,000	-
Maturity	-	50,000	50,000	-	-	-	-	-	-
Total	-	80,233	187,234	10,471	42,473	70,475	193,778	26,672	1,730
Loans Repaid									
Original	-	-	162,473	-	269,581	-	177,001	-	284,744
IAA	-	-	-	-	-	-	-	-	-
LGLF	-	-	239	-	824	-	1,114	-	1,289
Maturity	-	-	-	-	-	-	-	-	-
Total	-	-	162,712	-	270,405	-	178,115	-	286,033

continued on page 880

879

Loans Out-standing								
Original	15,186,679	15,186,679	15,024,206	15,024,206	14,754,624	14,754,624	14,577,624	14,577,624	14,292,879
IAA	46,655	46,888	94,123	94,593	95,066	155,542	334,319	345,991	347,721
LGLF	50,000	80,000	169,761	179,761	220,927	230,937	244,823	259,823	258,534
Maturity	50,000	100,000	150,000	150,000	150,000	150,000	150,000	150,000	150,000
Total	15,333,334	15,413,567	15,438,090	15,448,560	15,220,627	15,291,103	15,306,766	15,333,438	15,049,134
Interest								
Original	-	332,209	332,209	328,655	328,655	322,757	322,757	318,886	318,886
IAA	-	233	234	471	473	475	778	1,672	1,730
LGLF	-	1,250	2,000	4,244	4,494	5,523	5,773	6,121	6,496
Maturity	-	1,500	3,000	4,500	4,500	4,500	4,500	4,500	4,500
Total	-	335,192	337,443	337,870	338,122	333,255	333,808	331,179	331,612
Half-Year Interest	-	-	672,635	-	675,992	-	667,063	-	662,791
Average Loan Out-standing	-	-	15,373,451	-	15,443,325	-	15,255,865	-	15,320,102
Interest Rate	-	-	4.375302	-	4.377235	-	4.372513	-	4.326268
Management Expenses	-	-	5,360	-	5,693	-	5,879	-	6,028

Depreciation and Capital Funds

247 CAPITAL FUND CASH TRANSACTIONS

The cash transactions of the Capital Fund, including the transfers to and from the General Fund, are shown in the table beginning on page 877. The table is in two parts. First is shown the capital financing, resulting in a net change in cash balances. This is then adjusted by various revenue transactions, to show the final overall change in the cash position at the end of each quarter.

The capital cash transactions are straightforward. The most important feature is that in almost every period there is a reduction of capital cash balances. Each half-year, this draw-down is made good by the net result of the Capital Fund's other cash transactions. In particular, the transfers from the General Fund for depreciation and interest charges are more than enough to cover external debt service, thus providing internal funds towards capital expenditure. The net result has been to enable the Capital Fund to draw to the limit on grants, contributions, foreign low-interest loans and slightly concessional LGLF loans, before going into the market for maturity mortgages. In fact, it is doubtful if the maturity mortgages would be needed at all. They are included mainly for illustrative purposes. The cash requirements will, in any case, depend upon a longer-term view of capital fund operations.

The amounts shown as "Advances for Capital Expenditure" would, of course, be transferred to the General Fund or disbursed on its behalf.

248 EXTERNAL LOANS

The transactions of the Capital Fund with respect to external loans are shown by the following table. The loans brought forward at 31 December 19-6 are grouped as "Original". The loan transactions for 19-7 to 19-9 are shown separately.

The loans raised have been picked up from the cash-flow statement. The amounts shown against IAA(M) are the main loans raised to finance the two additional ambulances. The amounts shown under IAA(I) represent the interest charges which, instead of being paid in cash, are credited against the loan balance (capitalised). All other entries are self-explanatory.

Each half-year, the interest for the two quarters is totalled and a calculation is made of the average loan outstanding. The latter is the balance brought forward at the end of the previous half-year plus half the amount raised at the end of the first of the two quarters. The amount raised at the end of the second quarter is ignored in this calculation, because no interest is payable on it until the next half-year. Thus for the end of June 19-8 the average loan outstanding is U 15,333,334 + (80233 ÷ 2) = U 15,373,451.

Application of the interest payable (U 672,635) to this sum gives an average rate of:

$$\frac{672,635}{15,373,451} \times 100 = 4.375302\%$$

This interest rate forms the basis of charges to the General Fund. An adjustment will be made to allow for management expenses, shown as a footnote on the debt statement.

249   **CAPITAL FUND REVENUE ACCOUNT**

The Capital Fund revenue account, if made up half-yearly, would appear as follows:

KAMBALE COUNCIL

Capital Fund Revenue Account

	Jun. 19-8	Dec. 19-8	Jun. 19-9	Dec. 19-9
Income				
Investment Income	4,180	4,180	6,180	10,180
Interest Recovered	781,730	795,744	790,603	788,171
General Fund Transfers	-	10,000	-	15,000
Total Income	785,910	809,924	796,783	813,351
Expenditure				
Interest Payable	672,167	675,047	665,812	659,387
Interest Capitalized	467	944	1,253	3,402
Management Expenses	5,360	5,693	5,879	6,028
Total Expenditure	677,994	681,684	672,944	668,817
Revenue Surplus	107,916	128,240	123,839	144,534
Balance B/Forward	134,671	242,587	370,827	494,666
Balance C/Forward	242,587	370,827	494,666	639,200

The only significant point in the above statement is that capitalized interest payable to IAA is included as an expense of the Capital Fund, even though not paid in cash. Similarly, the Capital Fund takes credit for interest recovered or recoverable from the General Fund, including the interest charged against fixed assets (capitalized) and debited against advances.

250   **CAPITAL DISCHARGED**

As mentioned earlier, capital grants and other contributions will be credited direct to the equity capital of the Capital Fund, as capital discharged. The following statement shows how this would be done.

Depreciation and Capital Funds

KAMBALE COUNCIL

Statement of Capital Discharged

	Period Ended			
	Jun. 19-8	Dec. 19-8	Jun. 19-9	Dec. 19-9
Grants				
Sewage Disposal Works	60,000	40,000	35,000	15,000
Sewerage (Diwali Rd.)	50,000	-	-	-
Contributions				
Sewerage (Diwali Rd.)	50,000	-	-	-
Total	160,000	40,000	35,000	15,000
Balance B/Forward	2,424,650	2,584,650	2,624,650	2,659,650
Balance C/Forward	2,584,650	2,624,650	2,659,650	2,674,650

Some accountancy rules may require a different procedure, as explained below (section 255).

251 **CAPITAL FUND BALANCE SHEETS FOR SUBSEQUENT YEARS**

We are now in a position to set out the half-yearly balance sheets of the Capital Fund. The only balance sheet item not yet explained is that of "Advances". The balances on this account are the net difference between gross fixed asset balances and accumulated depreciation, (plus the unamortized deferred charges) as shown below, in the General Fund accounts. The Capital Fund balance sheets will, therefore, appear as follows:

KAMBALE COUNCIL
Balance Sheets As At

	Jun. 19-8	Dec. 19-8	Jun. 19-9	Dec. 19-9
Loans Outstanding				
Original	15,024,206	14,754,624	14,577,624	14,292,879
IAA	94,123	95,066	334,319	347,721
LGLF	169,761	220,937	244,823	258,534
Maturity	150,000	150,000	150,000	150,000
Total Loans	15,438,090	15,220,627	15,306,766	15,049,134
Equity				
Capital Discharged	2,584,650	2,624,650	2,659,650	2,674,650
Revenue Surplus	242,586	370,827	494,666	639,201
Total Equity	2,827,236	2,995,477	3,154,316	3,313,851
Total Liabilities & Equity	18,265,326	18,216,104	18,461,082	18,362,985
Long-Term Assets				
Advances to General Fund	18,031,585	17,896,750	18,018,930	17,901,356
Current Assets				
Investments	104,505	154,505	254,505	254,505
Cash	129,236	164,849	187,647	207,124
Total Current Assets	233,741	319,354	442,152	461,629
Total Assets	18,265,326	18,216,104	18,461,082	18,362,985

252 **CAPITAL EXPENDITURE**

To complete our review of transactions for 19-8 and 19-9 it is necessary to examine the capital expenditure transactions of the General Fund. A complete study of the general fund accounts is not necessary.

The table on page 885 shows the quarterly capital expenditure of the General Fund, together with the accumulated gross value of the fixed assets, before allowance for depreciation. The quarterly gross value of each fixed asset category and the total gross value, is arrived at by adding that quarter's capital expenditure to the balance at the end of the previous quarter. The capital expenditure figures are the same as those in the Capital Fund cash-flow statement, except for capitalised interest. This is calculated on the basis of accumulated capital expenditure on those assets not yet in service. Thus, for example, the amounts shown as "Admin. Bldgs (I)" represent the interest treated as a fixed asset (capitalised), calculated as shown on page 888.

KAMBALE COUNCIL

Capital Expenditure and Fixed Asset Balances

	Mar. 19-8 U	Jun. 19-8 U	Sep. 19-8 U	Dec. 19-8 U	Mar. 19-9 U	Jun. 19-9 U	Sep. 19-9 U	Dec. 19-9 U
CAPITAL EXPENDITURE								
Original	-	-	-	-	-	-	-	-
Admin. Buildings (C)	150,000	150,000	5,000	-	-	-	-	-
Admin. Buildings (I)	-	-	-	-	-	-	-	-
Ambulance	-	8,419	-	9,358	-	-	-	-
	-	47,000	-	-	-	-	-	-
Sewage Works (C)	60,000	60,000	30,000	30,000	30,000	30,000	30,000	-
Sewage Works (I)	-	12,069	-	17,240	-	20,628	-	11,638
Ambulance	-	-	-	-	-	48,000	-	-
Sewerage (Diwali Rd)	20,000	140,000	-	32,000	-	-	-	-
Clinic (C)	-	-	-	-	60,000	130,000	10,000	-
Clinic (I)	-	-	-	-	-	1,322	-	4,170
Street Lighting	-	-	-	-	10,000	60,000	80,000	30,000
Total	230,000	417,488	35,000	88,598	100,000	289,950	120,000	45,808
FIXED ASSETS								
Original	22,040,925	22,040,925	22,040,925	22,040,925	22,040,925	22,040,925	22,040,925	22,040,925
Admin. Building	266,099	424,518	429,518	438,876	438,876	438,876	438,876	438,876
Ambulance 1	46,833	46,833	46,833	46,833	46,833	46,833	46,833	46,833
Ambulance 2	-	47,000	47,000	47,000	47,000	47,000	47,000	47,000
Ambulance 3	-	-	-	-	-	48,000	48,000	48,000
Sewage Works	303,958	376,027	406,027	453,267	483,267	533,895	563,895	575,533
Sewers	20,000	160,000	160,000	192,000	192,000	192,000	192,000	192,000
Clinic	-	-	-	-	60,000	191,322	201,322	205,492
Street Lighting	-	-	-	-	10,000	70,000	150,000	180,000
Total	22,677,815	23,095,303	23,130,303	23,218,901	23,318,901	23,608,851	23,728,851	23,774,659

KAMBALE COUNCIL

Depreciation and Accrued Depreciation

PERIOD ENDED

	Jun. 19-8 U	Dec. 19-8 U	Jun. 19-9 U	Dec. 19-9 U
DEPRECIATION				
Original	201,178	209,224	217,594	226,297
Admin. Buildings	-	398	828	861
Ambulance (1)	4,057	4,219	4,388	4,564
Ambulance (2)	-	3,915	4,071	4,234
Ambulance (3)	-	-	-	3,998
Sewage Works	-	-	-	1,209
Sewers	42	676	837	871
Clinic	-	-	-	186
Street Lighting	-	-	53	1,162
Total	205,277	218,432	227,771	243,382
ACCRUED DEPRECIATION				
Original	5,255,718	5,464,942	5,682,536	5,908,833
Admin. Buildings	-	398	1,226	2,087
Ambulance 1	7,958	12,177	16,565	21,129
Ambulance 3	-	3,915	7,986	12,220
Ambulance 3	-	-	-	3,998
Sewage Works	-	-	-	1,209
Sewers	42	718	1,555	2,426
Clinic	-	-	-	186
Street Lighting	-	-	53	1,215
Total	5,263,718	5,482,150	5,709,921	5,953,303
Deferred Charges - Amortisation	40,000	40,000	40,000	40,000
Deferred Charges - Balance	200,000	160,000	120,000	80,000

KAMBALE COUNCIL

Advances, Recoveries, Revenue Charges and Interest

	Mar. 19-8 U	Jun. 19-8 U	Sep. 19-8 U	Dec. 19-8 U	Mar. 19-9 U	Jun. 19-9 U	Sep. 19-9 U	Dec. 19-9 U
ADVANCES	17,859,374	18,031,585	18,066,585	17,896,751	17,996,751	18,018,930	18,138,930	17,901,356
AVERAGE ADVANCES	-	17,744,374	-	18,049,085	-	17,946,751	-	18,078,930
INTEREST RECOVERED	-	776,370	-	790,051	-	784,724	-	782,143
MANAGEMENT EXPENSES RECOVERED	-	5,360	-	5,693	-	5,879	-	6,028
TOTAL RECOVERED	-	781,730	-	795,744	-	790,603	-	788,171
LESS CAPITALISED	-	20,488	-	26,598	-	21,950	-	15,808
CHARGED TO REVENUE	-	761,242	-	769,146	-	768,653	-	772,363
ADJUSTED INTEREST RATE	-	4.409%	-	4.409%	-	4.409%	-	4.360%

Municipal Accounting for Developing Countries

	CALCULATIONS	TOTALS
	U	U
Balance brought forward 1 Jan 19-8	116,099	116,099
Capital expenditure to 31 Mar 19-8	-	150,000
Equivalent for half-year	75,000	-
Capital expenditure to 30 Jun 19-8	-	150,000
Equivalent for half-year	-	-
Basis for interest charge	191,099	
Interest at 4.405509%	8,419	

Calculations for subsequent half-years will follow the same procedure. The other fixed assets where interest is capitalised, in the same way, are the sewage disposal works and the clinic. All other fixed assets are assumed to come into operation at the end of each quarter. This includes the sewers and the street lights.

The accumulated fixed asset values are those which would appear in the general fund balance sheet.

253 DEPRECIATION

The table on page 886 shows the depreciation charges for each half-year and the accumulated depreciation charges at the end of each half-year. It also shows the half-yearly amortisation of deferred charges and the reducing balance on this account. Again, these accumulated depreciation charges and deferred charge balances would appear in the General Fund balance sheet. The depreciation charges are assumed to follow the principle of a 4% half-yearly sinking fund method. So, for the original fixed assets brought forward from 19-7, the depreciation charge for each half-year is merely an increase of 4% over that of the previous half-year. For new assets coming into operation, the calculation must take account of partial periods. For example, the depreciation charge on the street lighting for June 19-9 would be calculated as follows:

	U
Fixed assets coming into operation 31 March	10,000
Equivalent for one quarter	5,000
Amount (from tables) required to accumulate to 1 in 40 half-years (20 years) at 4%	0.010523489
Annual depreciation charge 0.01052349 x 5000 =	53

The calculation for December 19-9 would be:

	U
Fixed assets coming into operation 30 June	60,000
Fixed assets coming into operation 30 Sept	80,000
Equivalent for one quarter	40,000
Depreciation charge on new assets equivalent to U 100,000: 0.01052349 x 100,000 =	1,052
Depreciation for 1 quarter on U 10,000 = 53	
Equivalent for full half-year = 53 x 2 = 106	
Depreciation for second period 106 + 4%	110
	1,162

Depreciation and Capital Funds

In practice, each group of fixed assets will be separately recorded in subsidiary records and depreciation on each group calculated separately.

254 INTEREST AND MANAGEMENT EXPENSES

The table on page 887 shows the advances outstanding at the end of each quarter, equal to gross fixed asset values minus depreciation. The table shows that for each half-year, interest is charged at the rate applicable to the Capital Fund - which is the weighted average rate of borrowings, as already explained. To this is added the management expenses, to provide a total to be recovered from the General Fund. The capitalised interest is then charged against the fixed assets, leaving the balance to be apportioned to the various revenue accounts within the General Fund.

An example of the entire process can be given for the period ended June 19-9, as follows:

	U
Loans outstanding 31 Dec 19-8	15,220,628
Loans outstanding 31 Mar 19-9	15,291,103
Average loans outstanding	15,255,865
Interest payable (including capitalised)	667,063

Average rate of interest:

$$\frac{667,063 \times 100}{15,255,865} \% = 4.372515$$

Advances outstanding 31 Dec 19-8	17,896,751
Advances outstanding 31 Mar 19-9	17,996,751
Average advances outstanding	17,946,751
Interest at 4.372515% on average advances outstanding	784,724
Management expenses	5,879
Total to be recovered	790,603

Adjusted interest rate:

$$\frac{790,603 \times 100}{17,946,751} \% = 4.405271$$

Total to be recovered	790,603
Interest capitalised	21,950
Balance charged to revenue	768,653

255 GRANTS AND CONTRIBUTIONS

In the examples given in this chapter, specific capital grants and consumer contributions have been treated as contributions towards the equity capital of the Capital Fund, to be used, in effect, in perpetuity. This treatment is rather similar to that of a commercial company. It is appropriate, because the grant or contribution is intended to provide the community with an increment to its fixed assets, which must subsequently be renewed, and replaced.

However, some accountancy authorities recommend a different practice. They assert that the capital grants and consumer contributions are, in effect, initial one-time payments in lieu of annual revenue (recurrent) grants which would otherwise be given to support the operation and maintenance of the fixed asset. Following this practice, it is necessary for the grant to be initially placed in an account which is, in effect, a suspense or holding account. Then, each year, an appropriate proportion of the grant, based upon the life of the fixed asset, would be transferred to the credit of the revenue account to which the fixed asset relates. The income would thus offset the expenditure incurred for the running expenses and capital charges of the fixed asset.

If this practice were followed in the case of Kambale, it would apply, for example, to the sewerage for Diwali Road. Here, it will be recalled, there was a U 50,000 government grant and also U 50,000 of consumer contributions received in the first half of 19-8. From the table on page 877 these transactions could be journalised as follows:

19-8				
Mar 31	Cash To Grants (Suspense) Being receipt of government grant for Diwali Road sewers	DR	20,000	20,000
Jun 30	Cash To Grants (Suspense) Being receipt of further government grants for Diwali Road sewers	DR	30,000	30,000
Jun 30	Cash To Consumer Contributions (Suspense) Being receipt of consumer contributions for Diwali Road sewers	DR	50,000	50,000

The sewers are deemed to have a working life of 30 years (60 half-years). Consequently, in its simplest form, an amount must be credited to the sewerage revenue account for each of the next 60 half-years, equal to 1/60 of U 100,000 = U 1667. The first such contribution would be journalised as follows:

19-8				
Dec 31	Consumer Contribs (Suspense) Grants (Suspense) To Sewerage Revenue Being half-yearly transfer of sewerage grant and consumer contributions to Revenue Account	DR DR	833 834	1,667

Depreciation and Capital Funds

This somewhat simplistic approach ignores the fact that the amounts received for capital grants and consumer contributions can be deemed to earn interest, by being used elsewhere in the Kambale Council's capital financing, until the half-yearly sums are transferred to the revenue account. Indeed, the sums may be invested in the Capital Fund, pending their appropriation. If this were done, the U 100,000 could be treated as an annuity loan made to the Capital Fund, repayable at (say) 8% per annum (4% half-yearly). In these circumstances, the half-yearly contribution to the sewerage revenue account of the General Fund would be:

Amount required to repay a loan of 1 over 60 periods at 4% (from tables) = 0.044201845.

Half-yearly payment for U 100,000
= 0.044201845 x 100,000
= U 4,420

The journal entries for the General Fund would be:

19-8 Jun 30	Investment DR
	    To Capital Fund
	        (Suspense)
	Being investment of proceeds of government grant and consumer contributions in the Capital Fund
		100,000	100,000

19-8 Dec 31	Capital Fund (Suspense) DR
	    To Investment
	      Grant/Contributions
	        (Suspense)
	Being withdrawal of first instalment of investment of sewerage grant and consumer contributions together with interest at 4% per half-year.
		4,420	420
			4,000

19-8 Dec 31	Grant/Contributions
	        (Suspense) DR
	    To Sewerage Revenue
	Being half-yearly transfer of sewerage grant and consumer contributions to Revenue Account
		4,420	4,420

It is not necessary to show the accounts for the Capital Fund, where the transaction would be a straightforward borrowing and repayment operation.

The above procedures introduce additional complications, both in terms of accounting practices and detailed record-keeping. Justification for this will depend upon circumstances, including legal requirements. The practice would seem more justified where grants were provided (or consumer contributions collected) as a regular procedure for financing certain classes of fixed assets. Where, however, the grants and contributions were specific ad hoc payments, not part of a regular pattern, the adoption of these alternative practices seems highly questionable. If possible, they should be avoided, in the interest of simplicity.

256 **MUNICIPAL BANKS AND LOANS FUNDS**

The accountancy procedures described in this chapter for the Capital Fund would be very appropriate for a municipal bank or a local government loans fund. Indeed, they could be adopted almost in their entirety, with very little modification. Detailed records would be required, of course, for individual borrowers. However, a bank or loans fund would not be very concerned with the fixed asset and depreciation records, which would be the responsibility of the borrowers themselves.

257 **ELECTRONIC DATA PROCESSING**

In the introduction to this book, it was stated that very little would be explained regarding computers. This practice has, indeed, been followed. It has not, it is hoped, affected an understanding of the basic accountancy procedures. Furthermore, as already explained, the accountancy practices illustrated in this book can easily be adapted for computer use. The enhanced use of computers is increasingly likely, especially as a result of the introduction of low-cost micro-computers more suitable and adaptable to the needs and circumstances of developing countries.

The rapidity with which computerisation has come about is well illustrated by the time-span for the production of this book. When the main material was first written, almost all the calculations were done manually. A few of the more complicated ones were made on a mechanical crank-handle calculator borrowed from time to time by the author from an engineer. This was all that was available.

Less than 20 years later, the financial tables in the final chapter were prepared, at the author's home, upon his own personal micro-computer.

Index

A

Abstract system - 151
Accountancy defined - 2
Accountancy practice - 283
Accountancy principles, application of to local and public authorities - 191
Accountancy procedures - 726
Accounts, normal financial period for - 60
Adjustment of loan charges - 744
Administrative overheads - 481
Advances and deposits - 402
Advances from external maturity mortgages - 763
Advances from internal sources - 711
Advances from loans pool for capital expenditure - 759
Advance payment of deferred premiums - 603
Alienation of fixed assets - 541
Application of internal borrowing to local authorities - 698
Appropriation of balances by the capital fund - 823
Appropriation of existing sinking funds - 756
Availability of funds - 698

B

Balance sheet - 14, 23, 238
Balancing - 12
Balancing the ledger accounts - 33
Bank deposits - 72
Bank overdraft - 85
Bank reconciliation - 110
Bank withdrawals - 72
Banking arrangements - 71
Basic rules of accounting - 19
Bin cards and stock book - 447
Book keeping information - 90
Book keeping procedures - 310
Books and records - 313
Budget - 284

C

Calculation of interest - 731
Capital accounts - 494
Capital accounts, commercial practices - 820
Capital and revenue - 279
Capital cash - 586
Capital discharged - 882
Capital expenditure - 281, 484, 884
Capital expenditure, financing new - 835
Capital finance - capital receipts - 494
Capital finance - fund contribution - 521
Capital finance - loans - 503
Capital fund - 822
Capital fund balance sheets for subsequent years - 883
Capital fund cash transactions - 881
Capital fund investments - 869
Capital fund management expenses - 849
Capital fund transactions in subsequent years - 876
Capital fund revenue account - 882
Capital programmes and capital budgets - 286
Capital project, use of reserves for - 699
Capital receipts and payments - 484
Capital register - 552
Capital statements - 678
Capital statements supporting final accounts - 618
Car Allowances - 381
Cash Book - 60, 343
Cash and credit income - 313
Cash book, analysis of - 144
Cash book as a prime record - 138
Cash forecasts - 302
Cash payments - 65
Cash receipts - 61
Cash receipts analysis - 413
Chargeable interest rate - 848
Cheque payments - 75, 362
Classification of ledger accounts - 22
Classified statement of receipts and payments - 203

INDEX

C (Continued)

Collection and deposit book - 344
Combined paying in book - 108
Complete final accounts - 208
Complete set of accounts - 165
Continuous inventory - 455
Contracts and professional fees - 384
Conversion of single entry to double entry - 151
Correction of errors - 127
Costing - 310
Costing and budgetary control - 458
Credit income - 314
Credit income analysis - 414
Current accounts - 74

D

Debit and credit, notes on - 88
Debt redemption, provision for - 723
Deferred charges - 536
Deferred payment of land premiums - 593
Deferred premiums, advance payment of - 603
Deposits, advances and - 402
Depreciation - 249, 888
Depreciation charges - 850
Disagreement of the trial balance - 126
Double account system - 239
Double entry, conversion from single entry - 151

E

Earmarked and pooled loans - 566
Effect of changes in financial position - 23
Eletronic data processing - 892
Elements of cost - 460
Errors and adjustments - 118
Errors, correction of - 127
Errors, types of - 119
Establishment of sinking fund - 738
Expenditure ledger - 439
Explanation of final adjustments - 615
Explanation of technical points - 236
External borrowing by the pool - 754
External loans - 881

F

Final accounts, complete - 53
Final accounts, conclusion - 619
Final accounts, introduction - 31, 611
Final adjustment, explanation of - 615
Financial period - 60
Financial position, effects of changes in - 23
Financial records, the ledger - 3
Fixed assets, alienation of - 541
Fixed assets, financing the cost of - 247
Funds, availability of - 698
Further advances financed from internal sources - 761
Further loan repayments - 745
Further notes on debit and credit - 88

G

Gains and losses - 15
Gains and losses, analysis - 100
Gains and losses account - 31, 36
Graduated personal tax - 349
Grants and contributions - 889
Gross trading profit - 37

I

Imprest system - 149
Income and expenditure analysis - 412
Income ledger - 415
Instalment and annuity loans - 569
Integration of accounting procedures - 706
Interest and management expenses - 889
Interest apportionment and recovery - 847
Interest calculation - 731
Interest charges amortisation and capital fund accounts - 851
Interest, payment of - 737
Internal borrowing, application of to local authorities - 698
Internal borrowing by the pool - 751
Internal borrowing, conclusion - 714

INDEX

I (Continued)

Internal borrowing from sinking fund - 748
Internal borrowing, introduction - 696
Internal investment of capital fund monies - 758
Issue prices - 451

J

Job costing - 462
Journalising - 97
Journal, ledger and - 97
Journal, main - 95
Journals - 94
Journals, special purpose - 97

L

Labour overheads - 466
Ledger accounts, balancing - 33
Ledger accounts - capital transactions - 772
Ledger accounts - classification - 22
Ledger accounts - detailed - 631
Ledger accounts - outline - 655
Ledger accounts - revenue transactions - 793
Ledger and journal - 97
Ledger, the opening the - 8
Ledger ruling, alternative form of - 106
Legal requirements of municipal budgets - 305
Licences, trading and liquor - 338
Light plant and tools - 479
Loan charges - 257
Loan charges, adjustment of - 744
Loans register - 560
Loan repayments - 740
Loans pooling - 750, 818
Loans pool transactions - subsequent years - 805
Loans, raising of internal - 700
Loans, raising of long-term - 725
Loans register - 560
Loans, repayment of internal - 704
Local and public accounts, an introduction to - 191
Local authority - abstracts - 198
Local authority cash books - 193
Local authority in practice - 283
Local authority receipts and payments - 71

M

Main ledger - 613
Main journal - 614, 666
Marginal costing - 465
Marshalling - 134
Manpower budgets - 298
Maturity loans - 570
Municipal banks and loan funds - 892
Maximum and minimum stocks - 448
Money values - 4

N

Net results and net resources - 5
New loans and sinking funds appropriations - 742

O

Occasional payments - 387
Official order systems - 377
Overheads, administrative - 481
Overseas indents - 406

P

Paying in book combined - 108
Payments analysis - 417
Payments in advance - 400
Payment of interest - 737
Payments, occasional - 387
Periodical income register - 326
Periodical payments - 381
Personal tax, graduated - 349
Petty cash payments - 365
Physical control of stores - 446
Posting - 10
Posting changes to the ledger - 24
Prime records and documents - 92
Pool loans, earmarked and - 566
Process costing - 462
Professional fees, contracts and - 384
Provision for debt redemption - 723
Published final accounts - 617, 673

INDEX

R

Raising of internal loan - 700
Raising of long-term loan - 725
Raising short-term maturity loans - 736
Rate book (property tax register) - 315
Rate (property tax) demand - 323
Receipt and payment of cash - 308
Receipts - 341
Receipts and payments book keeping - 140
Receipts and payments, classified statement of - 203
Records of the pool - 755
Refunds, paying - 388
Remittance list - 337
Renewals fund - 263
Rents - 334
Renewals provisions - 870
Reordering level - 449
Repayment of internal loan - 704
Repayment of loans at maturity - 740
Repayments of principal to the loans pool - 768
Replacement borrowing - 735
Reserves and provisions - 271
Results - 4
Revenue account, order of - 236
Revenue budget - 286
Revenue transactions - debt management expenses - 790
Revenue transactions - interest - 785
Review of half yearly balances - 844

S

Salaries and wages - 388
Single entry, conversion to double entry - 151
Sinking funds - 571, 738
Slip system - 331
Special purposes journal - 97
Standard costing - 464
Statement of receipts and payments - 202
State of balance - 4
Stock valuation - 134, 457
Stores analysis - 429
Stores ledger - 433
Stores overheads - 477
Surplus, analysis of - 165
Surplus and capital discharged - 239
Surpluses and deficiences - 456

S (Continued)

Surplus, types of 36
Sundry creditors - 365
Sundry debtors book - 327
Sundry debtors (miscellaneous receivables) invoices - 325
Suspense account - 127
Suspense account system - 490

T

Tables of postings - 443
Tax, graduated personal - 349
Temporary borrowing - 717
Temporary borrowing, capital purposes - 720
Ticket income - 336
Trading account - 39
Transfers and adjustments - 442
Trial balance - 14, 30, 612, 622
Trial balance, disagreement of - 126
Two-column cash book - 77

U

Unit costing - 463

V

Valuation of fixed assets - 824
Valuation of stock - 134, 457
Variations in financial position - 3
Vehicle and plant analysis - 421

W

Wages and salaries - 388
Wages and salaries analysis - 419
Working balance - 299
Working papers - 295, 614, 684

XYZ